Eighteenth Edition

Washington Real Estate Fundamentals

Kathryn J. Haupt
David L. Rockwell
David L. Jarman
Megan Dorsey
Jennifer Gotanda

Rockwell Publishing Company

Table of Contents

The Nature of Real Property

🏠🏢🏠🏢🏠 Chapter Overview

Real estate agents are concerned not just with the sale of land and houses, but with the sale of real property. Real property includes the land and improvements, and it also encompasses the rights that go along with ownership of land. The first part of this chapter explains those rights, which are known as appurtenances. It also explains natural attachments and fixtures, which are sold as part of the land, and the distinction between fixtures and personal property, the latter of which is not ordinarily transferred with the land. The second part of this chapter explains methods of legal description—the different ways in which a parcel of land may be identified in legal documents to prevent confusion about its boundaries or ownership.

What is Real Property?

There are two types of property: **real property** (realty) and **personal property** (personalty). Real property is commonly described as land, anything affixed to the land, and anything incidental or appurtenant to the land. Sometimes it is referred to as "that which is immovable." Personal property, on the other hand, is usually movable. A car, a sofa, and a hat are simple examples of personal property.

The distinction between real and personal property is very important in real estate transactions. When a piece of land is sold, anything that is considered part of the real property is transferred to the buyer along with the land, unless otherwise agreed. But if an item is considered personal property, the sellers can take it with them when they leave.

Of course, the principal component of real property is land. But real property is more than just the surface of the earth. It also includes everything beneath the surface down to the center of the earth, and everything above the surface, to the upper reaches of the sky.

A parcel of real property can be imagined as an inverted pyramid, with its tip at the center of the globe and its base above the earth's surface. The landowner owns not only the earth's surface within the boundaries of the parcel, but also everything under or over the surface.

The rights and privileges associated with land ownership are also considered part of the real property. Think of real property as the land plus a bundle of rights. The owner's bundle of rights includes the rights to possess, use, enjoy, encumber, will, sell, or do nothing at all with the land.

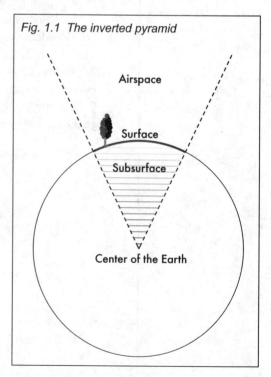

Fig. 1.1 The inverted pyramid

Airspace

Surface

Subsurface

Center of the Earth

Appurtenances

In addition to the basic bundle of ownership rights, a landowner has appurtenant rights. An **appurtenance** is a right or interest that goes along with or pertains to a piece of land. A landowner's property may include any or all of these appurtenances:

- air rights,
- water rights,
- solid mineral rights,
- oil and gas rights, and
- support rights.

Appurtenances are ordinarily transferred along with the land, but the landowner can sell certain appurtenant rights separately from the land. For example, the owner may keep the land but sell her mineral rights to a mining company.

Air Rights

In theory, a landowner's rights extend to the upper limits of the sky. In practice, however, this is no longer true. Congress gave the federal government complete control over the nation's airspace. A landowner still has the exclusive right to use the lower reaches of airspace over his property, but may do nothing that would interfere with normal air traffic.

On the other hand, sometimes air traffic interferes with a property owner's right to the normal use of his land. If aircraft overflights cause substantial damage to a landowner, he may sue the government for some form of reimbursement. The classic example is an airport built next door to a chicken farm. The noise and vibrations from overflights are so severe that the chickens no longer lay eggs. If the land cannot be used for any other reasonable purpose, the value of the land is significantly diminished. The landowner may be able to force the government to condemn the property and compensate him for its fair market value.

Water Rights

Water is found both on the surface of the earth and beneath the surface. Surface water may be confined to a channel or basin, or it may be unconfined water, such as run-off or flood water. The water beneath the surface may also be "confined" in the sense that it runs in recognizable underground streams, or it may collect in porous ground layers called aquifers.

In regard to confined surface waters, there are two types of property rights:

1. riparian rights, and
2. appropriative rights.

Riparian Rights. Riparian rights are the water rights of a landowner with respect to water that flows through or adjacent to her property. Such a landowner, called a riparian landowner, has a right to make reasonable use of the stream's natural flow. A riparian landowner also has the right to use stream water for domestic uses, such as drinking, bathing, and watering a personal-use produce garden. Upstream landowners are not allowed to substantially diminish the flow in quantity, quality, or velocity.

Whether a riparian owner also owns the land under the stream depends on whether the stream is considered navigable or not. A waterway is generally considered navigable if it is large enough to be used in commerce. If a stream that serves as the boundary of a property is not navigable, the property owner owns the land under the water to the midpoint of the streambed. If the stream is navigable, the government owns the land under the water and the riparian landowner owns only the land above the mean high water mark of the streambed. The general public has the right to use navigable waterways for transportation and recreation.

Property located beside a lake or ocean, as opposed to a river or stream, is called **littoral** property. The owner of lakeside littoral property is entitled to have the lake maintained at its natural level, and to use the lake for fishing or recreation. The owner is also entitled to have the natural purity of the lake's waters maintained. If the lake is non-navigable, each littoral owner owns a portion of the lake bed adjacent to his property. If the lake is navigable, each owner owns the land to the mean high water mark; this is also true with tidal (oceanfront) property.

There is one important restriction on a riparian or littoral owner's water rights. A riparian or littoral owner may never divert water from a stream or lake for use on non-riparian land—that is, land that does not adjoin the stream or lake from which the water is taken.

Example: Brown is a riparian landowner. She owns Parcel C, property that borders Swiftwater River. She also owns Parcel D, property that is about 300 feet inland. She cannot divert water from Swiftwater River to feed the livestock that graze on Parcel D, her non-riparian property.

In Washington, the riparian water rights system has been superseded by the appropriative rights system (discussed below). Thus, all riparian and littoral owners were required to register their water rights with the Department of Ecology by June 30, 1974. Any unregistered riparian or littoral rights were extinguished after that date.

Appropriative Rights. Riparian and littoral rights are tied to ownership of land beside a body of water. The second major type of water rights, appropriative rights, does not depend on land ownership. Instead, appropriative rights are based on a permit system called the **prior appropriation system**.

To establish appropriative rights, someone who wants to use water from a particular lake or stream applies to the state government (in Washington, the Department of Ecology) for a permit. It is not necessary for the applicant to own land beside the body of water. Water taken by a permit holder does not have to be used on property adjacent to the water source.

The prior appropriation system is primarily used in the western United States, where water resources are often scarce and therefore carefully controlled. If someone with appropriative rights fails to use the water for a certain period of time, he will lose those rights. Another person can apply for a permit to use the water.

Ground Water. Landowners have **overlying rights** in regard to the ground water in aquifers beneath their property. Overlying rights are similar to riparian rights; the landowner is allowed to make reasonable use of the ground water, but not to transport the water for use on land outside the ground water basin from which it was removed. The prior appropriation system may also be applied to ground water.

Solid Mineral Rights

A landowner owns all the solid minerals within the "inverted pyramid" under the surface of her property. These minerals are considered to be real property until they are extracted from the earth, at which point they become personal property.

Remember that a landowner can sell her mineral rights separately from the rest of the property. When the rights to a particular mineral are sold, the purchaser automatically acquires an implied easement—the right to enter the land in order to extract the minerals.

Oil and Gas Rights

Ownership of oil and gas is not as straightforward as ownership of solid minerals. In their natural state, oil and gas lie trapped beneath the surface in porous layers of earth. However, once an oil or gas reservoir has been tapped, the oil and gas begin to flow toward the point where the reservoir has been pierced by the well. A well on one parcel of land can attract all the oil and gas from the surrounding properties.

Ownership of oil and gas is governed by the "rule of capture." That is, a landowner owns all of the oil and gas produced from wells on his property. The oil and gas become the personal property of the landowner once they are "captured" and brought to the surface. The rule of capture has the effect of stimulating oil and gas production, since the only way for a landowner to protect his interest in the underlying gas and oil is to drill his own well to keep the oil and gas from migrating to the neighbor's wells.

Other Appurtenant Rights

In addition to rights concerning air, water, minerals, and oil and gas, there are some other important appurtenant rights.

A piece of land is physically supported by the other land that surrounds it. A landowner has **support rights**—the right to the natural support provided by the land beside and beneath her property. **Lateral support** is support from the adjacent land, which may be disturbed by construction or excavations on the adjacent property. **Subjacent support**, which is support from the underlying earth, may become an issue when a landowner sells her mineral rights.

Easements and restrictive covenants also create appurtenant rights. These are discussed in detail in Chapter 4.

Attachments

You have seen that the land and appurtenances are considered part of the real property. The third element of real property is attachments. There are two types of attachments:

1. natural, and
2. man-made.

Natural Attachments

Natural attachments are things attached to the earth by roots, such as trees and shrubs. This includes plants that grow spontaneously, without the help of humans, and also plantings cultivated by people. As a general rule, natural attachments are part of the real property. In some cases, however, crops to be harvested are treated as personal property. Thus, an orchard of cultivated apple trees would be realty, but the apples growing on the trees could be considered personalty under certain circumstances.

A special rule called the **doctrine of emblements** applies to crops planted by a tenant farmer. If the tenancy is for an indefinite period of time and the tenancy is terminated through no fault of the tenant before the crops are ready for harvest, the tenant has the right to re-enter the land and harvest the first crop that matures after the tenancy is terminated.

Man-made Attachments: Fixtures

Articles attached to the land by people are called **fixtures**. Houses, fences, and cement patios are all examples of fixtures. Fixtures are considered part of the real property.

Fixtures always start out as personal property—for example, lumber is personal property, but it becomes a fixture when it's used to build a fence. So it is sometimes difficult to determine whether a particular item has become a fixture or is still personal property. If the item remains personal property, the owner can remove it from the property when the land is sold. But if the item is a fixture, it's transferred to the buyer along with the land unless otherwise agreed.

Distinguishing Fixtures from Personal Property

Buyers and sellers often disagree as to exactly what has been purchased and sold. For instance, if an heirloom chandelier was installed by the seller, is it real property that's transferred to the buyer or can the seller remove it when he moves out?

The easiest way to avoid such a controversy is to put the intentions of the parties in writing. If there is a written agreement between a buyer and seller (or a landlord and tenant, or a lender and borrower) stipulating how a particular item will be treated—as part of the real estate or as personal property—then the court will respect and enforce that agreement. The stipulation between a buyer and seller would ordinarily be found in their purchase and sale agreement. For example, if a seller plans to take certain shrubs from the property before the transaction closes, a statement to that effect ought to be included in the purchase and sale agreement, since shrubs are usually considered part of the real property.

Similarly, if the seller intends to transfer personal property, such as a couch, to the buyer, that should also be stated in the purchase agreement. In addition to the deed conveying title to the real property, a separate document called a **bill of sale** may be needed. A bill of sale conveys title to personal property.

In the absence of a written agreement, courts apply a series of tests to classify the item in dispute. These tests include:

- the method of attachment,
- adaptation of the item to the realty,
- the intention of the annexor, and
- the relationship of the parties.

Method of Attachment. As a general rule, any item a person permanently attaches to the land becomes a part of the real estate. A permanent attachment occurs when the item is:

- annexed to the land by roots, as with trees and shrubs;
- embedded in the earth, like sewer lines or septic tanks;
- permanently resting on the land, like certain types of buildings; or
- attached by any other enduring method, such as by cement, plaster, nails, bolts, or screws.

It isn't absolutely necessary for an item to be physically attached to the real property in order to be considered a fixture. Often there is physical annexation even without actual attachment. The force of gravity alone may be sufficient, as in the case of a building with no foundation. Also, an article enclosed within a building may be considered annexed to the real property if it cannot be removed without dismantling it or tearing down part of the building.

Even easily movable articles may be considered "attached" to the real property, if they are essential parts of other fixtures. For example, the key to the front door of a house is a fixture. Also, fixtures that have been temporarily removed for servicing or repair remain legally attached to the real property. For example, a built-in dishwasher that has been sent to the repair shop is still considered to be a part of the house that it is ordinarily attached to.

Adaptation of the Item to the Realty. If an unattached article was designed or adapted specifically for use on a particular property, it is probably a fixture. Examples include the pews in a church, and storm windows made for a particular building.

Intention of the Annexor. The method of attachment was once regarded as the most important test in determining whether an item was a fixture, but over time the courts decided that test was too rigid. It did not allow for special situations where something permanently affixed would be more justly classified as personal property. Now, the intention of the annexor is considered a more important test. Courts try to determine what the person who annexed the item to the property intended. Did she intend the item to become part of the realty or to remain personal property? Each of the other tests (including method of attachment) is viewed as objective evidence of this intention. For instance, permanently embedding a birdbath in concrete indicates an intention to make the item a permanent fixture, while just setting a birdbath out in the yard does not.

Relationship of the Parties. Intent is also indicated by the relationship between the parties: landlord/tenant, buyer/seller, borrower/lender. For example, it is generally held that a tenant who installs an item, such as new lighting, probably does so with the intention of removing it at the expiration of the lease. On the other

Fig. 1.2 Fixture tests

Fixture Tests

- *Method of attachment*
- *Adaptation to the property*
- *Intention of the annexor*
- *Relationship of the parties*

hand, it's assumed that an owner making the same alteration is trying to improve the property and does not intend to remove the item. So an item that would be considered personal property if installed by a tenant might be considered a fixture if installed by an owner.

Items installed by a tenant so he can carry on a trade or business are called **trade fixtures**. Trade fixtures may be removed unless there is a contrary provision in the lease, or unless the fixtures have become an integral part of the land or improvements. In the latter case, if the tenant still wants to remove the fixtures, it is his responsibility to either restore the property to its original condition, or compensate the landlord for any physical damage resulting from the removal. Trade fixtures that are not removed by the tenant become the property of the landlord.

Manufactured Homes

The distinction between fixtures and personal property has special significance in connection with mobile or manufactured homes. At one time, mobile homes were simply wheeled trailers that could be set up inexpensively in mobile home parks, but the category has expanded to include manufactured homes, which are large structures that can be set permanently on a full-sized lot. Manufactured homes are assembled in a factory and transported to the property they'll occupy, in contrast to traditional homes that are built on the property (sometimes referred to as site-built or stick-built homes).

Manufactured homes leave the factory as personal property and only later become real property. As long as a manufactured home is classified as personal property, its sale is subject to sales tax and to the same title registration system that's used for motor vehicles. An agent involved in the sale doesn't need a real estate license, but is required to have a mobile home dealer's license.

In order for the manufactured home to become real property, it must go through a procedure called title elimination. This eliminates the vehicle title, and the home becomes part of the real property where it is located. The title elimination process is what determines whether a manufactured home is transferred and taxed as personal property or as real property. Once a manufactured home becomes real property, it is treated just like a site-built home, and an agent listing or selling it must have a real estate license.

Of course, a manufactured home that has become real property may later be sold separately from the land it occupies and moved away. Before that can happen, the consent of anyone with a security interest in the land must be obtained. The new owner of the home may either arrange to have the vehicle title reissued (so that the home becomes personal property again) or else reattach the home to another piece of land (so that it remains real property).

Methods of Legal Description

When real property is transferred from one party to another, an accurate description of the land being conveyed is essential. An ambiguous or uncertain land description could make a contract or a deed invalid. The resulting confusion could

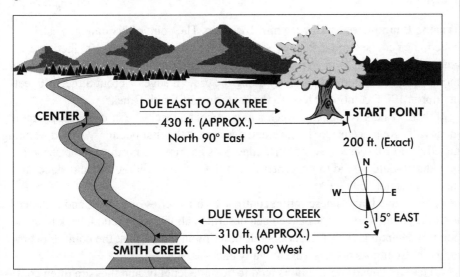

Fig. 1.3 Metes and bounds description

A tract of land located in Spokane County, described as follows: "Beginning at the oak tree, thence south 15° east, 200 feet, thence north 90° west, 310 feet more or less to the centerline of Smith Creek, thence northwesterly along the centerline of Smith Creek to a point directly west of the oak tree, thence north 90° east, 430 feet more or less to the point of beginning."

cause problems not only for the parties involved in the current transaction, but also for the parties in future transactions.

There are three major methods used to describe land in legal documents:

- metes and bounds,
- government survey, and
- lot and block.

Metes and Bounds

The metes and bounds method describes a parcel by establishing its boundaries. The boundaries are described by reference to three things:

- **monuments**, which may be natural objects such as rivers or trees, or man-made objects such as roads or survey markers;
- directions or **courses**, in the form of compass readings; and
- **distances**, measured in any convenient units of length.

Point of Beginning. A metes and bounds description begins at a convenient and well-defined point along the boundary of a tract of land (called the point of beginning). It then sets out directions that would allow a surveyor to trace the boundaries of the tract all the way back to the point of beginning. The point of beginning will always be described by reference to a monument, such as "the SW corner of the intersection of Front and Cherry," or "200 feet north of the old barn." Notice that the point of beginning does not have to be a monument itself, but can be described by referring to a monument.

Tracing Boundaries by Course and Distance. The point of beginning is established, then courses and distances are given. For example, "north, 100 feet" is a course and distance. Both the course and the distance may be described in terms of a monument; for example, "northerly along the eastern edge of Front Street 100 feet" or "north, 100 feet more or less, to the centerline of Smith Creek."

If there is a discrepancy between a monument and a course or distance, the monument will take precedence. In the examples above, the first boundary would be along the edge of Front Street, even if that edge does not run due north, and the second boundary would extend to the center of Smith Creek even if the actual distance to that point is not 100 feet.

A metes and bounds description continues with a series of courses and distances, until the parcel's boundaries have been described all the way around, back to the point of beginning. A metes and bounds description must end at the point of beginning, or else it does not describe a totally enclosed tract.

Metes and bounds descriptions tend to be quite lengthy, and they are often confusing. Furthermore, monuments and reference points do not always maintain their exact locations over the years. An actual survey of the property is usually necessary when dealing with a metes and bounds description.

Conflicting Directions. As noted above, discrepancies may occur between the various elements of a metes and bounds description. In resolving them, the order of priority is as follows:

1. natural monuments,
2. then man-made monuments,
3. then courses,
4. then distances,
5. then names (e.g., "Smith Farm"),
6. then areas (e.g., "40 acres").

If any two of these elements conflict, the one with higher priority will prevail.

Compass Bearings. Directions or courses in metes and bounds descriptions are given in a peculiar fashion. A direction is described by reference to its deviation from either north or south, whichever is closer. Thus, northwest or 315° is written as north 45° west, since it is a deviation of 45° to the west of north. Similarly, south southeast or 157½° is written as south 22½° east, since it is a deviation of 22½° to the east of south. East and west are both written relative to north: north 90° east and north 90° west, respectively.

Government Survey

The government survey system, also called the rectangular survey system, describes land by reference to a series of

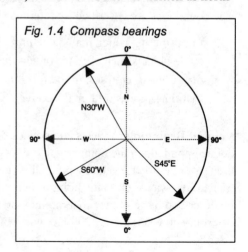

Fig. 1.4 Compass bearings

grids. This system of land description was established after many of the northeastern states were already surveyed. Thus, it is mainly used west of the Mississippi River.

The grids and terms used in the government survey system may seem confusing at first, and we recommend that you study the accompanying diagrams closely.

The grids are composed of two sets of lines, one set running north/south, the other east/west. Each grid is identified by a **principal meridian**, which is the original north/south line established in that grid, and by a **base line**, which is the original east/west line. In Washington, the principal meridian is the Willamette Meridian. (See Figure 1.6.)

Grid lines run parallel to the principal meridian and the base line at intervals of six miles. The east/west lines are called **township lines**, and they divide the land into rows or tiers called **township tiers**. The north/south lines, called **range lines**, divide the land into columns called **ranges**. Every fourth range line is a **guide meridian** and every fourth township line is a correction line. (See Figure 1.7.)

A particular area of land that is located at the intersection of a range and a township tier is called a **township**, and it is identified by its position relative to the principal meridian and base line. For example, the township that is located in the fourth tier north of the base line and the third range east of the principal meridian is called "Township 4 North Range 3 East." (See Figure 1.7.) This is often abbreviated "T4N, R3E."

Grid systems are identical across the country, so it is necessary to include in the description the name of the principal meridian that is being used as a reference. (Since each principal meridian has its own base line, it is not necessary to specify the base line.) It's also a good practice to mention the county and state where the land is situated, to avoid any possible confusion. Thus, for example, a complete description of a township might be T4N, R3E of the Willamette Meridian, Clark County, State of Washington.

Each township measures 36 square miles and contains 36 sections. Each section is one square mile, or 640 acres. (See Figure 1.8.) These sections are numbered in a special way, starting with the northeast corner and moving west, then down a row and eastward, snaking back and forth and ending with the southeast corner.

Fig. 1.5 Units of land measurement

UNITS OF MEASUREMENT FOR LAND	
UNITS OF AREA	1 Tract = 24 mi. × 24 mi. (576 sq. mi) = 16 townships 1 Township = 6 mi. × 6 mi. (36 sq. mi.) = 36 sections 1 Section = 1 mi. × 1 mi. (1 sq. mi.) = 640 acres 1 Acre = 43,560 sq. ft. 1 Square Acre = 208.71 ft. × 208.71 feet
UNITS OF LENGTH	1 Mile = 5,280 ft. 1 Yard = 3 ft.

Note: To determine the area of partial sections, simply multiply the fraction of the section by 640. For example:

$$1 \text{ half section} = \frac{1}{2} \times 640 = 320 \text{ acres}$$
$$1 \text{ quarter-section} = \frac{1}{4} \times 640 = 160 \text{ acres}$$
$$1 \text{ quarter-quarter section} = \frac{1}{4} \times \frac{1}{4} \times 640 = 40 \text{ acres}$$

Fig. 1.6 Principal meridians and baselines

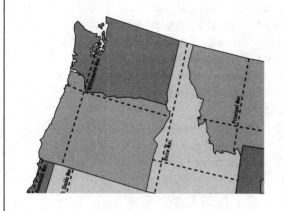

Fig. 1.7 East/west lines are township lines, north/south lines are range lines

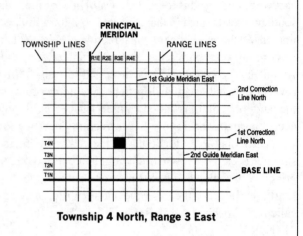

Township 4 North, Range 3 East

Fig. 1.8 A township contains 36 sections

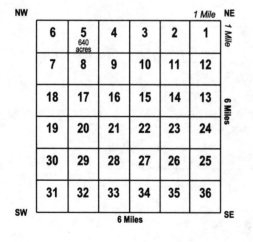

Fig. 1.9 A section can be divided into smaller parcels

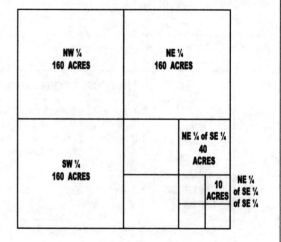

Smaller parcels of land can be identified by reference to sections and partial sections, as illustrated in Figure 1.9.

Government Lots. A government lot is a section of land of irregular shape or size that is referred to by a lot number. Because of the curvature of the earth, range lines converge, so it is impossible to keep all sections exactly one mile square. As a result, the sections along the north and west boundaries of each township are irregular in size. The quarter sections along the north and west boundaries of these sections are used to take up the excess or shortage. The quarter-quarter sections, then, along the north and west boundaries of a township are given government lot numbers.

Another situation in which government lots occur is when a body of water or some other obstacle makes it impossible to survey a square-mile section. The irregularly shaped sections are assigned government lot numbers.

Lot and Block

The lot and block method is sometimes referred to as the platting method or the maps and plats system. When land is subdivided, lots and blocks (groups of lots surrounded by streets) are mapped out by a surveyor on a subdivision map called a **plat**. The plat is then recorded in the county where the land is located.

After the plat has been recorded, a reference to one of the lot numbers on the specified plat is a sufficient legal description of the lot. Since a detailed description of the lot is already on file in the county recorder's office, that description may be incorporated into any legal document simply by reference to the lot number and subdivision plat.

To find the precise location and dimensions of the parcel, you would look at the plat map in the county records. Here is an example of a lot and block description:

Lot 2, Block 4 of Tract number 455, in the City of Vancouver, County of Clark, State of Washington, as per map recorded in Book 25, page 92, of maps, in the office of the recorder of said county.

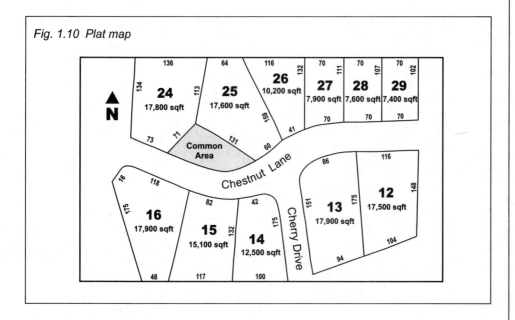

Fig. 1.10 Plat map

Plat maps frequently contain a considerable amount of useful information beyond a detailed description of lot boundaries. For example, they may include area measurements, the locations and dimensions of various easements, the location of survey markers, and a list of use restrictions applying to the land.

Other Methods of Land Description

There are other methods of describing land besides the three major systems discussed above. When an adequate description of property is already a matter of public record—contained in a recorded document—then a simple reference to that earlier document serves as an adequate property description in a new document. (For example, "All that land described in the grant deed recorded under recording number 92122401503 in Skagit County, Washington.") Also, generalized descriptions such as "all my lands" or "Smith Farm" can be adequate, as long as they make it possible to determine exactly what property is being described. But it's always best to use the least ambiguous description possible, to prevent future problems. It should be noted that a property's street address is usually not an adequate description for a legal document.

Air Lots. Not every parcel of real property can be described simply in terms of its position on the face of the earth. Some forms of real property (for example, condominium units) require description in terms of elevation above the ground as well. These descriptions are made by reference to an established plane of elevation, called a **datum**. Most large cities have their own official datum, and frequently subsidiary reference points, called bench marks, are also established. A **bench mark** is a point whose position relative to a datum has been accurately measured. Thereafter, surveyors can use the bench mark as a reference when it is more convenient than the datum.

Chapter Summary

1. There are two types of property: real property and personal property. Real property is the land, anything affixed to the land, and anything appurtenant to the land. Movable items, such as furniture, are usually personal property.

2. Appurtenances to land include air rights, water rights, mineral rights, oil and gas rights, and support rights.

3. Attachments may be natural (growing plants) or man-made (fixtures). In the absence of a written agreement, the tests used to distinguish fixtures from personal property include: the method of attachment, the adaptation of the item to the realty, the intention of the annexor, and the relationship of the parties.

4. Before property can be transferred, it must be adequately described. There are three major methods of legal description: metes and bounds, government survey, and lot and block.

Key Terms

Real property—Land, attachments, and appurtenances.

Personal property—Anything that is not real property; its main characteristic is movability.

Appurtenance—A right incidental to the land that is transferred with it.

Emblements—Crops, such as wheat, produced annually through the labor of the cultivator.

Trade fixtures—Personal property attached to real property by a tenant for use in a trade or business. Trade fixtures are removable by the tenant.

Riparian rights—The water rights of a landowner whose land borders on a stream or other surface water. Riparian rights allow only reasonable use of the water.

Littoral land—Land bordered by a stationary body of water, such as a lake or pond.

Appropriative rights—Water rights established by obtaining a government permit, and not based on ownership of land beside a body of water.

Lateral support—The physical support that a piece of land receives from the surrounding land.

Subjacent support—The physical support that a piece of land receives from the underlying earth.

Metes and bounds—A system of land description in which the boundaries of a parcel of land are described by reference to monuments, courses, and distances.

Monument—A visible marker (natural or artificial) used in a survey or a metes and bounds description to establish the boundaries of a piece of property.

Point of beginning—The starting point in a metes and bounds description; a monument or a point described by reference to a monument.

Course—In a metes and bounds description, a direction, stated in terms of a compass bearing.

Distance—In a metes and bounds description, the length of a boundary, measured in any convenient unit of length.

Government survey—A system of land description in which the land is divided into squares called townships, and each township is, in turn, divided up into 36 sections, each one square mile.

Principal meridian—In the government survey system, the main north-south line in a particular grid, used as the starting point in numbering the ranges and township tiers.

Range—In the government survey system, a strip of land six miles wide, running north and south.

Township—The intersection of a range and a township tier in the government survey system. It is a parcel of land that is six miles square and contains 36 sections.

Section—One square mile of land, containing 640 acres. There are 36 sections in a township.

Government lot—In the government survey system, a parcel of land that is not a regular section.

Lot and block—The system of description used for subdivided land. The properties within a subdivision are assigned lot numbers on a plat map, and the plat map is recorded; the location and dimensions of a particular lot can be determined by consulting the recorded plat.

Air lot—A parcel of property above the surface of the earth, not containing any land: for example, a condominium unit on the third floor.

Chapter Quiz

1. Real property is equivalent to:

   a) land

   b) personal property

   c) land, attachments, and appurtenances

   d) land and water

2. The most important consideration in determining whether an article is a fixture is:

   a) physical attachment

   b) the annexor's intention

   c) adaptation of the article to the realty

   d) intended use of article

3. Articles installed in or on realty by tenants for use in a business are called:

   a) personalty

   b) trade fixtures

   c) emblements

   d) easements

4. A right that goes with or pertains to real property is called:

   a) an attachment

   b) an appurtenance

   c) personal property

   d) a fixture

5. A landowner's rights regarding water in a stream flowing through her land are called:

   a) riparian rights

   b) littoral rights

   c) appropriative rights

   d) easement rights

6. Minerals become personal property when they are:

   a) surveyed

   b) extracted from the land

   c) taken to a refinery

   d) claimed

7. Rights to oil and gas are determined by:

   a) the rule of capture

   b) offset wells

   c) the Bureau of Land Management

   d) the Department of the Interior

8. Whether land borders on a lake or stream is irrelevant under the system of:

   a) riparian rights

   b) capture rights

   c) littoral rights

   d) appropriative rights

9. Ted's property is damaged by sinkholes caused by old coal mining tunnels beneath his land. The rights implicated in this situation are:

   a) riparian rights

   b) subjacent support rights

   c) proximate support rights

   d) lateral support rights

10. Which of the following is most likely to be considered part of the real property?

    a) Piano

    b) Dining room table

    c) Living room drapes

    d) Kitchen sink

11. Which of the following benefits tenant farmers?

    a) Doctrine of emblements

    b) Rule of capture

    c) Overlying rights

    d) Method of attachment test

12. A section of a township contains the following number of acres:

    a) 360

    b) 580

    c) 640

    d) 560

13. A parcel that measures $\frac{1}{4}$ of a mile by $\frac{1}{4}$ of a mile is:

   a) $\frac{1}{4}$ of a section
   b) $\frac{1}{8}$ of a section
   c) $\frac{1}{16}$ of a section
   d) $\frac{1}{36}$ of a section

14. The distance between the east and west boundary lines of a township is:

   a) one mile
   b) two miles
   c) six miles
   d) ten miles

15. A township contains 36 sections that are numbered consecutively 1 through 36. The last section in the township is located in the:

   a) southeast corner
   b) southwest corner
   c) northeast corner
   d) northwest corner

👉 Answer Key

1. c) Real property is made up of land, everything that is attached to the land (e.g., fixtures), and everything that is appurtenant to the land (e.g., water rights).

2. b) The intention of the party who attached the item is the primary consideration in determining whether it is a fixture. The other tests provide evidence of the party's intention.

3. b) An article installed by a tenant for use in a business is called a trade fixture, and it remains the tenant's personal property.

4. b) An appurtenance is a right or interest that goes with the property. Riparian rights are an example.

5. a) Riparian rights include the right to reasonable use of the water that flows through a property owner's land.

6. b) When minerals are extracted from the land, they become personal property.

7. a) The rule of capture determines ownership of oil and gas. The rule provides that the landowner owns all the oil and gas removed from a well on his property, even if the oil or gas was originally under someone else's property.

8. d) To obtain a water appropriation permit, it is not necessary to own riparian or littoral land.

9. b) Subjacent support rights involve support from the underlying earth.

10. d) Unlike the other items listed, the kitchen sink is a fixture, and therefore part of the real property.

11. a) The doctrine of emblements allows a tenant farmer to return and harvest crops after the lease expires.

12. c) In the government survey system of land description, one section contains 640 acres.

13. c) A section is one mile on each side, a quarter section is ½ mile on each side, and a quarter of a quarter section is ¼ mile on each side.

14. c) A township measures six miles by six miles.

15. a) Section 36 is always in the southeast corner of a township.

Chapter 2

Estates in Land and Methods of Holding Title

I. Estates
   A. Freehold estates
      1. Fee simple estate
      2. Qualified fee estate
      3. Life estate
   B. Leasehold estates
      1. Estate for years
      2. Periodic estate
      3. Estate at will
      4. Tenancy at sufferance
II. Methods of Holding Title
   A. In severalty
   B. Concurrently
      1. Tenancy in common
      2. Joint tenancy
      3. Community property
   C. Forms of business ownership
      1. Partnerships
      2. Corporations
      3. Limited liability companies
      4. Joint ventures
      5. Trusts
   D. Condominiums and cooperatives

🏠 Chapter Overview

Real property ownership can take many different forms. An owner typically has full title to the property and full possession of it, but that isn't necessarily the case. An owner may have a more limited interest instead of full title, or may allow someone else (a tenant) to take possession of the property without taking title. In addition, a property may be owned by more than one person at the same time, which is called concurrent ownership. The first part of this chapter explains the various types of ownership interests, and also the types of interests that tenants may have. The second part of this chapter explains concurrent ownership and the different ways co-owners may hold title.

Estates

The word "estate" refers to an interest in land that is or may become possessory. In other words, someone has now, or may have in the future, the right to possess the property—the right to exclusively occupy and use it.

There are several different types of estates, and they are distinguished from one another by differences in duration (how long the estate holder has the right of possession) and time of possession (whether the estate holder has the right to possess the property right now, or not until sometime in the future).

It is important to note that while all estates are interests in land, not every interest in land is an estate. Interests that are not estates are called nonpossessory interests. For example, a mortgage gives a lender a financial interest in the property (a lien), but this interest is not an estate, because it is not a possessory interest. Nonpossessory interests are covered in Chapter 4.

Estates fall into two categories:

1. freehold estates, and
2. leasehold (less-than-freehold) estates.

A **freehold** estate is an interest in real property that has an indeterminable (not fixed or certain) duration. The holder of such an estate is usually referred to as an owner. All other possessory interests are leasehold (less-than-freehold) estates. A **leasehold** estate has a limited duration (a one-year lease is an example). The holder of a leasehold estate is referred to as a tenant; a tenant has possession of the property but not title.

Freehold Estates

The freehold estate got its name back in the Middle Ages; it originally referred to the holdings of a freeman under the English feudal system. Freehold estates are subdivided into fee simple estates and life estates.

Fee Simple Estates. The fee simple estate (also called the "fee," the "fee simple," or the "fee simple absolute") is the greatest estate that can exist in land, the highest and most complete form of ownership. It is of potentially infinite duration and represents the whole "bundle of rights."

Fee simple estates are freely transferable and inheritable, so a fee simple is sometimes referred to as an **estate of inheritance**. A fee simple estate has no set termination point, and theoretically can be owned forever by the titleholder and his heirs. When a fee simple owner transfers title by deed, it is presumed that the grantee (the new owner) receives a fee simple absolute estate, unless the deed includes language that indicates an intent to confer a lesser estate (such as a life estate, described below).

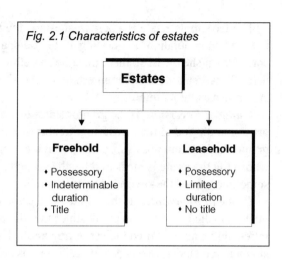

Fig. 2.1 Characteristics of estates

Qualified Fee Estates. A fee simple estate may be qualified when it is transferred from one owner to another. For example, in a deed, the grantor may specify that the grantee's estate will continue only as long as a certain condition is met, or until a certain event occurs.

> **Example:** Able conveys a parcel of land to "Barney and his heirs so long as it is used for church purposes, and if it is no longer used for church purposes it shall revert back to Able or his heirs."

This type of qualification creates a qualified fee estate (also known as a "defeasible fee," "base fee," or "conditional fee"). The owner of a qualified fee holds the same interest as the owner of a fee simple estate, but the qualified fee holder's interest is subject to termination.

There are two types of qualified fees: fee simple determinable, and fee simple subject to a condition subsequent. A **fee simple determinable** ends automatically if the condition is violated; the property reverts back to the grantor without legal action by the grantor. Language in a deed creating a fee simple determinable includes a phrase such as "so long as," "during," or "until." A **fee simple subject to a condition subsequent** doesn't end automatically when the condition is breached. The grantor must take some action to terminate the estate. This type of estate is created by the words "if" or "on the condition that."

Life Estates. An estate for life, or life estate, is a freehold estate whose duration is limited to the lifetime of a specified person or persons.

> **Example:** Noel gives a parcel of property to Beatrice for her lifetime, calling for a reversion of title to Noel upon Beatrice's death. Beatrice is the life tenant (holder of the life estate), and the duration of the life estate is measured by her lifetime.

The measuring life may be that of the life tenant (as in the example above, where Beatrice's life is the measuring life) or it may be the life of another person. If it is for the life of another person, it may be known as a life estate **pur autre vie** (which is French for "for another life"). Suppose Angie gives a parcel of property to Howard for the life of Charlie. Howard has a life estate that will end when Charlie dies.

The fee simple estate is a perpetual estate; the life estate is a lesser estate because it is limited in duration. In granting a life estate, a fee simple owner transfers only part of what she owns, so there must be something left over after the life estate terminates. What remains is either an estate in reversion or an estate in remainder. These are known as future interests.

Estate in Reversion. If the grantor states that the property will revert back to the grantor at the end of the measuring life, the grantor holds an estate in reversion. The grantor has a future possessory interest in the property. Upon the death of the person whose life the estate is measured by, the property will revert to the grantor (who is sometimes called the **reversioner**) or her heirs.

Estate in Remainder. If the grantor states that the property should go to a person other than the grantor upon the death of the life tenant, that other person has an estate in remainder and is called the **remainderman**. The only difference between reversion and remainder estates is that the former is held by the grantor and the latter by a third party. (If the grantor doesn't name a remainderman, an estate in reversion is created.) The interest that will pass to the designated party on the death of the life tenant is a fee simple estate.

Rights and Duties of Life Tenants. A life tenant has the same rights as a fee simple owner, including the right to profits or rents, and the right to lease or mortgage the property. A life tenant also has the same duties as a fee simple owner: to pay taxes, assessments, and liens. A life tenant has certain additional duties, because someone else has a future interest in the property:

- A life tenant must not commit **waste**, which means that the life tenant must not engage in acts that will permanently damage the property and harm the interests of the reversionary or remainder estate.
- A life tenant must also allow for the reasonable inspection of the property by the remainderman, who is permitted to check the property for possible waste.

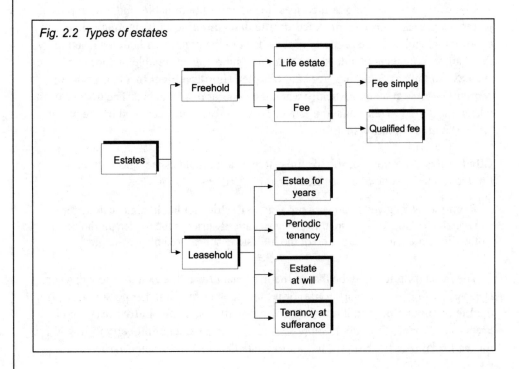

Fig. 2.2 Types of estates

The life tenant may transfer or lease his interest in the property. But it should be noted that the life tenant can give, sell, or lease only that which he owns. In other words, a lease given by a life tenant will terminate upon the death of the person designated as the measuring life. The lease need not be honored by a remainderman. Similarly, a mortgage on a life estate loses its status as a valid lien upon the death of the person named as the measuring life.

Leasehold Estates

Less-than-freehold estates are more commonly called **leasehold estates**. The holder of a leasehold estate is the tenant, who does not own the property, but rather has a right to exclusive possession of the property for a specified period.

The leasehold is created with a **lease**. The parties to a lease are the **landlord (lessor)**, who is the owner of the property, and the **tenant (lessee)**, the party with the right of possession. The lease creates the relationship of landlord and tenant. It grants the tenant the right of exclusive possession, with a reversion of the possessory rights to the landlord at the end of the rental period. The lease is a contract and its provisions are interpreted under contract law. Although it creates an interest in real property, the lease itself is classified as personal property.

There are four types of leasehold estates:

1. the estate for years (tenancy for years or term tenancy),
2. the periodic estate (periodic tenancy),
3. the estate at will (tenancy at will), and
4. the tenancy at sufferance.

Estate for Years. The estate for years is a tenancy for a fixed term. Its name is misleading in the sense that the duration need not be for a year or a period of years; it must only be for some fixed term.

> **Example:** Bob rents a cabin in the mountains from Clark for a period from June 1 through September 15. Bob has an estate for years because the rental term is fixed.

An estate for years can be created only by express agreement. It terminates automatically when the agreed-upon term expires; neither party has to give notice of termination. If either the landlord or the tenant wants to terminate an estate for years before the end of the lease period, he or she may do so only if the other party consents. Termination of a lease by mutual consent is called **surrender**.

Unless the lease includes a no-assignment clause, an estate for years is assignable—that is, the tenant can assign her interest to another person.

Periodic Estate. A periodic estate, more commonly called a periodic tenancy, has no fixed termination date. It lasts for a specific period (for example, one year, one month, or one week) and continues for successive similar periods (another year, month, or week) until either party gives the other proper notice of termination. Unlike an estate for years, which terminates automatically, a periodic tenancy automatically renews itself at the end of each period, unless one of the parties gives notice. Failure to give proper notice of termination results in the automatic extension of the lease for an additional period.

Like an estate for years, a periodic tenancy is assignable unless assignment is prohibited by the terms of the lease agreement.

Estate at Will. An estate at will is usually created after a periodic tenancy or estate for years has terminated. This estate is created with the agreement of both parties and can be terminated at the will of either. An estate at will often arises when a lease has expired and the parties are in the process of negotiating the terms of a new lease. The term of the tenancy is indefinite; it will continue until either party gives proper notice of termination. Note, however, that unlike an estate for years or periodic tenancy, which are not affected by the death of the landlord or tenant, an estate at will automatically expires upon the death of either the landlord or the tenant. Also, an estate at will is not assignable.

Tenancy at Sufferance. The tenancy at sufferance is the lowest type of estate; in fact, though it's sometimes called an "estate at sufferance," technically it isn't an estate at all. In a tenancy at sufferance, a tenant who came into possession of the property lawfully, under a valid lease, holds over after the lease has expired. The tenant continues in possession of the premises, but without the consent of the landlord.

> **Example:** Joe has a one-year lease with Landlord Sam. At the end of the term, Joe refuses to move out. Joe initially obtained possession of the property legally (under a valid lease), but he is remaining on the property without Sam's consent.

Tenancy at sufferance is simply a way to distinguish between someone who entered into possession of the property legally but no longer has a right to possession, and a trespasser, who never had permission to enter the land in the first place. Because a tenant at sufferance does not hold an estate (a possessory interest in the property), the landlord is not required to give the tenant notice of termination. Even so, the tenant cannot simply be forced off the property; the landlord must follow proper legal procedures for eviction.

Methods of Holding Title

Title to real property may be held by one person, which is ownership in severalty, or it may be held by two or more persons at the same time, which is concurrent ownership.

Ownership in Severalty

When one person holds title to property individually, the property is owned in severalty. The term is derived from the word "sever," which means to keep separate or apart. A sole owner is free to dispose of the property at will. Real property may be owned in severalty by a natural person (a human being) or an artificial person (such as a corporation, a city, or a state).

Concurrent Ownership

Concurrent ownership (also called co-ownership) exists where two or more people simultaneously share title to a piece of property. There are several forms of concurrent ownership, each with distinctive legal characteristics. Under Washington law, three forms of concurrent ownership are recognized:

- tenancy in common,
- joint tenancy, and
- community property.

Tenancy in Common. Tenancy in common is the most basic form of concurrent ownership. In a tenancy in common, two or more individuals each have an **undivided interest** in a single piece of property. This means that each tenant in common has a right to share possession of the whole property, not just a specified part of it. This is referred to as unity of possession.

Tenants in common may have equal or unequal interests. For example, if three people own property as tenants in common, they might each have a one-third interest in the property, or one of them might have a one-half interest in the property and each of the other two a one-quarter interest. But no matter how small a tenant in common's ownership interest is, he is still entitled to share possession of the whole property.

A tenant in common may deed his interest to someone else without obtaining the consent of the other co-tenants. A tenant in common may also mortgage his interest without the others' consent. At death, a tenant in common's interest is transferred according to the terms of his will, or to his legal heirs.

Termination of Tenancy in Common. A tenancy in common may be terminated by a **partition suit**, a legal action that divides the interests in the property and destroys the unity of possession. If possible, a court will actually divide the land into separate parcels. If the property cannot be divided fairly, the court will order the property to be sold and the proceeds divided among the tenants based on their fractional interests.

Joint Tenancy. The second form of concurrent ownership is joint tenancy. In a joint tenancy, two or more individuals are joint and equal owners of the property. The key feature that distinguishes joint tenancy from tenancy in common is the **right of survivorship**: on the death of one of the joint tenants, her interest automatically passes by operation of law to the other joint tenant(s). To create a joint tenancy, the "four unities of title" must exist. These unities are:

- unity of interest,
- unity of title,
- unity of time, and
- unity of possession.

These four unities signify that each joint tenant has an equal interest in the property (unity of interest), that each received title through the same deed or will (unity of title), which was executed and delivered at a single time (unity of time), and that each is entitled to undivided possession of the property (unity of possession). If any one of these unities does not exist when the tenancy is created, a joint tenancy is not established.

Since title passes directly to the other joint tenant(s) upon the death of one joint tenant (because of the right of survivorship), property held in joint tenancy can't be willed. The heirs of a deceased joint tenant have no interest in the joint tenancy property.

Fig. 2.3 Tenancy in common vs. joint tenancy: death of a co-owner

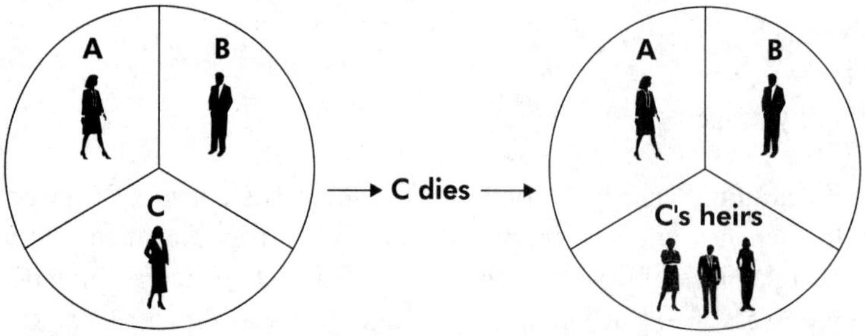

A, B, and C owned property as tenants in common. Then C died, and her heirs inherited her share of the property. Now the property is owned by A, B, and C's heirs as tenants in common.

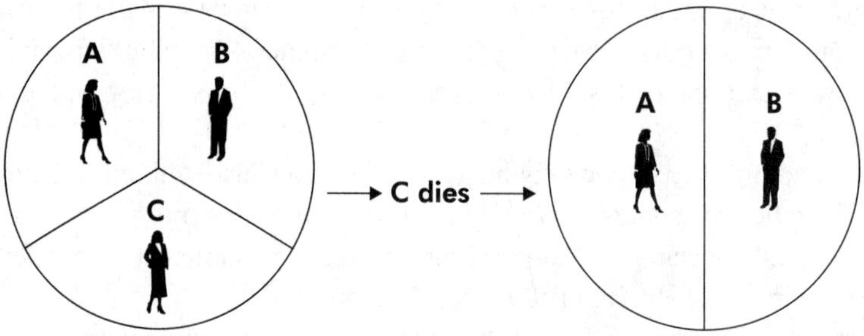

A, B, and C owned property as joint tenants, each with a 1/3 interest. Then C died. Now, by the right of survivorship A and B own the property as joint tenants, each with a 1/2 interest.

Example: Jim, Sue, and Bill own property as joint tenants. Jim dies. Sue and Bill now own the entire property fifty-fifty. Jim's heirs cannot make any legal claim to the property. On his death, it ceased to be a part of his estate. Accordingly, the property is not subject to probate and could not have been willed by Jim.

Avoiding the delay and cost of probate proceedings is one of the primary advantages of joint tenancy. Also, the survivors hold the property free from the claims of the deceased tenant's creditors and from any liens against his interest. The main disadvantage is that a joint tenant gives up the right to dispose of his property by will.

Termination of Joint Tenancy. Like a tenancy in common, a joint tenancy can be terminated through a partition suit. But a joint tenancy also terminates automatically if any one of the four unities is destroyed. A joint tenant is free to convey her interest in the property to someone else. However, a conveyance destroys the unities of time and title. This terminates the joint tenancy with respect to the ownership of the conveying joint tenant.

Example: Aaron, Bob, and Caroline own a piece of property as joint tenants. If Aaron conveys his interest to Alice, that terminates the joint tenancy with respect to that one-third interest. Since Alice did not receive title through the same deed or at the same time as Bob and Caroline, Alice can't be a joint tenant. Bob and Caroline are still joint tenants in relation to one another, but Alice holds title as a tenant in common.

Community Property. The community property system of ownership is of Spanish origin; for historical reasons, it is used in several western states, including Washington. In those states, all the property owned by a married couple is classified either as the **separate property** of one spouse or as the **community property** of both spouses.

A spouse's separate property is the property he or she owned before the marriage, and any property he or she acquires during the marriage by inheritance, will, or gift. All other property a spouse acquires during the marriage is community property. For example, property purchased with wages earned by either spouse during the marriage is community property. Each spouse has an undivided one-half interest in the community property.

The separate property of either spouse is free from the interests and claims of the other spouse; it may be transferred or encumbered without the approval or interference of the other spouse. A conveyance or encumbrance of community real property, however, requires the approval of both spouses. (With certain exceptions, such as household furnishings, community personal property can be transferred without spousal consent.)

In some states that do not have a community property system, married couples may hold title to property as tenants by the entireties. A **tenancy by the entireties** is quite similar to a joint tenancy, but there are some differences. A tenancy by the entireties can only be created by a married couple, and (unlike a joint tenant) a tenant by the entireties cannot convey his interest without the other tenant's consent. Tenancy by the entireties is not recognized in community property states such as Washington, and it has been abolished in a number of other states as well.

Forms of Business Ownership

The discussion so far has focused on real property ownership by individuals, whether in severalty or concurrently. Real property can also be owned by business entities.

A **syndicate** is a group of individuals who come together and pool their resources to carry out an enterprise. The syndicate, as such, is not a recognized legal entity. A syndicate may be a business association or a nonprofit organization, and it may be organized as one of the following legally recognized entities:

- partnership,
- corporation,
- limited liability company,
- joint venture, or
- trust.

The parties who create a syndicate usually decide which form of organization to use based on tax consequences and other considerations, such as the members' personal liability for the syndicate's debts. The form of organization affects how a syndicate holds title to real property.

Partnerships. A partnership is generally defined as an association of two or more persons, to carry on, as co-owners, a business for profit. There are two types of partnerships: general and limited.

A **general partnership** is formed by contract. The contract does not have to be in writing, although a written agreement is always advisable. If an aspect of the partnership is addressed in the partnership agreement, it is governed by that agreement. Any aspect not addressed by the agreement is governed by Washington's Uniform Partnership Act.

The partners in a general partnership all share in the profits and management of the partnership. Unless otherwise agreed, each one has an equal share of the profits and losses, and each has an equal voice in management and control of the business. Each partner can be held personally liable for the debts of the partnership.

Also, each partner is both a principal for and an agent of the general partnership for business purposes. Thus, the authorized acts of one partner (including the execution of legal documents) are binding on the partnership. A partnership is a fiduciary relationship; all the partners have a duty to act with utmost good faith toward one another. (See Chapter 7 for a discussion of agency.)

In general, property acquired for the partnership's business is **partnership property**. Title to partnership property may be held in the partnership's name. Alternatively, it may be held in the name of one or more of the partners, as long as the deed makes reference to the partnership.

Unless otherwise agreed, each partner has an equal right to possess and use all partnership property for partnership purposes. However, a partner is not a co-owner of the partnership property and has no transferable interest in it.

When title to partnership property is held in the partnership's name, it must also be conveyed in the partnership's name. Since each partner is an agent for the partnership, any authorized partner can sign the deed.

A **limited partnership** is a partnership with one or more general partners and one or more limited partners. Limited partnerships must conform to the statutory requirements of the Uniform Limited Partnership Act. To establish a limited partnership, a certificate of limited partnership must be filed with the secretary of state's office.

The general partners in a limited partnership have unlimited liability for the partnership's debts and obligations. By contrast, the limited partners have limited liability (that is, they cannot be held personally liable for the partnership's debts and obligations). The Uniform Limited Partnership Act originally allowed only the general partners to manage or control the partnership's business; limited partners would lose their limited liability if they participated in management or control. The act now allows limited partners full participation without affecting their limited liability.

Corporations. A corporation is owned by its shareholders, individuals who purchase shares of stock in the company as an investment. But the corporation is legally a separate entity from its shareholders. In the eyes of the law, a corporation is an "artificial person." It can enter into contracts, own property, and incur debts and liabilities, just like a natural person (a human individual).

Shares in a corporation are **securities**. A security is an investment interest; it gives an investor a financial interest in an enterprise without allowing direct managerial control. (Limited partnership interests may also be classified as securities.) Sales of securities are regulated by the federal Securities and Exchange Commission. They may also be subject to state securities regulations, commonly called "blue sky laws." Generally, only licensed securities dealers may sell securities.

A corporation is capable of perpetual existence; the death of a shareholder does not affect its operation. Corporate property is owned by the corporation in severalty, not by the shareholders. The shareholders own only a right to share in the profits of the business. Their liability is limited.

The main drawback to the corporate form of organization is the double taxation that applies to all but the smallest corporations. First the corporation must pay income taxes on any profits it generates. Then if the profits are distributed to the shareholders as dividends, the same money is taxed again as the personal income of the shareholders. Business investors can avoid double taxation by choosing a different form of organization, such as a partnership, a limited liability company, or a trust.

A corporation formed under the laws of Washington is called a **domestic corporation**. All other corporations, incorporated in other states or foreign countries, are called foreign corporations. Foreign corporations may conduct business in Washington, but they must obtain a certificate of good standing (also called a certificate of authority) from the secretary of state and abide by any conditions or limitations imposed.

Note that a corporation cannot co-own property in joint tenancy. Since a corporation has a potentially perpetual existence, the other joint tenant could not really have a right of survivorship. Thus, when a corporation co-owns real property with another entity or person, it holds title as a tenant in common.

Limited Liability Companies. A limited liability company (LLC) combines many of the advantages of a corporation with many of the advantages of a partnership.

To create an LLC, one or more business owners (called members) enter into an LLC agreement and file a certificate of formation with the state. In their agreement, members can specify virtually any manner of allocating income, losses, or appreciation among themselves.

LLC members have the flexibility of a general partnership when it comes to managing the business. Certain members may be appointed to manage the company, or all of the members may manage the company. All managing members can bind the LLC with their actions. However, unlike general partners, managing members are not personally liable for the company's contractual liabilities. LLC members have the same type of limited liability enjoyed by corporate stockholders or limited partners.

As explained above, a major disadvantage of the corporate form of ownership is the double taxation imposed on corporations and their stockholders. In contrast, income earned by an LLC is taxed at only one level—the member level. LLC income is taxed as the personal income of each member, in the same manner as partnership income.

Joint Ventures. A joint venture is similar to a partnership, except that it is created for a single business transaction or for a series of individual transactions. It is not intended to be an ongoing business of indefinite duration. Joint ventures are generally governed by the same rules as partnerships. An example of a joint venture would be a property owner, an architect, and a building contractor joining together to design and construct a particular building.

Trusts. In a trust, one or more trustees manage property for the benefit of one or more **beneficiaries**. A trust instrument vests title to the property in the trustees, who have only the powers expressly granted in the instrument.

Trusts are sometimes used as a form of business ownership. One example is a **real estate investment trust** (REIT). Investors form REITs to finance large real estate projects. REITs are not subject to double taxation if they meet certain requirements set by the IRS. For example, a real estate investment trust must have at least 100 investors, and at least 75% of its investment assets must be in real estate.

As long as a qualifying REIT distributes at least 90% of its income to its investors, the REIT pays income taxes only on the earnings it retains, avoiding double taxation. Yet the investors, like corporate shareholders, are shielded from liability for the REIT's debts. REIT shares are securities, subject to federal regulation.

Condominiums and Cooperatives

Condominiums and cooperatives provide alternatives to ownership of a traditional single-family home. In a sense, they combine aspects of individual ownership with aspects of concurrent ownership.

Condominiums. In Washington, the development and management of condominium properties are governed by a state statute called the Condominium Act.

Someone who buys a unit in a condominium owns the unit itself in severalty, but shares ownership of the common elements with other unit owners as tenants in common. **Common elements** (also called common areas) are aspects of the condominium property that all of the unit owners have the right to use, such as the driveway or the elevator.

Some features may be designated as **limited common elements**, which are reserved for the owners of certain units. For example, an assigned parking space would be a limited common element. A feature such as a balcony, which is designed for use with a particular unit but is outside of the unit itself, would also be a limited common element.

Each unit owner obtains separate financing to buy her unit, receives an individual property tax bill, and may acquire a title insurance policy for the unit. A lien can attach to a single unit, so that the unit can be foreclosed on separately, without affecting the other units in the condominium. The sale of a unit ordinarily doesn't require the approval of the other unit owners. The seller's interest in the common elements passes to the buyer.

All the unit owners in a condominium automatically belong to a homeowners association (sometimes called a unit or condo owners association). The association elects a board of directors to manage the condominium, and also votes on other major issues. For example, monthly fees are usually imposed on each unit owner to cover maintenance costs for the common elements. (Note that subdivisions of townhomes or single-family homes also have homeowners associations.)

A condominium usually involves one or more multi-family residential buildings, but commercial and industrial properties can also be developed as condominiums. To establish a condominium, the developer must record a condominium plan and declaration. A large condominium project may be regulated as a subdivision.

Sometimes the owner of an apartment complex will find it profitable to change the complex into a condominium. This process, called **conversion**, is regulated to protect renters who will be displaced.

Cooperatives. In a cooperative, ownership of the property is vested in a single entity—usually a corporation. The residents of the cooperative building own shares in the corporation, rather than owning the property itself. They are tenants with long-term proprietary leases on their units; they do not hold title to their units.

To establish a cooperative, the corporation gets a mortgage loan to buy or construct the building, and other funds are raised by selling shares in the corporation to prospective tenants. The rent that each tenant pays to the corporation is a pro rata share of the mortgage, taxes, operating expenses, and other debts for the whole property. The cooperative corporation is managed by an elected board of directors.

In many cooperatives, a tenant cannot transfer stock or assign his proprietary lease without the consent of the governing board or a majority of the members. This approval process is used to screen out undesirable tenants; however, discrimination in violation of fair housing laws is not allowed (see Chapter 15).

Differences Between Condominiums and Cooperatives. In a condominium, each unit is owned individually. In a cooperative, a corporation owns the whole project; the tenants own shares in the corporation and have proprietary leases on their units.

In a condominium, each unit owner secures individual financing to buy the unit. In a cooperative, the corporation takes out one blanket loan for the entire project. One advantage of condominiums over cooperatives is that a condominium owner is not responsible for any default on another unit owner's loan. In a cooperative, if one tenant defaults on her share of the mortgage payments, the other tenants must cure the default or risk having the mortgage on the entire project foreclosed. This is also true for tax assessments and other liens.

A condominium owner can usually sell his unit to anyone who can pay for it. In a cooperative, the corporation usually must approve of the proposed tenant.

Timeshares. Sometimes condominium units are offered for sale under a **timeshare** arrangement. Instead of purchasing a unit outright, a timeshare buyer purchases a right to occupy the unit during a particular time slot each year. Most timeshare condominiums are located in resort areas, where people often want a place to stay for a limited time on a regular basis.

> **Example:** The Garcias like to vacation in Ocean Shores for two weeks every year. Buying a condominium unit there would be expensive and unnecessary, so they decide to buy an interest in a timeshare condominium called the Sea Winds. This entitles them to occupy Unit 6 in the Sea Winds condo every year from July 1 through July 14. Other buyers have the right to occupy Unit 6 during the rest of the year.

The **Washington Timeshare Act** is a consumer protection law that governs the sale of timeshares in this state. It requires timeshare developments to be registered with the Department of Licensing, and also requires people involved in selling timeshares to be registered as **timeshare salespersons**.

Under the Timeshare Act, prospective buyers of timeshare interests must be given a disclosure statement. The law gives buyers a seven-day right of rescission—the right to cancel their purchase and sale agreement within seven days after signing the agreement or receiving the disclosure statement, whichever occurs later.

A real estate licensee is allowed to handle timeshare resales without registering under the Timeshare Act as a timeshare salesperson. The licensee must be acting solely in a brokerage capacity, not selling inventory that she owns herself or that's owned by her firm.

Even though real estate licensees are exempt from the Timeshare Act's registration requirement, they still have to comply with all of the other aspects of the law. For example, they must give buyers a disclosure statement and allow a seven-day right of rescission, just like registered timeshare sellers.

Chapter Summary

1. An estate is a possessory interest in real property. Someone who has a freehold estate has title to the property and is considered an owner. Someone who has a leasehold (less-than-freehold) estate has possession of the property, but does not have title.

2. Freehold estates include the fee simple absolute, the qualified fee, and the life estate. A life estate lasts only as long as a specified person is alive; then the property either reverts to the grantor or else passes to the remainderman. Leasehold estates include the estate for years, the periodic estate, and the estate at will. (The tenancy at sufferance, which arises when a tenant holds over without the landlord's permission, is not really an estate.)

3. Title to real property can be held in severalty or concurrently. In Washington, the methods of concurrent ownership are joint tenancy, tenancy in common, and community property. The distinguishing feature of joint tenancy is the right of survivorship.

4. Real property can be owned by a syndicate, which may be organized as a general or limited partnership, a corporation, a limited liability company, a joint venture, or a real estate investment trust.

5. In a condominium, each unit is separately owned, and all the unit owners own the common elements as tenants in common. A cooperative is owned by a corporation; a resident owns shares in the corporation, and has a proprietary lease for a particular unit. In a timeshare arrangement, a buyer purchases the right to occupy a condominium unit for a specified period each year.

🔑 Key Terms

Estate—An interest in land that is or may become possessory.

Freehold estate—A possessory interest that has an indeterminable duration.

Leasehold estate—A possessory interest that has a limited duration.

Fee simple absolute—The highest and most complete form of ownership, which is of potentially infinite duration.

Qualified fee—A fee simple estate that carries a qualification, so that ownership may revert to the grantor if a specified event occurs or a condition is not met. Also called a defeasible fee.

Life estate—A freehold estate whose duration is measured by the lifetime of one or more persons.

Waste—Permanent damage to real property caused by the party in possession, harming the interests of other estate holders.

Estate for years—A leasehold estate with a fixed term. Also called a term tenancy.

Periodic tenancy—A leasehold estate that is renewed at the end of each period unless one party gives notice of termination.

Estate at will—A leasehold estate without a definite termination date that may arise after a periodic tenancy or an estate for years terminates. Also called a tenancy at will.

Ownership in severalty—Sole ownership of property.

Tenancy in common—Joint ownership where there is no right of survivorship.

Joint tenancy—Joint ownership with right of survivorship.

Right of survivorship—The right by which the surviving joint tenant(s) acquire another joint tenant's interest in the property upon her death.

Community property—Property owned jointly by husband and wife (in Washington and other community property states).

Corporation—An artificial person; a legal entity separate from its shareholders.

Limited liability company—A form of business entity that offers limited liability and tax benefits.

Real estate investment trust—A real estate investment business that qualifies for tax advantages if certain requirements are met.

Condominium—A property that has been developed so that individual unit owners have separate title to their own units, but share ownership of the common elements as tenants in common.

Cooperative—A property that is owned by a corporation and tenanted by shareholders in the corporation who have proprietary leases for their units.

Timeshare—An interest in a condominium unit that entitles the holder to occupy the unit during a specified time slot every year.

Chapter Quiz

1. A fee simple title in real estate is of indefinite duration, and can be:

   a) freely transferred
   b) encumbered
   c) inherited
   d) All of the above

2. A conveyance of title with the condition that the land shall not be used for the sale of intoxicating beverages creates a:

   a) less-than-freehold estate
   b) qualified fee
   c) life estate
   d) reservation

3. Lewis was given real property for the term of his natural life. Which of the following statements is incorrect?

   a) Lewis has a freehold estate
   b) Lewis has a fee simple estate
   c) Lewis is the life tenant
   d) If Lewis leases the property to someone else, the lease will terminate if Lewis dies during its term

4. Baker sold a property to Lane, but reserved a life estate for himself and remained in possession. Later Baker sells his life estate to Clark and surrenders possession to Clark. Lane then demands immediate possession as fee owner. Which of the following is true?

   a) Lane is entitled to possession
   b) Clark should sue Baker for return of the purchase price
   c) Baker is liable for damages
   d) Clark can retain possession during Baker's lifetime

5. Cobb owns a property in fee simple; he deeds it to Smith for the life of Jones. Which of the following is true?

   a) Jones holds a life estate; Smith holds an estate in reversion
   b) Smith holds a life estate; Cobb holds an estate in remainder
   c) Smith holds a fee simple estate; Jones holds a life estate
   d) Smith holds a life estate; Cobb holds an estate in reversion

6. Johnston, a life tenant, decides to cut down all the trees on the property and sell them for timber. Mendez, the remainderman, can stop Johnston's actions because:

   a) a life tenant is never permitted to cut down any trees on the property for any reason
   b) a life tenant cannot commit waste
   c) Mendez's interest is superior to Johnston's, since it is a possessory estate
   d) None of the above; Mendez has no legal grounds for stopping Johnston

7. Jones and Adams signed an agreement for the use and possession of real estate, for a period of 120 days. This is a/an:

   a) estate for years
   b) estate at sufferance
   c) periodic tenancy
   d) estate at will

8. The four unities of title, time, interest, and possession are necessary for a:

   a) tenancy in common
   b) partnership
   c) mortgage
   d) joint tenancy

9. Which of the following is incorrect? Joint tenants always have:

   a) equal rights to possession of the property
   b) the right to will good title to heirs
   c) the right of survivorship
   d) equal interests in the property

10. A, B, and C own property as joint tenants. C dies and B sells her interest in the property to D. The property is now owned:

    a) as joint tenants by A, D, and C's widow E, his sole heir
    b) by A and D as joint tenants
    c) by A and D as tenants in common
    d) None of the above

11. Asher and Blake own real property together. Asher has a one-third interest and Blake has a two-thirds interest. How do they hold title?

    a) Community property
    b) Tenancy at will
    c) Joint tenancy
    d) Tenancy in common

12. All of the following statements about a corporation are true, except:

    a) A corporation has a potentially perpetual existence
    b) Each shareholder is individually liable for the corporation's acts
    c) Corporations are subject to double taxation
    d) A corporation can enter into contracts in essentially the same way as an individual person

13. A real estate investment trust is required to:

    a) invest at least 75% of its assets in real estate
    b) have at least 150 participating investors
    c) make sure all investors accept liability for the trust's acts
    d) be incorporated in the state in which it does business

14. In a condominium:

    a) individual units are owned in severalty, while common elements are owned in joint tenancy
    b) individual units are owned in joint tenancy, while common elements are owned in severalty
    c) individual units are owned in severalty, while common elements are owned in tenancy in common
    d) the entire building is owned in tenancy in common, with residents owning shares

15. A unit in a cooperative is owned:

    a) in severalty by its resident
    b) by the corporation that owns the building, in which the resident owns shares
    c) in tenancy in common among all residents of the building
    d) in partnership among all residents of the building

👉 Answer Key

1. d) A fee simple owner has the full bundle of rights.

2. b) A qualified fee (or defeasible fee) is an estate that will fail if a certain event occurs.

3. b) Although a life estate is a freehold estate, it is not a fee simple estate.

4. d) Baker was entitled to sell his life estate to Clark. Clark can retain possession during Baker's lifetime.

5. d) Smith has possession of the property for the duration of Jones's life, so Smith has a life estate. Cobb has an estate in reversion, because the property will revert to Cobb after Jones's death.

6. b) A life tenant cannot commit waste, which means that the life tenant cannot damage the property or harm the interests of the remainderman. Severely depleting the property's resources—for example, by cutting down all of the timber or extracting all of the minerals—would constitute waste.

7. a) An estate for years has a set termination date.

8. d) A valid joint tenancy requires all four unities: title, time, interest, possession.

9. b) A joint tenant cannot will his interest in the property. The right of survivorship means the surviving joint tenants acquire the deceased tenant's title.

10. c) When C dies, his interest in the property goes to the other joint tenants, A and B. When B sells her interest to D, the joint tenancy is terminated and a tenancy in common is created between A and D.

11. d) Because their interests in the property are unequal, Asher and Blake must be tenants in common.

12. b) A corporation's shareholders have limited liability for the corporation's actions.

13. a) A real estate investment trust must invest at least 75% of its assets in real estate. The minimum number of investors is 100, not 150.

14. c) In a condominium, residents own their individual units in severalty, but own the common elements as tenants in common.

15. b) A cooperative is owned by a business entity, usually a corporation. Residents purchase shares in the corporation and receive long-term leases, rather than title to their units.

Transfer of Real Property

⌂ Chapter Overview

*A property owner may transfer property to someone else by choice, as when
an owner deeds property to a buyer or wills it to a friend. Property may also be
transferred involuntarily, as in a foreclosure sale or a condemnation. This chapter describes both voluntary and involuntary transfers. It also discusses how and why deeds
and other documents are recorded, and how title insurance works.*

Alienation

A person who owns property is said to have **title** to it. The process of transferring title to real property (transferring ownership) from one party to another is called
alienation. Alienation may be either voluntary or involuntary. Voluntary alienation
includes transferring property by deed or will. Involuntary alienation, a transfer of
property without any action by the owner, can be the result of rules of law, accession,
or occupancy (adverse possession).

Voluntary Alienation

Patents

Title to all real property originates with the sovereign government. The government holds absolute title to all the land within its boundaries, except what it grants to
various other entities or persons. Title to land passes from the government to a private party by a document known as a **patent**. The patent is the ultimate source of title
for all the land under private ownership.

Deeds

The most common form of voluntary alienation is transfer by deed. With a deed,
the owner of real property, called the **grantor**, conveys all or part of his interest in
the property to another party, called the **grantee**. The process of transferring real
property by deed is known as conveyance. A grantor conveys real property to a grantee by means of a deed.

Types of Deeds. There are many different types of deeds. The ones used most often
in Washington are the warranty deed, special warranty deed, quitclaim deed, trustee's
deed, and deed executed under court order.

Warranty Deed. The warranty deed (also known as the general warranty deed)
gives the greatest protection to a real estate buyer. Under a warranty deed, the grantor
makes five basic promises, or covenants, to the grantee. These covenants warrant
against defects in the title that arose either before or during the grantor's period of
ownership (tenure). When a statutory warranty deed form is used, the covenants are
implied; they do not have to be expressly stated in the deed.

The first covenant is called the **covenant of seisin**. Seisin means peaceable possession under color of title. Color of title means a good faith belief in ownership. So the covenant of seisin promises that the grantor actually owns the property interest she is transferring to the grantee.

The second covenant is the **covenant of right to convey**. The grantor promises she has the power to make the conveyance. In other words, the grantor either has title to the interest, or is an agent of the owner with the authority to transfer the interest.

The **covenant against encumbrances** warrants that the property is not burdened by any easement, mortgage, lien, or other right of a third party. If such encumbrances do exist, they must be listed in the deed.

The fourth covenant is the **covenant of quiet enjoyment**. This covenant promises that the grantee's possession of the property will not be threatened by any lawful claim made by a third party. It does not protect the grantee from claims that have no legal basis, called spurious claims.

The final covenant in the warranty deed is the **covenant of warranty**. This is a promise that the grantor will defend the grantee's title against any claims superior to the grantee's that exist when the conveyance is made.

Special Warranty Deed. The special warranty deed contains the same covenants found in the general warranty deed, but the scope of the covenants is limited to defects that arose during the grantor's tenure. The grantor makes no assurances regarding defects that may have existed before he obtained title. This type of deed is most often used by entities such as corporations or trusts that hold land only temporarily for fiduciary purposes, and do not want to assume the level of liability imposed by a general warranty deed.

A warranty deed (general or special) conveys the "after-acquired title" of the grantor. This means that if the grantor's title was defective at the time of transfer, but the grantor later acquires a more perfect title, the additional interest passes automatically to the grantee under the original deed.

> **Example:** Warner conveyed her property to Meyers on June 1, by a warranty deed. However, Warner did not have valid title to the property on June 1 because she held title under a forged deed. On August 12, Warner received good title to the property under a properly executed deed. Meyers automatically acquired good title to the property on August 12.

Quitclaim Deed. The quitclaim deed contains no warranties of any sort, and it does not convey after-acquired title. It conveys only the interest the grantor has when the deed is delivered. It conveys nothing at all if the grantor has no interest at that time. But if the grantor does have an interest in the property, the quitclaim deed will convey it just as well as any other type of deed.

The usual reason for using a quitclaim deed is to cure "clouds" on the title; in such situations, a quitclaim deed may be referred to as a **reformation deed**. A cloud is a title defect, often the result of a technical flaw in an earlier conveyance. Perhaps one of the parties' names was misspelled, or the land was inaccurately described. A quitclaim deed is also used when the grantor is unsure of the validity of her title and wishes to avoid giving any warranties.

> **Example:** Smith holds title by virtue of an inheritance that is being challenged in probate court. If Smith wants to transfer the property, she will probably use a quitclaim deed, because she is not sure that her title is valid.

Fig. 3.1 Warranty deed

AFTER RECORDING MAIL TO:
Joseph and Hannah Shapiro
3406 N.W. 66th St.
Anytown 99999

Filed for Record at Request of
Acme Escrow Co.
Escrow Number: 001021SHA

Statutory Warranty Deed

Grantor(s): Alan S. Matsumoto
Grantee(s): Joseph R. Shapiro, Hannah L. Shapiro
Abbreviated Legal: Lot 12, Block 8, Jasperson Add., Vol. 10, p. 94
Additional Legal(s) on page: N/A
Assessor's Tax Parcel Number(s): 117600-0720-05

THE GRANTOR   Alan S. Matsumoto

for and in consideration of TEN DOLLARS AND OTHER GOOD AND VALUABLE CONSIDERATION

in hand paid, conveys and warrants to Joseph R. Shapiro and Hannah L. Shapiro,
a married couple
the following described real estate, situated in the County of Thurston , State of Washington:

LOT 12, BLOCK 8, JASPERSON ADDITION TO THE CITY OF ANYTOWN,
ACCORDING TO THE PLAT THEREOF RECORDED IN VOLUME 10 OF PLATS, PAGE 94,
RECORDS OF THURSTON COUNTY, WASHINGTON.
SITUATE IN THE COUNTY OF THURSTON, STATE OF WASHINGTON.

Dated this _21_ day of _____February_____ , 20 _15_

By _Alan S. Matsumoto_   By _____
   Alan S. Matsumoto
By _____   By _____

STATE OF WASHINGTON   }
County of THURSTON   } SS:

I certify that I know or have satisfactory evidence that _____ALAN S. MATSUMOTO_____

_IS_ the person(s) who appeared before me, and said person(s) acknowledged that _HE_ signed this instrument
and acknowledged it to be _HIS_ free and voluntary act for the uses and purposes mentioned in this instrument.

Dated: ___FEBRUARY 21, 2015___   _Claire M. Vincent_
                                         CLAIRE M. VINCENT
                                         Notary Public in and for the State of ___WASHINGTON___

| CLAIRE M. VINCENT |
| STATE OF WASHINGTON |
| NOTARY --[]-- PUBLIC |
| MY COMMISSION |
| EXPIRES 1-16-19 |

Residing at FIFE
My appointment expires: _01-16-19_

1502210094

In a quitclaim deed, words such as "grant" or "convey" should be avoided. The use of these words may imply that the grantor is warranting the title. A quitclaim deed should use only terms such as "release," "remise," or "quitclaim" to describe the transfer.

Trustee's Deed. When property is foreclosed under a deed of trust, the trustee conveys the property to the buyer at the foreclosure sale with a trustee's deed. The trustee's deed states that the conveyance is in accordance with the trustee's powers and responsibilities under the deed of trust. (Deeds of trust are discussed in Chapter 10.)

Deeds Executed by Court Order. Court-ordered deeds are used after a court-ordered sale of property. A common example is the sheriff's deed used to transfer property to the highest bidder at a court-ordered foreclosure sale (see Chapter 10). Court-ordered deeds usually state the exact amount of the purchase price approved by the court, and carry no warranties of title.

Requisites of a Valid Deed. A deed will transfer title only if it meets the requirements for validity. To be valid, a deed must:

- be in writing,
- identify the parties,
- be signed by a competent grantor,
- have a living grantee,
- contain words of conveyance (the granting clause), and
- include an adequate description of the property.

In Writing. The **statute of frauds** is a state law that requires certain contracts and other legal transactions to be in writing. With only a few minor exceptions, the statute of frauds applies to any transfer of an interest in real property. An unwritten deed cannot transfer title; it has no legal effect.

Identification of the Parties. Both the grantor and the grantee must be identified in the deed. The name of the grantee is not required, as long as an adequate description is given; for example, "John T. Smith's only sister."

Signed by a Competent Grantor. In addition to requiring a deed to be in writing, the statute of frauds also requires that the deed must be signed by the party who is to be bound by the transfer—the grantor.

A grantor must be legally competent when she signs the deed. This means she must be an adult (at least 18 years old) and of sound mind (not insane or mentally impaired in some other way). If the grantor is not competent, the deed is not valid.

If the grantor can't sign her full name (due to disability or illiteracy), she may sign by making a mark. But a signature by mark must be accompanied by the signatures of witnesses who can attest to the grantor's execution of the deed.

A deed can also be signed by the grantor's **attorney in fact**. The attorney in fact (not necessarily a lawyer) is someone the grantor has appointed to act on her behalf in a document called a **power of attorney**. The power of attorney must specifically authorize the attorney in fact to convey the property.

Deeds from corporations are usually signed by an authorized officer of the corporation.

If there is more than one grantor, all of the grantors must sign the deed. If a prior deed named several grantees, all of them must sign as grantors of a new deed. The signatures of both spouses are required to convey community property (see Chapter 2). For this reason, it is a good idea (although not required) to state the grantor's marital status in the deed and to obtain the spouse's signature if the grantor is married, even if the property is not community property.

Living Grantee. The grantee does not have to be competent in order for the deed to be valid. It is only necessary for the grantee to be alive (or, if the grantee is a corporation, legally in existence) and identifiable when the deed is executed.

Words of Conveyance. The requirement of words of conveyance, also called a granting clause, is easily satisfied. The single word "grant" or a similar word is sufficient. Additional technical language should be avoided, since it adds nothing to the validity of the deed and could do more harm than good.

Description of the Property. A valid deed must contain an adequate description of the property to be conveyed. A legal description of the property should always be included. (Land description is discussed in Chapter 1.)

Acknowledgment, Delivery, and Acceptance. To successfully convey real property, more than a valid deed is necessary; a proper conveyance also requires acknowledgment, delivery, and acceptance.

Acknowledgment occurs when the grantor swears before a notary public or other official witness that her signature is genuine and voluntary. The witness cannot be a person who has an interest in the transfer. For example, if Grandma deeds her property to Granddaughter, who is a notary public, Granddaughter should not be the one to notarize the deed.

Technically, a deed may be considered valid even if the grantor's signature is not acknowledged. However, an unacknowledged deed cannot be recorded.

To transfer title, a deed must be **delivered** to the grantee. Traditionally, delivery had to occur while the grantor was alive. However, Washington recently began allowing "transfer on death deeds." A transfer on death deed will transfer title to the grantee automatically and without probate when the grantor dies. The grantor can revoke the deed at any time before dying. The deed must state that the transfer will take place on the grantor's death, and it must be recorded.

Acceptance of a valid deed by the grantee completes a property transfer. A grantee may refuse to accept a deed (this occasionally happens because of liability concerns or tax considerations, for example). Note that the grantee may accept delivery through an agent.

> **Example:** Clark deeds his property to Martinez. Clark hands the deed to Martinez's attorney, with the intention of immediately transferring ownership to Martinez. This is considered delivery to an agent of the grantee, and the deed is valid.

Because delivery of a deed involves some complicated legal issues, a real estate lawyer should be consulted when there is a question concerning delivery.

Non-essential Terms. There are some elements that should be included in a deed, even though they aren't required. A deed should include a **habendum clause** (also called a "to have and to hold" clause), which states the nature of the interest the grantor is conveying. Is the grantor conveying a fee simple absolute or a life estate? Unless otherwise specified, the grantor's entire interest is presumed to pass to the grantee. If there is more than one grantee, the deed should say how they will hold title (for example, whether this is a tenancy in common or a joint tenancy).

Many deeds have an **exclusions and reservations clause**, which is a list of any encumbrances (easements, private restrictions, or liens) that the grantee will be taking title subject to. However, valid encumbrances usually remain in force even if they aren't listed in the deed.

A recital of the purchase price is helpful because it indicates that the transfer is a purchase instead of a gift. (If the transfer were a gift, the grantee might be vulnerable to the claims of the grantor's creditors.) The recital of consideration usually says something like, "for $1.00 and other valuable consideration."

The date of conveyance is standard, but not legally required. Other non-essential items include the grantor's seal, warranties, and technical terminology. "I hereby grant Greenacres Farm to Harry Carter. (signed) Sam Smith" is a valid deed, assuming that Sam Smith is legally competent. Note that the grantee does not ordinarily sign the deed.

Wills

The will (or testament) is another method of voluntary alienation. In general, a will must be:

1. in writing,
2. signed by the person making it (the testator), and
3. attested to by at least two competent witnesses.

The will must be signed by the testator in the presence of the witnesses. The witnesses must also sign an acknowledgment that the testator declared the document to be his will.

Although ordinarily a will must be in writing to be valid, under certain circumstances Washington will recognize an oral will, sometimes called a **nuncupative** will. An oral will can be valid if spoken while the testator is on her deathbed with two witnesses present. But if the testator recovers, the will is no longer valid. An oral will can transfer only personal property worth less than $1,000. Real estate can never be transferred by an oral will, since all transfers involving real property must be in writing.

Some states recognize **holographic** wills. A holographic will is an unwitnessed will written entirely in the testator's own handwriting. Washington law does not recognize holographic wills. A holographic will can be valid in Washington only if the testator executes it in a state where holographic wills are valid, then later moves to Washington and does not make out a new will.

Terminology. The person who makes a will is referred to as the **testator**. A testator **bequeaths** personal property to **legatees** and **devises** real property to **devisees**. An amendment to a will is called a **codicil**. The directions contained in the will are carried out by an **executor** named in the will, under the supervision of the probate court (in Washington, the superior court). **Probate** is the procedure by which a will is proved valid and the testator's directions are carried out. If no executor is

---

Fig. 3.2 Will terminology

> **Testator**: One who makes a will.
>
> **Bequeath**: To transfer personal property by will.
>
> **Devise**: To transfer real property by will.
>
> **Executor**: Appointed by the testator to carry out the instructions in the will.
>
> **Administrator**: Appointed by the court if no executor was named.
>
> **Probate**: Procedure to prove a will's validity.

named in the will, the court will appoint an **administrator** to manage and distribute the estate.

Probate Procedures. A will does not convey any interest until the testator has died and the will has been probated. Depending on the procedures followed, all conveyances of real property under the will may have to be approved by the probate court. The court also approves any brokerage commissions pertaining to such conveyances.

Involuntary Alienation

The patent, the deed, and the will are the three most common methods of transferring property voluntarily. We will now look at the different ways interests in real property can be transferred without any voluntary action on the part of the owner.

Involuntary alienation of real property can be the result of rule of law, adverse possession, or accession. Alienation by rule of law includes dedication, intestate succession and escheat, condemnation, and court decisions regarding real property.

Dedication

When a private owner gives real property to the public, it is called dedication. While dedication may be voluntary (for example, a philanthropist might deed land to the city for a park, as a gift), it is usually involuntary. Most often it is required in exchange for a benefit from a public entity.

> **Example:** The county requires a land developer to dedicate land within a new subdivision for public streets. Otherwise, the county will deny permission to subdivide.

This type of involuntary dedication is called **statutory dedication** because it involves compliance with relevant statutory procedures. In the example above, the subdivision statutes require that land for streets and utilities must be dedicated before a parcel can be subdivided.

A second type of involuntary dedication is called **common law dedication**. The usual requirement for common law dedication is the owner's acquiescence in the public's use of her property for a prolonged period of time. If property has been used by the public for long enough, a government entity can pass an ordinance accepting a common law dedication. The dedication may be treated as a transfer of ownership, or it may only establish a public easement, depending on the circumstances.

> **Example:** Barker owns some lakefront property. For many years, people from town have walked across a corner of the lot to gain access to the lake, and Barker has done nothing to prevent this. Barker's acquiescence to this public use might be considered a common law dedication.

Intestate Succession and Escheat

When someone dies without leaving a will, he is said to have died intestate. The law provides for the division of his property by a process called **intestate succession**.

The procedure varies from state to state, but in general the property passes first to the surviving spouse, then to any surviving children, then to various other relatives.

Persons who take property by intestate succession are called **heirs**. Those who receive property by intestate succession are said to have received property by **descent**, rather than by devise or bequest. Intestate succession is supervised by the probate court. The court appoints an administrator, who is responsible for distributing the property in the manner required by the intestate succession statutes.

If a person dies intestate and the probate court can't locate any heirs, then the intestate person's property will pass back to the state according to the law of **escheat**. Since the state is the ultimate source of title to property, it is also the ultimate heir when there are no intervening interested parties. The state may also take ownership of abandoned property through escheat.

Condemnation

The government has the constitutional power to take private property for public use, as long as it pays compensation to the owner of the property. Taking property in this way is called **condemnation**. The government's power to condemn property is called the power of **eminent domain**. Before the power of eminent domain can be exercised, the following requirements must be met:

- The proposed use must be a **public use**—that is, it must benefit the public. Taking property for a public park would qualify as a public use. In cases of mixed public and private benefit the question is more difficult, but generally there is no authority for the government to take one person's land for the sole purpose of turning it over to another person.
- The condemning entity must pay **just compensation** to the owner. As a general rule, just compensation is the fair market value of the property.

The power of eminent domain may be exercised by any government entity, and also by some semi-public entities, such as utility companies.

Inverse Condemnation. If a property owner feels that her property has been taken or damaged by a public entity, she may file a lawsuit called an inverse condemnation action to force the government to pay the fair market value of the taken or damaged property.

Court Decisions

Title to real property can also be transferred by court order in accordance with state statutes and the precedents of the common law. The most common forms of court action affecting title to real property are quiet title actions, suits for partition, and foreclosures.

Quiet Title. A quiet title action is used to remove a cloud on the title when the title cannot be cleared by the more peaceful means of an agreement and a quitclaim deed. In a quiet title action, the court decides questions of property ownership. The result is a binding determination of the various parties' interests in a particular piece of real estate.

Example: A seller has found a potential buyer for his property. However, a title search uncovers a gap in the title: the public record doesn't indicate who owned the property for a certain time period.

The seller brings a quiet title action. The defendants in the action are all persons who have a potential interest in the seller's property. This includes whoever the mystery person was who held title during the gap, even though his or her name is unknown.

The seller asks the court to declare his title valid, thereby "quieting title" to the land. If no defendants appear to challenge the seller's title, the court will grant the seller's request. The buyer can then safely rely on the court's decision and consummate the sale.

Partition. A suit for partition is a means of dividing property owned by more than one person when the co-owners cannot agree on how to divide it. For example, joint tenants may wish to end their joint tenancy but be unable to decide among themselves who gets what portion of the property. The court divides the property for them, and the owners are then bound by the court's decision. In many cases, the court will order the property sold and the proceeds divided among the co-owners.

Example: Green and Black are joint tenants. The joint tenancy property is a vacation home in the mountains. After a serious argument, Green and Black decide they want to terminate their joint tenancy. However, they can't agree on how to divide the property. Green wants to put the property up for sale and divide the proceeds. Black wants to buy out Green's interest and keep the vacation home for himself, but Green says Black isn't offering him enough money.

Finally, Green files a suit for partition. The court orders the vacation home sold and divides the proceeds between Green and Black. Black must abide by this decision, even though he doesn't like it.

Foreclosure. Persons holding liens against real property may force the sale of the property if the debts secured by their liens are not paid. Foreclosure is available for any type of lien that attaches to real property, including mortgages, deeds of trust, construction liens, and judgment liens. (See Chapter 10 for further discussion of foreclosure.)

Adverse Possession

Adverse possession, another form of involuntary alienation, is the process by which the possession and use of property can mature into title. The law of adverse possession encourages the fullest and most productive use of land. It provides that someone who actually uses property may eventually attain a greater interest in that property than the owner who does not use it. The precise requirements for obtaining title by adverse possession vary from state to state. These requirements are often highly technical, and they must be followed exactly in order to obtain title. Legal counsel should be obtained in transactions where title may be affected by adverse possession.

Requirements. In Washington, there are five basic requirements for adverse possession. Possession of the land must be:

1. actual,
2. open and notorious,

3. hostile to the owner's interest,
4. exclusive, and
5. continuous and uninterrupted for a specific period of time.

Actual. Actual possession means occupation and use of the property in a manner appropriate to the type of property. It does not require residence on the property unless residence is the appropriate use. Thus, actual possession of farmland may be achieved by fencing the land and planting crops, while actual possession of urban property would usually require a residential or commercial use of the property.

Open and Notorious. The requirement of "open and notorious" possession means that the possession must be obvious enough to put the average owner on notice that her interest in the property is threatened. This requirement overlaps with the actual possession requirement. Actual possession generally constitutes reasonable notice to the world that the adverse possessor is occupying the property.

Hostile. The adverse possessor must intend to claim ownership of the property and defend that claim against all parties. Hostile intent is proven by the adverse possessor's actions. If the adverse possessor uses the property in the same fashion as an owner would use it, then hostile intent exists. Hostile intent can also be proven by color of title. An example of an adverse possessor with color of title is one who takes possession under an invalid deed, with a good faith but mistaken belief that he is the owner of the land. Note that the hostility requirement cannot be satisfied if the possession is with the permission of the actual owner.

Exclusive. An adverse possessor must have exclusive possession of the property; in other words, the true owner must be excluded from possession. Someone who is sharing use of the property with the true owner (even without the owner's knowledge) cannot acquire title by adverse possession.

Continuous. An adverse possessor is required to have continuous and uninterrupted possession of the property for the length of time prescribed by state statute. In Washington, possession generally must be continuous and uninterrupted for ten years. The possession period is only seven years if an adverse possessor has color of title (has taken possession under an invalid deed and with the good faith belief that she owns the property) and pays property taxes on the parcel.

In some cases, intermittent use of the property may be enough to fulfill the continuity requirement. This is true if the property is a type that an owner would ordinarily use only at certain times of year, such as seasonal farmland or summer resort property. However, the continuity requirement is not met if the adverse possessor fails to use the property for a significant period when it would ordinarily be used, or if the true owner interrupts the period of exclusive possession.

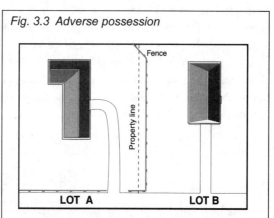

Fig. 3.3 *Adverse possession*

Use of property (here, the strip between Lot A's fence and the true property line) can mature into title by the process of adverse possession.

Periods of possession by successive adverse possessors can be added together to equal the statutory time period; this is called **tacking**.

> **Example:** Brown adversely possesses property for seven years, then transfers possession to White, who possesses the property for five years. White can claim title because the total period of adverse possession is more than ten years.

Note that title to government property can never be acquired by adverse possession.

Perfecting Title. Since the adverse possessor's interest is not recorded, she must take additional steps to acquire marketable title. Unless the true owner is willing to provide a quitclaim deed, the adverse possessor has to file a quiet title action. Note that once the adverse possessor has title to the property, she is responsible for paying any unpaid property taxes that accrued before she gained title.

Accession

Accession is any addition to real property from natural or artificial causes. It can result in involuntary alienation. Accession includes:

- accretion,
- reliction, and
- avulsion.

Accretion. When riparian or littoral land is slowly enlarged by waterborne soil deposits (called alluvion or alluvium), the riparian or littoral owner acquires title to the new land. A key feature of accretion is that the build-up of soil must be so gradual that the process is virtually imperceptible.

Reliction. When riparian or littoral land is enlarged by the gradual retreat of the body of water, the landowner acquires title to the newly exposed land. Like accretion, reliction must be very gradual. Reliction is also called dereliction.

Avulsion. Accretion and reliction are both gradual processes. By contrast, avulsion occurs when land is violently torn away by flowing water or waves and deposited somewhere else, or when land is exposed by a sudden change in a watercourse. Unlike accretion and reliction, avulsion does not necessarily result in involuntary alienation of the land that has been moved or exposed. The original owner still has title to that land, if there is some way to claim it. If unclaimed, it eventually becomes part of the property it is now attached to.

Recording

Once an interest in property has been transferred (voluntarily or involuntarily), the new owner protects his interest by recording the document of conveyance with the county clerk. Recording is a way to provide convenient access to information regarding ownership of a property to anyone who's interested.

The Recording Process

Recording is accomplished by filing a deed or other document at the county records office in the county where the property is located. Documents are recorded chronologically, in the order in which they were filed for recording. Each recorded document is assigned a recording number.

County property records are searchable by computer at the records office, and many counties also offer online searches. When someone is considering buying a property, a title search is performed to determine the validity of the seller's title and find what other claims there are against the property. By searching the records by grantor or grantee name, or using various other identifiers such as the property's tax parcel number, the prospective buyer or a title company employee can trace the chain of title (the series of recorded deeds that transferred the property from one owner to the next) back in time far enough to establish that the seller is the true owner. The title search can also help the buyer and the lender make sure the seller has not already conveyed the property to another party.

Almost any document affecting title to land may be recorded: a deed, a mortgage, an abstract of judgment, a lis pendens (a notice of pending legal proceedings that may affect property), and so on. A deed or other document of conveyance must be acknowledged before it can be recorded, mainly to protect against forgeries. Also, the federal Fair Housing Act prohibits the recording of any deed that contains a racially restrictive covenant (see Chapter 15).

The Effect of Recording

Recording has two significant consequences. Most importantly, it gives **constructive notice** of recorded interests to "the world." In other words, anyone who later acquires an interest in the property is held to know about all the other recorded interests, even if he does not check the record. (Constructive notice is contrasted with **actual notice**, which occurs when someone actually knows about some fact concerning the property.)

Example: Jones owns Haystack Farm. She sells the farm to Chin, who immediately records his deed. One week later, Jones sells Haystack Farm to Brown. Jones pretends she still owns the farm, and Brown simply takes her word for it; he doesn't do a title search. When Brown tries to record his deed, he discovers that Jones did not have title to Haystack Farm when she sold it to him.

Although Brown didn't actually know about the conveyance from Jones to Chin, he had constructive notice of that conveyance. He could have found out about it by checking the public record. As a result, he has no claim to the property. Chin owns Haystack Farm. Brown could sue Jones to get his money back, but she may be long gone.

A grantee who fails to record her deed can lose title to a subsequent good faith purchaser who did not have notice of the earlier conveyance. In a conflict between two purchasers, the one who records his deed first has good title to the property—even if the other purchaser's deed was executed first.

Example: Jones sells Haystack Farm to Chin, but Chin does not record his deed. One week later, Jones sells the same property to Brown. No one tells Brown about the previous conveyance to Chin.

Since Chin's deed isn't recorded, Brown doesn't have constructive notice of Chin's interest in the property. Even if Brown does a title search, there's nothing in the public record to indicate that Jones no longer owns the property.

Brown qualifies as a subsequent good faith purchaser without notice. If he records his deed before Chin records his, Brown has good title to the property.

In addition to providing constructive notice, recording also creates a presumption that the recorded instrument is valid and effective. Recording will not serve to validate an otherwise invalid deed, however, nor will it protect against interests that arise by operation of law, such as adverse possession.

Possession Provides Notice. A potential purchaser is also held to have constructive notice of the interests of parties in possession of the property, even if those interests aren't recorded. For example, if a tenant has possession under an unrecorded lease, a purchaser would have constructive notice of the lease, even if she never visited the property and is unaware of the tenant.

Wild Deeds. Sometimes it's possible for a deed to be undiscovered even though it was recorded.

Example: Atwood sells some land to Burns, but Burns does not record his deed. Burns later sells the land to Cooper, and Cooper does record her deed. But because the previous deed (the deed from Atwood to Burns) was not recorded, Cooper's deed is outside the chain of title. In a title search, if someone just looked up Atwood's name, he would find no indication that Atwood conveyed the property, and nothing would lead the searcher to Cooper's deed.

A deed that is outside the chain of title is called a **wild deed**. The general rule is that a subsequent purchaser is not held to have constructive notice of a wild deed. In the example, Cooper's title is unprotected against subsequent good faith purchasers. Suppose Atwood were to fraudulently sell the same property to another person, Dunn. A court could rule that Dunn has good title to the property, not Cooper.

Title Insurance

Given the complexity of real property law and the high cost of real estate, it's natural that a prospective buyer will want to do everything possible to make sure that he's going to have good title to the property. The warranties carried by a warranty deed offer some assurance about the seller's title, but warranties aren't very useful to the buyer if the seller can't back them up financially.

The buyer could also obtain a complete history of all the recorded interests in the property (called a **chain of title**) or a condensed history of those interests (called an **abstract of title**), and then have the history examined by an attorney who could render an opinion on the condition of the title. But the buyer would still have no protection against latent or undiscovered defects in the title. Therefore, most buyers will protect their interests with a title insurance policy.

In a title insurance policy, the title insurance company agrees to indemnify the policy holder against (in other words, reimburse the policy holder for) losses caused by defects in the title, except for defects specifically excluded from coverage. The title company will also handle the legal defense of any claims covered by the policy.

Obtaining Title Insurance

There are two steps to getting a title insurance policy. First, the buyer (or the seller, on the buyer's behalf) pays a fee to the title company to cover the cost of a title search. After the title search is completed, the title company issues a **title report** describing the condition of the title. The report lists all defects and encumbrances that have been discovered in the public record; these items will be excluded from the policy coverage. If the report is satisfactory to the buyer, the title company will issue a policy when the transaction closes.

The premium for a title insurance policy is paid at closing. A single payment covers the entire life of the policy, which lasts as long as the insured holds an interest in the property.

Title Insurance Coverage

Title insurance coverage is limited in a variety of ways. As mentioned above, all defects and encumbrances of record are listed in the policy and excluded from coverage. In addition, the liability of the title company cannot exceed the face value of the policy. The extent of protection also varies depending on what type of policy is purchased. Traditionally, the two most common types of policies have been the standard coverage policy and the extended coverage policy.

A **standard coverage** policy was traditionally used to insure the property owner (the buyer) against defects in title, including hidden risks such as forgery. (This is why it is sometimes called an owner's policy.) It does not insure against the claims of a person in actual possession of the property (such as an adverse possessor), nor against problems that would be disclosed by an inspection of the property (such as an encroachment).

An **extended coverage** policy insures against all matters covered by the standard policy, plus matters not of public record, such as the rights of parties in possession of the property, unrecorded construction liens, and encroachments. Extended coverage is often used for the mortgagee's policy, a policy insuring the buyer's lender (as opposed to an owner's policy, which is the policy insuring the buyer). Lenders require buyers to pay for a mortgagee's policy in virtually all transactions.

In addition to standard and extended coverage, title companies offer a third commonly used type of policy, **homeowner's coverage**, for transactions that involve residential property with up to four units. This policy provides the buyer with much more extensive coverage than a traditional standard coverage policy. In fact, a homeowner's title policy covers most of the same title problems that an extended coverage policy does, plus some additional ones, such as violations of restrictive covenants.

A buyer who wants coverage for a specific item not ordinarily covered by a particular type of policy may be able to purchase an **endorsement** to cover it.

Title insurance coverage is limited to losses resulting from defects in the particular interest covered. Thus, an owner's policy covers only defects in title, a mortgagee's

Fig. 3.4 *Types of title insurance coverage*

	Standard Coverage	Extended Coverage	Homeowner's Coverage
Unmarketable title	X	X	X
Latent defects in title (forged deed, incompetent grantor)	X	X	X
Incorrect legal descriptions or clerical errors in recorded documents	X	X	X
Undisclosed heirs in improperly probated wills	X	X	X
Nondelivery or improper delivery of deeds	X	X	X
Unrecorded liens		X	X
Claims of parties in possession (tenants, adverse possessors)		X	X
Matters discovered by survey (incorrect boundary lines, easements, incorrect area)		X	X
Subdivision regulation violations			X
Zoning or building code violations			X
Claims that arise post-closing			X

policy only insures the lender's lien priority, and a leaseholder's policy only insures the validity of a lease.

Note that title insurance does not protect a landowner from losses due to governmental action such as condemnation or zoning changes.

Chapter Summary

1. A transfer of ownership of property from one person to another is called alienation. Alienation may be either voluntary or involuntary.

2. Property may be transferred voluntarily by patent, deed, or will. The deed is the most common way of voluntarily transferring property. To be valid, a deed must be in writing, identify the parties, be signed by a competent grantor, have a living grantee, contain words of conveyance, and include an adequate description of the property. For property to be successfully conveyed, there must be delivery and acceptance as well as a valid deed. Once the deed is delivered and accepted, it should be recorded to protect the new owner's interest.

3. When a person dies, her real property may be transferred to devisees through a will, a trust, or a transfer on death deed, or to heirs by the rules of intestate succession. (A person who dies without a will is said to have died intestate.) Property from an estate is distributed under the jurisdiction of the probate court. If a person dies without a valid will and without heirs, the estate property escheats to the state.

4. In addition to intestate succession and escheat, there are several other methods of involuntary alienation, including dedication, condemnation, court decisions (quiet title, partition, foreclosure), and adverse possession. When someone uses property openly and continuously without the owner's permission for ten years, she may acquire title to it by adverse possession.

5. Ownership of property may be transferred by accession. Accession refers to an addition to real property by various natural means, including accretion, reliction, and avulsion.

6. Documents affecting real property are recorded to provide constructive notice of their contents to anyone interested in the property. Recording also creates a presumption that a document is valid.

7. Under a title insurance policy, the title insurance company will reimburse the insured for losses caused by covered title defects and will defend the title against legal claims. Most transactions involve two title insurance policies: one protecting the buyer (the owner's policy), and one protecting the buyer's lender (the mortgagee's policy).

O—̄ Key Terms

Alienation—The transfer of title, ownership, or an interest in property from one person to another. Alienation may be voluntary or involuntary.

Deed—A written instrument that, when properly executed, delivered, and accepted, conveys title or ownership of real property from the grantor to the grantee.

Warranty deed—The deed that provides the greatest protection to a purchaser of real property, because it contains five basic covenants against defects in the title.

Quitclaim deed—A deed that conveys and releases any interest in a piece of real property that the grantor may have. It contains no warranties of any kind, but does transfer any right, title, or interest the grantor has at the time the deed is executed.

Acknowledgment—A formal declaration made before an authorized official, such as a notary public or county clerk, by a person who has signed a document; he states that the signature is genuine and voluntary.

Will—The written declaration of an individual that designates how his estate will be disposed of after death.

Intestate—When a person dies without leaving a valid will, she dies intestate.

Escheat—The reversion of property to the state after no one with a legal claim to the property comes forward to claim it. (This may happen, for example, because the owner died without leaving a will and without heirs.)

Dedication—When a private owner voluntarily or involuntarily gives real property to the public.

Eminent domain—The power of the government to take (condemn) private property for public use, upon payment of just compensation to the owner.

Condemnation—The act of taking private property for public use under the power of eminent domain.

Adverse possession—A means by which a person may acquire title to property by using it openly and continuously without the owner's permission for the required statutory period.

Accession—Any addition to real property from natural or artificial causes.

Constructive notice—Notice of a fact that a person is held by law to have (as opposed to actual notice); he had the opportunity to discover the fact in question by searching the public record.

Title search—An inspection of the public record to determine all rights to a piece of property.

Chain of title—A complete history of all the recorded interests in a piece of real property.

Abstract of title—A condensed history of the recorded interests in a piece of real property.

Title report—A report issued after a title search by a title insurance company, listing all defects and encumbrances of record.

Wild deed—A recorded deed that cannot be located under the grantor-grantee system of indexing.

Chapter Quiz

1. The process of transferring real property is called:
   a) avulsion
   b) quitclaim
   c) alienation
   d) dereliction

2. The government transfers title to private parties by means of a/an:
   a) patent
   b) deed
   c) quitclaim
   d) escheat

3. In a deed, the promise that the grantor owns the property is called the covenant:
   a) of quiet enjoyment
   b) against encumbrances
   c) of seisin
   d) of warranty

4. Clouds on title are usually cleared by:
   a) a suit for partition
   b) title insurance
   c) adverse possession
   d) a quitclaim deed

5. A valid deed must refer to a grantee who is:
   a) competent
   b) over 21 years old
   c) identifiable
   d) intestate

6. Conveyance requires a valid deed, plus:
   a) recording
   b) delivery
   c) acceptance
   d) Both b) and c)

7. A person who makes a will is called:
   a) a grantor
   b) an executor
   c) a testator
   d) an escheat

8. An unwitnessed, handwritten will is called:
   a) a witnessed will
   b) a holographic will
   c) a nuncupative will
   d) None of the above

9. The process by which possession of property can result in ownership of the property is called:
   a) fee simple
   b) succession
   c) adverse possession
   d) reliction

10. A quitclaim deed conveys:
   a) whatever interest the grantor has
   b) only a portion of the interest held by the grantor
   c) only property acquired by adverse possession
   d) None of the above

11. A nuncupative will:
   a) must be entirely handwritten
   b) is invalid in Washington
   c) is an oral will
   d) is only valid for sailors and merchant marines

12. The five basic promises made by a grantor through a warranty deed include all of the following, except:
   a) covenant of right to convey
   b) covenant of quiet enjoyment
   c) covenant of habitability
   d) covenant of warranty

13. When a cloud on the title cannot be cleared with a quitclaim deed, this judicial proceeding decides ownership:
   a) quiet title action
   b) suit for partition
   c) interpleader action
   d) reformation action

14. All of the following are requirements for adverse possession, except:
    a) open and notorious possession
    b) exclusive possession
    c) hostile possession
    d) recorded claim of possession

15. A standard title insurance policy would protect against:
    a) adverse possession
    b) encroachments
    c) a forged deed
    d) condemnation

👉 Answer Key

1. c) The general term for a transfer of ownership of real property from one party to another is alienation.

2. a) The government transfers title to property with a patent.

3. c) The covenant of seisin is a promise that the grantor actually owns the interest that is being conveyed.

4. d) A quitclaim deed is commonly used to clear clouds on title.

5. c) The grantee only has to be identifiable. He does not have to be competent.

6. d) To successfully convey title, the deed must be delivered and accepted.

7. c) A testator is the person who makes a will.

8. b) A holographic will is one that is handwritten by the testator and not witnessed. Generally, holographic wills are not valid in Washington.

9. c) Adverse possession encourages the full use of land by providing a means by which a user may acquire ownership rights.

10. a) A quitclaim deed transfers whatever interest the grantor has. If the grantor has good title, it conveys good title. If the grantor has no interest in the property, it conveys nothing at all.

11. c) A nuncupative will is an oral will; it is valid in Washington under limited circumstances.

12. c) A warranty deed carries no promise that the property is habitable or otherwise suitable for the buyer.

13. a) A quiet title action provides a binding determination of the parties' interests in a piece of real estate.

14. d) All of these are among the requirements for adverse possession, except recording a claim. Although an adverse possessor may perfect title by recording a quitclaim deed after the statutory period ends, that isn't a requirement for adverse possession.

15. c) Standard title insurance coverage insures only against defects of title (such as a forged deed), not against matters that are not part of the public record, and not against governmental action.

Encumbrances

Chapter Overview

An interest in real property may be held by someone other than the property owner or a tenant; such an interest is called an encumbrance. Nearly every property has encumbrances against it. Some encumbrances represent another person's financial interest in the property. Other encumbrances involve another person's right to make use of the property or to restrict how the owner uses it.

The first part of this chapter explains financial encumbrances, including mortgages and other types of liens. The second part of this chapter covers the nonfinancial encumbrances, including easements and private restrictions, and some related concepts.

Encumbrances

An encumbrance is a nonpossessory right or interest in real property held by someone other than the property owner. The interest can be financial or nonfinancial in nature. A financial encumbrance only affects title; a nonfinancial encumbrance also affects the use or physical condition of the property.

Financial Encumbrances (Liens)

Financial encumbrances are commonly called **liens**. A lien is a security interest in property; it is held by a creditor of the property owner. If the owner doesn't pay off the debt owed to the creditor, the security interest allows the creditor to force the property to be sold, so that the creditor can collect the debt out of the sale proceeds. This is called **foreclosure**. The most familiar example of a lien is a mortgage.

A creditor who has a lien against (a security interest in) the debtor's property is called a **secured creditor**. The lien does not prevent the debtor from transferring the property, but the new owner takes title subject to the lien. The creditor can still foreclose if the debt is not repaid.

Liens may be voluntary or involuntary. A **voluntary lien** is one the debtor voluntarily gives to the creditor, usually as security for a loan. The two types of voluntary liens are mortgages and deeds of trust. **Involuntary liens** (sometimes called statutory liens) are given to creditors without the property owner's consent, by operation of law. Examples of involuntary liens are property tax liens and judgment liens.

> **Example:** Dunn sues Bronson for injuries sustained in a car crash and wins a $125,000 judgment. The judgment can become a lien against Bronson's property.

Liens may also be general or specific. A **general lien** attaches to all of the debtor's property. For instance, the judgment lien in the example is a general lien. Any property owned by Bronson could be encumbered by the judgment lien. On the other hand, a **specific lien** attaches only to a particular piece of property. A mortgage is an example of a specific lien. It is a lien against only the particular piece of property offered as security for the loan.

Types of Liens

The most common types of liens against real property include mortgages, deeds of trust, construction liens, judgment liens, attachment liens, and tax and assessment liens.

Mortgages. A mortgage is a specific, voluntary lien created by a contract between the property owner (the **mortgagor**) and the creditor (the **mortgagee**). The mortgagee is usually a lender, who will not loan money unless the borrower gives a lien as security for repayment.

Deeds of Trust. A deed of trust (also called a trust deed) is used for the same purpose as a mortgage. However, there are three parties to a trust deed rather than the two found in a mortgage transaction. The borrower is called the **trustor** (or sometimes the grantor); the lender or creditor is called the **beneficiary**; and there's an independent third party (often an attorney or a title insurance company) called the **trustee**. The most significant difference between mortgages and deeds of trust is in the foreclosure process. Mortgages and deeds of trust are discussed in more detail in Chapter 10.

Construction Liens. A person who provides labor, materials, or professional services for the improvement of real property may be entitled to claim a construction lien against the property. For example, if a plumber who is involved in remodeling a bathroom isn't paid, he can claim a lien against the property for the amount owed. Eventually, if necessary, the plumber could foreclose on the lien, forcing the property to be sold to pay the debt.

A construction lien is a specific, involuntary lien, attaching only to the property where work was performed or materials were supplied. Construction liens are often called **mechanic's liens**, and a construction lien claimed by someone who provides materials (as opposed to labor) is sometimes called a **materialman's lien**.

Many improvement projects involve a complex hierarchy of contractors, subcontractors, laborers, and materials suppliers, all of whom may be entitled to claim construction liens. In certain cases, a potential construction lien claimant is required to give the property owner a notice of right to claim a lien (also called a "pre-lien notice") within a certain time after she begins providing services or materials. This is not necessary when the claimant has a contract directly with the owner, however.

A claim of lien must be recorded no later than 90 days after the claimant has stopped working on or providing materials for the project. A potential claimant who misses this deadline loses the right to a construction lien. He is still entitled to be paid for services rendered, but does not have a security interest in the debtor's property.

To foreclose on a construction lien, the lienholder must file a court action within eight months after the claim of lien was recorded.

Fig. 4.1 Lien classifications		
	Voluntary	**Involuntary**
Specific	Mortgages Deeds of trust	Property taxes Special assessments Construction liens
General		Judgment liens IRS liens

Judgment Liens. Judgment liens are involuntary, general liens. If a lawsuit results in a money judgment against the loser, the winner (the judgment creditor) may obtain a lien against the loser's (the judgment debtor's) property. The lien attaches to all the property owned by the debtor in the county where the judgment was entered, and also attaches to any property acquired by the debtor during the lien period (the length of time the judgment creditor has to take action on the lien). If the debtor owns property in other counties, the judgment creditor can make the lien attach to that property by recording an **abstract of judgment** in those counties.

Once a judgment lien has attached, the debtor must pay the judgment to free the property from the lien. If it's not paid, the property can be sold by a designated official to satisfy the judgment. To do this, the court issues a **writ of execution**.

Attachment Liens. When someone files a lawsuit, there is a danger that by the time a judgment is entered, the **defendant** (the party sued) will have sold his property and disappeared, leaving the other party with little more than a piece of paper. To prevent this, the **plaintiff** (the person who started the lawsuit) can ask the court to issue a writ of attachment. A **writ of attachment** directs the sheriff to attach enough of the defendant's property to satisfy the judgment the plaintiff is seeking. When the writ of attachment is recorded, it creates a lien on the defendant's real property.

Also, when a lawsuit that may affect title to real property is pending, the plaintiff may record a document called a **lis pendens**, which is Latin for "action pending." While a lis pendens is not a lien, anyone who purchases the property identified in the lis pendens has constructive notice of the pending lawsuit and therefore is bound by any judgment that results from the suit.

Property Tax Liens. Property is assessed (appraised for tax purposes) and taxed according to its value (ad valorem). When property taxes are levied, a lien attaches to the property until they are paid. Property tax liens are involuntary, specific liens. (Property taxation is discussed in more detail in Chapter 5.)

Special Assessments. Special assessments result from local improvements, such as road paving or sewer lines, that benefit some, but not all, property owners within the county. The properties that have benefited from the improvement are assessed for their share of the cost of the improvement. The assessment creates an involuntary, specific lien against the property. (Special assessments are also discussed in Chapter 5.)

Other Tax Liens. Many other taxes, such as federal income taxes, estate or inheritance taxes, and gift taxes, can result in liens against property. These types of tax liens are general liens against all of a taxpayer's properties.

Lien Priority

It is not at all unusual for a piece of property to have more than one lien against it. In fact, the dollar amount of all the liens may add up to more than the property will bring at a foreclosure sale. When this happens, the sale proceeds are not allocated among all the lienholders in a "pro rata" fashion (proportionate distribution). Instead, the liens are paid according to their priority. This means that the lien with the highest priority is paid first. If any money is left over, the lien with the second highest priority is paid, and so forth.

As a general rule, lien priority is determined by the date a lien was recorded. The lien that was recorded first will be paid first, even though another lien may have been created first.

Example: Suppose Bakerman borrows money from two banks—$5,000 from National Bank on March 17, and $5,000 from State Bank on May 5 of the same year. Bakerman gives mortgages to both banks when the loan funds are received. If National Bank does not record its mortgage until July 14, but State Bank records its mortgage promptly on May 5, State Bank's lien will be paid before National Bank's in the event of foreclosure.

While "first in time (to record), first in right" is the general rule, there are important exceptions; some types of liens are given special priority. In Washington, special priority is given to property tax and special assessment liens; they have priority over all other liens. Construction liens are another exception. Their priority is determined by the date the claimant began working on the project, even though the claim of lien was recorded later on.

The Homestead Law

Homestead laws are state laws that give homeowners limited protection against lien foreclosure. In Washington, the homestead law offers protection only against general judgment liens. It does not apply to mortgages, deeds of trust, construction liens, liens for child support or spousal maintenance, or liens imposed by a condominium or homeowners association.

A **homestead** is an owner-occupied dwelling, together with any appurtenant buildings and land. Homestead protection is automatic, beginning as soon as the owner starts residing on the property.

An owner can obtain homestead protection in advance, for property he is planning to reside on, by recording a document called a "declaration of homestead" for that property. However, a person may have only one homestead at a time.

Exemption. Homestead protection consists of a limited exemption from foreclosure of judgment liens. In Washington, the exemption amount is $125,000.

A judgment creditor cannot foreclose unless the net value of the property is greater than the $125,000 exemption amount. The net value is the property's market value, minus all liens that are senior to the lien being foreclosed on.

Example: The Crenshaws own and occupy a home worth $275,000. The liens against the home, in order of priority, are a $2,500 property tax lien, a $130,000 mortgage, and a $15,000 judgment lien. The judgment creditor wants to foreclose on the judgment lien.

The net value of the home is $127,500 ($275,000 − $147,500 = $127,500). Because the net value is greater than the $125,000 exemption amount, the judgment creditor will be permitted to foreclose.

When the proceeds of the foreclosure sale are distributed, first the exemption amount is paid to the homeowner, then the remaining proceeds are paid to the lienholders in order of priority. For up to one year after foreclosure, money paid to the former homeowner as a result of the homestead exemption is protected from other creditors (just as it was protected while it was invested in the homestead). The former homeowner can reinvest the funds in a new homestead.

Termination. Homestead protection terminates automatically when the owner sells the property. However, out of the sale proceeds, the exemption amount is still protected from the claims of general creditors for one year following the sale. This allows the owner time in which to reinvest the exempt funds in a new home, which will then become her new homestead.

Nonfinancial Encumbrances

While financial encumbrances affect only title to property, nonfinancial encumbrances affect the physical use or condition of the property itself. Thus, a property owner can find the use of his land limited by a right or interest held by someone else. Nonfinancial encumbrances include easements, profits, and private restrictions. We'll also cover licenses, encroachments, and nuisances in this section; they too involve someone using another's property or affecting the owner's use of it, although they aren't actually interests in real property.

Easements

An easement is a right to use another person's land for a particular purpose. It is a nonpossessory interest in land. That means that the easement holder has a right to use the land, but has no title or right of possession. An easement is not an estate.

Example: A landowner has an easement across her neighbor's lot for access to the public road. She has a right to make reasonable use of that easement to get to and from her property. However, she does not have the right to build a shed on the easement, or to use the easement in any way other than as a driveway.

Types of Easements. There are two main types of easements: easements appurtenant and easements in gross.

Easements Appurtenant. An easement appurtenant burdens one parcel of land for the benefit of another parcel of land. The parcel with the benefit is called the **dominant tenement**; the one with the burden is called the **servient tenement**. The owner of the dominant tenement is called the **dominant tenant**; the owner of the servient tenement is the **servient tenant**. Do not confuse the term "tenement," which is the land, with "tenant," which is the landowner.

Probably the most common example of an easement appurtenant is a driveway easement providing access across one parcel of land to another. (A driveway easement is often called an easement for **ingress and egress**, which means entering

Fig. 4.2 Types of encumbrances	
Financial Encumbrances	**Nonfinancial Encumbrances**
• Mortgages • Deeds of trust • Construction liens • Judgment liens • Attachment liens • Property tax liens • Other tax liens	• Easements • Profits • Private restrictions

and exiting.) In Figure 4.3, Lot B has an easement appurtenant across Lot A. The easement provides access to a public road. Lot B is the dominant tenement. Lot A is the servient tenement.

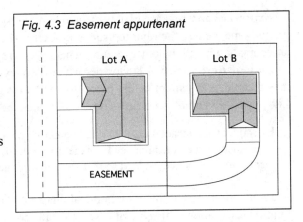

Fig. 4.3 Easement appurtenant

Lot A   Lot B

EASEMENT

An easement appurtenant "runs with the land." This means that if either the dominant or servient tenement is transferred to a new owner, the new owner also acquires the benefit or the burden of the easement. Refer to Figure 4.3 again. If Lot B were sold, the new owner would still have an easement across Lot A. If Lot A were sold, the new owner would still bear the burden of allowing the owner of Lot B to use the easement.

An easement that benefits a parcel of land is called an easement appurtenant because it goes along with ownership of the land like other appurtenances (air rights, for example). The easement is appurtenant to the dominant tenement.

Ordinarily, an easement agreement or a deed creating an easement must be in writing in order for the easement to be valid. To make the easement run with the land, the document usually must also be recorded. In some situations, though, if it would be immediately apparent to a person visiting the property that an easement is in use, the easement could run with the land even though it was never written down or recorded.

Easements in Gross. An easement in gross benefits a person (a dominant tenant) rather than a parcel of land. When someone has an easement in gross, there is no dominant tenement, only a servient tenement.

> **Example:** Wilson has the right to enter Able's land and fish in Able's stream. Wilson is a dominant tenant with an easement in gross over Able's land (the servient tenement). The easement serves Wilson, not a parcel of land.

Since an easement in gross belongs to an individual, and not a parcel of land, it is a personal right that is extinguished on the death of the dominant tenant. In the example above, when Wilson dies, the easement will disappear. A personal easement in gross may not be assigned by its owner to a third party.

Most easements in gross are commercial easements. The most common example is the easement held by a utility company, which allows company employees to enter property to install and service the lines. Because commercial easements in gross are considered more substantial interests than personal easements, they can be assigned from one utility company to another.

Creating an Easement. Easements (whether appurtenant or in gross) can be created in any of the following ways:

- express grant,
- express reservation,
- implication,
- prescription,
- dedication, or
- condemnation.

Express Grant. An easement is created by express grant when a property owner grants someone else the right to use the property. The grant must be put into writing and comply with all the other requirements for conveyance of an interest in land.

Express Reservation. A landowner who is conveying a portion of her property may reserve an easement in that parcel to benefit the parcel of land that is retained. Like an express grant, an express reservation must be in writing.

Example: Carmichael owns 100 acres bordering on a state highway. She sells 40 acres, including all the highway frontage. In the deed, she reserves to herself an easement across the conveyed land so that she will have access to her remaining 60 acres.

Implication. An easement by implication can be either an implied grant or an implied reservation. This type of easement can arise only when a property is divided into more than one lot, and the grantor neglects to grant or reserve an easement on one lot for the benefit of the other. When this happens, the easement is implied by law.

There are two requirements for an easement to be created by implication:

1. it must be reasonably necessary for the enjoyment of the property, and
2. there must have been apparent prior use.

The second requirement is fulfilled if the use was established before the property was divided, and would have been apparent to prospective purchasers from an inspection of the property. However, different rules apply if one of the parcels would be entirely landlocked without an easement. When an easement for ingress and egress is strictly necessary (not merely reasonably necessary) because there is no other way to reach the landlocked parcel, then a court may declare that there is an easement even though there was no apparent prior use. This subtype of easement by implication is called an easement by necessity.

Prescription. An easement by prescription is created through long-term use of land without the permission of the landowner. Acquiring an easement by prescription is similar to acquiring ownership through adverse possession. Here are the requirements for an easement by prescription:

- the use must be **open and notorious** (apparent to the landowner);
- the use must be **hostile** (without the permission of the landowner); and
- the use must be **reasonably continuous** for a statutory period of time (in Washington, ten years).

Note that although an adverse possessor's use of the property must be exclusive, that isn't a requirement for a prescriptive easement. A prescriptive easement may be created even if the landowner is also using the property.

Dedication. A private landowner may grant an easement to the public to use some portion of his property for a public purpose, such as a sidewalk. The dedication may be expressly stated or implied.

Condemnation. The government may exercise its power of eminent domain and condemn private property to gain an easement for a public purpose, such as a road. This power may also be exercised by private companies that serve the public, such as railroad and power companies.

Terminating an Easement. An easement can be terminated in any of these ways:

- release,
- merger,
- failure of purpose,
- abandonment, or
- prescription.

Release. The holder of the easement may release her rights in the servient tenement. This would be done by a written document, usually a quitclaim deed to the owner of the servient tenement.

Merger. Since an easement is, by definition, the right to make some use of another person's land, if the dominant and servient tenements come to be owned by the same person, the easement is no longer necessary and therefore is terminated. This is called merger; ownership of the dominant and servient tenements has merged.

Failure of Purpose. If the purpose for which the easement was created ceases, then the easement terminates. For example, if an easement was created for a railroad, and if the railroad company later discontinued its use and removed the rails, the easement would be terminated through failure of purpose.

Abandonment. An easement is also terminated if the easement holder abandons it. This requires acts by the holder indicating an intent to abandon the easement. Mere non-use is not abandonment.

Example: If the dominant tenant were to build a fence that blocked any further use of an easement that had been used for ingress and egress, it would be reasonable for the servient tenant to conclude that the easement had been abandoned.

Prescription. An easement is extinguished if the servient tenant prevents the dominant tenant from using the easement for the statutory period (ten years).

Example: The servient tenant builds a brick wall around his property. The dominant tenant can no longer use his easement for ingress and egress. If the wall remains undisturbed for ten years, the easement will be terminated.

Profits

A profit is the right to take something from land belonging to someone else. For example, it might be the right to take timber, peat, or gravel from someone else's land. The difference between a profit and an easement is that the easement is just a right to use another's land, but a profit allows the removal of something from the land. A profit must be created in writing or by prescription.

Licenses

Like an easement, a license gives someone the right to make some use of another person's land. However, easements and licenses are different in many ways. An easement is created in writing or through action of law. A license may be merely spoken permission to cross, hunt, fish on, or make some other use of a landowner's property. An easement is irrevocable, but a license can be revoked at the will of the landowner. In general, easements are permanent and licenses are temporary. A license is a personal right that does not run with the land. It cannot be assigned. Since the license is

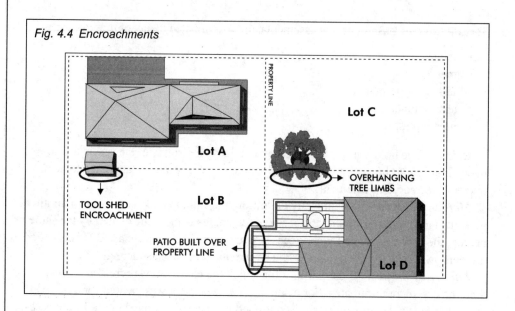

Fig. 4.4 Encroachments

revocable at the will of the landowner, it is not actually considered an encumbrance or an interest in the property.

Encroachments

An encroachment is a physical object that is wholly or partially on someone else's property, such as a fence or garage built partially over the property line onto the neighbor's land (see Figure 4.4). Most encroachments are unintentional, resulting from a mistake concerning the exact location of the property line.

An encroachment may be a **trespass** if it violates the neighboring owner's right to possession. A court can order an encroachment to be removed through a judicial action called an **ejectment,** or if the cost of the removal would be too high, order the encroacher to pay damages to the neighbor.

Technically, an encroachment is not an encumbrance, because it is not a right or interest held by the encroacher. However, if ignored for the statutory period, the encroachment could ripen into a prescriptive easement or even into title by adverse possession.

Nuisances

A nuisance is an activity or a condition on neighboring property that interferes with a property owner's reasonable use or enjoyment of his own property. Common examples include odors, noises, and interference with communication signals. Like an encroachment, a nuisance isn't truly an encumbrance, but rather a violation of an owner's possessory rights.

A private nuisance affects only a few surrounding people. For example, rotting garbage in a neighbor's back yard would be a private nuisance. A public nuisance affects a larger community's health or welfare; jet noise and industrial emissions are examples. A property owner may ask a court for an injunction against a private or public nuisance, or may sue for damages.

A related concept is the **attractive nuisance** doctrine. The owner of a property with a feature that is dangerous and attractive to children, such as an unfenced swimming pool or construction site, will be held liable for any harm resulting from failure to keep out trespassing children.

Private Restrictions

Private restrictions (also known as deed restrictions) are restrictions on the use of a property that were imposed by some previous owner. For example, when selling a house long ago, a previous owner might have stated in the deed that the poplar trees in the front yard must not be cut down. Like easements, private restrictions can "run with the land," binding all subsequent owners of the property.

As long as a private restriction isn't unconstitutional, in violation of a law, or contrary to a judicial determination of public policy, it can be enforced in court. (An example of an unenforceable restriction is one prohibiting the sale of property to non-white buyers; see Chapter 15.)

Most subdivision developers impose a list of restrictions on all lots within the subdivision, before they begin selling individual lots. This is called a declaration of restrictions, or **CC&Rs** (covenants, conditions, and restrictions). The CC&Rs typically include rules limiting all the lots to single-family residential use, requiring property maintenance, and preventing activities that would bother the neighbors. The rules are intended to ensure that the subdivision will remain a desirable place to live.

Covenants vs. Conditions. A private restriction is either a covenant or a condition. A **covenant** is a promise to do or not do something, as in a contract. A property owner who violates a covenant may be sued, leading to an injunction (a court order directing the owner to comply with the covenant) or to payment of damages for failure to comply. Violation of a **condition** can have more serious consequences. A condition in a deed makes the grantee's title conditional, so that she owns a qualified fee (rather than a fee simple absolute; see Chapter 2). Breach of the condition could result in forfeiture of title.

Whether a particular restriction is a covenant or a condition depends on the wording in the deed. Courts try to avoid forfeitures, so they will usually interpret a restriction as a covenant rather than a condition, if there is any ambiguity. (CC&Rs are virtually always covenants, even though the term includes the word "conditions.")

Termination of Restrictions. It is up to the property owners within a subdivision to enforce the CC&Rs, which they can do by obtaining an injunction, if necessary. However, if the residents have failed to enforce a particular restriction in the past, they may no longer be able to enforce it.

> **Example:** The subdivision's CC&Rs state that recreational vehicles may not be parked within view of the street. Over the years, however, many homeowners have broken this rule and their neighbors haven't complained. If someone tries to start enforcing the parking restriction now, a court might rule that it has been abandoned and is no longer enforceable.

A private restriction will also terminate if its purpose can no longer be achieved. For example, this might occur because zoning changes and other factors have dramatically altered the character of the neighborhood. If there is a private restriction limiting a property to single-family residential use, but most of the surrounding properties are now used for light industry, the restriction is probably no longer enforceable.

📖 Chapter Summary

1. An encumbrance is a nonpossessory right or interest in real property held by someone other than the property owner. Encumbrances may be financial or nonfinancial.

2. A financial encumbrance (a lien) affects title to property. It gives a creditor the right to foreclose and use the sale proceeds to pay off the debt. A lien may be voluntary or involuntary, general or specific. The most common types of liens include mortgages, deeds of trust, construction liens, tax liens, and judgment liens.

3. A nonfinancial encumbrance affects the use or condition of the property. Nonfinancial encumbrances include easements, profits, and private restrictions.

4. An easement gives the easement holder the right to use a portion of someone else's property for a specified purpose. An easement runs with the land, affecting the title of subsequent owners of the property or properties in question.

5. An easement appurtenant burdens one parcel of land (the servient tenement) for the benefit of another parcel (the dominant tenement). An easement in gross burdens a parcel of land for the benefit of a person, not another parcel of land.

6. Licenses, encroachments, and nuisances may also affect the use or condition of property. They are not classified as encumbrances, however, because they are not interests in real property.

7. Private restrictions affect how an owner may use his own property. Like easements, private restrictions run with the land. A declaration of CC&Rs recorded by a subdivision developer is binding on the future owners of the subdivision lots.

🔑 Key Terms

Encumbrance—An interest in real property held by someone other than the property owner.

Voluntary lien—A security interest in real property given voluntarily to a creditor by the owner. A voluntary lien is either a mortgage or a deed of trust.

Involuntary lien—A security interest given to a creditor by operation of law.

General lien—A lien that attaches to all of a debtor's property.

Specific lien—A lien that attaches only to one particular piece of property.

Construction lien—A lien on property in favor of someone who provided labor or materials to improve it; also called a mechanic's lien or materialman's lien.

Judgment lien—A lien held by someone who has won a judgment in a lawsuit, attaching to property owned by the person who lost the lawsuit.

Easement—The right to use another's land for a particular purpose.

Easement appurtenant—An easement that burdens one parcel of land (the servient tenement) for the benefit of another parcel (the dominant tenement).

Easement in gross—An easement that benefits a person rather than a parcel of land.

Easement by implication—An easement created automatically because it is necessary for the enjoyment of the benefited land.

Prescriptive easement—An easement created by continuous use for the statutory period, without the landowner's permission.

Merger—When both the dominant and servient tenements are acquired by one owner, resulting in termination of the easement.

Abandonment—A way in which an easement may terminate; it requires action by the easement holder, not simply non-use.

Profit—The right to take something (such as timber) from another's land.

License—Revocable permission to enter another's land, which does not create an interest in the property.

Encroachment—A physical object that intrudes onto another's property, such as a tree branch or a fence.

Nuisance—An activity or condition on nearby property that interferes with a property owner's reasonable use and enjoyment of her property.

CC&Rs—Covenants, conditions, and restrictions; private restrictions imposed by a subdivision developer.

Condition—A restriction on the use of land, the violation of which may result in forfeiture of title.

Covenant—A promise by a landowner to refrain from using her land in a particular manner.

Chapter Quiz

1. Real estate property taxes are:
   a) general, involuntary liens
   b) general, voluntary liens
   c) specific, voluntary liens
   d) specific, involuntary liens

2. A lawsuit against Thatcher is pending. The court rules that a lien should be placed on his farm, holding it as security in case of a negative judgment. This is:
   a) adverse possession
   b) prescription
   c) attachment
   d) appurtenance

3. A recorded document that informs potential buyers that the property may become subject to a judgment in a lawsuit is a:
   a) lis pendens
   b) writ of execution
   c) writ of attachment
   d) habendum clause

4. Which of the following has priority over a mortgage that has already been recorded?
   a) A deed of trust
   b) A judgment lien
   c) A property tax lien
   d) None of the above

5. If there were two deeds of trust against the same property and you needed to know which one had higher priority, you could find this information in the county records. The priority is usually established by the:
   a) printed trust deed forms, which have the words "first deed of trust" and "second deed of trust" on their face
   b) date and time of recording
   c) county auditor's stamp, which says "first trust deed" or "second trust deed"
   d) execution date of each document

6. When there's an easement appurtenant, the dominant tenement:
   a) can be used only for purposes of ingress and egress
   b) is burdened by the easement
   c) receives the benefit of the easement
   d) cannot be sold

7. You have the right to cross another's land to get to your house. You probably own:
   a) a dominant tenement
   b) a servient tenement
   c) Both of the above
   d) Neither of the above

8. An easement in gross benefits:
   a) a dominant tenement
   b) a servient tenement
   c) Both of the above
   d) Neither of the above

9. Unlike a personal easement in gross, a commercial easement in gross:
   a) is not an encumbrance
   b) is considered a possessory interest in real property
   c) can be assigned to another party
   d) can be revoked by the owner of the servient tenement

10. Which of the following is not a method of creating an easement?
    a) Implication
    b) Express grant in a deed
    c) Dedication
    d) Spoken grant

11. The creation of an easement by prescription is similar to acquiring ownership of property by:
    a) adverse possession
    b) escheat
    c) alluvium
    d) intestate succession

12. A has an easement over B's property. If A buys
    B's property, the easement:

    a) goes with the land
    b) is terminated
    c) is unaffected
    d) None of the above

13. A porch or balcony that hangs over the estab-
    lished boundary line of a parcel of land is called
    a/an:

    a) easement in gross
    b) encroachment
    c) easement appurtenant
    d) license

14. All of the following would be considered
    nuisances, except:

    a) fumes from a paper mill
    b) a house with regular drug-dealing activity
    c) radiation from a microwave tower
    d) a garage built on top of the property line

15. The private restrictions in a subdivision's
    CC&Rs:

    a) do not run with the land
    b) were most likely imposed by the developer
    c) can terminate only with the approval of a ma-
       jority of the lot owners
    d) create a lien against the property

☞ **Answer Key**

1. d) Property tax liens are specific (they attach only to the taxed property) and involuntary.

2. c) In an attachment, a lien is created against the defendant's property, pending the outcome of the lawsuit.

3. a) A lis pendens provides constructive notice of a pending lawsuit that may affect the property described in the document.

4. c) Property tax liens always have priority over other liens.

5. b) The date of recording governs lien priority, rather than the date of execution of the documents.

6. c) The dominant tenement is benefited by the easement; the servient tenement is burdened by the easement. An easement appurtenant is not necessarily an easement for ingress and egress.

7. a) Since you have the right to use another's property to reach your own, you probably own a dominant tenement.

8. d) An easement in gross benefits an individual (the dominant tenant) rather than any parcel of land.

9. c) A commercial easement in gross can be assigned to another party, but a personal easement in gross cannot be.

10. d) Like any other interest in land, an easement must be granted in writing, unless it is created by operation of law.

11. a) An easement by prescription is obtained in much the same way as ownership by adverse possession: the use must be open and notorious, hostile, and continuous for ten years. It does not have to be exclusive, however.

12. b) Merger occurs when one person acquires ownership of both the dominant tenement and the servient tenement. Merger terminates the easement.

13. b) An overhanging porch or balcony is an encroachment.

14. d) A structure built on the property line is an encroachment, not a nuisance. A nuisance is an activity or condition on neighboring property that negatively affects an owner's use and enjoyment of his property.

15. b) CC&Rs are usually imposed by the developer. They run with the land, which means that subsequent owners of the subdivision lots must abide by them.

Chapter 5

Public Restrictions on Land

I. Land Use Controls
   A. Comprehensive planning
   B. Zoning
      1. Nonconforming uses
      2. Variances
      3. Conditional uses
      4. Rezones
   C. Building codes
   D. Subdivision regulations
      1. Physical regulations
      2. Consumer protection laws
   E. Environmental laws
      1. Shoreline Management Act
      2. NEPA
      3. SEPA
      4. CERCLA
      5. Pollution control laws
      6. Environmental hazards
II. Eminent Domain
III. Taxation
   A. General real estate taxes
   B. Special assessments
   C. Real estate excise tax

Chapter Overview

Although property owners have many rights in regard to their property, those rights are limited by federal, state, and local governments. This chapter examines the ways in which governmental powers affect real property ownership most directly. It covers planning, zoning, and other public restrictions on land use; the taking of private property for public use; and the taxation of real property.

Land Use Controls

In the United States, the powers of government are restricted by the federal and state constitutions. Thus, efforts by the federal, state, and local governments to control the use of private property raise constitutional issues. When a property owner objects to a land use law, the central question is often whether the law is constitutional—whether the federal and state constitutions give the government the power to interfere with private property rights in this way.

The basis for land use control laws is the **police power**. This is the power vested in a state government to adopt and enforce laws and regulations necessary for the protection of the public's health, safety, morals, and general welfare. A state may delegate its police power to local governmental bodies.

It is the police power that allows state and local governments to regulate a private individual's use of her property. The Constitution does not give the federal government a general power to regulate for the public health, safety, morals, and welfare. But the federal government does have authority to use its other powers (such as the power to regulate interstate commerce) to advance police power objectives.

An exercise of the police power must meet constitutional limitations. As a general rule, a land use law or regulation is constitutional if it meets these four criteria:

1. It is reasonably related to the protection of the public health, safety, morals, or general welfare.
2. It applies in the same manner to all property owners who are similarly situated (in other words, it is not discriminatory).
3. It does not reduce a property's value so much that the regulation amounts to a confiscation—an uncompensated taking of property.
4. It benefits the public by preventing harm that would be caused by the prohibited use of the property.

Government land use controls take a variety of forms: comprehensive plans, zoning ordinances, building codes, subdivision regulations, and environmental laws. All of these are intended to protect the public from problems that unrestricted use of private property can cause.

Comprehensive Planning

To alleviate the problems caused by haphazard, unplanned growth, many states require cities and counties to have a planning agency, which is usually called a planning commission.

The planning commission is responsible for designing and adopting a comprehensive, long-term plan for all the development within the city or county. This is often called the "master plan" or "general plan." The purpose of the general plan is to outline the community's development goals and design an overall physical layout to achieve those goals. Once the general plan has been adopted, all development and all land use regulations (such as zoning laws) must conform to it.

The government uses both its police power and its power of eminent domain (discussed later) to implement the planning commission's general plan.

In Washington, land use planning and administration is governed by the **Growth Management Act**. The act's goals include:

1. reducing suburban sprawl by concentrating new development in already existing urban growth areas;
2. requiring thorough infrastructure planning, including an emphasis on transportation alternatives;
3. protecting critical areas from environmentally harmful activities, and protecting open space;
4. encouraging the availability of affordable housing; and
5. encouraging economic growth consistent with the act's other goals.

Zoning

Zoning ordinances divide a community into areas (or zones) that are set aside for specific types of uses, such as agricultural, residential, commercial, or industrial use. Each of these basic classifications typically has subcategories. For instance, industrial uses may be divided into light industry and heavy industry; residential uses may be divided into single-family, two- to four-family, and multifamily dwellings. Keeping different types of uses in separate zones helps ensure that only compatible uses are located in the same area. In addition, areas zoned for incompatible uses may be separated by undeveloped areas called **buffers**.

Zoning ordinances regulate the height, size, and shape of buildings, as well as their use. They also usually include setback and side yard requirements, which prescribe the minimum distance between a building and the property lines. These regulations control population density, provide aesthetic guidelines, and help preserve adequate open space and access to air and daylight. Certain subdivisions, known as planned unit developments, may be zoned with reduced setback and side yard requirements, creating smaller lots in exchange for commonly held green space. (In less urban areas, these subdivisions may be called rural cluster developments.)

Zoning Exceptions and Amendments. Complications inevitably arise when zoning regulations are administered and enforced. So zoning ordinances provide for certain exceptions and changes to their rules, including:

- nonconforming uses,
- variances,
- conditional uses, and
- rezones.

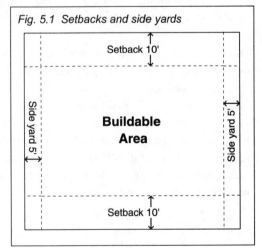

Fig. 5.1 Setbacks and side yards

Setback 10'

Side yard 5'

Buildable Area

Side yard 5'

Setback 10'

Nonconforming Uses. When an area is zoned for the first time, or when a zoning ordinance is amended, certain established uses that were lawful before may not conform to the new rules. These **nonconforming uses** will usually be permitted to continue.

Example: Smith has been lawfully operating a bakery for seven months when his property is rezoned for single-family residential use. Smith's bakery will be allowed to continue as a nonconforming use.

Even though nonconforming uses are allowed to remain, the local government wants all uses to conform to the current zoning laws at some point. In some cases, an ordinance requires nonconforming uses to be phased out by a certain deadline (for example, ten years after the ordinance is passed). And even in the absence of such a deadline, the owner of a nonconforming use property is often prohibited from enlarging the use, rebuilding if the property is destroyed, or resuming the use after abandoning it.

Example: Smith's bakery burns to the ground in a terrible fire. The zoning authority will not allow him to rebuild the bakery in this residential zone. He will have to sell the property and find a suitable property located in a commercial zone.

Variances. In some cases, if a zoning law were strictly enforced, the property owner's injury would far outweigh the benefit of enforcing the zoning requirement. Under these circumstances, a **variance** may be available. A variance is authorization to build or maintain a structure or use that is prohibited by the zoning ordinance. For example, a variance might authorize construction of a house even though the topography of the lot makes it virtually impossible to comply with normal setback requirements. In most communities, the property owner applies to the local zoning authority for a variance.

A variance usually will not be granted unless the property owner faces severe practical difficulties or undue hardship (not created by the property owner himself) as a result of the zoning. The owner is generally required to prove that the zoning prevents any reasonable use of the land, not merely the most profitable use.

Example: Corelli owns a piece of property that would make a perfect site for a convenience store, but it is in a residential zone. Corelli will not be able to get a variance by claiming that she could make much more money by building a convenience store than she could by building a single-family home.

Most variances authorize only minor deviations from the zoning law. A variance should not change the essential character of the neighborhood or conflict with the community's general plan.

Conditional Uses. Various special uses, such as schools, hospitals, and churches, don't fit into the ordinary zoning categories. These uses are necessary to the community, yet they may have adverse effects on neighboring properties. So in most communities the zoning authority can issue **conditional use permits** (also called special exception permits), allowing a limited number of these uses to operate in compliance with specified conditions. For example, a property owner might be given a conditional use permit to build a private school in a residential neighborhood, as long as the school meets certain requirements for parking, security, and so on.

Rezones. If a property owner believes that her property has been zoned improperly, she may petition the local appeals board for a **rezone** (sometimes called a zoning amendment). Usually, notice must be given to surrounding landowners and a hearing must be held before a decision is made on a petition.

When an area is rezoned to a more restrictive use (for example, a change from multifamily dwellings to single-family dwellings), it is referred to as **downzoning**. An **upzone** is the opposite: the zoning becomes less restrictive. For example, an upzone would include raising the building height limits in an urban area to help meet the housing density goals of a comprehensive plan.

Building Codes

The enactment of building codes is another exercise of the police power. Building codes protect the public from unsafe or unworkmanlike construction. They are generally divided into specialized codes, such as a fire code, an electrical code, and a plumbing code. The codes set standards for construction methods and materials. A structure that was built before a new, stricter standard is enacted may still be required to meet the new standard. However, if an older structure is protected as a historic landmark, a separate building code usually applies.

Enforcement of building codes is usually accomplished through the building permit system. A property owner must obtain a permit from the city or county before constructing a new building or repairing, improving, or altering an existing building. For example, it is usually necessary to have a building permit in order to add on to a home, to convert a carport into a garage, or even to build a fence over a certain height. The permit requirement allows officials to inspect the building plans to verify that building codes and zoning ordinances have been complied with. Once the completed building has been inspected and found satisfactory, a **certificate of occupancy** is issued.

Subdivision Regulations

Another way state and local governments control land use is by regulating subdivisions. A subdivision is a division of one parcel of land into two or more parcels.

There are two basic types of subdivision regulations in Washington. The first type establishes requirements concerning the physical aspects of subdivisions, such as access roads, utilities, lot size, and so on. The second type is embodied in the state's Land Development Act. This is actually a consumer protection law rather than a land use control law; it requires subdivision developers to disclose certain information to prospective lot purchasers.

Physical Regulations. Regulations concerning the physical aspects of subdivisions are adopted and administered by each county in Washington. Although the regulations vary from county to county, the procedures for compliance are fairly uniform throughout the state. Someone who wants to subdivide a parcel of land must first notify county officials by submitting a plat map. The plat shows the boundaries of the proposed lots and provides information about arrangements for utilities and other public services. If the property is within city limits or within one mile of a city, the plat map must also be submitted to the proper city officials (usually the planning commission).

The plat must include the legal description of the land to be subdivided. It must also provide for any dedications that the county or city requires, such as dedication of land within the subdivision for public streets. (Dedication is a transfer of property from private to public ownership; see Chapter 3.)

The county or city may approve the plat as submitted, or may require amendments. It is illegal for the subdivider to sell any lots until the plat has been approved.

Washington Land Development Act. The Land Development Act applies to anyone selling or advertising 26 or more unimproved lots to the general public in Washington as part of a common promotional plan. It applies even when the subdivision is located in another state, if it is promoted in this state.

Under the act, a subdivision developer must prepare a **public offering statement**, providing information about the development. The statement includes disclosures concerning liens against the subdivision, the physical condition of the land, compliance with land use laws, and warranties that apply to the purchase of a lot.

The developer should give a public offering statement to each prospective lot buyer at least two days before the buyer signs a purchase contract. Otherwise, the buyer has a right to back out of the transaction (rescind the contract) within two days after receiving the statement. If the developer fails to give the buyer a statement before the transaction closes, the buyer can sue for damages.

The Land Development Act has a number of exemptions. It doesn't apply to a subdivision if fewer than ten lots will be offered for sale in a 12-month period, or if all the subdivision lots:

- are five acres or more,
- have buildings on them (or the developer intends to build within two years),
- are sold to builders for development,
- are sold to one purchaser, or
- lie entirely within city limits.

ILSA. The **Interstate Land Sales Full Disclosure Act** (commonly referred to as ILSA) is a federal consumer protection law concerning subdivisions of vacant land offered for sale or lease in interstate commerce. It has registration requirements (requiring developers to register their projects with a federal agency) and anti-fraud provisions (requiring disclosure of information to buyers and prohibiting misleading sales practices and advertising). The anti-fraud provisions generally apply to subdivisions with 25 or more vacant lots, and the registration requirements generally apply to subdivisions with 100 or more vacant lots, but there are numerous exemptions. The Consumer Financial Protection Bureau enforces ILSA.

Environmental Laws

The federal and state governments have enacted a number of laws aimed at preserving and protecting the physical environment, and some local governments have additional environmental regulations. These laws can have a substantial impact on the ways in which a property owner is allowed to use his land.

Shoreline Management Act. The purpose of this law is to protect Washington's shorelines by regulating development within 200 feet of the high water mark. It applies to coastal shorelines, and to the shores of larger lakes and streams.

National Environmental Policy Act (NEPA). NEPA is a federal law that requires federal agencies to prepare an **environmental impact statement** (EIS) for any governmental action that would have a significant impact on the environment. NEPA also applies to private uses or developments that require the approval of a federal agency.

State Environmental Policy Act (SEPA). Washington's SEPA is similar to NEPA in that it requires preparation of environmental impact statements. Under the state law, an EIS is required in connection with all actions of state and local agencies that may have a significant effect on the environment. The act also applies to private uses and developments that require the approval of the state, county, or city. Thus, SEPA procedures must be followed before a city or county approves rezones, conditional use permits, variances, or building permits.

CERCLA. The Comprehensive Environmental Response, Compensation, and Liability Act, a federal law, concerns liability for environmental cleanup costs. In some cases, the current owners of contaminated property may be required to pay for cleanup, even if they did not cause the contamination. This law is enforced by the federal Environmental Protection Agency (the EPA).

Pollution Control Laws. Federal legislation sets national standards for air and water quality and requires the states to implement these objectives. Permits are required for the discharge of pollutants into the air or water.

Environmental Hazards. Real estate agents should also be aware of the dangers posed by environmental hazards, such as asbestos insulation, lead-based paint, and geologic hazards. Some of these hazards are addressed by federal or state laws.

Asbestos. Asbestos was used for many years in insulation on plumbing pipes and heat ducts, and as general insulation material. It can also be found in floor tile and roofing material. In its original condition, asbestos is considered relatively harmless; but when it gets old and starts to disintegrate into a fine dust, it can cause lung cancer and should be removed. Asbestos must be enclosed, covered with a permanent seal, or removed by an experienced professional.

Urea Formaldehyde. Adhesives containing urea formaldehyde are found in the pressed wood building materials used in furniture, kitchen cabinets, and some types of paneling. Urea formaldehyde can release formaldehyde gas, which can cause cancer, skin rashes, and breathing problems. However, these materials emit significant amounts of this gas only in the first few years. Older urea formaldehyde materials are not considered dangerous.

Radon. Radon, a colorless, odorless gas, is actually present almost everywhere. It is found wherever uranium is deposited in the earth's crust. As uranium decays, radon gas is formed and seeps from the earth, usually into the atmosphere. However, radon sometimes collects in buildings. For example, radon may enter a house through cracks in the foundation or through floor drains. Exposure to dangerous levels of radon gas may cause lung cancer.

Lead-Based Paint. Lead is extremely toxic to human beings, damaging the brain, the kidneys, and the central nervous system. The most common source of lead in the home is lead-based paint. Although lead is now banned in consumer paint, it is still found in many homes built before 1978. As lead-based paint deteriorates, or if it is sanded or scraped, it forms a lead dust that accumulates inside and outside the home. The dust can be breathed in or ingested, increasing the risk of toxic lead exposure. In some cases, a seller or landlord is required by law to make disclosures concerning lead-based paint to prospective buyers or tenants.

Underground Storage Tanks. Underground storage tanks are found not only on commercial and industrial properties, but also on residential properties. Older homes used underground storage tanks to store fuel oil. A storage tank is considered underground if at least 10% of its volume (including piping) is below the earth's surface. The principal danger from underground storage tanks is that when they grow old they begin to rust, leaking toxic products into the soil or, even more dangerously, into the groundwater. Removing underground storage tanks and cleaning up the contaminated soil can be time-consuming and expensive. Both federal and state laws regulate the removal of storage tanks and the necessary cleanup.

Water Contamination. Water can be contaminated by a variety of agents, including bacteria, viruses, nitrates, metals such as lead or mercury, fertilizers, pesticides, and radon. These contaminants may come from underground storage tanks, industrial discharge, urban area runoff, malfunctioning septic systems, and runoff from agricultural areas. Drinking contaminated water can cause physical symptoms that range from mild stomach upset to kidney and liver damage, cancer, and death. If a home uses a well as a water source, it should be tested by health authorities or private laboratories at least once a year.

Illegal Drug Manufacturing. If property has been the site of illegal drug manufacturing, there may be substantial health risks for subsequent occupants. The chemicals used to manufacture certain illegal drugs are highly toxic, and the effects of the contamination can linger for a long time. The government can seize any property being used to manufacture illegal drugs. Property should not be listed or sold until any conditions that could subject the property to seizure have been eliminated.

Example: Meyers owns a single-family home that has been used as a rental property for several years. Unknown to Meyers, the current tenants are manufacturing illegal drugs in the basement of the home. The property could be seized by the government, even though Meyers knows nothing about the drug activity.

Mold. Mold is a commonplace problem, especially in damp parts of houses such as basements and bathrooms. For most people, the presence of mold does not cause any adverse effects. However, for people who are allergic to mold or who have respiratory problems, the presence of mold may render a house unlivable. Mold can affect residential, commercial, or public buildings such as schools and government offices. Bear in mind that mold may grow out of sight, inside walls or heating ducts, and will not necessarily be discovered in an inspection.

Geologic Hazards. Geologic hazards are a significant concern for many property owners in the coastal regions of the country. Major potential geologic problems include landslides, flooding, subsidence, and earthquakes. When dealing with a property located on or near a steep slope, look for signs of ground movement. Tilting trees, active soil erosion, and cracking, dipping, or slumping ground are all indicators of slide activity. Subsidence is the collapse of ground into underground cavities, which may be natural or man-made. It is wise to consult with a geologist to assess the magnitude of a ground movement problem.

Flooding can also be a serious problem for property owners. Whenever property is located in a flood plain—the low-lying, flat areas immediately adjacent to a river— there is cause for concern. It is prudent to check for signs of previous flood damage to structures, particularly in basements and foundations. In some cases, it may be necessary to obtain flood insurance.

Earthquakes are the least predictable and least controllable of geologic problems. However, steps can be taken to protect buildings against earthquakes. Seismic retrofitting can make a property more desirable and increase its value. Many contractors are able to perform this type of work, and information about seismic retrofitting is widely available from state and local government agencies.

Eminent Domain

As you've seen, the government can regulate the use of private property with a variety of laws—zoning ordinances, building codes, and so on. These laws are based on the police power, the government's power to regulate for the public health, safety, morals, and general welfare. Another governmental power that can be used to control land use is the power of **eminent domain**.

The power of eminent domain is the federal or state government's power to take private property for a public purpose upon payment of **just compensation** to the owner (and to any others who hold an interest in the property, such as tenants). Just compensation for an owner is usually defined as the fair market value of the property. A state government may delegate the power of eminent domain to local governments, and to private entities that serve the public, such as utility companies and railroads.

Condemnation is the process by which the government exercises its power of eminent domain. When a particular property is needed for a public purpose, the government first offers to buy it from the owner. If the owner refuses to sell for the price offered, the government files a condemnation lawsuit. The court will order the property to be transferred to the government. The owner's only grounds for objection are that the intended use of the property is not a public use, or that the price offered is not just compensation.

A local government can use the power of eminent domain to implement its general plan. For example, to fulfill the plan's open space goals, several pieces of private property might be condemned for use as a public park.

It is important to understand the distinction between eminent domain and the police power. Eminent domain involves a "taking": property is taken away from the owner, and the Constitution requires the government to pay the owner compensation. In an exercise of the police power, private property is regulated, but not taken away from the owner. The government is usually not required to compensate the owner for a proper exercise of the police power, unless the action (such as a new environmental regulation) so significantly reduces the value of the property that a court finds it to be a taking.

Taxation

Real property taxes affect property ownership. The taxes create liens, and if the property owner fails to pay the taxes, the government can sell the property to collect them. Real property taxation has always been a popular method of raising revenue because land has a fixed location, is relatively indestructible, and is essentially impossible to conceal. Thus, there is a high degree of certainty that the taxes will be collected.

In this section, we will discuss these three types of taxes on real property:

- general real estate taxes (also called ad valorem taxes),
- special assessments (also called improvement taxes), and
- the real estate excise tax (also called the transfer tax).

General Real Estate Taxes

General real estate taxes are levied to support the general operation and services of government. Public schools and police and fire protection are examples of government services paid for with general real estate tax revenues. These taxes are levied by a number of governmental agencies, such as cities, counties, school districts, and water districts. Thus, a single property can be situated in five or six taxing districts.

Assessment. General real estate taxes are **ad valorem** taxes. That means the amount of tax owed depends on the value of the property. The valuation of property for purposes of taxation is called **assessment**. In Washington, all real property must be assessed at 100% of its "true and fair value" unless otherwise provided by law. True and fair value means market value: the most probable price that the property would sell for under normal market conditions.

Real property is assessed each year on January 1, although a physical examination of the property has to be performed only once every six years. In each county, a Board of Equalization hears appeals of property tax assessments from taxpayers.

Collection of Taxes. Tax bills are mailed to property owners each year in the middle of February. Payment of half the taxes is due on April 30, and the balance is due on October 31.

General real estate taxes become a lien on January 1 of the year in which they are levied. Taxes are levied in October of each year and payable the following year.

The county can foreclose on a property when the taxes have been delinquent for three years. The owner can redeem the property before the sale by paying the amount of delinquent taxes, interest, and any other accumulated costs.

Exemptions. State law exempts numerous types of property from general real estate taxes. For example, the taxes aren't levied against publicly owned property, property used for church purposes, or nonprofit hospitals and schools.

There are also some exemptions available to individual property owners. For example, there is a partial exemption for low-income homeowners who are 61 or older, or retired because of physical disability. In some cases, these owners may also be allowed to defer payment of the partial taxes they owe until their property is sold.

Open Space. Washington has a special rule for taxation of open space, which shows how the power to tax can be used for land use control. Certain land that qualifies as open space is eligible to be assessed not at its market value (which might mean how much it would be worth if developed) but at its value as it is currently being used. This results in a lower assessment, and therefore in lower taxes, providing an incentive to preserve the property as open space instead of developing it. To have property assessed in this way, the owner must agree that if the property is developed or sold for development, additional taxes will be paid at that point.

Special Assessments

Special assessments, also called local improvement taxes, are levied to pay for improvements that benefit particular properties, such as the installation of streetlights or the widening of a street. Only the properties that benefit from the improvement are taxed, on the theory that the value of those properties is increased by the improvement. A special assessment is usually a one-time tax, although the property owners may be allowed to pay the assessment off in installments.

Like general real estate taxes, special assessments create liens against the taxed properties. If an owner fails to pay the assessment, the government can foreclose on the property.

Here is a summary of the distinctions between general real estate taxes and special assessments:

1. General real estate taxes are levied to pay for ongoing government services, such as police protection. A special assessment is levied to pay for a specific improvement, such as adding sidewalks to a section of street.

2. General real estate taxes are levied against all taxable real property within a taxing district, for the benefit of the entire community. A special assessment, on the other hand, is levied against only those properties that benefit from the improvement in question.

3. General real estate taxes are levied every year. A special assessment is a one-time tax, levied only when a property is benefited by a public improvement.

Real Estate Excise Tax

An excise tax is levied on each sale of real property in Washington. The tax is based on the property's selling price. The state's share of the tax is 1.28% of the selling price, and an additional percentage is owed to the local government. This additional percentage varies depending on the city or county where the property is located.

The excise tax is ordinarily collected when the buyer's deed is recorded; the recorder's office will not accept a deed for recording unless the tax is paid and a real estate excise tax affidavit is executed. By law, the seller is liable for payment of the excise tax. Yet the tax creates a lien against the transferred property (now owned by the buyer). Thus, even though payment is the seller's responsibility, a buyer should always make sure the excise tax is paid, so that the deed can be recorded and lien foreclosure avoided.

📖 Chapter Summary

1. The police power—the government's power to adopt and enforce laws for the protection of the public health, safety, morals, and general welfare—is the basis for land use control laws.

2. Many communities have a general plan—a comprehensive, long-term plan for development—and some counties and cities are required by law to have one. A local government implements its general plan with zoning ordinances and other laws.

3. Zoning ordinances provide for certain exceptions to their rules: nonconforming uses, variances, and conditional uses. They also have procedures for rezones.

4. Building codes set standards for construction materials and practices, to protect the public. The codes are enforced through the building permit system.

5. Someone who subdivides land must submit a plat map to the county and comply with local subdivision regulations. In some cases, a developer will also be required to comply with consumer protection laws regulating the sale of subdivision lots.

6. There are a number of important federal and state environmental laws that affect land use, including the Shoreline Management Act, NEPA, SEPA, and CERCLA.

7. Along with environmental laws, real estate agents need to be aware of environmental hazards such as asbestos, urea formaldehyde, radon, lead-based paint, underground storage tanks, water contamination, illegal drug manufacturing, mold, and geologic hazards.

8. A government entity can use the power of eminent domain to implement its general plan. When property is taken under the power of eminent domain, the government must pay just compensation to the owner. (Compensation is not required when property is merely regulated under the police power.)

9. The government's power to tax also affects property ownership. General real estate taxes are levied each year to pay for ongoing government services. Special assessments are levied to pay for improvements that benefit specific properties. The real estate excise tax must be paid on each sale of real property in Washington.

🔑 Key Terms

Police power—The power of state governments to regulate for the protection of the public health, safety, morals, and general welfare.

General plan—A comprehensive, long-term plan of development for a community, which is implemented by zoning and other laws.

Zoning—A method of controlling land use by dividing a community into zones for different types of uses.

Nonconforming use—A formerly legal use that does not conform to a new zoning ordinance, but is nonetheless allowed to continue.

Variance—An authorization to deviate from the rules in a zoning ordinance, granted because strict enforcement would cause undue hardship for the property owner.

Conditional use permit—A permit that allows a special use, such as a school or hospital, to operate in a neighborhood where it would otherwise be prohibited by the zoning.

Rezone—An amendment to a zoning ordinance; a property owner who feels her property has been zoned improperly may apply for a rezone.

Building codes—Regulations that set minimum standards for construction methods and materials.

Eminent domain—The government's power to take private property for public use, upon payment of just compensation to the owner.

Condemnation—The process of taking property pursuant to the power of eminent domain.

General real estate taxes—Taxes levied against real property annually to pay for general government services; based on the value of the property taxed (ad valorem).

Special assessment—A tax levied against property that benefits from a local improvement project, to pay for the project.

Real estate excise tax—A tax levied when a piece of real property is sold; based on the selling price of the property.

Chapter Quiz

1. The police power is the government's power to:
   a) take private property for public use
   b) enact laws for the protection of the public health, safety, morals, and general welfare
   c) tax property to pay for police protection
   d) None of the above

2. Which of the following is likely to be controlled by a zoning ordinance?
   a) Use of the property
   b) Building height
   c) Placement of a building on a lot
   d) All of the above

3. Which of the following is NOT likely to be one of the goals of a land use control law?
   a) Ensuring that properties are put to their most profitable use
   b) Controlling growth and population density
   c) Ensuring that neighboring uses are compatible
   d) Preserving access to light and air

4. As a general rule, when a new zoning ordinance goes into effect, nonconforming uses:
   a) must comply with the new law within 90 days
   b) must shut down within 90 days
   c) will be granted conditional use permits
   d) are allowed to continue, but not to expand

5. An owner who feels that his property was improperly zoned should apply for a:
   a) conditional use permit
   b) variance
   c) rezone
   d) nonconforming use permit

6. A property owner is generally required to show undue hardship in order to obtain a:
   a) nonconforming use permit
   b) special exception permit
   c) rezone
   d) variance

7. Which of these is an example of a variance?
   a) Authorizing a hospital to be built in a residential zone
   b) Authorizing a structure to be built only 12 feet from the lot's boundary, although the zoning ordinance requires 15-foot setbacks
   c) Allowing a grocery store to continue in operation after the neighborhood is zoned residential
   d) Approving the subdivision of a parcel of land into two or more lots

8. Which of these is NOT an exercise of the police power?
   a) Condemnation
   b) Building code
   c) Zoning ordinance
   d) Subdivision regulations

9. Eminent domain differs from the police power in that:
   a) the government is required to compensate the property owner
   b) it can be exercised only by the state government, not a city or county government
   c) it affects only the use of the property, not the title
   d) the property must be unimproved

10. Which of the following hazardous substances is a natural product of the decay of radioactive matter?
    a) Radon
    b) Urea formaldehyde
    c) Mold
    d) Carbon monoxide

11. A special assessment is the same thing as a/an:
    a) general real estate tax
    b) improvement tax
    c) real estate excise tax
    d) ad valorem tax

12. General real estate taxes are:
    a) used to support the general operation and services of government
    b) levied annually
    c) based on the value of the taxed property
    d) All of the above

13. Which of these is a federal law concerning liability for environmental cleanup costs?
    a) ILSA
    b) CERCLA
    c) SEPA
    d) NEPA

14. The real estate excise tax is based on the property's:
    a) selling price
    b) fair market value
    c) current use
    d) highest and best use

15. Under the State Environmental Policy Act (SEPA), an environmental impact statement is required:
    a) for every building project
    b) only for state or federal projects
    c) for all actions of state and local agencies that may have a significant impact on the environment
    d) for all actions of state and local agencies on an annual basis

👉 Answer Key

1. b) The police power is the government's power to pass laws (such as zoning ordinances) for the protection of the public health, safety, morals, and general welfare.

2. d) Zoning ordinances typically control the height and placement of buildings, as well as type of use.

3. a) Land use controls are not aimed at encouraging the most profitable use of particular properties. In some cases they prohibit more profitable uses that would be detrimental to the public health, safety, or welfare.

4. d) A nonconforming use (a use established before new zoning rules go into effect, which does not comply with those rules) is ordinarily allowed to continue, but the use cannot be expanded, rebuilt after destruction, or resumed after abandonment.

5. c) A rezone is an amendment to the zoning ordinance, giving a particular area a new zoning designation.

6. d) A variance is granted when the property owner shows that strict enforcement of the zoning law would result in undue hardship.

7. b) A variance authorizes the improvement of property in a manner not ordinarily allowed by the zoning ordinance. Most variances permit only minor deviations from the rules.

8. a) Condemnation is an exercise of the power of eminent domain, not the police power.

9. a) When a government body takes property under the power of eminent domain, it is required to pay compensation to the owner. Compensation is not required if a property loses value due to regulation under the police power.

10. a) Radon is an environmental hazard that occurs where uranium deposits are found. As uranium decays, radon gas is released, which can seep into buildings, often through foundation cracks.

11. b) A special assessment is also called an improvement tax; it is levied to pay for a particular public improvement.

12. d) All of these statements concerning general real estate taxes are true.

13. b) CERCLA is the Comprehensive Environmental Response, Compensation, and Liability Act, a federal law enforced by the EPA.

14. a) The real estate excise tax is levied only when title to property is transferred, and it is based on the selling price.

15. c) An EIS is required for all actions by state or local agencies that may have a significant impact on the environment, including state or local approval of private projects.

Chapter 6

Contract Law

I. Legal Classifications of Contracts
  A. Express vs. implied
  B. Unilateral vs. bilateral
  C. Executory vs. executed
II. Elements of a Valid Contract
  A. Capacity
  B. Mutual consent
  C. Lawful objective
  D. Consideration
  E. Writing requirement
III. Legal Status of Contracts
  A. Void
  B. Voidable
  C. Unenforceable
  D. Valid
IV. Discharging a Contract
  A. Full performance
  B. Agreement between the parties
V. Breach of Contract
  A. Remedies for breach of contract
    1. Rescission
    2. Compensatory damages
    3. Liquidated damages
    4. Specific performance
  B. Tender
VI. Types of Real Estate Contracts
  A. Listing agreements
  B. Buyer representation agreements
  C. Purchase and sale agreements
  D. Land contracts
  E. Leases
  F. Escrow instructions
  G. Option agreements

🏠 Chapter Overview

Contracts are a significant part of the real estate business. Almost everyone has a basic understanding of what a contract is, but real estate agents need more than that. This chapter explains the requirements that must be met in order for a contract to be valid and binding; how a contract can be terminated; what is considered a breach of contract; and what remedies are available when a breach occurs.

Introduction

Real estate licensees deal with contracts on a daily basis: listing agreements, purchase and sale agreements, option agreements, and leases are all contracts. Thus, it is essential for a licensee to understand the basic legal requirements and effects of contracts.

Keep in mind, however, that a real estate licensee may not draft the original language for a contract. Anyone other than a lawyer who drafts a contract for someone else may be charged with the unauthorized practice of law.

Here is a general definition of a **contract**: an agreement between two or more competent persons to do or not do certain things in exchange for consideration. An agreement to sell a car, deliver lumber, or rent an apartment is a contract. If the contract meets minimum legal requirements, it can be enforced in court.

Legal Classifications of Contracts

There are certain basic classifications that apply to any contract, no matter what type it is. Every contract is either express or implied, either unilateral or bilateral, and either executory or executed.

Express vs. Implied

An **express** contract is one that has been put into words. It may be written or oral. Each party to the contract has stated what he or she is willing to do and has been told what to expect from the other party. Most contracts are express. On the other hand, an **implied** contract, or contract by implication, is created by the actions of the parties, not by express agreement.

> **Example:** A written lease agreement expires, but the tenant continues to make payments and the landlord continues to accept them. Both parties have implied their consent to a new lease contract.

Unilateral vs. Bilateral

A contract is **unilateral** if only one of the contracting parties is legally obligated to perform. That party has promised to do a particular thing if the other party does something else; but the other party has not promised to do anything, and is not legally obligated to do anything.

Fig. 6.1 Contract classifications

Express	OR	Implied
Written or oral		Actions of the parties
Unilateral	OR	Bilateral
One promise		Two promises
Executory	OR	Executed
Not yet fully performed		Fully performed

Example: In an open listing agreement, a seller promises to pay a real estate brokerage a commission if the firm finds a buyer for the property. The firm does not promise to try to find a buyer, but if it does, the seller is obligated to pay. An open listing agreement is a unilateral contract.

A **bilateral** contract is formed when each party promises to do something, so that both parties are legally obligated to perform. Most contracts are bilateral.

Example: In a purchase and sale agreement, the seller promises to transfer title to the buyer, and the buyer promises to pay the agreed price to the seller. This is a bilateral contract. Each party has made a promise, and both are obligated to perform.

Executory vs. Executed

An **executory** contract is one that has not yet been performed, or is in the process of being performed. An **executed** contract has been fully performed; the parties have fulfilled the terms of their agreement. In this sense, the terms "executed" and "performed" mean the same thing.

Note, however, that "executed" also has another meaning in connection with contracts. Execution of a contract (or execution of a will, a deed, or some other type of legal document) can simply refer to signing it, not to performing or fulfilling it. The party or parties who execute a document have signed it and taken any other steps needed to make it legally binding (for example, in the case of a will, having it witnessed). Which meaning is intended in a particular case will usually be clear from the context.

Elements of a Valid Contract

To make any type of contract valid and binding, so that it will be enforced by a court, four elements are needed:

1. legal capacity to contract,
2. mutual consent,
3. a lawful objective, and
4. consideration.

Capacity

The first requirement for a valid contract is that the parties have the legal capacity to enter into a contract. A person must be at least 18 years old to enter into a valid contract, and she must also be competent.

Age Eighteen. Eighteen years of age is the age of majority in Washington. Minors (those under the age of 18) do not have capacity to contract. If a minor signs a contract, it is voidable by the minor; in other words, it cannot be enforced against him.

> **Example:** A 16-year-old signs a purchase and sale agreement, agreeing to buy a house. The seller cannot enforce the contract against the minor, although the minor could compel the seller to honor the terms of the agreement.

The purpose of this rule is to prevent people from entering into legally binding agreements when they may be too young to understand the consequences.

Competent. A person must also be mentally competent to have capacity to contract. If a person has been declared incompetent by a court, any contract she signs is void. If someone is declared incompetent after signing a contract, the contract may be voidable at the discretion of the court-appointed guardian.

A contract entered into by a person who was temporarily incompetent (for example, under the influence of alcohol or drugs) may be voidable if he takes legal action within a reasonable time after regaining mental competency.

Representing Another. Often, one person has the capacity to represent another person or entity in a contract negotiation. For instance, the affairs of minors and incompetent persons are handled by parents or court-appointed guardians; corporations are represented by properly authorized officers; partnerships are represented by individual partners; deceased persons are represented by executors or administrators; and a competent adult can appoint another competent adult to act on her behalf through a power of attorney. In each of these cases, the authorized representative can enter into a contract on behalf of the person represented.

Mutual Consent

Mutual consent is the second requirement for a valid contract. Each party must consent to the agreement. Once someone has signed a contract, consent is presumed, so no contract should be signed until its contents are fully understood. A person can't use failure or inability to read an agreement as an excuse for nonperformance. An illiterate person should have a contract explained thoroughly by someone trustworthy.

Mutual consent is sometimes called mutual assent, mutuality, or "a meeting of the minds." It is achieved through the process of **offer and acceptance**.

Offer. A contract offer shows the willingness of the person making it (the **offeror**) to enter into a contract on the stated terms. To be valid, an offer must meet two requirements:

1. It must express a willingness to contract. Whatever words make up the offer, they must clearly indicate that the offeror intends to enter into a contract.

2. It must be definite and certain in its terms. A vague offer that does not clearly state what the offeror is proposing is unenforceable.

Note that an advertisement that lists a property's price is not considered a contract offer; it is merely an invitation to negotiate.

Terminating an Offer. Sometimes circumstances change after an offer has been made, or perhaps the offeror has had a change of heart. If an offer terminates before it is accepted, no contract is formed. There are many things that can terminate an offer before it is accepted, including:

- revocation by the offeror,
- lapse of time,
- death or incompetency of the offeror,
- rejection of the offer, or
- a counteroffer.

The offeror can **revoke** the offer at any time until he is notified that the offer has been accepted. To effect a proper "offer and acceptance," the accepting party must not only accept the offer, but must also communicate that acceptance to the offeror before the offer is revoked. (See the discussion of acceptance, below.)

Many offers include a deadline for acceptance. If a deadline is set and acceptance is not communicated within the time allotted, the offer terminates automatically. If a time limit is not stated in the offer, a reasonable amount of time is allowed. What is reasonable is determined by the court if a dispute arises.

If the offeror dies or is declared incompetent before the offer is accepted, the offer terminates.

A **rejection** also terminates an offer. Once the **offeree** (the person to whom the offer was made) rejects the offer, she cannot go back later and create a contract by accepting the offer.

Example: Howard offers to purchase Maria's house for $235,000. Maria rejects the offer the next day. The following week, Maria changes her mind and decides to accept Howard's offer. But her acceptance at this point does not create a contract, because the offer terminated with her rejection.

A **counteroffer** is sometimes called a qualified acceptance. It is actually a rejection of the offer and a tender of a new offer. Instead of either accepting or rejecting the offer outright, the offeree "accepts" with certain modifications. This happens when some, but not all, of the original terms are unacceptable to the offeree. When there is a counteroffer, the roles of the parties are reversed: the original offeror becomes the offeree and can accept or reject the revised offer. If he chooses to accept the counteroffer, there is a binding contract. If the counteroffer is rejected, the party making the counteroffer cannot go back and accept the original offer. The original offer was terminated by the counteroffer.

Example: Palmer offers to buy Harrison's property on the following terms: the purchase price will be $450,000, the downpayment will be $30,000, and the closing date will be January 15. Harrison agrees to all of the terms except the closing date, which she wants to be February 1. By changing one of the terms, Harrison has rejected Palmer's initial offer and made a counteroffer. Now it is up to Palmer to either accept or reject Harrison's counteroffer.

Fig. 6.2 Mutual consent is achieved through the process of offer and acceptance

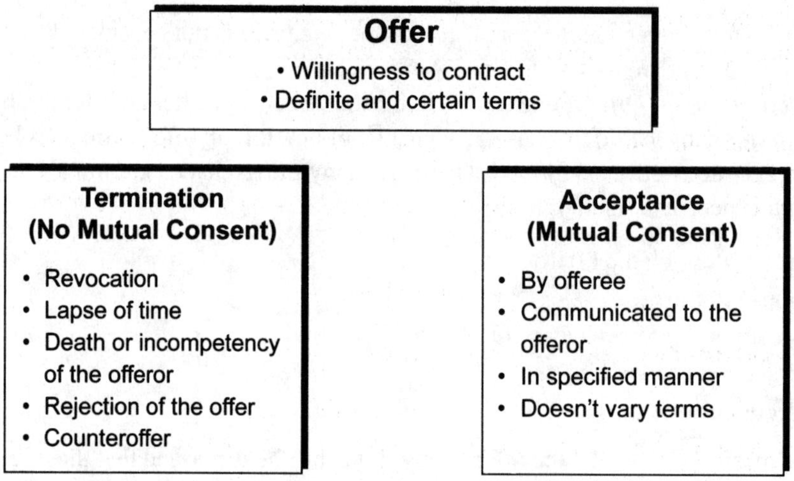

Offer
- Willingness to contract
- Definite and certain terms

Termination (No Mutual Consent)
- Revocation
- Lapse of time
- Death or incompetency of the offeror
- Rejection of the offer
- Counteroffer

Acceptance (Mutual Consent)
- By offeree
- Communicated to the offeror
- In specified manner
- Doesn't vary terms

Acceptance. An offer can be revoked at any time until acceptance has been communicated to the offeror. To create a binding contract, the offeree must communicate acceptance to the offeror in the manner and within the time limit stated in the offer (or before the offer is revoked). If no time or manner of acceptance is stated in the offer, a reasonable time and manner is implied.

The offeree's acceptance must also be free of any negative influences, such as fraud, undue influence, or duress. If an offer or acceptance is influenced by any of these negative forces, the contract is voidable by the injured party.

Fraud is misrepresentation of a material fact to another person who relies on the misrepresentation as the truth in deciding to enter into a transaction.

- **Actual fraud** occurs when the person making the statement either knows the statement is false and makes it with an intent to deceive, or doesn't know whether or not the statement is true but makes it anyway. For example, a seller who paints over cracks in the basement and then tells the buyer that the foundation is completely sound is committing actual fraud.
- **Constructive fraud** occurs when a person who occupies a position of confidence and trust, or who has superior knowledge of the subject matter, makes a false statement with no intent to deceive. For example, if a seller innocently points out incorrect lot boundaries, it may be constructive fraud.

Undue influence is using one's influence to pressure a person into making a contract, or taking advantage of another's distress or weakness of mind to induce her to enter into a contract.

Duress is compelling someone to do something—such as enter into a contract—against his will, by using or threatening to use force or constraint.

Lawful Objective

The third requirement for a valid contract is a lawful objective. Both the purpose of the contract and the consideration for the contract (discussed below) must be lawful. Examples of contracts with unlawful objectives are a contract requiring payment of an interest rate in excess of the state's usury limit, or a contract relating to unlawful gambling. If a contract does not have a lawful objective, it is void.

A contract may contain some lawful provisions and some unlawful provisions. In this situation, it may be possible to sever the unlawful portions of the contract and enforce the lawful portions.

Example: Callahan and Baker enter into a contract for the purchase and sale of an apartment house. A clause in the contract prohibits the buyer from renting the apartments to persons of a certain race. The contract concerning the sale of the property would probably be enforceable, but the racially restrictive clause would be void because it is unlawful.

Consideration

The fourth element of a valid contract is **consideration**. Consideration is something of value exchanged by the contracting parties. It might be money, goods, or services, or a promise to provide money, goods, or services. Whatever form it takes, the consideration must be either a benefit to the party receiving it or a detriment to the party offering it. The typical real estate purchase and sale contract involves a promise by the purchaser to pay a certain amount of money to the seller at a certain time, and a promise by the seller to convey title to the purchaser when the price has been paid. Both parties have given and received consideration.

While consideration is usually the promise to do a particular act, it can also be a promise to not do a particular act. For example, Aunt Martha might promise to pay her nephew Charles $1,000 if he promises not to smoke.

As a general rule, a contract is enforceable as long as the consideration has value, even though the value of the consideration exchanged is unequal. A contract to sell a piece of property worth $120,000 for $105,000 is enforceable. However, in cases where the disparity in value is quite large (for example, a contract to sell a piece of property worth $185,000 for $55,000), a court may refuse to enforce the contract. This is particularly likely to happen if the parties have unequal bargaining power (for instance, if the buyer is a real estate developer and the seller is elderly, uneducated, and inexperienced in business).

The Writing Requirement

The requirements we've covered so far—capacity, mutual consent, a lawful objective, and consideration—apply to any kind of contract. For most contracts used in real estate transactions, there's a fifth requirement: they must be put into writing, as required by the statute of frauds.

The **statute of frauds** is a state law that requires certain types of contracts to be in writing and signed. Only the types of contracts covered by the statute of frauds have to be in writing; other contracts may be oral.

Each state has its own statute of frauds, and the requirements vary

Fig. 6.3 Real estate contract requirements

A Valid Real Estate Contract

- Capacity
- Mutual consent
- Lawful objective
- Consideration
- In writing

slightly from state to state. As a general rule, however, almost all of the contracts typically used in a real estate transaction are covered by the statute of frauds. In Washington, the statute of frauds applies to:

- any agreement to convey an interest in real property (such as a purchase and sale agreement);
- any agreement that, by its terms, will not be performed within one year after it is made (such as a two-year lease);
- any agreement to assume the debts of another (such as the assumption of a mortgage); and
- any agreement to employ an agent for compensation to sell, buy, lease, or exchange real property (such as a listing agreement).

The "writing" required by the statute of frauds does not have to be in any particular form, nor does it have to be contained entirely in one document. A note or memorandum about the agreement or a series of letters will suffice, as long as the writing:

1. identifies the subject matter of the contract,
2. indicates an agreement between the parties and its essential terms, and
3. is signed by the party or parties to be bound.

If the parties fail to put a contract that falls under the statute of frauds in writing, the contract is usually unenforceable. However, occasionally a court will enforce such an unwritten agreement. This might occur if there is evidence that the contract exists and evidence of its terms, and if the party trying to enforce the contract has completely or substantially performed her contractual obligations. This is a relatively rare occurrence; the safest course is to put a contract in writing.

Legal Status of Contracts

Four terms are used to describe the legal status of a contract: a contract is void, voidable, unenforceable, or valid. We've already used these terms in our discussion, and now we'll look more closely at what each one means.

Void

A void contract is no contract at all; it has no legal effect. This most often occurs because one of the essential elements, such as mutual consent or consideration, is absent.

Example: Talbot signed a contract promising to deed some property to Worth, but Worth did not offer any consideration in exchange for Talbot's promise. Since the contract is not supported by consideration, it is void.

However, certain required elements can be missing without making the contract void. If an agreement to purchase real estate is not in writing, the contract is unenforceable rather than void. Or if one of the parties to a contract is a minor, then the contract is voidable for the minor and unenforceable for the other party; the minor's lack of full contractual capacity does not automatically make the contract void.

A void contract may be disregarded. Neither party is required to take legal action to withdraw from the agreement.

Voidable

A voidable contract appears on its face to be valid, but has some defect giving one or both of the parties the power to withdraw from the agreement. Contracts entered into by minors or as a result of fraud are normally voidable by the injured party (the minor or the one defrauded).

It is important to note that action must be taken to rescind a voidable contract. Unlike a contract that is void from the outset, a voidable contract cannot simply be ignored. Failure to take action within a reasonable time may result in a court declaring that the contract was ratified. Alternatively, the injured party may decide to continue with the agreement; in that case, he may expressly ratify it.

Unenforceable

An unenforceable contract is one that cannot be enforced in court for one of the following reasons:

1. its contents cannot be proved,
2. it is voidable by the other party, or
3. the statute of limitations has expired.

Contents Cannot Be Proved. This is most often a problem associated with oral agreements, where it may be impossible to prove who said what. Even if the statute of frauds does not require a certain kind of contract to be written, it is a good idea to put it in writing because it avoids confusion and misunderstanding.

Contract Voidable by Other Party. If a contract is voidable by one of the parties, it is unenforceable by the other party. (Note that the party who has the option of voiding the contract can choose instead to enforce the contract against the other party.)

Statute of Limitations Expired. A statute of limitations is a law that sets a deadline for filing a lawsuit. Unless an injured party files suit before the deadline set by the applicable statute of limitations, his legal claim is lost forever. The purpose of a statute

---

Fig. 6.4 *Legal status of contracts*

Type of Contract	Legal Effect	Example
Void	No contract at all	An agreement for which there is no consideration
Voidable	Valid until rescinded by one party	A contract with a minor
Unenforceable	One or both parties cannot sue to enforce	A contract after the limitations period expires
Valid	Binding and enforceable	An agreement that meets all the legal requirements

of limitations is to prevent one person from suing another too many years after an event, when memories have faded and evidence has been lost.

Every state has a statute of limitations for contracts. If one of the parties to a contract fails to perform her obligations (breaches the contract), the other party has to sue within a certain number of years after the breach. Otherwise, the statute of limitations will run out and the contract will become unenforceable.

In Washington, the statute of limitations generally requires lawsuits concerning written contracts to be filed within six years after their breach, and lawsuits concerning oral contracts to be filed within three years after their breach.

Valid

If an agreement contains all of the essential elements, its contents can be proved, and it is free of any negative influences, it is a valid contract and can be enforced in a court of law.

Discharging a Contract

Once there is a valid, enforceable contract, it may be discharged by:

1. full performance, or
2. agreement between the parties.

Full Performance

Full performance means that the parties have performed all their obligations; the contract is executed. For example, once the deed to the property has been transferred to the buyer, and the seller has received the purchase price, the purchase and sale agreement has been discharged by full performance.

Agreement Between the Parties

The parties to a contract can agree to discharge the contract in any of the following ways:

- rescission,
- cancellation,
- assignment, or
- novation.

Rescission. Sometimes the parties to a contract agree that they would be better off if the contract had never been signed. In such a case, they may decide to rescind the contract.

The buyer and the seller sign an agreement that terminates their previous agreement and puts them as nearly as possible back in the positions they were in before entering into the agreement. If money or other consideration has changed hands, it will be returned.

In certain circumstances, a contract may be rescinded by court order (rather than by agreement). Court-ordered rescission is discussed later in this chapter.

Cancellation. A cancellation does not go as far as a rescission. The parties agree to terminate the contract, but previous acts are unaffected. For example, money that was paid prior to the cancellation is not returned.

When contracting to purchase real property, a buyer generally gives the seller a deposit to show that she is acting in good faith and intends to fulfill the terms of their agreement. This is called an **earnest money deposit**, and the seller is entitled to keep it if the buyer defaults (breaches the contract). If the buyer and seller agree to terminate the contract and the seller refunds the earnest money deposit to the buyer, the contract has been rescinded. If the parties agree that the seller will keep the deposit, the contract has been cancelled.

Assignment. Sometimes one of the parties to a contract wants to withdraw by assigning his interest in the contract to another person. As a general rule, a contract can be assigned to another unless a clause in the contract prohibits assignment. Technically, assignment does not discharge the contract. The new party (the assignee) assumes primary liability for the contractual obligations, but the withdrawing party (the assignor) is still secondarily liable.

> **Example:** A buyer is purchasing a home under a 15-year land contract. In the absence of any prohibitive language in the contract, she can sell the home, accept a cash downpayment, and assign her contract rights and liabilities to the new buyer. The new buyer would assume primary liability for the contract debt, but the original buyer would retain secondary liability.

One exception to the rule that a contract can be assigned unless otherwise agreed: a personal services contract can't be assigned without the other party's consent.

> **Example:** A nightclub has a contract with a singer for several performances. The singer cannot assign his contract to another singer, because it is a personal services contract. The nightclub management has a right to choose who will be singing in their establishment.

Novation. The term "novation" has two generally accepted meanings. One type of novation is the substitution of a new party into an existing contract obligation. If a seller releases the original buyer from a purchase and sale agreement in favor of a new buyer under the same contract, there has been a novation. The first buyer is relieved of all liability connected with the contract.

Novation may also be the substitution of a new obligation for an old one. If a landlord and tenant agree to tear up a three-year lease in favor of a new ten-year lease, it is a novation.

Assignment vs. Novation. The difference between assignment and novation concerns the withdrawing party's liability. When a contract is assigned, there is continuing liability for the assignor. In a novation, on the other hand, the withdrawing party is released from liability, because she was replaced with someone else who was approved by the other original party. Novation, unlike assignment, always requires the other party's consent.

Breach of Contract

A **breach of contract** occurs when one of the parties fails, without legal excuse, to perform any of the promises contained in the agreement. The injured party can seek a remedy in court only if the breach is a **material breach**. A breach is material when the promise that has not been fulfilled is an important part of the contract.

Many contracts state that "**time is of the essence**." That phrase is used to warn the parties that timely performance is crucial and failure to meet a deadline would be a material breach. If one party misses a deadline, the other party may choose whether to proceed with the contract or use the "time is of the essence" clause as the basis for ending it.

Remedies for Breach of Contract

There are four possible legal remedies for a breach of contract:

- rescission,
- compensatory damages,
- liquidated damages, or
- specific performance.

Rescission. As previously explained, a rescission is a termination of the contract in which the parties are returned to their original positions. In the case of a purchase and sale agreement, the seller refunds the buyer's earnest money deposit and the buyer gives up her equitable interest in the property. The rescission can be by agreement, or it can be ordered by a court at the request of one party when the other party has breached the contract.

Compensatory Damages. Financial losses that a party suffers as a result of a breach of contract are referred to as **damages**.

> **Example:** Able, a manufacturer, contracts to buy 50,000 hinges from Baker for $12,000, and Baker promises to deliver the hinges by April 22.
> As it turns out, Baker fails to deliver the hinges on time, and Able (in order to fulfill commitments to her customers) must quickly purchase the hinges from another supplier. This other supplier charges Able $17,000, which is $5,000 more than Baker was charging. Able has suffered $5,000 in damages as a result of Baker's breach of contract.

The most common remedy for a breach of contract is an award of **compensatory damages**. This is a sum of money that a court orders the breaching party to pay to the other party, to compensate the other party for losses suffered as a result of the breach of contract. Compensatory damages are generally intended to put the nonbreaching party in the financial position she would have been in if the breaching party had fulfilled the terms of the contract.

> **Example:** Continuing with the previous example, suppose Able sues Baker for breach of contract. The court orders Baker to pay Able $5,000 in damages. When Baker pays Able the $5,000, that puts Able in the financial position she would have been in if Baker had delivered the hinges on time.

Liquidated Damages. The parties to a contract sometimes agree in advance to an amount that will serve as full compensation to be paid in the event that one of the parties breaches the contract. This sum is called **liquidated damages**.

> **Example:** Let's return to the previous example. Now suppose that Able and Baker included a liquidated damages provision in their contract. The provision states that if Baker breaches the agreement, he will pay Able $3,000, and that will serve as full compensation for the breach.
>
> Baker fails to deliver the hinges to Able on time, Able must purchase them from another supplier, and that costs her an extra $5,000. But because of the liquidated damages provision in the contract, Able is only entitled to receive $3,000 from Baker. She can't sue for any additional amount, even though her actual damages were greater than $3,000.

Although a liquidated damages provision limits the amount of compensation the nonbreaching party will receive, it benefits both parties by making it easier to settle their dispute without going to court. It's sometimes difficult for the nonbreaching party to prove the extent of the actual damages she suffered; a liquidated damages provision makes that unnecessary.

In a real estate transaction, the buyer's earnest money deposit is often treated as liquidated damages. If the buyer breaches the purchase and sale agreement, the seller is entitled to keep the deposit as liquidated damages. The seller usually can't sue the buyer for an additional amount.

On the other hand, a typical purchase and sale agreement doesn't have a liquidated damages provision that applies if it's the seller who breaches instead of the buyer. If the seller breaches the contract, the buyer can sue for compensatory damages.

Specific Performance. Specific performance is a legal action designed to compel a breaching party to perform the contract as agreed. For example, if a seller breaches a purchase and sale agreement, a court could issue an order of specific performance, requiring the seller to sign and deliver a deed to the buyer, fulfilling the terms of their contract.

Specific performance is usually available as a remedy only when monetary damages would not be sufficient compensation. For instance, in our example involving failure to deliver hinges as agreed, the court wouldn't order Baker to deliver the hinges to Able, because hinges could be obtained from another supplier and financial compensation was really all Able needed. In contrast, specific performance may be an appropriate remedy for a seller's breach of a purchase and sale agreement, because a piece of real estate is unique; there's no other property that's exactly like the one the seller agreed to sell. Payment of damages would not enable the buyer to purchase another property just like it.

Tender

A tender is an unconditional offer by one of the contract parties to perform her part of the agreement. It is sometimes referred to as "an offer to make an offer good." A tender is usually made when it appears that the other party is going to default; it is necessary before legal action can be taken to remedy the breach of contract.

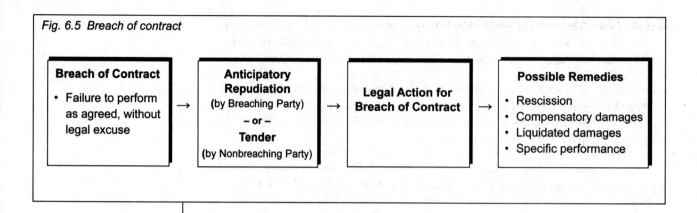

Fig. 6.5 Breach of contract

Example: A seller suspects that the buyer does not plan to complete the purchase, and he intends to sue the buyer if this happens. Before he can sue, the seller must attempt to deliver the deed to the buyer as promised in the purchase and sale agreement. When the tender is made, if the buyer refuses to pay the agreed price and accept the deed, the buyer is placed in default and the seller may then file a lawsuit.

If a buyer has reason to believe the seller doesn't plan to complete the sale, the buyer tenders by attempting to deliver to the seller the full payment promised in the purchase and sale agreement. When the seller refuses to accept the money and deliver the deed, she is in default.

Sometimes there is an **anticipatory repudiation** by one of the parties. An anticipatory repudiation is a positive statement by the defaulting party indicating that he will not or cannot fulfill the terms of the agreement. When this happens, no tender is necessary as a basis for a legal action.

Types of Real Estate Contracts

This section provides a brief overview of some of the contracts a real estate agent should be familiar with: listing agreements, buyer representation agreements, purchase and sale agreements, land contracts, leases, escrow instructions, and options. Each of these except the option is discussed in more detail in a later chapter, as noted below.

Listing Agreements

A listing agreement is a written contract between a property owner and a real estate firm. The owner hires the firm to find a buyer or tenant who is ready, willing, and able to buy or lease on the owner's terms.

In Washington and many other states, a firm can't sue to collect a commission unless it has a written listing agreement with the property owner. What the firm must do in order to earn the commission depends on what type of listing has been used—open, exclusive agency, or exclusive right to sell—and on the terms of the contract. Listing agreements are discussed in more detail in Chapter 8.

Buyer Representation Agreements

A buyer representation agreement is a written contract between a prospective property buyer and a real estate firm. The buyer hires the firm to locate a suitable property for the buyer to purchase. In Washington, although a firm may act as a buyer's agent without a written agreement, the firm can't sue the buyer for compensation unless their agreement is in writing. Buyer agency and buyer representation agreements are discussed in more detail in Chapter 7.

Purchase and Sale Agreements

The purchase and sale agreement is a written contract between a buyer and a seller, stating the terms on which a piece of real property is going to be sold. It should spell out the details of the sale (such as price, closing and possession dates, any liens or encumbrances to be assumed, and any contingencies), and it must be signed by both parties.

In most cases, the prospective buyer is the offeror, and the property seller is the offeree.

- A buyer makes an offer to purchase by filling out a standard purchase and sale agreement form with the terms of her offer. The buyer then signs the form and submits it to the seller or the seller's agent.
- If the seller is willing to sell on the buyer's term, he signs the purchase and sale agreement form and delivers it to the buyer or the buyer's agent, thus communicating to the buyer his acceptance of the offer.
- If the seller wants to change any of the terms offered, he can make a counteroffer to the buyer. Now the seller is the offeror and the buyer is the offeree.

Once a purchase and sale agreement has been signed by both parties, it is a binding contract, assuming that all of the other requirements for a valid contract have been met. The terms of the agreement cannot be modified unless both parties consent and sign a written amendment to the original contract. Purchase and sale agreements are discussed in more detail in Chapter 9.

Land Contracts

Under a land contract (also called a real estate contract, installment sales contract, or contract for deed), the buyer purchases the seller's property on an installment basis. The parties to the contract are called the **vendor** (the seller) and the **vendee** (the buyer). Periodic payments toward the purchase price are made over a span of years, and during that time the vendor retains legal title to the property. The deed is not delivered to the vendee until the full purchase price has been paid. In the meantime, the vendee has **equitable title** to the property, which is the right to possess and enjoy the property while paying off the purchase price.

Example: Bender agrees to buy Jones's property for $250,000, to be paid at the rate of $25,000 per year, plus 9% interest, for ten years. Jones allows Bender to take possession of the property, and she promises to convey legal title to Bender when he's paid the full purchase price. Bender and Jones have entered into a land contract.

Land contracts are discussed in more detail in Chapter 10.

Leases

A lease is an agreement that transfers the right of possession and use of real property from the landlord (the property owner) to the tenant. A lease is both a conveyance and a contract. As a conveyance, the lease transfers the right of possession. As a contract, it sets forth the terms of the occupancy: the amount of rent, the rights and responsibilities of the parties, and the duration of the tenancy.

Leases are categorized according to their duration and manner of termination. Many of the terms of a residential lease are governed by the Washington Landlord-Tenant Act. Leases are discussed in more detail in Chapter 16.

Escrow Instructions

Escrow instructions authorize an escrow agent to close a transaction. They set forth the obligations of the parties and the conditions that must be fulfilled before a sale can be finalized. The buyer and the seller generally use joint escrow instructions to avoid giving conflicting directives; however, in some commercial transactions the parties issue separate sets of instructions. Escrow instructions are discussed in more detail in Chapter 13.

Option Agreements

An option agreement is essentially a contract to make a contract; it is an agreement that gives a party the right to buy, sell, or lease property for a fixed price within a set period of time. The parties to an option agreement are the **optionor** (the property owner who grants the option) and the **optionee** (the one who has the option right). In an option to purchase, the optionor is the seller and the optionee is the buyer.

> **Example:** Jensen is offering to sell her property for $400,000. Conners isn't yet sure that he wants to buy the property, but he doesn't want to lose the opportunity to do so. Jensen agrees to give him a three-week option to purchase. They execute a written option agreement, and Conners pays Jensen $1,000 as consideration for the option. The option gives Conners the right to buy the property at the stated price during the next three weeks, but does not in any way obligate him to buy it.

The optionor is bound to keep the offer open for the period specified in the option agreement. She is not allowed to sell or lease the property to anyone other than the optionee until the option expires.

If the optionee decides to exercise the option (that is, to buy or lease the property on the stated terms), he must give written notice of acceptance to the optionor. If the optionee fails to exercise the option within the specified time, the option expires automatically.

An option agreement may be considered a unilateral contract, because the optionee is not obligated to exercise the option. However, when the option is exercised, the parties have a bilateral contract. (If the option is exercised, but the underlying sale is not yet closed, the parties have an executory bilateral contract.)

Requirements. Because an option is a contract, it must have all the necessary elements of a contract, including consideration. The consideration may be a nominal amount—there's no set minimum. But some consideration must, in fact, pass from the optionee to the optionor; a mere statement of consideration in the agreement is not sufficient. (There is an exception to this rule for lease/option agreements: the provisions of the lease are treated as sufficient consideration to support the option.)

An option contract must be in writing; oral options are unenforceable. Furthermore, since an option to purchase anticipates that a sale may take place, the underlying terms of the sale (such as price and financing) should be spelled out in the option agreement.

Contract Rights. An option agreement gives the optionee a contract right, but does not create an interest in real property. An option is not a lien, and it also cannot be used as security for a mortgage loan.

If the optionor dies during the option period, that will not affect the rights of the optionee, who may still exercise the right to purchase or lease. The option contract is binding on the heirs and assignees of the optionor.

An option can be assigned, unless the agreement includes a provision prohibiting assignment. One exception is when the consideration paid by the optionee is in the form of an unsecured promissory note. In that case, the optionee must obtain the optionor's written permission before the option may be assigned.

Recording. An option agreement may be recorded to give third parties constructive notice of the option. In that case, if the optionee exercises the option, her interest in the property will relate back to the date the option was recorded, taking priority over the rights of intervening third parties.

A recorded option that is not exercised creates a cloud on the optionor's title. The optionor should obtain a release from the optionee, and then record the release to remove the cloud.

Right of First Refusal. An option should not be confused with a right of first refusal, which gives a person the first opportunity to purchase or lease real property when it becomes available. For instance, a lease might give the tenant a right of first refusal to purchase the property if the landlord decides to sell it.

Once the property owner offers the property for sale or receives an offer to buy from a third party, the holder of the right of first refusal must be given a chance to match the offer. If the right-holder does not want the property or is unwilling to match the offer, the property may be sold to a third party.

Chapter Summary

1. A contract is an agreement between two or more competent persons to do or not do certain things for consideration. Every contract is either express or implied, either unilateral or bilateral, and either executory or executed.

2. For a contract to be valid and binding, the parties must have the legal capacity to contract, and there must be mutual consent (offer and acceptance), a lawful objective, and consideration. The statute of frauds requires real estate contracts to be in writing.

3. A contract may be void, voidable, unenforceable, or valid.

4. An existing contract can be discharged by full performance or by agreement between the parties. The parties can agree to terminate the contract by rescission or cancellation, or there can be an assignment or a novation.

5. A breach of contract occurs when a party fails, without legal excuse, to perform any material promise contained in the agreement. When a breach occurs, the four possible remedies are rescission, compensatory damages, liquidated damages, or specific performance.

6. In an option to purchase, the optionee has a right to buy the property at a specified price, but is under no obligation to buy. The optionor is not allowed to sell the property to anyone other than the optionee during the option period.

🔑 Key Terms

Contract—An agreement between two or more competent persons to do or not do certain things for consideration.

Capacity—A person must be mentally competent and at least 18 years of age to have the capacity to contract.

Mutual consent—The agreement of both parties to the terms of the contract, demonstrated by offer and acceptance.

Offer—A communication that shows the willingness of the person making it (the offeror) to enter into a contract, and that has definite and certain terms.

Acceptance—A communication showing the willingness of the offeree to be bound by the terms of the offer.

Counteroffer—A qualified acceptance; technically a rejection of the offer, with a new offer made on slightly different terms.

Fraud—The misrepresentation of a material fact to someone who relies on the misrepresentation as the truth in deciding whether to enter into a contract.

Undue influence—Pressuring someone or taking advantage of his weakness or distress to induce him to enter into a contract.

Duress—Compelling someone to enter into a contract with the use or threat of force or constraint.

Consideration—Something of value exchanged by the parties to a contract; either a benefit to the party receiving it or a detriment to the party offering it.

Statute of frauds—A state law that requires certain types of contracts (including most contracts related to real estate transactions) to be in writing and signed.

Valid—When a contract contains all of the required elements and is enforceable in court.

Void—When a contract lacks an essential element, so that it has no legal force or effect.

Voidable—When one of the parties can choose to rescind the contract, because of lack of capacity, fraud, etc.

Unenforceable—When a contract cannot be enforced in a court of law because its contents cannot be proved, or it is voidable by the other party, or the statute of limitations has expired.

Rescission—When a contract is terminated and any consideration given is returned, putting the parties as nearly as possible back into the position they were in prior to entering into the contract.

Cancellation—When a contract is terminated but previous contractual acts are unaffected.

Assignment—When one party transfers her rights and obligations under the contract to another party, but remains secondarily liable.

Novation—When one party is completely replaced with another, or one contract is completely replaced with another, and all liability under the original contract ends.

Compensatory damages—An amount that a court orders one party in a lawsuit to pay to the other party as compensation for a breach of contract or other injury.

Liquidated damages—An amount that the parties agree in advance will serve as full compensation if one of them defaults.

Specific performance—A remedy for breach of contract in which the court orders the defaulting party to perform as agreed in the contract.

Tender—An unconditional offer by one of the parties to perform his part of the agreement, made when it appears that the other party is going to default.

Option agreement—An agreement that gives one party the right to buy or lease property at a set price within a certain period of time.

Chapter Quiz

1. A contract can be valid and binding even though:

   a) it is not supported by consideration

   b) it does not have a lawful objective

   c) it is not put into writing

   d) there was no offer and acceptance

2. To have legal capacity to contract, a person must have:

   a) reached the age of majority

   b) been declared competent by a court

   c) a high school diploma or general equivalency certificate

   d) All of the above

3. An offer to purchase property would be terminated by any of the following, except:

   a) failure to communicate acceptance of the offer within the prescribed period

   b) revocation after acceptance has been communicated

   c) a qualified acceptance of the offer by the offeree

   d) death or insanity of the offeror

4. A counteroffer:

   a) terminates the original offer

   b) will result in a valid contract if accepted by the other party

   c) Both of the above

   d) None of the above

5. Tucker sends Johnson a letter offering to buy his property for $120,000 in cash, with the transaction to close in 60 days. Johnson sends Tucker a letter that says, "I accept your offer; however, the closing will take place in 90 days." Which of the following is true?

   a) Johnson's statement is not a valid acceptance

   b) Johnson's statement is a counteroffer

   c) There is no contract unless Tucker accepts the counteroffer

   d) All of the above

6. Which of these could be consideration for a contract?

   a) $63,000

   b) A promise to convey title

   c) A promise to not sell property during the next 30 days

   d) All of the above

7. An executory contract is one that:

   a) is made by the executor of an estate for the sale of probate property

   b) has not yet been performed

   c) has been completely performed

   d) has been proposed but not accepted by either party

8. A void contract is one that:

   a) lacks an essential contract element

   b) needs to be rescinded by the injured party

   c) can be rescinded by agreement

   d) can no longer be enforced because the deadline set by the statute of limitations has passed

9. A voidable contract is:

   a) not enforceable by either party

   b) enforceable unless action is taken to rescind it

   c) void unless action is taken to rescind it

   d) None of the above

10. The statute of frauds is a law that requires:

    a) all contracts to be supported by consideration

    b) unlawful provisions to be severed from a contract

    c) certain contracts to be unilateral

    d) certain contracts to be in writing and signed

11. A contract can be discharged by all of the following except:

    a) novation
    b) performance
    c) cancellation
    d) breach

12. Brown and Murdock have a five-year contract.
After two years, they agree to tear up that con-
tract and replace it with a new ten-year contract.
This is an example of:

    a) novation
    b) rescission
    c) duress
    d) specific performance

13. Graves and Chung are parties to a contract that
doesn't prohibit assignment. If Chung assigns his
interest in the contract to Stewart:

    a) Graves is not required to fulfill the
       contract
    b) Graves can sue for anticipatory repudiation
    c) Chung remains secondarily liable to Graves
    d) Chung is relieved of all further liability under
       the contract

14. A clause in the contract provides that if one party
breaches, the other will be entitled to $3,500 and
cannot sue for more than that. This is a:

    a) just compensation provision
    b) compensation cap
    c) satisfaction clause
    d) liquidated damages provision

15. The McClures agreed in writing to sell their
house to Jacobsen, but then they refused to go
through with the sale. If Jacobsen wants a court
order requiring the McClures to convey the house
to her as agreed, she should sue for:

    a) damages
    b) specific performance
    c) liquidated damages
    d) rescission

👉 Answer Key

1. c) Only certain types of contracts are required to be in writing, but all contracts require consideration, a lawful objective, and offer and acceptance.

2. a) A person has capacity to contract if he has reached the age of majority (in Washington, age 18) and is mentally competent. It isn't necessary to be declared competent by a court, however.

3. b) If the offeree accepts the offer before the offeror revokes it, a binding contract is formed.

4. c) A counteroffer terminates the original offer (operating as a rejection), but if the counteroffer is then accepted, a valid contract is formed.

5. d) All of the options are true statements.

6. d) Consideration is almost anything of value: money, goods, services, or a promise to do or not do something.

7. b) An executory contract has not yet been performed; an executed contract is one that has been fully performed.

8. a) A contract that lacks an essential element (such as consideration) is void. It has no legal force or effect, so there is nothing to rescind.

9. b) A voidable contract can be rescinded by the injured party, but unless it is rescinded it will be enforceable.

10. d) The statute of frauds requires certain contracts to be in writing and signed by the party or parties to be bound.

11. d) Performance, cancellation, and novation are all ways of discharging a contract. Breach does not discharge the contract; the breaching party is liable to the other party.

12. a) Novation is the replacement of an existing contract with a new contract, or the replacement of a party to a contract with a new party.

13. c) A contract can be assigned unless otherwise agreed, but the assignor remains secondarily liable to the other party.

14. d) Liquidated damages are an amount the contracting parties agree in advance will be paid as full compensation if one of them breaches the contract.

15. b) If the court granted Jacobsen specific performance, the McClures would be ordered to convey the house as agreed in the contract (as opposed to merely having to pay Jacobsen damages as compensation).

Real Estate Agency

Chapter Overview

Agency is a special legal relationship that involves certain duties and liabilities. The law of agency governs many aspects of a real estate agent's relationships with clients and customers. The first part of this chapter explains what an agency relationship is and how one is created, then discusses real estate agency duties and liabilities. The second part of this chapter describes the various types of agency relationships that are possible under Washington's real estate agency law. Agency disclosure requirements and the designated broker/broker relationship are also covered.

Introduction to Agency

We'll begin our discussion of real estate agency with some basic definitions and some information about the framework of agency law.

The Agency Relationship

An agency relationship arises when one person authorizes another to represent her, subject to her control, in dealings with third parties. The parties in an agency relationship are the **agent**, the person authorized to represent another, and the **principal**, the person who authorizes and controls the actions of the agent. Persons outside the agency relationship who seek to deal with the principal through the agent are called **third parties**.

There is usually an agency relationship between a property seller and the real estate firm that he has listed the property with. The seller is the principal, who employs the firm to act as his agent. The agent/firm represents the seller/principal's interests in negotiations with potential buyers/third parties. The seller/principal is referred to as the licensee's **client**.

A buyer is also likely to have an agency relationship with a real estate firm. As a general rule, when a real estate licensee works with a buyer—for example, by showing the buyer homes, preparing offers to purchase, and negotiating on the buyer's behalf—then the firm that employs that licensee becomes the agent of the buyer, and the buyer is the firm's principal and client. A firm's principal is whoever has authorized the firm to act as her representative.

There is also an agency relationship between a real estate firm and the affiliated licensees who work for the firm. In other words, an affiliated licensee is the brokerage firm's agent. To the firm's principal (the seller or the buyer), a licensee representing the firm would be a **subagent**—an agent of an agent.

Agency Law

An agency relationship has significant legal implications. For a third party, dealing with the agent can be the legal equivalent of dealing with the principal. For instance, when an agent who is authorized to do so signs a document or makes a promise, it's as if the principal signed or promised. And in some cases, if the agent does something wrong, the principal may be held liable to third parties for harm resulting from the agent's actions.

Those rules are part of general agency law, a body of law that applies to agency relationships in nearly any context. For example, it governs the relationship between lawyer and client, or between trustee and beneficiary. Traditionally, general agency law also governed the relationship between a real estate licensee and her client. In Washington, however, real estate agency relationships are now subject to the Real Estate Brokerage Relationships Act, which went into effect in 1997. This statute grew out of general agency law, but made important changes to address agency problems that were specific to the real estate field.

We will cover both general agency law and the Washington real estate agency statute, since both are tested on the state licensing examination. General agency law questions appear on the national portion of the exam, while questions concerning Washington's Real Estate Brokerage Relationships Act and agency disclosure rules appear on the state portion of the exam.

Creating an Agency Relationship

No particular formalities are required to create an agency relationship; the only requirement is the consent of both parties. Under general agency law, an agency relationship may be formed in four ways: by express agreement, by ratification, by estoppel, or by implication.

Express Agreement

Most agencies are created by express agreement: the principal appoints someone to act as his agent, and the agent accepts the appointment. The agreement does not need to be in writing in order to create a valid agency relationship.

The agency agreement also does not have to be supported by consideration. Agency rights, responsibilities, and liabilities arise even when the principal has no contractual obligation to compensate the agent for the services rendered.

For example, if a licensee doesn't have a written listing agreement with a seller, that licensee cannot sue the seller for compensation. Yet even without a written agreement, the licensee still may be the seller's agent, with all of the duties and liabilities that agency entails.

Ratification

An agency is created by ratification when the principal gives approval after the fact to acts performed by:

- a person who had no authority to act for the principal, or
- an agent whose actions exceeded the authority granted by the principal.

The principal may ratify unauthorized acts expressly, or by accepting the benefits of the acts. For example, if the principal accepts a contract offer negotiated by someone who wasn't authorized to negotiate on her behalf, the principal has ratified the agency.

Estoppel

Under the legal doctrine of estoppel, a person cannot take a position that contradicts his previous conduct, if someone else has relied on the previous conduct. An agency can be created by estoppel when it would be unfair to a third party to deny the agent's authority, because the principal has allowed the third party to believe there was an agency relationship.

Implication

An agency may be created by implication when one person behaves toward another in a way that suggests or implies that she is acting as that other person's agent. If the other person reasonably believes that there is an agency relationship, and the supposed agent fails to correct that impression, she may owe the other person agency duties.

So, for example, an agent who takes a buyer to see a house without discussing representation may become the buyer's agent by implication. This is sometimes referred to as an **implied buyer agency**. Similarly, an agent's actions in helping a seller without an express agreement to represent him may create an **implied seller agency**.

Although agency by implication resembles agency by estoppel, there's a significant difference between them. An agency by estoppel requires the principal to acknowledge that an agency relationship exists, to protect the interests of a third party. An agency by implication requires the agent to acknowledge that an agency relationship exists, to protect the principal's interests.

Creating a Real Estate Agency

In Washington, under the Real Estate Brokerage Relationships Act, an agency relationship between a real estate firm and a client begins when a licensee affiliated with the firm undertakes to provide real estate services for the client.

An agency relationship with a seller ordinarily begins with the execution of a written listing agreement. On the other hand, an agency relationship with a buyer begins automatically when a licensee performs real estate brokerage services for the buyer.

Example: Booth, a prospective buyer, walks into Thompson Realty and is greeted by Broker Dickerson. Booth tells Dickerson that she wants to buy a home. She tells him her general price range and the kind of house she wants. Dickerson goes to his computer and keys in some information, then prints out a list of homes that Booth may be interested in. After making some phone calls, Dickerson and Booth go and look at three of the homes.

Under the real estate agency statute, Dickerson and his designated broker, Thompson, are Booth's agents. This agency relationship is created automatically, without a written agreement, because Dickerson is performing brokerage services for Booth.

There is an important exception to this rule concerning buyer agency. A licensee working with a buyer does not automatically become the buyer's agent if there's a written agreement to the contrary. This might be a listing agreement with the seller, a written subagency agreement with the seller, or a written non-agency agreement.

Example: To return to the previous scenario, suppose Dickerson shows Booth one of his own listings. Because Thompson Realty already has a written agreement with the seller, Dickerson and Thompson won't be representing Booth if she decides to buy this house. They'll be acting as the seller's agents, not the buyer's.

The Legal Effects of Agency

Once an agency relationship has been established, the principal is bound by acts of the agent that are within the scope of the agent's actual or apparent authority. Under general agency law, the principal may be held liable for harm caused by the agent's negligent or wrongful acts. In addition, the principal may be held to know information that is known to the agent. We will now examine these legal effects of agency.

Scope of Authority

The extent to which the principal can be bound by the agent's actions depends first of all on the scope of authority granted to the agent. There are three basic types of agents:

- universal agents,
- general agents, and
- special agents.

A **universal agent** is authorized to do anything that can be lawfully delegated to a representative. This type of agent has the greatest degree of authority.

A **general agent** is authorized to handle all of the principal's affairs in one or more specified areas. He has the authority to conduct a wide range of activities on an ongoing basis on behalf of the principal. For example, a business manager who has the authority to handle personnel matters, enter into contracts, and manage the day-to-day operations of the business is considered to be a general agent.

A **special agent** has limited authority to do a specific thing or conduct a specific transaction. For instance, an attorney who is hired to litigate a specific legal matter, such as a person's divorce, is a special agent.

In most cases, a real estate licensee is a special agent, because the licensee has only limited authority. A seller hires a licensee to find a buyer for a particular piece of property, and the licensee is only authorized to negotiate with third parties, not to sign a contract on the seller's behalf. A real estate licensee can be granted broader powers, but usually is not.

Actual vs. Apparent Authority

An agent may have actual authority to perform an action on the principal's behalf, or else may have only apparent authority.

Actual authority is authority granted to the agent by the principal, either expressly or by implication. Express actual authority is communicated to the agent in

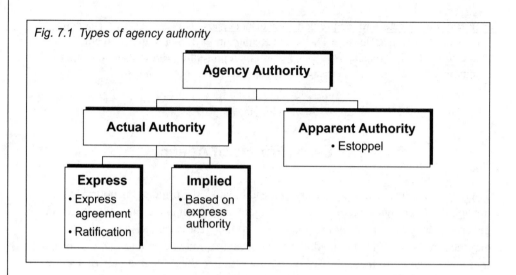

Fig. 7.1 Types of agency authority

express terms, either orally or in writing. Implied actual authority is the authority to do what is necessary to carry out actions that were expressly authorized.

> **Example:** When a seller lists property with a brokerage firm, the designated broker is given express actual authority to find a buyer for the property. Based on custom in the real estate industry, the designated broker also has the implied actual authority to delegate certain tasks to an affiliated licensee. In contrast, the authority granted to the designated broker does not imply the power to enter into a contract or execute a deed on the seller's behalf.

A person has **apparent authority** when she has no actual authority to act, but the principal negligently or deliberately allows it to appear that the person's actions are authorized. In other words, the principal's words or conduct lead a third party to believe that this person (the **apparent agent** or **ostensible agent**) has authority to act on behalf of the principal. In this way, apparent authority corresponds to an agency created by estoppel, which was explained earlier.

A principal is bound by acts performed within the scope of an ostensible agent's apparent authority. However, declarations of the agent alone cannot establish apparent authority; the principal must be aware of the declarations or acts and make no effort to deny that they are authorized.

A third party has a duty, when dealing with an agent, to make a reasonable effort to discover the scope of the agent's authority. The third party will not be able to hold the principal liable when an agent acts beyond the scope of his actual authority and the principal's conduct does not indicate approval of those acts. Especially when a contract between the principal and a third party limits the agent's authority to make representations, the third party is on notice that any representations made by the agent beyond the written terms of the agreement are unauthorized and not binding on the principal.

Vicarious Liability

A **tort** is a negligent or intentional wrongful act involving breach of a duty imposed by law (as opposed to breach of a contractual duty). It is a mistake, accident, or misconduct that results in an injury or financial harm to another person. For example, negligent driving that results in an accident and injures another driver is a tort. Someone who commits a tort may be sued by the injured party and required to compensate her.

Under general agency law, a principal may be held liable for his agent's negligent or wrongful acts. This is referred to as **vicarious liability**. The Washington Real Estate Brokerage Relationships Act provides that, as a general rule, there's no vicarious liability between a real estate agent and her principal. This means that a seller or buyer is ordinarily not liable for any act, error, or omission by his designated broker, a licensee working for the designated broker, or another subagent.

There are two exceptions to this exclusion from liability. The principal may be liable for his real estate agent's actions if:

1. the principal participated in or authorized the act, error, or omission; or
2. the principal benefited from the act, error, or omission, and a court determines that it is highly probable that the injured party would be unable to enforce a judgment against the agent or subagent.

Likewise, under the Washington statute, an agent is not liable for an act, error, or omission of a subagent, unless the agent participated in or authorized the act, error, or omission. Note that a designated broker or branch manager may still be held liable for the actions of her affiliated licensees, however.

Imputed Knowledge

Under general agency law, a principal is considered to have notice of information that the agent knows, even if the agent never actually tells the principal. In other words, the agent's knowledge is automatically imputed to the principal. As a result, the principal could be held liable for failing to disclose a problem to a third party, even if the agent never informed the principal of the problem.

However, under Washington's real estate agency statute, the imputed knowledge rule no longer applies in the real estate context. A principal in a real estate transaction is not automatically held to have notice of facts known by his real estate agent.

Duties in an Agency Relationship

An agency relationship is a **fiduciary** relationship. A fiduciary is a person who stands in a special position of trust and confidence in relation to someone else. Under general agency law, an agent owes fiduciary duties to her principal. These include the duty of reasonable skill and care, obedience and utmost good faith, accounting, loyalty, and disclosure of material facts. By contrast, an agent's duties to third parties are much more limited.

Washington's real estate agency statute has modified agency duties for real estate licensees. While licensees still owe special duties to their principals, their duties to third parties have been expanded.

The Licensee's Duties in General

In Washington, a real estate licensee owes certain statutory duties to any party to whom she renders services, whether that person is her principal or a third party. These duties are:

- reasonable skill and care,
- honesty and good faith,
- presenting all written communications,
- disclosure of material facts,
- accounting for trust funds,
- providing an agency law pamphlet, and
- making an agency disclosure.

Reasonable Skill and Care. A licensee has a duty to use reasonable skill and care in the performance of his duties. If a licensee claims to possess certain skills or abilities, he must act as a competent person having those skills and abilities would act. In other words, a person who holds himself out as a real estate licensee must exercise the skill and care that a competent licensee would bring to the transaction. If the licensee causes a party harm due to carelessness or incompetence, the licensee will be liable to that party.

Honesty and Good Faith. A licensee must act toward any party with honesty and good faith. She must avoid inaccuracies in statements to prospective buyers or sellers. As was explained in Chapter 6, any intentional misrepresentation may constitute actual fraud, and even an unintentional misrepresentation may be considered constructive fraud. In either case, the party to whom the misrepresentation was made would have the right to rescind the transaction and/or sue for damages.

Misrepresentations, which may give rise to a lawsuit, should not be confused with mere opinions, predictions, or puffing. These are nonfactual or exaggerated statements that a party should realize he can't rely on. Since it isn't reasonable to rely on them, opinions, predictions, and puffing generally can't be the basis of a lawsuit.

Examples:
Opinion: "*I think this is the best buy on the market.*"
Prediction: "*This house is solid—it'll still be standing a hundred years from now.*"
Puffing: "*This is a dream house; it has a fabulous view.*"

Present Written Communications. A licensee is obligated to present all types of written communications to or from either party in a timely manner. Written communications include written offers.

A real estate licensee must present all offers and counteroffers to the parties, regardless of how unacceptable a particular one may appear to be. The offeree, not the licensee, decides whether or not to accept a particular offer or counteroffer. Failing to inform a party of an offer (perhaps because its acceptance would mean a smaller commission for the licensee) is a breach of duty.

This duty to present all offers continues even after the property is subject to an existing contract, or when the offeree is already a party to an existing contract.

Example: Seller Howard has just accepted an offer from Buyer Carmichael. Trent, a real estate licensee, receives another written offer for the same property. Trent has a duty to present this offer to Howard, even though Howard has already accepted Carmichael's offer.

Disclosure of Material Facts. A licensee must disclose any material fact she knows to the appropriate party, if the fact is not apparent or readily ascertainable by that party. A **material fact** is defined by Washington's real estate agency statute as information that has a substantial adverse (negative) effect on the value of the property or on a party's ability to perform her contractual duties, or that defeats the purpose of the transaction.

Latent property defects are material facts. A **latent defect** is one that is not discoverable by ordinary inspection. A licensee must disclose any known latent defects to the parties. (The principle of "caveat emptor," or "let the buyer beware," is limited in real estate transactions.) A seller also has this duty to prospective buyers.

While some states have gone so far as to require real estate licensees to physically inspect the property and report all findings to the buyer, Washington's real estate agency law states that licensees do not have the duty to investigate any matters they have not specifically agreed to investigate. A licensee has no duty to inspect the property, investigate either party's financial position, or independently verify the seller's statements.

Washington does require sellers of real property to give their buyers a disclosure statement. The purpose of the statement is to disclose the seller's knowledge regarding the condition of the property, including the condition of the buildings and utilities, the existence of any easements and encumbrances, and other material information. The statement is for disclosure purposes only, and is not to be considered a part of the sales agreement. Property disclosure statements are discussed in more detail in Chapter 9.

Stigmatized Properties. The seller's property is considered stigmatized if the property (or a neighboring property) was or may have been the site of a violent crime, a suicide or other death, drug- or gang-related activity, political or religious activity, or any other negative occurrence. Generally, these problems aren't considered material facts unless they adversely affect the property's physical condition or title. So, for example, if the drug-related activity involved methamphetamine production, that would be a material fact that has to be disclosed because making this drug generally leaves harmful residues on a property.

While not strictly an issue of stigmatization, neither a licensee nor a seller has a legal duty to disclose the presence of a sex offender in the neighborhood. In response to a buyer's questions about the presence of a sex offender, an agent's best response is to refer the buyer to online resources where the buyer can investigate further.

Accounting. A licensee must account for any funds or other valuable items received on behalf of a party to a transaction. The licensee is required to report to the party on the status of those funds (called **trust funds**) and avoid mixing (**commingling**) them with her own money. In most states, a real estate agent is required to deposit all trust funds in a special trust or escrow account in order to prevent improper use of the funds. Washington's trust fund requirements are discussed in Chapter 17.

Real Estate Agency Law Pamphlet. A licensee must give an agency law pamphlet to each party to whom he renders services. The pamphlet sets forth the provisions of the Real Estate Brokerage Relationships Act. Each party must receive the pamphlet before signing an agency agreement with the licensee, before signing an offer in a transaction handled by the licensee, before consenting to a dual agency, or before waiving any agency rights, whichever of these events comes first.

Agency Disclosure. Before a party signs an offer in a real estate transaction handled by a licensee, the licensee must disclose in writing to that party whether the licensee represents the buyer, the seller, both, or neither. The purpose of this disclosure is to help make clear who is representing whom. The specific disclosure requirements are discussed later in this chapter.

Agent's Duties to the Principal

In addition to the general duties owed by licensees to any party they render services to, there are specific duties that licensees owe to the parties they represent. If the licensee represents the seller, these duties are owed to the seller. If the licensee represents the buyer, these duties are owed to the buyer. If the licensee is acting as a dual agent, these duties are owed to both the seller and the buyer.

Loyalty. Loyalty is essential to an agency relationship. The agent must place the principal's interests above the interests of a third party. For instance, the seller's agent must try to negotiate with the buyer to get the highest possible price for the seller, because the agent's loyalty is owed to the seller.

An agent should disclose her opinion of the property's true value to her principal. Misleading a principal as to the value of the property or withholding information that affects its value breaches the agent's duty of loyalty.

The agent must also place the principal's interests above her own interests. This means that the agent must not make any **secret profits** from the agency. A secret profit is a financial benefit that an agent receives without the principal's consent, such as a kickback for referring the principal's business to a contractor.

Conflicts of Interest. A licensee must disclose to the principal any conflicts of interest. For instance, a seller's agent must inform the seller if there is any relationship between the agent and a prospective buyer—before the seller decides whether to accept the buyer's offer. If the buyer is a friend, relative, or business associate of the agent, or a company in which the agent has an interest, there may be a conflict of interest. The seller has the right to have this information when making his decision.

Of course, a seller's agent must also let the seller know if the agent is buying the property herself. It would be a gross breach of duty for a licensee to list a property for less than it is worth, secretly buy it through an intermediary, and then sell it for a profit. This is sometimes called **self-dealing**.

Confidentiality. An agent may not disclose any confidential information about the principal, even after the termination of the agency relationship. **Confidential infor-**

mation is defined in Washington's real estate agency law as information from or concerning a principal that:

1. the licensee acquired during the course of an agency relationship with the principal;
2. the principal reasonably expects to be kept confidential;
3. the principal has not disclosed or authorized to be disclosed to third parties;
4. would, if disclosed, operate to the detriment of the principal; and
5. the principal personally would not be obligated to disclose to the other party.

The last item on this list puts an important limitation on the principal's right to confidentiality. For instance, information about a latent defect known to the agent must be disclosed to a third party no matter how "confidential" the principal may consider it, because the principal (as well as the agent) is legally obligated to disclose latent defects. On the other hand, the principal's need to sell the property quickly would be considered confidential information that must not be disclosed.

Expert Advice. A licensee must advise the principal to seek expert advice on any matters relating to the transaction that are beyond the agent's expertise. For instance, if the principal has questions about the property's structural soundness, the agent should advise the principal to contact a home inspector.

Good Faith and Continuous Effort. In general, real estate licensees have a duty to make a good faith and continuous effort to fulfill the terms of their agency agreement. This means that a seller's agent must make a good faith and continuous effort to find a buyer for the property. A buyer's agent must make a good faith and continuous effort to find a suitable property for the buyer to purchase.

Once the seller's agent finds a buyer and a purchase and sale agreement has been signed, the seller's agent doesn't have to seek additional offers to purchase, as long as the property remains subject to that contract. (However, any additional offers received still must be presented to the seller.) Similarly, the buyer's agent doesn't have to seek additional properties while the buyer is a party to an existing contract.

Breach of Duty

If a licensee breaches any duties owed to either a principal or a third party, it is considered a tort. (A tort, as we explained earlier, is a wrongful act resulting from a breach of a duty imposed by law.) The party injured by the tort, whether it is the principal or a third party, is then entitled to sue for redress.

The most common remedy in a tort suit is compensatory damages. A court will order the licensee to compensate the injured party for the value of the loss that the injured party suffered. This might include repaying any commission collected in a transaction.

Most breaches of duty by a licensee are also violations of the real estate license law. The Department of Licensing may take disciplinary action against the licensee even if the injured party does not pursue a lawsuit. Disciplinary action may include fines as well as suspension or revocation of the licensee's real estate license. (See Chapter 17.)

Terminating an Agency

Once an agency relationship has terminated, the agent is no longer authorized to represent the principal. Under general agency law, an agency may be terminated either by acts of the parties or by operation of law. (Following our discussion of termination under general agency law, we'll address how a real estate agency is terminated under the Brokerage Relationships Act.)

Termination by Acts of the Parties

Under general agency law, the ways in which the parties can terminate an agency relationship include:

- mutual agreement,
- revocation by the principal, and
- renunciation by the agent.

Mutual Agreement. The parties may terminate the agency by mutual agreement at any time. If the original agreement was in writing, the termination agreement should also be in writing.

Principal Revokes. The principal may revoke the agency by firing the agent whenever he wishes. (Remember that an agency relationship requires the consent of both parties.) However, in some cases revoking an agency breaches a contractual agreement, and the principal may be liable for any damages suffered by the agent because of the breach.

An **agency coupled with an interest** cannot be revoked. An agency is coupled with an interest if the agent has a financial interest in the subject matter of the agency. For instance, if a real estate licensee co-owns a property with other people, and they've authorized her to represent them in selling the property, it's an agency coupled with an interest. The co-owners can't revoke it.

Agent Renounces. An agent can renounce the agency at any time. Like revocation, renunciation may be a breach of contract, in which case the agent could be liable for the principal's damages resulting from the breach. But since an agency contract is a personal services contract (the agent has agreed to provide personal services to the

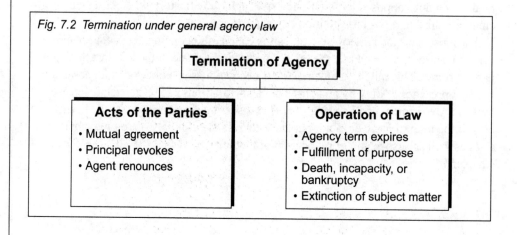

Fig. 7.2 *Termination under general agency law*

principal), the principal could not demand specific performance as a remedy. The courts will not force a person to perform personal services, because that would violate the constitutional prohibition against involuntary servitude.

Termination by Operation of Law

Several events terminate an agency relationship automatically, without action by either party. These events include:

- expiration of the agency term;
- fulfillment of the purpose of the agency;
- the death, incapacity, or bankruptcy of either party; and
- extinction of the subject matter.

Expiration of Agency Term. An agency terminates automatically when its term expires. If the agency agreement did not include an expiration date, it is deemed to expire within a reasonable time (which would vary, depending on the type of agency in question). If there is no expiration date, either party may terminate the agency without liability for damages, although the other party might be able to demand reimbursement for expenses incurred before the termination.

Fulfillment of Purpose. An agency relationship terminates when its purpose has been fulfilled. For example, if a licensee is hired to sell the principal's property and the licensee does so, the agency is terminated by fulfillment.

Death, Incapacity, or Bankruptcy. An agency is terminated before it expires if either the agent or the principal dies. Most states provide that the agency also terminates if either party becomes mentally incompetent. Generally, the agent has no authority to act after the death or incompetency of the principal, even if the agent is unaware of the principal's death or incompetency. An agency is also terminated by the bankruptcy of either party.

Extinction of Subject Matter. The subject matter of a real estate agency is the property in question. If the property is in any way extinguished (for example, by being sold or destroyed), the agency automatically terminates.

Terminating a Real Estate Agency

Under the terms of Washington's real estate agency law, a real estate agency relationship commences when the licensee undertakes to provide real estate brokerage services to a principal and continues until the earliest of the following:

1. Completion of performance by the licensee (the terms of the agency agreement are fulfilled).
2. Expiration of the agency term as agreed by the parties. (Note that an exclusive listing agreement should always specify a termination date. That is even a legal requirement in some states, although not in Washington.)
3. Termination of the relationship by mutual consent.
4. Notification from one party to the other that the agency is terminated.

When an agency relationship has terminated, the agent can no longer represent the principal. However, the agent still owes two statutory duties to the principal after the relationship terminates:

1. The agent must account for all money and property received during the relationship.
2. The agent must not disclose confidential information about the principal that was learned during the agency relationship.

Real Estate Agency Relationships

Washington's real estate agency statute fundamentally changed how agency relationships work in real estate transactions. Before discussing real estate agency relationships under the current law, we're going to examine how they used to work. This historical perspective will help you understand why the law developed as it did. We'll start by describing a typical residential transaction and reviewing some terminology.

Agents in a Typical Transaction

A typical residential real estate transaction is likely to involve more than one real estate agent. Someone who wants to find a home in a particular area contacts a real estate firm in that area. A licensee who works for that firm will interview the prospective buyer to find out what kind of a home he wants and can afford, and then will show the buyer various suitable properties. Most firms belong to a multiple listing service, so the licensee can show the buyer not only homes that are listed directly with her own firm, but also homes that are listed with other MLS members. If the buyer becomes interested in a particular home, negotiations for the purchase of that home will involve the listing agent as well as the licensee who has been showing properties to the buyer.

Meanwhile, other real estate agents may be showing the same house to other prospective buyers. By the time the transaction closes, it may involve a listing firm, a listing agent, a selling firm, and a selling agent, in addition to other cooperating agents who showed the home to buyers who decided they didn't want it or didn't offer enough for it.

Understanding the agency relationships in this transaction means understanding which party each of these real estate licensees is representing. As a first step, you should be familiar with all of the following terms.

- **Real estate agent:** Real estate agent is the generic term used to refer to real estate licensees. In fact, only real estate firms are authorized to represent a buyer or a seller directly; real estate brokers and managing brokers act on behalf of the firm they work for.

- **Client:** A client is the person who has engaged the services of an agent. A client may be a real estate seller, buyer, landlord, or tenant.

- **Customer:** In transactions where the agent is representing a seller or a landlord, third parties are generally referred to as customers. A customer may be a buyer or a tenant.

- **Listing agent:** The licensee who takes the listing on a home is referred to as the listing agent. (He may or may not be the one who eventually procures a buyer for the listed home.) The real estate firm (or the firm's designated broker) that this licensee works for may also be referred to as the listing agent.

- **Selling agent:** The licensee who actually procures the buyer for a home is referred to as the selling agent. (She may or may not have taken the listing on the home.) The real estate firm (or the firm's designated broker) that this licensee works for may also be referred to as the selling agent. (Don't confuse "selling agent" with "seller's agent." In most transactions the selling agent represents the buyer, while the listing agent represents the seller.)

- **Cooperating agent:** All the members of the listing firm's multiple listing service (and the members of any other MLS that is participating in the transaction) are considered to be "cooperating agents." A cooperating agent may be the agent of either the buyer or the seller, or act in some other capacity as agreed to by the parties. (The cooperating agent who procures a buyer is the selling agent.)

Agency Relationships: a Historical Perspective

Until the 1990s, most listing agreements in Washington (and elsewhere in the country) stated that cooperating agents were subagents of the seller. This meant that in nearly all transactions not only the listing agent but also the selling agent represented the seller, not the buyer. This was confusing for buyers, who often assumed (understandably) that the agent who was helping them find a house was representing their interests rather than the seller's. Based on that assumption, a buyer would often tell the selling agent confidential information. Yet because the selling agent actually represented the seller, the agent had a duty to pass that information along to the seller.

If the selling agent went ahead and disclosed this confidential information to the seller and the buyer found out, the buyer naturally felt betrayed—and sometimes sued. But if the selling agent protected the buyer's confidence and failed to give the information to the seller, the agent was effectively violating her duty of loyalty to the seller. Reform was needed.

Real Estate Agency Statute. In an effort to clear up the confusion over who was representing whom, many states (including Washington) passed agency disclosure laws. These laws require real estate agents to disclose to both the buyer and the seller, in writing, the identity of the party they represent. However, the Washington State Legislature decided that an agency disclosure law was not enough, and so it passed the Real Estate Brokerage Relationships Act.

As we discussed earlier, under the terms of this legislation a real estate licensee who works with a buyer is presumed to be the buyer's agent, unless there is a written agreement to the contrary. This rule has two important benefits. First, it turns the buyer's natural assumption—that the licensee the buyer is working with is acting as her agent—into reality. Second, it significantly reduces the danger of inadvertent, undisclosed dual agency (discussed below). Because a licensee represents the buyer he is working with, there is no conflict between the licensee's desire to help the buyer and the licensee's agency duties.

Types of Agency Relationships

Under the Real Estate Brokerage Relationships Act, there are four types of real estate agency relationships:

- seller agency,
- buyer agency,
- dual agency, and
- non-agency.

Seller Agency. Whereas traditionally real estate agents nearly always represented the seller, under the Washington statute the only licensees who represent the seller are the listing broker, the listing designated broker, and the listing firm. The listing agreement creates a seller agency relationship.

Under the terms of the listing agreement, the primary task of a seller's agent is to find a buyer for the seller's property at a price that is acceptable to the seller. To accomplish this, the seller's agent advises the seller about preparing the property for sale, helps the seller decide on the listing price, markets the property, and negotiates on the seller's behalf with selling agents and buyers.

Seller's Agents and Buyers. Throughout a transaction, a seller's agent must use her best efforts to promote the interests of the seller. Yet the seller's agent may also provide some services to a prospective buyer. For example, the seller's agent may help a buyer who doesn't have his own agent fill out a purchase offer form and apply for financing. These services are considered to be in the best interests of the seller, and thus do not violate the agent's duties to the seller. Of course, the seller's agent must disclose to the buyer that she is acting as the seller's agent.

A seller's agent must be very careful to treat the buyer fairly, but the agent must not act as if she is representing the buyer. In other words, the agent must fully disclose all known material facts and answer the buyer's questions honestly. However, the agent should not give the buyer certain kinds of advice, such as how much to offer for the listed property.

> **Example:** Harrison, who works for Yates Real Estate, recently listed Tilden's house. The listing price is $315,000, but Harrison has reason to believe that Tilden would accept an offer of $306,000. Harrison shows the listed house to Markham, who asks Harrison, "How low do you think the seller will go?" Harrison should make it clear to Markham that he is representing Tilden and cannot divulge confidential information to Markham. If Harrison were to do so, Tilden could sue Harrison and Yates Real Estate for breach of agency duties.

In some cases, the seller's agent has had a previous agency relationship with the buyer. In this situation it may be difficult for the agent to represent the seller's interests without feeling some loyalty to the buyer as well.

> **Example:** Suppose Tilden listed her home with Harrison and liked him so well that she wanted Harrison to help her find another home. Harrison shows Tilden one of his own listings.
>
> Under these circumstances, it would be easy for Tilden to think that Harrison is acting as her agent. However, because of the listing agreement, Harrison is the seller's agent, and he should emphasize this fact to Tilden. Tilden should be reminded that Harrison is obligated to disclose any material information Tilden tells him to

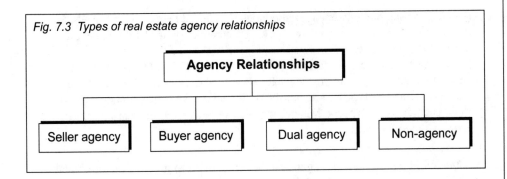

Fig. 7.3 Types of real estate agency relationships

Agency Relationships

Seller agency   Buyer agency   Dual agency   Non-agency

the seller, and that in all negotiations Harrison will be representing the seller's best interests.

However, a real estate agent is not permitted to disclose confidential information about a principal even after the termination of the agency relationship. Thus, Harrison cannot disclose to the seller any confidential information about Tilden that he learned during his agency relationship with Tilden.

In transactions like the one in this example, where the listing agent is also the selling agent, the licensee risks creating an inadvertent dual agency. **Inadvertent dual agency** occurs if an agent unintentionally leads each party to believe that he or she (rather than the other party) is the agent's principal, while failing to make the required agency disclosures and obtain the parties' written consent to a dual agency.

Example: Returning to the first part of our example involving the agent Harrison, let's suppose that Harrison fails to disclose his seller agency to the buyer Markham. Instead, Harrison behaves as if he's the buyer's agent. He tells Markham that a full-price offer may be necessary, but that the seller is in a hurry to sell and could be willing to accept significantly less.

Markham reasonably believes that Harrison is his agent because of this negotiation advice, and also because there was no agency disclosure to the contrary.

By his conduct, Harrison has created an inadvertent dual agency. This violates the license law because he didn't make the proper agency disclosures and failed to obtain written consent to a dual agency. Also, in this particular case, Harrison has violated his duty of loyalty to the seller by disclosing the seller's negotiating position. Thus, the seller could sue Harrison for damages.

Buyer Agency. Even before passage of Washington's real estate agency law, buyers were beginning to realize the benefits of having their own agent, and taking the trouble to find someone to represent them. Now that buyers are automatically represented by the agent they're working with (unless there is a written agreement to the contrary), the majority of buyers are able to benefit from buyer agency. The advantages of buyer agency include confidentiality and loyalty, objective advice, help with negotiations, and access to more homes.

Confidentiality and Loyalty. A buyer's agent owes agency duties to the buyer, including the duties of confidentiality and loyalty. For many buyers, these two duties make up the most important advantage of buyer agency.

Example: Broker Mendez is helping Buyer Jackson find a home. She shows Jackson many houses, and there are two that interest him. One is a large fixer-upper selling for $250,000. The other is a smaller, newer house in mint condition that's selling for $236,000. Because Mendez must put Jackson's interests before her own, she advises him to purchase the smaller house because it better suits his needs. She does this even though she would earn a bigger commission if Jackson bought the more expensive house.

Mendez advises Jackson to offer $229,900 for the $236,000 house. Jackson agrees to, although he tells Mendez that he's willing to pay the full listing price. Because Mendez is Jackson's agent, she is obligated to keep that confidential. (If she'd been the seller's agent, Mendez would have been required to disclose that information to the seller.)

Objective Advice. A buyer's agent can be relied upon to give the buyer objective advice about the pros and cons of purchasing a particular home. He will point out various issues the buyer should be aware of, such as energy costs, the need for future repairs, and property value trends. By contrast, a seller's agent will present the property in the most positive light and may use expert sales techniques to convince the buyer to sign on the dotted line.

Help with Negotiating. Buyers often feel uncomfortable negotiating for a property, especially one they really want to buy. They may be afraid to make a mistake through ignorance, or they may feel pressured to make a high offer quickly before someone else snaps up the property. A buyer's agent can use her negotiating skills and intimate knowledge of the real estate market to help the buyer get the property on the best possible terms.

Access to More Properties. A buyer's agent may arrange to be compensated if the buyer purchases any home, even one that isn't listed with a brokerage. So a buyer's agent may pursue less traditional means of searching for properties, and show the buyer properties that are for sale by owner, properties with open listings, and properties in foreclosure or probate proceedings.

Creation of Buyer Agency. Although buyer agency relationships are created automatically under the terms of the real estate agency law, a buyer and a real estate licensee may also enter into a written **representation agreement**. (An example is shown in Figure 7.4.) While the terms of buyer representation agreements vary, they generally include the following:

- the duration of the agency,
- the general characteristics of the property the buyer wants,
- the price range,
- the conditions under which a fee will be earned,
- who will pay the fee, and
- a description of the licensee's duties.

Buyer's Agent's Compensation. There are a variety of ways in which a buyer's agent may be compensated. The three most common are:

- a retainer,
- a seller-paid fee, and/or
- a buyer-paid fee.

A **retainer** is a fee paid up front, before services are provided. Some buyer's agents collect a retainer when they enter into a buyer agency relationship, to ensure that their services won't go entirely uncompensated. The retainer is usually nonrefundable, but it will be credited against any fee or commission that the agent becomes entitled to.

Fig. 7.4 Buyer representation agreement

Form 41A
Buyer's Agency Agreement
Rev. 7/10
Page 1 of 2

©Copyright 2010
Northwest Multiple Listing Service
ALL RIGHTS RESERVED

BUYER'S AGENCY AGREEMENT

This Buyer's Agency Agreement is made this _____ between 1

_____ ("Real Estate Firm" or "Firm") 2

and _____ ("Buyer"). 3

1. **AGENCY.** Firm appoints _____ ("Selling Broker") 4
to represent Buyer. This Agreement creates an agency relationship with Selling Broker and any of Firm's brokers 5
who supervise Selling Broker's performance as Buyer's agent ("Supervising Broker"). No other brokers affiliated 6
with Firm are agents of Buyer, except to the extent that Firm, in its discretion, appoints other brokers to act on 7
Buyer's behalf as and when needed. Buyer acknowledges receipt of the pamphlet entitled "The Law of Real 8
Estate Agency." 9

2. **EXCLUSIVE OR NON-EXCLUSIVE.** This Agreement creates a ❑ sole and exclusive; ❑ non-exclusive (non- 10
exclusive if not checked) agency relationship. 11

3. **AREA.** Selling Broker will search for real property for Buyer located in the following geographical areas: 12
_____ 13
_____ (unlimited if not filled in) ("Area"). 14

4. **FIRM'S LISTINGS/SELLING BROKER'S OWN LISTINGS/DUAL AGENCY.** If Selling Broker locates a property 15
listed by one of Firm's brokers other than Selling Broker ("Listing Broker"), Buyer consents to any Supervising 16
Broker, who also supervises Listing Broker, acting as a dual agent. Further, if Selling Broker locates a property 17
listed by Selling Broker, Buyer consents to Selling Broker and Supervising Broker acting as dual agents. 18

5. **TERM OF AGREEMENT.** This Agreement will expire _____ (120 days from signing if not filled in) or by 19
prior written notice by either party. Buyer shall be under no obligation to Firm except for those obligations existing 20
at the time of termination. 21

6. **NO WARRANTIES OR REPRESENTATIONS.** Firm makes no warranties or representations regarding the value 22
of or the suitability of any property for Buyer's purposes. Buyer agrees to be responsible for making all inspections 23
and investigations necessary to satisfy Buyer as to the property's suitability and value. 24

7. **INSPECTIONS RECOMMENDED.** Firm recommends that any offer to purchase a property be conditioned on 25
Buyer's inspection of the property and its improvements. Firm and Selling Broker have no expertise on these 26
matters and Buyer is solely responsible for interviewing and selecting all inspectors. 27

8. **COMPENSATION.** Buyer shall pay Firm compensation as follows: 28
_____ 29
_____ 30
_____ 31

  a. **Exclusive**. If the parties agree to an exclusive relationship in Paragraph 2 above and if Buyer shall, during the 32
  course of this Agreement, purchase a property located in the Area, then Buyer shall pay to Firm the 33
  compensation provided for herein. If Buyer shall, within six (6) months after the expiration or termination of 34
  this Agreement, purchase a property located in the Area that was first brought to the attention of Buyer by the 35
  efforts or actions of Firm, or through information secured directly or indirectly from or through Firm, then Buyer 36
  shall pay to Firm the compensation provided for herein. 37

  b. **Non-Exclusive**. If the parties agree to non-exclusive relationship in Paragraph 2 above and if Buyer shall, 38
  during the course of or within six (6) months after the expiration or termination of this Agreement, purchase a 39
  property that was first brought to the attention of Buyer by the efforts or actions of Firm, or through information 40
  secured directly or indirectly from or through Firm, then Buyer shall pay to Firm the compensation provided for 41
  herein. 42

BUYER: _____   BUYER: _____

Form 41A
Buyer's Agency Agreement
Rev. 7/10
Page 2 of 2

BUYER'S AGENCY AGREEMENT
Continued

    c. **MLS.** Firm will utilize a multiple listing service ("MLS") to locate properties and MLS rules may require the 43
seller to compensate Firm by apportioning a commission between the Listing Firm and Firm. Firm will disclose 44
any such commission or bonuses offered by the seller prior to preparing any offer. Buyer will be credited with 45
any commission or bonus so payable to Firm. In the event that said commission and any bonus is less than 46
the compensation provided in this Agreement, Buyer will pay the difference to Firm at the time of closing. In 47
the event that said commission and any bonus is equal to or greater than the compensation provided for by 48
this Agreement, no compensation is due to Firm herein. If any of Firm's brokers act as a dual agent, Firm 49
shall receive the listing and selling commission paid by the seller plus any additional compensation Firm may 50
have negotiated with the seller. All such compensation shall be credited toward the fee specified above. 51

9. **V.A. TRANSACTIONS.** Due to VA regulations, VA financed transactions shall be conditioned upon the full 52
commission being paid by the seller. 53

10. **NO DISTRESSED HOME CONVEYANCE.** Firm will not represent or assist Buyer in a transaction that is a 54
"Distressed Home Conveyance" as defined by Chapter 61.34 RCW unless otherwise agreed in writing. A 55
"Distressed Home Conveyance" is a transaction where a buyer purchases property from a "Distressed 56
Homeowner" (defined by Chapter 61.34 RCW), allows the Distressed Homeowner to continue to occupy the 57
property, and promises to convey the property back to the Distressed Homeowner or promises the Distressed 58
Homeowner an interest in, or portion of the proceeds from a resale of the property. 59

11. **ATTORNEYS' FEES.** In the event of suit concerning this Agreement, including claims pursuant to the Washington 60
Consumer Protection Act, the prevailing party is entitled to court costs and a reasonable attorney's fee. The 61
venue of any suit shall be the county in which the property is located. 62

12. **OTHER AGREEMENTS (none if not filled in).** 63

_____ 64

_____ 65

_____ 66

Buyer has read and approves this Agreement and hereby acknowledges receipt of a copy. 67

_____	_____	_____
Buyer	Date	Firm (Company)

68

_____	_____	_____
Buyer	Date	By: (Selling Broker)

69

_____
Address

70

_____
City, State, Zip

71

_____
Phone   Fax

72

_____
E-mail Address

73

In many cases, a buyer's agent is paid by the seller through a **commission split**. The commission split is based on a provision found in most MLS listing agreements, whereby any cooperating licensee who procures a buyer is entitled to the selling agent's portion of the commission, regardless of which party that cooperating licensee represents. Note that the source of the agent's commission does not determine who his principal is; a buyer's agent who accepts a seller-paid fee does not then owe agency duties to the seller.

> **Example:** Helman lists his property with Thurston Realty and agrees to pay Thurston 6% of the sales price. The listing agreement includes a clause that entitles any cooperating licensee who procures a buyer to the selling agent's portion of the commission.
>
> Adams Realty has a buyer agency agreement with Gray. Gray offers $350,000 for Helman's house, and Helman accepts the offer.
>
> When the transaction closes, Helman pays a $21,000 commission; $10,500 goes to Thurston Realty and $10,500 goes to Adams Realty.

Most buyer representation agreements also provide for payment by means of a commission split when the buyer purchases a home that is listed through a multiple listing service. However, a buyer representation agreement may provide for a **buyer-paid fee** instead. The buyer-paid fee might be based on an hourly rate, which essentially makes the agent a consultant. Alternatively, a buyer's agent may charge a percentage fee, so that the commission is a percentage of the purchase price. A third possibility is a flat fee—a specified sum that is payable if the buyer purchases a property found by the agent.

Some buyer agency agreements provide that the buyer's agent will accept a commission split if one is available, but the buyer will pay the fee if the purchased property was unlisted (for example, if it was for sale by owner).

Dual Agency. A dual agency relationship exists whenever a real estate agent represents both the seller and the buyer in the same transaction. Because the interests of the buyer and the seller usually conflict, it is difficult to represent them both without being disloyal to one or both.

> **Example:** Davis represents both the buyer and the seller in a transaction. The seller informs Davis that she's in a big hurry to sell and will accept any reasonable offer. The buyer tells Davis that he's very interested in the house and is willing to pay the full listing price. Should Davis tell the buyer of the seller's eagerness to sell? Should Davis tell the seller about the buyer's willingness to pay the full price?

In fact, it's really impossible for a dual agent to fully represent both parties. Thus, instead of the duty of loyalty, Washington law imposes on a dual agent the duty to refrain from acting to the detriment of either party. The dual agent must do his best to act impartially and treat both clients equally.

Each party to a dual agency should be informed that he or she will not receive full representation. Certain facts must necessarily be withheld from each party; the dual agent cannot divulge confidential information about one party to the other party. Returning to the previous example, the dual agent must not tell the buyer the seller's bottom line price, nor tell the seller how much the buyer is willing to pay.

Before acting as a dual agent, a licensee must have a buyer agency agreement with the buyer and a seller agency agreement with the seller. Acting as a dual agent without the agency agreements, full disclosure, and written consent to the dual agency may give rise to a lawsuit by one or both parties. It's also grounds for disciplinary action by the Department of Licensing (see Chapter 17). Statutory agency disclosure requirements and the consent requirement for dual agency are discussed in the next section of this chapter.

In-house Transactions. Under the Real Estate Brokerage Relationships Act, dual agency occurs most often in in-house transactions. It's an **in-house transaction** when the listing agent and the selling agent both work for the same brokerage firm. In this situation, the listing agent represents only the seller, the selling agent represents only the buyer, and the designated broker is a dual agent, representing both parties. This arrangement is sometimes referred to as a **split agency**, since the brokerage is serving both parties. It may also be called a **designated**, **assigned**, or **appointed agency**, referring to the fact that one agent in the brokerage is assigned or appointed to represent one party, while another agent with the same firm represents the other party (with the designated broker representing both parties).

> **Example:** Winston works for Roberts, a designated broker. Winston has shown King several houses over the course of a few weeks. Finally, Winston shows King a house listed by Vincent, who also works for Roberts. King decides to make an offer on the house. In this transaction, Winston is the buyer's agent, Vincent is the seller's agent, and Roberts is a dual agent.

Non-Agency. In some transactions, a real estate licensee might choose to act only as a facilitator and refuse to act as an agent for either principal. This is called **non-agency**, and it is legal under Washington's real estate agency law. However, a non-agent still owes general statutory duties to any party she works with. There's no way for a licensee to opt out of the duties of disclosure, reasonable skill and care, honesty and good faith, and so on.

Agency Disclosure Requirements

As we explained earlier, licensees must give anyone they render services to a pamphlet setting forth the provisions of Washington's real estate agency statute. In addition, they must disclose to anyone they render services to in a transaction which party (or parties) they're representing in the transaction.

A licensee must make the required agency disclosures to a party before that party signs an offer in the transaction. The disclosures must be in writing. They may be in a paragraph in the purchase and sale agreement entitled "Agency Disclosure"; in that case, the parties' signatures on the agreement indicate their acceptance and understanding of the stated agency relationships (see Chapter 9). Alternatively, a licensee may make the disclosures in a separate disclosure document, which must be signed by the parties as well as the licensee. An example is shown in Figure 7.5.

Dual Agency Disclosure. Before acting as a dual agent, a licensee must obtain the informed written consent of both parties. The dual agent must disclose to both parties that she will be acting as a dual agent. The terms of the dual agent's compensation must also be revealed. The parties will then sign the confirmation of the agency disclosure in the purchase and sale agreement.

Fig. 7.5 Agency disclosure form

Form 42
Agency Disclosure
Rev. 7/10
Page 1 of 1

AGENCY DISCLOSURE

Washington State law requires real estate brokers to disclose to all parties to whom the broker renders real estate   1
brokerage services whether the broker represents the seller (or lessor), the buyer (or lessee), both the seller/lessor   2
and buyer/lessee, or neither.   3

This form is for use when the transaction forms **do not** otherwise contain an agency disclosure provision.   4

THE UNDERSIGNED BROKER REPRESENTS: _____   5

THE UNDERSIGNED BUYER / LESSEE OR SELLER / LESSOR ACKNOWLEDGES RECEIPT   6
OF A COPY OF THE PAMPHLET ENTITLED "THE LAW OF REAL ESTATE AGENCY"   7

_____ DATE _____   8
Signature

_____ DATE _____   9
Signature

_____ DATE _____   10
Signature

_____ DATE _____   11
Signature

BROKER _____   12
Print/Type

BROKER'S SIGNATURE _____   13

FIRM NAME AS LICENSED _____   14
Print/Type

FIRM'S ASSUMED NAME (if applicable) _____   15
Print/Type

SAMPLE

Real estate licensees should be extra careful with their disclosures in the context of dual agency. Buyers and sellers, eager to get on with the business of buying and selling a home, may agree to a dual agency without really understanding what it means. They may accept the agent's explanation at face value and sign a disclosure form without question. Later, one party might feel that the licensee breached his agency duties. This kind of disappointment often leads to legal action.

Designated Broker/Broker Relationship

Finally, let's discuss the legal relationship between a real estate broker and the designated broker for whom that broker works. (In this discussion, the term "broker" will generally encompass managing brokers, too.) As you know, the broker is an agent of the designated broker and a subagent of the designated broker's client. The broker is not licensed to represent members of the public directly, and the designated broker is responsible for supervising the broker's actions.

For certain purposes, a real estate broker is classified either as the designated broker's **employee** or as an **independent contractor**. An independent contractor is hired to perform a particular job, and he uses his own judgment to decide how the job should be completed. In contrast, an employee is hired to perform whatever tasks the employer requires, and is given instructions on how to accomplish each task. An employee is supervised and controlled much more closely than an independent contractor. Various employment and tax laws apply only when someone is hired as an employee, and not when someone is hired as an independent contractor.

A designated broker is virtually always an independent contractor in relation to his principal (the buyer and/or the seller). When it comes to the relationship between a designated broker and a broker, however, the distinction between employee and independent contractor may be an issue.

Whether a broker is her designated broker's employee or an independent contractor depends on the degree of control the designated broker exercises over the broker. If the designated broker closely directs the activities of the broker and controls how she carries out her work, the broker may be considered an employee. For example, if the designated broker requires the broker to work on a set schedule, tells the broker when to go where, and decides what steps the broker should take in marketing each property, the broker is probably the designated broker's employee.

Most designated brokers exercise much less control over their brokers' work than that. They generally focus on the end results—listings, closings, and satisfied clients—and not on the details of how the broker accomplishes those results. A designated broker usually isn't concerned with where the broker is or what she is doing at any given time. The broker is paid on the basis of results (by commission) rather than hours spent on the job. Thus, in most cases, a real estate broker is an independent contractor, not the designated broker's employee. (Note that managing brokers who receive salaries for administrative duties might be considered employees.)

If a broker were an employee, the real estate firm would be required to withhold money from the broker's compensation for certain federal and state taxes (income tax, social security, and unemployment insurance) and also contribute a share of some of these taxes. By contrast, an independent contractor is responsible for paying her own social security and income taxes. In Washington, an important exception to this rule is industrial insurance (commonly called workers' compensation), which is insurance to help cover the costs of work-related injuries. A real estate firm must pay industrial insurance premiums to the state Department of Labor and Industries for all of the firm's workers, both employees and independent contractors. However, the firm may require the workers to pay a portion of this cost.

The Internal Revenue Code provides that a real estate agent will be considered an independent contractor for federal income tax purposes if three conditions are met:

1. the individual is a licensed real estate agent;
2. substantially all of his or her compensation is based on commission rather than hours worked; and
3. the services are performed under a written contract providing that the individual will not be treated as an employee for federal tax purposes.

Bear in mind that even when a real estate broker meets the criteria for independent contractor status, the license law makes the designated broker responsible for a broker's conduct.

Chapter Summary

1. In an agency relationship, the agent represents the principal in dealings with third parties. An agent may be a universal, general, or special agent, depending on the scope of authority granted.

2. Most agency relationships are created by express agreement (oral or written), but they can also be created by ratification, estoppel, or implication. Acts performed by an agent or an ostensible agent are binding on the principal if they fall within the scope of the agent's actual or apparent authority.

3. A real estate licensee who performs real estate brokerage services for a buyer automatically becomes the buyer's agent, unless there is a written agreement to the contrary.

4. A licensee owes a number of statutory duties to any party to whom the licensee renders real estate services, whether or not there is an agency relationship. These duties are reasonable skill and care, honesty and good faith, presenting all written communications, disclosure of material facts, accounting, providing an agency law pamphlet, and making an agency disclosure.

5. A licensee who enters into an agency relationship owes certain additional duties to the principal, including loyalty, disclosure of conflicts of interest, confidentiality, advising the principal to seek expert advice, and a good faith and continuous effort to fulfill the terms of the agency agreement.

6. Under general agency law, an agency relationship may be terminated by mutual agreement; revocation; renunciation; expiration; fulfillment of purpose; the death, incapacity, or bankruptcy of either party; or extinction of the subject matter.

7. Under Washington law, a real estate licensee may act as the seller's agent, the buyer's agent, a dual agent, or a non-agent.

8. A seller agency is usually created with a listing agreement. A seller's agent owes agency duties to the seller and general licensee duties to the buyer. A listing agent must be careful to avoid any actions that might give rise to an agency relationship with the buyer.

9. A buyer agency relationship is created automatically by providing services to the buyer (unless the agent is already bound by a listing agreement). However, the licensee and the buyer may also enter into a representation agreement. A buyer's agent may be paid by the seller (through a commission split) or by the buyer (with a commission, an hourly fee, or a flat rate).

10. A licensee is a dual agent when she represents both the seller and the buyer in the same transaction. Dual agency is unlawful without the informed written consent of both parties and written agency agreements with both the buyer and the seller. Dual agency most commonly arises in in-house transactions.

11. A licensee is required to disclose to each party which party he represents in the transaction. The disclosure must be made to each party before that party signs an offer to purchase (a purchase and sale agreement). The disclosure must be in writing; it may take the form of a provision included in the purchase and sale agreement, or it may be a separate document.

12. For the purposes of certain tax and employment laws, a real estate broker may be classified either as her brokerage firm's employee or as an independent contractor. In most cases, a broker is considered to be an independent contractor, even though the designated broker has legal responsibility for the broker's conduct.

🔑 Key Terms

Principal—The person who authorizes an agent to act on his behalf.

Agent—A person authorized to represent another in dealings with third parties.

Third party—A person seeking to deal with the principal through the agent.

Fiduciary—Someone who holds a special position of trust and confidence in relation to another.

Ratification—When the principal gives approval to unauthorized actions after they are performed, creating an agency relationship after the fact.

Estoppel—When the principal allows a third party to believe an agency relationship exists, so that the principal is legally precluded (estopped) from denying the agency.

Actual authority—Authority the principal grants to the agent either expressly or by implication.

Apparent authority—Where no actual authority has been granted, but the principal allows it to appear that the agent is authorized, and therefore is estopped from denying the agency. Also called ostensible authority.

Material facts—Information that has a substantial negative impact on the value of the property or on a party's ability to perform, or that would defeat the purpose of the transaction.

Confidential information—Information from or concerning a principal that was acquired during the course of an agency relationship, that the principal reasonably expects to be kept confidential, that the principal has not disclosed to third parties, that would operate to the detriment of the principal, and that the principal is not legally obligated to disclose to the other party.

Secret profit—Any profit an agent receives as a result of the agency relationship and does not disclose to the principal.

Listing agent—The agent that takes the listing on a property, and who may or may not be the agent who procures a buyer.

Selling agent—The agent who procures a buyer for a property, and who may or may not have taken the listing.

Subagent—An "agent of an agent." A broker is generally considered to be a subagent of her designated broker's principal.

In-house transaction—A sale in which the buyer and the seller are brought together by licensees working for the same brokerage firm.

Employee—Someone who works under the direction and control of another.

Independent contractor—A person who contracts to do a job for another, but retains control over how he will carry out the task, rather than following detailed instructions.

Chapter Quiz

1. An agency relationship can be created in any of the following ways, except:
   a) written agreement
   b) oral agreement
   c) ratification
   d) verification

2. After an agency relationship terminates, the agent still owes the principal the duty of:
   a) loyalty
   b) confidentiality
   c) reasonable skill and care
   d) disclosure of material facts

3. Garcia acted on behalf of Hilton without her authorization. At a later date, Hilton gave her approval to Garcia's actions. This is an example of:
   a) express agreement
   b) ratification
   c) estoppel
   d) assumption of authority

4. A seller lists his home with a brokerage at $290,000; he asks for a quick sale. When the listing broker shows the home to a buyer, he says the seller is financially insolvent and will take $280,000. The buyer offers $280,000 and the seller accepts. The broker:
   a) did not violate his duties to the seller, because the seller accepted the offer
   b) did not violate his duties to the seller, since he fulfilled the purpose of his agency
   c) violated his duties to the seller by disclosing confidential information to the buyer
   d) was unethical, but did not violate his duties to the seller, since he did not receive a secret profit

5. Stark lists his property with Agent Bell. Bell shows the property to her cousin, who decides he would like to buy it. Which of the following is true?
   a) Bell can present her cousin's offer to Stark, as long as she tells Stark that the prospective buyer is one of her relatives
   b) Bell violated her duties to Stark by showing the property to one of her relatives
   c) It was not unethical for Bell to show the property to a relative, but it would be a violation of her duties if she presented her cousin's offer to Stark
   d) It is not necessary for Bell to tell Stark that the buyer is related to her, as long as he is offering the full listing price for the property

6. A principal can be held liable for harm caused by a real estate licensee if the:
   a) act resulting in harm was authorized by the principal
   b) licensee has a reputation for unethical practices
   c) licensee has many assets that could be awarded to the injured party
   d) licensee assured the third party that the principal would be liable for any harm caused by the transaction

7. A real estate agent tells potential buyers: "This is a wonderful house—way better than anything else on the market." This statement would be considered:
   a) a misrepresentation
   b) actual fraud
   c) self-dealing
   d) puffing

8. In most cases, a listing agent:

    a) is authorized to enter into contracts on behalf of the seller

    b) is considered a special agent

    c) Both of the above

    d) Neither of the above

9. Dual agency is:

    a) no longer legal in Washington State

    b) legal as long as both principals consent to the arrangement in writing

    c) unlawful unless the agent has a written agency agreement with each party

    d) Both b) and c)

10. Able listed Glover's property. Able:

    a) cannot give a buyer any information about Glover's property without being considered a dual agent

    b) may give a buyer information about Glover's property without owing agency duties to the buyer

    c) must sign a disclaimer of liability if he presents a buyer's offer to purchase to Glover

    d) is a non-agent

11. Grant, who works for Carter (his designated broker), is showing Manning a property listed by Lee, who also works for Carter. Who is most likely to be acting as a dual agent?

    a) Grant

    b) Carter

    c) Manning

    d) Lee

12. Broker Kelley works for Designated Broker Forrest. A good friend wants Kelley to try to find a house for her. Kelley shows her a house listed by one of Forrest's other sales agents. Kelley:

    a) is in danger of becoming a dual agent

    b) is automatically acting as a buyer's agent in this situation

    c) should request special approval of the sale from the Real Estate Commission

    d) is the seller's agent, no matter how she behaves towards her friend

13. A buyer's agent:

    a) may not accept compensation paid by the seller

    b) must have a written buyer agency agreement in order to be compensated

    c) may be paid through a commission split

    d) may not receive compensation that is based on the property's sales price

14. A licensee must disclose which party she is representing:

    a) to anyone she renders services to, before that person signs an offer

    b) to anyone she renders services to, before the services are rendered

    c) to the buyer, before showing the buyer any properties

    d) to the seller, before presenting an offer to the seller

15. A dual agent must:

    a) keep each party's negotiating position confidential

    b) disclose all material facts to both parties, no matter how confidential

    c) act only as a facilitator, with no agency duties to either party

    d) refer all conflicts of interest to the Board of Equalization

👉 Answer Key

1. d) An agency relationship may be created by express agreement (written or oral), ratification, estoppel, or implication.

2. b) After an agency relationship terminates, the agent still owes the principal the duty of confidentiality.

3. b) An agency relationship is created by ratification when the principal gives approval to unauthorized actions after the fact.

4. c) The broker was disloyal to his principal and violated his duties by disclosing confidential information to a third party.

5. a) A seller's real estate agent is required to tell the seller if the prospective buyer is related to the agent.

6. a) A principal can't be held liable for harm caused by a licensee unless the act that resulted in harm was authorized by the principal, or unless the principal benefited from the act and there is little chance that the third party will be able to recover damages from the licensee.

7. d) This is an example of puffing, an exaggerated statement that the buyers should realize they can't depend on.

8. b) A listing agent is usually a special agent, with limited authority to represent the principal in a particular transaction. A listing agent is ordinarily not authorized to sign contracts on behalf of the principal.

9. d) Dual agency is legal, but only if the seller and the buyer are informed that the agent is representing both of them, and each party has a written agency agreement with the agent.

10. b) A seller's agent can give a buyer information about the seller's property without becoming a dual agent.

11. b) Carter would be considered a dual agent in this situation. Grant (the selling agent) is the buyer's agent. Lee (the listing agent) is the seller's agent.

12. b) Kelley is representing the buyer only, although Designated Broker Forrest is considered a dual agent.

13. c) Buyer's agents often accept a share of the commission that the listing firm receives from the seller. This arrangement does not create an agency relationship between the buyer's agent and the seller.

14. a) A licensee is required to disclose which party she's representing to anyone she renders services to in connection with a transaction. The disclosure must be made before that person signs an offer in the transaction.

15. a) A dual agent must not disclose confidential information about one party to the other party. This includes information on each party's negotiating position.

Listing Agreements

🏘 Chapter Overview

A listing agreement is a written contract between a property owner and a real estate firm. The owner hires the firm to find a buyer or a tenant who is ready, willing, and able to buy or lease the property on the owner's terms. The listing agreement defines the rights and responsibilities of both the owner and the firm. This chapter explains what a real estate firm is required to do in order to earn a commission, the distinctions between the different types of listings, and the elements of a typical listing agreement.

Introduction

When a seller hires a real estate firm to help sell a piece of property, they enter into a contract called a **listing agreement**. Even though the listing agreement form is frequently filled out and signed by the individual agent who is working with the seller, the contract is between the seller and the real estate brokerage, not the individual agent.

The listing agreement creates an agency relationship between the real estate firm (as well as the licensee who takes the listing) and the seller. As you saw in Chapter 7, agency carries with it a high level of responsibility. The licensee/agent is a fiduciary, required to act in the best interests of her client, the seller/principal, in carrying out the agency.

Fiduciary duties are imposed on the agent by law; in addition, the agent and the seller agree to take on certain contractual duties in their listing agreement. The terms of the listing agreement determine what the agent is obligated to do, and under what circumstances the seller will be obligated to pay the agent a commission.

Earning a Commission

The standard form of payment for a real estate agent is the commission, also called a **brokerage fee**. The commission is usually computed as a percentage of the sales price (the price that the property is sold for), as opposed to the listing price.

A real estate agent cannot sue a seller for compensation unless three criteria are met. First, there must be a written employment agreement. Second, the agent and her firm must have been properly licensed before the agent offered to provide real estate services or procured a promise of compensation (see Chapter 17). Finally, the agent must have fulfilled the terms of the listing agreement.

A listing agreement can make payment of the commission depend on any conditions that are mutually acceptable to the agent and the seller. For example, the seller might ask to include a "no sale, no commission" provision in the agreement. This would make the commission payable only if the transaction actually closes and the seller receives full payment from the buyer.

Unless otherwise agreed, however, certain standard rules are followed regarding payment of the commission. These include the rules concerning a ready, willing, and able buyer, and those concerning the three types of listings.

Ready, Willing, and Able Buyer

As a general rule, a listing agreement obligates the seller to pay the agent (the listing firm) a commission if a ready, willing, and able buyer is found during the listing period. A buyer is considered "ready and willing" if he makes an offer that meets the seller's stated terms. (In the listing agreement, the seller should state the price and any other essential terms—for instance, if the seller requires a specific closing date or downpayment amount.) A ready and willing buyer is considered "able" if he has the capacity to contract and the financial ability to complete the purchase. The buyer must have enough cash to buy the property on the agreed terms, or be eligible for the necessary financing.

Since the obligation to pay the commission arises when the listing agent finds a ready, willing, and able buyer, if a seller decides not to accept that buyer's offer, she still owes the commission. Furthermore, if the offer is accepted, the obligation to pay the commission does not terminate just because the sale falls through, at least not if that failure was the seller's fault. For example, if the seller changes her mind about selling or can't deliver marketable title, she still owes the commission. (However, the firm or firms involved may decide against demanding payment.)

Note that if the buyer causes the sale to terminate—for example, because he can't get financing—that might mean the buyer wasn't actually "able" and therefore no commission is owed.

Types of Listing Agreements

Whether a seller is required to pay the agent's commission also depends on the type of listing agreement that they have. The three basic types of listing agreements are the:

- open listing,
- exclusive agency listing, and
- exclusive right to sell listing.

Open Listing. Under an open listing agreement, the seller is obligated to pay the agent a commission only if the agent was the **procuring cause** of the sale. The procuring cause is the person who was primarily responsible for bringing about the agreement between the parties. To be the procuring cause, an agent must have personally obtained the offer from the ready, willing, and able buyer.

An open listing is also called a non-exclusive listing, because a seller is free to give open listings to any number of agents. If a seller signs two open listing agreements with two different agents, and one of the agents sells the property, only the agent who made the sale is entitled to a commission. The other agent is not compensated for her efforts. Or if the seller sells the property directly, without the help of either agent, then the seller does not have to pay any commission at all. The sale of the property terminates all outstanding listings.

The open listing arrangement has obvious disadvantages. If two competing agents both negotiate with the person who ends up buying the property, there may be a dispute over which agent was the procuring cause of the sale. Also, because an agent with an open listing agreement is not assured of a commission when the property sells, he may not put as much effort into marketing the property, so it may take longer to sell. For the most part, open listing agreements are used only when a seller is unwilling to execute an exclusive listing agreement. (Many multiple listing services do not allow agents to submit open listings.)

Exclusive Agency Listing. In an exclusive agency listing, the seller agrees to list with only one agent, but retains the right to sell the property herself without being obligated to pay the agent a commission. The agent is entitled to a commission if anyone other than the seller finds a buyer for the property, but not if the seller finds the buyer without the help of an agent.

Exclusive Right to Sell Listing. Under an exclusive right to sell listing, the seller agrees to list with only one agent, and that agent is entitled to a commission if the property sells during the listing term, regardless of who finds the buyer. Even if the seller makes the sale directly, the agent is still entitled to the commission.

In spite of the designation "exclusive right to sell," this type of listing agreement does not actually authorize the agent to sell the property. As with the other types of listings, the agent is authorized only to submit offers to purchase to the seller.

The exclusive right to sell listing is preferred by agents because it gives them the best chance of earning a commission. It's the type of listing that's most commonly used.

Due Diligence. An important distinction between open and exclusive listings concerns the agent's contractual obligations. An open listing is a unilateral contract: the seller promises to pay the agent a commission if the agent finds a buyer, but the agent does not promise to make any effort to do so. If the agent does nothing at all, it is not a breach of contract.

On the other hand, an exclusive listing is a bilateral contract. In exchange for the seller's promise to pay a commission no matter who finds a buyer, the agent (by implication, if not expressly) promises to market the property and make a diligent effort to find a buyer. If the seller can prove that the listing agent did nothing to help sell the property, a court might not require the seller to pay the agent's commission.

Elements of a Listing Agreement

Although an agent and a seller can draw up their listing agreement from scratch, that's rare, at least for residential listings. Most brokerages use one of several available listing agreement forms and make few—if any—modifications to it. If a firm belongs to a multiple listing service (discussed below), it is usually required to use the listing form provided by the MLS (which generally cannot be modified by the firm).

In this section of the chapter, we will first discuss the basic requirements for any listing agreement, and then look at the provisions of a typical listing agreement form.

Basic Requirements

Under Washington law, a listing agreement must comply with the statute of frauds. It must be in writing and signed by the seller. The listing agreement must also include authorization for the agent to market the property and state the agent's commission. The commission may be given as a percentage of the sales price (which is the standard practice) or as a set dollar amount. The listing agreement must also adequately describe the property to be sold. A complete legal description of the property is not absolutely required by Washington law, as long as the agreement clearly identifies the property in question. Certainly the best practice is to use a legal description.

In a **net listing**, the seller states what net amount he will accept as the proceeds from the sale of the property. If the sales price exceeds that net figure, the agent is entitled to keep the excess as her compensation—no matter how much it may amount to. (Net listings are generally frowned upon; an unscrupulous agent can use them to take advantage of clients. In some states, they are entirely illegal.)

A slip of paper that says "I will pay Diaz Realty $1,000 for helping me to sell Claraway Farm" could be an enforceable listing agreement in Washington, as long as it is signed by a competent seller. Of course, it is much better to have a formal legal document that sets forth all of the terms of the agreement. All listing agreements should, at a minimum, contain the following:

1. a description of the property;
2. an authorization of the real estate firm to act as the seller's agent;
3. the seller's agreement to pay the firm a commission, along with the commission rate or amount;
4. the terms of sale the seller will accept;
5. the conditions under which the commission will be payable; and
6. the seller's warranties as to the accuracy of the information given to the agent and included in the listing agreement.

In addition, best practice is to include a termination date in an exclusive listing agreement. Since exclusive agency agreements prevent the seller from hiring other agents, a fixed termination date lets the seller know when he can move on if the listing agent isn't satisfactory. That said, Washington doesn't require agency agreements to have a termination date. A listing (exclusive or open) with no ending date will terminate after a reasonable time.

Provisions of a Typical Listing Agreement Form

In Washington (as in most other states), there's no single listing agreement form that agents are legally required to use. However, the Northwest Multiple Listing Service (NWMLS) has a uniform listing agreement that's used by most of the multiple listing services throughout the state. Various other listing forms are available through multiple listing services, professional associations, and general publishers of legal forms. Although most listing forms have many common elements, there may also be significant differences between them. A real estate licensee should use only the forms chosen by her brokerage firm, and should become familiar with the provisions of those particular forms. We'll present a general discussion of provisions likely to appear in a typical form, but any given form might omit some of these and include others not discussed here.

Most residential listings are exclusive right to sell agreements with a multiple listing authorization. As an example, the NWMLS listing agreement form is shown in Figure 8.1. An NWMLS listing input form is shown in Figure 8.2.

Brokerage's Authority. The first lines in a listing agreement form usually identify the brokerage, establish the firm's agency authority, and specify the date on which the listing period will expire.

The clause in the listing agreement that establishes agency authority usually says something like, "The agent shall have the sole and exclusive right to submit offers to purchase." Again, note that the agent is not given authority to sell the property—in other words, he is not given authority to enter into a purchase and sale agreement on the seller's behalf. (To grant an agent the right to sell the property, the seller would have to execute a power of attorney.)

The agent is usually also given the authority to "receipt for deposits," to accept earnest money deposits from any prospective buyers on behalf of the seller. As a result of this authorization, if the agent were to misappropriate a buyer's deposit, the seller rather than the buyer would suffer the loss. Without this authorization, the agent would be acting on behalf of the buyer in accepting the earnest money, and any misappropriation would be the buyer's loss.

Listing Period. The listing agreement form usually provides that the listing period begins on the date that the agreement is executed and lasts until a specific termination date chosen by the parties. It may prohibit advertising the property during the period between signing the listing agreement and the official "list date."

Multiple Listing Provision. A multiple listing service (MLS) is a regional cooperative made up of real estate firms (and their licensees) who exchange information about their exclusive listings to increase exposure of the properties to the public. Any member may try to secure buyers for any of the listed properties. The listing agreement forms used by an MLS include a provision authorizing the agent to submit the listing to the MLS for publication.

The members of the listing firm's multiple listing service are typically considered to be "cooperating agents." A cooperating agent may act as the agent of the buyer, the agent of the seller, or in some other capacity as agreed to by the parties. The MLS provision in a listing agreement form generally includes a clause that makes this clear. The cooperating agent who finds the buyer (the selling agent) is ordinarily entitled to receive a share of the listing agent's commission, regardless of which party she is representing. (See Chapter 7 for further discussion of cooperating agents.)

MLS forms include a disclaimer provision stating that the information given in the listing is not confidential and will be available to third parties, and that the MLS is not a party to the listing contract. An MLS assumes no responsibility with respect to particular transactions beyond gathering and circulating information about the properties. It assumes no responsibility for verifying that the information is accurate.

Fig. 8.1 Exclusive right to sell listing agreement

Form 1A
Exclusive Sale
Rev. 6/13
Page 1 of 2

EXCLUSIVE SALE AND LISTING AGREEMENT

_____ ("Seller") 1

hereby grants to _____ , ("Real Estate Firm" or "Firm") 2

from date hereof until midnight of _____ ("Listing Term"), the sole and exclusive right 3

to submit offers to purchase, and to receipt for deposits in connection therewith, the real property ("the Property") 4

commonly known as _____ 5

in the City of _____ , County of _____ , State of Washington, Zip _____ ; 6

to be listed at $ _____ and legally described as: LOT _____ , BLOCK _____ , 7

DIVISION _____ , VOL _____ , PAGE _____ 8

_____ . 9

1. **DEFINITIONS.** For purposes of this Agreement: (a) "MLS" means the Northwest Multiple Listing Service; and (b) "sell" 10
    includes a contract to sell; an exchange or contract to exchange; an option to purchase; and/or a lease with option to 11
    purchase. 12

2. **AGENCY/DUAL AGENCY.** Seller authorizes Firm to appoint _____ 13
    as Seller's Listing Broker. This Agreement creates an agency relationship with Listing Broker and any of Firm's brokers 14
    who supervise Listing Broker's performance as Seller's agent ("Supervising Broker"). No other brokers affiliated with 15
    Firm are agents of Seller, except to the extent that Firm, in its discretion, appoints other brokers to act on Seller's behalf 16
    as and when needed. If the Property is sold to a buyer represented by one of Firm's brokers other than Listing Broker 17
    ("Buyer's Broker"), Seller consents to any Supervising Broker, who also supervises Buyer's Broker, acting as a dual 18
    agent. If the Property is sold to a buyer who Listing Broker also represents, Seller consents to Listing Broker and 19
    Supervising Broker acting as dual agents. If any of Firm's brokers act as a dual agent, Firm shall be entitled to the entire 20
    commission payable under this Agreement plus any additional compensation Firm may have negotiated with the buyer. 21
    Seller acknowledges receipt of the pamphlet entitled "The Law of Real Estate Agency." 22

3. **LIST DATE.** Firm shall submit this listing, including the Property information on the attached pages and photographs of 23
    the Property (collectively, "Listing Data"), to be published by MLS by 5:00 p.m. on _____ ("List Date"), 24
    which date shall not be more than 30 days from the effective date of the Agreement. Seller acknowledges that exposure 25
    of the Property to the open market through MLS will increase the likelihood that Seller will receive fair market value for 26
    the Property. Accordingly, prior to the List Date, Firm and Seller shall not promote or advertise the Property in any 27
    manner whatsoever, including, but not limited to yard or other signs, flyers, websites, e-mails, texts, mailers, magazines, 28
    newspapers, open houses, previews, showings, or tours. 29

4. **COMMISSION.** If during the Listing Term (a) Seller sells the Property and the buyer does not terminate the agreement 30
    prior to closing; or (b) after reasonable exposure of the Property to the market, Firm procures a buyer who is ready, 31
    willing, and able to purchase the Property on the terms in this Agreement, Seller will pay Firm a commission of (fill in 32
    one and strike the other) _____% of the sales price, or $ _____ ("Total Commission"). From the 33
    Total Commission, Firm will offer a cooperating member of MLS representing a buyer ("Selling Firm") a commission of 34
    (fill in one and strike the other) _____% of the sales price, or $ _____. Further, if Seller shall, within six 35
    months after the expiration of the Listing Term, sell the Property to any person to whose attention it was brought 36
    through the signs, advertising or other action of Firm, or on information secured directly or indirectly from or through 37
    Firm, during the Listing Term, Seller will pay Firm the above commission. Provided, that if Seller pays a commission to a 38
    member of MLS or a cooperating MLS in conjunction with a sale, the amount of commission payable to Firm shall be 39
    reduced by the amount paid to such other member(s). Provided further, that if Seller cancels this Agreement without 40
    legal cause, Seller may be liable for damages incurred by Firm as a result of such cancellation, regardless of whether 41
    Seller pays a commission to another MLS member. Selling Firm is an intended third party beneficiary of this Agreement. 42

5. **SHORT SALE / NO DISTRESSED HOME CONVEYANCE.** If the proceeds from the sale of the Property are insufficient 43
    to cover the Seller's costs at closing, Seller acknowledges that the decision by any beneficiary or mortgagee, or its 44
    assignees, to release its interest in the Property, for less than the amount owed, does not automatically relieve Seller of 45
    the obligation to pay any debt or costs remaining at closing, including fees such as Firm's commission. Firm will not 46
    represent or assist Seller in a transaction that is a "Distressed Home Conveyance" as defined by Chapter 61.34 RCW 47
    unless otherwise agreed in writing. A "Distressed Home Conveyance" is a transaction where a buyer purchases 48
    property from a "Distressed Homeowner" (defined by Chapter 61.34 RCW), allows the Distressed Homeowner to 49
    continue to occupy the property, and promises to convey the property back to the Distressed Homeowner or promises 50
    the Distressed Homeowner an interest in, or portion of, the proceeds from a resale of the property. 51

_____   _____
Seller   Seller

Form 1A
Exclusive Sale
Rev. 6/13
Page 2 of 2

EXCLUSIVE SALE AND LISTING AGREEMENT
Continued

6. **KEYBOX.** Firm is authorized to install a keybox on the Property. Such keybox may be opened by a master key held by 52
    members of MLS and their brokers. A master key also may be held by affiliated third parties such as inspectors and 53
    appraisers who cannot have access to the Property without Firm's prior approval which will not be given without Firm 54
    first making reasonable efforts to obtain Seller's approval. 55

7. **SELLER'S WARRANTIES AND REPRESENTATIONS.** Seller warrants that Seller has the right to sell the Property on 56
    the terms herein and that the Property information on the attached pages to this Agreement is correct. Further, Seller 57
    represents that to the best of Seller's knowledge, there are no structures or boundary indicators that either encroach on 58
    adjacent property or on the Property. Seller authorizes Firm to provide the information in this Agreement and the 59
    attached pages to prospective buyers and to other cooperating members of MLS who do not represent the Seller and, 60
    in some instances, may represent the buyer. Seller agrees to indemnify and hold Firm and other members of MLS 61
    harmless in the event the foregoing warranties and representations are incorrect. 62

8. **CLOSING COSTS.** Seller shall furnish and pay for a buyer's policy of title insurance showing marketable title to the 63
    Property. Seller shall pay real estate excise tax and one-half of any escrow fees or such portion of escrow fees and any 64
    other fees or charges as provided by law in the case of a FHA or VA financed sale. Rent, taxes, interest, reserves, 65
    assumed encumbrances, homeowner fees and insurance are to be prorated between Seller and the buyer as of the 66
    date of closing. 67

9. **MULTIPLE LISTING SERVICE.** Seller authorizes Firm and MLS to publish the Listing Data and distribute it to other 68
    members of MLS and their affiliates and third parties for public display and other purposes. This authorization shall 69
    survive the termination of this Agreement. Firm is authorized to report the sale of the Property (including price and all 70
    terms) to MLS and to its members, financial institutions, appraisers, and others related to the sale. Firm may refer this 71
    listing to any other cooperating multiple listing service at Firm's discretion. Firm shall cooperate with all other members 72
    of MLS, or of a multiple listing service to which this listing is referred, in working toward the sale of the Property. 73
    Regardless of whether a cooperating MLS member is the agent of the buyer, Seller, neither or both, such member shall 74
    be entitled to receive the selling firm's share of the commission. MLS is an intended third party beneficiary of this 75
    agreement and will provide the Listing Data to its members and their affiliates and third parties, without verification and 76
    without assuming any responsibility with respect to this agreement. 77

10. **DISCLAIMER/SELLER'S INSURANCE.** Neither Firm, MLS, nor any members of MLS or of any multiple listing 78
    service to which this listing is referred shall be responsible for loss, theft, or damage of any nature or kind whatsoever to 79
    the Property and/or to any personal property therein, including entry by the master key to the keybox and/or at open 80
    houses. Seller is advised to notify Seller's insurance company that the Property is listed for sale and ascertain that the 81
    Seller has adequate insurance coverage. If the Property is to be vacant during all or part of the Listing Term, Seller 82
    should request that a "vacancy clause" be added to Seller's insurance policy. 83

11. **FIRM'S RIGHT TO MARKET THE PROPERTY.** Seller shall not commit any act which materially impairs 84
    Firm's ability to market and sell the Property under the terms of this Agreement. In the event of breach of the foregoing, 85
    Seller shall pay Firm a commission in the above amount, or at the above rate applied to the listing price herein, 86
    whichever is applicable. Unless otherwise agreed in writing, Firm and other members of MLS shall be entitled to show 87
    the Property at all reasonable times. Firm need not submit to Seller any offers to lease, rent, execute an option to 88
    purchase, or enter into any agreement other than for immediate sale of the Property. 89

12. **SELLER DISCLOSURE STATEMENT.** Unless Seller is exempt under RCW 64.06, Seller shall provide to Firm 90
    as soon as reasonably practicable a completed and signed "Seller Disclosure Statement" (Form 17 (Residential), Form 91
    17C (Unimproved Residential), or Form 17 Commercial). Seller agrees to indemnify, defend and hold Firm harmless 92
    from and against any and all claims that the information Seller provides on Form 17, Form 17C, or Form 17 Commercial 93
    is inaccurate. 94

13. **DAMAGES IN THE EVENT OF BUYER'S BREACH.** In the event Seller retains earnest money as liquidated 95
    damages on a buyer's breach, any costs advanced or committed by Firm on Seller's behalf shall be paid therefrom and 96
    the balance divided equally between Seller and Firm. 97

14. **ATTORNEYS' FEES.** In the event either party employs an attorney to enforce any terms of this Agreement and 98
    is successful, the other party agrees to pay reasonable attorneys' fees. In the event of trial, the successful party shall be 99
    entitled to an award of attorneys' fees and expenses; the amount of the attorneys' fees and expenses shall be fixed by 100
    the court. The venue of any suit shall be the county in which the Property is located. 101

DATED THIS _____ DAY OF_____, _____ . Are the undersigned the sole owner(s)? ❑ YES ❑ NO 102

FIRM (COMPANY) _____   SELLER: _____ 103

BY: _____   SELLER: _____ 104

Fig. 8.2 Listing input sheet

NWMLS Form 1 Rev. 6/14
Copyright 2014
Northwest Multiple Listing Service
All Rights Reserved

RESIDENTIAL Exclusive Listing Agreement (page 1 of 4)
LISTING INPUT SHEET

PROPERTY TYPE **1**

• Indicates Required information   ( ) Indicates Maximum Choice   *Indicates "Yes" By Default   **LISTING #**

ADDRESS

• County   • City   • ZIP Code   + 4

• Area   • Community/District

Direction
• Street # (HSN)   **Modifier**   ❑N ❑S ❑E ❑W   • Street Name
                                   ❑NE ❑NW ❑SE ❑SW

Suffix   **Post Direction**   Unit #
❑ Ave   ❑ Blvd   ❑ Ct Av ❑ Drive Ct ❑ Lane ❑ Pkwy ❑ Street ❑ St Pl ❑ Way   ❑N   ❑S   ❑E ❑W
❑ Ave Ct ❑ Cir   ❑ Ct St ❑ Hwy   ❑ Loop ❑ Place ❑ St Ct ❑ Terr   ❑NE ❑NW ❑SE ❑SW
❑ Ave Pl ❑ Court ❑ Drive ❑ Junction ❑ Park ❑ Road ❑ St Dr ❑ Trail   ❑KPN ❑KPS

LISTING

$
• **Listing Price**   • **Listing Date**   • **Expiration Date**   • **Tax ID#**   • **Preliminary Title Ordered**
                                                                                          ❑ Yes ❑ No

LOCATION

Lot Number   **Block**   Plat/Subdivision/Building Name
MAP BOOK
❑ Thomas   ❑ RR-Jeff   ❑ RR-Thurs ❑ RR-Clallam ❑ Totem ❑ P-Kittitas ❑ Yellow Pgs ❑ Unknown **Map Page**   **Top Map**   **Side Map**
❑ RR-Kitsap ❑ RR-Mason ❑ RR-Lewis ❑ RR-Grays ❑ P-Grant ❑ P-Yakima   ❑ R A-Clark   Coord.   Coord.

PROPERTY INFORMATION

• **Prohibit Blogging**   • **Allow Automated Valuation**   • **Show Map Link**   • **Internet Advertising**   • **Show Address to Public**
❑ *Yes ❑ No   ❑ *Yes ❑ No   ❑ *Yes ❑ No   ❑ *Yes ❑ No   ❑ *Yes ❑ No

• **SOC** (Selling Office Com.)   **Selling Office Commission Comments** (40 characters maximum)

                                   Effective Year Built Source
• **Year Built**   **Effective Year Built**   ❑ Public Records ❑ See Remarks

• **ASF - Total** (Square Feet)   • **Lot Size** (Square Feet)   • **Lot Size Source**

Virtual Tour URL (Please include http://)

BROKER INFORMATION

• **LAG**   **Broker Name and Phone**   **Listing Firm** - ID# **Firm Name and Phone**
Listing Broker ID#

Co Broker - ID#   **CO Broker Name and Phone**   **Co Firm** - ID# **Co Firm Name and Phone**

LISTING INFORMATION

• **Possession** (3)   • **Showing Information** (10)   • **Potential Terms** (10)
❑ Closing   ❑ Appointment   ❑ Other Keybox   ❑ Security System ❑ Assumable   ❑ Lease/Purchase   ❑ USDA
❑ Negotiable   ❑ Call Listing Office ❑ Owner-Call First ❑ See Remarks   ❑ Cash Out   ❑ Owner Financing ❑ VA
❑ See Remarks   ❑ Day Sleeper   ❑ Pet in House   ❑ Vacant   ❑ Conventional   ❑ Rehab Loan
❑ Sub. Tenant's Rights   ❑ Gate Code Needed ❑ Power Off   ❑ Farm Home Loan ❑ See Remarks
                          ❑ MLS Keybox   ❑ Renter-Call First   ❑ FHA   ❑ State Bond

                                                         • **Senior Exemption**   **Right of First Refusal**
                          $ ❑ Yes ❑ No   ❑ Yes ❑ No
• **Tax Year**   • **Annual Taxes**

                          $ $ • **Form 17** (1)
                          Monthly H.O. Dues **Monthly Rent**   ❑ Exempt   ❑ Provided
                                                                    ❑ Not Provided

INITIALS: _____ _____ _____ _____ _____ _____
          Seller   Date   Seller   Date   Broker   Date

NWMLS Form 1 Rev. 6/14
Copyright 2014
Northwest Multiple Listing Service
All Rights Reserved

RESIDENTIAL Exclusive Listing Agreement (page 2 of 4)
LISTING INPUT SHEET

PROPERTY **1**
TYPE

Listing Address: _____   LAG # _____

SCHOOL & OWNER INFO.

• **School District** _____   **Elementary School** _____   **Junior High/Middle School** _____   **Senior High School** _____

• **Owner's Name** _____   • **Owner's Phone** _____   • **Occupant Type** _____
(Owner/Presale/Tenant /Vacant)

• **Phone to Show** _____

• **Owner's City and State** _____   • **Occupant's Name** _____

• **Bank Owned/REO**
☐ Yes ☐ No

• **3rd Party Aprvl Req. (2)**
☐ None ☐ Short Sale
☐ Other - See Remarks

• **Auction**
☐ Yes ☐ No

SITE INFORMATION

Lot Dimensions _____

Waterfront Footage (Feet) _____

Pool (1)
☐ Above Ground ☐ Indoor
☐ Community ☐ In-Ground

Zoning Code _____

Zoning Jurisdiction (1)
☐ City ☐ See Remarks
☐ County

Lot Topog./Veg. (7)
☐ Brush ☐ Pasture
☐ Dune ☐ Rolling
☐ Equestrian ☐ Sloped
☐ Fruit Trees ☐ Steep Slope
☐ Garden Sp. ☐ Terraces
☐ Level ☐ Wooded
☐ Partial Slope

View (6)
☐ Bay ☐ Ocean
☐ Canal ☐ Partial
☐ City ☐ River
☐ Golf Course ☐ See Remarks
☐ Jetty ☐ Sound
☐ Lake ☐ Strait
☐ Mountain ☐ Territorial

Waterfront (5)
☐ Bank-High ☐ Lake
☐ Bank-Low ☐ No Bank
☐ Bank Medium ☐ Ocean
☐ Bay ☐ River
☐ Bulkhead ☐ Saltwater
☐ Canal ☐ Sound
☐ Creek ☐ Strait
☐ Jetty ☐ Tideland
Rights

Site Features (14)
☐ Arena-Indoor ☐ Deck ☐ Gated Entry ☐ Propane
☐ Arena-Outdoor ☐ Disabled Access ☐ Green House ☐ RV Parking
☐ Athletic Court ☐ Dock ☐ High Speed Internet ☐ Shop
☐ Barn ☐ Dog Run ☐ Hot Tub/Spa ☐ Sprinkler System
☐ Boat House ☐ Fenced-Fully ☐ Moorage ☐ Stable
☐ Cabana/Gazebo ☐ Fenced-Partially ☐ Outbuildings
☐ Cable TV ☐ Gas Available ☐ Patio

Lot Details (7)
☐ Alley ☐ High Voltage Line
☐ Corner Lot ☐ Open Space
☐ Cul-de-sac ☐ Paved Street
☐ Curbs ☐ Secluded
☐ Dead End St. ☐ Sidewalk
☐ Drought Res Landscape ☐ Value in Land

BUILDING INFORMATION

• **Sewer** (2)
☐ Available ☐ Sewer Connected
☐ None
☐ Septic

Basement (3)
☐ Daylight ☐ Partially Finished
☐ Fully Finished ☐ Roughed In
☐ None ☐ Unfinished

• **Parking Type** (4)
☐ Carport-Attached ☐ Garage-Detached
☐ Carport-Detached ☐ None
☐ Garage-Attached ☐ Off Street

Aprvd # of Bedrooms (septic) _____

• **Total Covered Parking** _____

Builder _____

• **New Construction**
☐ Yes ☐ No

New Construction State (1)
☐ Completed
☐ Presale
☐ Under Construction

• **Building Information** (3)
☐ Addl. Dwelling ☐ Modular
☐ Built on Lot ☐ Planned Unit Dev
☐ Manufd. Home ☐ Zero Lot Line

• **Style Code** _____

Manufactured Home Serial No. _____

Manufactured Home Manufacturer _____

Manufactured Home Model Number _____

• **Exterior** (4)
☐ Brick ☐ See Remarks
☐ Cement Planked ☐ Stone
☐ Cement/Concrete ☐ Stucco
☐ Log ☐ Wood
☐ Metal/Vinyl ☐ Wood Products

Foundation (3)
☐ Concrete Block ☐ See Remarks
☐ Concrete Ribbon ☐ Slab
☐ Post & Block ☐ Tie down
☐ Post & Pillar
☐ Poured Concrete

Building Condition (1)
☐ Average ☐ Restored
☐ Fair ☐ Under Construction
☐ Fixer ☐ Very Good
☐ Good
☐ Remodeled

• **Roof** (3)
☐ Built-up ☐ Flat ☐ See Remarks
☐ Cedar Shake ☐ Green (Living) ☐ Tile
☐ Composition ☐ Metal ☐ Torch Down

Architecture (1)
☐ A-Frame/Dome ☐ Colonial ☐ Modern ☐ Spanish/SW ☐ Victorian
☐ Cabin ☐ Contemporary ☐ NW Contemporary ☐ Traditional
☐ Cape Cod ☐ Craftsman ☐ See Remarks ☐ Tudor

INITIALS: _____

Seller _____ Date _____   Seller _____ Date _____   Broker _____ Date _____

NWMLS Form 1 Rev. 6/14
Copyright 2014
Northwest Multiple Listing Service
All Rights Reserved

RESIDENTIAL Exclusive Listing Agreement (page 3 of 4)
LISTING INPUT SHEET

PROPERTY TYPE **1**

Listing Address: _____   LAG # _____

GREEN BUILDING INFO

Green Certification (4)
- ❑ Built Green™
- ❑ LEED™
- ❑ Northwest ENERGY STAR®
- ❑ Other - See Remarks

Built Green™ (1)
- ❑ 1 Star   ❑ 4 Stars
- ❑ 2 Stars   ❑ 5 Stars
- ❑ 3 Stars

LEED™ (1)
- ❑ Platinum
- ❑ Gold
- ❑ Silver
- ❑ Certified

Northwest ENERGY STAR® (1)
- ❑ NWESH Certified
- ❑ NWESH Presale
- ❑ NWESH Under Construction

Construction Methods (2)
- ❑ Advanced Wall
- ❑ Double Wall
- ❑ Ins. Concrete Form (ICF)
- ❑ Post & Beam
- ❑ Standard Frame
- ❑ Steel & Concrete
- ❑ Strawbale
- ❑ Structural Ins. Panel (SIPs)
- ❑ Tilt-up

EPS Energy Score (0-99,999kWh) _____

HERS Index Score (0-150) _____

INTERIOR FEATURES

(Approximate Square Footage Excluding Garage)

Finished _____   **Unfinished** _____   • **Square Footage Source** _____

Lower Fireplaces _____   **Upper Fireplaces** _____   **Main Fireplaces** _____

Type of Fireplace (1)
- ❑ Both
- ❑ Gas
- ❑ Wood

Leased Equipment _____   **Water Heater Type** _____   **Water Heater Location** _____

• Energy Source (6)
- ❑ Electric
- ❑ Geothermal
- ❑ Ground Source
- ❑ Natural Gas
- ❑ Oil
- ❑ Pellet
- ❑ Propane
- ❑ See Remarks
- ❑ Solar (Unspecified)
- ❑ Solar Hot Water
- ❑ Solar PV
- ❑ Wood

• Heating/Cooling (8)
- ❑ 90%+ High Efficiency
- ❑ Baseboard
- ❑ Central A/C
- ❑ Ductless HP-Mini Split
- ❑ Forced Air
- ❑ Heat Pump
- ❑ HEPA Air Filtration
- ❑ High Efficiency (Unspecified)
- ❑ Hot Water Recirc Pump
- ❑ HRV/ERV System
- ❑ Insert
- ❑ None
- ❑ Other - See Remarks
- ❑ Radiant
- ❑ Radiator
- ❑ Stove/Free Standing
- ❑ Tankless Water Heater
- ❑ Wall

Floor Covering (5)
- ❑ Bamboo/Cork
- ❑ Ceramic Tile
- ❑ Concrete
- ❑ Fir/Softwood
- ❑ Hardwood
- ❑ Laminate
- ❑ Other Renewable
- ❑ See Remarks
- ❑ Slate
- ❑ Vinyl
- ❑ Wall to Wall Carpet

Interior Features (16)
- ❑ 2nd Kitchen
- ❑ 2nd Mstr BR
- ❑ Bath Off Master
- ❑ Built-in Vacuum
- ❑ Ceiling Fan(s)
- ❑ Dbl Pane/Strm Windw
- ❑ Dining Room
- ❑ Disabled Access
- ❑ FP in Mstr BR
- ❑ French Doors
- ❑ High Tech Cabling
- ❑ Hot Tub/Spa
- ❑ Jetted Tub
- ❑ Loft
- ❑ Sauna
- ❑ Security System
- ❑ Skylights
- ❑ Solarium/Atrium
- ❑ Vaulted Ceilings
- ❑ Walk-in Pantry
- ❑ Walk-in Closet
- ❑ Wet Bar
- ❑ Wine Cellar
- ❑ Wired for Generator

Appliances That Stay (10)
- ❑ Dishwasher
- ❑ Double Oven
- ❑ Dryer
- ❑ Garbage Disposal
- ❑ Microwave
- ❑ Range/Oven
- ❑ Refrigerator
- ❑ See Remarks
- ❑ Trash Compactor
- ❑ Washer

UTILITY/COMMUNITY

Community Features (8)
- ❑ Age Restriction
- ❑ Airfield
- ❑ Boat Launch
- ❑ CCRs
- ❑ Clubhouse
- ❑ Community Waterfront / Pvt Beach Access
- ❑ Golf Course
- ❑ Tennis Courts

• Water Source (3)
- ❑ Community
- ❑ Individual Well
- ❑ Lake
- ❑ Private
- ❑ Public
- ❑ See Remarks
- ❑ Shared Well
- ❑ Shares
- ❑ Well Needed

Water Company _____   **Power Company** _____   **Sewer Company** _____

Bus Line Nearby _____
- ❑ Yes ❑ No   **Bus Route Number** _____

INITIALS: _____
Seller _____ Date _____ Seller _____ Date _____ Broker _____ Date _____

NWMLS Form 1 Rev. 6/14
Copyright 2014
Northwest Multiple Listing Service
All Rights Reserved

RESIDENTIAL Exclusive Listing Agreement (page 4 of 4)
LISTING INPUT SHEET

PROPERTY **1**
TYPE

ROOM LOCATION

Listing Address:

LAG #

Level (1)   U for Upper   M for Main   L for Lower   S for Split   G for Garage

Entry	U	M	L	S	**Kit w/o Eating Space**	U	M	L	**Extra Fin. Room**	U	M	L	G
Living Room	U	M	L		**Master Bedroom**	U	M	L	**Rec Room**	U	M	L	
Dining Room	U	M	L		**Bonus Room**	U	M	L	**Family Room**	U	M	L	
Kit with Eating Space	U	M	L		**Den/Office**	U	M	L	**Great Room**	U	M	L	

No. of Bedrooms   U____ M____ L____

No. of Full Baths   U____ M____ L____ G____

No. of ¾ Baths   U____ M____ L____ G____

No. of ½ Baths   U____ M____ L____ G____

Utility Room   U____ M____ L____ G____

Approved Accessory   U____ M____ L____
Dwelling Unit

REMARKS

Marketing Remarks. CAUTION! The comments you make in the following lines are limited to descriptions of the land and improvements only. These remarks will appear in the client handouts and websites. (500)

_____
_____
_____
_____
_____
_____
_____
_____
_____

Confidential Broker-Only Remarks. Comments in this category are for broker's use only. (250)

_____
_____
_____
_____

• **Driving Directions to Property** (200)

_____
_____
_____
_____
_____

INITIALS: _____ _____   _____ _____   _____ _____
            Seller   Date   Seller   Date   Broker   Date

Agency Disclosure. Listing agreement forms often include an agency disclosure provision, to help licensees comply with Washington's agency disclosure law. In this provision, the seller authorizes the brokerage to appoint the listing licensee to act as a subagent of the seller. The provision also states that other licensees affiliated with the firm do not represent the seller, and may represent the buyer. If another affiliated licensee finds the buyer, then the firm will be a dual agent.

Short Sales and Distressed Properties. In a short sale, the proceeds from a property's sale aren't enough to repay the debt secured by the property; nevertheless, the lender agrees to accept the sale proceeds and release the borrower from the debt. (Short sales are also discussed in Chapter 10.) When a potential short sale is being listed, the listing agent should give the seller a written disclosure explaining that the lender's approval of a short sale won't necessarily relieve the seller of liability for costs owed at closing, including the brokerage commission. This disclosure may be included in the listing form itself.

The listing form should also include a provision in which the seller warrants that her home is not distressed—that is, the seller's residence isn't in foreclosure or in imminent danger of foreclosure (see the discussion later in this chapter).

Access and Keyboxes. A listing form typically provides that the agent will have access to the property at reasonable times, so that he can show it to prospective buyers.

MLS listing forms usually include a provision authorizing the installation of a keybox on the property and permitting MLS agents to enter and show the home when the seller isn't there. A **keybox** is a device that holds a copy of the house key, which the seller can padlock to a porch railing or some other appropriate place outside when she isn't going to be home; cooperating agents open the keybox with a master key or a combination from the MLS. The listing agreement form may provide that affiliated third parties, such as appraisers or inspectors, are also authorized to use the keybox to gain access to the home. The listing form will typically have a disclaimer of liability on the part of the MLS or the agents for any loss or damage to the seller's property— the listed home itself and personal property on the premises.

Commission. The percentage or amount of the brokerage commission for a given transaction is set in the listing agreement, not by law. Commissions must be negotiable between the seller and the listing agent; it is a violation of antitrust laws for agents to set uniform commission rates. (See Chapter 17 for a discussion of antitrust laws and how they affect licensees.) So an amount or percentage can't be pre-printed on the listing agreement form; instead, there is a blank to be filled in when the form is executed for a particular transaction.

Beyond setting the commission amount or rate, the listing agreement should spell out how and when the listing agent will earn the commission. An exclusive right to sell listing form typically provides that the listing agent will earn a commission if any of the following events occur:

1. During the listing period, the listing agent (or another agent in the MLS) secures a buyer who is willing and able to buy on the exact terms specified by the seller in the listing agreement or on other terms acceptable to the seller (in other words, a ready, willing, and able buyer).
2. The seller sells, exchanges, or enters into a contract to sell or exchange the property during the term of the listing agreement.

3. The seller sells the property within a certain period (for example, six months) after the expiration date of the listing agreement, to anyone who first became aware of the property through any advertising or other marketing activities of the listing agent (or other agents in the MLS).

Extender Clause. The third condition listed above is an example of an **extender clause** (sometimes called a "safety," "protection," or "carryover" clause). It is intended to prevent the seller from delaying acceptance of a buyer's offer until after the listing expires in order to avoid paying a commission.

Most listing agreements contain an extender clause, but the specific terms differ. For example, sometimes the obligation to pay a commission after the listing has expired is only triggered when the property is sold to a buyer that the agent actually negotiated with during the listing period. Or the clause may be broader, obligating the seller to pay a commission if the property is sold within the extension period to anyone who first learned about it in any way that could be traced to the listing agent or another MLS agent. Under such a broad provision, the seller could become liable for a commission unwittingly, since it can be very difficult for a seller to know the names of all potential buyers who viewed the property during the listing period.

Sometimes if a property fails to sell during the listing period, the seller then lists it with another brokerage. In that case, it's possible for the seller to become liable for a commission to two different firms. If the sale occurs during the first listing's extension period and the buyer was introduced to the property during the first listing period, the first firm is entitled to a commission under the extender clause, and the second firm is entitled to a commission under the terms of the second listing. If both firms are members of the same MLS, they could agree to split one commission rather than make the seller pay twice.

Often extender clauses include safeguards for the seller. The listing brokerage may be required to give the seller a list of the potential buyers she negotiated with during the listing period. Or the extender clause might state that a commission will not be due if the property is listed with another real estate firm during the extension period, protecting the seller from becoming liable for two commissions.

Rental or Option by the Seller. Under the terms of many listing forms, the seller agrees not to lease the property, grant an option, or enter into any other agreement that might interfere with the marketing or sale of the property. If the seller breaches this agreement, he will be liable to the brokerage for the full commission.

The form may also state that the listing agent is not obligated to submit any offers to the seller other than offers for immediate purchase, so that offers to lease the property or requests for an option to purchase need not be relayed to the seller.

Property Description. A listing agreement should include a full and accurate description of the property—preferably a legal description. The agent filling out the form might ask to see the seller's deed and copy the description from that document. If it is something more than a lot and block description, the parties should date and initial a photocopied attachment. When the description is long and complicated, it's better to photocopy it instead of writing or typing it.

It is useful to include the property's street address on the listing form, but as a general rule the address alone is not a sufficient description for an enforceable listing agreement. Land descriptions are discussed in Chapter 1.

Closing Costs. The listing agreement form is likely to provide that the seller will pay for the buyer's title insurance policy and certain other closing costs, such as the excise tax and half of the escrow fee. Keep in mind that these provisions in the listing agreement do not create any obligation toward potential buyers. These are promises that the seller makes to her listing agent, and failure to fulfill them can lead only to liability for the commission, not to liability toward a buyer.

Seller's Warranties. Most listing forms include some warranties by the seller, which allow the listing agent to rely on certain information the seller provides. Most fundamentally, the seller warrants that he has the right to sell the property on the stated terms. The seller also warrants the accuracy of the property information that is made part of the listing agreement (see the discussion of the listing input sheet, below).

The listing agreement form may include additional warranties; for example, the seller may warrant that there are no encroachments, or that the property conforms to applicable zoning regulations.

The listing agreement form usually states that the seller takes responsibility for the information given and will indemnify the listing agent against any losses caused by errors or omissions. This statement is called a "hold harmless agreement."

Seller Disclosure Statement. A listing form may include a provision concerning the disclosure statement that Washington law requires a seller in a real estate transaction to give to the buyer upon the execution of a purchase and sale agreement (see Chapter 9). Such a provision in the listing usually states that the seller will give the listing agent a completed and signed disclosure statement, unless the transaction is exempt from the disclosure law.

Although the law doesn't require the seller to give the buyer a disclosure statement until a purchase and sale agreement is signed, this provision in the listing obligates the seller to fill out a disclosure statement and give it to the listing agent as soon as possible. This makes it possible for the listing agent to learn about any potential problems with the property early on in the selling process.

The listing provision typically also states that the seller will take full responsibility for the information given in the disclosure statement. The seller agrees to defend the listing agent against any claims based on inaccuracies in the statement.

Damages in the Event of Buyer's Breach. Listing agreement forms often provide that the listing agent is entitled to half of any damages that the seller receives as a result of the buyer's default. In practical terms, this usually means that the listing agent will get half of the forfeited earnest money (see Chapter 9).

Attorneys' Fees. Many listing agreement forms provide that if either party has to employ an attorney to enforce the contract, the attorneys' fees of the winning party must be paid by the losing party.

Signatures. The listing agreement form is signed by both parties, the listing agent and the seller. When filling out the form, the listing agent should write in the name of the brokerage firm and then sign his own name on the "By" line underneath the firm's name.

If the property is owned by more than one person, all co-owners should sign the listing agreement. If a seller is married, the seller's spouse should sign the document as well as the seller.

Listing Information. The listing forms used by multiple listing services include one or more pages for information about the property and the listing, such as the NWMLS "Listing Input Sheet" shown in Figure 8.2. The purpose of a listing input sheet is to generate detailed information for distribution by the MLS. Much of the information is coded to make computer input easier.

All of the following information is generally required on a listing input sheet:

- property address,
- location on a coded map,
- architectural style of the home,
- listing price,
- identity of the listing agent,
- expiration date of the listing,
- age of the home,
- number of bedrooms,
- number of baths,
- county tax ID number,
- selling office commission,
- name of the occupant, and
- name, address, and phone number of the owner.

The rest of the input sheet has spaces to fill in or boxes to check to describe a wide variety of property features and amenities. There is also a place for information about existing encumbrances and property taxes.

Receipt of Copy. Real estate licensees are required to give a copy of any document they prepare to the parties at the time of signature. So a listing agreement form may include the seller's acknowledgment of receipt of a copy of the agreement.

Receipt of Agency Pamphlet. When the parties enter into a listing agreement, the agent is legally obligated to provide the seller with a pamphlet on Washington's real estate agency law (see Chapter 7). Many listing agreements include a provision in which the seller acknowledges the receipt of this pamphlet.

Distressed Property Listings

If a licensee is taking a listing on a distressed property, he must be careful to comply with Washington's **Distressed Property Law**. This law helps protect homeowners from foreclosure rescue scams by strictly regulating distressed home consultants.

The law defines a distressed home consultant as anyone who offers to help the owner of a personal residence stop or slow a foreclosure sale, purchases the home within 20 days of the foreclosure sale (unless the homeowner is represented by a real estate licensee), or arranges for the homeowner to rent the home so the homeowner can remain in the home. (The law specifically excludes real estate licensees who are providing routine brokerage services to clients from the definition of a distressed home consultant.)

If a distressed home consultant is engaged in a distressed home conveyance, he must complete a distressed home consultant agreement with the homeowner. A distressed home conveyance is one where a buyer purchases property from a distressed homeowner, allows the homeowner to continue to occupy the property for more than 20 days past the closing date, and promises to convey the property back to the homeowner (or promises the homeowner an interest in or a portion of the proceeds from a resale of the property).

The distressed home consultant agreement must disclose the services that will be provided as well as the consultant's compensation. The agreement must also clearly state that the consultant owes fiduciary duties to the homeowner, including the duty of loyalty, the duty to disclose material facts, the duty to use reasonable care, and the duty to do a full accounting.

Chapter Summary

1. The listing agreement is an employment contract between the seller and the real estate firm. The seller agrees to pay the listing agent a stated commission if a ready, willing, and able buyer is found during the listing period.

2. The three basic types of listing agreements are the open listing, the exclusive agency listing, and the exclusive right to sell listing. The type of listing determines the circumstances under which the firm is entitled to be paid a commission.

3. A written listing agreement is an enforceable contract if it adequately identifies the property to be sold, includes a promise to pay compensation to the listing agent, and is signed by the seller.

4. The listing agreement should also state the terms of sale the seller will accept, the conditions under which the commission would be paid, the duration of the contract, and the seller's warranties regarding the accuracy of the information provided about the property.

5. A multiple listing service is a cooperative association of licensed firms and agents who exchange information about their exclusive listings and help sell property listed by other members.

6. An extender clause provides that the seller will be liable for the listing agent's commission if the property is sold during a certain period after the listing expires to a buyer the listing firm dealt with during the listing period.

7. Special rules apply to the sale of distressed properties. Under state law, a person who participates in a transaction with a distressed property owner may be required to have a special agreement if their activities meet the definition for a "distressed home consultant." In most cases, real estate licensees are exempt from the requirements of this law.

🔑 Key Terms

Open listing—A non-exclusive listing under which the real estate firm earns a commission only if it is the procuring cause of the sale.

Procuring cause—The person who directly or indirectly brings about a sale.

Exclusive agency listing—A listing under which the real estate firm is entitled to a commission if any agent sells the property, but the owner may sell the property directly without being obligated to pay a commission.

Exclusive right to sell listing—A listing under which the owner must pay the brokerage a commission on the sale of the property, no matter who was the procuring cause.

Multiple listing service—A regional cooperative of real estate firms and licensees who exchange listing information and help market the listings of other members.

Net listing—A listing in which the commission is any amount received from the sale over and above the "net" required by the seller.

Extender clause—A provision in a listing agreement that obligates the seller to pay a commission if the property is sold within a certain period after the listing expires to someone the agent introduced to the property during the listing period. Also called a safety clause or carryover clause.

Distressed home consultant—Anyone who offers to help the owner of a personal residence stop or slow a foreclosure sale, purchases the home within 20 days of the foreclosure sale (unless the homeowner is represented by a real estate licensee), or arranges for the homeowner to rent the home so the homeowner can remain in the home. Real estate licensees who are providing routine brokerage services to clients are usually not considered to be distressed home consultants.

Chapter Quiz

1. The type of listing that provides for payment of a commission to the listing firm regardless of who sells the property is a/an:

    a) open listing
    b) exclusive agency listing
    c) exclusive right to sell listing
    d) net listing

2. The type of listing that provides for the payment of a commission to the listing firm only if it was the procuring cause of the sale is a/an:

    a) open listing
    b) exclusive agency listing
    c) exclusive right to sell listing
    d) net listing

3. A type of listing that provides for the payment of a commission that consists of any proceeds from the sale over a specified amount is a/an:

    a) open listing
    b) exclusive agency listing
    c) exclusive right to sell listing
    d) net listing

4. A listing agreement must contain all of the following, except:

    a) a specific dollar amount for compensation
    b) the signature of the seller
    c) an adequate description of the property
    d) an authorization to sell the property in exchange for compensation

5. A type of listing that provides for the payment of a commission to the listing firm if anyone other than the seller finds the buyer is a/an:

    a) open listing
    b) exclusive agency listing
    c) exclusive right to sell listing
    d) net listing

6. The listing agent has negotiated an offer from a ready, willing, and able buyer that matches the seller's terms of sale set forth in the listing agreement. Which of the following is true?

    a) The seller is required to accept the offer and pay the listing agent a commission
    b) The seller is required to accept the offer, but not required to pay the listing agent a commission
    c) The listing agent has earned the commission, whether or not the seller accepts the offer
    d) The listing agent has not earned the commission unless this is an exclusive agency listing

7. Which of these is a basic requirement for an enforceable listing agreement in Washington?

    a) An adequate description of the property
    b) A multiple listing provision
    c) An extender clause
    d) A warranty that the seller owns the property

8. An extender clause provides that:

    a) the listing agent is entitled to a commission whether or not she is the procuring cause
    b) the buyer must pay part of the listing agent's commission
    c) the seller warrants the safety of the premises
    d) the listing agent may be entitled to a commission if the property is sold after the listing expires

9. Matthews, a property owner, entered into an exclusive right to sell listing agreement with Ferris Realty. Ferris negotiated a sale between Matthews and Buyer Swanson. Both Matthews and Swanson signed a purchase and sale agreement. Two weeks later, Matthews and Swanson mutually agreed to cancel their agreement. Under the circumstances:

    a) Matthews is still obligated to pay Ferris Realty the full sales commission
    b) Matthews owes Ferris Realty half of the sales commission
    c) Swanson owes Ferris Realty the full sales commission
    d) Ferris Realty is not entitled to a commission, because the sale did not close

10. Under an exclusive right to sell listing, the listing agent:

    a) has the authority to accept an offer on the seller's behalf
    b) is authorized to reject offers that do not meet the seller's stated terms
    c) will earn the sales commission only if someone other than the owner procures a buyer
    d) has the exclusive right to submit offers to purchase to the seller

11. A multiple listing provision in a listing agreement generally:

    a) makes other members of the MLS cooperating agents
    b) authorizes the listing agent to submit the listing to the MLS for publication
    c) includes a disclaimer provision that states that the MLS is not a party to the listing agreement
    d) All of the above

12. Which of these types of listings is considered to be a unilateral contract?

    a) Open listing
    b) Exclusive agency listing
    c) Exclusive right to sell listing
    d) Net listing

13. Under the terms of most listings, the seller will owe the listing agent the commission even if the:

    a) seller turns down a reasonable offer for less than the listing price
    b) prospective buyer is not ready, willing, and able
    c) sale fails to close because the seller's title is not marketable
    d) listing agent terminates the agreement

14. Under the terms of an exclusive listing agreement, the listing agent is:

    a) under no obligation to make an effort to find a buyer
    b) required to find at least three ready, willing, and able buyers during the listing period
    c) obligated to market the property and make a diligent effort to find a buyer
    d) None of the above

15. In the listing agreement, the seller agrees to pay certain closing costs. This creates a legal obligation to:

    a) the buyer only
    b) the listing agent only
    c) both the buyer and the listing agent
    d) neither the buyer nor the listing agent

Answer Key

1. c) An exclusive right to sell listing obligates the seller to pay the listing agent a commission if the property sells during the listing period, regardless of who brings about the sale.

2. a) An open listing obligates the seller to pay a commission to the listing agent only if the listing agent was the procuring cause of the sale.

3. d) A net listing is a way of determining the amount of the commission, rather than the circumstances under which a commission is owed.

4. a) Compensation may be expressed as a percentage of the sales price, rather than a set dollar amount.

5. b) An exclusive agency listing obligates the seller to pay the listing agent a commission if any agent (anyone other than the seller herself) sells the property.

6. c) When the listing agent presents an offer that matches the seller's terms of sale, the listing agent has earned the commission whether or not the seller accepts the offer. The seller is under no obligation to accept the offer.

7. a) In Washington, a listing agreement is not enforceable unless it includes a description of the property that is adequate to identify it.

8. d) An extender clause entitles the listing agent to a commission if the property is sold within a certain time after the listing expires to someone he introduced to the property or negotiated with during the listing period.

9. a) Because the parties voluntarily backed out of the transaction, Ferris Realty is still legally entitled to collect a full commission from Matthews.

10. d) The listing agent under an exclusive right to sell listing has the exclusive right to submit offers to the seller.

11. d) A multiple listing provision typically makes all other MLS members cooperating agents, authorizes the listing agent to submit the listing to the MLS for publication, and states that the MLS is not a party to the contract.

12. a) An open listing is considered to be a unilateral contract, because only the seller promises performance.

13. c) The seller owes the listing agent a commission even when a transaction fails to close, if the failure was the seller's fault. This rule applies in the situation described in the question, where the seller's title turns out to be unmarketable.

14. c) Unlike an open listing, an exclusive listing obligates the listing agent to make a diligent effort to find a buyer for the property.

15. b) The listing agreement is a contract between the seller and the listing agent; it does not create any legal obligations to prospective buyers.

Purchase and Sale Agreements

◣▣◣▣◣ Chapter Overview

Most real estate sales are initiated by a written contract between the buyer and the seller, who agree on a price and the other terms of sale. The contract between the buyer and the seller of real property is the purchase and sale agreement, which may also be called an earnest money agreement. This chapter will describe the purpose and effect of a purchase and sale agreement, preparation of the agreement, the elements required to make it a binding contract, and the operation of contingency clauses. The final section of the chapter covers laws requiring certain information to be disclosed when property is sold, including Washington's seller disclosure law and the federal law concerning lead-based paint.

Purpose and Effect of a Purchase and Sale Agreement

The contract between a buyer and a seller to purchase and sell real property is more than a preliminary agreement. If it contains the necessary elements and is properly executed, the parties are legally bound by all of the terms of the agreement. Neither may change or add any terms without the written consent of the other, and neither may withdraw from the transaction without legal consequences. In fact, the whole purpose of a purchase and sale agreement is to hold the buyer and the seller to the original terms of their agreement until the transaction is ready to close.

To be a valid and enforceable contract, the purchase and sale agreement must be created by offer and acceptance and supported by consideration (see Chapter 6). In most cases, the buyer is the offeror, offering to buy the seller's property on specific terms. The buyer usually provides an **earnest money deposit**, to show the seller that she is serious about the purchase. The buyer's written offer is set forth on a purchase and sale agreement form, which the buyer signs before it is presented to the seller. If the seller decides to accept the buyer's offer, he also signs the form, and it becomes a binding contract. The mutual promises of the parties (the promise to buy and the promise to sell) are the consideration supporting the contract.

The basic requirements for a valid purchase and sale agreement are relatively simple. The agreement must identify the parties and the property, state the price and the method of payment, and state the time for delivery of title and possession. Despite this basic simplicity, most purchase and sale agreements are quite detailed. It is important that the agreement between the parties be stated clearly and accurately; anything that isn't made absolutely clear at the outset can give rise to a dispute later on, and may prevent the transaction from closing.

In practical terms, the buyer and the seller need a document that preserves their agreement while other matters are attended to that will enable the sale to close. For instance, most buyers do not have the cash necessary to close the sale, so they have to arrange to borrow all or part of the money for the purchase. The buyer also needs to make sure that the seller actually owns the property (through a title search), and may want to arrange for a physical inspection of the property. There might be liens or other encumbrances that need to be dealt with, and the seller may be required to repair the property to satisfy the requirements of the buyer's lender.

All of these things cost time and money. Neither party wants to spend time or money without the assurance that the original agreement is still in effect. As long as the purchase and sale agreement is a valid contract, it protects both parties by providing legal recourse if one fails to perform. Either party could file a lawsuit against the other for breach of contract. The court could order the breaching party to pay the other party damages as compensation for losses resulting from the breach, or even issue an order of specific performance, requiring the seller to fulfill his side of the bargain (see Chapter 6). Because a court could order the seller to deed the property to the buyer, the buyer is considered to have equitable title to the property as soon as the purchase and sale agreement is executed, even though she won't acquire legal title until closing.

Who May Prepare a Purchase and Sale Agreement

It is legal—though often unwise—for the parties to an agreement to write their own contract. But when someone who is not a party draws up a contract on behalf of the parties, that is considered to be the practice of law. As a general rule, only a licensed attorney at law is allowed to write a contract for others.

However, there is a limited exception to that rule that applies to certain real estate agreements. A real estate agent can prepare routine real estate agreements using standard printed forms. This is because the provisions of these contract forms were originally written and approved by attorneys with expertise in real estate law.

In the typical residential real estate transaction, the real estate agent fills in the blanks of a standard purchase and sale agreement form and obtains the signatures of the parties. In filling out the form, the agent is held to the same standard of care that is demanded of an attorney. An agent who prepared a purchase and sale agreement improperly could be held liable for any damages caused to either party.

Real estate agents run into trouble when they go beyond merely filling in the blanks. Sometimes an agent writes a special clause to insert into the preprinted form to meet an unusual situation. Or an agent might give the parties his opinion of the meaning or effect of provisions in the document. Actions like these go beyond what the law generally allows real estate agents to do and may constitute the unauthorized practice of law. The unauthorized practice of law is a criminal offense, and a real estate agent can be prosecuted even if he gave accurate legal advice. It is also grounds for suspension or revocation of the agent's real estate license (see Chapter 17).

A real estate agent may only fill out forms in connection with a transaction actually being handled by that agent. And an agent is not allowed to charge a separate fee (in addition to the brokerage commission) for completing the forms.

> **Example:** Suppose Agent Dahl is involved in a complicated commercial real estate transaction. He is confused by some of the paperwork, so he gets Agent Merrick (a friend of his) to fill out the purchase and sale agreement. Merrick charges the client a separate fee for her work. This is the unauthorized practice of law, because Merrick filled out forms for a transaction that she was not handling and accepted separate compensation for her work.

Available Forms and Guidance

In Washington and most other states, there is no single purchase and sale agreement form that all real estate agents use. A variety of forms are available from multiple listing services, other professional organizations, and legal form publishers.

A residential purchase and sale agreement form from the Northwest Multiple Listing Service (NWMLS) is shown in Figure 9.1 as an example.

The organizations that provide forms sometimes offer line-by-line guidance for filling in each provision. A real estate agent should read any explanatory materials provided and obtain advice for any aspects of the form that she does not understand. Relying on advice from professional sources helps ensure that the agent will meet the required standard of care.

Here are two basic precautions to take when filling out a purchase and sale agreement:

- A form must be used only for the purpose intended. For instance, the NWMLS purchase and sale agreement form in Figure 9.1 is intended for residential sales only. It shouldn't be used for anything else.
- Forms should always be filled in completely. If an entry isn't applicable to a given transaction, the agent should write in "N/A," rather than leaving the space blank. All boxes should be checked where appropriate.

Elements of a Purchase and Sale Agreement

As explained in Chapter 6, the statute of frauds requires every real estate purchase and sale agreement to be in writing. An enforceable purchase and sale agreement generally must contain all of the following elements:

- identification of the parties,
- an adequate description of the property,
- the total price and the method of payment,
- the closing date,
- the date of possession,
- the type of deed and the condition of title,
- liens or other encumbrances the buyer will take title subject to, and
- any conditions or contingencies (such as a financing contingency).

We will look at several of these elements more closely, and then discuss contingency clauses in detail, since they play a crucial role in many real estate transactions.

The Parties

Of course, the parties to the purchase and sale agreement are the buyer and the seller. When preparing a purchase and sale agreement, there are two key questions to ask about the parties. First, does everyone who is signing have the capacity to contract? If any of the parties is underage or mentally incompetent, the purchase and sale agreement—like any contract—will be voidable or void. (See Chapter 6.)

Second, is everyone with an ownership interest in the property signing the contract? If not, the buyer may only be able to force the sale of a partial interest in the property. In some cases, the buyer would not be able to enforce the contract at all.

Particular care should be taken with married parties. In Washington and other community property states, the law requires both spouses to join in any sale, encumbrance,

Fig. 9.1 *Purchase and sale agreement*

Form 21
Residential Purchase & Sale Agreement
Rev. 5/14
Page 1 of 5

©Copyright 2014
Northwest Multiple Listing Service
ALL RIGHTS RESERVED

RESIDENTIAL REAL ESTATE PURCHASE AND SALE AGREEMENT
SPECIFIC TERMS

1. **Date:** _____ **MLS No.:** _____

2. **Buyer:** _____
   Buyer   Buyer   Status

3. **Seller:** _____
   Seller   Seller

4. **Property:** Tax Parcel No(s).: _____ (_____ County)

   _____
   Address   City   State   Zip

   Legal Description: Attached as Exhibit A.

5. **Included Items**: ❑ stove/range; ❑ refrigerator; ❑ washer; ❑ dryer; ❑ dishwasher; ❑ hot tub; ❑ fireplace insert; ❑ wood stove; ❑ satellite dish; ❑ security system; ❑ attached television(s); ❑ attached speaker(s); ❑microwave ❑ other _____

6. **Purchase Price:** $ _____ Dollars

7. **Earnest Money:** (To be held by ❑ Selling Firm; ❑ Closing Agent)

   Personal Check: $_____; Note: $_____; Other (_____): $_____

8. **Default:** (check only one) ❑ Forfeiture of Earnest Money; ❑ Seller's Election of Remedies

9. **Title Insurance Company:** _____

10. **Closing Agent:** ❑ a qualified closing agent of Buyer's choice; ❑ _____

11. **Closing Date:** _____

12. **Possession Date:** ❑ on Closing; ❑ Other _____

13. **Offer Expiration Date:** _____

14. **Services of Closing Agent for Payment of Utilities:** ❑ Requested (attach NWMLS Form 22K); ❑ Waived

15. **Charges and Assessments Due After Closing:** ❑ assumed by Buyer; ❑ prepaid in full by Seller at Closing

16. **Agency Disclosure:**   Selling Broker represents: ❑ Buyer; ❑ Seller; ❑ both parties; ❑ neither party
                     Listing Broker represents: ❑ Seller; ❑ both parties

17. **Addenda:** _____

    _____

    _____

    _____

Buyer's Signature	Date	Seller's Signature	Date
Buyer's Signature	Date	Seller's Signature	Date
Buyer's Address		Seller's Address	
City, State, Zip		City, State, Zip	
Phone No.	Fax No.	Phone No.	Fax No.
Buyer's E-mail Address		Seller's E-mail Address	
Selling Firm	MLS Office No.	Listing Firm	MLS Office No.
Selling Broker (Print)	MLS LAG No.	Listing Broker (Print)	MLS LAG No.
Phone No.	Firm Fax No.	Phone No.	Firm Fax No.
Selling Firm Document E-mail Address		Listing Firm Document E-mail Address	
Selling Broker's E-mail Address		Listing Broker's E-mail Address	

Reprinted courtesy of Northwest Multiple Listing Service. All rights reserved.

Form 21
Residential Purchase & Sale Agreement
Rev. 5/14
Page 2 of 5

©Copyright 2014
Northwest Multiple Listing Service
ALL RIGHTS RESERVED

RESIDENTIAL REAL ESTATE PURCHASE AND SALE AGREEMENT
GENERAL TERMS
Continued

a. Purchase Price. Buyer shall pay to Seller the Purchase Price, including the Earnest Money, in cash at Closing, unless 1
otherwise specified in this Agreement. Buyer represents that Buyer has sufficient funds to close this sale in accordance 2
with this Agreement and is not relying on any contingent source of funds, including funds from loans, the sale of other 3
property, gifts, retirement, or future earnings, except to the extent otherwise specified in this Agreement. 4

b. Earnest Money. Buyer shall deliver the Earnest Money within 2 days after mutual acceptance to Selling Broker or to 5
Closing Agent. If Buyer delivers the Earnest Money to Selling Broker, Selling Broker will deposit any check to be held 6
by Selling Firm, or deliver any Earnest Money to be held by Closing Agent, within 3 days of receipt or mutual 7
acceptance, whichever occurs later. If the Earnest Money is held by Selling Firm and is over $10,000.00 it shall be 8
deposited into an interest bearing trust account in Selling Firm's name provided that Buyer completes an IRS Form W-9. 9
Interest, if any, after deduction of bank charges and fees, will be paid to Buyer. Buyer shall reimburse Selling Firm for 10
bank charges and fees in excess of the interest earned, if any. If the Earnest Money held by Selling Firm is over 11
$10,000.00 Buyer has the option to require Selling Firm to deposit the Earnest Money into the Housing Trust Fund 12
Account, with the interest paid to the State Treasurer, if both Seller and Buyer so agree in writing. If the Buyer does not 13
complete an IRS Form W-9 before Selling Firm must deposit the Earnest Money or the Earnest Money is $10,000.00 or 14
less, the Earnest Money shall be deposited into the Housing Trust Fund Account. Selling Firm may transfer the Earnest 15
Money to Closing Agent at Closing. If all or part of the Earnest Money is to be refunded to Buyer and any such costs 16
remain unpaid, the Selling Firm or Closing Agent may deduct and pay them therefrom. The parties instruct Closing 17
Agent to provide written verification of receipt of the Earnest Money and notice of dishonor of any check to the parties 18
and Brokers at the addresses and/or fax numbers provided herein. 19

Upon termination of this Agreement, a party or the Closing Agent may deliver a form authorizing the release of Earnest 20
Money to the other party or the parties. The party(s) shall execute such form and deliver the same to the Closing Agent. 21
If either party fails to execute the release form, the other party may make a written demand to the Closing Agent for the 22
Earnest Money. If only one party makes such a demand, Closing Agent shall promptly deliver notice of the demand to 23
the other party. If the other party does not object to the demand within 10 days of Closing Agent's notice, Closing Agent 24
shall disburse the Earnest Money to the party making the demand. If Closing Agent complies with the preceding 25
process, each party shall be deemed to have released Closing Agent from any and all claims or liability related to the 26
disbursal of the Earnest Money. The parties are advised that, notwithstanding the foregoing, Closing Agent may require 27
the parties to execute a separate agreement before disbursing the Earnest Money. If either party fails to authorize the 28
release of the Earnest Money to the other party when required to do so under this Agreement, that party shall be in 29
breach of this Agreement. Upon either party's request, the party holding the Earnest Money shall commence an 30
interpleader action in the county in which the Property is located. For the purposes of this section, the term Closing 31
Agent includes a Selling Firm holding the Earnest Money. The parties authorize the party commencing an interpleader 32
action to deduct up to $500.00 for the costs thereof. 33

c. Included Items. Any of the following items, including items identified in Specific Term No. 5 if the corresponding box is 34
checked, located in or on the Property are included in the sale: built-in appliances; wall-to-wall carpeting; curtains, 35
drapes and all other window treatments; window and door screens; awnings; storm doors and windows; installed 36
television antennas; ventilating, air conditioning and heating fixtures; trash compactor; fireplace doors, gas logs and gas 37
log lighters; irrigation fixtures; electric garage door openers; water heaters; installed electrical fixtures; lighting fixtures; 38
shrubs, plants and trees planted in the ground; and other fixtures; and all associated operating remote controls. If any of 39
the above Included Items are leased or encumbered, Seller shall acquire and clear title at or before Closing. 40

d. Condition of Title. Unless otherwise specified in this Agreement, title to the Property shall be marketable at Closing. 41
The following shall not cause the title to be unmarketable: rights, reservations, covenants, conditions and restrictions, 42
presently of record and general to the area; easements and encroachments, not materially affecting the value of or 43
unduly interfering with Buyer's reasonable use of the Property; and reserved oil and/or mining rights. Monetary 44
encumbrances or liens not assumed by Buyer, shall be paid or discharged by Seller on or before Closing. Title shall be 45
conveyed by a Statutory Warranty Deed. If this Agreement is for conveyance of a buyer's interest in a Real Estate 46
Contract, the Statutory Warranty Deed shall include a buyer's assignment of the contract sufficient to convey after 47
acquired title. 48

e. Title Insurance. Seller authorizes Buyer's lender or Closing Agent, at Seller's expense, to apply for the then-current 49
ALTA form of Homeowner's Policy of Title Insurance for One-to-Four Family Residence, from the Title Insurance 50
Company. If Seller previously received a preliminary commitment from a Title Insurance Company that Buyer declines 51
to use, Buyer shall pay any cancellation fees owing to the original Title Insurance Company. Otherwise, the party 52
applying for title insurance shall pay any title cancellation fee, in the event such a fee is assessed. If the Title Insurance 53
Company selected by the parties will not issue a Homeowner's Policy for the Property, the parties agree that the Title 54
Insurance Company shall instead issue the then-current ALTA standard form Owner's Policy, together with 55
homeowner's additional protection and inflation protection endorsements, if available. The Title Insurance Company 56
shall send a copy of the preliminary commitment to Seller, Listing Broker, Buyer and Selling Broker. The preliminary 57
commitment, and the title policy to be issued, shall contain no exceptions other than the General Exclusions and 58
Exceptions in the Policy and Special Exceptions consistent with the Condition of Title herein provided. If title cannot be 59

Buyer's Initials	Date	Buyer's Initials	Date	Seller's Initials	Date	Seller's Initials	Date

Form 21
Residential Purchase & Sale Agreement
Rev. 5/14
Page 3 of 5

RESIDENTIAL REAL ESTATE PURCHASE AND SALE AGREEMENT
GENERAL TERMS
Continued

made so insurable prior to the Closing Date, then as Buyer's sole and exclusive remedy, the Earnest Money shall, 60
unless Buyer elects to waive such defects or encumbrances, be refunded to the Buyer, less any unpaid costs described 61
in this Agreement, and this Agreement shall thereupon be terminated. Buyer shall have no right to specific performance 62
or damages as a consequence of Seller's inability to provide insurable title. 63

f.   **Closing and Possession**. This sale shall be closed by the Closing Agent on the Closing Date. If the Closing Date falls 64
on a Saturday, Sunday, legal holiday as defined in RCW 1.16.050, or day when the county recording office is closed, 65
the Closing Agent shall close the transaction on the next day that is not a Saturday, Sunday, legal holiday, or day when 66
the county recording office is closed. "Closing" means the date on which all documents are recorded and the sale 67
proceeds are available to Seller. Seller shall deliver keys and garage door remotes to Buyer on the Closing Date or on 68
the Possession Date, whichever occurs first. Buyer shall be entitled to possession at 9:00 p.m. on the Possession Date. 69
Seller shall maintain the Property in its present condition, normal wear and tear excepted, until the Buyer is entitled to 70
possession. Seller shall not enter into or modify existing leases or rental agreements, service contracts, or other 71
agreements affecting the Property which have terms extending beyond Closing without first obtaining Buyer's consent, 72
which shall not be unreasonably withheld. If possession transfers at a time other than Closing, the parties agree to 73
execute NWMLS Form 65A (Rental Agreement/Occupancy Prior to Closing) or NWMLS Form 65B (Rental 74
Agreement/Seller Occupancy After Closing) (or alternative rental agreements) and are advised of the need to contact 75
their respective insurance companies to assure appropriate hazard and liability insurance policies are in place, as 76
applicable. 77

RCW 19.27.530 requires the seller of any owner-occupied single-family residence to equip the residence with a carbon 78
monoxide alarm(s) in accordance with the state building code before a buyer or any other person may legally occupy 79
the residence following the sale. The parties acknowledge that the Brokers are not responsible for ensuring that Seller 80
complies with RCW 19.27.530. Buyer and Seller shall hold the Brokers and their Firms harmless from any claim 81
resulting from Seller's failure to install a carbon monoxide alarm(s) in the Property. 82

g.   **Section 1031 Like-Kind Exchange**. If either Buyer or Seller intends for this transaction to be a part of a Section 1031 83
like-kind exchange, then the other party shall cooperate in the completion of the like-kind exchange so long as the 84
cooperating party incurs no additional liability in doing so, and so long as any expenses (including attorneys' fees and 85
costs) incurred by the cooperating party that are related only to the exchange are paid or reimbursed to the cooperating 86
party at or prior to Closing. Notwithstanding the Assignment paragraph of this Agreement, any party completing a 87
Section 1031 like-kind exchange may assign this Agreement to its qualified intermediary or any entity set up for the 88
purposes of completing a reverse exchange. 89

h.   **Closing Costs and Prorations and Charges and Assessments**. Seller and Buyer shall each pay one-half of the 90
escrow fee unless otherwise required by applicable FHA or VA regulations. Taxes for the current year, rent, interest, 91
and lienable homeowner's association dues shall be prorated as of Closing. Buyer shall pay Buyer's loan costs, 92
including credit report, appraisal charge and lender's title insurance, unless provided otherwise in this Agreement. If any 93
payments are delinquent on encumbrances which will remain after Closing, Closing Agent is instructed to pay such 94
delinquencies at Closing from money due, or to be paid by, Seller. Buyer shall pay for remaining fuel in the fuel tank if, 95
prior to Closing, Seller obtains a written statement as to the quantity and current price from the supplier. Seller shall pay 96
all utility charges, including unbilled charges. Unless waived in Specific Term No. 14, Seller and Buyer request the 97
services of Closing Agent in disbursing funds necessary to satisfy unpaid utility charges in accordance with RCW 60.80 98
and Seller shall provide the names and addresses of all utilities providing service to the Property and having lien rights 99
(attach NWMLS Form 22K Identification of Utilities or equivalent). 100

Buyer is advised to verify the existence and amount of any local improvement district, capacity or impact charges or 101
other assessments that may be charged against the Property before or after Closing. Seller will pay such charges that 102
are encumbrances at the time of Closing, or that are or become due on or before Closing. Charges levied before 103
Closing, but becoming due after Closing shall be paid as agreed in Specific Term No. 15. 104

i.   **Sale Information**. Listing Broker and Selling Broker are authorized to report this Agreement (including price and all 105
terms) to the Multiple Listing Service that published it and to its members, financing institutions, appraisers, and anyone 106
else related to this sale. Buyer and Seller expressly authorize all Closing Agents, appraisers, title insurance companies, 107
and others related to this Sale, to furnish the Listing Broker and/or Selling Broker, on request, any and all information 108
and copies of documents concerning this sale. 109

j.   **FIRPTA - Tax Withholding at Closing**. The Closing Agent is instructed to prepare a certification (NWMLS Form 22E or 110
equivalent) that Seller is not a "foreign person" within the meaning of the Foreign Investment In Real Property Tax Act. 111
Seller shall sign this certification. If Seller is a foreign person, and this transaction is not otherwise exempt from FIRPTA, 112
Closing Agent is instructed to withhold and pay the required amount to the Internal Revenue Service. 113

k.   **Notices**. In consideration of the license to use this and NWMLS's companion forms and for the benefit of the Listing 114
Broker and the Selling Broker as well as the orderly administration of the offer, counteroffer or this Agreement, the 115
parties irrevocably agree that unless otherwise specified in this Agreement, any notice required or permitted in, or 116

| Buyer's Initials | Date | Buyer's Initials | Date | Seller's Initials | Date | Seller's Initials | Date |

Form 21
Residential Purchase & Sale Agreement
Rev. 5/14
Page 4 of 5

RESIDENTIAL REAL ESTATE PURCHASE AND SALE AGREEMENT
GENERAL TERMS
Continued

related to, this Agreement (including revocations of offers or counteroffers) must be in writing. Notices to Seller must be 117 signed by at least one Buyer and shall be deemed given only when the notice is received by Seller, by Listing Broker or 118 at the licensed office of Listing Broker. Notices to Buyer must be signed by at least one Seller and shall be deemed 119 given only when the notice is received by Buyer, by Selling Broker or at the licensed office of Selling Broker. Receipt by 120 Selling Broker of a Form 17, Disclosure of Information on Lead-Based Paint and Lead-Based Paint Hazards, Public 121 Offering Statement or Resale Certificate, homeowners' association documents provided pursuant to NWMLS Form 122 22D, or a preliminary commitment for title insurance provided pursuant to NWMLS Form 22T shall be deemed receipt 123 by Buyer. Selling Broker and Listing Broker have no responsibility to advise of receipt of a notice beyond either phoning 124 the party or causing a copy of the notice to be delivered to the party's address shown on this Agreement. Buyer and 125 Seller must keep Selling Broker and Listing Broker advised of their whereabouts in order to receive prompt notification 126 of receipt of a notice. 127

l.   Computation of Time. Unless otherwise specified in this Agreement, any period of time measured in days and stated 128 in this Agreement shall start on the day following the event commencing the period and shall expire at 9:00 p.m. of the 129 last calendar day of the specified period of time. Except for the Possession Date, if the last day is a Saturday, Sunday 130 or legal holiday as defined in RCW 1.16.050, the specified period of time shall expire on the next day that is not a 131 Saturday, Sunday or legal holiday. Any specified period of 5 days or less shall not include Saturdays, Sundays or legal 132 holidays. If the parties agree that an event will occur on a specific calendar date, the event shall occur on that date, 133 except for the Closing Date, which, if it falls on a Saturday, Sunday, legal holiday as defined in RCW 1.16.050, or day 134 when the county recording office is closed, shall occur on the next day that is not a Saturday, Sunday, legal holiday, or 135 day when the county recording office is closed. If the parties agree upon and attach a legal description after this 136 Agreement is signed by the offeree and delivered to the offeror, then for the purposes of computing time, mutual 137 acceptance shall be deemed to be on the date of delivery of an accepted offer or counteroffer to the offeror, rather than 138 on the date the legal description is attached. Time is of the essence of this Agreement. 139

m. Facsimile and E-mail Transmission. Facsimile transmission of any signed original document, and retransmission of 140 any signed facsimile transmission, shall be the same as delivery of an original. At the request of either party, or the 141 Closing Agent, the parties will confirm facsimile transmitted signatures by signing an original document. E-mail 142 transmission of any signed original document, and retransmission of any such e-mail, shall be the same as delivery of 143 an original, provided that the e-mail is sent to both Selling Broker and Selling Firm or both Listing Broker and Listing 144 Firm at the e-mail addresses on page one of this Agreement. At the request of either party, or the Closing Agent, the 145 parties will confirm e-mail transmitted signatures by signing an original document. 146

n.   Integration and Electronic Signatures. This Agreement constitutes the entire understanding between the parties and 147 supersedes all prior or contemporaneous understandings and representations. No modification of this Agreement shall 148 be effective unless agreed in writing and signed by Buyer and Seller. The parties acknowledge that a signature in 149 electronic form has the same legal effect and validity as a handwritten signature. 150

o.   Assignment. Buyer may not assign this Agreement, or Buyer's rights hereunder, without Seller's prior written consent, 151 unless the parties indicate that assignment is permitted by the addition of "and/or assigns" on the line identifying the 152 Buyer on the first page of this Agreement. 153

p.   Default. In the event Buyer fails, without legal excuse, to complete the purchase of the Property, then the following 154 provision, as identified in Specific Term No. 8, shall apply: 155

i.   Forfeiture of Earnest Money. That portion of the Earnest Money that does not exceed five percent (5%) of the 156 Purchase Price shall be forfeited to the Seller as the sole and exclusive remedy available to Seller for such failure. 157

ii. Seller's Election of Remedies. Seller may, at Seller's option, (a) keep the Earnest Money as liquidated damages 158 as the sole and exclusive remedy available to Seller for such failure, (b) bring suit against Buyer for Seller's actual 159 damages, (c) bring suit to specifically enforce this Agreement and recover any incidental damages, or (d) pursue 160 any other rights or remedies available at law or equity. 161

q.   Professional Advice and Attorneys' Fees. Buyer and Seller are advised to seek the counsel of an attorney and a 162 certified public accountant to review the terms of this Agreement. Buyer and Seller agree to pay their own fees incurred 163 for such review. However, if Buyer or Seller institutes suit against the other concerning this Agreement the prevailing 164 party is entitled to reasonable attorneys' fees and expenses. 165

r.   Offer. Buyer shall purchase the Property under the terms and conditions of this Agreement. Seller shall have until 9:00 166 p.m. on the Offer Expiration Date to accept this offer, unless sooner withdrawn. Acceptance shall not be effective until a 167 signed copy is received by Buyer, by Selling Broker or at the licensed office of Selling Broker. If this offer is not so 168 accepted, it shall lapse and any Earnest Money shall be refunded to Buyer. 169

s.   Counteroffer. Any change in the terms presented in an offer or counteroffer, other than the insertion of the Seller's 170 name, shall be considered a counteroffer. If a party makes a counteroffer, then the other party shall have until 9:00 p.m. 171 on the counteroffer expiration date to accept that counteroffer, unless sooner withdrawn. Acceptance shall not be 172

_____   _____   _____   _____   _____   _____   _____   _____
Buyer's Initials   Date   Buyer's Initials   Date   Seller's Initials   Date   Seller's Initials   Date

Form 21
Residential Purchase & Sale Agreement
Rev. 5/14
Page 5 of 5

RESIDENTIAL REAL ESTATE PURCHASE AND SALE AGREEMENT
GENERAL TERMS
Continued

effective until a signed copy is received by the other party, the other party's broker, or at the licensed office of the other 173
party's broker. If the counteroffer is not so accepted, it shall lapse and any Earnest Money shall be refunded to Buyer.   174

t. Offer and Counteroffer Expiration Date. If no expiration date is specified for an offer/counteroffer, the 175
offer/counteroffer shall expire 2 days after the offer/counteroffer is delivered by the party making the offer/counteroffer, 176
unless sooner withdrawn.   177

u. Agency Disclosure. Selling Firm, Selling Firm's Designated Broker, Selling Broker's Branch Manager (if any) and 178
Selling Broker's Managing Broker (if any) represent the same party that Selling Broker represents. Listing Firm, Listing 179
Firm's Designated Broker, Listing Broker's Branch Manager (if any), and Listing Broker's Managing Broker (if any) 180
represent the same party that the Listing Broker represents. If Selling Broker and Listing Broker are different persons 181
affiliated with the same Firm, then both Buyer and Seller confirm their consent to Designated Broker, Branch Manager 182
(if any), and Managing Broker (if any) representing both parties as dual agents. If Selling Broker and Listing Broker are 183
the same person representing both parties then both Buyer and Seller confirm their consent to that person and his/her 184
Designated Broker, Branch Manager (if any), and Managing Broker (if any) representing both parties as dual agents. All 185
parties acknowledge receipt of the pamphlet entitled "The Law of Real Estate Agency."   186

v. Commission. Seller and Buyer agree to pay a commission in accordance with any listing or commission agreement to 187
which they are a party. The Listing Firm's commission shall be apportioned between Listing Firm and Selling Firm as 188
specified in the listing. Seller and Buyer hereby consent to Listing Firm or Selling Firm receiving compensation from 189
more than one party. Seller and Buyer hereby assign to Listing Firm and Selling Firm, as applicable, a portion of their 190
funds in escrow equal to such commission(s) and irrevocably instruct the Closing Agent to disburse the commission(s) 191
directly to the Firm(s). In any action by Listing or Selling Firm to enforce this paragraph, the prevailing party is entitled to 192
court costs and reasonable attorneys' fees. Seller and Buyer agree that the Firms are intended third party beneficiaries 193
under this Agreement.   194

w. Cancellation Rights/Lead-Based Paint. If a residential dwelling was built on the Property prior to 1978, and Buyer 195
receives a Disclosure of Information on Lead-Based Paint and Lead-Based Paint Hazards (NWMLS Form 22J) after 196
mutual acceptance, Buyer may rescind this Agreement at any time up to 3 days thereafter.   197

x. Information Verification Period and Property Condition Disclaimer. Buyer shall have 10 days after mutual 198
acceptance to verify all information provided from Seller or Listing Firm related to the Property. This contingency shall 199
be deemed satisfied unless Buyer gives notice identifying the materially inaccurate information within 10 days of mutual 200
acceptance. If Buyer gives timely notice under this section, then this Agreement shall terminate and the Earnest Money 201
shall be refunded to Buyer.   202

Buyer and Seller agree, that except as provided in this Agreement, all representations and information regarding the 203
Property and the transaction are solely from the Seller or Buyer, and not from any Broker. The parties acknowledge that 204
the Brokers are not responsible for assuring that the parties perform their obligations under this Agreement and that 205
none of the Brokers has agreed to independently investigate or confirm any matter related to this transaction except as 206
stated in this Agreement, or in a separate writing signed by such Broker. In addition, Brokers do not guarantee the 207
value, quality or condition of the Property and some properties may contain building materials, including siding, roofing, 208
ceiling, insulation, electrical, and plumbing, that have been the subject of lawsuits and/or governmental inquiry because 209
of possible defects or health hazards. Some properties may have other defects arising after construction, such as 210
drainage, leakage, pest, rot and mold problems. Brokers do not have the expertise to identify or assess defective 211
products, materials, or conditions. Buyer is urged to use due diligence to inspect the Property to Buyer's satisfaction 212
and to retain inspectors qualified to identify the presence of defective materials and evaluate the condition of the 213
Property as there may be defects that may only be revealed by careful inspection. Buyer is advised to investigate 214
whether there is a sufficient water supply to meet Buyer's needs. Buyer is advised to investigate the cost of insurance 215
for the Property, including, but not limited to homeowner's, flood, earthquake, landslide, and other available coverage. 216
Buyer and Seller acknowledge that home protection plans may be available which may provide additional protection 217
and benefit to Buyer and Seller. Brokers may assist the parties with locating and selecting third party service providers, 218
such as inspectors or contractors, but Brokers cannot guarantee or be responsible for the services provided by those 219
third parties. The parties agree to exercise their own judgment and due diligence regarding third-party service providers. 220

_____   _____   _____   _____   _____   _____   _____   _____
Buyer's Initials   Date   Buyer's Initials   Date   Seller's Initials   Date   Seller's Initials   Date

or purchase of community real property. Since it can be difficult to know for certain whether a particular piece of property is community property or separate property, it's advisable to obtain the signature of the spouse in every transaction involving a married person, just in case.

Business Entities. When a partnership is a party to a purchase and sale agreement, the names of all general partners (and their spouses) and the name of the partnership itself should be listed in the contract. For all types of business entities (partnerships, corporations, and LLCs), the company's address and the state in which it is organized or incorporated should also be shown.

A business entity's legal authority to enter into the transaction must be established. Before closing, the escrow agent (or other closing agent) will require documentation proving that the partner, corporate officer, or other representative who is signing on behalf of the entity has the authority to do so. The documentation could take the form of a power of attorney or a resolution of the board of directors.

Note that even if the closing agent is specific about what documentation and signatures are required to close the transaction, that doesn't necessarily mean that those will, in fact, make the transaction legally valid. A closing agent does not give legal advice. So if there is doubt about who needs to sign the documents, it's necessary to consult a lawyer.

Property Description

A purchase and sale agreement is not enforceable unless it includes an adequate description of the property, one that would be sufficient in a deed (see Chapter 1). A complete legal description should be used whenever possible. The NWMLS form states that the legal description will be attached to the agreement as "Exhibit A." Like any attachment to a contract, it should be signed or initialed by the parties.

Price and Method of Payment

The full purchase price should be stated in the agreement. The amount of the earnest money should be noted as well. If the buyer is going to assume the seller's existing mortgage or if seller financing is involved, a payment terms addendum should be attached to the purchase and sale agreement. In the payment terms addendum, you include specific information about how the purchase price will be paid.

If the seller will be financing all or part of the purchase, the interest rate and payment amount for the seller financing must be stated, and a copy of the financing documents that the parties will be executing must be attached to the purchase and sale agreement. The amount of any downpayment should also be stated. (For more information about financing arrangements, see Chapters 10 and 11.)

Included Items

An "Included Items" paragraph states that certain items are included in the sale unless otherwise noted in the agreement. The list usually includes carpeting, built-in appliances, window coverings, air conditioning equipment, shrubs, and so forth.

Even without this provision in the agreement, many of the items listed would be considered fixtures or attachments and included in the sale (see Chapter 1), but the provision prevents disputes over this issue.

If there is an item on the list that the seller does not want to include in the sale, the real estate agent should be sure to attach an addendum to the agreement stating that the item is excluded. Similarly, if items that do not appear on the list will be included in the sale, those should be specified in an addendum.

Closing Date

The closing date is the date when the proceeds of the sale are disbursed to the seller, the deed is delivered to the buyer, and all the appropriate documents are recorded.

The purchase and sale agreement must provide a specific date for closing. The lender should be consulted as to when the funds will be available to close the transaction. In setting a closing date, it is also important to consider how long it will take to meet any conditions that have been set. The buyer may have to obtain a loan and sell his current home. The seller will have to obtain title insurance, clear any liens, and perhaps make some repairs. (These conditions are discussed in more detail later in this chapter.) The chosen closing date must allow the parties sufficient time for all these obligations and conditions to be met.

> **Example:** The purchase and sale agreement is going to be conditioned on the buyer obtaining a VA-guaranteed loan. A lender tells the real estate agent that it currently takes about two weeks to obtain VA loan approval, and the agent knows it normally takes four or five business days after loan approval and the satisfaction of any other conditions for the closing officer to finish the necessary work and close the transaction. So the agent suggests that the parties choose a closing date at least 20 days after the date the purchase and sale agreement is signed.

If the closing date is approaching and an inspection report is not yet available, or it looks like some other contingency will not be satisfied in time, the parties may want to change the closing date by executing a written extension agreement. The purchase and sale agreement will terminate on the date set for closing, so it is important to get an extension agreement signed as soon as possible. Failure to extend the closing date by amending the agreement may result in a contract that cannot be enforced.

Closing Agent and Closing Costs

It's a good idea for an escrow agent or other closing agent to be appointed in the purchase and sale agreement. Closing agents perform a wide variety of tasks connected with closing a real estate transaction, such as ordering inspections and title insurance, arranging for liens to be paid off and released, and preparing and recording documents on behalf of both the buyer and the seller. They may also hold funds and documents in escrow for the parties, distributing them only when specified conditions have been fulfilled. (Escrow and the closing process are discussed in more detail in Chapter 13.)

The purchase and sale agreement should also state which party is responsible for paying the closing agent's fees (typically, they are split between the parties) and various other closing costs (such as costs connected with the buyer's loan). In addition, the agreement should set forth how certain property expenses (such as taxes and homeowner's association dues) and any property income (rent from tenants, for example) will be shared. These are ordinarily prorated as of the closing date, unless otherwise agreed (see Chapter 13).

A federal law, the Foreign Investment in Real Property Tax Act (FIRPTA), applies to some transactions in which the seller is a "foreign person"—in other words, not a U.S. citizen or resident alien. FIRPTA requires the buyer or the closing agent to withhold a certain percentage of the price and then turn the money over to the Internal Revenue Service. The purchase and sale agreement may include a provision concerning compliance with this law. Many residential transactions are exempt from FIRPTA.

Possession

Unless the parties make other arrangements, possession of the property is usually transferred to the buyer when the transaction closes. If the buyer wants to take possession earlier, or if the seller wants a few extra days to vacate the property, that should be provided for in the purchase and sale agreement; the parties should also execute a separate rental agreement.

The seller usually agrees that the property will be maintained in its present condition until the buyer takes possession.

Casualty Loss

Another issue that may be addressed in the purchase and sale agreement is casualty loss. For instance, what happens if the house burns down after the agreement is executed, but before closing? Unless the buyer has already taken possession of the property, the seller ordinarily bears the risk of loss until closing. So if the property is destroyed or substantially damaged before the transaction closes, the buyer is generally not required to go through with the purchase. (However, the purchase and sale agreement may allocate the risk of loss in some other fashion.)

Conveyance and Title

Almost every purchase and sale agreement includes provisions pertaining to the conveyance of the property and the condition of title. The type of deed that the seller will execute in favor of the buyer (ordinarily a warranty deed) is specified. There is usually a clause in which the seller agrees to provide marketable title, free of undisclosed encumbrances, with a homeowner's title insurance policy. The seller also agrees to pay off (at or before closing) any liens that the buyer is not assuming. Any unusual encumbrances that will remain after closing must be disclosed in the purchase and sale agreement.

Many agreements go into more detail about what will be considered marketable title. For example, an agreement might say that CC&Rs that apply to the entire neighborhood or subdivision will not make the title unmarketable, nor will easements that do not significantly interfere with the buyer's use of the property (an easement for underground wiring, for instance). There will be no problem if encumbrances of that type show up as exceptions on the preliminary title report. However, if the report reveals other undisclosed encumbrances (such as an access easement that would interfere with the buyer's use of the property) and the seller cannot remove them before closing, then the title will be considered unmarketable, and the buyer can refuse to go through with the purchase.

Time is of the Essence

A purchase and sale agreement usually states that "time is of the essence of this agreement." This phrase means more than simply that the parties hope the sale progresses as quickly as possible; it means they are legally required to meet all deadlines set in the agreement.

A contract in which time is of the essence is one in which performance on or before the exact dates specified (not just within a reasonable time thereafter) is considered one of the essential terms of the agreement. Failure to meet any of the deadlines is a breach of contract.

Since time is of the essence in a purchase and sale agreement, the closing must take place on the date stated in the agreement. It's possible for either party to waive this clause, allowing the other party to perform after the deadline. But as a general rule, meeting all deadlines is an essential part of fulfilling a purchase and sale agreement.

Default

Another issue addressed in a purchase and sale agreement is the seller's remedies in the event that the buyer defaults, or breaches the contract. (The buyer's remedies in case the seller defaults usually aren't specifically listed; they include the right to sue for damages or specific performance, as explained in Chapter 6.)

A purchase and sale agreement form typically allows the parties to specify either that the earnest money will be treated as liquidated damages if the buyer defaults, or that the seller will be permitted an election of remedies. An election of remedies means that after the buyer has defaulted, the seller can decide whether to simply keep the buyer's earnest money deposit, sue for actual damages, sue for specific performance, or pursue some other legal remedy.

In most cases, however, the parties agree in advance that instead of allowing the seller an election of remedies, the earnest money will serve as liquidated damages. In that case, the seller will be entitled to keep the earnest money without having to prove that she suffered a financial loss as a result of the buyer's default. But the seller also gives up the right to sue the buyer for any additional damages or for specific performance. Keeping the earnest money will be the seller's only remedy.

Under Washington law, no more than 5% of the property's purchase price can be treated as liquidated damages in a purchase and sale agreement. So if the buyer's earnest money deposit was more than 5% of the price, the seller is required to return the excess to the buyer.

A purchase and sale agreement also typically includes an attorneys' fees provision. If one of the parties must resort to a lawsuit to enforce the contract and wins the lawsuit, then the losing party is obligated to pay the winning party's attorneys' fees.

Agency Disclosure

In Washington, a purchase and sale agreement usually includes an agency disclosure provision. In this provision, the real estate agents involved in the transaction specify which party each of them is representing. Washington law requires this information to be disclosed in writing to each party before he or she signs an offer (see Chapter 7), and the provision in the purchase and sale agreement fulfills this requirement. The parties' signatures on the agreement indicate their acceptance and understanding of the stated agency relationships.

Addenda

A paragraph that may be labeled "Addenda" or "Additional Provisions" indicates whether there are attachments to the agreement that contain additional contract provisions. There might be addenda concerning payment terms, fixtures to be excluded from the sale, FHA/VA financing, inspections, and so on. In order to incorporate additional provisions into the agreement, the attachments should be listed in the space provided, and the parties must initial and date each page of the attachments.

Earnest Money

A purchase and sale agreement form will provide space to fill in the amount of the buyer's earnest money deposit. It should also have a place to indicate what form the deposit takes (personal check, cash, promissory note, or some other form) and explain how the deposit will be held while the transaction is pending.

Sometimes the buyer gives the selling agent a check for the deposit when the purchase and sale agreement form is filled out, before the agent submits the buyer's offer to the listing agent. In this situation, the purchase and sale agreement usually provides that the selling agent will hold the buyer's check undeposited until the seller has accepted the buyer's offer (or, if the seller makes a counteroffer, until a final agreement is reached). That makes it easy to return the deposit to the buyer if the seller rejects the offer.

More commonly, however, the purchase and sale agreement form provides that the buyer won't give the earnest money check to the selling agent until the seller has accepted the offer or, if there are counteroffers, until a final agreement has been reached.

Once the parties have a binding agreement, the selling agent will either turn the buyer's check over to the closing agent for deposit into escrow, or else deposit the check into one of her real estate firm's trust accounts. The rules concerning real estate firm trust accounts are explained in Chapter 17. Briefly, if a check is for $10,000 or less, it has to be kept in the firm's housing trust fund account (a pooled trust account), with the interest paid to the state. If the check is for more than $10,000, the parties may choose instead to have it deposited in a separate trust account, with the interest paid either to the buyer or to the seller, as agreed. (The NWMLS residential purchase and sale agreement provides that the interest will be paid to the buyer.)

The appropriate amount for an earnest money deposit varies according to local custom; it can be any amount that both parties agree on. (Remember, however, that the seller can keep no more than 5% of the purchase price as liquidated damages if the buyer defaults.) Naturally, the buyer wants to make a small deposit, while the seller wants to receive a large deposit. The deposit is supposed to express the buyer's commitment to the purchase, and it should not be so small that forfeiting it would be painless. If the buyer goes through with the transaction, the deposit is ordinarily applied to the purchase price.

If a transaction falls through after the earnest money has been deposited into escrow or into a real estate firm's trust account, there may be a dispute over the earnest money; the buyer and the seller may each feel entitled to it. In some states, the escrow agent or the real estate firm that holds the funds in trust would file an **interpleader** action in this situation, turning the matter over to a court. The court would decide which party is the rightful owner of the funds.

Under Washington law, if the parties can't agree on who is entitled to funds held by a real estate firm, the designated broker must notify them in writing that the firm intends to disburse the funds. The notice must include the names and addresses of all parties, the amount of money involved, and when and to whom the disbursement will be made. Disbursement must occur no more than 30 days after the notice was given.

Brokerage Fee

Nearly all purchase and sale agreement forms also have a clause in which the buyer and seller agree to pay the real estate commission, as stated in any representation or commission agreement they entered into earlier.

Signatures

Of course, space is provided on the form for the signatures of the parties. The buyer's signature turns the form into an offer to purchase, and the seller's signature turns it into a binding contract.

Offer and Acceptance. The purchase and sale agreement form has a provision in which to set a deadline for acceptance of the offer. The manner in which the seller is required to communicate acceptance may also be specified. For example, it might say the seller's acceptance is not effective until a copy of the agreement signed by the seller has been returned to the selling agent (the agent who presented the buyer's offer). If the seller fails to accept in the prescribed manner by the deadline, the offer terminates and the earnest money is returned to the buyer. (Note that in addition to meeting any other requirements specified by the buyer, the seller's acceptance must be in writing to satisfy the statute of frauds.)

Counteroffers

The purchase and sale agreement form may include a provision concerning counteroffers, in case the seller wants to modify the buyer's offer instead of accepting it outright. The provision may set a deadline for the buyer's acceptance of the counteroffer. Remember that a counteroffer is not an acceptance; the buyer isn't bound unless he accepts the seller's counteroffer.

When a seller wants to make a counteroffer, it's best to write it on another form or a separate attachment, rather than crossing out or writing over the terms on the original form. Printed counteroffer forms are available for this purpose.

Amendments

After the buyer and the seller have signed the purchase and sale agreement, the terms of the contract can only be modified in writing. All parties who signed the original agreement must also sign the amendment for it to be binding.

Don't confuse an amendment with an addendum. An amendment is a written modification that occurs after the parties have signed the purchase and sale agreement, while an addendum is an attachment added to the agreement prior to signature.

Backup Offers

A prospective buyer may be so enthusiastic about a property that she decides to submit an offer even though the seller has already accepted an offer from another buyer. The second offer, known as a **backup offer**, would be contingent on the failure of the existing sales contract. If the seller accepts the backup offer, the parties will have a deal in place should the original sale fail to close.

Contingency Clauses

Most of the time, the agreement between a buyer and a seller is conditional; in other words, it is legally binding only if certain conditions are fulfilled. These conditions are called "contingency clauses," or simply "contingencies." The contract is contingent on fulfillment of the conditions.

The most common type of contingency clause is a financing contingency, which makes the contract depend on whether the buyer is able to obtain financing. Other common contingencies concern the sale of the buyer's present home, or the satisfactory completion of some type of inspection (for example, a structural, pest, or septic tank inspection).

If a contract contains a contingency clause, the contract will be enforceable if—and only if—that contingent event occurs. If it does not occur, the contract is terminated. When a purchase and sale agreement terminates because a contingent event does not occur, the buyer is usually entitled to a refund of the earnest money deposit.

The parties are obligated to make a reasonable effort to fulfill the condition set forth in a contingency clause. For instance, the buyer must apply for financing, or the seller must order the required inspections. As with every contract, the parties to a purchase and sale agreement have an obligation to act in good faith; each must cooperate so that both can benefit from the contract. It is best to make this obligation of good faith explicit in the contingency clause.

The party who benefits from the contingency clause usually has the right to waive it. For example, a buyer could waive a pest inspection contingency. In that case the parties would be bound by the agreement whether or not the results of the pest inspection were satisfactory, or even if no pest inspection were performed.

In some purchase and sale agreement forms, the closing date is expressly tied to fulfillment of a contingency. If a real estate agent believes that fulfillment of a condition in a purchase and sale agreement may affect the closing date, the agent should point that out to the parties.

All contingencies must be spelled out in the purchase and sale agreement or in attached addenda that are incorporated into the agreement. If a printed form contains boxes to be checked for each of the different kinds of contingencies, the agent filling out the form must be sure that all appropriate boxes are checked.

Any contingency clause should include these four things:

1. exactly what the condition is and what has to be done to meet it;
2. the procedure for notifying the other party of either satisfaction or waiver of the condition;
3. a date by which the condition must be satisfied or waived; and
4. the rights of the parties in the event the condition is not satisfied or waived by the specified date.

As with the purchase and sale agreement itself, there are attorney-approved contingency addendum forms that can be attached to the agreement. A real estate agent should use one of those forms instead of writing a complicated provision.

Financing Contingencies

Nearly all residential transactions are contingent on whether the buyer is able to obtain financing. That's why it's particularly important to describe the financing arrangements in the purchase and sale agreement. The buyer is required to make a diligent, good faith effort to obtain financing on the terms stated in the agreement. But if, despite the buyer's best efforts, no lenders are willing to make a loan on those terms, then the buyer can terminate the agreement without forfeiting the deposit.

A financing contingency should contain enough information to clearly identify the type of loan that the buyer wants. It isn't possible to include the details of all loan programs a buyer might qualify for, but the contingency clause should include the following basic information:

1. the type of the loan;
2. the amount of the downpayment;
3. the deadline by which the buyer must apply for a loan, and the consequences for missing that deadline;
4. the deadline for obtaining a loan commitment, and the consequences of a failure to obtain a loan commitment; and
5. the party who is to pay the costs and fees associated with the loan application (normally the buyer).

FHA, VA, and RD Financing. A financing contingency often includes special provisions concerning FHA, VA, and RD (rural development) financing. The regulations that govern these financing programs prohibit the buyer from paying certain loan and closing costs, and so the financing contingency provides that the seller agrees to pay these costs if the buyer is applying for an FHA, VA, or RD loan.

Note that if there is a low appraisal in an FHA, VA, or RD transaction, the buyer can't be required to go through with the purchase, even if the seller is willing to reduce the price (although the buyer may choose to buy the property at the reduced price). There is an exception to this rule, however: if the seller can get a reappraisal that indicates the property is worth the originally agreed-on price, the buyer must proceed with the transaction. This reappraisal has to be made by the same appraiser who initially submitted the low appraisal.

Contract Conditioned on Sale of Buyer's Home

Purchase and sale agreements are often contingent on the buyer's ability to sell her current home. In fact, even when this is not an express condition, it may be a hidden one. Most buyers are planning to use part of the proceeds from the sale of the current home for a downpayment on the new home, and won't be able to qualify for the loan described in the financing contingency clause without selling the current home.

Under those circumstances, the sale of the current home should be an express condition in the purchase and sale agreement. Otherwise the seller may be misled into believing that the buyer has a much better chance of being able to complete the purchase than she actually has. It's generally a waste of time for the seller to accept a contingent offer from a buyer who is unlikely to fulfill the condition.

The contract clause should specify what will fulfill a condition concerning sale of the current home. Is it fulfilled when the buyer accepts an offer on the current home? Or is it fulfilled only when the sale of the current home actually closes? The parties and the agent should carefully consider how much time is allowed for this contingency. There's a natural conflict between the desires of the buyer and the seller. The buyer wants as much time as possible in order to get the highest possible price for her current home. The seller wants the present transaction to close as soon as possible.

Bump Clauses. To deal with these conflicting interests, the **bump clause** has evolved. A bump clause enables the seller to keep the property on the market pending fulfillment of a contingency. It's now common to include one in the purchase and sale agreement when the transaction depends on the sale of the buyer's current home.

Fig. 9.2 Sample contingency clause concerning sale of buyer's home

Sale of Buyer's Home. This agreement is contingent upon Buyer's accepting an offer to sell Buyer's present residence, located at _____. Buyer must notify Seller, in writing, within _____ days after the date of the Seller's signature on this agreement that Buyer has accepted a written offer to sell Buyer's home. The price and terms of that sale agreement must be such that Buyer will receive sufficient net proceeds to make completion of this transaction possible. If Buyer fails to provide Seller with such notice within said _____-day period, then this purchase and sale agreement shall become null and void and Buyer's earnest money deposit shall be refunded.

This purchase and sale agreement is also conditioned upon the closing of and distribution of the proceeds from the sale of the Buyer's home on or before the closing date of this agreement. If the sale of Buyer's home fails to close by that date through no fault of Buyer, then this agreement becomes null and void and Buyer's earnest money shall be refunded.

If the seller receives another offer before the buyer's home is sold, the seller can demand that the buyer waive the condition or rescind the contract. A bump clause can be used with any type of contingency, and one is most likely to be used when there is a good chance that the contingency will not be fulfilled on time.

Time Frame. Although it's difficult, if not impossible, to predict how long it will take a buyer to sell her home, there is one practical detail to keep in mind. The agent must make sure that there isn't a conflict in the terms of the purchase and sale agreement. For example, the buyer should not be given 60 days to find a buyer for her home if the original sale is supposed to close in 45 days.

Inspection Contingencies

Another kind of contingency clause concerns an expert inspection of the property. For example, a purchase and sale agreement might include provisions making the contract contingent upon a structural inspection, a geological inspection, or a pest control inspection. In fact, if an appraiser notes that pests might be a problem, then the buyer's lender may require a pest control inspection to be performed before the buyer's loan is approved.

Contingency clauses dealing with inspections sometimes simply state that they can be met only with "satisfactory" test results, leaving what is satisfactory to the buyer's discretion. In other cases, an inspection contingency includes some objective standard, such as a determination that no immediate repairs are needed, or that necessary repairs can't exceed a set cost, such as $1,000.

Any objective standards set in an inspection contingency clause should be ones that will satisfy the buyer's personal standards. For example, a particular buyer might not want to buy a house that has ever had a termite infestation. Even if there's no immediate need for repairs, or if the damage is negligible, that buyer simply doesn't want a house that is susceptible to termite infestation. In that case, the clause should allow the buyer to withdraw from the transaction if the inspection reveals any past or present infestation.

An inspection contingency clause is often a separate page attached to the purchase and sale agreement as an addendum. It should establish:

- who is responsible for ordering and paying for the inspection;
- when and how the buyer must give the seller notice of disapproval of the inspection report;
- the seller's option to either perform repairs or terminate the purchase and sale agreement, refunding the buyer's earnest money; and
- a time limit for re-inspection by the buyer if the seller performs repairs.

The seller should be aware that if an inspection reveals building code violations or certain other problems, public authorities could order the seller to correct the violations, whether or not the transaction proceeds.

Second Buyer Contingencies

When it appears that a transaction might fail because a condition is not met, the seller may want to accept an offer from a second buyer. To allow this, a provision is usually included in the second purchase and sale agreement making it contingent on the failure of the first transaction, and on the first buyer's release of all claims. The best way to accomplish this is by asking the first buyer to execute a rescission agreement in which the parties agree to rescind the first contract.

Property Disclosure Laws

In many transactions, sellers are required by law to make certain disclosures to buyers about the property being transferred. In this section, we'll explain Washington's seller disclosure law and a federal law requiring disclosures concerning lead-based paint.

Seller Disclosure Law

Washington law requires a seller of real property to give the buyer a **seller disclosure statement**. This requirement generally applies to the sale of any type of real property except agricultural or timber land.

However, certain types of transactions are exempt from this law. For example, a seller disclosure statement is not required:

- in a foreclosure sale or when a borrower gives a lender a deed in lieu of foreclosure;
- when property is transferred as a gift to a family member; or
- when property is transferred pursuant to bankruptcy proceedings or the settlement of an estate.

A transaction may also be exempt because another disclosure requirement applies instead. That's true for sales that are subject to disclosure requirements under the Condominium Act or the Timeshare Act.

Disclosures. The information that must be included in a seller disclosure statement is set forth in the state statute. Different disclosures are required for unimproved residential property, improved residential property, and commercial property. A seller disclosure form for improved residential property is shown in Figure 9.3.

The purpose of the disclosure statement is to disclose the seller's knowledge about the condition of the property, including the condition of the buildings, the availability of utilities, the existence of any easements and encumbrances, and other material information. The statement is for disclosure purposes only; it is not a part of the purchase and sale agreement.

The seller disclosure form specifically states that the disclosures are made by the seller and may not be regarded as representations made by any of the real estate licensees involved in the transaction. Furthermore, the law provides that the statement is not a warranty from either the seller or the real estate agents. Neither the seller nor the agents will be liable for any inaccuracies in the statement unless they had personal knowledge of the inaccuracies.

Deadlines and Right of Rescission. The seller must give the buyer the disclosure statement within **five business days** after a purchase and sale agreement is signed, unless the parties agree in writing to another time frame, or the buyer signs a written waiver of the right to receive the statement. However, a waiver is not allowed for the Environmental section of the form, if any of the questions in that section would be answered "Yes."

Within **three business days** after receiving the statement (or another time frame agreed to in writing), the buyer can either "approve and accept" the disclosure statement or rescind the purchase and sale agreement. The choice between acceptance and rescission is at the complete discretion of the buyer. There are no objective standards that can be applied to the disclosure statement to measure its adequacy. If the buyer doesn't like something revealed in the disclosure statement, however trivial, the buyer can rescind the agreement. In fact, the buyer can rescind the agreement simply because he's decided he doesn't want the property after all, even if the decision isn't actually based on information disclosed by the seller.

If the buyer decides to rescind the agreement, he must deliver a written notice of rescission to the seller or the seller's agent before the three-day period expires. The buyer will then be entitled to a refund of the earnest money deposit.

After delivery of the disclosure statement, information may later come to light that makes the disclosure statement inaccurate.

Example: The seller filled out the seller disclosure statement and gave it to the buyer within the five-day time frame. The buyer examined the statement, was satisfied with it, and waived the right to rescind the agreement. Two weeks later, the seller realizes that there's an encroachment on the property. The disclosure statement given to the buyer is no longer accurate.

When this happens, the seller must either give the buyer an amended disclosure statement or else take corrective action so that the original disclosure statement is accurate again. If the seller provides an amended statement, the buyer has three business days to either accept the amended statement or rescind the purchase and sale agreement.

Example: The seller in the previous example gives the buyer an amended disclosure statement. The buyer, who has had second thoughts about buying the property anyway, decides to rescind the purchase and sale agreement.

If the seller neither provides an amended statement nor takes corrective action—or if the seller never provided a disclosure statement in the first place—the buyer can rescind the contract at any time before closing. Once the sale closes, however, the buyer's right of rescission ends. Even if new information comes to light after closing, the buyer doesn't have the right to rescind the transaction.

Lead-Based Paint Disclosure Law

In transactions involving housing built before 1978, federal law requires a seller to disclose information concerning lead-based paint to potential buyers. A landlord is also required to make these disclosures to potential tenants. Many of the homes built before 1978 contain some lead-based paint. The paint is usually not dangerous if

Fig. 9.3 Seller disclosure statement

Form 17
Seller Disclosure Statement
Rev. 6/12
Page 1 of 5

SELLER DISCLOSURE STATEMENT †
IMPROVED PROPERTY

©Copyright 2012
Northwest Multiple Listing Service
ALL RIGHTS RESERVED

SELLER: _____ 1

† To be used in transfers of improved residential real property, including residential dwellings up to four units, new construction, condominiums 2
not subject to a public offering statement, certain timeshares, and manufactured and mobile homes. See RCW Chapter 64.06 and Section 3
43.22.432 for further explanations. 4

INSTRUCTIONS TO THE SELLER 5

Please complete the following form. Do not leave any spaces blank. If the question clearly does not apply to the property write "NA." If the 6
answer is "yes" to any asterisked (*) item(s), please explain on attached sheets. Please refer to the line number(s) of the question(s) when you 7
provide your explanation(s). For your protection you must date and initial each page of this disclosure statement and each attachment. Delivery 8
of the disclosure statement must occur not later than five (5) business days, unless otherwise agreed, after mutual acceptance of a written 9
purchase and sale agreement between Buyer and Seller. 10

NOTICE TO THE BUYER 11

THE FOLLOWING DISCLOSURES ARE MADE BY THE SELLER ABOUT THE CONDITION OF THE PROPERTY LOCATED AT 12

_____, 13
CITY _____, COUNTY _____ ("THE PROPERTY")14
OR AS LEGALLY DESCRIBED ON THE ATTACHED EXHIBIT A. SELLER MAKES THE FOLLOWING DISCLOSURES OF EXISTING 15
MATERIAL FACTS OR MATERIAL DEFECTS TO BUYER BASED ON SELLER'S ACTUAL KNOWLEDGE OF THE PROPERTY AT 16
THE TIME SELLER COMPLETES THIS DISCLOSURE STATEMENT. UNLESS YOU AND SELLER OTHERWISE AGREE IN 17
WRITING, YOU HAVE THREE (3) BUSINESS DAYS FROM THE DAY SELLER OR SELLER'S AGENT DELIVERS THIS 18
DISCLOSURE STATEMENT TO YOU TO RESCIND THE AGREEMENT BY DELIVERING A SEPARATELY SIGNED WRITTEN 19
STATEMENT OF RESCISSION TO SELLER OR SELLER'S AGENT. IF THE SELLER DOES NOT GIVE YOU A COMPLETED 20
DISCLOSURE STATEMENT, THEN YOU MAY WAIVE THE RIGHT TO RESCIND PRIOR TO OR AFTER THE TIME YOU ENTER 21
INTO A PURCHASE AND SALE AGREEMENT. 22

THE FOLLOWING ARE DISCLOSURES MADE BY SELLER AND ARE NOT THE REPRESENTATIONS OF ANY REAL ESTATE 23
LICENSEE OR OTHER PARTY. THIS INFORMATION IS FOR DISCLOSURE ONLY AND IS NOT INTENDED TO BE A PART OF 24
ANY WRITTEN AGREEMENT BETWEEN BUYER AND SELLER. 25

FOR A MORE COMPREHENSIVE EXAMINATION OF THE SPECIFIC CONDITION OF THIS PROPERTY YOU ARE ADVISED TO 26
OBTAIN AND PAY FOR THE SERVICES OF QUALIFIED EXPERTS TO INSPECT THE PROPERTY, WHICH MAY INCLUDE, WITHOUT 27
LIMITATION, ARCHITECTS, ENGINEERS, LAND SURVEYORS, PLUMBERS, ELECTRICIANS, ROOFERS, BUILDING INSPECTORS, ON- 28
SITE WASTEWATER TREATMENT INSPECTORS, OR STRUCTURAL PEST INSPECTORS. THE PROSPECTIVE BUYER AND SELLER 29
MAY WISH TO OBTAIN PROFESSIONAL ADVICE OR INSPECTIONS OF THE PROPERTY OR TO PROVIDE APPROPRIATE 30
PROVISIONS IN A CONTRACT BETWEEN THEM WITH RESPECT TO ANY ADVICE, INSPECTION, DEFECTS OR WARRANTIES. 31

Seller ❑ is/ ❑ is not occupying the property. 32

I.   SELLER'S DISCLOSURES: 33

* If you answer "Yes" to a question with an asterisk (*), please explain your answer and attach documents, if available and not otherwise 34
publicly recorded. If necessary, use an attached sheet. 35

		YES	NO	DON'T KNOW	
1.	**TITLE**				36
A.	Do you have legal authority to sell the property? If no, please explain.	❑	❑	❑	37 / 38
*B.	Is title to the property subject to any of the following?				39
	(1) First right of refusal	❑	❑	❑	40
	(2) Option	❑	❑	❑	41
	(3) Lease or rental agreement	❑	❑	❑	42
	(4) Life estate?	❑	❑	❑	43
*C.	Are there any encroachments, boundary agreements, or boundary disputes?	❑	❑	❑	44
*D.	Is there a private road or easement agreement for access to the property?	❑	❑	❑	45
*E.	Are there any rights-of-way, easements, or access limitations that may affect the Buyer's use of the property?	❑	❑	❑	46 / 47
*F.	Are there any written agreements for joint maintenance of an easement or right-of-way?	❑	❑	❑	48
*G.	Is there any study, survey project, or notice that would adversely affect the property?	❑	❑	❑	49
*H.	Are there any pending or existing assessments against the property?	❑	❑	❑	50
*I.	Are there any zoning violations, nonconforming uses, or any unusual restrictions on the property that would affect future construction or remodeling?	❑	❑	❑	51 / 52
*J.	Is there a boundary survey for the property?	❑	❑	❑	53
*K.	Are there any covenants, conditions, or restrictions recorded against the property?	❑	❑	❑	54

PLEASE NOTE: Covenants, conditions, and restrictions which purport to forbid or restrict the conveyance, encumbrance, occupancy, or 55
lease of real property to individuals based on race, creed, color, sex, national origin, familial status, or disability are void, unenforceable, and 56
illegal. RCW 49.60.224. 57

SELLER'S INITIALS: _____ Date: _____ SELLER'S INITIALS: _____ Date: _____

Form 17
Seller Disclosure Statement
Rev. 06/12
Page 2 of 5

SELLER DISCLOSURE STATEMENT
IMPROVED PROPERTY
(Continued)

	YES	NO	DON'T KNOW

2. **WATER**

A. Household Water

  (1) The source of water for the property is: ☐ Private or publicly owned water system
    ☐ Private well serving only the subject property *☐ Other water system
    *If shared, are there any written agreements? .... ☐ ☐ ☐

  *(2) Is there an easement (recorded or unrecorded) for access to and/or maintenance
    of the water source? .... ☐ ☐ ☐

  *(3) Are there any problems or repairs needed? .... ☐ ☐ ☐

  (4) During your ownership, has the source provided an adequate year-round supply
    of potable water? .... ☐ ☐ ☐

    If no, please explain: _____

  *(5) Are there any water treatment systems for the property? .... ☐ ☐ ☐
    If yes, are they: ☐ Leased ☐ Owned

  *(6) Are there any water rights for the property associated with its domestic water supply,
    such as a water right permit, certificate, or claim? .... ☐ ☐ ☐

    (a) If yes, has the water right permit, certificate, or claim been assigned, transferred,
      or changed? .... ☐ ☐ ☐

    *(b) If yes, has all or any portion of the water right not been used for five or more
      successive years? .... ☐ ☐ ☐

  *(7) Are there any defects in the operation of the water system (e.g. pipes, tank, pump, etc.)? ☐ ☐ ☐

B. Irrigation Water

  (1) Are there any irrigation water rights for the property, such as a water right permit,
    certificate, or claim? .... ☐ ☐ ☐

    *(a) If yes, has all or any portion of the water right not been used for five or more
      successive years? .... ☐ ☐ ☐

    *(b) If so, is the certificate available? (If yes, please attach a copy.) .... ☐ ☐ ☐

    *(c) If so, has the water right permit, certificate, or claim been assigned,
      transferred, or changed? .... ☐ ☐ ☐

  *(2) Does the property receive irrigation water from a ditch company, irrigation district, or other entity?....... ☐ ☐ ☐
    If so, please identify the entity that supplies water to the property:

    _____

C. Outdoor Sprinkler System

  (1) Is there an outdoor sprinkler system for the property? .... ☐ ☐ ☐

  *(2) If yes, are there any defects in the system? .... ☐ ☐ ☐

  *(3) If yes, is the sprinkler system connected to irrigation water? .... ☐ ☐ ☐

3. **SEWER/ON-SITE SEWAGE SYSTEM**

A. The property is served by:
  ☐ Public sewer system ☐ On-site sewage system (including pipes, tanks, drainfields, and all other component parts)
  ☐ Other disposal system
  Please describe: _____

B. If public sewer system service is available to the property, is the house
  connected to the sewer main? .... ☐ ☐ ☐

  If no, please explain: _____

*C. Is the property subject to any sewage system fees or charges in addition to those covered
  in your regularly billed sewer or on-site sewage system maintenance service?........................ ☐ ☐ ☐

D. If the property is connected to an on-site sewage system:

  *(1) Was a permit issued for its construction, and was it approved by the local health
    department or district following its construction?........................ ☐ ☐ ☐

  (2) When was it last pumped? _____

  *(3) Are there any defects in the operation of the on-site sewage system?........................ ☐ ☐ ☐

  (4) When was it last inspected? _____

    By whom: _____

  (5) For how many bedrooms was the on-site sewage system approved? _____ bedrooms

SELLER'S INITIALS: _____ Date: _____ SELLER'S INITIALS: _____ Date: _____

Line numbers: 58, 59, 60, 61, 62, 63, 64, 65, 66, 67, 68, 69, 70, 71, 72, 73, 74, 75, 76, 77, 78, 79, 80, 81, 82, 83, 84, 85, 86, 87, 88, 89, 90, 91, 92, 93, 94, 95, 96, 97, 98, 99, 100, 101, 102, 103, 104, 105, 106, 107, 108, 109, 110, 111

SELLER DISCLOSURE STATEMENT
IMPROVED PROPERTY
(Continued)

	YES	NO	DON'T KNOW	
E. Are all plumbing fixtures, including laundry drain, connected to the sewer/on-site sewage system?	☐	☐	☐	112 / 113 / 114
If no, please explain:				115
*F. Have there been any changes or repairs to the on-site sewage system?	☐	☐	☐	116
G. Is the on-site sewage system, including the drainfield, located entirely within the boundaries of the property?	☐	☐	☐	117 / 118
If no, please explain:				119
*H. Does the on-site sewage system require monitoring and maintenance services more frequently than once a year?	☐	☐	☐	120 / 121

NOTICE: IF THIS RESIDENTIAL REAL PROPERTY DISCLOSURE IS BEING COMPLETED FOR NEW CONSTRUCTION WHICH HAS NEVER BEEN OCCUPIED, SELLER IS NOT REQUIRED TO COMPLETE THE QUESTIONS LISTED IN ITEM 4 (STRUCTURAL) OR ITEM 5 (SYSTEMS AND FIXTURES). (122 / 123 / 124)

4. **STRUCTURAL** (125)

	YES	NO	DON'T KNOW	
*A. Has the roof leaked within the last 5 years?	☐	☐	☐	126
*B. Has the basement flooded or leaked?	☐	☐	☐	127
*C. Have there been any conversions, additions or remodeling?	☐	☐	☐	128
*(1) If yes, were all building permits obtained?	☐	☐	☐	129
*(2) If yes, were all final inspections obtained?	☐	☐	☐	130
D. Do you know the age of the house?	☐	☐	☐	131
If yes, year of original construction:				132
*E. Has there been any settling, slippage, or sliding of the property or its improvements?	☐	☐	☐	133
*F. Are there any defects with the following: (If yes, please check applicable items and explain.)	☐	☐	☐	134

☐ Foundations ☐ Decks ☐ Exterior Walls (135)
☐ Chimneys ☐ Interior Walls ☐ Fire Alarms (136)
☐ Doors ☐ Windows ☐ Patio (137)
☐ Ceilings ☐ Slab Floors ☐ Driveways (138)
☐ Pools ☐ Hot Tub ☐ Sauna (139)
☐ Sidewalks ☐ Outbuildings ☐ Fireplaces (140)
☐ Garage Floors ☐ Walkways ☐ Wood Stoves (141)
☐ Siding ☐ Other _____ (142)

	YES	NO	DON'T KNOW	
*G. Was a structural pest or "whole house" inspection done?	☐	☐	☐	143
If yes, when and by whom was the inspection completed?				144 / 145
H. During your ownership, has the property had any wood destroying organism or pest infestation?	☐	☐	☐	146
I. Is the attic insulated?	☐	☐	☐	147
J. Is the basement insulated?	☐	☐	☐	148

5. **SYSTEMS AND FIXTURES** (149)

*A. If any of the following systems or fixtures are included with the transfer, are there any defects? (150)
If yes, please explain: _____ (151)

	YES	NO	DON'T KNOW	
Electrical system, including wiring, switches, outlets, and service	☐	☐	☐	152
Plumbing system, including pipes, faucets, fixtures, and toilets	☐	☐	☐	153
Hot water tank	☐	☐	☐	154
Garbage disposal	☐	☐	☐	155
Appliances	☐	☐	☐	156
Sump pump	☐	☐	☐	157
Heating and cooling systems	☐	☐	☐	158
Security system ☐ Owned ☐ Leased	☐	☐	☐	159
Other _____	☐	☐	☐	160

*B. If any of the following fixtures or property is included with the transfer, are they leased? (161)
(If yes, please attach copy of lease.) (162)

	YES	NO	DON'T KNOW	
Security System _____	☐	☐	☐	163
Tanks (type): _____	☐	☐	☐	164
Satellite dish _____	☐	☐	☐	165
Other: _____	☐	☐	☐	166

SELLER'S INITIALS: _____ Date: _____ SELLER'S INITIALS: _____ Date: _____

Form 17
Seller Disclosure Statement
Rev. 06/12
Page 4 of 5

SELLER DISCLOSURE STATEMENT
IMPROVED PROPERTY
(Continued)

	YES	NO	DON'T KNOW	
*C. Are any of the following kinds of wood burning appliances present at the property?				167
				168
(1) Woodstove?	❑	❑	❑	169
(2) Fireplace insert?	❑	❑	❑	170
(3) Pellet stove?	❑	❑	❑	171
(4) Fireplace?	❑	❑	❑	172
If yes, are all of the (1) woodstoves or (2) fireplace inserts certified by the U.S. Environmental				173
Protection Agency as clean burning appliances to improve air quality and public health?	❑	❑	❑	174
D. Is the property located within a city, county, or district or within a department of natural resources				175
fire protection zone that provides fire protection services?	❑	❑	❑	176
E. Is the property equipped with carbon monoxide alarms? (Note: Pursuant to RCW 19.27.530, Seller				177
must equip the residence with carbon monoxide alarms as required by the state building code.)	❑	❑	❑	178
F. Is the property equipped with smoke alarms?	❑	❑	❑	179

6. HOMEOWNERS' ASSOCIATION/COMMON INTERESTS

				180
A. Is there a Homeowners' Association?	❑	❑	❑	181
Name of Association and contact information for an officer, director, employee, or other authorized				182
agent, if any, who may provide the association's financial statements, minutes, bylaws, fining policy,				183
				184
and other information that is not publicly available: _____				
B. Are there regular periodic assessments?	❑	❑	❑	185
				186
$_____ per ❑ month ❑ year				187
❑ Other _____				
*C. Are there any pending special assessments?	❑	❑	❑	188
*D. Are there any shared "common areas" or any joint maintenance agreements (facilities				189
such as walls, fences, landscaping, pools, tennis courts, walkways, or other areas co-owned				190
in undivided interest with others)?	❑	❑	❑	191

7. ENVIRONMENTAL

				192
*A. Have there been any flooding, standing water, or drainage problems on the property				193
that affect the property or access to the property?	❑	❑	❑	194
*B. Does any part of the property contain fill dirt, waste, or other fill material?	❑	❑	❑	195
*C. Is there any material damage to the property from fire, wind, floods, beach movements,				196
earthquake, expansive soils, or landslides?	❑	❑	❑	197
D. Are there any shorelines, wetlands, floodplains, or critical areas on the property?	❑	❑	❑	198
*E. Are there any substances, materials, or products in or on the property that may be environmental				199
concerns, such as asbestos, formaldehyde, radon gas, lead-based paint, fuel or chemical storage				200
tanks, or contaminated soil or water?	❑	❑	❑	201
*F. Has the property been used for commercial or industrial purposes?	❑	❑	❑	202
*G. Is there any soil or groundwater contamination?	❑	❑	❑	203
*H. Are there transmission poles or other electrical utility equipment installed, maintained,				204
or buried on the property that do not provide utility service to the structures on the property?	❑	❑	❑	205
*I. Has the property been used as a legal or illegal dumping site?	❑	❑	❑	206
*J. Has the property been used as an illegal drug manufacturing site?	❑	❑	❑	207
*K. Are there any radio towers in the area that cause interference with cellular telephone reception?	❑	❑	❑	208

8. LEAD BASED PAINT (Applicable if the house was built before 1978.)

	209
A. Presence of lead-based paint and/or lead-based paint hazards (check one below):	210
❑ Known lead-based paint and/or lead-based paint hazards are present in the housing	211
(explain). _____	212
❑ Seller has no knowledge of lead-based paint and/or lead-based paint hazards in the housing.	213
B. Records and reports available to the Seller (check one below):	214
❑ Seller has provided the purchaser with all available records and reports pertaining to	215
lead-based paint and/or lead-based paint hazards in the housing (list documents below).	216
_____	217
❑ Seller has no reports or records pertaining to lead-based paint and/or lead-based paint hazards in the housing.	218

9. MANUFACTURED AND MOBILE HOMES

				219
If the property includes a manufactured or mobile home,				220
*A. Did you make any alterations to the home?	❑	❑	❑	221
If yes, please describe the alterations: _____				222
*B. Did any previous owner make any alterations to the home?	❑	❑	❑	223
*C. If alterations were made, were permits or variances for these alterations obtained?	❑	❑	❑	224

SELLER'S INITIALS: _____ Date: _____ SELLER'S INITIALS: _____ Date: _____

**SELLER DISCLOSURE STATEMENT
IMPROVED PROPERTY**
(Continued)

10. FULL DISCLOSURE BY SELLERS

	YES	NO	DON'T KNOW

225
A. Other conditions or defects: 226
   *Are there any other existing material defects affecting the property that a prospective buyer 227
   should know about? .... ☐ ☐ ☐ 228

B. Verification 229
   The foregoing answers and attached explanations (if any) are complete and correct to the best of Seller's knowledge and Seller has 230
   received a copy hereof. Seller agrees to defend, indemnify and hold real estate licensees harmless from and against any and all claims 231
   that the above information is inaccurate. Seller authorizes real estate licensees, if any, to deliver a copy of this disclosure statement to 232
   other real estate licensees and all prospective buyers of the property. 233
   Date: _____ Date: _____ 234
   Seller: _____ Seller: _____ 235

NOTICES TO THE BUYER 236

SEX OFFENDER REGISTRATION 237

INFORMATION REGARDING REGISTERED SEX OFFENDERS MAY BE OBTAINED FROM LOCAL LAW ENFORCEMENT 238
AGENCIES. THIS NOTICE IS INTENDED ONLY TO INFORM YOU OF WHERE TO OBTAIN THIS INFORMATION AND IS 239
NOT AN INDICATION OF THE PRESENCE OF REGISTERED SEX OFFENDERS. 240

PROXIMITY TO FARMING 241

THIS NOTICE IS TO INFORM YOU THAT THE REAL PROPERTY YOU ARE CONSIDERING FOR PURCHASE MAY LIE IN 242
CLOSE PROXIMITY TO A FARM. THE OPERATION OF A FARM INVOLVES USUAL AND CUSTOMARY AGRICULTURAL 243
PRACTICES, WHICH ARE PROTECTED UNDER RCW 7.48.305, THE WASHINGTON RIGHT TO FARM ACT. 244

II. BUYER'S ACKNOWLEDGEMENT 245
   Buyer hereby acknowledges that: 246
   A. Buyer has a duty to pay diligent attention to any material defects that are known to Buyer or can be known to Buyer by utilizing 247
      diligent attention and observation. 248
   B. The disclosures set forth in this statement and in any amendments to this statement are made only by the Seller and not by any real 249
      estate licensee or other party. 250
   C. Buyer acknowledges that, pursuant to RCW 64.06.050 (2), real estate licensees are not liable for inaccurate information provided by 251
      Seller, except to the extent that real estate licensees know of such inaccurate information. 252
   D. This information is for disclosure only and is not intended to be a part of the written agreement between the Buyer and Seller. 253
   E. Buyer (which term includes all persons signing the "Buyer's acceptance" portion of this disclosure statement below) has received a 254
      copy of this Disclosure Statement (including attachments, if any) bearing Seller's signature(s). 255
   F. If the house was built prior to 1978, Buyer acknowledges receipt of the pamphlet *Protect Your Family From Lead in Your Home*. 256

DISCLOSURES CONTAINED IN THIS DISCLOSURE STATEMENT ARE PROVIDED BY SELLER BASED ON SELLER'S ACTUAL 257
KNOWLEDGE OF THE PROPERTY AT THE TIME SELLER COMPLETES THIS DISCLOSURE. UNLESS BUYER AND SELLER 258
OTHERWISE AGREE IN WRITING, BUYER SHALL HAVE THREE (3) BUSINESS DAYS FROM THE DAY SELLER OR SELLER'S 259
AGENT DELIVERS THIS DISCLOSURE STATEMENT TO RESCIND THE AGREEMENT BY DELIVERING A SEPARATELY SIGNED 260
WRITTEN STATEMENT OF RESCISSION TO SELLER OR SELLER'S AGENT. YOU MAY WAIVE THE RIGHT TO RESCIND PRIOR 261
TO OR AFTER THE TIME YOU ENTER INTO A SALE AGREEMENT. 262

BUYER HEREBY ACKNOWLEDGES RECEIPT OF A COPY OF THIS DISCLOSURE STATEMENT AND ACKNOWLEDGES THAT 263
THE DISCLOSURES MADE HEREIN ARE THOSE OF THE SELLER ONLY, AND NOT OF ANY REAL ESTATE LICENSEE OR 264
OTHER PARTY. 265
DATE: _____ DATE: _____ 266
BUYER: _____ BUYER: _____ 267

BUYER'S WAIVER OF RIGHT TO REVOKE OFFER 268
Buyer has read and reviewed the Seller's responses to this Seller Disclosure Statement. Buyer approves this statement and waives Buyer's right 269
to revoke Buyer's offer based on this disclosure. 270
DATE: _____ DATE: _____ 271
BUYER: _____ BUYER: _____ 272

BUYER'S WAIVER OF RIGHT TO RECEIVE COMPLETED SELLER DISCLOSURE STATEMENT 273
Buyer has been advised of Buyer's right to receive a completed Seller Disclosure Statement. Buyer waives that right. However, if the answer to 274
any of the questions in the section entitled "Environmental" would be "yes," Buyer may not waive the receipt of the "Environmental" section of 275
the Seller Disclosure Statement. 276
DATE: _____ DATE: _____ 277
BUYER: _____ BUYER: _____ 278

If the answer is "Yes" to any asterisked (*) items, please explain below (use additional sheets if necessary). Please refer to the line number(s) of 279
the question(s). 280

_____ 281
_____ 282
_____ 283

SELLER'S INITIALS: _____ Date: _____ SELLER'S INITIALS: _____ Date: _____

properly maintained, but if it deteriorates, it may cause brain damage and organ damage in young children.

The law requires the seller or landlord of a dwelling built before 1978 to do all of the following:

- disclose the location of any lead-based paint that he is aware of in the home (in both the dwelling unit and the common areas, if applicable);
- provide a copy of any report concerning lead-based paint in the home, if it has been inspected; and
- give buyers or tenants a copy of a pamphlet on lead-based paint prepared by the U.S. Environmental Protection Agency.

In addition, buyers (but not tenants) must be offered at least a ten-day period in which to have the home tested for lead-based paint.

Specific warnings must be included in the purchase agreement or lease, along with signed statements from the parties acknowledging that the requirements of this law have been fulfilled. The signed acknowledgments must be kept for at least three years as proof of compliance.

Agent's Responsibilities. The law also imposes responsibilities on real estate agents in transactions involving pre-1978 housing. An agent is required to ensure that the seller or landlord knows his obligations under the disclosure law and fulfills those obligations. It is also the agent's responsibility to make sure that the purchase agreement or lease contains the required warnings, disclosures, and signatures.

Penalties. Sellers, landlords, or real estate agents who fail to fulfill their obligations under this law may be ordered to pay the buyer or tenant treble damages (three times the amount of any actual damages suffered by the buyer or tenant). Civil and criminal penalties may also be imposed. Although a real estate agent may be held liable for a seller or landlord's failure to provide the documents required by the law, the agent isn't responsible for information withheld by the seller or landlord.

Exemptions. Some transactions are exempt from the provisions of the lead-based paint disclosure law. This includes transactions involving zero-bedroom units (such as efficiency or studio apartments, dormitories, and room rentals); leases for less than 100 days; housing for the elderly or disabled (unless young children live there); rental housing that has been inspected by a certified inspector and found to be free of lead-based paint; and foreclosure sales.

Home Warranty Plans

Regardless of what information is disclosed in the seller disclosure statement, home buyers may choose to protect themselves against the risk of unexpected and potentially expensive repairs by purchasing a home warranty plan (also called a home protection plan). This is a short-term insurance policy, usually in effect only for the first few years of home ownership, that will reimburse the owner for the cost of repairing or replacing covered systems, components, or appliances, such as the heating or electrical system or the dishwasher. Sometimes a seller or a real estate agent offers to purchase home warranty coverage for prospective buyers to help sell the home.

📖 Chapter Summary

1. A properly executed purchase and sale agreement is a binding contract that holds the parties to the terms of their agreement until all conditions have been fulfilled and the transaction is ready to close.

2. A real estate agent may prepare a purchase and sale agreement form if the agent is representing one of the parties in the transaction. The agent is limited to filling in the blanks on standard forms that have been drafted by attorneys. No separate fee for completing the documents may be charged. The agent preparing the purchase and sale agreement will be held to the same standard of care as an attorney.

3. The parties to a purchase and sale agreement are the buyer(s) and the seller(s); all parties must have capacity to contract. Everyone with an interest in the property must sign the agreement. Signatures of both spouses should be obtained in a transaction involving married parties.

4. Every purchase and sale agreement must have an adequate description of the property, specify the total purchase price and method of payment, set a closing date and date of possession, and state by what type of deed and in what condition title will be conveyed.

5. Because a purchase and sale agreement typically contains a "time is of the essence" clause, the closing date is a material term of the contract. Closing must take place on the date stated in the agreement, unless the parties agree in writing to an extension.

6. The purchase and sale agreement will include provisions concerning the earnest money deposit, including the amount and form of the deposit, and how it will be handled while the transaction is pending. In the event that the buyer defaults, the earnest money usually serves as liquidated damages.

7. A purchase and sale agreement often has a provision that makes it contingent on whether one or more events occur. It's common for a transaction to be contingent on financing, inspections, and/or the sale of the buyer's current home. Contingency clauses must clearly state the condition to be fulfilled, notification procedures, time limits, and the rights of the parties if the conditions are not met.

8. In Washington, a real property seller is required to give the buyer a disclosure statement providing information about the property based on the seller's own knowledge. The buyer can rescind the purchase and sale agreement within three business days after receiving the statement.

🔑 Key Terms

Purchase and sale agreement—A binding contract between a buyer and a seller of real property, setting forth the terms of the sale.

Earnest money—A sum the buyer gives to the seller when making an offer to purchase, as a sign of good faith; it is applied to the purchase price if the buyer goes through with the transaction, and forfeited to the seller if the buyer defaults.

Time is of the essence clause—A contract provision that imposes a legal duty to meet all of the deadlines in the contract.

Closing—When the transaction documents are recorded, the deed is delivered to the buyer, and the sale proceeds are made available for disbursement to the seller.

Contingency clause—A contract clause which provides that unless some specified event occurs, the contract is not binding.

Bump clause—A clause that allows the seller to demand that the buyer waive the "sale of the buyer's home" contingency or rescind the contract, if the seller receives another offer.

Home warranty plan—An insurance policy that reimburses a home owner for expenses related to the failure of covered systems, components, or appliances on the property. Also called a home protection plan.

Chapter Quiz

1. In most transactions, a purchase and sale agreement form is initially filled out as a/an:

   a) option to purchase offered by a seller to a potential buyer

   b) buyer's offer to purchase, for submission to the property seller

   c) agent's preliminary proposal to a seller

   d) property owner's offer to sell on specified terms

2. Which of the following may NOT fill out a purchase and sale agreement form?

   a) An attorney at law

   b) A real estate agent representing one of the parties

   c) A real estate agent who is not a party and is not representing either party

   d) The seller

3. A purchase and sale agreement should state:

   a) only the essential terms of the sale, leaving other details to be worked out in the final contract

   b) the listing price as well as the purchase price

   c) the total purchase price, the method of payment, and the basic financing terms

   d) the seller's reasons for selling the property

4. The purchase and sale agreement states that it will not be binding unless the buyer can obtain financing. This is a:

   a) contingency clause

   b) defeasibility clause

   c) bump clause

   d) lender's clause

5. An earnest money deposit is:

   a) 10% of the purchase price, unless otherwise agreed

   b) usually treated as liquidated damages if the buyer defaults

   c) not applied to the purchase price if the transaction closes

   d) always returned if the sale falls through

6. In a purchase and sale agreement, the phrase "time is of the essence" means that the:

   a) contract provisions must be performed on or before the specified date(s)

   b) seller is in a hurry to sell the property

   c) buyer must obtain the necessary financing within 30 days

   d) closing must take place as soon as possible

7. The closing date specified in the purchase and sale agreement:

   a) is just an estimate, without real significance

   b) should allow time for all contingencies to be satisfied

   c) can be changed (if necessary) by the real estate agent without the parties' consent

   d) should be the same as the closing date set forth in the listing agreement

8. A bump clause:

   a) allows the closing to be delayed for 30 days at either party's option

   b) increases the purchase price at closing to reflect the inflation rate

   c) prevents the buyer from waiving any contingencies

   d) allows the seller to keep the property on the market after accepting the buyer's offer

9. The purchase and sale agreement includes a financing contingency. If the buyer applies to lenders but cannot obtain financing on the specified terms:

   a) the seller is required to finance the purchase

   b) the buyer is required to accept less favorable terms

   c) the buyer may terminate the transaction, and the seller will return the buyer's earnest money

   d) the transaction is terminated, and the seller is allowed to keep the earnest money

10. When a contract includes a contingency clause:
    a) the parties are required to make a good faith effort to fulfill the condition
    b) the contingency can be waived by the party for whose benefit it was included
    c) Both of the above
    d) Neither of the above

11. If the seller is going to finance the purchase:
    a) the financing section of the purchase and sale agreement can be left blank
    b) a copy of the financing documents the parties will be using should be attached to the purchase and sale agreement
    c) the real estate agent should oversee the finance arrangements
    d) the purchase and sale agreement should include a bump clause

12. Sam is purchasing a home from Hal, a married man. Hal assures Sam that title to the property is in Hal's name alone, and that Hal's wife, Rita, does not need to sign the purchase and sale agreement. Which of the following is true?
    a) Sam should insist that both Hal and Rita sign the purchase and sale agreement
    b) Sam should insist that both Hal and the listing agent sign the purchase and sale agreement
    c) Only Hal needs to sign the purchase and sale agreement
    d) If only Hal signs the purchase and sale agreement, Sam should purchase additional title insurance

13. If the seller rejects the buyer's offer and presents the buyer with a counteroffer, the agent's best course of action would be to:
    a) cross out the old terms on the purchase and sale agreement, fill in the new terms, and have the buyer initial the changes
    b) cross out the old terms on the purchase and sale agreement, fill in the new terms, and have the seller initial the changes
    c) use a counteroffer form, signed by the seller, to present the seller's counteroffer to the buyer
    d) relay the counteroffer to the buyer by phone

14. An inspection contingency clause should include all of the following, except:
    a) who is responsible for paying for the inspection
    b) the method for notifying the seller of disapproval of the inspection report
    c) the amount of the penalty the buyer must pay for rejecting the inspection report
    d) the seller's option to perform the repairs or terminate the contract

15. The brokerage fee:
    a) is often provided for in a purchase and sale agreement (as agreed to in any representation agreement entered into by the parties at an earlier date)
    b) should never be included in a purchase and sale agreement, since the amount of the commission should not be disclosed to the buyer
    c) must be set out in the purchase and sale agreement in extra large type
    d) will be forfeited completely if the parties default on the purchase and sale agreement

Answer Key

1. b) The purchase and sale agreement form is used to set forth the buyer's offer. If the seller signs the form, it becomes a binding contract.

2. c) A real estate agent is not allowed to complete a purchase and sale agreement unless she is representing the buyer or the seller (or both parties).

3. c) A purchase and sale agreement should state all of the terms of sale, including the total purchase price, the method of payment, and the terms on which the buyer will finance the purchase.

4. a) A provision that makes the purchase and sale agreement contingent on the occurrence of a certain event is a contingency clause.

5. b) If the buyer defaults on the purchase and sale agreement, the seller often retains the earnest money deposit as liquidated damages.

6. a) "Time is of the essence" means that the parties must perform by the exact dates specified; failure to meet a deadline in the agreement is a breach of contract.

7. b) The closing date should be far enough off so that all contingencies can be met. If a transaction does not close by the specified date, the contract becomes unenforceable.

8. d) A bump clause allows the seller to keep the property on the market until a contingency is satisfied or waived by the buyer. If a second buyer makes an offer, the seller can ask the first buyer to waive the contingency or terminate their agreement.

9. c) When a contingency in the purchase and sale agreement is not fulfilled, the contract terminates, and the buyer is usually entitled to have the earnest money refunded.

10. c) The parties are required to make a good faith effort to fulfill the conditions in their contract; one party can't deliberately avoid fulfilling a condition and then use that as an excuse for terminating the contract. A contingency clause can usually be waived by the party for whose benefit it was included in the contract.

11. b) It is important to attach to the purchase and sale agreement copies of any financing documents that will be used in a seller-financed transaction.

12. a) When one of the parties to a purchase and sale agreement is married, his or her spouse should always sign the agreement, even if the spouse's signature may not be necessary.

13. c) When a counteroffer is presented, it is much less confusing to use a counteroffer form than to try to change the terms on the original purchase and sale agreement.

14. c) A buyer does not have to pay a penalty for rejecting an inspection report.

15. a) A clause reaffirming the obligation to pay the brokerage fee is often included in the purchase and sale agreement.

Principles of Real Estate Financing

⌂ Chapter Overview

Financing—lending and borrowing money—is essential to the real estate industry. If financing weren't available, buyers would have to pay cash for their property, and very few people could afford to do so. Real estate agents often help their clients and customers with the financing process, so they need a thorough understanding of the subject. This chapter starts with background information about real estate cycles, how the government influences real estate finance, and the secondary market. The chapter then goes on to explain how mortgages and other financing instruments work, the foreclosure process, and the various types of mortgage loans. The process of applying for a mortgage loan is covered in Chapter 11.

The Economics of Real Estate Finance

Nearly every buyer needs to borrow money in order to purchase real estate. Whether a particular buyer will be able to obtain a loan depends in part on her personal financial circumstances, and in part on national and local economic conditions. In this section, we're going to discuss real estate cycles and the government's role in the economy, to help you understand the economic factors that affect real estate lending.

Real Estate Cycles

From a lender's point of view, a loan is an investment. A lender loans money in the expectation of a return on the investment. The borrower will repay the money borrowed, plus interest; the interest is the lender's return.

As a general rule, investors demand a higher return on risky investments than they do on comparatively safe ones. That holds true for loan transactions: the greater the risk that the borrower won't repay the loan, the higher the interest rate charged. But the interest rate a lender charges on a particular loan also depends on market forces and real estate cycles.

The real estate market is cyclical: it goes through active periods followed by slumps. These periodic shifts in the level of activity in the real estate market are called **real estate cycles**. Residential real estate cycles can be dramatic or moderate, and they can be local or regional. At any given time and place, there may be a buyer's market, where few people are buying and homes sit on the market for a long time, or there may be a seller's market, where many people are buying and homes sell rapidly.

These cycles obey the **law of supply and demand**. When demand for a product exceeds the supply (a seller's market), the price charged for the product tends to rise, and the price increase stimulates more production. As production increases, more of the demand is satisfied, until eventually the supply outstrips demand and a buyer's market is created. At that point, prices fall and production tapers off until demand catches up with supply, and the cycle begins again.

Real estate cycles are caused in part by changes in the supply of and demand for mortgage loan funds. The supply of mortgage funds depends on how much money investors have available and choose to invest in real estate loans. The demand for mortgage funds depends on how many people want to purchase real estate and can afford to borrow enough money to do so.

Interest rates represent the price of mortgage funds. They affect supply and demand, and they also fluctuate in response to changes in supply and demand. Interest is sometimes called "the cost of money."

In a healthy economy, supply and demand are more or less in balance. This is the ideal; in reality, the forces affecting supply and demand are constantly changing, and so is the balance between them. But as long as supply and demand are reasonably close, the economy functions well. When supply far exceeds demand, or vice versa, the economy suffers.

Real estate cycles can be moderated, though not eliminated, by factors that either help keep interest rates under control or directly affect the supply of mortgage funds. Federal economic policy plays a key role in moderating real estate cycles.

Interest Rates and Federal Policy

Economic stability is directly tied to the supply of and demand for money. If money is plentiful and can be borrowed cheaply (that is, interest rates are low), increased economic activity is often the result. On the other hand, if funds are scarce or expensive to borrow, an economic slowdown will result.

Thus, manipulation of the availability and cost of money can help achieve economic balance. The federal government influences real estate finance, as well as the rest of the U.S. economy, through its **fiscal policy** and its **monetary policy**.

Fiscal Policy. Fiscal policy refers to the way in which the federal government manages its money. Congress and the president determine fiscal policy through tax legislation and the federal budget. The U.S. Treasury implements fiscal policy by managing tax revenues, expenditures, and the national debt.

When the federal government spends more money than it takes in, a shortfall called the **federal deficit** results. It is the Treasury's responsibility to borrow enough money to cover the deficit. It does this by issuing interest-bearing securities that are backed by the U.S. government and purchased by private investors. These securities include Treasury bills, notes, and bonds. Investors often prefer to invest in these government securities instead of other investments because they are comparatively low-risk.

When the government borrows money, it competes with private industry for available investment funds. Economists and politicians debate what impact this has on the economy. According to some, by draining the number of dollars in circulation, heavy government borrowing may lead to an economic slowdown. The greater the federal deficit, the more money the government has to borrow, and the greater the effect on the economy. Other economists claim that the federal deficit has little effect on interest rates.

The government's taxation policies also affect the supply of and demand for money. As with the deficit, the effect of taxation on the economy is controversial. Basically, when taxes are low, taxpayers have more money to lend and invest. When taxes are high, taxpayers not only have less money to lend or invest, they also may be more likely to invest what money they do have in tax-exempt securities instead of taxable investments. Since real estate and real estate mortgages are taxable investments, this may have a significant impact on the real estate finance industry.

Monetary Policy. Monetary policy refers to the direct control the federal government exerts over the money supply and interest rates. The main goal of monetary policy is to keep the U.S. economy healthy.

Monetary policy is determined by the Federal Reserve, commonly called "the Fed." The Federal Reserve System, established in 1913, is the nation's central banking system. It is governed by the Federal Reserve Board and the board's chairman. It has 12 districts nationwide, with a Federal Reserve Bank in each district. Thousands of commercial banks across the country are members of the Federal Reserve.

The Fed is responsible for regulating commercial banks and providing financial services to member banks. But setting and implementing the government's monetary policy is perhaps the Fed's most important function.

The major objectives of monetary policy are high employment, economic growth, price stability, interest rate stability, and stability in financial and foreign exchange markets. Although these goals are interrelated, we are most concerned with the Federal Reserve policies that affect the availability and cost of borrowed money (interest rates), since those have the most direct impact on the real estate industry.

The Fed uses three tools to implement its monetary policy and influence the economy:

- key interest rates,
- reserve requirements, and
- open market operations.

Key Interest Rates. The Fed has control over two interest rates, the federal funds rate and the discount rate. These are the interest rates charged when a bank borrows money, either from another bank or from a Federal Reserve Bank. When the Fed works to raise or lower the interest rates that its member banks have to pay, the banks will typically raise or lower the interest rates they charge their customers. Lower interest rates tend to stimulate the economy, and higher rates tend to slow it down. (The Fed may increase rates if it decides that a slower pace is desirable to keep price inflation in check.)

Reserve Requirements. Commercial banks are required to maintain a certain percentage of their customers' funds on deposit at the Federal Reserve Bank. These reserve requirements help prevent financial panics (a "run on the bank") by assuring depositors that their funds are safe and accessible; the bank will always have enough money available to meet unusual customer demand.

Reserve requirements also give the Fed some control over the growth of credit. By increasing reserve requirements, the Fed can reduce the amount of money banks have available to lend. On the other hand, a reduction in reserve requirements frees more money for investment or lending. So an increase in reserve requirements tends to decrease available loan funds and increase interest rates. Conversely, a decrease in reserve requirements tends to increase available loan funds and decrease interest rates.

Open Market Operations. The Fed also buys and sells government securities; these transactions are called open market operations. They are the Fed's chief method of controlling the money supply, and, indirectly, controlling inflation and interest rates. Only money in circulation is considered part of the money supply, so actions by the Fed that put money into circulation increase the money supply, and actions that take money out of circulation decrease it.

When the Fed buys government securities from an investor, it increases the money supply, because the money that the Fed uses to pay for the securities goes into circulation. When the Fed sells government securities to an investor, the money that the buyer uses to pay for the securities is taken out of circulation, decreasing the money supply. Interest rates tend to fall with increases in the money supply, and to rise with decreases in the money supply.

Other Agencies that Affect Finance. Aside from the Federal Reserve, there are a number of other federal agencies and programs that have an impact on real estate finance.

Federal Home Loan Bank System. The Federal Home Loan Bank System (FHLB) is made up of twelve regional, privately owned wholesale banks. The banks loan funds to FHLB members—local community lenders—and accept their mortgages and other loans as collateral. The FHLB, which is headed by the Federal Housing Finance Agency, is active in promoting affordable housing.

Federal Deposit Insurance Corporation. The FDIC was created in 1933 to insure bank deposits against bank insolvency. If a bank or other lending institution fails, the FDIC will step in to protect the institution's customers against the loss of their deposited funds, up to specified limits.

HUD. The Department of Housing and Urban Development (HUD) is a federal cabinet-level department. Among many other things, HUD's responsibilities include urban renewal projects, public housing, FHA-insured loan programs, and enforcement of the federal Fair Housing Act (see Chapter 15). Ginnie Mae (discussed later in this chapter) and the Federal Housing Administration (discussed in Chapter 11) are both part of HUD.

Rural Housing Service. The Rural Housing Service is an agency within the Department of Agriculture. To help people living in rural areas build, purchase, or improve their homes, the Rural Housing Service makes loans and grants; it also guarantees loans made by lending institutions. In addition, it finances the construction of affordable housing in rural areas.

Real Estate Finance Markets

There are two "markets" that supply the funds available for real estate loans: the primary market and the secondary market. In addition to using monetary policy to control the money supply and interest rates, another way in which the federal government has helped moderate the severity and duration of real estate cycles is by establishing a strong, nationwide secondary market. The secondary market limits the adverse effects of local economic circumstances on real estate lending. We'll look first at the primary market, then at the secondary market.

Primary Market

The **primary market** is the market in which mortgage lenders make loans to home buyers. When buyers apply for a loan to finance their purchase, they're seeking a loan in the primary market.

Originally, the primary market was entirely local. It was made up of the various lending institutions in a community—the local banks and savings and loan associations. (Today the primary market is considerably more complicated, since there are interstate lenders, online lenders, nationwide mortgage companies, and so on.) The traditional source of funds for the primary market was the savings of individuals and businesses in the local area. A bank or savings and loan would use the savings deposits of members of the local community to make mortgage loans to members of that same community.

The local economy has a significant effect on the amount of deposited funds available to a lender, and on the local demand for them. When employment is high, consumers are more likely to borrow money for cars, vacations, or homes. Businesses expand and borrow to finance their growth. At the same time, fewer people are saving. This decrease in deposits means that less local money is available for lending, making it difficult to meet the increased demand for loans. On the other hand, when an area is in an economic slump, consumers are more inclined to save than to borrow. Businesses suspend plans for growth. The result is a drop in the demand for money, and the local lending institutions' deposits grow.

From a lender's point of view, either too little or too much money on deposit is cause for concern. In the first case, with little money to lend, a lender's primary source of income is affected. In the second case, the lender is paying interest to its depositors, and if it is unable to reinvest the deposited funds quickly, it will lose money.

The solution to these problems has been for lenders to look beyond their local area. When local savings deposits are low, a lender needs to get funds from other parts of the country to lend locally. When local demand for loans is low, a lender needs to send funds to other parts of the country where demand is higher. This is where the secondary market comes in. The secondary market makes it easy for lenders to transfer funds around the country.

Secondary Market

The **secondary market** is a national market. In the secondary market, private investors, government agencies, and government-sponsored enterprises buy and sell mortgages secured by real estate in all parts of the United States.

Buying and Selling Loans. Mortgage loans can be bought and sold just like other investments—stocks or bonds, for example. The value of a loan is influenced by the rate of return on the loan compared to the market rate of return, as well as the degree of risk associated with the loan (the likelihood of default). Investors generally buy mortgage loans at a discount, for less than their face value.

The availability of funds in the primary market (a local lender's ability to lend money to prospective borrowers) now depends a great deal on the existence of the national secondary market. As explained above, a particular lender may have either too much or too little money to lend, depending on conditions in the local economy. It's the secondary market that provides balance by transferring funds from areas where there is an excess to areas where there is a shortage. When local demand for funds is high, lenders can take loans they've already made, sell them on the secondary market, and use the proceeds of those sales to make more loans. When local demand for loan funds is low, lenders can use their excess funds to purchase loans on the secondary market.

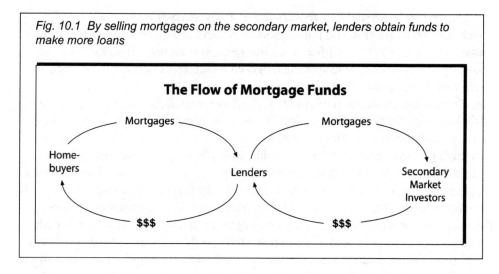

Fig. 10.1 By selling mortgages on the secondary market, lenders obtain funds to make more loans

The secondary market has a stabilizing effect on local mortgage markets. Lenders are willing to commit themselves to long-term real estate loans even when local funds are scarce, because they can raise more funds by liquidating their loans on the secondary market.

Secondary Market Entities. The federal government has played a central role in developing the secondary market for mortgage loans. It's done this by establishing three secondary market entities: Fannie Mae, Freddie Mac, and Ginnie Mae. We'll describe each of these entities shortly, after a general description of what they do.

A secondary market entity buys large numbers of mortgage loans from primary market lenders, and then issues securities using the loans as collateral ("securitizes" the loans). The entity sells these **mortgage-backed securities** to private investors. As the underlying loans are repaid by the borrowers, the secondary market entity passes the payments through to the investors, providing a return on their investment. The securities are guaranteed by the secondary market entity, so the investors will receive their payments from the entity even if borrowers default on some of the underlying loans.

Of course, the secondary market entities don't want to buy loans that carry a high risk of default. To prevent that, the entities have established their own **underwriting standards**. Underwriting standards are the criteria used to evaluate a loan applicant and the property offered as security, to determine if the loan would be a good investment or would involve too much risk. Lenders may apply their own underwriting standards when they make loans, but they generally won't be able to sell the loans to a secondary market entity unless the loans conform to the entity's underwriting standards. Because lenders generally want to have the option of selling their loans on the secondary market, the majority of home mortgage loans in the U.S. are now made in accordance with the entities' standards. (Underwriting standards are discussed in more detail in Chapter 11.)

Fannie Mae. The most prominent of the secondary market entities is the Federal National Mortgage Association (FNMA), often referred to as "Fannie Mae." Fannie Mae started out as a federal agency in 1938. Its original purpose was to provide a secondary market for FHA-insured loans.

Fannie Mae was eventually reorganized as a private corporation, but it is still chartered by the government. It is sometimes referred to as a **government-sponsored enterprise,** or GSE. Fannie Mae now purchases conventional, FHA, and VA loans to use as the collateral for its mortgage-backed securities. (These different types of loans are discussed in Chapter 11.)

Freddie Mac. Congress created the Federal Home Loan Mortgage Corporation (FHLMC), nicknamed "Freddie Mac," in 1970. Its original purpose was to assist savings and loan associations (which had been hit particularly hard by a recession) by buying their conventional loans. Freddie Mac is now authorized to buy conventional, FHA, and VA loans from any type of lender. Like Fannie Mae, Freddie Mac is a government-sponsored enterprise, chartered by the federal government.

Ginnie Mae. The Government National Mortgage Association (GNMA), nicknamed "Ginnie Mae," is one of the federal agencies that make up HUD. Ginnie Mae guarantees securities backed by loans made through the FHA and VA loan programs. It also provides assistance to urban renewal and housing programs. Note that unlike the other secondary market entities, Ginnie Mae is a government agency, not a private corporation.

Current Status of Secondary Market Entities. Because of severe financial problems brought on by the recession that began in 2007, the federal government placed both Fannie Mae and Freddie Mac into conservatorship toward the end of 2008. This was essentially a government takeover of both entities, and it will continue until their solvency is restored.

As part of the takeover, Congress also created a new government regulator for the two entities, the Federal Housing Financing Agency (FHFA). Prior to that, Fannie Mae and Freddie Mac had been supervised by HUD; now HUD has authority over Ginnie Mae only.

Real Estate Finance Documents

Now let's turn to the legal aspects of real estate financing. Once a buyer has found a lender willing to finance his purchase on acceptable terms, the buyer is required to sign the finance documents. The legal documents used in conjunction with most real estate loans are a promissory note and a security instrument, which is either a mortgage or a deed of trust.

We'll look first at promissory notes, then at security instruments and foreclosure procedures, and then at the land contract, a document used in some seller-financed transactions.

Promissory Notes

A **promissory note** is a written promise to repay a debt. One person loans another money, and the other signs a promissory note, promising to repay the loan (plus interest, in most cases). The borrower who signs the note is called the **maker**, and the lender is called the **payee**.

Basic Provisions. A promissory note states the loan amount (the **principal**), the amount of the payments, when and how the payments are to be made, and the matu-

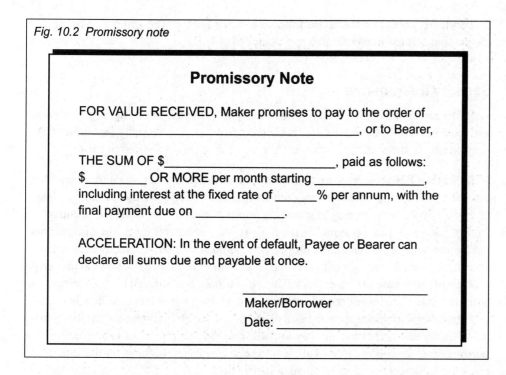

Fig. 10.2 Promissory note

Promissory Note

FOR VALUE RECEIVED, Maker promises to pay to the order of
_____, or to Bearer,

THE SUM OF $_____, paid as follows:
$_____ OR MORE per month starting _____,
including interest at the fixed rate of _____% per annum, with the
final payment due on _____.

ACCELERATION: In the event of default, Payee or Bearer can
declare all sums due and payable at once.

_____
Maker/Borrower
Date: _____

rity date—when the loan is to be repaid in full. The note also states the interest rate, and whether it is fixed or variable. (In some situations, the state usury law may prohibit the interest rate charged from exceeding a specified maximum.)

A promissory note used in a real estate transaction does not need to contain a legal description of the property, because the note concerns only the debt, not the property. The legal description is instead included in the security instrument.

The note usually explains the consequences of a failure to repay the loan as agreed. Real estate lenders often protect themselves with late charges, acceleration clauses, and similar provisions; these will be discussed later in this chapter.

Types of Notes. There are various types of promissory notes, classified according to the way the principal and interest is paid off. With a **straight note** (also called a **term note**), the periodic payments are interest only, and the full amount of the principal is due in a lump sum (called a **balloon payment**) when the loan term ends. With an **installment note**, the periodic payments include part of the principal as well as interest. If the installment note is **fully amortized**, the periodic payments are enough to pay off the entire loan, both principal and interest, by the end of the term. (Amortization is discussed in Chapter 11.)

Whether the payments are interest-only or amortized, the interest paid on a real estate loan is virtually always **simple interest**. This means it is computed annually on the remaining principal balance.

Negotiable Instrument. A promissory note is usually a **negotiable instrument**, which means that the payee (the lender) has the option of assigning the debt to someone else by endorsing the note. A note is endorsed to transfer the right to payment to another party in the same way that a check is endorsed. A check is another example of a negotiable instrument.

The payee transferring the note may state that the endorsement is "without recourse." This means that the issue of future payments is strictly between the maker (the borrower) and the purchaser of the note; the original payee will not be liable to the purchaser if the maker fails to pay as agreed.

Security Instruments

When someone borrows money to buy real estate, in addition to signing a promissory note in favor of the lender, she is also required to sign a **security instrument**. As we said earlier, the security instrument is either a mortgage or a deed of trust.

Relationship Between Note and Security Instrument. It's important to understand the relationship between the promissory note and the security instrument. The promissory note is the borrower's binding promise to repay the loan. The security instrument is a contract that makes the real property collateral for the loan; it secures the loan by creating a lien on the property. If the borrower doesn't repay the loan as agreed, the security instrument gives the lender the right to foreclose on the property.

A promissory note can be enforced even if it is not accompanied by a security instrument. If the borrower does not repay as agreed, then the lender can file a lawsuit and obtain a judgment against the defaulting borrower. But without a security instrument, the lender might have no way of collecting the judgment. For example, the borrower may have already sold all of his property, leaving nothing for the lender (now the judgment creditor) to obtain a lien against.

Title Theory vs. Lien Theory. To understand how security instruments work, it's useful to know how they developed. Historically, to protect the lender against default, a real estate borrower was required to transfer title to the property to the lender for the term of the loan. The borrower remained in possession of the property and had the full use of it, but the lender held title until the loan was paid off. If it wasn't paid off as agreed, the lender could take possession of the property.

This arrangement—in which title to property is given as collateral, but the borrower retains possession—is called **hypothecation**. When title is transferred only as collateral, unaccompanied by possessory rights, it is called **legal title**, bare title, or naked title. The property rights the borrower retains (without legal title) are referred to as equitable rights or **equitable title**.

Today, a handful of states (called "title theory" states) still technically regard the execution of a mortgage or a deed of trust as a transfer of legal title to the lender or trustee. However, most states (including Washington) now follow "lien theory." In these states, a mortgage or a deed of trust only creates a lien against the property; it doesn't transfer title. The borrower retains full title to the property throughout the term of the loan, and the lender simply has the right to foreclose on the lien if the borrower defaults.

Note that while the license exam might include a question about title theory vs. lien theory, the distinction has lost practical importance. Under either theory, the borrower will lose the property if the loan isn't repaid.

Fig. 10.3 Purpose of a security instrument

Security Instrument
Mortgage or Deed of Trust

- Makes the borrower's property collateral for the loan
- Gives the lender the power to foreclose if the debt is not repaid

Mortgage vs. Deed of Trust. Now let's consider the two types of real property security instruments, mortgages and deeds of trust. Both are contracts in which a property owner gives someone else a security interest in the property, usually as collateral for a loan. The most important difference between a mortgage and a deed of trust concerns the procedures for foreclosure if the borrower defaults. We will discuss the foreclosure process later in this chapter.

There are two parties to a mortgage: the **mortgagor** and the **mortgagee**. The mortgagor is the property owner and borrower. The mortgagee is the lender.

A deed of trust (sometimes called a trust deed) has three parties: the **trustor** or **grantor** (the borrower), the **beneficiary** (the lender), and the **trustee**. The trustee is a neutral third party who will handle the foreclosure process, if that proves necessary.

Foreclosure can be considerably easier with a deed of trust than with a mortgage, which makes deeds of trust popular with lenders. In Washington and a number of other states, deeds of trust are now much more widely used than mortgages.

The terminology used in a deed of trust has its roots in title theory. The document is called a "deed," and it purports to convey legal title to the trustee. The trustee holds the deed "in trust" pending repayment of the debt. When the loan has been repaid, the trustee "reconveys" title to the trustor. In spite of this language, in a lien theory state like Washington a deed of trust (like a mortgage) only creates a lien against the property.

Note that the terms "mortgage" and "mortgage loan" are often used to refer to any type of loan secured by real property, whether the security instrument actually used in the transaction is a mortgage or a deed of trust.

Recording. Whether it's a mortgage or a deed of trust, the lender should always have the security instrument recorded immediately after the loan is made. The security instrument does not have to be recorded to create a valid lien on the property, but without recording the public would not have constructive notice of the lien. Other parties who acquired an interest in the property without notice of the lender's security interest would not be subject to it, and subsequent liens would have priority over the lender's.

Provisions in Finance Documents

There is no standard mortgage or deed of trust form, but any security instrument must contain certain provisions and should contain certain others. Many of the following provisions will be found in nearly every mortgage or deed of trust; some of them may also appear in the promissory note. In a few cases (noted below), there is a distinction between the type of provision found in a mortgage and the type found in a deed of trust.

Mortgaging or Granting Clause. Every security instrument is required to include a statement expressing what the instrument is designed to do, indicating that the property is being promised as security for the loan. This is sometimes called the mortgaging clause or (in a deed of trust) the granting clause. The clause may include the words "grant, bargain, sell, and convey," much like a deed, even if the transaction takes place in a lien theory state, where no actual transfer of title occurs.

Property Description. Like a deed or any other document that transfers an interest in real estate, the security instrument must contain a complete and unambiguous description of the collateral property.

Taxes and Insurance. Security instruments invariably require the borrower to pay general real estate taxes, special assessments, and hazard insurance premiums when due. If the borrower were to allow the taxes to become delinquent or the insurance to lapse, the value of the lender's security interest could be severely diminished—by tax lien foreclosure or by a fire, for example.

Acceleration Clause. An **acceleration clause** states that if the borrower defaults, the lender has the option of declaring the entire loan balance (all the principal still owed) due and payable immediately. Sometimes this is referred to as "calling the note." If the borrower fails to pay the balance as demanded, the lender can sue to enforce the promissory note or foreclose on the lien.

An acceleration clause is likely to appear in both the promissory note and in the security instrument. Acceleration can be triggered by failure to make loan payments as agreed in the note, or by breach of a provision in the security instrument, such as failure to keep the property insured.

Alienation Clause. An **alienation clause** is also called a **due-on-sale clause**. This provision gives the lender the right to accelerate the loan—demanding immediate payment of the entire loan balance, as described above—if the borrower sells the property or otherwise alienates an interest in it. (Alienation refers to any transfer of an interest in real estate. See Chapter 3.) An alienation clause does not prohibit the sale of the property, but it allows the lender to force the borrower to pay off the loan if the property is sold without the lender's approval.

Whether or not there's an alienation clause in the security instrument, a sale of the property doesn't extinguish the lender's lien. If the loan isn't paid off at closing, the buyer will take title subject to the lien. The buyer may also arrange to assume the lien.

In an **assumption**, the borrower sells the security property to a buyer who agrees to take legal responsibility for the loan and pay it off according to its terms. The buyer becomes primarily liable to the lender for repayment of the loan, but the seller (original borrower) retains secondary liability in case the buyer defaults.

By contrast, when a buyer simply takes title **subject to** an existing mortgage or deed of trust (without assuming it), the original borrower remains fully liable for the debt. The buyer is not personally liable to the lender, although in case of default the lender can still foreclose.

Even though the sale of the property doesn't extinguish the mortgage or deed of trust lien, lenders prefer to have the opportunity to approve or reject a prospective buyer. Thus, most mortgages and deeds of trust include an alienation clause. When a lender evaluates a buyer and concludes that she is creditworthy, the lender may agree to an assumption of the loan. The lender will usually charge an assumption fee, and may also raise the interest rate on the loan. In most cases, the lender will release the original borrower from any further liability. (When the original borrower is released from liability, it's technically a novation—see Chapter 6—but it's still usually called an assumption.)

A buyer assuming a loan should ask the lender to provide a **certificate of reduction**, which states the principal balance as of the assumption date.

Late Payment Penalty. If the lender wants to impose penalties for late payments, the charges must be clearly defined in the finance documents. Late payment charges are not considered interest on the loan and so are not deductible on income tax statements. For most federally insured or high-cost loans, the law limits late penalties to 4% of the overdue amount. With high-cost mortgages, the payment must be at least 15 days late.

Prepayment Penalty. Some lenders do not impose any restrictions on prepayment. This is usually addressed in the promissory note; for example, a note might call for a payment of "$500.00 or more." The words "or more" indicate that prepayment is allowed.

In other notes, there is a provision that allows prepayment of a certain percentage of the principal each year, but imposes a penalty if the borrower prepays more than that percentage. For example, a note might state, "The borrower may prepay up to 15% of the original loan amount during any 12-month period without penalty. If the borrower prepays more than 15%, a prepayment fee equal to six months' interest on the excess will be charged."

Federal law prohibits charging prepayment penalties for certain loans after the first three to five years of the loan term. Federal law also limits the amount of the penalty. Washington law limits prepayment penalties too, but only for adjustable-rate mortgages.

Many mortgages don't have prepayment penalty provisions, although they aren't uncommon in subprime loans. A mortgage loan without a prepayment penalty is sometimes referred to as an **open mortgage**.

Subordination Clause. Occasionally a security instrument includes a **subordination clause**, which states that the instrument will have lower lien priority than another mortgage or deed of trust to be executed in the future. The clause makes it possible for a later security instrument to have a higher priority position—usually first lien position—even though this earlier security instrument was executed and recorded first.

Subordination clauses are common in mortgages and deeds of trust that secure purchase loans for unimproved land, when the borrower is planning to get a construction loan later on. The construction lender will demand first lien position for its loan because of the risk of loss associated with uncompleted work. Lien priority is ordinarily determined by recording date ("first in time is first in right"), but the subordination clause in the earlier land loan allows the later construction loan to have first lien position.

Defeasance Clause. A **defeasance clause** states that the borrower will regain title and the security instrument will be canceled when the debt has been paid.

When a debt secured by a mortgage has been paid in full, a document called a **satisfaction of mortgage** (or a "satisfaction piece") is used to release the mortgage lien. The lender must deliver the satisfaction of mortgage to the borrower after the final loan payment has been made. The mortgage will be a cloud on the borrower's title until he has the satisfaction recorded.

When a debt secured by a deed of trust has been paid in full, the lien is removed by means of a **deed of reconveyance**, also called a reconveyance deed. Like a satisfaction of mortgage, the deed of reconveyance should be recorded to clear the title. Either a satisfaction of mortgage or a deed of reconveyance may be referred to as a **lien release**.

Foreclosure Procedures

If the borrower doesn't repay a secured loan as agreed, the lender may foreclose on the property and collect the debt from the proceeds of a forced sale. Establishing the lender's right to foreclose is the basic purpose of a security instrument. There are two main forms of foreclosure: judicial and nonjudicial. As a general rule, mortgages are foreclosed judicially, and deeds of trust are foreclosed nonjudicially.

Judicial Foreclosure. As the term suggests, a judicial foreclosure is carried out through the court system. Upon default, the lender files a lawsuit against the borrower in a court in the county where the collateral property is located. Any **junior lienholders** (those who have liens with lower priority than the mortgage) are notified of the foreclosure action, so that they can take steps to protect their interests. (A junior lienholder may be adversely affected by foreclosure of a senior lien if the sale proceeds aren't sufficient to pay off all of the liens against the property.)

When the complaint is heard in court, in the absence of unusual circumstances the judge will issue a **decree of foreclosure**, ordering the property to be sold to satisfy the debt. The sale takes the form of an auction, and since it is usually the county sheriff's office that conducts the auction, it is referred to as a **sheriff's sale**. The property is sold to the highest bidder, who is given a **certificate of sale**.

Between the time the lawsuit is filed and the actual sale of the property, the borrower is entitled to redeem the property by paying off the mortgage debt in full, plus any costs incurred. This is referred to as the **equitable redemption** period. After the sale, the borrower is given an additional period to redeem the property, which is called the **statutory redemption** period. In Washington, the statutory redemption period is one year, unless the lender has waived her rights to a deficiency judgment. In that case, the statutory redemption period is eight months. A **deficiency judgment** is a judgment against the borrower for the difference between the debt and the proceeds of the sheriff's sale, if the proceeds weren't sufficient to pay off the debt in full.

In some cases, a lender isn't entitled to a deficiency judgment even though the foreclosure sale proceeds didn't completely pay off the debt. When a deficiency judgment isn't allowed, the mortgage is referred to as a **non-recourse mortgage**.

During the statutory redemption period, the holder of the certificate of sale does not have title to the property. If the borrower doesn't redeem the property, a **sheriff's deed** is provided to the holder of the certificate of sale when the redemption period expires. At that point, the borrower has no further claim to the property.

The redemption period makes bidding at a judicial foreclosure sale unappealing to many investors; they don't want to wait so long to gain title to the property. For this reason, there are often no outside bidders at a judicial foreclosure sale, and the lender acquires the property by bidding the amount the borrower owes.

When there are outside bidders at the auction, if the proceeds from the sale exceed the amount necessary to satisfy all valid liens against the property, the surplus belongs to the foreclosed owner (the borrower).

Nonjudicial Foreclosure. Every deed of trust has a **power of sale clause**. This is a provision that authorizes the trustee to sell the property if the trustor defaults, through a process known as nonjudicial foreclosure. Without having to obtain a decree of foreclosure from a court, the trustee can conduct an auction called a **trustee's sale** and use the sale proceeds to pay off the debt owed to the beneficiary. As with a sheriff's

Fig. 10.4 Comparison of mortgages and deeds of trust

Security Instruments	
Mortgage	**Deed of Trust**
• Mortgagor and mortgagee • Judicial foreclosure • Equitable redemption before decree of foreclosure • Statutory redemption after sheriff's sale • Deficiency judgment allowed (subject to limitations)	• Trustor, beneficiary, and trustee • Nonjudicial foreclosure • Reinstatement before trustee's sale • No post-sale redemption • No deficiency judgment

sale, if the trustee's sale results in a surplus, the excess amount belongs to the foreclosed owner.

Nonjudicial foreclosure must be conducted in accordance with procedures prescribed by statute. These procedures are designed to give the borrower an opportunity to **cure** the default and **reinstate** the loan. First, the trustee must give a **notice of default** to the borrower. A month after the notice of default, the trustee issues a **notice of sale** to the borrower and also records a notice of sale in the county where the property is located. The notice of sale must also be sent to junior lienholders and to anyone who recorded a request for notice.

Until shortly before the sale, if the borrower pays the lender the delinquent amount plus late charges and costs incurred, the default is cured. The foreclosure is terminated and the loan is reinstated. This is very different from the right of equitable redemption in a judicial foreclosure, where the borrower has to pay off the entire debt (not just the delinquent amount) in order to prevent foreclosure.

Many lenders prefer a deed of trust to a mortgage because it enables them to bypass court proceedings, which are often slow. Also, the trustee's sale is final; there is no statutory redemption period afterward. The successful bidder at a trustee's sale is given a **trustee's deed**. The disadvantage of a deed of trust from the lender's point of view is that after nonjudicial foreclosure there is no right to a deficiency judgment. If the proceeds of the trustee's sale are insufficient to satisfy the debt, the lender takes a loss; the lender is not allowed to sue the borrower to make up the deficiency.

Alternatives to Foreclosure

There are three alternatives to foreclosure for a defaulting homeowner: loan workouts, deeds in lieu of foreclosure, and short sales. A lender might agree to one of these alternatives to save time, money, and aggravation.

Loan Workouts. A loan workout from the lender can sometimes be the simplest way to avoid a foreclosure. Some workouts involve a repayment plan—an adjustment in the repayment schedule, often referred to as a forbearance. The borrower gets extra time to make up a missed payment or is allowed to skip a few payments. (The skipped payments are added on to the repayment period.) If a forbearance wouldn't solve the problem (for instance, if the payment amount is about to increase dramatically, far beyond the borrower's means), the lender may agree to modify the terms of the loan. A **loan modification** might involve changing an ARM to a fixed-rate mortgage (to prevent it from resetting to a higher rate), reducing the interest rate, or reducing the amount of principal owed.

Deed in Lieu of Foreclosure. A defaulting borrower who can't negotiate a loan workout might offer to give the lender a deed in lieu of foreclosure, sometimes called a **deed in lieu**. The deed in lieu transfers title from the borrower to the lender; this satisfies the debt and stops foreclosure proceedings. The borrower will want to make sure that the lender doesn't have the right to sue for a deficiency following the sale.

The lender takes title subject to any other liens that encumber the property. Thus, before accepting a deed in lieu, the lender will determine what other liens have attached to the property since the original loan was made.

Short Sales. Another alternative to foreclosure is a short sale. In a short sale, the owner sells the house for whatever it will bring (something "short" of the amount owed because the home's market value has decreased). The lender receives the sale proceeds and, in return, releases the borrower from the debt. As when arranging a deed in lieu, the borrower will want to avoid the possibility of a deficiency judgment. State law requires the lender to send a notice informing the borrower whether it waives or reserves the right to collect a deficiency judgment.

The existence of secondary liens won't necessarily prevent a lender from approving a short sale. This is because—unlike with a deed in lieu—the lender isn't taking responsibility for the property or its liens. However, the presence of multiple liens will complicate matters, since all of the lienholders must consent to the sale. The junior lienholders (or creditors) aren't likely to get much, if anything, from a short sale and may not be willing to approve the transaction. In this situation, a foreclosure may be inevitable.

Land Contracts

Most real estate buyers finance their purchases with a loan from an institutional lender. But some transactions are financed by the seller; the seller extends credit to the buyer, accepting a downpayment and arranging to be paid over time, instead of requiring full payment at closing. In certain cases a seller offers more favorable terms than institutional lenders are offering (such as an exceptionally low interest rate), in order to attract a wider range of potential buyers and obtain a higher price for the property.

In a seller-financed transaction, the seller may ask the buyer to execute a mortgage or a deed of trust, just like an institutional lender. Sellers also have the option of using a third type of security instrument: the **land contract**, also called a contract for deed, installment sales contract, real estate contract, or contract of sale.

The parties to a land contract are the **vendor** (the seller) and the **vendee** (the buyer). The vendee agrees to pay the purchase price (plus interest) in installments over a specified number of years. The vendee takes possession of the property right away, but the vendor retains legal title until the full price has been paid. In the meantime, the vendee has equitable title to the property. When the contract is finally paid off, the vendor delivers the deed to the vendee.

The vendee should have the contract recorded promptly after signing it, to protect his equitable interest. While the contract is being paid off, the vendee is usually required to pay the property taxes and keep the property insured. The vendor may use the legal title to the property for any purpose that does not impair the vendee's interest. The vendor is not allowed to encumber the property in any way that would prevent the transfer of clear title to the vendee as agreed.

Forfeiture. If a vendee defaults on a land contract, the vendor can foreclose judicially. Alternatively, the vendor may choose to declare a **forfeiture**, which is a remedy available only in connection with a land contract. In a forfeiture, the vendor terminates the contract without having to go to court, and without having to refund any of the payments the vendee has made. Washington law allows this only if there is a forfeiture clause in the contract (nearly all land contracts have one) and the contract is recorded. The law also includes provisions that give a vendee with substantial equity in the property some protection against forfeiture.

Types of Mortgage Loans

You will often hear "mortgage" or "deed of trust" coupled with an adjective that serves to describe the particular function of the security instrument or the circumstances in which it is used. For example, a "construction mortgage" is a mortgage used to secure a construction loan; a "blanket mortgage" is one that secures a loan with two or more parcels of property as collateral. Below are explanations of some of the most common of these terms. For the most part, we will use the term "mortgage" here, rather than the more cumbersome phrase "mortgage or deed of trust." In each case, however, a deed of trust could be (and today often would be) used instead of a mortgage.

First Mortgage. A first mortgage is simply the security instrument that holds first lien position; it has the highest lien priority of any security instrument. A second mortgage is one that holds second lien position, and so on.

Senior and Junior Mortgages. Any mortgage that has a higher lien position than another is called a senior mortgage in relation to that other one, which is called a junior mortgage. A first mortgage is senior to a second mortgage; a second mortgage is junior to a first mortgage, but senior to a third.

As was explained in Chapter 4, lien priority is important in the event of a foreclosure, because the sale proceeds are used to pay off the first lien first. If any money remains, the second lien is paid; then the third is paid, and so on, until the money is exhausted. Obviously, it is much better to be in first lien position than in third.

Purchase Money Mortgage. This term is used in two ways. Sometimes it means any mortgage loan used to finance the purchase of the property that is the collateral for the loan: a buyer borrows money to buy property and gives the lender a mortgage on that same property to secure the loan.

In other cases, "purchase money mortgage" is used more narrowly, to mean a mortgage that a buyer gives to a seller in a seller-financed transaction. Instead of paying the full price in cash at closing, the buyer gives the seller a mortgage on the property and pays the price off in installments.

Example: The sales price is $180,000. The buyer makes a $20,000 downpayment and signs a note and purchase money mortgage in favor of the seller for the remaining $160,000. The buyer will pay the seller in monthly installments at 7% interest over the next 15 years.

In this narrower sense, a purchase money mortgage is sometimes called a **soft money mortgage**, because the borrower receives credit instead of actual cash. If a borrower gives a lender a mortgage and receives cash in return (as with a bank loan), it is called a **hard money mortgage**.

Budget Mortgage. The monthly payment on a budget mortgage includes not just principal and interest on the loan, but one-twelfth of the year's property taxes and hazard insurance premiums as well. The lender holds the tax and insurance payments in a reserve account (impound account) until they're due. Many residential loans are secured by budget mortgages. This is the safest and most practical way for lenders to make sure the property taxes and insurance premiums are paid on time.

Package Mortgage. When personal property is included in the sale of real estate and financed along with the real estate with one loan, the security instrument is called a package mortgage. For example, if a buyer bought ovens, freezers, and other equipment along with a restaurant building, the purchase might be financed with a package mortgage.

Construction Loan. A construction loan (sometimes called an **interim loan**) is a temporary loan used to finance the construction of improvements on the land. When the construction is completed, the construction loan is replaced by permanent financing, which is called a **take-out loan**.

Construction loans can be profitable, but they are considered quite risky. Accordingly, lenders charge high interest rates and loan fees on construction loans, and they supervise the progress of the construction. There is always a danger that the borrower will overspend on a construction project and exhaust the loan proceeds before construction is completed. If the borrower cannot afford to finish, the lender is left with a security interest in a partially completed project.

Lenders have devised a variety of plans for disbursement of construction loan proceeds that guard against overspending by the borrower. Perhaps the most common is the **fixed disbursement plan**. This calls for a series of predetermined disbursements, called obligatory advances, at various stages of construction. Interest begins to accrue with the first disbursement.

Example: The construction loan agreement stipulates that the lender will release 10% of the proceeds when the project is 20% complete, and thereafter 20% draws will be available whenever construction has progressed another 20% toward completion.

The lender will often hold back 10% or more of the loan proceeds until the period for claiming construction liens has expired, to protect against unpaid liens that could affect the marketability of the property. The construction loan agreement usually states that if a valid construction lien is recorded, the lender may use the undisbursed portion of the loan to pay it off.

Blanket Mortgage. Sometimes a borrower mortgages several pieces of property as security for one loan. For example, a ten-acre parcel subdivided into twenty lots might be used to secure one loan made to the subdivider. Blanket mortgages usually have a **partial release clause** (also called a partial satisfaction clause, or in a blanket deed of trust, a partial reconveyance clause). This provision requires the lender to release certain parcels from the blanket lien when specified portions of the overall debt have been paid off.

> **Example:** A ten-acre parcel subdivided into twenty lots secures a $500,000 loan. After selling one lot for $50,000, the subdivider pays the lender $45,000 and receives a release for the lot that is being sold. The blanket mortgage is no longer a lien against that lot, so the subdivider can convey clear title to the lot buyer.

Participation Mortgage. A participation mortgage allows the lender to participate in the earnings generated by the mortgaged property, usually in addition to collecting interest payments on the principal. In some cases the lender participates by becoming a part-owner of the property. Participation loans are most common on large commercial projects where the lender is an insurance company or other large investor.

Shared Appreciation Mortgage. Real property usually appreciates (increases in value) over time. Appreciation usually benefits only the property owner, by adding to her equity. (**Equity** is the difference between a property's market value and the liens against it.) With a shared appreciation mortgage, however, the lender is entitled to a specified share of the increase in the property's value. Thus, a shared appreciation mortgage is actually a variation on the participation mortgage discussed above.

Wraparound Mortgage. A wraparound mortgage is a new mortgage that includes or "wraps around" an existing first mortgage on the property. Wraparounds are generally used only in seller-financed transactions.

> **Example:** A home is being sold for $600,000; there is an existing $440,000 mortgage on the property. Instead of assuming that mortgage, the buyer merely takes title subject to it. The buyer gives the seller a $120,000 downpayment and a second mortgage for the remaining $480,000 of the purchase price. The $480,000 second mortgage is a wraparound mortgage. Each month, the buyer makes a payment on the wraparound to the seller, and the seller uses part of that payment to make the monthly payment on the underlying $440,000 mortgage.

Wraparound financing works only if the underlying loan does not contain an alienation clause (see the discussion earlier in this chapter). Otherwise the lender would require the seller to pay off the underlying loan at the time of sale. A wraparound arrangement should always be designed so that the underlying loan will be paid off before the wraparound, to ensure that the buyer's title will not still be encumbered with the seller's debt after the buyer has paid the full purchase price.

Open-end Mortgage. An open-end mortgage sets a borrowing limit, but allows the borrower to reborrow, when needed, any part of the debt that has been repaid without having to negotiate a new mortgage. The interest rate on the loan is usually a variable rate that rises and falls with market interest rates. The open-end mortgage is often used as a business tool by builders and farmers.

Graduated Payment Mortgage. A graduated payment mortgage allows the borrower to make smaller payments at first and gradually step up to larger payments. For example, the payments might increase annually for the first three to five years of the loan, and then remain level for the rest of the loan term. This arrangement can benefit borrowers who expect their earnings to increase during the next few years.

Swing Loan. It often happens that a buyer is ready to purchase a new home before he's succeeded in selling his current home. The buyer needs funds for the downpayment and closing costs right away, without waiting for the proceeds from the eventual sale of his current home. In this situation, the buyer may be able to obtain a swing loan. A swing loan is usually secured by equity in the property that is for sale, and it will be paid off when that sale closes. A swing loan is also called a **gap loan** or **bridge loan**.

Home Equity Loan. A borrower can obtain a mortgage loan using the equity in property she already owns as collateral. This is called an **equity loan**; when the property is the borrower's residence, it's called a **home equity loan**.

As mentioned earlier, equity is the difference between a property's market value and the liens against it. In other words, it's the portion of the property's current value that the owner owns free and clear, which is therefore available to serve as collateral for another loan. With an equity loan, the lender agrees to loan a sum of money to the property owner in exchange for a second mortgage against the property. (The existing first mortgage is the loan the owner used to purchase the property.)

Sometimes a home equity loan is used to finance remodeling or other improvements to the property. In other cases, it's used for expenses unrelated to the property, such as a major purchase, college tuition, medical bills, or paying off credit cards.

Instead of having to apply for a home equity loan when they need money for a particular purpose, some homeowners have a home equity line of credit (or HELOC) that they can draw on when the need arises. This works in much the same way as a credit card—with a credit limit and minimum monthly payments—except that the debt is automatically secured by the borrower's home. A HELOC is a revolving credit account, in contrast to a home equity loan, which is an installment loan with regular payments made over a certain term.

Reverse Mortgage. Reverse mortgages, sometimes called reverse annuity mortgages or reverse equity mortgages, are designed to provide income to older homeowners. The owner borrows against the home's equity but will receive a monthly check from the lender, rather than making monthly payments. Typically, a reverse equity borrower must be over a certain age (for example, 62 or 65) and must own the home with little or no outstanding mortgage balance. The home usually must be sold when the owner dies in order to pay back the mortgage.

Subprime Mortgage. A subprime mortgage is a loan made to a borrower who wouldn't qualify for an ordinary mortgage loan, perhaps because her credit history or debt-to-income ratio doesn't meet the usual standards, or because she's unable or unwilling to provide the documentation usually required. A subprime lender typically charges higher interest rates and fees to offset the extra risk the loan entails. Subprime lending is discussed in more detail in Chapter 11.

Refinancing. Borrowers who refinance their mortgage are obtaining an entirely new mortgage loan to replace the existing one. The funds from the refinancing loan are used to pay off the existing loan. The refinancing might be from the same lender that made the existing loan, or from a different lender.

Borrowers often choose to refinance when market interest rates drop; refinancing at a lower interest rate can result in substantial savings over the long run. Another situation in which borrowers are likely to refinance is when the payoff date of the existing mortgage is approaching and a large balloon payment will be required.

In some cases, borrowers get a refinance loan for more than the amount needed to pay off their existing loan, which means that they also receive cash from the transaction. This is called **cash-out refinancing**. Depending on the terms of the refinance loan, the additional funds might be used for property improvements, debt consolidation, or other purposes.

📖 Chapter Summary

1. The federal government influences real estate finance directly and indirectly through its fiscal and monetary policy. The federal deficit may affect the availability of investment funds. The Federal Reserve Board uses reserve requirements, the discount rate, and open market operations to implement monetary policy, influencing the pace of economic growth and market interest rates.

2. The primary market is the local finance market, in which lenders make mortgage loans to borrowers. In the secondary market, mortgages are bought and sold by investors. The federal government created the major secondary market entities, Fannie Mae, Freddie Mac, and Ginnie Mae, to help moderate local real estate cycles.

3. A promissory note is a written promise to repay a debt. For a real estate loan, the borrower is required to sign a negotiable promissory note along with a security instrument, which makes the borrower's property collateral for the loan.

4. The two main types of security instruments are mortgages and deeds of trust. The central difference between the two types is that a deed of trust always includes a power of sale clause, which allows the trustee to foreclose nonjudicially in the event of default.

5. Most security instruments include an acceleration clause and an alienation clause; some also have a prepayment provision or a subordination clause. If there is no alienation clause, the loan can be assumed without the lender's consent.

6. A mortgage is foreclosed judicially. The borrower has an equitable right of redemption before the sheriff's sale and a statutory right of redemption for a certain period afterwards. The lender may be entitled to a deficiency judgment.

7. A deed of trust can be foreclosed nonjudicially, by the trustee, which is usually much faster and less expensive than judicial foreclosure. Until shortly before the trustee's sale, the borrower has the right to cure the default and reinstate the loan. After the sale, the borrower has no right of redemption. The lender cannot obtain a deficiency judgment.

8. With a land contract, the buyer takes possession of the property and makes installment payments to the seller; the seller retains legal title until the contract is paid off. If the buyer breaches the contract, the seller may declare a forfeiture.

9. There are many different types of mortgage loans, including purchase money, budget, package, construction, blanket, participation, shared appreciation, wraparound, open-end, graduated payment, swing, home equity, reverse mortgages, subprime, and refinance loans.

O—⚷ Key Terms

Federal Reserve Board—The body that regulates commercial banks and sets and implements the federal government's monetary policy; commonly called "the Fed."

Reserve requirements—The percentages of customer deposits commercial banks must keep on reserve with a Federal Reserve Bank.

Discount rate and federal funds rate—Two interest rates controlled by the Fed that have an effect on market interest rates.

Open market operations—The Fed's activities in buying and selling government securities.

Primary market—The local finance market, where individuals obtain loans from banks, savings and loans, and other types of mortgage lenders.

Secondary market—The national finance market, where mortgages are bought and sold as investments.

Promissory note—A written promise to repay a debt.

Mortgage—A two-party security instrument that gives the lender (mortgagee) the right to foreclose on the security property by judicial process if the borrower (mortgagor) defaults.

Deed of trust—A three-party security instrument that includes a power of sale clause, allowing the trustee to foreclose nonjudicially if the borrower (trustor) fails to pay the lender (beneficiary) or otherwise defaults.

Acceleration clause—A provision in loan documents that gives the lender the right to demand immediate payment in full if the borrower defaults.

Alienation clause—A provision in a security instrument that gives the lender the right to accelerate the loan if the borrower transfers the property; also called a due-on-sale clause.

Assumption—When a borrower sells the security property to a buyer who agrees to take on personal liability for repayment of the existing mortgage or deed of trust.

Defeasance clause—A provision giving the borrower the right to regain title to the security property when the debt is repaid.

Satisfaction of mortgage—The document a mortgagee gives to the mortgagor when the mortgage debt is paid off, releasing the property from the lien. Also called a satisfaction piece.

Deed of reconveyance—The document the trustee gives the trustor when the debt secured by a deed of trust is paid off, releasing the property from the lien.

Land contract—A contract between a seller (vendor) and a buyer (vendee) of real estate, in which the seller retains legal title to the property while the buyer pays off the purchase price in installments.

Chapter Quiz

1. In a tight money market, when business is slow, a reduction in interest rates would be expected to cause:

    a) an increase in real estate sales
    b) more bank lending activity
    c) increased business activity
    d) All of the above

2. Which of the following actions by the Federal Reserve Board would tend to increase the money supply?

    a) Selling government securities on the open market
    b) Buying government securities on the open market
    c) Increasing the federal discount rate
    d) Increasing reserve requirements

3. Funds for single-family mortgage loans are supplied by:

    a) Fannie Mae
    b) savings and loan associations
    c) Both a) and b)
    d) Neither a) nor b)

4. With an installment note, the periodic payments:

    a) include both principal and interest
    b) are interest only
    c) are principal only
    d) are called balloon payments

5. A mortgage loan provision that permits the lender to declare the entire loan balance due upon default by the borrower is a/an:

    a) acceleration clause
    b) escalator clause
    c) forfeiture clause
    d) subordination clause

6. A mortgage loan provision that permits the lender to declare the entire loan balance due if the property is sold is a/an:

    a) escalator clause
    b) subordination clause
    c) alienation clause
    d) prepayment provision

7. After a sheriff's sale, the mortgagor has a certain period in which to redeem the property. This period is called the:

    a) lien period
    b) equitable redemption period
    c) statutory redemption period
    d) reinstatement period

8. After a trustee's sale, if there are any sale proceeds left over after paying off liens and foreclosure expenses, the money belongs to the:

    a) sheriff
    b) beneficiary
    c) trustee
    d) foreclosed owner

9. The document that a mortgagee gives a mortgagor after the debt has been completely paid off is called a:

    a) partial release
    b) satisfaction of mortgage
    c) deed of reconveyance
    d) sheriff's deed

10. In a nonjudicial foreclosure, the borrower is entitled to:

    a) a statutory redemption period following the sheriff's sale
    b) a deficiency judgment
    c) a deed in lieu of foreclosure
    d) cure the default and reinstate the loan before the trustee's sale

11. When a buyer gives a mortgage to the seller instead of an institutional lender, it may be referred to as a:

    a) purchase money mortgage
    b) land contract
    c) shared appreciation mortgage
    d) reverse mortgage

12. A budget mortgage:

    a) is a loan made to a low-income borrower
    b) is a construction loan with a fixed disbursement plan
    c) is secured by personal property as well as real property
    d) has monthly payments that include taxes and insurance as well as principal and interest

13. The owner of five parcels of real property wants a loan. She offers all five parcels as security. She will be required to execute a:

    a) soft money mortgage
    b) participation mortgage
    c) package mortgage
    d) blanket mortgage

14. Victor is borrowing money to buy some land, and he plans to build a home on the property later on. To ensure that he will be able to get a construction loan when the time comes, Victor should make sure the mortgage he executes for the land loan includes a/an:

    a) lien waiver
    b) subordination clause
    c) acceleration clause
    d) wraparound clause

15. Under a fixed disbursement plan for a construction loan, the contractor is entitled to her final draw when:

    a) the project has been satisfactorily completed
    b) 80% of the work has been completed
    c) the building department issues a certificate of occupancy
    d) the period for claiming construction liens expires

Answer Key

1. d) The Fed lowers interest rates in times of economic downturn in an attempt to stimulate the economy.

2. b) When the Fed buys government securities back from private investors, it puts more money into circulation (increases the money supply).

3. c) Mortgage money comes from the primary market (in the form of savings deposits) and from the secondary market (when investors like Fannie Mae buy mortgages).

4. a) An installment note involves periodic payments that include some of the principal as well as interest.

5. a) An acceleration clause gives the lender the right to declare the entire debt immediately due and payable if the borrower defaults.

6. c) An alienation clause allows the lender to accelerate the loan if the borrower transfers the security property without the lender's approval.

7. c) The statutory redemption period is the period of time after the sheriff's sale in which the borrower has the right to redeem the property by paying off the entire debt, plus costs.

8. d) Any excess proceeds from a foreclosure sale belong to the borrower—that is, to the foreclosed owner.

9. b) When the debt has been fully paid off, a mortgagee gives the mortgagor a satisfaction of mortgage, releasing the property from the lien.

10. d) In the nonjudicial foreclosure of a deed of trust, the trustor is permitted to cure the default and reinstate the loan (as opposed to paying off the loan) before the trustee's sale is held.

11. a) A mortgage given by a buyer to a seller is sometimes called a purchase money mortgage.

12. d) A budget mortgage payment includes a share of the property taxes and hazard insurance as well as principal and interest.

13. d) A blanket mortgage has more than one parcel of property as collateral.

14. b) A subordination clause in the mortgage for the land loan would give it a lower priority than a mortgage executed later on for a construction loan. Lenders generally require first lien position for construction loans, because they are considered especially risky.

15. d) Construction lenders usually delay the final disbursement until no more construction liens can be filed.

Applying for a Residential Loan

Chapter Overview

When it's time to arrange financing, a home buyer must shop for a loan and choose a lender. Next, the buyer fills out a loan application and supplies supporting documentation. Then the lender evaluates the application and decides whether or not to approve the loan. The first part of this chapter describes the different types of lenders in the primary market, explains loan fees, and discusses the Truth in Lending Act, a law that helps prospective borrowers compare loans. The second part of the chapter covers the loan application form and the underwriting process. The next part of the chapter explains various features of a home purchase loan, and provides an overview of the major residential finance programs. The chapter ends with a discussion of predatory lending.

Choosing a Lender

Many home buyers look to their real estate agent for guidance in choosing a lender. Agents should be familiar with the lenders in their area and know how to help buyers compare the loans that different lenders are offering. We're going to discuss the various types of lenders that make home purchase loans, the fees that lenders charge, and the Truth in Lending Act.

Types of Mortgage Lenders

There are several major sources of residential financing in the primary market. Residential mortgage lenders include:

- commercial banks,
- thrift institutions,
- credit unions, and
- mortgage companies.

Commercial Banks. A commercial bank is either a national bank, chartered (authorized to do business) by the federal government, or a state bank, chartered by a state government. Commercial banks are the largest source of investment funds in the United States. As their name implies, they were traditionally oriented toward commercial lending activities, supplying capital for business ventures and construction activities on a comparatively short-term basis.

In the past, residential mortgages weren't a major part of the business of commercial banks. That was partly because most of their deposits were demand deposits (checking accounts), and the government limited the amount of long-term investments they could make. But eventually commercial banks began accepting more long-term deposits, and demand deposits now represent a considerably smaller share of banks' total deposits than they once did.

While commercial banks have continued to emphasize commercial loans, they have also diversified their lending, with a substantial increase in personal loans and home mortgages. They now have a significant share of the residential finance market.

Thrift Institutions. Savings and loan associations and savings banks are often grouped together and referred to as **thrift institutions** (or thrifts).

Savings and Loans. Savings and loan associations (S&Ls) are chartered by either the federal government or a state government.

Savings and loans started out in the nineteenth century strictly as residential real estate lenders. Over the years they carried on their original function, investing the majority of their assets in purchase loans for single-family homes. By the mid-1950s, they dominated local residential mortgage markets, becoming the nation's largest single source of funds for financing homes.

Many factors contributed to the dominance of savings and loans; one of the most important was that home purchase loans had become long-term loans (often with 30-year terms). Since most of the funds held by S&Ls were long-term deposits, S&Ls were comfortable making long-term home loans.

While savings and loans have branched out into different types of lending, they continue to focus on home mortgage loans. Yet S&Ls no longer dominate the residential finance market, because other types of lenders have become more involved in it.

Savings Banks. Savings banks started out in the nineteenth century offering financial services to small depositors, especially immigrants and members of the working class. They were called mutual savings banks (MSBs) because they were organized as mutual companies, owned by and operated for the benefit of their depositors (as opposed to stockholders).

Traditionally, MSBs were similar to savings and loans. They served their local communities. Their customers were individuals rather than businesses, and most of their deposits were savings deposits. Although the MSBs made many residential mortgage loans, they did not concentrate on them to the extent that S&Ls did. The MSBs were also involved in other types of lending, such as personal loans.

Today, savings banks can be organized as mutual companies or stock companies. Residential mortgages continue to be an important part of their business.

Credit Unions. Credit unions are depository institutions, like banks and S&Ls; however, they are set up as not-for-profit financial cooperatives, democratically controlled by their members. Credit unions were originally intended to serve only members of a particular group, such as the members of a labor union or a professional association, or the employees of a large company. Today, many credit unions allow anyone in their geographic area to join.

Credit unions traditionally provided small personal loans to their members. Many now emphasize home equity loans, which tend to be short-term, and they may also make home purchase loans.

Mortgage Companies. Unlike banks, S&Ls, and credit unions, mortgage companies are not depository institutions, so they don't lend out depositors' funds. Instead, they often act as **loan correspondents**, intermediaries between large investors and home buyers applying for financing.

A loan correspondent lends an investor's money to buyers and then **services** the loans (collecting and processing the loan payments on behalf of the investor) in exchange for servicing fees. In some cases a bank or an S&L will act as a loan correspondent, but mortgage companies have specialized in this role.

Mortgage companies frequently act on behalf of large investors such as life insurance companies and pension funds. These investors control vast amounts of capital in the form of insurance premiums and employer contributions to employee pensions. That money generally isn't subject to sudden withdrawal, so it's well suited to investment in long-term mortgages. Since these large investors typically operate on a national scale, they have neither the time nor the resources to understand the particular risks of local real estate markets or to deal with the day-to-day management of their loans. So they hire local loan correspondents.

Mortgage companies also borrow money from banks on a short-term basis and use the money to make (or **originate**) loans, which they then sell to the secondary market agencies and other private investors. Using short-term financing to originate loans before selling them to permanent investors is referred to as **warehousing**.

Banks and S&Ls generally keep some of the loans they make "in portfolio," instead of selling them to investors. In contrast, mortgage companies don't keep any of the loans they make. The loans are either made on behalf of an investor or else sold to an investor. In many cases, insurance companies, pension funds, and other large investors now simply buy loans from mortgage companies instead of using them as loan correspondents.

The number of mortgage companies increased rapidly during the 1990s, and they eventually came to dominate the residential finance market as savings and loans once had. Mortgage companies played a major role in the subprime lending boom, and recent problems in the subprime market have had a greater impact on mortgage companies than on other types of residential lenders. (Subprime lending is discussed later in this chapter.)

Traditionally, a distinction was made between mortgage bankers and mortgage brokers. A **mortgage broker** referred to someone who negotiated loans, bringing borrowers together with lenders in exchange for a commission. Once the loan was arranged, the mortgage broker's involvement ended. In contrast, a **mortgage banker** actually made loans (using an investor's funds or borrowed funds), sold or delivered the loans to an investor, and then (in many cases) serviced the loans to the end of their terms, in exchange for servicing fees. As a result of recent changes in the mortgage industry, there is no longer a clear-cut distinction between the two, and the more general term of mortgage company is typically used instead.

Private Lenders. Real estate limited partnerships, real estate investment trusts (see Chapter 2), and other types of private investment groups put a great deal of money into real estate. They often finance large residential developments and commercial ventures, such as shopping centers and office buildings. They don't offer loans to individual home buyers, however.

From the home buyer's point of view, the most important type of private lender is the home seller. Sometimes sellers provide all the financing for the purchase of their homes, and it's quite common for sellers to supplement the financing their buyers obtain from an institutional lender. Sellers are an especially important source of financing when institutional loans are hard to come by or market interest rates are high.

Comparing Types of Lenders. At one time, financial institutions in the United States were quite specialized. It was almost as if each type of institution had its own function—its own types of deposits, its own types of services, and its own types of loans. That is no longer true. To a great extent, all of the major depository institutions can now be regarded as "financial supermarkets," offering a wide range of services and loans.

There still are differences between the types of institutions, in terms of lending habits and government regulations, but these generally won't affect a loan applicant who wants to finance the purchase of a home.

Loan Costs

For the majority of buyers, the primary consideration in choosing a lender is how much the loan they need is going to cost. While the interest rate has the greatest impact, lenders impose other charges that can greatly affect the cost of a loan. Most important among these are origination fees and discount points. These are often grouped together and referred to as **points**. The term "point" is short for "percentage point." A point is one percentage point (one percent) of the loan amount. For example, on a $100,000 loan, one point would be $1,000; six points would be $6,000.

Origination Fees. Processing loan applications and making loans is called loan origination. A **loan origination fee** is designed to pay administrative costs the lender incurs in processing a loan; it is sometimes called a service fee, an administrative charge, or simply a loan fee. An origination fee is charged in most residential loan transactions. It's ordinarily paid by the buyer.

> **Example:** The buyer is borrowing $200,000, and the lender is charging 1.5 points (1.5% of the loan amount, or $3,000) as an origination fee. The buyer will pay this $3,000 fee to the lender at closing.

Discount Points. Lenders charge **discount points** to increase their upfront yield (their return) on a loan. With discount points, a lender not only gets interest throughout the loan term, it also collects an additional sum of money up front, when the loan is funded. As a result, the lender is willing to make the loan at a lower interest rate than it would have without the discount points. In effect, the lender is paid a lump sum at closing so the borrower can avoid paying more interest later. A lower interest rate also translates into a lower monthly payment.

Discount points aren't charged in all residential loan transactions, but they are quite common. The number of discount points charged usually depends on how the loan's interest rate compares to market interest rates; typically, a lender that offers an especially low rate charges more points to make up for it.

The number of discount points required to increase the lender's yield by one percentage point on a 30-year loan varies. One lender offering an interest rate one percentage point below market rates might charge six points to make up the difference, while another lender may charge four points. To find out exactly how many points a particular lender will charge for a specified interest rate reduction under current market conditions, it's necessary to ask the lender.

In some cases, the seller is willing to pay the discount points on the buyer's loan in order to help the buyer qualify for financing. Even when the lender isn't charging discount points, the seller may offer to pay points to make the loan more affordable. This type of arrangement is called a **buydown**: the seller pays the lender points to "buy down" the interest rate on the buyer's loan.

Truth in Lending Act. An origination fee, discount points, and other charges may increase the cost of a mortgage loan significantly. They also make it more difficult to compare the costs of loans offered by different lenders. For example, suppose one lender charges 7% interest, a 1% origination fee, and no discount points, while another charges 6.75% interest, a 1% origination fee, and two discount points. It isn't easy to tell at a glance which of these loans will cost the borrower more in the long term. (The second loan is just slightly less expensive.)

The **Truth in Lending Act** (TILA) is a federal consumer protection law that addresses this problem of comparing loan costs. The act requires lenders to disclose the complete cost of credit to consumer loan applicants, and also regulates the advertisement of consumer loans. The Truth in Lending Act is implemented by **Regulation Z**, a regulation enforced by the Consumer Financial Protection Bureau.

Loans Covered by TILA. A loan is a **consumer loan** if it's used for personal, family, or household purposes. A consumer loan is covered by the Truth in Lending Act if it is to be repaid in more than four installments, or is subject to finance charges, and is either:

- for $54,600 or less (the dollar figure is adjusted annually), or
- secured by real property.

Thus, any mortgage loan is covered by the Truth in Lending Act as long as the proceeds are used for personal, family, or household purposes (such as buying a home or sending children to college).

Loans Exempt from TILA. The Truth in Lending Act applies only to loans made to natural persons, so loans made to corporations or organizations aren't covered. Loans for business, commercial, or agricultural purposes are also exempt. So are loans in excess of the maximum dollar amount shown above, unless they are secured by real property. (Real estate loans for personal, family, or household purposes are covered regardless of the loan amount.)

TILA only applies to loans from lenders who regularly extend consumer credit. Most seller financing is exempt, because extending credit isn't in the seller's ordinary course of business.

Disclosure Requirements. The primary disclosures that the Truth in Lending Act requires a lender to make to a loan applicant are the total finance charge and the annual percentage rate.

The **total finance charge** is the sum of all fees and charges the borrower pays in connection with the loan. In addition to the interest on the loan, all of the following would be included in the total finance charge: origination fee, discount points paid by the borrower, finder's fee, mortgage broker's fee, service fees, and mortgage insurance premiums.

In real estate loan transactions, appraisal fees, credit report charges, inspection fees, and title fees aren't included in the total finance charge. Also, any charges that will be paid by someone other than the borrower—points paid by the seller, for example—aren't included.

The **annual percentage rate** (APR) expresses the total cost of the loan as an annual percentage of the loan amount. This key figure enables a prospective borrower to compare loans more accurately than the interest rate alone.

In addition to the total finance charge and the APR, the disclosure statement must list the amount financed, the total of all payments, the number of payments, and the payment amount(s). It must also provide other information, such as whether the borrower will be charged a prepayment penalty if the loan is paid off early.

Fig. 11.1 Truth in Lending Act disclosure statement

TRUTH IN LENDING DISCLOSURE STATEMENT

Creditor	Applicant(s)
Mailing Address	Property Address
Loan Number	Preparation Date

ANNUAL PERCENTAGE RATE The cost of your credit as a yearly rate.	FINANCE CHARGE The dollar amount the credit will cost you.	Amount Financed The amount of credit provided to you or on your behalf.	Total of Payments The amount you will have paid after you have made all payments as scheduled.
E %	E$	E$	E$

PAYMENT SCHEDULE:

NUMBER OF PAYMENTS	* AMOUNT OF PAYMENTS	MONTHLY PAYMENTS ARE DUE BEGINNING	NUMBER OF PAYMENTS	* AMOUNT OF PAYMENTS	MONTHLY PAYMENTS ARE DUE BEGINNING

* Includes mortgage insurance premiums, excludes taxes, hazard insurance or flood insurance.

DEMAND FEATURE: ☐ This loan does not have a Demand Feature   ☐ This loan has a Demand Feature.

ITEMIZATION: You have a right at this time to an ITEMIZATION OF AMOUNT FINANCED.

     I/We ☐ do ☐ do not want an itemization.

REQUIRED DEPOSIT:

     ☐ The annual percentage rate does not take into account your required deposit.

VARIABLE RATE FEATURE:

     ☐ This Loan has a Variable Rate Feature. Variable Rate Disclosures have been provided to you earlier.

SECURITY: You are giving a security interest in:

ASSUMPTION: Someone buying this property

     ☐ cannot assume the remaining balance due under original mortgage terms.

     ☐ may assume, subject to lender's conditions, the remaining balance due under original mortgage terms.

FILING / RECORDING FEES: $

PROPERTY INSURANCE:

     ☐ Property / hazard insurance is a required condition of this loan. Borrower may purchase this insurance from any insurance company acceptable to the lender.

Hazard insurance ☐ is ☐ is not available through the lender at an estimated cost of   for a   month term.

LATE CHARGES: If your payment is more than   days late, you will be charged a late charge of   % of the overdue payment.

PREPAYMENT: If you prepay this loan in full or in part, you

     ☐ may ☐ will not   have to pay a penalty.

     ☐ may ☐ will not   be entitled to a refund of part of the finance charge.

See your contract documents for any additional information regarding non-payment, default, required repayment in full before scheduled date, and payment refunds and penalties.

E means estimate.

I/We hereby acknowledge reading and receiving a complete copy of this disclosure. I/We understand there is no commitment for the creditor to make this loan and there is no obligation for me/us to accept this loan upon delivery or signing of this disclosure.

_____   Date   _____   Date

_____   Date   _____   Date

GENESIS 2000, INC. * V9.3/W11.0 * (818) 223-3260   Form RegZD (03/95)

Timing of Disclosures. In mortgage transactions that are secured by a borrower's dwelling and subject to the Real Estate Settlement Procedures Act (RESPA), a lender must deliver or mail a disclosure statement to the borrower within three days of receiving a written loan application. The disclosure statement must contain good faith estimates of the loan costs. This requirement applies to most purchase, refinancing, and home equity loans. (A sample disclosure form is shown in Figure 11.1.)

The borrower must receive the TILA disclosure statement at least seven business days before closing. The lender may not impose any loan fees on the borrower before the borrower has received the disclosure statement, except the fee for obtaining the borrower's credit report. If there are significant changes to the original cost estimates, the lender must give the borrower corrected information at least three business days before closing. Starting in August of 2015, the TILA disclosure statement will be combined with the good faith estimate of closing costs required under the Real Estate Settlement Procedures Act; the timetable requiring disclosure within three days of the loan application and at least seven days before closing will still apply.

Right of Rescission. The Truth in Lending Act provides for a right of rescission in connection with certain types of mortgage loans. When the security property is the borrower's principal residence, the borrower may rescind the loan agreement up until three days after signing it, receiving the disclosure statement, or receiving notice of the right of rescission, whichever comes latest. If the borrower never receives the statement or the notice, the right of rescission doesn't expire for three years.

The right of rescission generally applies only to home equity loans and to refinancing with a new lender. There's no right of rescission for a loan financing the purchase or construction of the borrower's residence. Nor is there a right of rescission for refinancing when the same lender that made the original loan is making the new loan, unless that lender is advancing additional funds (beyond the original loan amount). In that case, the right of rescission applies only to the additional amount.

Advertising Under TILA. The Truth in Lending Act strictly controls advertising of credit terms. Its advertising rules apply to anyone who advertises consumer credit, not just lenders. For example, a real estate agent advertising financing terms for a listed home has to comply with TILA and Regulation Z.

It's always legal to state the cash price or the annual percentage rate in an ad. If the APR is stated, the interest rate may also be given, as long as it isn't more prominent than the APR. But if the ad contains other specific loan terms known as **triggering terms** (the downpayment amount or percentage, the repayment period or number of payments, the amount of any payment, or the amount of any finance charge), then other information must also be disclosed. For example, if an ad says, "Assume seller's payments—only $1,525 a month," it will violate the Truth in Lending Act if it does not go on to reveal the APR, any required downpayment, and the repayment schedule, with the number and timing of the payments and all payment amounts, including any balloon payment. However, general statements such as "low monthly payment," "easy terms," or "affordable interest rate" do not trigger the full disclosure requirement.

Rate Lock-ins. There's one other issue concerning loan costs that we should mention. A prospective borrower may want to have the interest rate quoted by the lender "locked in" for a specified period. Unless the interest rate is locked in, the lender can change it at any time until the transaction closes. If market interest rates are rising, the lender is likely to increase the interest rate on the loan. That could cost the borrower a lot of money over the long term, or else actually price the borrower out of the transaction altogether.

Locking in the interest rate is generally not desirable when market interest rates are expected to go down. A lender will typically charge the borrower the locked-in rate even if market rates drop in the period before closing.

Some lenders charge the borrower a fee to lock in the interest rate. The fee is typically applied to the borrower's closing costs if the transaction closes. If the lender rejects the borrower's application, the fee is refunded; it will be forfeited to the lender, though, if the borrower withdraws from the transaction.

The Loan Application Process

Once a buyer has compared loan costs and selected a lender, the next step is applying for the loan. The buyer fills out a loan application form and provides the lender with supporting documentation. The application is then submitted to the lender's underwriting department, which evaluates the application and ultimately approves or rejects the proposed loan.

Preapproval

Traditionally, a buyer would first find the house she wanted, then apply for a loan. Now, however, getting **preapproved** for a loan is considered the standard practice in most areas. To get preapproved, a prospective buyer submits a loan application to a lender before starting to house-hunt. If the lender approves the application, the buyer is preapproved for a specified maximum loan amount.

Preapproval lets the buyer know in advance, before shopping, just how expensive a house she can afford. If a house meets the lender's standards and is in the established price range, the buyer will be able to buy it. This spares the buyer the disappointment of initially choosing a house that turns out to be too expensive and having the loan request turned down. Preapproval also helps streamline the closing process once the buyer has found the right house.

The Application Form

A mortgage loan application form asks the prospective borrower for detailed information about his finances. The lender requires this information because it wants its loans to be profitable investments. A loan is unlikely to be profitable if the borrower doesn't have the financial resources to make the payments reliably, or if the borrower has a habit of defaulting on debts. The application helps the lender identify and turn down potential borrowers who are likely to create collection problems.

Most mortgage lenders use a standard residential loan application form developed by Fannie Mae and Freddie Mac. The form requires all of the following information:

1. **Personal information**, such as the applicant's social security number, age, education, marital status, and number of dependents.

2. **Current housing expense** (monthly rent or house payment).

3. **Employment information** (such as job title, type of business, and duration of employment) concerning the applicant's current position and, if he's been with the current employer for less than two years, concerning previous jobs.

4. **Income** from all sources, including employment (salary, wages, bonuses, and/or commissions), investments (dividends and interest), and pensions.

5. **Assets,** which may include money in bank accounts, stocks and bonds, real estate, life insurance, retirement funds, cars, jewelry, and other personal property.

6. **Liabilities,** including credit card debts, car loans, real estate loans, alimony or child support payments, and unpaid taxes.

The lender will verify the applicant's information concerning income, assets, and liabilities (for example, by sending verification forms to the applicant's employer and bank).

Underwriting the Loan

Once a loan application has been submitted and the information has been verified, the loan is ready for underwriting. **Loan underwriting** is the process of evaluating both the applicant and the property she wants to buy to determine whether they meet the lender's minimum standards. The person who conducts the evaluation is called a loan underwriter or credit underwriter. The guidelines that the underwriter uses to decide whether a proposed loan would be an acceptable risk are called **underwriting standards** or **qualifying standards**.

A lender is generally free to set its own underwriting standards. In practice, however, most lenders apply underwriting standards set by the major secondary market agencies, Fannie Mae and Freddie Mac. And for FHA and VA loans, standards set by HUD or the VA must be used.

Qualifying the Buyer. In evaluating a loan applicant's financial situation, an underwriter must consider many factors. These factors fall into three main groups: credit history, income, and net worth.

Credit History. The first major component of creditworthiness is an applicant's credit history, or credit reputation. The loan underwriter analyzes the applicant's credit history by using credit reports obtained from credit reporting agencies. The credit reports indicate how reliably the applicant has paid bills and other debts, and whether there have been any severe problems such as bankruptcy or foreclosure.

Credit scores have become increasingly important as a way to assess how likely it is that a loan applicant will default on the proposed loan. A credit reporting agency calculates an individual's credit score using the credit report and a statistical model that correlates different types of negative credit information with actual loan defaults.

Credit problems can be an indication of financial irresponsibility, but in some cases they result from a personal crisis such as loss of a job, divorce, or hospitalization. A loan applicant with a poor credit history should explain any extenuating circumstances to the lender.

Incorrect information sometimes becomes part of a consumer's credit report, which can pose serious problems for a person trying to get a loan. The federal **Fair Credit Reporting Act** (FCRA) helps protect consumers against erroneous credit reporting. If a lender takes an adverse action (such as denying a loan application) because of information in a credit report, the lender must give the applicant written notice about the action and disclose which credit reporting agency provided the report. The FCRA entitles consumers to one free credit report per year, to enable them to check for errors. Creditors and credit reporting agencies must investigate disputed information and correct any errors. The act also sets limits on how long negative information may remain on credit reports; the limit is seven years for most information, but it's ten years for bankruptcies.

Income. Another primary consideration for the underwriter is whether the loan applicant's monthly income is enough to cover the proposed monthly mortgage payment in addition to all of the applicant's other expenses. So the underwriter needs to determine how much income the applicant has.

Not all income is equal in an underwriter's eyes, however. To be taken into account in deciding whether the applicant qualifies for the loan, income must meet standards of quality and durability. In other words, it must be from a dependable source, such as an established business, and it must be likely to continue for some time. Income that meets the tests of quality and durability is generally referred to as the loan applicant's **stable monthly income**.

Once the underwriter has calculated the loan applicant's stable monthly income, the next step is to measure its adequacy: Is the stable monthly income enough so that the applicant can afford the proposed monthly mortgage payment? To answer this question, underwriters use **income ratios**. The rationale behind the ratios is that if a borrower's expenses exceed a certain percentage of his monthly income, the borrower may have a difficult time making the payments on the loan.

There are two main types of income ratios:

- A **housing expense to income ratio** measures the proposed monthly mortgage payment against the applicant's stable monthly income.

- A **debt to income ratio** (also called a **debt service ratio**) measures all of the applicant's monthly obligations (the proposed mortgage payment, plus car payments, child support payments, etc.) against the stable monthly income.

For these calculations, the monthly mortgage payment includes principal, interest, taxes, insurance, and any homeowners association dues (often abbreviated as PITI or PITIA). Each ratio is expressed as a percentage; for example, a loan applicant's housing expense to income ratio would be 29% if her proposed mortgage payment represented 29% of her stable monthly income. Whether that ratio would be considered too high would depend on the lender and on the type of loan applied for. Each of the major residential loan programs (conventional, FHA-insured, or VA-guaranteed) has its own income ratio limits.

Net Worth. The third prong of the underwriting process is evaluating the borrower's net worth. An individual's net worth is determined by subtracting her total personal liabilities from her total personal assets. If a loan applicant has built up a significant net worth from earnings, savings, and other investments, that's an indication of creditworthiness. The applicant apparently knows how to manage her financial affairs.

Getting an idea of the loan applicant's financial skills isn't the only reason for investigating her net worth, however. The underwriter needs to make sure the applicant has sufficient funds to cover the downpayment, the closing costs, and other expenses incidental to the purchase of the property.

In addition, it's desirable for a loan applicant to have cash reserves left over after closing. Reserves provide some assurance that she would be able to handle a financial emergency, such as unexpected bills or a temporary interruption of income, without defaulting on the mortgage. Some lenders require an applicant to have sufficient reserves to cover a certain number of mortgage payments. Even when reserves aren't specifically required, they strengthen the loan application.

Qualifying the Property. In addition to deciding whether the buyer is a good risk, the underwriter also has to consider whether the property that the buyer wants to purchase is a good risk. Is the property worth enough to serve as collateral for the loan amount in question? In other words, if foreclosure became necessary, would the property sell for enough money to pay off the loan? To answer these questions, the underwriter relies on an appraisal report commissioned by the lender. The appraisal provides an expert's estimate of the property's value. We'll discuss appraisal in Chapter 12.

Automated Underwriting. Within the limits set by the underwriting standards they apply, underwriters draw on their own experience and judgment in deciding whether to recommend that a particular loan be approved or denied. For this reason, underwriting is often described as an art, not a science. However, **automated underwriting** (AU) has moved the underwriting process at least somewhat closer to the scientific end of the spectrum. In automated underwriting, a computer program performs a preliminary analysis of the loan application and the applicant's credit report and makes a recommendation for or against approval. A human underwriter then evaluates the application in light of the AU recommendation.

AU systems are based on statistics regarding the performance of millions of loans—whether the borrowers made the payments on time or defaulted. Analysis of these statistics provides strong evidence of which factors in a loan application make default more or less likely.

AU can streamline the underwriting process, as it often requires significantly less paperwork. This enables lenders to make approval decisions more quickly.

Subprime Lending. What happens to home buyers whose credit history doesn't meet standard underwriting requirements? Some of them may be able to obtain a loan by applying to a **subprime** lender. Subprime lending involves making riskier loans than prime (or standard) lending.

Although many of the buyers who obtain subprime mortgages have blemished credit histories and mediocre credit scores, that's not always the case. Subprime financing may also be necessary for buyers who:

- can't (or would rather not have to) meet the income and asset documentation requirements of prime lenders;
- have good credit but carry more debt than prime lenders allow; or
- want to purchase nonstandard properties that prime lenders don't regard as acceptable collateral.

Subprime lenders apply more flexible underwriting standards and, in exchange, typically charge much higher interest rates and fees than prime lenders. In addition to having high interest rates and fees, subprime loans are more likely than prime loans to have features such as prepayment penalties, balloon payments, and negative amortization. These features help subprime lenders counterbalance some of the extra risks involved in their loans, although they can also cause trouble for the borrowers. (See the discussion of predatory lending later in this chapter.)

A boom in subprime lending began in the late 1990s and continued into the new century. However, a significant number of these subprime loans turned out to be poor risks, and many of the borrowers defaulted on their loans. The resulting foreclosure epidemic in 2008 and 2009 affected not just the mortgage industry but the economy as a whole. As a result, it is now much more difficult to get subprime loans.

Mortgage Fraud. Mortgage fraud causes many millions of dollars in losses each year. Common types of mortgage fraud include borrowers lying on loan applications and loan professionals misleading secondary market investors. For instance, loan applicants may lie about their employment, assets, or liabilities in order to secure loans that they wouldn't otherwise qualify for. Investors may falsely claim to be purchasing property as their principal residence in order to qualify for lower interest rates and fees. Lenders may misrepresent the quality of poor loans when selling them to investors in the secondary market.

Both federal and state law prohibit mortgage fraud. In 2009, in response to the mortgage crisis, Congress passed the Fraud Enforcement and Recovery Act, which toughened up existing federal antifraud provisions and took particular aim at mortgage fraud. At about the same time, the state of Washington enacted the Mortgage Lending and Homeownership statute, which contains various provisions concerning mortgage fraud. Both the federal and state laws provide for significant jail time and fines for violations.

Basic Loan Features

In this section, we'll look at the basic features of a home mortgage loan. These include the loan term; the amortization; the loan-to-value ratio; a secondary financing arrangement (in some cases); and a fixed or adjustable interest rate. A lender is likely to present a home buyer with a number of options concerning these various loan features. Each of them affects how large a loan the buyer will qualify for, and ultimately how expensive a home the buyer can purchase.

Loan Term

A mortgage loan's **term** (also known as the **repayment period**) has a significant impact on both the monthly mortgage payment and the total amount of interest paid over the life of the loan. The longer the term, the lower the monthly payment, and the more interest paid.

Since the 1930s, the standard term for a mortgage loan has been 30 years. This long repayment period makes the monthly payments affordable, which reduces the risk of default.

Although 30-year loans continue to predominate, 15-year loans have also become popular. A 15-year loan has higher monthly payments than a comparable 30-year loan, but the 15-year loan offers substantial interest savings for the borrower. Lenders frequently offer lower interest rates on 15-year loans, because the shorter term means less risk for the lender. And the borrower will save thousands of dollars in total interest charges over the life of the loan (see Figure 11.2). A 15-year loan also offers free and clear ownership of the property in half the time.

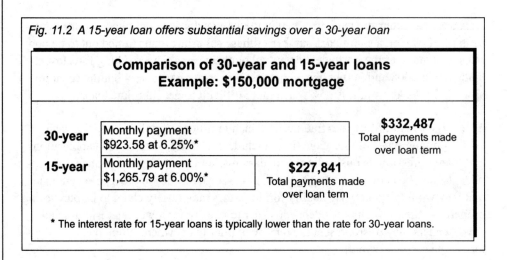

Fig. 11.2 A 15-year loan offers substantial savings over a 30-year loan

However, the monthly payments are significantly higher for a 15-year loan, and in some cases a much larger downpayment would be necessary to reduce the monthly payments to a level the borrower can afford.

Example: Bob has a choice between a 30-year loan at 6.5% and a 15-year loan at 6.25%. Based on his stable monthly income, he can afford to make monthly principal and interest payments of about $2,000. This is enough to amortize a $316,000 loan at 6.5% over 30 years, but it will amortize only about $233,000 at 6.25% over 15 years. In other words, Bob could qualify for a $316,000 loan under the 30-year plan, but will be able to borrow only $233,000 if he chooses the 15-year option.

There are alternatives to 15- and 30-year loans. For some borrowers, a 20-year loan is a good compromise between the two, with some of the advantages of each. And while 30 years is the maximum repayment period in many loan programs, some programs allow borrowers to choose a 40-year term, to maximize their purchasing power.

Amortization

Most mortgage loans are **fully amortized**. A fully amortized loan is repaid within a certain period of time by means of regular payments that include a portion for principal and a portion for interest. As each payment is made, the appropriate amount of principal is deducted from the debt and the remainder of the payment, which represents the interest, is retained by the lender as earnings or profit. With each payment, the amount of the debt is reduced and the interest due with the next payment is recalculated based on the lower balance. The total payment remains the same throughout the term of the loan, but every month the interest portion of the payment is reduced and the principal portion is increased. (See Figure 11.3.) The final payment pays off the loan completely; the principal balance is zero and no further interest is owed.

Example: A $190,000 loan at 6% interest can be fully amortized over a 30-year term with monthly principal and interest payments of $1,139.15. If the borrower pays $1,139.15 each month, then the loan will be fully repaid (with interest) after 30 years.

There are two alternatives to fully amortized loans: partially amortized loans and interest-only loans. A **partially amortized** loan requires regular payments of both interest and principal, but those payments are not enough to repay all of the principal; the borrower is required to make a large balloon payment (the remaining principal balance) at the end of the loan term.

Example: A $190,000 partially amortized mortgage at 6% interest calls for regular monthly payments of $1,296.13 for principal and interest, with a loan term of five years. Because the monthly payments are more than enough to cover the interest on the loan, some of the principal will be repaid during the five-year term. But since it would take 30 years to fully repay the loan at this rate, a substantial amount of principal (roughly $167,000) will still be unpaid after five years. This amount will be due as a balloon payment. To pay it, the borrower will have to refinance the property or come up with the funds from some other source.

With an **interest-only** loan (also called a **term mortgage**), the borrower's regular payments during the loan term cover the interest accruing on the loan, without paying any of the principal off. The entire principal amount—the amount originally borrowed—is due at the end of the term.

Example: A five-year, $190,000, interest-only loan at 5.5% interest requires monthly payments of $870.84, the amount needed to cover the monthly interest accruing on the loan. At the end of the five-year term, the borrower owes the lender the full amount of the principal ($190,000).

The term "interest-only loan" is also used to refer to a loan that's structured to allow interest-only payments during a specified period at the beginning of the loan term. At the end of the initial period, the borrower must begin making amortized payments that will pay off all of the principal and interest by the end of the term. This type of interest-only loan was very popular during the subprime boom, since the low initial payments enabled buyers to purchase a more expensive home than they otherwise could have. For many buyers, however, these loans eventually backfire. When the interest-only period ends, they can't afford the amortized payments, and the payment shock ultimately results in foreclosure. These loans are now rarely used.

Fig. 11.3 Payments for a fully amortized loan

Example: $190,000 loan @ 6.00%, 30-year term, monthly payments

Payment No.	Beginning Balance	Total Payment	Interest Portion	Principal Portion	Ending Balance
1	$190,000.00	$1,139.15	$950.00	$189.15	$189,810.85
2	$189,810.85	$1,139.15	$949.05	$190.09	$189,620.76
3	$189,620.76	$1,139.15	$948.10	$191.04	$189,429.72
4	$189,429.72	$1,139.15	$947.15	$192.00	$189,237.72
5	$189,237.72	$1,139.15	$946.19	$192.96	$189,044.74

Loan-to-Value Ratios

The loan-to-value ratio (LTV) for a particular transaction expresses the relationship between the loan amount and the value of the property. The lower the LTV, the smaller the loan amount and the bigger the downpayment.

Example: If a lender makes an $80,000 loan secured by a home appraised at $100,000, the loan-to-value ratio is 80%. The loan amount is 80% of the property's value, and the buyer makes a 20% downpayment. If the lender loaned $75,000 secured by the same property, the LTV would be 75% and the downpayment would be 25%.

The downpayment represents the borrower's initial investment or equity in the property. The lower the loan-to-value ratio, the greater the borrower's equity.

The loan-to-value ratio affects the degree of risk involved in the loan—both the risk of default and the risk of loss in the event of default. A borrower who has a substantial investment in the property will try harder to avoid foreclosure; and when foreclosure is necessary, the lender is more likely to recover the entire debt if the LTV is relatively low.

The higher the LTV, the greater the lender's risk. (In fact, lenders may apply special rules to high-LTV loans because of the extra risk they pose.) So lenders use loan-to-value ratios to set maximum loan amounts.

Example: If a lender's maximum LTV for a certain type of loan is 75%, and the property's appraised value is $100,000, then $75,000 would be the maximum loan amount.

Lenders actually base the maximum loan amount on the sales price or the appraised value, whichever is less. Thus, if the $100,000 property in the example above was selling for $95,000, the maximum loan amount would be $71,250 (75% of $95,000).

Secondary Financing

Sometimes a buyer obtains two mortgage loans at once: a primary loan to pay for most of the purchase price, and a second loan to pay part of the downpayment or closing costs required for the first loan. This supplementary second loan is called **secondary financing**. Secondary financing may come from an institutional lender, the seller, or a private third party.

In most cases, the primary lender will allow secondary financing only if it complies with certain requirements. For example, the borrower must be able to qualify for the combined payment on the first and second loans. The borrower is usually required to make a minimum downpayment out of her own funds. And the second loan must be payable at any time, without a prepayment penalty.

Fixed and Adjustable Interest Rates

A fixed-rate loan is repaid over its term at an unchanging rate of interest. For example, the interest rate is set at 6.25% when the loan is made, and the borrower pays 6.25% interest on the unpaid principal throughout the loan term.

When market interest rates are relatively low and stable, fixed-rate loans work well for borrowers and lenders. But in periods when market rates are high and volatile, neither borrowers nor lenders are comfortable with fixed-rate loans. High interest rates price many borrowers out of the market. And if market rates are fluctuating rapidly, lenders prefer not to tie up their funds for long periods at a set interest rate.

A type of loan that addresses both of these issues is the **adjustable-rate mortgage** (ARM). An ARM permits the lender to periodically adjust the loan's interest rate so that it accurately reflects changes in the cost of money. With an ARM, it's the borrower who is affected by interest rate fluctuations. If rates climb, the borrower's monthly payment goes up; if they decline, the payment goes down.

How an ARM Works. With an ARM, the borrower's interest rate is determined initially by the cost of money at the time the loan is made. Once the rate has been set, it's tied to one of several widely recognized indexes, and future interest adjustments are based on the upward and downward movements of the index.

Index and Margin. An **index** is a published statistical rate that is a reliable indicator of changes in the cost of money. Examples include the one-year Treasury bill index and the Eleventh District cost of funds index. At the time a loan is made, the lender selects the index it prefers, and thereafter the loan's interest rate will rise and fall with the rates reported for the index.

Since the index is a reflection of the lender's cost of money, it is necessary to add a **margin** to the index to ensure sufficient income for administrative expenses and profit. The lender's margin is usually 2% or 3%, or somewhere in between. The index plus the margin equals the interest rate charged to the borrower.

Example:

5.25%	Current index value
+ 2.00%	Margin
7.25%	Borrower's interest rate

It is the index that fluctuates during the loan term and causes the borrower's interest rate to increase and decrease; the lender's margin remains constant.

Adjustment Periods. The borrower's interest rate is not adjusted every time the index changes. Each ARM has a **rate adjustment period**, which determines how often its interest rate is adjusted. A rate adjustment period of one year is the most common.

An ARM also has a **payment adjustment period**, which determines how often the borrower's monthly mortgage payment is increased or decreased (reflecting changes in the interest rate). For most ARMs, payment adjustments are made at the same intervals as rate adjustments.

Caps. If market interest rates rise rapidly, so will an ARM's index, which could lead to a sharp increase in the interest rate the lender charges the borrower. Of course, a higher interest rate translates into a higher monthly payment. This creates the potential for payment shock. In other words, the monthly payments on an ARM might increase so dramatically that the borrower can't afford to pay them.

To help protect borrowers from payment shock and lenders from default, ARMs have interest rate and payment caps. An **interest rate cap** limits how much the lender can raise the interest rate on the loan, even if the index goes way up. A **mortgage payment cap** limits how much the lender can increase the monthly payment.

Negative Amortization. If an ARM has certain features, payment increases may not keep up with increases in the loan's interest rate, so that the monthly payments don't cover all the interest owed. The lender usually handles this by adding the unpaid interest to the loan's principal balance; this is called **negative amortization**. Ordinarily, a loan's principal balance declines steadily, although gradually. But negative amortization causes the principal balance to go up instead of down. The borrower may owe the lender more money than he originally borrowed. Today, lenders usually structure their ARMs to avoid negative amortization, which lessens the chance of ultimate default and foreclosure.

Hybrid ARMs. With a **hybrid ARM**, the interest rate is fixed for a specified number of years at the start of the loan term, and then the rate becomes adjustable. For example, a 3/1 hybrid ARM has a fixed rate during the first three years, with annual rate adjustments after that. A 5/1 ARM has a five-year fixed-rate period, and so on. As a general rule, the longer the initial fixed-rate period, the higher the initial interest rate.

Residential Financing Programs

Residential financing programs can be divided into two main groups: conventional loans and government-sponsored loans. In this section, we'll look first at conventional loans, and then at the most important loan programs sponsored by the federal government: the FHA-insured loan program, the VA-guaranteed loan program, and the Rural Housing Service loan program. As you'll see, each program has its own qualifying standards and its own rules concerning the downpayment and other aspects of the loan.

Conventional Loans

A conventional loan is simply any institutional loan that is not insured or guaranteed by a government agency. For example, FHA-insured and VA-guaranteed loans are not conventional loans, because they are backed by a government agency.

The rules for conventional loans presented here reflect the criteria established by the secondary market entities that purchase conventional loans, Fannie Mae and Freddie Mac (see Chapter 10). When a loan does not meet secondary market criteria it is considered **nonconforming** and cannot be sold to the major secondary market entities. Most lenders want to be able to sell their loans on the secondary market, so they tailor their standards for conventional loans to match those set by Fannie Mae or Freddie Mac.

Conventional LTVs. Traditionally, the standard loan-to-value ratio for a conventional loan has been 80% of the appraised value or sales price of the home, whichever is less. Lenders feel confident that a borrower who makes a 20% downpayment with his own funds is unlikely to default; the borrower has too much to lose. And even if the borrower were to default, a foreclosure sale would be fairly likely to generate at least 80% of the purchase price.

While an 80% LTV may still be regarded as the traditional standard, today many conventional loans have much higher loan-to-value ratios. Many lenders allow LTVs up to 95%, and loans with a 97% LTV may be available through special programs (although loans with such high LTVs are increasingly rare).

Because the lender's risk is greater when the borrower's downpayment is smaller, lenders require borrowers to obtain private mortgage insurance for any conventional loan with an LTV over 80%. (Private mortgage insurance is discussed below.) Some lenders also charge higher interest rates and larger loan fees for conventional loans with higher LTVs. The rules for loans with LTVs over 90% tend to be especially strict.

Owner-Occupancy. Residential lenders make a distinction between owner-occupied homes and investment properties. An owner-occupied home, as the term suggests, is one that the owner (the borrower) plans to live in herself, either as her principal residence or a second home. An investment property is a house that the owner/investor intends to rent out to tenants. Owner-occupants are considered less likely to default than non-occupant borrowers.

Owner-occupancy isn't a requirement for conventional loans, except for loans made through certain special programs (affordable housing programs, for example). In some cases, however, a lender will apply stricter rules to investors than to owner-occupants. For instance, a lender might set 95% as its maximum LTV for owner-occupants, but limit investors to a 90% LTV.

Private Mortgage Insurance. Private mortgage insurance (PMI) is designed to protect lenders from the greater risk of high-LTV loans; PMI makes up for the reduced borrower equity. PMI is usually required on all conventional loans that have an LTV over 80% (in other words, whenever the borrower is making a downpayment of less than 20%).

When insuring a loan, the mortgage insurance company actually assumes only a portion of the risk of default. It typically covers the upper 20% or 25% of the loan amount, not the entire loan amount. The higher the LTV, the higher the coverage requirements and the premiums, since the risk of default is greater. For example, a 95% loan will have a higher coverage requirement and higher premiums than a 90% loan.

In the event of default and foreclosure, the lender, at the insurer's option, will either sell the property or relinquish it to the insurer, then make a claim for reimbursement of actual losses (if any) up to the policy limit. Losses incurred by the lender may take the form of unpaid interest, property taxes and hazard insurance, attorney's fees, and the cost of preserving the property during the period of foreclosure and resale, as well as the expense of selling the property itself.

As the borrower pays off the loan, and as the value of the security property increases, the loan-to-value ratio decreases. With a lower LTV, the risk of default and foreclosure loss is reduced, and eventually the private mortgage insurance has fulfilled its purpose. Under the federal Homeowners Protection Act, lenders are required to cancel a loan's PMI once the loan has been paid down to 80% of the property's original value, if the borrower formally requests the cancellation. And once the loan balance reaches 78% of the original value, cancellation is automatically required, even if the borrower doesn't request it.

Conventional Qualifying Standards. Fannie Mae and Freddie Mac's underwriting standards include detailed guidelines for evaluation of a loan applicant's income, net worth, and credit history. To determine whether the applicant's stable monthly income is sufficient, an underwriter may calculate both a housing expense to income ratio and a total debt to income ratio.

Example: Suppose the lender's maximum housing expense to income ratio is 28% and maximum debt to income ratio is 36%. If a loan applicant's housing expense to income ratio is 26% (under the lender's limit), but her debt to income ratio is 41% (over the lender's limit), then the lender probably would not approve the loan unless there were special considerations.

In some cases, the underwriter will consider only the total debt to income ratio. Because the debt to income ratio takes all of the applicant's monthly obligations into account, it is considered a more reliable indicator of creditworthiness than the housing expense to income ratio.

Some lenders require an applicant for a conventional loan to have the equivalent of two months of mortgage payments in reserve after making the downpayment and paying all their closing costs. For loans with LTVs over 90%, a lender might require three months of mortgage payments in reserve.

Assumption. Most conventional loan agreements include an alienation clause, which means the borrower can't sell the property and arrange for the buyer to assume the loan without the lender's permission. Typically, the lender will evaluate the buyer with the same qualifying standards that it applies in a new loan transaction. If the lender approves the assumption, it will charge an assumption fee, and it may also adjust the interest rate to the current market rate.

FHA-Insured Loans

The Federal Housing Administration (FHA) was created by Congress in 1934 in the National Housing Act. The purpose of the act, and of the FHA, was to generate new jobs through increased construction activity, to exert a stabilizing influence on the mortgage market, and to promote the financing, repair, improvement, and sale of real estate nationwide.

Today the FHA is part of the Department of Housing and Urban Development (HUD). Its primary function is insuring mortgage loans; the FHA compensates lenders who make loans through its programs for losses that result from borrower default. The FHA does not build homes or make loans.

In effect, the FHA serves as a giant mortgage insurance agency. Its insurance program, known as the Mutual Mortgage Insurance Plan, is funded with premiums paid by FHA borrowers.

Under the plan, lenders who have been approved by the FHA to make insured loans either submit applications from prospective borrowers to the local FHA office for approval or, if authorized by the FHA to do so, perform the underwriting functions themselves. Lenders who are authorized to underwrite their own FHA loan applications are called "direct endorsement lenders."

Lenders who don't underwrite their own FHA loans forward applications to the local FHA office for underwriting and approval. Note that the FHA does not accept applications directly from borrowers; borrowers must begin by applying to a lender such as a bank or a mortgage company.

As the insurer, the FHA is liable to the lender for the full amount of any losses resulting from default and foreclosure. In exchange for insuring a loan, the FHA regulates many of the terms and conditions on which the loan is made.

Characteristics of FHA Loans. The typical FHA-insured loan has a 30-year term, although the borrower may have the option of a shorter term. The property purchased with the most common type of FHA loan, a **203(b)** loan, may have up to four dwelling units, and it must be the borrower's primary residence. The FHA requires all the loans it insures to have first lien position.

The downpayment required for an FHA loan is often considerably less than it would be for a conventional loan financing the same purchase (see below). Regardless of the size of the downpayment, mortgage insurance is required on all FHA loans.

Prepayment penalties are not allowed. An FHA loan can be paid off at any time without penalty.

FHA Loan Amounts. FHA programs are primarily intended to help low- and middle-income home buyers. So HUD sets maximum loan amounts, limiting the size of the loans that can be insured under a particular program. FHA maximum loan amounts vary from one place to another because they are based on median housing costs in each area. An area where housing is expensive has a higher maximum loan amount than a low-cost area does.

However, there's also a "ceiling" for FHA loan amounts that applies nationwide; no matter how high prices are in a particular area, FHA loans can't exceed that ceiling. As a result, FHA financing tends to be less useful in areas where housing is exceptionally expensive. The FHA ceiling is tied to Fannie and Freddie's loan amount limits for conforming loans, and it is subject to annual adjustment.

Loan-to-Value Ratios. The loan amount for a particular transaction is determined not just by the FHA loan ceiling for the local area, but also by the FHA's rules concerning loan-to-value ratios.

The maximum loan-to-value ratio for an FHA loan depends on the borrower's credit score. If the borrower's credit score is 580 or above, the maximum LTV is 96.5%. If his score is 500 to 579, the maximum LTV is 90%. Someone with a score below 500 isn't eligible for an FHA loan.

The difference between the maximum loan amount for a transaction and the appraised value or sales price (whichever is less) is called the borrower's **minimum cash investment**. In a transaction with maximum financing (a 96.5% LTV), the borrower must make a minimum cash investment of 3.5%.

FHA Qualifying Standards. As with any institutional loan, the underwriting for an FHA-insured loan involves the analysis of the applicant's income, net worth, and credit history. But the FHA's underwriting standards are not as strict as the Fannie Mae/Freddie Mac standards used for conventional loans. The FHA standards make it easier for low- and middle-income home buyers to qualify for a mortgage.

Income. Just as with a conventional loan, an underwriter evaluating an application for an FHA loan will apply two ratios to determine the adequacy of the applicant's income. However, the FHA's maximum income ratios are higher than the ones typically set for conventional loans. This means that an FHA borrower's mortgage payment and other monthly obligations can be a larger percentage of his income than a conventional borrower's.

Although FHA programs are targeted toward low- and middle-income buyers, there is no maximum income level. A person with a high income could qualify for an FHA loan, as long as the requested loan didn't exceed the maximum loan amount for the area.

Funds for Closing. At closing, an FHA borrower must have sufficient funds to cover the minimum cash investment, any discount points she has agreed to pay, and certain other closing costs. (Note that secondary financing generally can't be used for the minimum cash investment, unless the source of the second loan is a nonprofit or governmental agency, or a family member.) An FHA borrower is usually not required to have reserves after closing.

FHA Insurance Premiums. Mortgage insurance premiums for FHA loans are commonly referred to as the **MIP**. For most programs, an FHA borrower pays both a one-time premium and annual premiums. The one-time premium may be paid at closing, or else financed along with the loan amount and paid off over the loan term.

For most FHA loans, the annual MIP used to be canceled once the loan's principal balance reached a certain percentage of the property's original value. Since June 2013 the FHA has taken a different approach. For loans with an original loan-to-value ratio over 90%, the annual MIP now must be paid for the entire loan term. For loans with an original LTV of 90% or less, the annual MIP will be canceled after 11 years.

Assumption of FHA Loans. Loans made since 1990 can be assumed only by a buyer who meets FHA underwriting standards. The buyer must intend to occupy the home as his primary residence.

VA-Guaranteed Loans

The VA-guaranteed home loan program was established to help veterans finance the purchase of their homes with affordable loans. VA financing offers many advantages over conventional financing and has few disadvantages. The program is administered by the U.S. Department of Veterans Affairs (the VA).

Eligibility for VA Loans. Eligibility for a VA home loan is based on length of continuous active duty service in the U.S. armed forces. The minimum requirement varies from 90 days to 24 months, depending on when the veteran served. (Longer periods are required for peacetime service.) Eligibility may also be based on longtime service in the National Guard or reserves. Military personnel who receive a dishonorable discharge are not eligible for VA loans.

A veteran's surviving spouse may be eligible for a VA loan if he or she has not remarried and the veteran was killed in action or died of service-related injuries. A veteran's spouse may also be eligible if the veteran is listed as missing in action or is a prisoner of war.

Application Process. To apply for a VA-guaranteed loan, a veteran must apply to an institutional lender and provide a **Certificate of Eligibility** issued by the VA. The lender will process the veteran's loan application and forward it to the VA. Note that the Certificate of Eligibility isn't a guarantee that the veteran will qualify for a loan.

The property that the veteran wants to purchase must be appraised in accordance with VA guidelines. The appraised value is set forth in a document called a **Notice of Value**, or NOV (also referred to as a Certificate of Reasonable Value, or CRV).

When a lender approves a VA loan, the loan is guaranteed by the federal government. If the borrower defaults, the VA will reimburse the lender for part or all of any resulting loss. The loan guaranty works essentially like mortgage insurance; it protects the lender against a large loss if the borrower fails to repay the loan.

Characteristics of VA Loans. A VA loan can be used to finance the purchase or construction of a single-family residence or a multifamily residence with up to four units. The veteran must intend to occupy the home. (In the case of a multifamily property, the veteran must occupy one of the units.)

VA-guaranteed loans are attractive to borrowers for a number of reasons, including the following:

- Unlike most loans, a typical VA loan does not require a downpayment. The loan amount can be as large as the sales price or appraised value, whichever is less. In other words, the loan-to-value ratio can be 100%.
- The VA doesn't set a maximum loan amount or impose any income restrictions. (In other words, VA loans aren't limited to low- or middle-income buyers.)
- VA underwriting standards are less stringent than conventional underwriting standards.
- VA loans don't require mortgage insurance.

Traditionally, the interest rate for VA loans was set by the VA, but that's no longer the case. The interest rate for a VA loan is now negotiated between the lender and the borrower in the usual way. The lender may charge discount points, and the points may be paid by the borrower, the seller, or a third party. The lender cannot charge a prepayment penalty.

A VA borrower must pay a funding fee (currently 2.15% of the loan amount, for most borrowers). The fee is reduced if the borrower makes a downpayment of 5% or more.

VA Guaranty. Like private mortgage insurance, the VA guaranty covers only part of the loan amount, up to a maximum set by the government. The maximum guaranty amount is increased periodically. The amount of the guaranty available to a particular veteran is sometimes called the vet's "entitlement."

Because the guaranty amount is limited, a large loan amount presents some risk for the lender. Many lenders require the VA borrower to make at least a small downpayment if the loan amount exceeds a certain limit (typically four times the guaranty amount). This is a limit set by the lender, however, not by the VA.

Restoration of Entitlement. If a veteran sells property that was financed with a VA loan and repays the loan in full from the proceeds of the sale, the veteran is entitled to a full restoration of guaranty rights for future use. (Restoration of entitlement is also referred to as reinstatement.)

Substitution of Entitlement. If a home purchased with a VA loan is sold and the loan is assumed instead of repaid, the veteran's entitlement can be restored under certain circumstances. The buyer who assumes the loan must be an eligible veteran and must agree to substitute her entitlement for the seller's. The loan payments must be current, and the buyer must be an acceptable credit risk. If these conditions are met, the veteran can formally request a substitution of entitlement from the VA.

Note that a VA loan can be assumed by a non-veteran who meets the VA's standards of creditworthiness. But the entitlement of the veteran seller will not be restored if the buyer assuming the loan is not a veteran.

Default. If a VA borrower defaults and the foreclosure sale results in a loss, the borrower may be liable to the VA for the amount the VA pays the lender based on the guaranty. Also, the borrower's guaranty entitlement won't be restored (and he won't be eligible for another VA loan) until he reimburses the VA for the full amount paid out.

Qualifying Standards. Lenders must follow guidelines established by the VA to evaluate a VA loan applicant's creditworthiness. The VA's rules for income analysis are quite different from those used for conventional or FHA loans.

Instead of using both a housing expense to income ratio and a total debt to income ratio, the VA uses only a total debt to income ratio. The VA's maximum debt to income ratio is considerably higher than the maximum usually allowed for a conventional loan.

In addition to the total debt to income ratio, the underwriter will also consider the veteran's **residual income**. This is calculated by subtracting the proposed mortgage payment, all other recurring obligations, and certain taxes from the veteran's gross monthly income. The veteran's residual income must meet the VA's minimum requirements, which vary based on the region of the country where the veteran lives, family size, and the size of the proposed loan.

At least for some loan applicants, it can be considerably easier to qualify for a VA loan than for a conventional loan. Home buyers who are eligible veterans should keep the option of VA financing in mind.

Rural Housing Service Loans

The Rural Housing Service (RHS) is a federal agency within the U.S. Department of Agriculture that makes and guarantees loans used to purchase, build, or rehabilitate homes in rural areas. These loans are often referred to as rural development (or RD) loans. A rural area is generally defined as open country or a town with a rural character and a population of 10,000 or less. (Under special circumstances, a town with a population of up to 20,000 may be considered rural.)

To qualify for an RHS program, a borrower must currently be without adequate housing. The borrower must also be able to afford the proposed mortgage payments and have a reasonable credit history. A home purchased, built, or improved with a Rural Housing Service loan must be modest in both size and design.

Direct Loans. Low-income borrowers (whose income is no more than 80% of the area median income) may obtain financing from RHS for 100% of the purchase price. The loan term may be as long as 38 years, depending on the borrower's income level. The interest rate is set by RHS, and the loan is serviced by RHS.

Guaranteed Loans. The Rural Housing Service also guarantees loans made by approved lenders to borrowers whose income is no more than 115% of the area median income. Approved lenders include any state housing agency, FHA- and VA-approved lenders, and lenders participating in RHS-guaranteed loan programs. The loan amount may be 100% of the purchase price. The loan term is 30 years, and the interest rate is set by the lender.

Predatory Lending

Predatory lending refers to practices that unscrupulous mortgage lenders and mortgage brokers use to take advantage of (prey upon) unsophisticated borrowers for their own profit. Real estate agents and appraisers sometimes participate in predatory lending schemes, and in some cases a buyer or seller may play a role in deceiving the other party.

Predatory lending is especially likely to occur in the subprime market. It tends to be more common in refinancing and home equity lending, but home purchase loans are also affected.

There are many different predatory lending practices. Here are some examples:

- **Predatory steering:** Steering a buyer toward a more expensive loan when the buyer could qualify for a less expensive one.

- **Fee packing:** Charging interest rates, points, or processing fees that far exceed the norm and aren't justified by the cost of the services provided.

- **Loan flipping:** Encouraging a home owner to refinance repeatedly in a short period, when there's no real benefit to the borrower for doing so (but the lender collects loan fees on each new loan).

- **Predatory property flipping:** Buying property at a discount (because the seller needs a quick sale) and then rapidly reselling it to an unsophisticated buyer for an inflated price. (This is illegal when a real estate agent, an appraiser, and/or a lender commit fraud to deceive the seller and/or the buyer about the true value of the property.)

- **Disregarding borrower's ability to pay:** Making a loan based on the property's value, without using appropriate qualifying standards to determine the borrower's ability to afford the loan payments.

- **Balloon payment abuses:** Making a partially amortized or interest-only loan with low monthly payments, without disclosing to the borrower that a large balloon payment will be required after a short period.

- **Fraud:** Misrepresenting or concealing unfavorable loan terms or excessive fees, falsifying documents, or using other fraudulent means to induce a prospective borrower to enter into a loan agreement.

- **Excessive or unfair prepayment penalties:** Imposing an unusually large penalty, and/or failing to limit the penalty period to the first few years of the loan term.

Predatory lenders and mortgage brokers deliberately target borrowers who aren't able to understand the transaction they're entering into, or don't know that better alternatives are available to them. Potential borrowers are especially likely to be targeted if they're elderly, have a limited income, are poorly educated, or speak limited English.

As public awareness of predatory lending has grown, laws intended to prevent it have been implemented, but it remains a serious problem. Although the majority of subprime lenders are legitimate, predatory lending may have contributed to the foreclosure epidemic and the crisis in the subprime market that we discussed earlier.

📖 Chapter Summary

1. Real estate lenders in the primary market include savings and loan associations, commercial banks, savings banks, mortgage companies, credit unions, and private lenders.

2. Lenders charge an origination fee to cover their administrative costs, and sometimes charge discount points to increase the yield on the loan. One point is 1% of the loan amount.

3. The Truth in Lending Act applies to any consumer loan that is secured by real property. It requires lenders and credit arrangers to give loan applicants a disclosure statement about loan costs. It also regulates how financing information is presented in advertising.

4. In qualifying a buyer for a real estate loan, an underwriter examines the buyer's income, net worth, and credit history to determine if he can be expected to make the proposed monthly mortgage payments. Income ratios measure the adequacy of the buyer's stable monthly income.

5. The traditional loan term for a mortgage loan is 30 years, but loans with terms of 15, 20, and 40 years are also available. A 15-year loan requires higher payments than a comparable 30-year loan, but it saves the borrower thousands of dollars in interest.

6. A fully amortized loan has equal payments that pay off all of the principal and interest by the end of the loan term. Most mortgage loans are fully amortized, but partially amortized loans and interest-only loans are also available in some cases.

7. The loan-to-value ratio for a particular transaction expresses the relationship between the loan amount and the property's appraised value or sales price, whichever is less. The higher the loan-to-value ratio, the greater the lender's risk.

8. Secondary financing may be used to cover part of the downpayment and closing costs required for the primary loan. A secondary financing arrangement must comply with rules set by the primary lender.

9. The interest rate on a mortgage loan may be either fixed or adjustable. An ARM's interest rate is tied to an index, and it is adjusted at specified intervals to reflect changes in the index.

10. A conventional loan is an institutional loan that is not insured or guaranteed by the government. Private mortgage insurance is required for loans with LTVs over 80%.

11. FHA-insured loans are distinguished from conventional loans by less stringent qualifying standards, lower downpayments, and less cash needed for closing. The maximum loan amount available for an FHA loan depends on housing costs in the area where the property is located. FHA mortgage insurance is required on all FHA loans.

12. Eligible veterans may obtain a VA-guaranteed home loan. No downpayment is required for a VA loan. The VA sets a maximum guaranty amount, but does not set a maximum loan amount. The qualifying standards for a VA loan are considerably less stringent than the standards for conventional loans.

13. The federal Rural Housing Service makes and guarantees loans for homes in rural areas. Low- or moderate-income borrowers may qualify if they can afford the mortgage payments and have reasonable credit histories.

14. Predatory lending refers to lending practices used by lenders and other parties to take advantage of unsophisticated borrowers. Examples of predatory lending practices include predatory steering, fee packing, loan flipping, and disregarding the borrower's ability to afford the payments.

🔑 Key Terms

Mortgage company—A type of lender that is not a depository institution and that makes loans on behalf of large investors or using borrowed funds. Sometimes called a mortgage banker.

Mortgage broker—An individual or company that arranges loans between borrowers and investors, but does not make or service the loans.

Point—One percent of the amount of a loan.

Origination fee—A fee that a lender charges to cover the administrative costs of processing a loan.

Discount points—A fee that a lender may charge to increase the yield on the loan, over and above the interest rate.

Annual percentage rate (APR)—Under the Truth in Lending Act, the relationship of the total finance charge to the loan amount, expressed as an annual percentage.

Loan underwriting—Evaluating the creditworthiness of the buyer and the value of the property to determine if a loan should be approved.

Stable monthly income—Income that satisfies the lender's standards of quality and durability.

Income ratios—Percentages used to determine whether a loan applicant's stable monthly income is sufficient.

Housing expense to income ratio—A percentage that measures a loan applicant's proposed monthly mortgage payment against the applicant's stable monthly income.

Debt to income ratio—A percentage that measures all of a loan applicant's monthly obligations (including the proposed mortgage payment) against the stable monthly income.

Net worth—An individual's total personal assets minus her total personal liabilities.

Credit score—A number that is calculated by applying a statistical model to a loan applicant's credit report, used as an indication of how likely the applicant is to default on the proposed loan.

Automated underwriting (AU)—Analysis of a loan application with a computer program that makes a preliminary recommendation for or against approval.

Fully amortized loan—A loan that is fully paid off by the end of its term by means of regular principal and interest payments.

Loan-to-value ratio—The relationship between the loan amount and the property's appraised value or sales price, whichever is less.

Secondary financing—A second loan to help pay the downpayment or closing costs associated with the primary loan.

Fixed-rate loan—A loan repaid over its term at an unchanging rate of interest.

Truth in Lending Act (TILA)—A federal consumer protection law that requires lenders to give borrowers information about loan costs.

Adjustable-rate mortgage—A loan that allows the lender to periodically adjust the loan's interest rate to reflect changes in market interest rates.

Index—A published rate that is a reliable indicator of the current cost of money.

Margin—The difference between the index value on an ARM and the interest rate the borrower is charged.

Negative amortization—When unpaid interest is added to a loan's principal balance.

Conventional loan—An institutional loan that is not insured or guaranteed by a government agency.

Nonconforming loan—A loan that does not meet the underwriting standards of the major secondary market entities.

PMI—Private mortgage insurance; insurance designed to protect lenders from the greater risks of high-LTV conventional loans.

MIP—The mortgage insurance premiums required for FHA-insured loans.

Certificate of Eligibility—The document that establishes a veteran's eligibility to apply for a VA home loan.

Notice of Value (NOV)—The document issued when a home is appraised in connection with the underwriting of a VA loan.

Residual income—The amount of monthly income a VA borrower has left over after deducting monthly expenses and taxes.

Rural Housing Service—A federal agency that makes and guarantees loans to low- or moderate-income borrowers to purchase, build, or rehabilitate homes in rural areas.

Predatory lending—Lending practices used by unscrupulous lenders and mortgage brokers to take advantage of unsophisticated borrowers.

Chapter Quiz

1. Which one of the following bodies would be most likely to make a 90% conventional loan for the purchase of a residence?
   a) Federal Housing Administration
   b) Federal National Mortgage Association
   c) Farm Home Loan Administration
   d) Acme Mortgage Bankers

2. To increase its yield on the loan, the lender is charging 2% of the loan amount, to be paid at closing. This charge is called:
   a) the origination fee
   b) PMI
   c) the index
   d) discount points

3. The Truth in Lending Act and Regulation Z:
   a) place restrictions on how much a lender can charge for a consumer loan
   b) require lenders to give loan applicants a disclosure statement concerning loan costs
   c) prohibit lenders from advertising specific financing terms
   d) All of the above

4. A loan's APR expresses the relationship between:
   a) the total finance charge and the loan amount
   b) the interest rate on the loan and the discount rate
   c) the downpayment and the total finance charge
   d) the monthly payment and the interest rate

5. After determining the quantity of the loan applicant's stable monthly income, the underwriter measures the adequacy of the income using:
   a) the consumer price index
   b) income ratios
   c) credit scoring
   d) federal income tax tables

6. Fifteen-year mortgages typically have all of the following disadvantages, except:
   a) a higher interest rate
   b) higher monthly payments
   c) a larger downpayment
   d) All of these are disadvantages of a 15-year mortgage

7. The house was appraised for $293,000 and the sales price is $290,000. If the loan-to-value ratio is 90%, how much is the loan amount?
   a) $254,400
   b) $261,000
   c) $263,700
   d) $283,000

8. With an adjustable-rate mortgage, the interest rate:
   a) is adjusted at specified intervals, and so is the payment amount
   b) is adjusted monthly, and so is the payment amount
   c) increases and decreases, but the payment amount remains the same
   d) may increase periodically, but does not decrease

9. Unpaid interest added to the loan balance is referred to as:
   a) payment shock
   b) partial amortization
   c) negative amortization
   d) participation interest

10. For conventional loans, private mortgage insurance is required when the loan-to-value ratio is:
    a) 75% or higher
    b) 90% or higher
    c) over 95%
    d) over 80%

11. The FHA:
    a) makes loans
    b) insures loans
    c) buys and sells loans
    d) All of the above

12. All of the following statements about FHA loans
    are true, except:
    a) no downpayment is required
    b) the borrower is usually not required to have
       reserves after closing
    c) mortgage insurance is required on all loans
    d) the borrower must occupy the property as his
       or her primary residence

13. A VA loan can be assumed:
    a) only by an eligible veteran
    b) only by an eligible veteran who agrees to a
       substitution of entitlement
    c) by any buyer who passes the credit check
    d) by any buyer, without regard to credit-
       worthiness

14. A veteran may obtain a VA-guaranteed loan on a:
    a) single-family residence only
    b) four-plex, as long as all of the units are
       rented out to tenants
    c) residence with up to two units, as long as the
       veteran occupies one unit
    d) residence with up to four units, as long as the
       veteran occupies one unit

15. Which of the following statements about preda-
    tory lending is true?
    a) Most subprime lenders engage in predatory
       practices
    b) Predatory lending does not occur in connec-
       tion with home purchase loans
    c) Predatory lenders are especially likely to
       target the elderly and people who speak only
       limited English
    d) All of the above

☞ Answer Key

1. d) The mortgage banker is the only primary market lender listed among the options.

2. d) Discount points are a percentage of the loan amount paid at closing to increase the lender's yield on the loan.

3. b) TILA and Regulation Z require lenders to disclose loan costs to loan applicants, but they do not restrict how much a lender can charge in connection with a loan. And while these laws regulate how financing terms are presented in advertising, they do not prohibit advertisement of financing terms.

4. a) The APR is the annual percentage rate, which indicates the relationship between the total finance charge and the loan amount.

5. b) Income ratios are used to measure the adequacy or sufficiency of a loan applicant's stable monthly income.

6. a) Fifteen-year mortgages usually have lower interest rates than 30-year mortgages.

7. b) The loan amount is $261,000, because the loan-to-value ratio is based on the appraised value or the sales price, whichever is less. $290,000 × 90% = $261,000.

8. a) Both the interest rate and the payment amount for an ARM are adjusted at specified intervals. The rate and the payment amount may increase or decrease to reflect changes in the index.

9. c) Negative amortization is unpaid interest that is added to the loan balance.

10. d) When the LTV of a conventional loan is more than 80%, PMI is required.

11. b) The FHA only insures loans made by institutional lenders. It does not make loans itself, nor does it buy and sell loans on the secondary market.

12. a) A downpayment is required for an FHA loan.

13. c) A VA loan can be assumed by any buyer, whether or not he's an eligible veteran. The buyer is required to pass a credit check, however.

14. d) An eligible veteran can get a VA loan on a residence with up to four units, as long as the veteran occupies one of the units.

15. c) Predatory lenders are especially likely to target elderly people and other vulnerable groups. Predatory lending is a problem in connection with home purchase loans as well as home equity loans and refinancing. It's especially likely to occur in the subprime market, but most subprime lenders don't engage in predatory practices.

Real Estate Appraisal

Chapter Overview

The foundation of every real estate transaction is the value placed on the property in question. The value of a home affects its selling price, financing terms, rental rate, property tax assessment, and insurance coverage, and the income tax consequences of owning it. The parties to a transaction need to know what the property is worth aside from any emotional or other subjective considerations, and for this they rely on an appraisal. This chapter examines the concept of value and explains the various methods appraisers use to estimate value.

Introduction to Appraisal

An **appraisal** is an estimate or an opinion of value. It usually takes the form of a written **appraisal report**, which sets forth the appraiser's opinion of the value of a piece of property as of a given date. An appraisal is sometimes called a **valuation**.

An appraiser may be asked to help a seller decide on a fair asking price, or a buyer may seek an opinion as to how much to pay for the property. Most often, an appraisal is requested by a mortgage lender, when a buyer has applied for a loan. The lender uses the appraisal to decide whether the property the buyer has chosen is suitable security for a loan, and if so, what the maximum loan amount should be.

Most appraisals are performed by **fee appraisers**—independent appraisers hired to value a particular property in exchange for a fee. Fee appraisers are either self-employed or work for an appraisal firm. (Other appraisers are employed by government agencies, financial institutions, insurance companies, or other businesses.)

In addition to helping to determine a fair price or a maximum loan amount, an appraiser's services are regularly required in order to:

- identify raw land's highest and best use;
- estimate a property's value for purposes of taxation (assessment);
- establish rental rates;
- estimate the relative values of properties being exchanged;
- determine the amount of hazard insurance coverage necessary;
- estimate remodeling costs or their contribution to value;
- help establish just compensation in a condemnation proceeding; or
- estimate the value of properties involved in the liquidation of estates, corporate mergers and acquisitions, or bankruptcies.

Regardless of the situation, whoever employs the appraiser is the client. The appraiser is the client's agent. A principal/agent relationship exists and agency law applies (see Chapter 7).

An appraiser's fee is determined in advance, based on the expected difficulty of the appraisal and the amount of time it is likely to take. The fee cannot be calculated as a percentage of the appraised value of the property, nor can it be based on the client's satisfaction with the appraiser's findings.

To help ensure their independence and impartiality, appraisers in home loan transactions are subject to special rules. For example, if a loan will be secured by the borrower's home, federal law prohibits the appraiser from having any financial interest in the property. If a loan will be sold to Fannie Mae or Freddie Mac, the appraiser can't have any substantive communication with the mortgage loan originator; the appraisal must be arranged through an independent appraisal management company or through a separate department within the lender's organization. In addition, a real estate agent can't select or compensate the appraiser.

Under both federal and state law, it's illegal for an appraiser's client or anyone else with an interest in a transaction to attempt to improperly influence the appraisal through coercion, extortion, or bribery. However, it is permissible to ask the appraiser to consider additional property information, explain the basis for her value estimate more fully, or correct errors in the appraisal report.

The state of Washington licenses and certifies appraisers, and state law requires anyone who appraises real estate located in Washington to be licensed or certified, or registered as an appraiser trainee. (That requirement does not apply to a real estate licensee preparing a price opinion for a client, however. A broker's price opinion or competitive market analysis is not considered an appraisal.)

Under federal law, only appraisals prepared by state-licensed or state-certified appraisers in accordance with the **Uniform Standards of Professional Appraisal Practice** (USPAP) can be used in federally related loan transactions. The USPAP are guidelines adopted by the Appraisal Foundation, a nonprofit organization. The majority of residential real estate loans are federally related, since the category includes loans made by any financial institution regulated or insured by the federal government and loans sold to the federal secondary market agencies. Transactions for $250,000 or less are exempt from the licensed or certified appraiser requirement, however.

Value

Value is a term with many meanings. One common definition is "the present worth of future benefits." Value is usually measured in terms of money. For appraisal purposes, value falls into two general classifications: value in use and value in exchange. **Value in use** is the subjective value that a particular person places on a property, while **value in exchange** is the objective value of a property as viewed by any disinterested person. A property's value in use and value in exchange may be quite different, depending on the circumstances.

> **Example:** A large, expensive, one-bedroom home, designed, built, and occupied by its owner, would undoubtedly be worth more to the owner than to the average buyer. Most buyers would look at the property objectively and expect more than one bedroom for the price.

Value in exchange is the more significant of the two types of value. Value in exchange is better known as **market value**. Estimating a property's market value is the purpose of most appraisals.

Market Value

For something to have market value, four elements are required: utility, scarcity, transferability, and demand. In other words, the item must render a service or fill a need; it must not be universally available; it must be possible to transfer it from one owner to another; and there must be a desire to own it. This holds true for real property as well as other commodities.

Here is the most widely accepted definition of market value, the one used by the federal financial institution regulatory agencies:

The most probable price which a property should bring in a competitive and open market under all conditions requisite to a fair sale, the buyer and seller each acting prudently and knowledgeably, and assuming the price is not affected by undue stimulus.

Notice that according to this definition, market value is the *most probable* price (not "the highest price") that the property *should bring* (not "will bring"). Appraisal is a matter of estimation and likelihood, not certainty.

The Federal Housing Administration offers this succinct explanation of market value: "The price which typical buyers would be warranted in paying for the property for long-term use or investment, if they were well informed and acted intelligently, voluntarily, and without necessity."

Market Value vs. Market Price. There's an important distinction between market value and market price. Market price is the price actually paid for a property, regardless of whether the parties to the transaction were informed and acting free of unusual pressure. Market value is what should be paid if a property is purchased and sold under all the conditions requisite to a fair sale. These conditions include an open and competitive market, prudent and informed parties, and no undue stimulus (that is, no unusual pressure to sell or buy immediately).

Principles of Value

Of the major forces that influence our attitudes and behavior, three interact to create, support, or erode property values:

- social ideals and standards,
- economic fluctuations, and
- government regulations.

A change in attitudes regarding family size and the emergence of the two-car family are examples of social forces that affect the value of homes (in this case, homes with too many bedrooms or with one-car garages). Economic forces include employment levels, interest rates, and any other factors that affect the community's purchasing power. Government regulations, such as zoning ordinances, serve to promote, stabilize, or discourage the demand for property.

Over the years, appraisers have developed a reliable body of principles, referred to as the **principles of value**, that take these factors into account and guide appraisers in making decisions in the valuation process. Let's take a look at each of these principles.

Principle of Highest and Best Use. A property's **highest and best use** is the most profitable use that is legally permissible, physically possible, and financially feasible; in other words, it is the use that will provide the greatest net return to the owner over a period of time. **Net return** usually refers to net income, but it can't always be measured in terms of money. With residential properties, for example, net return might

Fig. 12.1 Evaluating highest and best use

Highest and Best Use (Alternative Use Considerations)		
	Annual Income	**Estimated Value**
Present Use: Warehouse	$30,250 (actual)	$275,000
Alternative Use 1: Parking lot	$29,500 (estimated)	$268,000
Alternative Use 2: Gas station	$31,500 (estimated)	$285,000
Alternative Use 3: Triplex	$34,200 (estimated)	$310,000

manifest itself in the form of amenities—the pleasure and satisfaction derived from living on the property.

Determining a property's highest and best use may simply be a matter of confirming that deed restrictions or an existing zoning ordinance limit the property to its present use. It's often true that the present use of a property is its highest and best use. But change is constant, and a warehouse site that was once profitable might now generate a greater net return as a parking lot. Figure 12.1 presents an example of alternative use considerations for a warehouse.

Principle of Change. The principle of change holds that real estate values are constantly in flux, moving up and down in response to changes in the various social, economic, and governmental forces that affect value. A property's value also changes as the property itself improves or deteriorates. A property that was worth $300,000 last year may be worth $325,000 today, and its value is likely to change in the coming year as well. Because value is always subject to change, an estimate of value must be tied to a specific point in time, which is called the **effective date** of the appraisal.

Related to the principle of change is the idea that property has a four-phase life cycle: **integration, equilibrium, disintegration,** and **rejuvenation**. Integration (also called development) is the early stage, when the property is being developed. Equilibrium is a period of stability, when the property undergoes little, if any, change. Disintegration is a period of decline, when the property's economic usefulness is near an end and constant upkeep is necessary. And rejuvenation (also known as revitalization) is a period of renewal, when the property is reborn, perhaps with a different highest and best use.

Every property has both a physical life cycle and an economic life cycle. It's invariably the property's **economic life**—the period when the land and its improvements are profitable—that ends first. An appraiser must take these life cycle stages into account when estimating a property's present worth.

Principle of Anticipation. It's the future, not the past, that's important to appraisers. Knowing that property values change, an appraiser asks: What is happening to this property? What is its future? How do prospective buyers view its potential? The appraiser must be aware of the social, economic, and governmental factors that will affect the future value of the property.

Value is created by the anticipated future benefits of owning a property. It is future benefits, not past benefits, that arouse a desire to own.

Anticipation can help or hurt value, depending on what informed buyers and sellers expect to happen to the property in the future. They usually expect property values to increase, but in certain situations they anticipate that values will decline, as when the community is experiencing a severe recession.

Principle of Supply and Demand. The principle of **supply and demand** affects almost every commodity, including real estate. Values tend to rise as demand increases and supply decreases, and to diminish when the reverse is true. It's not so much the demand for or supply of real estate in general that affects values, but the demand for or supply of a particular type of property. For instance, a generally depressed community may have one or two very attractive, sought-after neighborhoods. The value of homes in those neighborhoods remains high, no matter what the general trend is for the rest of the community.

Principle of Substitution. The principle of substitution states that no one will pay more for a property than they would have to pay for an equally desirable substitute property, provided that there would be no unreasonable delay in acquiring the substitute property. Explained another way, the principle of substitution holds that if two properties for sale are alike in every respect, the least expensive will be in greater demand.

Principle of Conformity. The maximum value of land is achieved when there is an acceptable degree of social and economic conformity (similarity) in the area. Conformity should be reasonable, not carried to an extreme.

In a residential appraisal, aspects of conformity that the appraiser considers are similarities in the age, size, style, and quality of the homes in the neighborhood. Nonconformity can work either to the benefit or to the detriment of the nonconforming home. The value of a home of much lower quality than those around it is increased by its association with the higher-quality homes; this is the principle of **progression**.

> **Example:** A small, unkempt home surrounded by large, attractive homes will be worth more in this neighborhood than it would be if it were situated in a neighborhood of other small homes in poor condition.

Conversely, the value of a large, expensive home in a neighborhood of small, inexpensive homes will suffer because of its surroundings; this is the principle of **regression**.

Principle of Contribution. The principle of contribution concerns the value that an improvement contributes to the overall value of the property. Most improvements contribute less to value than they cost to make. For example, a remodeled basement can increase the value of a home, but usually doesn't increase the home's value by as much as it cost to carry out the remodeling.

Principle of Competition. Competition can have a dramatic impact on the value of property, especially income property. For example, if one convenience store in a neighborhood is extremely profitable, its success is likely to bring a competing convenience store into the area. This competition will probably mean lower profits for the first store (as some of its customers begin doing business with the second store), and lower profits will reduce the property's value.

The Appraisal Process

Properly done, the appraisal process is orderly and systematic. While there's no official procedure, appraisers generally carry out the appraisal process using the following eight steps.

1. **Define the problem.** Each client wants an appraiser to solve a specific problem: to estimate the value of a particular property as of a particular date and for a particular purpose. The first step in the appraisal process is to define the problem to be solved. This involves identifying the **subject property**— what property and which aspect(s) of it are to be appraised—and establishing the purpose of the appraisal and how the client intends to use it. Unless instructed to do otherwise, the appraiser will estimate the property's value as of the date the appraisal is performed.

2. **Determine the scope of work.** Determining the scope of work refers to figuring out what work is needed to solve the appraisal problem: in other words, the type and extent of research and analyses required by the assignment. Together, defining the appraisal problem and determining the scope of work are sometimes called the appraiser's preliminary analysis.

3. **Collect and verify the data.** The data on which the value estimate is based is divided into two categories: general and specific.

    General data concerns matters outside the subject property that affect its value. It includes population trends, prevailing economic circumstances, zoning, and proximity of amenities (such as shopping, schools, and transportation), as well as the condition and quality of the neighborhood.

Fig. 12.2 The appraisal process

Steps in the Appraisal Process

1. Define the problem
2. Determine scope of work
3. Collect and verify data
4. Analyze data
5. Determine site value
6. Apply the approaches to value
7. Reconcile value indicators
8. Issue appraisal report

Specific data concerns the subject property itself. The appraiser will gather information about the title, the buildings, and the site. (General and specific data will be discussed in more detail in the next section of the chapter.)

4. **Analyze the data.** Data analysis actually occurs throughout the appraisal process. As data is collected, the appraiser analyzes its relevance: how reliable it is as an indicator of the subject property's value.

5. **Determine site value.** A site valuation is an estimate of the value of the land, excluding the value of any existing or proposed improvements. In the case of unimproved property, site valuation is the same as appraising the property as is. For improved property, site valuation means appraising the property as if vacant. Site valuation is necessary to determine the highest and best use of the property, but it's also important in tax assessment appraisal and other situations.

6. **Apply the approaches to value.** In some cases, the appraiser will approach the problem of estimating value three different ways: with the sales comparison approach, the cost approach, and the income approach. In other cases, she will use only the method that seems most appropriate for the problem to be solved. Whether one, two, or three approaches are used is a matter of judgment.

   Sometimes a particular method cannot be used. Raw land, for example, cannot be appraised using the cost approach. A public library, on the other hand, must be appraised by the cost approach because it does not generate income and no market exists for it.

7. **Reconcile value indicators for the final value estimate.** The figures yielded by each of the three approaches are called **value indicators**; they give indications of what the property is worth, but are not final estimates themselves.

   The appraiser will take into consideration the purpose of the appraisal, the type of property being appraised, and the reliability of the data gathered for each of the three approaches. She will place the greatest emphasis on the approach that seems to be the most reliable indication of value.

8. **Issue appraisal report.** The appraisal report contains the formal presentation of the value estimate and an explanation of what went into its determination.

Gathering Data

Once the appraiser knows what property he is to appraise, what the purpose of the appraisal is, and what work will be needed to produce the opinion of value, he begins to gather the necessary data. As mentioned above, data is broken down into general data (about the neighborhood and other external influences) and specific data (about the subject property itself).

General Data

General data includes both general economic data about the community and information about the subject property's neighborhood.

Economic Trends. The appraiser examines economic trends for hints as to the direction the property's value might take in the future. Economic trends can take shape at the local, regional, national, or international level, although local trends have the most significant impact on a property's value. Generally, prosperous conditions tend to have a positive effect on property values; economic declines have the opposite effect.

Economic forces include population growth shifts, employment and wage levels (purchasing power), price levels, building cycles, personal tax and property tax rates, building costs, and interest rates.

An appraiser might project future economic growth by looking at economic activity in basic industries, which are the local economy's foundation, as well as non-basic (service) industries, which support the basic industries. This type of projection is known as **economic-base analysis**.

Neighborhood Analysis. A property's value is inevitably tied to its surrounding neighborhood. A **neighborhood** is a residential, commercial, industrial, or agricultural area that contains similar types of properties. Its boundaries are determined by physical barriers (such as highways and bodies of water), land use patterns, the age or value of homes or other buildings, and the economic status of the residents.

Neighborhoods are continually changing and, like the individual properties that make them up, they have a four-phase life cycle of integration, equilibrium, disintegration, and rejuvenation. When evaluating the future of a neighborhood, the appraiser must consider its physical, social, and economic characteristics, and also governmental influences.

Here are some of the specific factors appraisers look at when gathering data about a residential neighborhood:

1. **Percentage of home ownership.** Is there a high degree of owner-occupancy, or do rental properties predominate? Owner-occupied neighborhoods are generally better maintained and less susceptible to deterioration.

2. **Vacant homes and lots.** An unusual number of vacant homes or lots suggests a low level of interest in the area, which has a negative effect on property values. On the other hand, significant construction activity in a neighborhood signals strong interest in the area.

3. **Conformity.** The homes in a neighborhood should be reasonably similar to one another in style, age, size, and quality. Strictly enforced zoning and private restrictions promote conformity and protect property values.

4. **Changing land use.** Is the neighborhood in the midst of a transition from residential use to some other type of use? If so, the properties may be losing their value.

5. **Contour of the land.** Mildly rolling topography is preferred to terrain that is either monotonously flat or excessively hilly.

6. **Streets.** Wide, gently curving streets are more appealing than narrow or straight ones. Streets should be hard-surfaced and well maintained.

7. **Utilities.** Is the neighborhood adequately serviced by electricity, water, gas, sewers, telephones, Internet, and cable TV?

8. **Nuisances.** Nuisances in or near a neighborhood (odors, eyesores, industrial noises or pollutants, or exposure to unusual winds, smog, or fog) hurt property values.

Fig. 12.3 Neighborhood data form

NEIGHBORHOOD DATA FORM

Property adjacent to:
NORTH _____ *Plum Boulevard, garden apartments* _____
SOUTH _____ *Cherry Boulevard, single-family residences* _____
EAST _____ *14th Avenue, single-family residences* _____
WEST _____ *12th Avenue, single-family residences* _____

Population: ☐ increasing   ☐ decreasing   ☑ stable

Stage of Life Cycle: ☐ integration ☑ equilibrium ☐ disintegration ☐ rebirth

Tax Rate: ☐ higher   ☐ lower   ☑ same as competing areas

Services: ☑ police   ☑ fire   ☑ garbage   ☐ other

Average family size: _____ *3.5* _____
Predominant occupations: _____ *white collar, skilled tradesman* _____

Distance from:
Commercial areas _____ *3 miles* _____
Primary schools _____ *6 blocks* _____
Secondary schools _____ *1 mile* _____
Recreational areas _____ *2 miles* _____
Cultural areas _____ *3 miles* _____
Places of worship _____ *Methodist, Catholic, Baptist* _____
Public transportation _____ *Bus stops nearby, excellent service* _____
Freeways/highways _____ *10 blocks* _____

Typical Properties	%	Age	Price Range	% Owner-Occupied
vacant lots	0			
single-family residences	80%	10 years	$275,000-$280,000	93%
2- to 4-unit apartments	15%	15 years		
over 4-unit apartments	5%	5 years		
non-residential	0			

Nuisances in neighborhood (odors, noise, etc.) _____ *none* _____
Hazards in neighborhood (chemical storage, pollution, etc.) _____ *none* _____

9. **Prestige.** Is the neighborhood considered prestigious, in comparison to others in the community? If so, that will increase property values.

10. **Proximity.** How far is it to traffic arterials and to important points such as downtown, employment centers, and shopping centers?

11. **Schools.** What schools serve the neighborhood? Are they highly regarded? Are they within walking distance? The quality of a school or school district can make a major difference in property values in a residential neighborhood.

12. **Public services.** Is the neighborhood properly serviced by public transportation, police, and fire units?

13. **Government influences.** Does zoning in and around the neighborhood promote residential use and insulate the property owner from nuisances? How do the property tax rates compare with those of other neighborhoods nearby?

Specific Data

Specific data has to do with the property itself. Often the appraiser will evaluate the site (the land and utilities) and the improvements (the buildings) separately. For example, when a property is being assessed for tax purposes, most states require the assessment to show the distribution of value between the land and the improvements. Another reason for appraising the land separately is to see if it is worth too much or too little compared to the value of the improvements. When an imbalance exists, the land is not serving its highest and best use. The primary purpose of site analysis is to determine highest and best use.

Site Analysis. A thorough site analysis calls for accumulation of a good deal of data concerning the property's physical characteristics, as well as factors that affect its use or the title. A site's physical characteristics include all of the following:

1. **Width.** This refers to the lot's measurements from one side boundary to the other. Width can vary from front to back, as in the case of a pie-shaped lot on a cul-de-sac.

2. **Frontage.** Frontage is the length of the front boundary of the lot, the boundary that abuts a street or a body of water. The amount of frontage is often a more important consideration than width because it measures the property's accessibility, or its access to something desirable.

3. **Area.** Area is the size of the site, usually measured in square feet or acres. Comparisons between lots often focus on the features of frontage and area.

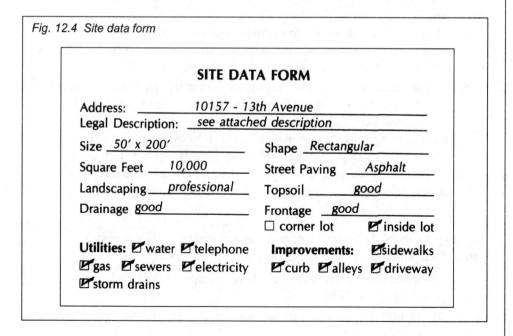

Fig. 12.4 Site data form

SITE DATA FORM

Address: _____ 10157 - 13th Avenue _____
Legal Description: __ see attached description __

Size _50' x 200'_   Shape _Rectangular_
Square Feet ___10,000___   Street Paving ___Asphalt___
Landscaping _professional_ Topsoil ___good___
Drainage _good_   Frontage _good_
                           ☐ corner lot   ☑ inside lot

Utilities: ☑ water ☑ telephone   Improvements: ☑ sidewalks
☑ gas ☑ sewers ☑ electricity   ☑ curb ☑ alleys ☑ driveway
☑ storm drains

Commercial land is usually valued in terms of frontage; that is, it is worth a certain number of dollars per front foot. Industrial land, on the other hand, tends to be valued in terms of square feet or acreage. Residential lots are measured both ways: by square feet or by acreage in most instances, but by front foot when the property abuts a lake or a river, or some other desirable feature.

4. **Depth.** Depth is the distance between the site's front boundary and its rear boundary. Greater depth (more than the norm) can mean greater value, but it doesn't always. For example, suppose Lot 1 and Lot 2 have the same amount of frontage along a lake, but Lot 2 is deeper; Lot 2 is not necessarily more valuable than Lot 1. The additional square footage of Lot 2 might simply be considered **excess land**. Each situation must be analyzed individually to determine whether more depth translates into greater value.

   Under certain circumstances, combining two or more adjoining lots to achieve greater width, depth, or area will make the larger parcel more valuable than the sum of the values of its component parcels. The increment of value that results when two or more lots are combined to produce greater value is called **plottage**. The process of assembling lots to increase their total value is most frequently part of industrial or commercial land development.

5. **Shape.** Lots with uniform width and depth (such as rectangular lots) are almost always more useful than irregularly shaped lots. This is true for any kind of lot—residential, commercial, or industrial.

6. **Topography.** A site is generally more valuable if it is aesthetically appealing. Rolling terrain is preferable to flat, monotonous land. On the other hand, if the site would be costly to develop because it sits well above or below the street or is excessively hilly, then that lessens its value.

7. **Utilities.** Site analysis includes an investigation into the availability and cost of utility connections. Remote parcels lose value because the cost of bringing utility lines to the site is high or even prohibitive. The site must also be evaluated for adding utilities. For instance, in areas not served by sewers, a **percolation test** might be required to measure how quickly water dissipates through the soil. The results of the test will determine whether a septic system can be added to the property.

8. **Site in relation to area.** How a lot is situated in relation to the surrounding area influences its value. For instance, a retail store is often worth more if it is located on a corner, because it enjoys more exposure and its customers have access from two different streets. The effect the corner location has on the value of a business site is called **corner influence**.

   By contrast, a corner location has a negative effect on the value of a residential property. A corner lot is more exposed to through traffic than a lot in the middle of the block.

Building Analysis. The improvements to the site must also be analyzed. Here are some of the primary considerations in a residential appraisal:

1. **Construction quality.** Is the quality of the materials and workmanship good, average, or poor?

2. **Age/condition.** How old is the home? Is its overall condition good, average, or poor?

Fig. 12.5 Building data form

BUILDING DATA FORM

Address: _____ 10157 - 13th Avenue _____

Age: _____ 7 yrs. _____   Square feet: _____ 1,350 _____

Number of rooms: __ 7 __ Quality of construction: __ excellent __

Style: __ ranch __

	Good	Bad	Fair
Exterior (general condition)	✔		
Foundation(slab/bsmt./crawl sp.)	✔		
Exterior (brick/frame/veneer/stucco/aluminum)	✔		
Garage(attached/detached/single/double)	✔		
Patio/porch/shed/other	✔		
Interior (general condition)	✔		
Walls (drywall/wood/plaster)	✔		
Ceilings	✔		
Floor (wood/tile/carpet/concrete)	✔		
Electrical wiring	✔		
Heating (electrical/gas/oil/other)	✔		
Air conditioning	✔		
Fireplace(s) one	✔		
Kitchen	✔		
Bathroom(s) two	✔		
Bedroom(s) three	✔		

Additional amenities _____ none _____

Design advantages _____ convenient, sunny kitchen _____

Design flaws _____ none _____

Energy efficiency ___ insulation, weather-stripping, storm windows, heat pump ___

	Living Rm.	Dining Rm.	Ktchn.	Bdrm.	Bath	Family Rm.
Basement						
1st Floor	✔	✔	✔	✔	✔	
2nd Floor						
Attic						

Depreciation:

    Deferred Maintenance _____ normal wear _____

    Functional Obsolescence _____ none _____

    External Obsolescence _____ none _____

3. **Size of house (square footage).** Square footage generally refers to the improved living area, excluding the garage, basement, and porches. (Note that an appraiser will exclude the square footage of any addition that was built without a permit.)

4. **Basement.** A functional basement, especially a finished basement, contributes to value. (As we mentioned earlier, however, the amount a finished basement contributes to value is often not enough to recover the cost of the finish work.)

5. **Interior layout.** Is the floor plan functional and convenient? It should not be necessary to pass through a public room (such as the living room) to reach other rooms, or to pass through one of the bedrooms to reach another.

6. **Number of rooms.** The appraiser will add up the total number of rooms in the house, excluding bathrooms and (usually) basement rooms.

7. **Number of bedrooms.** The number of bedrooms has a major impact on value. For instance, if all else is equal, a two-bedroom home is worth considerably less than a three-bedroom home.

8. **Number of bathrooms.** A full bath is a lavatory (wash basin), toilet, bathtub, and shower; a three-quarters bath is a lavatory, toilet, and tub or shower; a half bath is a lavatory and toilet only. The number of bathrooms can have a noticeable effect on value.

9. **Air conditioning.** The presence or absence of an air conditioning system is important in hot regions.

10. **Energy efficiency.** An energy-efficient home is more valuable than a comparable one that is not. Energy-efficient features such as double-paned windows, good insulation, and weather stripping increase value.

11. **Garage/carport.** As a general rule, an enclosed garage is considered better than a carport. How many cars can the garage accommodate? Is there work or storage space in addition to parking space? Is it possible to enter the home directly from the garage or carport, protected from the weather?

Approaches to Value

Once the appraiser has accumulated the necessary general and specific data, she will begin applying one or more of the three methods of appraising property:

- the sales comparison approach,
- the cost approach, and
- the income approach.

Different types of properties lend themselves to different appraisal methods. For example, appraisers rely most on the sales comparison approach in valuing older residential properties. Churches and public buildings, such as libraries or courthouses, aren't sold on the open market, nor do they generate income, so the cost approach is invariably used. On the other hand, the income approach is usually the most reliable method for appraising an apartment complex.

Sales Comparison Approach to Value

The **sales comparison approach** (also known as the market data approach) is the best method for appraising residential property, and the most reliable method for appraising raw land. It involves comparing the subject property to similar properties that have recently sold, referred to as **comparable sales** or **comparables**. The appraiser gathers pertinent information about comparables and makes feature-by-feature comparisons with the subject property. The appraiser then translates his findings into an estimate of the market value of the subject property. Appraisers use this method whenever possible because the sales prices of comparables—which reflect the actions of informed buyers and sellers in the marketplace—are excellent indicators of market value.

For residential property, an appraiser needs at least three reliable comparable sales to have enough data for the sales comparison approach. It's usually possible to find three good comparables, but when it isn't, the appraiser will turn to the alternative appraisal methods—the cost approach and the income approach.

Elements of Comparison. To determine whether a particular sale can legitimately be used as a comparable, the appraiser checks the following aspects of the transaction, sometimes called the primary elements of comparison.

Date of Comparable Sale. The sale should be recent, within the past six months if possible. Recent sales give a more accurate indication of what is happening in the marketplace today. If the market has been inactive and there are not three legitimate comparable sales from the past six months, the appraiser can go back further, as long as he provides justification in the appraisal report for doing so. When the market is going through a major shift, such as a rapid downswing during a recession, comparable sales should be no more than three months old.

When using an older comparable, the appraiser must adjust the sales price for inflationary or deflationary trends or any other forces that have affected prices in the area.

> **Example:** A comparable residential property sold ten months ago for $280,000. Local property values have risen by 5% over the past ten months. The comparable property, then, should be worth approximately 5% more than it was ten months ago.
>
> | $280,000 | Value ten months ago |
> |---|---|
> | × 105% | Inflation factor |
> | $294,000 | Approximate present value |

Location of Comparable Sale. Whenever possible, the appraiser should select comparables from the same neighborhood as the subject property. Absent any legitimate comparables in the neighborhood, the appraiser can look elsewhere, but the properties selected should at least come from comparable neighborhoods.

If a comparable selected from an inferior neighborhood is structurally identical to the subject property, it is probably less valuable; conversely, a structurally identical comparable in a superior neighborhood is probably more valuable than the subject property. Location generally contributes more to the value of real estate than any other characteristic. A high-quality property cannot overcome the adverse effects on value that a low-quality neighborhood causes. On the other hand, the value of a relatively weak property is enhanced by a stable and desirable neighborhood.

Physical Characteristics. To qualify as a comparable, a property should have physical characteristics (construction quality, design, amenities, etc.) that are similar to those of the subject property. When a comparable has a feature that the subject property lacks, or lacks a feature that the subject property has, the appraiser will adjust the comparable's price.

Example: One of the comparables the appraiser is using is quite similar to the subject property overall, but there are several significant differences. The subject property has a two-car garage, while the comparable has only a one-car garage. Based on experience, the appraiser estimates that space for a second car adds approximately $5,000 to the value of a home in this area. The comparable actually sold for $322,500. The appraiser will add $5,000 to the comparable's price, to estimate what the comparable would have been worth with a two-car garage.

On the other hand, the comparable has a fireplace and the subject property does not. The appraiser estimates that a fireplace adds approximately $1,400 to the value of a home. She will subtract $1,400 from the comparable's price, to estimate what the comparable would have sold for without a fireplace.

After adjusting the comparable's price up or down for each difference in this way, the appraiser can identify what the comparable would have sold for if it had been identical to the subject property. When the appraiser repeats this process for each comparable, the value of the subject property becomes evident.

Terms of Sale. The terms of sale can affect the price a buyer will pay for a property. Attractive financing concessions (such as seller-paid discount points or seller financing with an especially low interest rate) can make a buyer willing to pay a higher price than she would otherwise be willing to pay.

An appraiser has to take into account the influence the terms of sale may have had on the price paid for a comparable property. If the seller offered the property on very favorable terms, there's an excellent chance the sales price did not represent the true market value of the comparable.

Under the Uniform Standards of Professional Appraisal Practice, an appraiser giving an estimate of market value must state whether it's the most probable price:

1. in terms of cash,
2. in terms of financial arrangements equivalent to cash, or
3. in other precisely defined terms.

If the estimate is based on financing with special conditions or incentives, those terms must be clearly set forth, and the appraiser must estimate their effect on the property's value. Market data supporting the value estimate (comparable sales) must be explained in the same way.

Conditions of Sale. Last but not least, a comparable sale can be relied on as an indication of what the subject property is worth only if it occurred under normal conditions. That is, the sale was between unrelated parties (an "arm's length transaction"); both the buyer and the seller were informed of the property's attributes and deficiencies; both were acting free of unusual pressure; and the property was offered for sale on the open market for a reasonable length of time.

Thus, the appraiser must investigate the circumstances of each comparable sale to determine whether the price paid was influenced by a condition that would render it unreliable as an indication of value. For example, if the property sold only days before a scheduled foreclosure sale, the sales price probably reflects the pressure under

Fig. 12.6 Comparable sales comparison chart

	Subject Property	Comparables			
Comparable Sales Comparison Chart					
		1	2	3	4
Sales price		$391,750	$396,500	$387,000	$388,500
Location	quiet street				
Age	7 yrs.				
Lot size	50'x200'				
Construction	frame			+6,000	
Style	ranch				
Number of Rooms	7		−5,000		
Number of Bedrooms	3				
Number of Baths	2	+3,500			+3,500
Square feet	1,350				
Exterior	good				
Interior	good				
Garage	1 car attached				
Other improvements		−4,000			
Financing					
Date of sale		−3,000	−3,000		
Net Adjustments		−3,500	−8,000	+6,000	+3,500
Adjusted Price		$388,250	$388,500	$393,000	$392,000

which the seller was acting. Or if the buyer and seller were relatives, it's possible that the price was less than it would have been between two strangers. Or if the property sold the same day it was listed, it may have been underpriced. In each of these cases, there's reason to suspect that the sales price did not reflect the property's true value, so the appraiser would not use the transaction as a comparable sale.

Comparing Properties and Making Adjustments. A proper comparison between the subject property and each comparable is essential to an accurate estimate of value. The more similar the properties, the easier the comparison. A comparable property that is the same design and in the same condition as the subject property, on a very similar site in the same neighborhood, which sold under typical financing terms the previous month, will give an excellent indication of the market value of the subject property. However, except perhaps in a new subdivision where the houses are nearly identical, the appraiser usually cannot find such ideal comparables. There are likely to be at least some significant differences between the comparables and the subject property. So, as you've seen, the appraiser has to make adjustments, taking into account differences in time, location, physical characteristics, and terms of sale, in order to arrive at an **adjusted selling price** for each comparable.

It stands to reason that the more adjustments an appraiser has to make, the less reliable the resulting estimate of value will be. These adjustments are an inevitable part of the sales comparison approach, but appraisers try to keep them to a minimum by selecting the best comparables available.

Although the appraiser bases his estimate of the subject property's value on the adjusted prices of the comparables, it's important to understand that the value estimate is never merely an average of those prices; careful analysis is required. Also note that the original cost of the subject property (how much the current owners paid for it) is irrelevant to the appraisal process.

Use of Listings. When comparable sales are scarce (as when the market is just emerging from a dormant period), the appraiser may compare the subject property to properties that are presently listed for sale. The appraiser must keep in mind, however, that listing prices tend to be high and frequently represent the ceiling of the market value range. The appraiser might also use prices offered by buyers, though these can be difficult to confirm, since records of offers aren't always kept. Offers are usually at the low end of the market value range. Actual market value is typically somewhere between offers and listing prices.

Cost Approach to Value

The second method of appraisal, the **cost approach**, is based on the premise that the value of a property is limited by the cost of replacing it. (This follows from the principle of substitution: if the asking price for a home was more than it would cost to build a new one just like it, no one would buy it.)

The cost approach involves estimating how much it would cost to replace the subject property's existing buildings, and then adding to that the estimated value of the site. Because the cost approach involves estimating the value of land and buildings separately, then adding the estimates together, it is sometimes called the **summation method**.

There are three steps to the cost approach:

1. Estimate the cost of replacing the improvements.
2. Estimate and deduct any accrued depreciation.
3. Add the value of the lot to the depreciated value of the improvements.

We'll look at each of these steps. First, however, it's important to distinguish between replacement cost and reproduction cost. **Reproduction cost** is the cost of constructing an exact duplicate—a replica—of the subject building, at current prices. **Replacement cost**, on the other hand, is the current cost of constructing a building with a utility equivalent to the

Fig. 12.7 Calculating value with the cost approach

Cost Approach

　　Replacement cost of improvements
－ Depreciation
＋ Value of land
　　Value of subject property

subject's—that is, a building that can be used in the same way as the subject. Reproduction cost and replacement cost may be the same if the subject property is a new home. But if the structure is older, and was built with the detailed workmanship and expensive materials of earlier times, then the reproduction cost and the replacement cost will be quite different. So the appraiser must base her estimate of value on the replacement cost. The reproduction cost would be prohibitive, and it would not represent the current market value of the improvements.

Estimating Replacement Cost. The replacement cost of a building can be estimated in three different ways:

1. the square foot method,
2. the unit-in-place method, and
3. the quantity survey method.

Square Foot. The simplest way to estimate replacement cost is the **square foot method** (also known as the comparative cost or comparative unit method). By analyzing the average cost per square foot of construction for recently built comparable homes, the appraiser can calculate what the square foot cost of replacing the subject home would be. The number of square feet in a home is determined by measuring the outside dimensions of each floor of the structure.

To calculate the cost of replacing the subject property's improvements, the appraiser multiplies the estimated cost per square foot by the number of square feet in the subject.

Example: The subject property is a ranch-style house with a wood exterior, containing 1,600 square feet. Based on an analysis of the construction costs of three recently built homes of comparable size and quality, the appraiser estimates that it would cost $115.38 per square foot to replace the home.

1,600	Square feet
× 115.38	Cost per square foot
$184,608	Estimated cost of replacing improvements

Of course, a comparable structure (or "benchmark" building) is unlikely to be exactly the same as the subject property. Variations in design, shape, and grade of construction will affect the square-foot cost, either moderately or substantially. When recently built comparable homes aren't available, then the appraiser relies on current cost manuals to estimate the basic construction costs.

Unit-in-Place. The **unit-in-place method** involves estimating the cost of replacing specific components of the building, such as the floors, roof, plumbing, and foundation. For example, one of the estimates might be a certain number of dollars per one hundred square feet of roofing. Another component estimate would be a certain amount per cubic yard of concrete for an installed foundation. Then the appraiser adds all the estimates together to determine the replacement cost of the structure itself.

Quantity Survey. The **quantity survey method** involves a detailed estimate of the quantities and prices of construction materials and labor, which are added to the indirect costs (building permit, survey, etc.) to arrive at what is generally regarded as the most accurate replacement cost estimate. Because it's complex and time consuming, this method is generally used only by experienced contractors and price estimators.

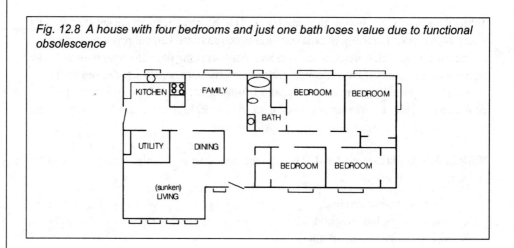

Fig. 12.8 A house with four bedrooms and just one bath loses value due to functional obsolescence

Estimating Depreciation. When the property being appraised is a used home, the presumption is that it is not as valuable as a comparable new home; it has depreciated in value. So, after estimating replacement cost—which indicates what the improvements would be worth if they were new—the appraiser's next step is to estimate the depreciation.

Depreciation is a loss in value due to any cause. Value can be lost as a result of physical deterioration, functional obsolescence, or external obsolescence.

- **Physical deterioration** is a loss in value due to wear and tear, damage, or structural defects. It's easier to spot this type of depreciation than the other types, and easier to estimate its impact on value.

   Physical deterioration may be curable or incurable. Depreciation is considered **curable** if the cost of correcting it could be recovered in the sales price when the property is sold. Depreciation is **incurable** if it is impossible to correct, or if it would cost so much to correct that it would be impractical to do so. Curable physical deterioration is often referred to as **deferred maintenance**.

- **Functional obsolescence** is a loss in value due to functional inadequacies, often caused by age or by poor design. Examples include a poor floor plan, an unappealing design, outdated fixtures, or too few bathrooms in relation to the number of bedrooms. Like physical deterioration, functional obsolescence may be curable or incurable.

- **External obsolescence** (also referred to as economic obsolescence) is caused by conditions outside the property itself, such as zoning changes, neighborhood deterioration, traffic problems, or exposure to nuisances, like noise from airport flight patterns. Identifying external obsolescence is the primary purpose of an appraiser's neighborhood analysis. External obsolescence is beyond a property owner's control, so it's virtually always incurable.

Estimating depreciation accurately is the most difficult phase of the replacement cost method of appraisal. Depreciation estimates are often highly subjective, and they are never any more reliable than the judgment and skill of the appraiser who is making them.

Adding Land Value. The last step in the replacement cost process is to add the value of the land to the depreciated value of the improvements. The value of the land is estimated by the sales comparison method. Prices recently paid for lots similar to the subject lot are compared and used as indications of what the subject lot is worth.

Keep in mind that the value of the land is not depreciated. An appraiser regards land as indestructible; it does not lose value.

Income Approach to Value

The **income approach** (also known as the capitalization method) is based on the idea that there is a relationship between the income a property generates and its market value to an investor. In effect, the income approach seeks to determine the present value of a property's future income.

Gross Income. When using the income approach, the appraiser first finds the property's gross income. She does this by estimating the rent the property would command if it were presently available for lease on the open market. What it would earn on the open market is called the **economic rent**, as distinguished from what it is actually earning now, which is called the **contract rent** or **historical rent**. Contract rent can be used to gauge the property's earnings potential. A pattern of rent increases or decreases is a strong indication of whether the contract rent is above or below the economic rent.

The economic rent is the property's **potential gross income**, what it could earn if it were fully occupied and all rents owed were collected. But it is unrealistic to expect a rental property to be fully occupied throughout its productive life; vacancies must be expected. Also, there are going to be tenants who do not pay their rent. So the appraiser must make a deduction from potential gross income to allow for occasional vacancies and unpaid rents. Called a **vacancy factor**, this deduction is expressed as a percentage of the potential gross income. For example, the appraiser might deduct 5% from potential gross income as a vacancy factor. Once the vacancy factor is deducted, the appraiser is left with a more reliable income figure, called **effective gross income**.

Operating Expenses. From the effective gross income, the appraiser deducts the expenses connected with operating the building. They fall into three classifications: fixed expenses, maintenance expenses, and reserves for replacement.

- **Fixed expenses:** Property taxes and hazard insurance.
- **Maintenance expenses:** Services for tenants, utilities, supplies, cleaning, repairs, administrative costs, and building employee wages.
- **Reserves for replacement:** Regular allowances set aside to replace structures and equipment that are expected to wear out, such as roofs, heating equipment, air conditioners, and (in a residential building) kitchen ranges and refrigerators.

The income that is left when operating expenses are deducted from effective gross income is called **net operating income**. It is net operating income that is capitalized to determine the property's value (see the next section).

Some expenses, such as the owner's income taxes, the depreciation reserves, and the mortgage payments (called **debt service**) are not deducted from the effective gross income to arrive at the net income. These are not considered operating expenses from an appraisal standpoint.

Capitalization. The process of converting net operating income into a meaningful value is called **capitalization**. The mathematical procedure is expressed in this formula:

Annual Net Operating Income ÷ Capitalization Rate = Value

Example: The property's annual net operating income is $55,700 and the capitalization rate is 11%. According to the capitalization formula, the property's value is $506,364.

$$\$55,700 \div 0.11 = \$506,364$$

The **capitalization rate** is the rate of return an investor (a potential purchaser) would want to receive on the money he invests in the property (the purchase price). When the investor chooses the rate of return, it is plugged into the formula shown above. By dividing the net operating income by the desired rate of return, the investor can determine how much she can pay for the property and still realize that desired return.

Example: The property's annual net operating income is $45,000 and the investor's desired return is 12%.

$$\$45,000 \div 0.12 = \$375,000$$

The investor can pay up to $375,000 for a property earning $45,000 in net income and realize her desired yield of 12%.

Selecting a Capitalization Rate. To appraise property using the income approach, the appraiser must be familiar with the rate of return that investors generally demand for similar properties.

There are a number of ways for an appraiser to determine a property's capitalization rate. For instance, the appraiser could analyze recent sales of comparable income properties and assume that the subject property would have a capitalization rate similar to theirs. This is known as the **direct comparison method**.

Regardless of the method used for selecting the capitalization rate, two very important considerations are the quality and the durability of the investment property's income. Quality (how reliable the tenants are) and durability (how long the income can be expected to last) influence the risk factor. The greater the risk, the higher the capitalization rate and the lower the property's value. On the other hand, the smaller the risk, the lower the capitalization rate and the higher the value.

Gross Income Multipliers. Residences generally aren't thought of as income-producing properties, so traditional income analysis techniques do not apply. If a residential appraiser uses an income method at all, she will use a simplified version called the **gross income multiplier method**. As a rule, this method is applied only when appraising single-family rental properties. It's sometimes called the **gross rent multiplier method**, since rents are typically the only form of income generated by residential rental properties.

In the gross income multiplier method, the appraiser looks at the relationship between a rental property's income and the price paid for the property.

Example:

Sales price:	$275,000
Monthly rent:	$1,675
Conclusion:	The monthly rent is equal to 0.61% of the sales price; the sales price is approximately 165 times the monthly rent.

Monthly rents may run about 1% of selling prices in one market, and more or less in another. A market exists where specific rental properties compete with each other for tenants. For competitive reasons, rents charged for similar properties tend to be much alike within the same market. As a result, if one rental property has a monthly income that is 1% of its sales price, comparable properties will have similar income-to-price ratios.

A monthly multiplier is established by dividing the sales price by the monthly rental income. An annual multiplier is calculated by dividing the sales price by the annual rental income.

Example:

Sales Price		Monthly Rent		Monthly Multiplier
$240,000	÷	$1,475	=	162.71

Sales Price		Annual Rent		Annual Multiplier
$240,000	÷	$17,700	=	13.56

After locating at least four comparable residential rental properties, the appraiser can determine their monthly or annual gross income multipliers (either is acceptable—it's a matter of the appraiser's preference) by dividing the rents into their respective selling prices.

Example:

Comp No.	Sales Price	Monthly Rent	Monthly Multiplier
1	$235,000	$1,450	162.07
2	$237,500	$1,460	162.67
3	$242,000	$1,500	161.33
4	$245,000	$1,525	160.66

The appraiser uses the multipliers of the comparables to determine an appropriate multiplier for the subject property, taking into account the similarities and differences between the properties. Then the appraiser multiplies the rent that the subject property generates by the chosen multiplier for a rough estimate of its value as income-producing property.

The principal weakness of the gross income multiplier method is that it is based on gross income figures and does not take into account vacancies or operating expenses. If two rental homes have the same rental income, the gross income multiplier method would indicate they are worth the same amount; but if one is older and has higher maintenance costs, the net return to the owner would be less, and so would the value of the property. Unless the appraiser knows the comparables are truly similar (having

Fig. 12.9 Uniform Residential Appraisal Report

Uniform Residential Appraisal Report   File

The purpose of this summary appraisal report is to provide the lender/client with an accurate, and adequately supported, opinion of the market value of the subject property.

SUBJECT

Property Address		City		State	Zip Code

Borrower ____ Owner of Public Record ____ County ____

Legal Description

Assessor's Parcel # ____ Tax Year ____ R.E. Taxes $ ____

Neighborhood Name ____ Map Reference ____ Census Tract ____

Occupant ☐ Owner ☐ Tenant ☐ Vacant   Special Assessments $ ____ ☐ PUD   HOA $ ____ ☐ per year ☐ per month

Property Rights Appraised ☐ Fee Simple ☐ Leasehold ☐ Other (describe)

Assignment Type ☐ Purchase Transaction ☐ Refinance Transaction ☐ Other (describe)

Lender/Client ____ Address ____

Is the subject property currently offered for sale or has it been offered for sale in the twelve months prior to the effective date of this appraisal? ☐ Yes ☐ No

Report data source(s) used, offering price(s), and date(s).

CONTRACT

I ☐ did ☐ did not analyze the contract for sale for the subject purchase transaction. Explain the results of the analysis of the contract for sale or why the analysis was not performed.

Contract Price $ ____ Date of Contract ____ Is the property seller the owner of public record? ☐ Yes ☐ No Data Source(s)

Is there any financial assistance (loan charges, sale concessions, gift or downpayment assistance, etc.) to be paid by any party on behalf of the borrower? ☐ Yes ☐ No
If Yes, report the total dollar amount and describe the items to be paid.

NEIGHBORHOOD

Note: Race and the racial composition of the neighborhood are not appraisal factors.

Neighborhood Characteristics			One-Unit Housing Trends				One-Unit Housing		Present Land Use %	
Location ☐ Urban ☐ Suburban ☐ Rural			Property Values ☐ Increasing ☐ Stable ☐ Declining				PRICE	AGE	One-Unit	%
Built-Up ☐ Over 75% ☐ 25–75% ☐ Under 25%			Demand/Supply ☐ Shortage ☐ In Balance ☐ Over Supply				$ (000)	(yrs)	2-4 Unit	%
Growth ☐ Rapid ☐ Stable ☐ Slow			Marketing Time ☐ Under 3 mths ☐ 3–6 mths ☐ Over 6 mths				Low		Multi-Family	%
Neighborhood Boundaries							High		Commercial	%
							Pred.		Other	%

Neighborhood Description

Market Conditions (including support for the above conclusions)

SITE

Dimensions	Area	Shape	View

Specific Zoning Classification ____ Zoning Description

Zoning Compliance ☐ Legal ☐ Legal Nonconforming (Grandfathered Use) ☐ No Zoning ☐ Illegal (describe)

Is the highest and best use of the subject property as improved (or as proposed per plans and specifications) the present use? ☐ Yes ☐ No If No, describe

Utilities	Public	Other (describe)		Public	Other (describe)	Off-site Improvements—Type	Public	Private
Electricity	☐	☐	Water	☐	☐	Street	☐	☐
Gas	☐	☐	Sanitary Sewer	☐	☐	Alley	☐	☐

FEMA Special Flood Hazard Area ☐ Yes ☐ No FEMA Flood Zone ____ FEMA Map # ____ FEMA Map Date ____

Are the utilities and off-site improvements typical for the market area? ☐ Yes ☐ No If No, describe

Are there any adverse site conditions or external factors (easements, encroachments, environmental conditions, land uses, etc.)? ☐ Yes ☐ No If Yes, describe

IMPROVEMENTS

General Description		Foundation		Exterior Description	materials/condition	Interior	materials/condition
Units ☐ One ☐ One with Accessory Unit		☐ Concrete Slab ☐ Crawl Space		Foundation Walls		Floors	
# of Stories		☐ Full Basement ☐ Partial Basement		Exterior Walls		Walls	
Type ☐ Det. ☐ Att. ☐ S-Det./End Unit		Basement Area ____ sq. ft.		Roof Surface		Trim/Finish	
☐ Existing ☐ Proposed ☐ Under Const.		Basement Finish ____ %		Gutters & Downspouts		Bath Floor	
Design (Style)		☐ Outside Entry/Exit ☐ Sump Pump		Window Type		Bath Wainscot	
Year Built		Evidence of ☐ Infestation		Storm Sash/Insulated		Car Storage ☐ None	
Effective Age (Yrs)		☐ Dampness ☐ Settlement		Screens		☐ Driveway # of Cars	
Attic ☐ None		Heating ☐ FWA ☐ HWBB ☐ Radiant		Amenities ☐ Woodstove(s) #		Driveway Surface	
☐ Drop Stair ☐ Stairs		☐ Other ____ Fuel		☐ Fireplace(s) # ☐ Fence		☐ Garage # of Cars	
☐ Floor ☐ Scuttle		Cooling ☐ Central Air Conditioning		☐ Patio/Deck ☐ Porch		☐ Carport # of Cars	
☐ Finished ☐ Heated		☐ Individual ☐ Other		☐ Pool ☐ Other		☐ Att. ☐ Det. ☐ Built-in	

Appliances ☐ Refrigerator ☐ Range/Oven ☐ Dishwasher ☐ Disposal ☐ Microwave ☐ Washer/Dryer ☐ Other (describe)

Finished area above grade contains: ____ Rooms ____ Bedrooms ____ Bath(s) ____ Square Feet of Gross Living Area Above Grade

Additional features (special energy efficient items, etc.)

Describe the condition of the property (including needed repairs, deterioration, renovations, remodeling, etc.).

Are there any physical deficiencies or adverse conditions that affect the livability, soundness, or structural integrity of the property? ☐ Yes ☐ No If Yes, describe

Does the property generally conform to the neighborhood (functional utility, style, condition, use, construction, etc.)? ☐ Yes ☐ No If No, describe

Freddie Mac Form 70 March 2005   Page 1 of 6   Fannie Mae Form 1004 March 2005

Uniform Residential Appraisal Report

File #

There are	comparable properties currently offered for sale in the subject neighborhood ranging in price from $		to $	.
There are	comparable sales in the subject neighborhood within the past twelve months ranging in sale price from $		to $	.

FEATURE	SUBJECT	COMPARABLE SALE # 1		COMPARABLE SALE # 2		COMPARABLE SALE # 3	
Address							
Proximity to Subject							
Sale Price	$		$		$		$
Sale Price/Gross Liv. Area	$ sq. ft.	$ sq. ft.		$ sq. ft.		$ sq. ft.	
Data Source(s)							
Verification Source(s)							
VALUE ADJUSTMENTS	DESCRIPTION	DESCRIPTION	+(-) $ Adjustment	DESCRIPTION	+(-) $ Adjustment	DESCRIPTION	+(-) $ Adjustment
Sale or Financing Concessions							
Date of Sale/Time							
Location							
Leasehold/Fee Simple							
Site							
View							
Design (Style)							
Quality of Construction							
Actual Age							
Condition							
Above Grade	Total Bdrms. Baths	Total Bdrms. Baths		Total Bdrms. Baths		Total Bdrms. Baths	
Room Count							
Gross Living Area	sq. ft.	sq. ft.		sq. ft.		sq. ft.	
Basement & Finished Rooms Below Grade							
Functional Utility							
Heating/Cooling							
Energy Efficient Items							
Garage/Carport							
Porch/Patio/Deck							
Net Adjustment (Total)		☐ + ☐ -	$	☐ + ☐ -	$	☐ + ☐ -	$
Adjusted Sale Price of Comparables		Net Adj. % Gross Adj. %	$	Net Adj. % Gross Adj. %	$	Net Adj. % Gross Adj. %	$

I ☐ did ☐ did not research the sale or transfer history of the subject property and comparable sales. If not, explain

My research ☐ did ☐ did not reveal any prior sales or transfers of the subject property for the three years prior to the effective date of this appraisal.

Data source(s)

My research ☐ did ☐ did not reveal any prior sales or transfers of the comparable sales for the year prior to the date of sale of the comparable sale.

Data source(s)

Report the results of the research and analysis of the prior sale or transfer history of the subject property and comparable sales (report additional prior sales on page 3).

ITEM	SUBJECT	COMPARABLE SALE # 1	COMPARABLE SALE # 2	COMPARABLE SALE # 3
Date of Prior Sale/Transfer				
Price of Prior Sale/Transfer				
Data Source(s)				
Effective Date of Data Source(s)				

Analysis of prior sale or transfer history of the subject property and comparable sales

Summary of Sales Comparison Approach

Indicated Value by Sales Comparison Approach $

Indicated Value by: Sales Comparison Approach $ Cost Approach (if developed) $ Income Approach (if developed) $

This appraisal is made ☐ "as is", ☐ subject to completion per plans and specifications on the basis of a hypothetical condition that the improvements have been completed, ☐ subject to the following repairs or alterations on the basis of a hypothetical condition that the repairs or alterations have been completed, or ☐ subject to the following required inspection based on the extraordinary assumption that the condition or deficiency does not require alteration or repair:

Based on a complete visual inspection of the interior and exterior areas of the subject property, defined scope of work, statement of assumptions and limiting conditions, and appraiser's certification, my (our) opinion of the market value, as defined, of the real property that is the subject of this report is $, as of   , which is the date of inspection and the effective date of this appraisal.

Uniform Residential Appraisal Report

File #

ADDITIONAL COMMENTS

COST APPROACH TO VALUE (not required by Fannie Mae)

Provide adequate information for the lender/client to replicate the below cost figures and calculations.

Support for the opinion of site value (summary of comparable land sales or other methods for estimating site value)

ESTIMATED ☐ REPRODUCTION OR ☐ REPLACEMENT COST NEW	OPINION OF SITE VALUE .... = $
Source of cost data	Dwelling Sq. Ft. @ $ .... =$
Quality rating from cost service Effective date of cost data	Sq. Ft. @ $ .... =$
Comments on Cost Approach (gross living area calculations, depreciation, etc.)	
	Garage/Carport Sq. Ft. @ $ .... =$
	Total Estimate of Cost-New .... = $
	Less Physical Functional External
	Depreciation =$( )
	Depreciated Cost of Improvements................................. =$
	"As-is" Value of Site Improvements................................. =$
Estimated Remaining Economic Life (HUD and VA only) Years	Indicated Value By Cost Approach .... =$

INCOME APPROACH TO VALUE (not required by Fannie Mae)

Estimated Monthly Market Rent $ X Gross Rent Multiplier   = $ Indicated Value by Income Approach

Summary of Income Approach (including support for market rent and GRM)

PROJECT INFORMATION FOR PUDs (if applicable)

Is the developer/builder in control of the Homeowners' Association (HOA)? ☐ Yes ☐ No   Unit type(s) ☐ Detached ☐ Attached

Provide the following information for PUDs ONLY if the developer/builder is in control of the HOA and the subject property is an attached dwelling unit.

Legal name of project

Total number of phases   Total number of units   Total number of units sold

Total number of units rented   Total number of units for sale   Data source(s)

Was the project created by the conversion of an existing building(s) into a PUD? ☐ Yes ☐ No If Yes, date of conversion

Does the project contain any multi-dwelling units? ☐ Yes ☐ No Data source(s)

Are the units, common elements, and recreation facilities complete? ☐ Yes ☐ No If No, describe the status of completion.

Are the common elements leased to or by the Homeowners' Association? ☐ Yes ☐ No If Yes, describe the rental terms and options.

Describe common elements and recreational facilities

Uniform Residential Appraisal Report   File

This report form is designed to report an appraisal of a one-unit property or a one-unit property with an accessory unit; including a unit in a planned unit development (PUD). This report form is not designed to report an appraisal of a manufactured home or a unit in a condominium or cooperative project.

This appraisal report is subject to the following scope of work, intended use, intended user, definition of market value, statement of assumptions and limiting conditions, and certifications. Modifications, additions, or deletions to the intended use, intended user, definition of market value, or assumptions and limiting conditions are not permitted. The appraiser may expand the scope of work to include any additional research or analysis necessary based on the complexity of this appraisal assignment. Modifications or deletions to the certifications are also not permitted. However, additional certifications that do not constitute material alterations to this appraisal report, such as those required by law or those related to the appraiser's continuing education or membership in an appraisal organization, are permitted.

SCOPE OF WORK: The scope of work for this appraisal is defined by the complexity of this appraisal assignment and the reporting requirements of this appraisal report form, including the following definition of market value, statement of assumptions and limiting conditions, and certifications. The appraiser must, at a minimum: (1) perform a complete visual inspection of the interior and exterior areas of the subject property, (2) inspect the neighborhood, (3) inspect each of the comparable sales from at least the street, (4) research, verify, and analyze data from reliable public and/or private sources, and (5) report his or her analysis, opinions, and conclusions in this appraisal report.

INTENDED USE: The intended use of this appraisal report is for the lender/client to evaluate the property that is the subject of this appraisal for a mortgage finance transaction.

INTENDED USER: The intended user of this appraisal report is the lender/client.

DEFINITION OF MARKET VALUE: The most probable price which a property should bring in a competitive and open market under all conditions requisite to a fair sale, the buyer and seller, each acting prudently, knowledgeably and assuming the price is not affected by undue stimulus. Implicit in this definition is the consummation of a sale as of a specified date and the passing of title from seller to buyer under conditions whereby: (1) buyer and seller are typically motivated; (2) both parties are well informed or well advised, and each acting in what he or she considers his or her own best interest; (3) a reasonable time is allowed for exposure in the open market; (4) payment is made in terms of cash in U. S. dollars or in terms of financial arrangements comparable thereto; and (5) the price represents the normal consideration for the property sold unaffected by special or creative financing or sales concessions* granted by anyone associated with the sale.

*Adjustments to the comparables must be made for special or creative financing or sales concessions. No adjustments are necessary for those costs which are normally paid by sellers as a result of tradition or law in a market area; these costs are readily identifiable since the seller pays these costs in virtually all sales transactions. Special or creative financing adjustments can be made to the comparable property by comparisons to financing terms offered by a third party institutional lender that is not already involved in the property or transaction. Any adjustment should not be calculated on a mechanical dollar for dollar cost of the financing or concession but the dollar amount of any adjustment should approximate the market's reaction to the financing or concessions based on the appraiser's judgment.

STATEMENT OF ASSUMPTIONS AND LIMITING CONDITIONS: The appraiser's certification in this report is subject to the following assumptions and limiting conditions:

1. The appraiser will not be responsible for matters of a legal nature that affect either the property being appraised or the title to it, except for information that he or she became aware of during the research involved in performing this appraisal. The appraiser assumes that the title is good and marketable and will not render any opinions about the title.

2. The appraiser has provided a sketch in this appraisal report to show the approximate dimensions of the improvements. The sketch is included only to assist the reader in visualizing the property and understanding the appraiser's determination of its size.

3. The appraiser has examined the available flood maps that are provided by the Federal Emergency Management Agency (or other data sources) and has noted in this appraisal report whether any portion of the subject site is located in an identified Special Flood Hazard Area. Because the appraiser is not a surveyor, he or she makes no guarantees, express or implied, regarding this determination.

4. The appraiser will not give testimony or appear in court because he or she made an appraisal of the property in question, unless specific arrangements to do so have been made beforehand, or as otherwise required by law.

5. The appraiser has noted in this appraisal report any adverse conditions (such as needed repairs, deterioration, the presence of hazardous wastes, toxic substances, etc.) observed during the inspection of the subject property or that he or she became aware of during the research involved in performing this appraisal. Unless otherwise stated in this appraisal report, the appraiser has no knowledge of any hidden or unapparent physical deficiencies or adverse conditions of the property (such as, but not limited to, needed repairs, deterioration, the presence of hazardous wastes, toxic substances, adverse environmental conditions, etc.) that would make the property less valuable, and has assumed that there are no such conditions and makes no guarantees or warranties, express or implied. The appraiser will not be responsible for any such conditions that do exist or for any engineering or testing that might be required to discover whether such conditions exist. Because the appraiser is not an expert in the field of environmental hazards, this appraisal report must not be considered as an environmental assessment of the property.

6. The appraiser has based his or her appraisal report and valuation conclusion for an appraisal that is subject to satisfactory completion, repairs, or alterations on the assumption that the completion, repairs, or alterations of the subject property will be performed in a professional manner.

Uniform Residential Appraisal Report   File

APPRAISER'S CERTIFICATION: The Appraiser certifies and agrees that:

1. I have, at a minimum, developed and reported this appraisal in accordance with the scope of work requirements stated in this appraisal report.

2. I performed a complete visual inspection of the interior and exterior areas of the subject property. I reported the condition of the improvements in factual, specific terms. I identified and reported the physical deficiencies that could affect the livability, soundness, or structural integrity of the property.

3. I performed this appraisal in accordance with the requirements of the Uniform Standards of Professional Appraisal Practice that were adopted and promulgated by the Appraisal Standards Board of The Appraisal Foundation and that were in place at the time this appraisal report was prepared.

4. I developed my opinion of the market value of the real property that is the subject of this report based on the sales comparison approach to value. I have adequate comparable market data to develop a reliable sales comparison approach for this appraisal assignment. I further certify that I considered the cost and income approaches to value but did not develop them, unless otherwise indicated in this report.

5. I researched, verified, analyzed, and reported on any current agreement for sale for the subject property, any offering for sale of the subject property in the twelve months prior to the effective date of this appraisal, and the prior sales of the subject property for a minimum of three years prior to the effective date of this appraisal, unless otherwise indicated in this report.

6. I researched, verified, analyzed, and reported on the prior sales of the comparable sales for a minimum of one year prior to the date of sale of the comparable sale, unless otherwise indicated in this report.

7. I selected and used comparable sales that are locationally, physically, and functionally the most similar to the subject property.

8. I have not used comparable sales that were the result of combining a land sale with the contract purchase price of a home that has been built or will be built on the land.

9. I have reported adjustments to the comparable sales that reflect the market's reaction to the differences between the subject property and the comparable sales.

10. I verified, from a disinterested source, all information in this report that was provided by parties who have a financial interest in the sale or financing of the subject property.

11. I have knowledge and experience in appraising this type of property in this market area.

12. I am aware of, and have access to, the necessary and appropriate public and private data sources, such as multiple listing services, tax assessment records, public land records and other such data sources for the area in which the property is located.

13. I obtained the information, estimates, and opinions furnished by other parties and expressed in this appraisal report from reliable sources that I believe to be true and correct.

14. I have taken into consideration the factors that have an impact on value with respect to the subject neighborhood, subject property, and the proximity of the subject property to adverse influences in the development of my opinion of market value. I have noted in this appraisal report any adverse conditions (such as, but not limited to, needed repairs, deterioration, the presence of hazardous wastes, toxic substances, adverse environmental conditions, etc.) observed during the inspection of the subject property or that I became aware of during the research involved in performing this appraisal. I have considered these adverse conditions in my analysis of the property value, and have reported on the effect of the conditions on the value and marketability of the subject property.

15. I have not knowingly withheld any significant information from this appraisal report and, to the best of my knowledge, all statements and information in this appraisal report are true and correct.

16. I stated in this appraisal report my own personal, unbiased, and professional analysis, opinions, and conclusions, which are subject only to the assumptions and limiting conditions in this appraisal report.

17. I have no present or prospective interest in the property that is the subject of this report, and I have no present or prospective personal interest or bias with respect to the participants in the transaction. I did not base, either partially or completely, my analysis and/or opinion of market value in this appraisal report on the race, color, religion, sex, age, marital status, handicap, familial status, or national origin of either the prospective owners or occupants of the subject property or of the present owners or occupants of the properties in the vicinity of the subject property or on any other basis prohibited by law.

18. My employment and/or compensation for performing this appraisal or any future or anticipated appraisals was not conditioned on any agreement or understanding, written or otherwise, that I would report (or present analysis supporting) a predetermined specific value, a predetermined minimum value, a range or direction in value, a value that favors the cause of any party, or the attainment of a specific result or occurrence of a specific subsequent event (such as approval of a pending mortgage loan application).

19. I personally prepared all conclusions and opinions about the real estate that were set forth in this appraisal report. If I relied on significant real property appraisal assistance from any individual or individuals in the performance of this appraisal or the preparation of this appraisal report, I have named such individual(s) and disclosed the specific tasks performed in this appraisal report. I certify that any individual so named is qualified to perform the tasks. I have not authorized anyone to make a change to any item in this appraisal report; therefore, any change made to this appraisal is unauthorized and I will take no responsibility for it.

20. I identified the lender/client in this appraisal report who is the individual, organization, or agent for the organization that ordered and will receive this appraisal report.

Uniform Residential Appraisal Report   File

21. The lender/client may disclose or distribute this appraisal report to: the borrower; another lender at the request of the borrower; the mortgagee or its successors and assigns; mortgage insurers; government sponsored enterprises; other secondary market participants; data collection or reporting services; professional appraisal organizations; any department, agency, or instrumentality of the United States; and any state, the District of Columbia, or other jurisdictions; without having to obtain the appraiser's or supervisory appraiser's (if applicable) consent. Such consent must be obtained before this appraisal report may be disclosed or distributed to any other party (including, but not limited to, the public through advertising, public relations, news, sales, or other media).

22. I am aware that any disclosure or distribution of this appraisal report by me or the lender/client may be subject to certain laws and regulations. Further, I am also subject to the provisions of the Uniform Standards of Professional Appraisal Practice that pertain to disclosure or distribution by me.

23. The borrower, another lender at the request of the borrower, the mortgagee or its successors and assigns, mortgage insurers, government sponsored enterprises, and other secondary market participants may rely on this appraisal report as part of any mortgage finance transaction that involves any one or more of these parties.

24. If this appraisal report was transmitted as an "electronic record" containing my "electronic signature," as those terms are defined in applicable federal and/or state laws (excluding audio and video recordings), or a facsimile transmission of this appraisal report containing a copy or representation of my signature, the appraisal report shall be as effective, enforceable and valid as if a paper version of this appraisal report were delivered containing my original hand written signature.

25. Any intentional or negligent misrepresentation(s) contained in this appraisal report may result in civil liability and/or criminal penalties including, but not limited to, fine or imprisonment or both under the provisions of Title 18, United States Code, Section 1001, et seq., or similar state laws.

SUPERVISORY APPRAISER'S CERTIFICATION: The Supervisory Appraiser certifies and agrees that:

1. I directly supervised the appraiser for this appraisal assignment, have read the appraisal report, and agree with the appraiser's analysis, opinions, statements, conclusions, and the appraiser's certification.

2. I accept full responsibility for the contents of this appraisal report including, but not limited to, the appraiser's analysis, opinions, statements, conclusions, and the appraiser's certification.

3. The appraiser identified in this appraisal report is either a sub-contractor or an employee of the supervisory appraiser (or the appraisal firm), is qualified to perform this appraisal, and is acceptable to perform this appraisal under the applicable state law.

4. This appraisal report complies with the Uniform Standards of Professional Appraisal Practice that were adopted and promulgated by the Appraisal Standards Board of The Appraisal Foundation and that were in place at the time this appraisal report was prepared.

5. If this appraisal report was transmitted as an "electronic record" containing my "electronic signature," as those terms are defined in applicable federal and/or state laws (excluding audio and video recordings), or a facsimile transmission of this appraisal report containing a copy or representation of my signature, the appraisal report shall be as effective, enforceable and valid as if a paper version of this appraisal report were delivered containing my original hand written signature.

APPRAISER

Signature_____
Name _____
Company Name _____
Company Address_____

_____
Telephone Number _____
Email Address _____
Date of Signature and Report_____
Effective Date of Appraisal _____
State Certification #_____
or State License #_____
or Other (describe) _____ State # _____
State _____
Expiration Date of Certification or License _____

ADDRESS OF PROPERTY APPRAISED

_____
_____

APPRAISED VALUE OF SUBJECT PROPERTY $ _____

LENDER/CLIENT

Name _____
Company Name _____
Company Address_____

_____
Email Address _____

SUPERVISORY APPRAISER (ONLY IF REQUIRED)

Signature_____
Name _____
Company Name _____
Company Address_____

_____
Telephone Number _____
Email Address _____
Date of Signature _____
State Certification #_____
or State License #_____
State _____
Expiration Date of Certification or License _____

SUBJECT PROPERTY

☐ Did not inspect subject property
☐ Did inspect exterior of subject property from street
   Date of Inspection _____
☐ Did inspect interior and exterior of subject property
   Date of Inspection _____

COMPARABLE SALES

☐ Did not inspect exterior of comparable sales from street
☐ Did inspect exterior of comparable sales from street
   Date of Inspection _____

similar vacancy rates and operating expenses), the appraiser must take into account the rough nature of the value indicated by this method.

If possible, the appraiser should use the subject property's economic rent, as opposed to the contract rent (the rent the owner is actually receiving), in calculating the gross income multiplier.

Example: The owner leased the home two years ago for $1,600 a month, and the lease contract has another year to go. Market rents have risen sharply over the past two years, so that the property could now command a much higher rent—probably about $1,875 a month. If the appraiser were to use the $1,600 contract rent in the gross income multiplier method instead of the $1,875 economic rent, it would distort the estimate of value.

Reconciliation and Final Estimate of Value

Throughout the appraisal process, the appraiser is gathering facts on which he will base the ultimate conclusion, the final estimate of the property's value. In many cases, the facts require nothing beyond simple verification; their meaning is self-evident. In other cases, they require expert interpretation. Nowhere in the appraisal process does the appraiser's experience and judgment play a more critical role.

The final value estimate is not simply the average of the results yielded by the three approaches to value—sales comparison, cost, and income. Rather, it is the figure that represents the appraiser's expert opinion of the subject property's value after all the data has been assembled and analyzed. Usually the values indicated by the different approaches vary at least somewhat. The process of deriving a single estimate of value from the differing indicators is called **reconciliation**.

Once the appraiser has determined the final estimate of value, he presents it to the client in an appraisal report. The two most common types of reports are the narrative report and the form report. A **narrative report** is a thorough, detailed, written presentation of the facts and reasoning behind the appraiser's estimate of value. A **form report** is a brief, standard form used by lending institutions and government agencies (for example, the FHA and VA), presenting only the key data and the appraiser's conclusions. This is the most common type of appraisal report. The Uniform Residential Appraisal Report form, used in most residential transactions, is shown in Figure 12.9.

Chapter Summary

1. An appraisal is an estimate or an opinion of value. Most real estate appraisals concern the property's market value, the price it is likely to bring on the open market in a sale under normal conditions.

2. Appraisers have developed many "principles of value" that guide them in the valuation process. These include the principles of highest and best use, change, supply and demand, substitution, conformity, contribution, anticipation, and competition.

3. The steps in the appraisal process include defining the problem, determining the scope of work, collecting and verifying the data, analyzing the data, valuing the site, applying the approaches to value, reconciling the value indicators, and issuing the appraisal report.

4. General data concerns factors outside the subject property itself that influence the property's value; the appraiser gathers general data by evaluating economic and social trends and by performing a neighborhood analysis. Specific data (about the subject property itself) is gathered through site analysis and building analysis.

5. In the sales comparison approach to value (which is the most important method of appraisal for residential properties), the appraiser compares the subject property to comparable properties that were sold recently, and uses the adjusted selling prices of the comparables to estimate the value of the subject property.

6. In the cost approach to value, the appraiser estimates the cost of replacing the improvements, deducts any depreciation, and adds the estimated value of the land to arrive at an estimate of the value of the whole property. The three types of depreciation are physical deterioration, functional obsolescence, and external obsolescence. Depreciation is curable if the cost of correcting it could be recovered in the sales price when the property is sold. Curable physical deterioration is also called deferred maintenance.

7. In the income approach to value, the appraiser divides the property's net income by a capitalization rate to estimate its value to an investor. The appraiser first estimates the property's potential gross income (economic rent), then deducts a vacancy factor to determine the effective gross income, then deducts operating expenses to determine net operating income, and finally divides net operating income by a capitalization rate to find the property's value. The gross income multiplier method is a simplified version of the income approach that is sometimes used in appraising residential rental properties.

🔑 Key Terms

Market value—The most probable price that a property should bring in a competitive and open market under all conditions requisite to a fair sale, the buyer and seller each acting prudently and knowledgeably, and assuming the price is not affected by undue stimulus.

Highest and best use—The most profitable use of the property; the one that provides the greatest net return over time.

Principle of change—Real property is in a constant state of change; it goes through a four-phase life cycle of integration, equilibrium, disintegration, and rejuvenation.

Principle of substitution—No one will pay more for a piece of property than they would have to pay for an equally desirable substitute.

Sales comparison approach—The method of appraisal in which the appraiser compares the subject property to recently sold comparable properties.

Arm's length transaction—A transaction in which there is no pre-existing family or business relationship between the parties.

Cost approach—The method of appraisal in which the appraiser estimates the replacement cost of the building, deducts depreciation, and adds the value of the site.

Depreciation—Loss in value due to any cause. Depreciation is curable if the cost of correcting it could be recovered in the sales price when the property is sold.

Physical deterioration—Depreciation caused by wear and tear, damage, or structural defects. Curable physical deterioration is called deferred maintenance.

Functional obsolescence—Depreciation caused by functional inadequacies or outmoded design.

External obsolescence—Depreciation caused by forces outside the property, such as neighborhood decline or proximity to nuisances; also called economic obsolescence.

Income approach—The method of appraising property in which net income is converted into value using a capitalization rate.

Effective gross income—A property's potential gross income, minus a vacancy factor.

Net operating income—A property's effective gross income, minus operating expenses. Also called net income.

Capitalization rate—The rate of return an investor wants on her investment in the property.

Economic rent—The rent that a property would earn on the open market if it were currently available for rent, as distinguished from the rent it is actually earning now (the contract rent).

Chapter Quiz

1. An appraisal is a/an:
   a) scientific determination of a property's value
   b) property's average value, as indicated by general and specific data
   c) estimate of a property's value as of a specific date
   d) mathematical analysis of a property's value

2. The focus of most appraisals is the subject property's:
   a) market value
   b) market price
   c) sales price
   d) value in use

3. A property's highest and best use is the use that:
   a) will generate the greatest net return
   b) will generate the highest gross return
   c) best promotes the public health, safety, and welfare
   d) is best suited to the present owner's plans

4. The earliest phase of a property's life cycle, when it is being developed, is called:
   a) substitution
   b) regression
   c) integration
   d) disintegration

5. Developers have announced plans to build a multimillion dollar shopping center next door to a vacant commercial lot you own. Property values in the area will tend to increase as a result of this announcement. This is an example of the principle of:
   a) highest and best use
   b) supply and demand
   c) substitution
   d) anticipation

6. The owner of an apartment building has asked an appraiser to determine if it would make financial sense to put in a swimming pool for the tenants' use. The appraiser will be most concerned with the principle of:
   a) regression
   b) substitution
   c) conformity
   d) contribution

7. If someone were to build a high-quality home costing $450,000 in a neighborhood where all of the other homes were valued at around $175,000, the expensive home would suffer a loss in value. This illustrates the principle of:
   a) regression
   b) supply and demand
   c) progression
   d) aversion

8. An appraiser gathers general data in a:
   a) site analysis
   b) building analysis
   c) neighborhood analysis
   d) None of the above

9. The sales comparison approach would be much more important than the other two methods (the cost approach and the income approach) in the appraisal of a/an:
   a) six-unit apartment building
   b) industrial building
   c) shopping center
   d) single-family home

10. A residential appraiser looking for good comparables is most likely to consider homes that:
    a) have not changed hands within the past three years
    b) are currently listed for sale
    c) were sold within the past six months
    d) were listed for less than they eventually sold for

11. In which of the following situations would the sales comparison method of appraisal be least reliable?

   a) When all the comparables are in the same price range
   b) When the real estate market has been inactive for quite a while
   c) When some of the comparables are located in another neighborhood
   d) When the subject property is in better condition than the comparables

12. When applying the sales comparison method to appraise a single-family home, an appraiser would never use as a comparable a similar home that:

   a) sold over six months ago
   b) sold recently but is located in another neighborhood
   c) was sold by owners who were forced to sell because of financial difficulties
   d) is situated on a corner lot

13. When using the replacement cost approach, which of the following would be least important?

   a) Current construction cost per square foot
   b) Rental cost per square foot
   c) Depreciation
   d) Estimated land value

14. An appraiser is applying the cost approach in valuing an elegant building that was built in 1894. Which of the following is most likely to be true?

   a) The building's replacement cost is the same as its reproduction cost
   b) The building's replacement cost is a better indicator of its market value than its reproduction cost
   c) The building's reproduction cost is a better indicator of its market value than its replacement cost
   d) The building's replacement cost is much greater than its reproduction cost

15. In the income approach to value, which of the following is not considered to be one of the property's operating expenses?

   a) General real estate taxes
   b) Maintenance expenses
   c) Reserves for replacement
   d) Mortgage payments

Answer Key

1. c) An appraisal is only an estimate or opinion of value, and it is valid only in regard to a specified date.

2. a) An appraiser is usually asked to determine the subject property's market value (value in exchange).

3. a) The highest and best use is the use that would produce the greatest net return over time, given the current zoning and other restrictions on use.

4. c) Integration is the period during which the property is being developed.

5. d) This is an example of the principle of anticipation, which holds that value is created by the expectation of future benefits to be derived from owning a property.

6. d) The appraiser will be concerned with the principle of contribution. Will the proposed improvement—the swimming pool—contribute enough to the property's value (in the form of higher rents from tenants, and, ultimately, net income to the owner) to justify the expense of installing it?

7. a) The principle of regression holds that association with properties of much lower quality reduces a property's value.

8. c) General data is data concerning factors outside the subject property itself that affect the property's value. A neighborhood analysis involves collection of general data, whereas the site and building analysis involve collection of specific data about the subject property itself.

9. d) In the appraisal of single-family homes, the sales comparison approach is given the most weight.

10. c) A sales comparison appraisal of residential property is usually based on the sales prices of homes that sold within the past six months.

11. b) There is little data available in an inactive market. (However, the appraiser can use older comparable sales if she determines the rate of appreciation or depreciation and adjusts the prices accordingly.)

12. c) Forced sales are never used as comparables for appraisal purposes. Comparable sales must occur under normal market conditions, where neither party was acting under unusual pressure.

13. b) The cost approach involves estimating the current cost of construction, subtracting the amount of accrued depreciation, then adding back in the estimated value of the land. How much the property rents for is irrelevant in the cost approach.

14. b) The cost of producing a replica of an old building at current prices (reproduction cost) is invariably much higher than the cost of constructing a building with the equivalent utility using modern materials (replacement cost). Reproduction cost is not a good indicator of an old building's market value.

15. d) The mortgage payments—referred to as the property's debt service—are not considered operating expenses for the purposes of the income approach.

Closing Real Estate Transactions

Chapter Overview

The real estate agent's job doesn't end when the parties sign the purchase and sale agreement. Many matters must be taken care of before the sale can be finalized, and the service provided by the real estate agent during the closing process is just as important as the agent's marketing efforts before the sale. Guiding the parties through closing prevents unnecessary delays and earns the agent a reputation for professionalism. This chapter explains the purpose of escrow, the steps involved in closing, and Washington's Escrow Agent Registration Act. It also discusses how settlement statements work, how closing costs are allocated and prorated, income tax aspects of closing, and the requirements of the federal Real Estate Settlement Procedures Act.

Introduction

Once a buyer and a seller have signed a purchase agreement, the parties and their agents begin making preparations to finalize the transaction. Finalizing a real estate transaction is called **closing** or **settlement**.

The closing process varies considerably from one state to another. In some states, all of the parties involved in the transaction get together to sign and exchange documents and transfer funds. In many other states (including Washington), the closing process is handled by a third party, through the creation of an escrow.

Escrow

Escrow is an arrangement in which money and documents are held by a third party (the **escrow agent**) on behalf of the buyer and the seller. The parties usually give the escrow agent written **escrow instructions**, which determine under what conditions and at what time the agent will distribute the money and documents to the proper parties. The escrow agent is a dual agent, representing both the buyer and the seller, with fiduciary duties to both parties (see Chapter 7).

The purpose of escrow is to ensure that the seller receives the purchase price, the buyer receives clear title to the property, and the lender's security interest in the property is perfected. Escrow protects each party from the other's change of mind. For example, if the seller suddenly doesn't want to sell the property as agreed, he can't just refuse to deliver the deed to the buyer. Once a deed has been given to an escrow agent, if the buyer fulfills all the conditions specified in the escrow instructions and deposits the purchase price into escrow, the escrow agent is required to deliver the deed to the buyer. An added advantage of escrow is convenience: the parties do not have to be present to close the transaction.

Escrow agents perform a wide variety of services to prepare a transaction for closing. Most escrow closings involve all of the following steps:

- gathering the information necessary to prepare escrow instructions;
- obtaining a preliminary title report from the title insurance company;
- paying off existing loans secured by the property;
- preparing documents, such as the deed;
- depositing funds from the buyer (and seller if necessary);

- prorating expenses and allocating closing costs;
- preparing a uniform settlement statement;
- obtaining title insurance policies;
- recording documents; and
- disbursing funds and delivering documents.

Escrow Agent Registration Act

Washington's Escrow Agent Registration Act requires escrow agents to be licensed and registered with the Department of Financial Institutions. A company that is licensed to engage in the escrow business under the Registration Act is called a **licensed escrow agent**. The individuals that a licensed escrow agent employs to handle transactions must be **licensed escrow officers**, and they must be supervised by the company's **designated escrow officer**. The designated escrow officer is a licensed escrow officer; he is also either a partner, a corporate officer, or the sole proprietor of the company, depending on how the company is organized.

To become a licensed escrow agent, a company must comply with bonding requirements and have errors and omissions insurance. The company's owners and managers must submit proof of good character, fingerprints, and personal credit reports.

To become a licensed escrow officer, an individual must pass a state exam and submit proof of good character, fingerprints, and a personal credit report.

A licensed escrow agent is responsible for keeping adequate transaction records and maintaining a trust account for clients' funds in a recognized Washington depository. The director of the Department of Financial Institutions may investigate the actions of licensed escrow agents and escrow officers and suspend or revoke their licenses if they have committed dishonest or prohibited acts.

Exemptions. There are several significant exemptions from the Escrow Agent Registration Act's licensing requirements. Attorneys, title insurance companies, other insurance companies, banks, savings and loans, credit unions, and federally approved lenders are allowed to perform escrow services without being licensed or registered under the act; so are those acting under the supervision of a court, such as receivers, trustees in bankruptcy, guardians, executors, and probate administrators. A real estate licensee handling the escrow for her own transaction (one for which she is providing brokerage services) is also exempt, provided that she does not charge an additional fee for the escrow services.

Throughout this chapter, we refer to the person who handles the closing process for a transaction as the escrow agent, in accordance with common usage. Keep in mind, however, that the closing agent is not necessarily a licensed escrow agent or a licensed escrow officer. In some transactions, the closing agent is the real estate licensee or one of the other parties that are exempt from the Registration Act.

Closing Costs and Settlement Statements

Most real estate transactions involve a wide variety of costs in addition to the purchase price: inspection fees, title insurance charges, loan fees, and so on. These are known as **closing costs**. Some of these closing costs are paid by the buyer, and some are paid by the seller. Some are paid by one party to the other; for example, the buyer may have to reimburse the seller for property taxes the seller already paid. Other closing costs are paid by one of the parties to a third party; the seller may be required to pay a pest inspector's fee, for instance.

There are also other payments to be made in connection with closing. For example, the seller often has to pay off an existing mortgage or other liens. Determining who is required to pay how much to whom at closing can be a complicated matter.

So for each transaction, the escrow agent prepares a **settlement statement**. A settlement statement (also known as a closing statement) sets forth all the financial aspects of the transaction in detail. It shows exactly how much the buyer will have to pay at closing, and exactly how much the seller will take away from closing. A simplified example of a settlement statement is shown in Figure 13.1.

Preparing a Settlement Statement

The items listed on the settlement statement are either **debits** or **credits**. A debit is a charge payable by a party; the purchase price is a debit to the buyer, for example, and the sales commission is a debit to the seller. Credits are items payable to a party; the buyer is credited for her new loan, and the seller for the purchase price.

Preparing a settlement statement involves little more than determining what charges and credits apply to a given transaction and making sure each one is allocated to the right party. When allocating expenses, an escrow agent is generally guided by the terms of the purchase and sale agreement or the escrow instructions. The allocation can also be determined by custom (local or general), provided the custom doesn't conflict with the terms of the parties' contract. For example, in most places the buyer usually pays the cost of an appraisal, so that cost would ordinarily be a debit to the buyer at closing. But if the purchase and sale agreement stipulated that the seller would pay the appraisal fee, the agreement would take precedence over custom and the expense would be a debit to the seller at closing.

Of course, neither custom nor the agreement between the parties will be honored if they are contrary to local, state, or federal law.

Although a real estate agent typically won't be called upon to prepare a formal settlement statement, every agent should know what closing costs are likely to be involved in a transaction and how they are customarily allocated. The buyer and the seller may want to negotiate the allocation of particular costs, and in any case they should have a good idea of their costs before signing a contract. A real estate agent should be able to prepare a preliminary estimate of closing costs for each party.

Guide to Settlement Statements

The simplified settlement statement in Figure 13.1 uses the double entry accounting method, so each party has a credit column and a debit column. The sum of the buyer's credits must equal the sum of the buyer's debits. The sum of the seller's credits must equal the sum of the seller's debits. Think of the settlement statement as a check register for a bank account. Debits are like checks written against the account, and credits are the equivalent of deposits into the account. When the transaction closes, the balance in each party's account should be zero.

When an item is payable by one party to the other, it will appear on the settlement statement as a debit to the paying party and as a credit to the party paid. An obvious example is the purchase price, which is debited to the buyer and credited to the seller.

Fig. 13.1 Simplified settlement statement

	Buyer		Seller	
	Debits	**Credits**	**Debits**	**Credits**
Purchase price	175,000.00			175,000.00
Deposit		8,750.00		
Excise tax			2,240.00	
Sales commission			12,250.00	
Payoff of seller's loan			92,950.00	
Assumption of seller's loan				
New loan		140,000.00		
Seller financing				
Owner's title insurance			120.00	
Lender's title insurance	456.00			
Origination/assumption fee	2,100.00			
Discount points				
Property taxes				
In arrears				
Paid in advance	684.50			684.50
Hazard insurance				
Assumption of policy				
New policy	260.00			
Interest				
Payoff of seller's loan			382.86	
Assumption				
New loan (prepaid)	161.08			
Reserve account				
Payoff of seller's loan				286.05
Assumption				
Credit report	40.00			
Appraisal	275.00			
Survey				
Pest inspection and repairs			150.00	
Personal property				
Recording fees	50.00		25.00	
Escrow fee	147.00		147.00	
Balance due from buyer		30,423.58		
Balance due to seller			67,705.69	
TOTALS	179,173.58	179,173.58	175,970.55	175,970.55

If an item is paid by one of the parties to a third party, it appears on the settlement statement in the paying party's debit column, and it does not appear in the other party's columns at all. For example, the seller is customarily charged for the state excise tax, which is paid to the county treasurer. The tax is a debit to the seller, but it is not a credit to the buyer.

Similarly, certain items are shown as a credit to one party, but not as a debit to the other. The seller's reserve balance is a case in point. If the sale calls for the payoff of the seller's existing mortgage, any property tax and insurance reserves held by the seller's lender are refunded. They are a credit to the seller, but not a debit to the buyer.

Settlement Charges. Here is a list of the items that appear on the settlement statements for most standard transactions.

Purchase Price. Paid by the buyer to the seller, the purchase price is listed as a debit to the buyer and a credit to the seller.

Earnest Money Deposit. In most transactions, the buyer provides an earnest money deposit. If the transaction closes, the earnest money is applied to the purchase price. Since the buyer has already paid the earnest money, it appears on the settlement statement as a credit to the buyer. And since the full purchase price has already been debited to the buyer and credited to the seller, no entry for the earnest money is made on the seller's side of the statement.

Sales Commission. The real estate sales commission is normally paid by the seller, so it is entered as a debit to the seller.

New Loan. If the buyer secures a new loan to finance part or all of the sale, the loan amount is listed as a credit to the buyer. Like the deposit, the buyer's loan is part of the purchase price already credited to the seller, so no entry is made on the seller's side of the statement.

Assumed Loan. If the buyer assumes the seller's existing loan, it is part of the money used to finance the transaction, so (like a new loan) it is credited to the buyer. The assumed loan balance is a debit to the seller.

Seller Financing. If the seller accepts a mortgage or deed of trust from the buyer for part of the purchase price, that shows up in the buyer's credit column, just like an institutional loan. At the same time, a seller financing arrangement reduces the amount of cash the seller will receive at closing, so it is listed as a debit to the seller.

If the property is sold under a land contract, the contract price (less the down-payment) is credit extended by the seller. It reduces the seller's net at closing and is used by the buyer to finance the purchase, so it's a debit to the seller and a credit to the buyer.

Payoff of Seller's Loan. If the seller pays off an existing mortgage loan, his net is reduced by that amount. The payoff is a debit to the seller. No entry is made on the buyer's side of the statement.

Prepayment Penalty. A prepayment penalty is a charge the seller's lender may impose on the seller for paying the loan off before the end of its term. It would be a debit to the seller on the settlement statement.

Seller's Reserve Account. As was mentioned earlier, the seller often has reserves on deposit with his lender to cover property taxes and hazard insurance premiums. When the seller's loan is paid off, the unused balance in the reserve account (also called an **impound account**) is refunded to the seller. It appears as a credit on the seller's side of the settlement statement. If the buyer is assuming the loan and the reserve account, the reserves would appear as a credit to the seller and a debit to the buyer.

Appraisal Fee. The appraisal is usually required by the buyer's lender, so the fee is ordinarily a debit to the buyer.

Credit Report. The buyer's lender charges the buyer for the credit investigation, so this is also a debit to the buyer.

Survey. Sometimes a lender requires a survey as a condition for making the loan. Unless otherwise agreed, the cost of the survey is a debit to the buyer.

Origination Fee. This is the lender's one-time charge to the borrower for setting up the loan (see Chapter 11). It's a debit to the buyer.

Discount Points. The discount points are a debit to the buyer, unless the seller has agreed to pay for a buydown (see Chapter 11). In that case, the points are a debit to the seller.

Assumption Fee. A lender charges an assumption fee when the buyer is assuming the seller's existing loan. The assumption fee is a debit to the buyer.

Owner's Title Insurance Premium. The premium for the owner's title insurance policy (which protects the buyer) is customarily paid by the seller. So this is a debit to the seller, unless otherwise agreed.

Lender's Title Insurance Premium. The lender requires the buyer to provide an extended coverage policy to protect the lender's lien priority. The premium for this policy is a debit to the buyer, unless otherwise agreed.

Sale of Personal Property. If the seller is selling the buyer some personal property along with the real property, the price of these items should be credited to the seller and debited to the buyer. (The seller should sign a bill of sale to be delivered to the buyer at closing along with the deed.)

Inspection Fees. The cost of an inspection is allocated by agreement between the parties. For example, the buyer might agree to pay for the cost of a pest inspection, while the seller agrees to pay for repairs if the inspection shows that any are necessary.

Hazard Insurance Policy. The lender generally requires the buyer to pay for one to three years of hazard insurance coverage in advance. This is a debit to the buyer.

Excise Tax. This is a tax imposed on every sale of real property in Washington (see Chapter 5). It is customarily paid by the seller, so it would usually be listed in the seller's debit column.

Attorney's Fees. A buyer or seller who is represented by an attorney in the transaction is responsible for his own attorney's fees. On the settlement statement, the fees will show up as a debit to the appropriate party.

Recording Fees. The fees for recording the various documents involved in the transaction are usually charged to the party who benefits from the recording. For example, the fees for recording the deed and the new mortgage or deed of trust are debits to the buyer; the fee for recording a satisfaction of the old mortgage is a debit to the seller.

Escrow Fee. Also called a settlement fee or closing fee, the escrow fee is the escrow agent's charge for her services. The buyer and the seller commonly agree to split the escrow fee; in that case, half the fee will be debited to each party.

Prorations. There are, of course, certain recurring expenses connected with ownership of real estate, including property taxes, hazard insurance premiums, and mortgage interest payments. As a general rule, the seller is responsible for these expenses during his period of ownership, but not beyond. In preparing a settlement statement, the escrow agent checks to see whether the seller will be current, in arrears (late), or paid in advance with respect to these expenses on the closing date. The escrow agent then prorates the expenses, determining what portion the seller is responsible for. To

prorate an expense is to divide and allocate it proportionately, according to time, interest, or benefit.

If, in regard to a particular expense, the seller will be in arrears on the closing date, the amount that he owes is entered as a debit on the settlement statement. If the seller has paid in advance, he is entitled to a partial refund, which appears as a credit on the statement. If the expense is one that will continue after closing (as in the case of property taxes), the buyer is responsible for it once her period of ownership begins. That will show up on the buyer's side of the settlement statement as a credit (if the seller is in arrears) or as a debit (if the seller has paid in advance).

The first step in prorating an expense is to divide it by the number of days it covers to determine the **per diem** (daily) rate. So an annual expense would be divided by 365 days (366 in a leap year); the per diem rate would be $1/365$ of the annual amount. A monthly expense would be divided by the number of days in the month in question (28, 29, 30, or 31).*

The next step is to determine the number of days during which a particular party is responsible for the expense. The final step is to multiply that number of days by the per diem rate, to arrive at the share of the expense that party is responsible for. Examples appear below. (See Chapter 18 for further discussion of proration calculations.)

Property Taxes. The seller is responsible for property taxes up to the day of closing; the buyer is responsible for them thereafter. The parties will agree on (or rely on local custom to settle) which party pays the taxes for the closing date itself; more often than not, the buyer is responsible. If the seller has already paid the property taxes for the year, he is entitled to a prorated refund at closing. On the settlement statement, this will appear as a credit to the seller and a debit to the buyer.

> **Example:** Sharon is selling her house to Ben. The transaction will close July 14. This year the property taxes on the house are $2,200.95. The escrow agent calculates the per diem rate by dividing the property tax figure by 365, the number of days in the year.
>
> $$\$2,200.95 \div 365 = \$6.03 \text{ per diem}$$
>
> Sharon, the seller, is responsible for the property taxes through July 13—in other words, for the first 194 days of the year. The buyer, Ben, is responsible for the taxes from July 14 forward—the remaining 171 days in the year.
>
> Sharon has already paid the full year's taxes, so at closing she'll be entitled to a credit for the share that is Ben's responsibility. The escrow agent multiplies the number of days for which Ben is responsible by the per diem rate to determine the amount Ben will owe Sharon at closing.
>
> $$171 \text{ days} \times \$6.03 = \$1,031.13$$
>
> This $1,031.13 will appear as a credit on the seller's side of the settlement statement, and as a debit on the buyer's side of the statement.

---

* It was once a common practice to simplify proration calculations by using a 360-day year and 30-day months (regardless of how many days there actually were in a particular year or month). But when calculators became widely available, most closing agents started using the exact number of days in the year or month in question. Also note that in order for the result of a proration to be completely accurate, the per diem rate must be calculated to an accuracy of at least four decimal places for monthly amounts, and five decimal places for annual amounts.

If the taxes are in arrears, the amount the seller should have paid for the period before closing will be a debit to the seller on the settlement statement.

Hazard Insurance. Hazard insurance is commonly paid in advance. At closing, the seller is entitled to a refund for the unused portion of the policy. For example, if the seller has paid the premium for the year, and there are three months left in the year, the seller gets a refund of one-fourth of the premium. This would show up as a credit to the seller on the settlement statement. Hazard insurance policies typically cannot be assumed, but if one is assumed, the seller will be credited and the buyer will be debited for the appropriate amount.

Interest on Seller's Loan. Interest on a real estate loan is almost always paid in arrears. In other words, the interest accruing during a given month is paid as part of the next month's payment. For instance, a loan payment due on September 1 includes the interest that accrued during August. If a transaction closes in the middle of the payment period, the seller owes the lender some interest.

> **Example:** The closing date is August 15. Although the seller made a payment on his loan on August 1, that payment did not include any of the interest that is accruing during August. At closing, the seller will owe the lender interest for the period from August 1 through August 15. The escrow agent prorates the interest, charging the seller only for those days, rather than the whole month's interest. The prorated amount is entered on the settlement statement as a debit to the seller.
>
> If the buyer assumes the loan, her first payment will be due on September 1, and it will pay all of the interest for August. The seller will be debited for the interest owed up to August 15, and the buyer will be credited for the same amount.

Prepaid Interest on Buyer's Loan. Another expense that the escrow agent prorates (one that does not concern the seller) is the interest on the buyer's new mortgage loan. As a general rule, the first payment date of a new loan is not the first day of the month immediately following closing, but rather the first day of the next month after that.

> **Example:** A buyer is financing the purchase of a home with a new institutional loan. Closing takes place on January 23. The buyer is not required to make a payment on the new loan on February 1. Instead, the first payment isn't due until March 1.

Even though the first payment isn't due for an extra month, interest begins accruing on the loan on the closing date. As was explained above, the first regular payment will cover the interest for the preceding month. So if the transaction closes on January 23, the first payment will be due on March 1, and that payment will cover the interest accrued in February. However, it will not cover the interest accrued between January 23 and January 31. Instead, the lender requires the buyer to pay the interest for those nine days in January at closing. This is called **prepaid interest** or **interim interest**. It will appear as a debit to the buyer on the settlement statement.

> **Example:** The buyer is borrowing $418,500 at 7% interest to finance the purchase. The annual interest on the loan during the first year will be $29,295 ($418,500 × 7% = $29,295). The escrow agent divides that annual figure by 365 to determine the per diem interest rate.

$$\$29,295 \div 365 = \$80.26 \text{ per diem}$$

There are nine days between the closing date (January 23) and the first day of the following month, so the lender will expect the buyer to prepay nine days' worth of interest at closing.

$$\$80.26 \times 9 \text{ days} = \$722.34 \text{ prepaid interest}$$

The escrow agent will enter $722.34 as a debit to the buyer on the settlement statement.

The buyer and seller both typically pay interest for the closing date (unless a loan is being assumed). The seller pays interest on the existing loan, which ends on the closing date, and the buyer pays interest on the purchase loan, which begins on the closing date. If the buyer is assuming the seller's existing loan, the parties need to agree on which party is responsible for interest on the closing date.

Rent. So far we've only discussed prorated expenses. In some transactions, there is also income to be prorated at closing. If the property generates rental income and the tenants have paid for some period beyond the closing date, the seller is debited and the buyer credited for the rent paid in advance. If the rent is paid in arrears, the seller will be credited for the amount due up to closing, and the buyer will be debited for the same amount.

Note that tenants' security deposits are not prorated. The seller must transfer all of the deposits to the buyer, since the leases will continue after closing.

Cash at Closing. As we said earlier, on a settlement statement the sum of one party's credits should equal the sum of that party's debits, so that the final balance in each party's "account" is zero. In order for the statement to work this way, it must list the amount of cash that the buyer will have to bring to closing, and also the amount of cash the seller will take away from closing.

Balance Due from Buyer. Add up all of the buyer's credits, then add up all of the buyer's debits. Subtract the buyer's credits from the buyer's debits to find the balance due, which is the amount of cash the buyer will have to pay at closing. Enter this amount as a credit for the buyer. Now the buyer's credits column should add up to exactly the same amount as the buyer's debits column.

Balance Due to Seller. Add up all of the seller's credits, then add up all of the seller's debits. Subtract the seller's debits from the seller's credits. The result is the amount of cash the seller will receive at closing (if any). Enter this amount as a debit if credits exceed debits, but as a credit if debits exceed credits. Now the seller's credits column should add up to exactly the same amount as the seller's debits column.

Income Tax Aspects of Closing

Nearly all real estate transactions have tax implications for the parties (see Chapter 14) and, naturally, it is up to each party to fulfill his or her own tax obligations. However, there are certain requirements related to income taxes that must be met when a transaction closes.

Form 1099-S Reporting

The IRS generally requires an escrow agent to report real property sales on Form 1099-S. The form is used to report the seller's name and social security number and the gross proceeds from the sale. However, the form doesn't have to be filed for the sale of a principal residence if: 1) the seller certifies in writing that none of the gain is taxable; and 2) the sale is for $250,000 or less ($500,000 or less if the seller is married). Certain other types of transactions are also exempt from the requirement.

An escrow agent may not charge the parties a separate fee for complying with 1099-S reporting requirements.

Form 8300 Reporting

The IRS requires an escrow agent who receives more than $10,000 in cash to report the cash payment on Form 8300, in order to help detect money laundering. This rule applies whether the cash was received in a single transaction or in a series of related transactions.

Example: ABC Escrow is handling the closing for buyer Sam. As part of the process, Sam will bring $12,000 cash to closing. He gives ABC Escrow $8,000 on Thursday, and the remaining $4,000 on Friday. Although the individual amounts are less than $10,000, ABC Escrow will need to submit Form 8300 to the IRS because the transactions are related.

The escrow agent must file Form 8300 within 15 days of receiving the cash. A copy of the form should be kept on file for five years.

FIRPTA

The Foreign Investment in Real Property Tax Act (FIRPTA) is a federal law designed to help prevent foreign investors from evading their tax liability on income generated from the sale of real estate. FIRPTA requires the property buyer to determine whether the seller is a "foreign person," defined as someone who is not a U.S. citizen or resident alien. If the seller is a foreign person, the buyer must withhold 10% of the amount realized from the sale and forward those funds to the IRS. (In most cases, the amount realized is simply the sales price.) The closing agent usually handles these requirements on behalf of the buyer. Payment must be made within 20 days after the transfer date. Note that many residential transactions are exempt from FIRPTA.

Real Estate Settlement Procedures Act

The Real Estate Settlement Procedures Act (**RESPA**) is a federal law that affects how closing is handled in most residential transactions financed with institutional loans. The law has two main goals:

- to provide borrowers with information about their closing costs; and
- to eliminate kickbacks and referral fees that unnecessarily increase the costs of settlement.

Transactions Covered by RESPA

RESPA applies to "federally related" loan transactions. A loan is federally related if:

1. it will be secured by a mortgage or deed of trust against:
   * property on which there is (or on which the loan proceeds will be used to build) a dwelling with four or fewer units;
   * a condominium unit or a cooperative apartment; or
   * a lot with (or on which the loan proceeds will be used to place) a mobile home; and
2. the lender is federally regulated, has federally insured accounts, is assisted by the federal government, makes loans in connection with a federal program, sells loans to Fannie Mae, Ginnie Mae, or Freddie Mac, or makes real estate loans totaling more than $1,000,000 per year.

In short, the act applies to most institutional lenders and to most residential loans.

Exemptions. RESPA does not apply to the following loan transactions:

* a loan used to purchase 25 acres or more;
* a loan used primarily for a business, commercial, or agricultural purpose;
* a loan used to purchase vacant land, unless there will be a one- to four-unit dwelling built on it or a mobile home placed on it;
* temporary financing, such as a construction loan; or
* an assumption for which the lender's approval is neither required nor obtained.

Note that RESPA also does not apply to seller-financed transactions, since they are not federally regulated.

RESPA Requirements

RESPA has these requirements for federally related loan transactions:

1. Within three days after receiving a written loan application, the lender must give all loan applicants:
   * a copy of "Shopping For Your Home Loan," a HUD **booklet about settlement procedures**, which explains RESPA, closing costs, and the settlement statement;
   * a **mortgage servicing disclosure statement**, which discloses whether the lender intends to service the loan or transfer it to another lender; and
   * a **good faith estimate of closing costs** (see Figure 13.2) the borrower is expected to pay; a lender or loan originator may not charge a loan applicant any fees other than a credit report fee until the good faith estimate (GFE) has been provided and the applicant has expressed an intent to continue with the loan transaction.

   If the lender turns down the loan within three days, these documents do not need to be provided.
2. If the lender or another settlement service provider requires the borrower to use a particular attorney, credit reporting agency, or appraiser, that requirement must be disclosed to the borrower when the loan application or service agreement is signed.

Fig. 13.2 Good faith estimate of closing costs

OMB Approval No. 2502-0265

Good Faith Estimate (GFE)

Name of Originator		Borrower	
Originator Address		Property Address	
Originator Phone Number			
Originator Email		Date of GFE	

Purpose

This GFE gives you an estimate of your settlement charges and loan terms if you are approved for this loan. For more information, see HUD's *Special Information Booklet* on settlement charges, your *Truth-in-Lending Disclosures*, and other consumer information at www.hud.gov/respa. If you decide you would like to proceed with this loan, contact us.

Shopping for your loan

Only you can shop for the best loan for you. Compare this GFE with other loan offers, so you can find the best loan. Use the shopping chart on page 3 to compare all the offers you receive.

Important dates

1. The interest rate for this GFE is available through [_____]. After this time, the interest rate, some of your loan Origination Charges, and the monthly payment shown below can change until you lock your interest rate.

2. This estimate for all other settlement charges is available through [_____].

3. After you lock your interest rate, you must go to settlement within [__] days (your rate lock period) to receive the locked interest rate.

4. You must lock the interest rate at least [__] days before settlement.

Summary of your loan

Your initial loan amount is	$
Your loan term is	years
Your initial interest rate is	%
Your initial monthly amount owed for principal, interest, and any mortgage insurance is	$ per month
Can your interest rate rise?	☐ No ☐ Yes, it can rise to a maximum of %. The first change will be in .
Even if you make payments on time, can your loan balance rise?	☐ No ☐ Yes, it can rise to a maximum of $
Even if you make payments on time, can your monthly amount owed for principal, interest, and any mortgage insurance rise?	☐ No ☐ Yes, the first increase can be in and the monthly amount owed can rise to $. The maximum it can ever rise to is $.
Does your loan have a prepayment penalty?	☐ No ☐ Yes, your maximum prepayment penalty is $
Does your loan have a balloon payment?	☐ No ☐ Yes, you have a balloon payment of $ due in years.

Escrow account information

Some lenders require an escrow account to hold funds for paying property taxes or other property-related charges in addition to your monthly amount owed of $[_____].

Do we require you to have an escrow account for your loan?

☐ No, you do not have an escrow account. You must pay these charges directly when due.

☐ Yes, you have an escrow account. It may or may not cover all of these charges. Ask us.

Summary of your settlement charges

A	**Your Adjusted Origination Charges** *(See page 2.)*	$
B	**Your Charges for All Other Settlement Services** *(See page 2.)*	$
A + B	Total Estimated Settlement Charges	$

Good Faith Estimate (HUD-GFE) 1

Understanding your estimated settlement charges

Some of these charges can change at settlement. See the top of page 3 for more information.

Your Adjusted Origination Charges

1. Our origination charge
This charge is for getting this loan for you.

2. Your credit or charge (points) for the specific interest rate chosen

☐ The credit or charge for the interest rate of [＿＿] % is included in "Our origination charge." (See item 1 above.)

☐ You receive a credit of $[＿＿＿＿] for this interest rate of [＿＿] %. This credit **reduces** your settlement charges.

☐ You pay a charge of $[＿＿＿＿] for this interest rate of [＿＿] %. This charge (points) **increases** your total settlement charges.

The tradeoff table on page 3 shows that you can change your total settlement charges by choosing a different interest rate for this loan.

| **A** | **Your Adjusted Origination Charges** | $ |

Your Charges for All Other Settlement Services

3. Required services that we select
These charges are for services we require to complete your settlement. We will choose the providers of these services.

Service   *Charge*

4. Title services and lender's title insurance
This charge includes the services of a title or settlement agent, for example, and title insurance to protect the lender, if required.

5. Owner's title insurance
You may purchase an owner's title insurance policy to protect your interest in the property.

6. Required services that you can shop for
These charges are for other services that are required to complete your settlement. We can identify providers of these services or you can shop for them yourself. Our estimates for providing these services are below.

Service   *Charge*

7. Government recording charges
These charges are for state and local fees to record your loan and title documents.

8. Transfer taxes
These charges are for state and local fees on mortgages and home sales.

9. Initial deposit for your escrow account
This charge is held in an escrow account to pay future recurring charges on your property and includes ☐ all property taxes, ☐ all insurance, and ☐ other [＿＿＿＿＿＿＿].

10. Daily interest charges
This charge is for the daily interest on your loan from the day of your settlement until the first day of the next month or the first day of your normal mortgage payment cycle. This amount is $[＿＿＿＿] per day for [＿＿] days (if your settlement is [＿＿＿＿]).

11. Homeowner's insurance
This charge is for the insurance you must buy for the property to protect from a loss, such as fire.

Policy   *Charge*

| **B** | **Your Charges for All Other Settlement Services** | $ |

| **A + B** | **Total Estimated Settlement Charges** | $ |

 Good Faith Estimate (HUD-GFE) 2

Instructions

Understanding which charges can change at settlement

This GFE estimates your settlement charges. At your settlement, you will receive a HUD-1, a form that lists your actual costs. Compare the charges on the HUD-1 with the charges on this GFE. Charges can change if you select your own provider and do not use the companies we identify. (See below for details.)

These charges **cannot increase** at settlement:	The total of these charges **can increase up to 10%** at settlement:	These charges **can change** at settlement:
■ Our origination charge ■ Your credit or charge (points) for the specific interest rate chosen *(after you lock in your interest rate)* ■ Your adjusted origination charges *(after you lock in your interest rate)* ■ Transfer taxes	■ Required services that we select ■ Title services and lender's title insurance *(if we select them or you use companies we identify)* ■ Owner's title insurance *(if you use companies we identify)* ■ Required services that you can shop for *(if you use companies we identify)* ■ Government recording charges	■ Required services that you can shop for *(if you do not use companies we identify)* ■ Title services and lender's title insurance *(if you do not use companies we identify)* ■ Owner's title insurance *(if you do not use companies we identify)* ■ Initial deposit for your escrow account ■ Daily interest charges ■ Homeowner's insurance

Using the tradeoff table

In this GFE, we offered you this loan with a particular interest rate and estimated settlement charges. However:

■ If you want to choose this same loan with **lower settlement charges,** then you will have a **higher interest rate.**
■ If you want to choose this same loan with a **lower interest rate,** then you will have **higher settlement charges.**

If you would like to choose an available option, you must ask us for a new GFE.

Loan originators have the option to complete this table. Please ask for additional information if the table is not completed.

	The loan in this GFE	The same loan with lower settlement charges	The same loan with a lower interest rate
Your initial loan amount	$	$	$
Your initial interest rate[1]	%	%	%
Your initial monthly amount owed	$	$	$
Change in the monthly amount owed from this GFE	No change	You will pay $ **more** every month	You will pay $ **less** every month
Change in the amount you will pay at settlement with this interest rate	No change	Your settlement charges will be **reduced** by $	Your settlement charges will **increase** by $
How much your total estimated settlement charges will be	$	$	$

[1] For an adjustable rate loan, the comparisons above are for the initial interest rate before adjustments are made.

Using the shopping chart

Use this chart to compare GFEs from different loan originators. Fill in the information by using a different column for each GFE you receive. By comparing loan offers, you can shop for the best loan.

	This loan	Loan 2	Loan 3	Loan 4
Loan originator name				
Initial loan amount				
Loan term				
Initial interest rate				
Initial monthly amount owed				
Rate lock period				
Can interest rate rise?				
Can loan balance rise?				
Can monthly amount owed rise?				
Prepayment penalty?				
Balloon payment?				
Total Estimated Settlement Charges				

If your loan is sold in the future

Some lenders may sell your loan after settlement. Any fees lenders receive in the future cannot change the loan you receive or the charges you paid at settlement.

 Good Faith Estimate (HUD-GFE)   3

3. If a settlement service provider refers a borrower to an affiliated provider, that business relationship must be fully disclosed, along with the fact that the referral is optional. Fee estimates for the services in question must also be given.

4. The closing agent (whoever handles closing, whether it's an escrow agent, the lender's employee, a real estate licensee, a lawyer, etc.) must itemize all loan settlement charges on a **uniform settlement statement** form (discussed below and shown in Figure 13.3).

5. If the borrower will have to make deposits into a reserve account (impound account) to cover taxes, insurance, and other recurring costs, the lender cannot require excessive deposits (more than necessary to cover the expenses when they come due, plus a two-month cushion).

6. A lender, title company, real estate agent, or other settlement service provider may not:
   • pay or receive a **kickback** or a referral fee (a payment from one settlement service provider to another for referring customers);
   • pay or receive an **unearned fee** (a charge that one settlement service provider shares with another provider who hasn't actually performed any services in exchange for the payment); or
   • charge a fee for the preparation of the uniform settlement statement, a reserve account statement, or the disclosure statement required by the Truth in Lending Act.

   Note that RESPA's prohibition against kickbacks does not apply to referral fees that one real estate licensee or firm pays to another for referring potential customers or clients.

7. The seller may not require the buyer to use a particular title company.

Uniform Settlement Statement. The escrow agent (or other closing agent) must provide completed uniform settlement statement forms to the borrower, the seller, and the lender on or before the closing date. (The borrower may sign a written waiver of the right to receive the statement by closing, in which case the forms must be provided to the parties as soon as practicable after closing.) If the borrower requests it, the escrow agent must allow the borrower to inspect the statement one business day before closing. The escrow agent may not charge a fee specifically for the preparation of the settlement statement.

A copy of the uniform settlement statement form (sometimes called a HUD-1 form) is shown in Figure 13.3. It does not have the same format as the simplified settlement statement shown earlier in this chapter (with buyer's credit and debit columns and seller's credit and debit columns side by side), but it presents the same information.

On the uniform settlement statement, each party's closing costs are itemized on the second page of the form, with the buyer's costs in the left column and the seller's costs in the right column. Each party's costs are added up, and the total is transferred to the first page of the form. The buyer's total costs are entered on line 103, and the seller's total costs are entered on line 502.

On the first page of the uniform settlement statement form, lines 101 through 120 correspond to the "Buyer's Debits" column on the simplified version. Lines 201 through 220 correspond to the "Buyer's Credits" column. Lines 401 through 420 are the same as the "Seller's Credits" column, and lines 501 through 520 represent the

"Seller's Debits" column. The amount of cash the buyer must bring to closing appears on line 303, and the amount of cash the seller will receive at closing is on line 603.

Estimates vs. Actual Charges. Some of the charges listed on the good faith estimate form given to the buyer at the beginning of the loan application process are in fact only estimates, so they won't necessarily match the buyer's actual charges at closing. However, RESPA doesn't allow certain charges on the GFE to be increased, and it limits how much certain others may be increased. There are three categories:

1. Charges that cannot increase at closing. This includes all of the lender's or loan originator's points and fees, and also the transfer taxes.
2. Charges for required services, such as the appraisal and title insurance, if the service provider was chosen or recommended by the lender. The total amount of these charges can increase no more than 10%.
3. Charges that can change any amount, because they're difficult to predict at the outset, such as hazard insurance.

The categories are explained in more detail on the third page of the good faith estimate form itself. The third page of the uniform settlement statement provides a side-by-side comparison of the estimated and actual charges.

Integrated Disclosure Forms. Starting August 1, 2015, the Consumer Financial Protection Bureau will require the use of integrated forms that satisfy the disclosure requirements of both RESPA and the Truth in Lending Act. The RESPA good faith estimate and the initial TILA disclosure will be combined into a single loan estimate form. The estimate form must be given to consumers no later than three days after a loan application is submitted. Similarly, the HUD-1 form and the final TILA disclosure will be merged into a closing disclosure form, which must be given to consumers at least three days before closing. (This is a change from RESPA's previous requirement that the settlement statement be delivered on or before the closing date.)

Fig. 13.3 Uniform settlement statement (HUD-1 form)

OMB Approval No. 2502-0265

A. Settlement Statement (HUD-1)

B. Type of Loan

| 1. ☐ FHA | 2. ☐ RHS | 3. ☐ Conv. Unins. | 6. File Number: | 7. Loan Number: | 8. Mortgage Insurance Case Number: |
| 4. ☐ VA | 5. ☐ Conv. Ins. | | | | |

C. Note: This form is furnished to give you a statement of actual settlement costs. Amounts paid to and by the settlement agent are shown. Items marked "(p.o.c.)" were paid outside the closing; they are shown here for informational purposes and are not included in the totals.

D. Name & Address of Borrower:	E. Name & Address of Seller:	F. Name & Address of Lender:
G. Property Location:	H. Settlement Agent:	I. Settlement Date:
	Place of Settlement:	

J. Summary of Borrower's Transaction		K. Summary of Seller's Transaction	
100. Gross Amount Due from Borrower		**400. Gross Amount Due to Seller**	
101. Contract sales price		401. Contract sales price	
102. Personal property		402. Personal property	
103. Settlement charges to borrower (line 1400)		403.	
104.		404.	
105.		405.	
Adjustment for items paid by seller in advance		**Adjustments for items paid by seller in advance**	
106. City/town taxes to		406. City/town taxes to	
107. County taxes to		407. County taxes to	
108. Assessments to		408. Assessments to	
109.		409.	
110.		410.	
111.		411.	
112.		412.	
120. Gross Amount Due from Borrower		**420. Gross Amount Due to Seller**	
200. Amounts Paid by or in Behalf of Borrower		**500. Reductions In Amount Due to Seller**	
201. Deposit or earnest money		501. Excess deposit (see instructions)	
202. Principal amount of new loan(s)		502. Settlement charges to seller (line 1400)	
203. Existing loan(s) taken subject to		503. Existing loan(s) taken subject to	
204.		504. Payoff of first mortgage loan	
205.		505. Payoff of second mortgage loan	
206.		506.	
207.		507.	
208.		508.	
209.		509.	
Adjustments for items unpaid by seller		**Adjustments for items unpaid by seller**	
210. City/town taxes to		510. City/town taxes to	
211. County taxes to		511. County taxes to	
212. Assessments to		512. Assessments to	
213.		513.	
214.		514.	
215.		515.	
216.		516.	
217.		517.	
218.		518.	
219.		519.	
220. Total Paid by/for Seller		**520. Total Reduction Amount Due Seller**	
300. Cash at Settlement from/to Borrower		**600. Cash at Settlement to/from Seller**	
301. Gross amount due from borrower (line 120)		601. Gross amount due to seller (line 420)	
302. Less amounts paid by/for borrower (line 220)	( )	602. Less reductions in amount due seller (line 520)	( )
303. Cash ☐ From ☐ To Borrower		**603. Cash ☐ To ☐ From Seller**	

The Public Reporting Burden for this collection of information is estimated at 35 minutes per response for collecting, reviewing, and reporting the data. This agency may not collect this information, and you are not required to complete this form, unless it displays a currently valid OMB control number. No confidentiality is assured; this disclosure is mandatory. This is designed to provide the parties to a RESPA covered transaction with information during the settlement process.

Previous editions are obsolete   Page 1 of 3   HUD-1

L. Settlement Charges

700. Total Real Estate Broker Fees	Paid From Borrower's Funds at Settlement	Paid From Seller's Funds at Settlement
Division of commission (line 700) as follows:		
701. $ to		
702. $ to		
703. Commission paid at settlement		
704.		

800. Items Payable in Connection with Loan			
801. Our origination charge	$	(from GFE #1)	
802. Your credit or charge (points) for the specific interest rate chosen $		(from GFE #2)	
803. Your adjusted origination charges		(from GFE A)	
804. Appraisal fee to		(from GFE #3)	
805. Credit report to		(from GFE #3)	
806. Tax service to		(from GFE #3)	
807. Flood certification		(from GFE #3)	
808.			

900. Items Required by Lender to Be Paid in Advance			
901. Daily interest charges from to @ $ /day		(from GFE #10)	
902. Mortgage insurance premium for months to		(from GFE #3)	
903. Homeowner's insurance for years to		(from GFE #11)	
904.			

1000. Reserves Deposited with Lender			
1001. Initial deposit for your escrow account		(from GFE #9)	
1002. Homeowner's insurance months @ $ per month $			
1003. Mortgage insurance months @ $ per month $			
1004. Property taxes months @ $ per month $			
1005. months @ $ per month $			
1006. months @ $ per month $			
1007. Aggregate Adjustment –$			

1100. Title Charges			
1101. Title services and lender's title insurance		(from GFE #4)	
1102. Settlement or closing fee	$		
1103. Owner's title insurance		(from GFE #5)	
1104. Lender's title insurance	$		
1105. Lender's title policy limit $			
1106. Owner's title policy limit $			
1107. Agent's portion of the total title insurance premium	$		
1108. Underwriter's portion of the total title insurance premium	$		

1200. Government Recording and Transfer Charges			
1201. Government recording charges		(from GFE #7)	
1202. Deed $ Mortgage $ Releases $			
1203. Transfer taxes		(from GFE #8)	
1204. City/County tax/stamps Deed $ Mortgage $			
1205. State tax/stamps Deed $ Mortgage $			
1206.			

1300. Additional Settlement Charges			
1301. Required services that you can shop for		(from GFE #6)	
1302. $			
1303. $			
1304.			
1305.			

1400. Total Settlement Charges (enter on lines 103, Section J and 502, Section K)		

Comparison of Good Faith Estimate (GFE) and HUD-1 Charges		Good Faith Estimate	HUD-1
Charges That Cannot Increase	**HUD-1 Line Number**		
Our origination charge	# 801		
Your credit or charge (points) for the specific interest rate chosen	# 802		
Your adjusted origination charges	# 803		
Transfer taxes	#1203		

Charges That in Total Cannot Increase More Than 10%		Good Faith Estimate	HUD-1
Government recording charges	# 1201		
	#		
	#		
	#		
	#		
	#		
	#		
	#		
Total			
Increase between GFE and HUD-1 Charges		$ or	%

Charges That Can Change		Good Faith Estimate	HUD-1
Initial deposit for your escrow account	#1001		
Daily interest charges	# 901 $ /day		
Homeowner's insurance	# 903		
	#		
	#		
	#		

Loan Terms

Your initial loan amount is	$
Your loan term is	▮▮▮ years
Your initial interest rate is	▮▮▮ %
Your initial monthly amount owed for principal, interest, and and any mortgage insurance is	$ ▮▮▮▮ includes ☐ Principal ☐ Interest ☐ Mortgage Insurance
Can your interest rate rise?	☐ No. ☐ Yes, it can rise to a maximum of ▮▮%. The first change will be on ▮▮▮▮ and can change again every ▮▮▮▮ after ▮▮▮▮ . Every change date, your interest rate can increase or decrease by ▮▮%. Over the life of the loan, your interest rate is guaranteed to never be **lower** than ▮▮% or **higher** than ▮▮%.
Even if you make payments on time, can your loan balance rise?	☐ No. ☐ Yes, it can rise to a maximum of $ ▮▮▮▮ .
Even if you make payments on time, can your monthly amount owed for principal, interest, and mortgage insurance rise?	☐ No. ☐ Yes, the first increase can be on ▮▮▮▮ and the monthly amount owed can rise to $ ▮▮▮▮ . The maximum it can ever rise to is $ ▮▮▮▮ .
Does your loan have a prepayment penalty?	☐ No. ☐ Yes, your maximum prepayment penalty is $ ▮▮▮▮ .
Does your loan have a balloon payment?	☐ No. ☐ Yes, you have a balloon payment of $ ▮▮▮▮ due in ▮▮▮ years on ▮▮▮▮ .
Total monthly amount owed including escrow account payments	☐ You do not have a monthly escrow payment for items, such as property taxes and homeowner's insurance. You must pay these items directly yourself. ☐ You have an additional monthly escrow payment of $ ▮▮▮▮ that results in a total initial monthly amount owed of $ ▮▮▮▮ . This includes principal, interest, any mortgage insurance and any items checked below: ☐ Property taxes ☐ Homeowner's insurance ☐ Flood insurance ☐ ▮▮▮▮ ☐ ▮▮▮▮ ☐ ▮▮▮▮

Note: If you have any questions about the Settlement Charges and Loan Terms listed on this form, please contact your lender.

Chapter Summary

1. After a purchase and sale agreement has been signed, the next stage of the transaction is the closing process. Closing is often handled through escrow, an arrangement in which money and documents are held by a third party (the escrow agent) on behalf of the buyer and the seller, and distributed when all of the conditions in the escrow instructions have been fulfilled.

2. In Washington, escrow agents and escrow officers must be licensed, but many groups (including lawyers, title companies, and lenders) are exempt from those requirements. A real estate licensee is exempt while handling escrow for a transaction in which she is also providing brokerage services, as long as no special fee is charged.

3. The escrow agent prepares a settlement statement, detailing all the charges payable by (debits) and payable to (credits) each of the parties at closing. Who pays which closing costs may be determined by agreement or by local custom. Certain expenses must be prorated as of the closing date.

4. Certain requirements related to income taxes must be fulfilled when a real estate transaction closes. These include the 1099-S and 8300 reporting requirements, and the FIRPTA tax withholding requirements.

5. RESPA applies to most residential purchase loan transactions involving institutional lenders. It requires a lender to give a loan applicant a good faith estimate of closing costs within three days after a written loan application is submitted. RESPA also requires the closing agent to complete a uniform settlement statement.

🔑 Key Terms

Closing—The final stage of a real estate transaction, in which documents are signed and delivered and funds are transferred.

Escrow—An arrangement in which money and documents are held by a third party on behalf of the buyer and the seller.

Escrow agent—A third party who holds money and documents in trust and carries out the closing process. Also called a closing agent.

Licensed escrow agent—A business that is licensed to provide escrow services under Washington's Escrow Agent Registration Act.

Licensed escrow officer—An individual who is licensed under the Escrow Agent Registration Act to perform escrow services as an employee of a licensed escrow agent.

Escrow instructions—A written document that tells the escrow agent how to proceed and states the conditions each party must fulfill before the transaction can close.

Settlement statement—A statement that sets forth all the financial aspects of a real estate transaction in detail and indicates how much cash each party will be required to pay or will receive at closing.

Debit—An amount payable by a party.

Credit—An amount payable to a party.

Reserve account—Funds on deposit with a lender to pay the property taxes and insurance premiums when due. Also called an impound account.

Prorate—To divide and allocate an expense proportionately, according to time, interest, or benefit, determining what share of it a particular party is responsible for.

Prepaid interest—Interest on the buyer's new mortgage loan that the lender requires to be paid at closing, covering the period from the closing date through the last day of the month.

Uniform settlement statement—The settlement statement form that closing agents are required to use in transactions covered by the Real Estate Settlement Procedures Act. Also called a HUD-1 form.

Chapter Quiz

1. The Henrys listed their home with Louise, a licensed real estate agent, who found them a buyer. Now Louise is handling the closing for this transaction. She's exempt from the licensing requirements of the Washington Escrow Agent Registration Act only if:

   a) this is a residential transaction

   b) the sales price is $100,000 or less

   c) she doesn't charge a separate fee for her escrow services

   d) the escrow fee she charges doesn't exceed the limits set by the Registration Act

2. Every debit on the buyer's side of the settlement statement is a charge that:

   a) will be paid to the buyer at closing

   b) must be paid by the buyer at closing

   c) the buyer must pay to the seller at closing

   d) the seller must pay to the buyer at closing

3. On a settlement statement, the purchase price will be listed as:

   a) a debit to the buyer

   b) a debit to the seller

   c) Both of the above

   d) Neither of the above

4. The transaction is closing on September 16. The seller has already paid the annual premium for hazard insurance, and the buyer will not be assuming the policy. On the settlement statement, part of the insurance premium will be listed as:

   a) a debit to the buyer and a credit to the seller

   b) a debit to the seller and a credit to the buyer

   c) a credit to the buyer

   d) a credit to the seller

5. How does the buyer's earnest money deposit show up on a settlement statement?

   a) It's listed as a debit on the buyer's side of the statement, and as a credit on the seller's side of the statement

   b) It's listed as a credit on the buyer's side of the statement, but it isn't listed on the seller's side because it's included in the purchase price

   c) It's listed as a credit on the seller's side of the statement, but it isn't listed on the buyer's side because it will be refunded at closing

   d) It's listed as a debit on both the buyer's side and the seller's side of the statement

6. When a buyer assumes a mortgage, how does the mortgage balance appear on the settlement statement?

   a) Only as a credit to the seller

   b) Only as a debit on the seller's side of the statement

   c) As a credit to the buyer and a debit to the seller

   d) As a credit to the seller and a debit to buyer

7. Which of the following is ordinarily one of the seller's closing costs?

   a) Sales commission

   b) Credit report fee

   c) Appraisal fee

   d) Origination fee

8. Which of the following is ordinarily one of the buyer's closing costs?

   a) Sales commission

   b) Lender's title insurance premium

   c) Excise tax

   d) None of the above

9. On a settlement statement, prepaid interest would usually appear as a:

    a) seller's debit

    b) buyer's credit

    c) seller's credit

    d) buyer's debit

10. The Matsons are selling their home. They are current on their mortgage payments, having made their most recent payment on May 1. They will be paying off their mortgage when the sale closes on May 17. At closing, the Matsons will probably be:

    a) entitled to a refund of the mortgage interest accruing in May

    b) required to pay the mortgage interest accruing in May

    c) entitled to a refund of the prepayment penalty

    d) required to pay part of the mortgage interest that accrued in April

11. A settlement statement:

    a) is given to the buyer but not the seller

    b) sets out the charges to be paid by each party or to each party at closing

    c) is given only to the buyer's lender

    d) is required only in transactions closed by licensed escrow agents

12. When an item is prorated, it means that:

    a) it is deleted from the cost of the sale

    b) it is calculated on the basis of a particular time period

    c) it is not paid until closing

    d) the escrow agent must pay the fee

13. Under RESPA, a loan is considered federally related if:

    a) it will be used to finance the purchase of real property

    b) the property has up to four dwelling units

    c) the lender is federally regulated

    d) All of the above

14. Under FIRPTA:

    a) a foreign investor can never buy or sell property without special authorization

    b) if a seller is not a U.S. citizen or resident alien, the escrow agent will have to deduct 10% of the amount realized and send it to the IRS

    c) the escrow agent must notify the real estate broker if the buyer is a foreign investor

    d) a foreign investor purchasing property in the U.S. must pay an additional 10% over and above the purchase price and submit it to the IRS

15. Tim, a real estate agent, has a friend who is purchasing a property through another agent. The purchase price is $95,000. Tim offers to act as escrow agent for the transaction for a small fee. Tim:

    a) is exempt from the Escrow Agent Registration Act because he is a real estate agent

    b) is violating the Escrow Agent Registration Act, because he isn't acting as a real estate agent in the transaction and he's charging a fee for escrow services

    c) is exempt from the Escrow Agent Registration Act because he is acting for a personal acquaintance

    d) is exempt from the Escrow Agent Registration Act because the sales price is less than $100,000

☞ Answer Key

1. c) A real estate licensee is exempt from the Escrow Agent Registration Act when handling closing for a transaction in which she is providing brokerage services, as long as the licensee does not charge a separate fee for escrow services.

2. b) A debit on the buyer's side of the statement is a charge that the buyer must pay. In some cases, it is a charge that the buyer must pay to the seller (a refund for taxes paid in advance, for example), but in other cases the buyer owes it to a third party (the loan fee paid to the lender, for example).

3. a) The purchase price is a debit to the buyer and a credit to the seller.

4. d) The seller is entitled to a refund for the insurance he paid in advance, and this will show up as a credit on the seller's side of the settlement statement. Since the buyer is not assuming the policy, the seller's insurance is not listed on the buyer's side of the statement.

5. b) The earnest money deposit is a credit to the buyer, since it has already been paid. It does not appear on the seller's side of the statement, because the full purchase price is listed as a credit to the seller, and the deposit is included in the price.

6. c) A loan the buyer uses to finance the transaction is listed as a credit to the buyer, whatever its source. When the financing comes through the seller (either through an assumption of the seller's loan, or through seller financing) it is a debit to the seller as well as a credit to the buyer.

7. a) The seller almost always pays the real estate commission. The other expenses listed relate to the buyer's loan, and they are ordinarily paid by the buyer.

8. b) The buyer is usually required to pay the premium for the lender's extended coverage title insurance policy.

9. d) Prepaid interest—interest on a new loan to cover the period from the closing date through the last day of the month—is one of the buyer's debits.

10. b) Because mortgage interest is paid in arrears—the month after it accrues—at closing the sellers will be required to pay the interest that has accrued during May. (Their May 1 mortgage payment included the interest that accrued in April.)

11. b) A settlement statement sets forth the charges that must be paid by each party and to each party at closing.

12. b) Prorating an expense is calculating it on the basis of a particular time period, such as number of days.

13. d) All of these are elements of a federally related loan under RESPA.

14. b) FIRPTA requires the escrow agent to deduct 10% of the amount realized and send it to the IRS when the seller is a foreign investor.

15. b) A real estate agent who isn't also a licensed escrow officer would be violating the Escrow Agent Registration Act if he handled escrow in a transaction he wasn't already involved in as a real estate agent. Also, it would be illegal for the real estate agent to charge a separate fee for escrow services.

Federal Income Taxation and Real Estate

Chapter Overview

Almost every business transaction has tax consequences, and real estate transactions are no exception. Not only are there taxes that arise at the time of sale (such as the real estate excise tax discussed in Chapter 5), there are also income tax ramifications for the parties involved. This chapter provides an overview of how federal income taxation affects the transfer and ownership of real estate. It explains some income tax terminology, discusses certain types of transactions that receive special treatment, and also covers tax deductions available to real estate owners.

Basic Taxation Concepts

As you no doubt know, in the United States the federal government taxes the income of individuals and businesses on an annual basis. Before discussing how the transfer or acquisition of real estate can affect the federal income taxes a seller or a buyer is required to pay, we need to explain some basic terms and concepts.

Progressive Tax

A tax may be "proportional," "regressive," or "progressive," depending on how its burden is distributed among taxpayers. A tax is proportional if the same tax rate is applied to all levels of income. A tax is regressive if the rate applied to higher levels of income is lower than the rate applied to lower levels. Our federal income tax is a **progressive** tax. This means that the more a taxpayer earns in a given tax year, the higher his tax rate will be. In other words, someone who earns a large income is generally required not just to pay more taxes than someone who earns a small income, but to pay a greater percentage of his income in taxes.

Tax rates increase in uneven steps called **tax brackets**. An additional dollar earned by a given taxpayer may be taxed at a higher rate than the dollar earned just before it, because it crosses the line into a higher bracket. But the additional dollar earned will not increase the tax this taxpayer is required to pay on dollars previously earned.

Income

When asked about their income, many people tend to think only in terms of the wages or salary they earn at a job. The Internal Revenue Service (IRS) takes a much broader view of income, however. It regards any economic benefit realized by a taxpayer as part of her income, unless it is a type of benefit specifically excluded from income by the tax code. (The concept of realization is discussed below.)

For certain purposes, the IRS classifies income received by an investor from an enterprise in which he doesn't materially participate (such as a limited partnership) as **passive income**.

Deductions and Tax Credits

The tax code authorizes certain expenses to be deducted from income. For example, if a business loses money in a particular tax year, the owner may be allowed to deduct the loss. A taxpayer who's entitled to a **deduction** can subtract a specified amount from his income before it is taxed. By reducing the amount of income that's taxed, the deduction also reduces the amount of tax the taxpayer owes.

In contrast to deductions, **tax credits** are subtracted directly from the amount of tax owed. The taxpayer's income is added up, the tax rate is applied, and then any applicable tax credits are subtracted to determine how much the taxpayer will actually have to pay. An example of a tax credit is the Child Tax Credit, which is worth $1,000 per child.

The government often uses deductions and tax credits to implement social and economic policy. For example, allowing homeowners to deduct mortgage interest from their taxable income helps make homeownership more affordable. (The mortgage interest deduction is explained later in this chapter.)

Gains and Losses

The sale or exchange of an asset (such as real estate) nearly always results in either a **gain** or a **loss**. Gains are treated as income, so any gain is taxable unless the tax code specifically says otherwise. On the other hand, a loss may be deducted from income only if the deduction is specifically authorized by the tax code. Most deductible losses are losses incurred in a trade or business or in transactions entered into for profit. A business entity (such as a corporation) can deduct all of its losses. An individual taxpayer can deduct a loss only if it was incurred in connection with:

1. the taxpayer's trade or business,
2. a transaction entered into for profit, or
3. a casualty loss or theft of the taxpayer's property.

No deduction is allowed for a loss suffered on the sale of the taxpayer's principal residence or other real property owned for personal use.

A gain or loss on the sale of an asset held for personal use or as an investment is considered a **capital gain** or a **capital loss**. Capital gains and losses are netted against each other. If there is a net gain, it is taxed as a capital gain. (The maximum tax rate applied to most capital gains is considerably lower than the rate for other income.) If there is a net loss, it may be deducted, but there is an annual limit on how much may be deducted. Losses in excess of the limit may be carried forward and deducted in future years.

Investments that allow a taxpayer to reduce her taxes by deducting losses from income from another source are referred to as **tax shelters**.

Basis

For income tax purposes, a property owner's **basis** in the property is her investment in it. In most cases, a taxpayer's initial basis is equal to the actual amount of her investment—that is, how much it cost to acquire the property. For instance, if she paid $280,000 for a rental house plus $12,000 in closing costs, she has an initial basis of $292,000 in the property.

If a taxpayer sells an asset, her gain on the sale is the amount by which the sale proceeds exceed her basis. To determine the amount of a gain or a loss, it's necessary to know the taxpayer's basis in the property. In our example, the seller could turn around and sell the house for $292,000 without having to report a gain to the IRS. If she sold the house for $300,000, though, she would have to report a gain of $8,000.

Adjusted Basis

A taxpayer's initial basis in a property may be increased or decreased to arrive at an **adjusted basis,** which reflects capital expenditures and, in some cases, depreciation deductions. **Capital expenditures** are expenditures made to improve the property, such as money a homeowner spends on adding a new room or remodeling the kitchen. Capital expenditures increase the value of the property or significantly extend its useful life. They are added to the initial basis in calculating the adjusted basis.

> **Example:** Greene buys an investment property for $345,000 plus $11,000 in closing costs. Four years later, she spends $45,000 on improvements to the property, remodeling the bathrooms and the kitchen in both units. Her adjusted basis in the property is now $401,000.

Maintenance expenses, such as repainting or replacing a broken window, are not capital expenditures. Maintenance expenses do not affect basis. (However, the owner of rental or business real estate can deduct maintenance expenses, as we'll discuss shortly.)

With rental or business real estate, a taxpayer's initial basis is also adjusted to take into account depreciation deductions, which we'll discuss in more detail later in this chapter. These deductions are subtracted from the initial basis in calculating the adjusted basis.

$$
\begin{array}{l}
 \text{Initial basis} \\
+\ \text{Capital expenditures} \\
-\ \underline{\text{Depreciation deductions}} \\
 \text{Adjusted basis}
\end{array}
$$

Realization

Not every gain is immediately taxable. A gain is not considered taxable income until it is **realized.** Ownership of an asset involves gain if the asset is appreciating in value. But for tax purposes, a gain is realized only when a sale or exchange occurs; the gain is then separated from the asset.

> **Example:** Referring back to the example given above, suppose that during Greene's six years of ownership property values have been increasing steadily. Her improved property (which she bought for $356,000 and invested another $45,000 in) now has a market value of $489,000. She has enjoyed an economic gain or benefit: she now owns property that is worth $88,000 more than what she put into it. However, that $88,000 is not realized—and therefore is not treated as income subject to taxation—until she sells the property.

The gain or loss realized on a transaction is the difference between the net sales price (referred to as the **amount realized**) and the adjusted basis of the property:

$$
\begin{array}{l}
 \text{Amount realized (net sales price)} \\
-\ \underline{\text{Adjusted basis}} \\
 \text{Gain or loss}
\end{array}
$$

In calculating the amount realized, the sales price includes money or other property received in exchange for the property, plus the amount of any mortgage debt that is eliminated. This means that if the buyer takes the property subject to the seller's mortgage or assumes it, the amount of that debt is treated as part of the sales price for tax purposes.

The sales price is reduced by selling expenses (such as the brokerage commission and the seller's other closing costs) to arrive at the amount realized.

> Money received
> + Market value of other property received
> + Mortgage debt disposed of
> − Selling expenses
> _____
> Amount realized (net sales price)

Recognition and Deferral

A gain is said to be **recognized** in the year it is taxed. A gain will be recognized in the same year it is realized, unless there is a specific exception in the tax code that allows the taxpayer to defer payment of taxes on the gain until a later tax year or a later transaction, or to exclude the gain from income and avoid paying taxes on it altogether. For example, the tax code permits an individual selling his rental property on an installment basis to defer taxation of part of the gain to the year in which it is actually received (rather than the year the sale takes place). The tax code provisions that allow recognition of a gain to be deferred are called "nonrecognition provisions."

Nonrecognition provisions (including the rule already mentioned concerning installment sales) and exclusion provisions are discussed in detail later in this chapter.

Classifications of Real Property

The particular tax rules that apply to a piece of real estate depend on the type of property involved. Here are some basic property types:

1. principal residence property,
2. personal use property,
3. unimproved investment property,
4. property held for the production of income,
5. property used in a trade or business, and
6. dealer property.

Principal Residence Property. A principal residence (also called a main home) is the home the taxpayer owns and occupies as her primary dwelling. It might be a single-family home, a duplex, a condominium unit, a cooperative apartment, or a mobile home. If the taxpayer owns two homes and lives in both of them, the one in which she lives most of the time is the principal residence. A taxpayer cannot have two principal residences at the same time.

Personal Use Property. Real property that a taxpayer owns for personal use, other than the principal residence, is classified as personal use property. A second home or a vacation cabin would belong in this category.

Unimproved Investment Property. Unimproved investment property is vacant land that produces no rental income. The land is held simply as an investment, in the expectation that it will appreciate in value.

Property Held for Production of Income. Property held for the production of income includes residential, commercial, and industrial property that is used to generate rental income for the owner.

Property Used in a Trade or Business. This category (also called business property) includes land and buildings that the taxpayer owns and uses in his trade or business, such as a factory owned by the manufacturer, or a small building the owner uses for his own retail business.

Dealer Property. This is property held primarily for sale to customers rather than for long-term investment. If a developer subdivides land for sale to the public, the lots will usually be included in this classification until they are sold.

Nonrecognition Transactions

As was explained earlier, when a nonrecognition provision in the tax code applies to a particular transaction, the taxpayer isn't required to pay taxes on a gain in the year it is realized. The following types of real estate transactions are covered by nonrecognition provisions:

- installment sales,
- involuntary conversions, and
- "tax-free" exchanges.

Keep in mind that nonrecognition provisions do not completely exclude the gain from taxation, but merely defer the tax consequences to a later tax year. These are not really "tax-free" transactions. The realized gain is simply recognized and taxed in a subsequent year.

Installment Sales

The tax code considers a sale to be an installment sale if less than 100% of the sales price is received in the year of sale. Nearly all seller-financed transactions are installment sales. Installment sale reporting allows the taxpayer/seller to defer recognition of part of the gain to the year(s) in which it is actually received. In effect, taxes are paid only on the portion of the profit received each year. Installment sale reporting is permitted for all classes of property, except that dealer property is eligible only under special circumstances.

In installment sales, the gain recognized in any given year is calculated based on the ratio of gross profit to the contract price. The **gross profit** is essentially the difference between the sales price and the adjusted basis.

To calculate the gross profit, take the seller's adjusted basis at

Fig. 14.1 *Eligibility for installment sale reporting*

Installment Sale Reporting

1. Less than 100% of sales price received in year of sale

2. All classifications of real property eligible except dealer property

the time of sale, add the amount of the commission and other selling expenses, and subtract this sum from the sales price.

Example: Once again, we'll use Greene as an example. Her adjusted basis in her investment property was $401,000. She sold the property for $489,000. She had to pay a $29,000 commission and $8,200 in other selling expenses.

$489,000	Sales price

$401,000	Seller's adjusted basis
+ 37,200	Commission and other selling expenses
$438,200	Adjusted basis plus selling expenses

$489,000	Sales price
− 438,200	Adjusted basis plus selling expenses
$50,800	Gross profit

The next step is to compare the gross profit to the contract price to arrive at the **gross profit ratio** (also called the gross profit percentage). The contract price is the total amount of all principal payments the buyer will pay the seller. In most cases, unless the buyer assumes an existing loan, the contract price is the same as the sales price.

Example:

Gross Profit	÷	Contract Price	=	Gross Profit Ratio
$50,800	÷	$489,000	=	10.39%

The gross profit ratio is applied to the principal payments received in each year to determine how much of the principal is gain to be taxed that year. Note that the gross profit ratio is not applied to the interest the buyer pays the seller; all of the interest payments are treated as taxable income in the year received.

If the seller in the example above received a $48,900 downpayment, $2,500 in principal installment payments, and $30,500 in interest the first year, the taxable income would be calculated as follows:

$48,900	Downpayment
+ 2,500	Installment principal payments
$51,400	Total principal payments

$51,400	Total principal payments
× 10.39%	Gross profit ratio
$5,340	Recognized gain
+ 30,500	Interest income
$35,840	Total taxable income

Sometimes a buyer assumes a seller's existing mortgage or deed of trust and also gives the seller a second mortgage or deed of trust for part of the purchase price. If the loan being assumed is larger than the seller's basis in the property, the excess is treated as payment received from the buyer in the year of sale.

If the property is subject to recapture provisions because of depreciation deductions (discussed later in this chapter), the amount recaptured is also treated as a payment received in the year of sale.

Involuntary Conversions

An involuntary conversion occurs when an asset is turned into cash without the voluntary action of the owner, as when an asset is condemned, destroyed, stolen, or lost, and the owner receives a condemnation award or insurance proceeds. Since the award or proceeds usually represent the property's replacement cost or market value, the owner often realizes a gain on an involuntary conversion.

However, recognition of a gain on an involuntary conversion can be deferred if the taxpayer uses the money received to replace the property within the replacement period set by the IRS. Generally, the replacement period lasts for two years after the date the property was destroyed or lost (or in the case of a condemnation, two years after the end of the tax year in which the gain was realized). Recognition of the gain is deferred only to the extent that the condemnation award or insurance proceeds are reinvested in the replacement property. Any part of the gain used for purposes other than purchase of replacement property will be taxed as income.

"Tax-Free" Exchanges

Section 1031 of the tax code concerns property exchanges. Although 1031 exchanges are commonly called "tax-free" exchanges, they're really just tax-deferred exchanges. If unimproved investment property, income-producing property, or property used in a trade or business is exchanged for **like-kind property**, recognition of any realized gain will be deferred. This reduces or eliminates current tax expenses, essentially giving the investor more buying power. A principal residence, personal use property, and dealer property are not eligible for this type of deferral.

The property the taxpayer receives in the exchange must be like-kind—that is, the same kind as the property given. This requirement refers to the general nature of the properties rather than their quality. Most real estate is considered to be of like kind for the purposes of a 1031 exchange, without regard to whether it is improved, unimproved, residential, commercial, or industrial. For example, if a taxpayer exchanges a strip shopping center for an apartment complex, the transaction can qualify as a tax-free exchange. Both of the exchanged properties must be located in the United States to be considered like-kind property.

If nothing other than like-kind property is received in the exchange, no gain or loss is recognized in the year of the exchange. However, anything other than like-kind property that the taxpayer receives is called **boot** and recognized in the year of the exchange. In a real estate exchange, boot might be cash, stock, other types of personal property, or the difference between mortgage balances.

Example: A taxpayer trades a property with a mortgage debt of $120,000 for a property with a mortgage debt of $100,000. The taxpayer has received $20,000 in boot because of the reduction in debt (regardless of whether or

---

Fig. 14.2 Eligibility for tax-free exchanges

"Tax-Free" Exchanges

1. Only property held for production of income, property used in a trade or business, or unimproved investment property is eligible.

2. Must be exchanged for like-kind property.

3. Any boot is taxed in the year it is received.

not there has been a formal assumption of the loan). The taxpayer will have to pay taxes on a gain of $20,000, just as if she had received $20,000 in cash along with the real property.

The taxpayer's basis in the property exchanged is transferred to the property she receives. If nothing other than like-kind property is exchanged, no adjustments are necessary. But if the exchange involved boot, the basis must be adjusted for any boot that was paid or received, and for any gain or loss that was recognized because of the boot.

Originally, 1031 exchanges were limited to simultaneous transfers of ownership (trades of property). Now, however, 1031 tax deferral benefits also apply when a taxpayer sells a property to one party and then buys a like-kind property from another party, in two separate transactions. Time limits apply: once the taxpayer has sold the original (relinquished) property, he has 45 days to identify a replacement property. Then, the purchase of the replacement property must close within 180 days of the sale of the relinquished property.

If a real estate licensee arranges an exchange of properties between two parties that qualifies as a 1031 exchange, she may receive compensation from both parties.

Exclusion of Gain from the Sale of a Principal Residence

We will discuss only one exclusion from capital gains taxation, the one that will be of greatest interest to most homeowners: the exclusion of gain on the sale of a principal residence.

A taxpayer may exclude the entire gain on the sale of his principal residence, up to $250,000 if the taxpayer is filing a single return, or $500,000 if the taxpayer is married and filing a joint return.

Example:

$275,000	Amount realized (after selling costs)
− 80,000	Seller's basis in home
$195,000	Gain realized

Whether filing singly or jointly, the seller will be able to exclude the entire amount of gain—$195,000—from taxation.

If the amount of the gain on the sale of the home exceeds the $250,000 or $500,000 limit, the amount in excess of the limit will be taxed at the capital gains rate.

Example:

$375,000	Amount realized (after selling costs)
− 70,000	Seller's basis in home
$305,000	Gain realized

If the seller is filing singly, only $250,000 of the $305,000 gain will be excluded from taxation. The seller will have to pay capital gains taxes on the $55,000 that exceeded the exclusion limit.

Eligibility. To qualify for this exclusion, the seller must have both owned and used the property as a principal residence for at least two years during the five-year period ending on the date of sale. Because of this rule, this exclusion is available only once every two years.

Note that if the sellers are married and filing a joint return, only one spouse has to meet the ownership test, but both spouses must meet the use test. If only one spouse meets both the ownership test and the use test, the maximum exclusion the married couple can claim is $250,000, even if they file a joint return.

If the seller owned and used the property as a principal residence for less than two years because of special circumstances (for example, if she sold the home after only a year because of a change in health or employment), she may be able to claim a reduced exclusion.

Deductions Available to Property Owners

As was explained earlier, a **deduction** is subtracted from a taxpayer's income before the tax rate is applied. The income tax deductions allowed to real property owners are a significant benefit of ownership. There are deductions for:

- depreciation,
- repairs,
- real property taxes, and
- mortgage interest.

Depreciation Deductions

Depreciation deductions (sometimes called **cost recovery deductions**) permit a taxpayer to recover the cost of an asset over a period of years. Only property used for the production of income or used in a trade or business is eligible for depreciation deductions. They cannot be taken in connection with a principal residence, personal use property, unimproved investment property, or dealer property.

Depreciable Property. In general, only property that wears out and will eventually have to be replaced is **depreciable**—that is, eligible for depreciation deductions. For example, apartment buildings, business or factory equipment, and the trees in commercial fruit orchards all have to be replaced, so they are depreciable. But land does not wear out, so it is not depreciable (which is why unimproved investment property cannot be depreciated).

Time Frame. The entire expense of acquiring depreciable property cannot be deducted in the year it is incurred (although that is permitted with many other business expenses, such as wages, supplies, and utilities). However, the expense can be deducted over a number of years; for most real estate, the recovery period is between 27½ and 39 years. The length of the recovery period is a reflection of legislative policy and has little, if any, relationship to the actual length of time that the property will be economically useful. The whole field of depreciation deductions has been subject to frequent modification by Congress.

Fig. 14.3 *Favorable tax treatment for real property*

Eligibility for Favorable Income Tax Treatment			
	Installment Sale	"Tax-Free" Exchange	Depreciation Deductions
Principal Residence	Yes	No	No
Personal Use	Yes	No	No
Unimproved Investment	Yes	Yes	No
Trade or Business	Yes	Yes	Yes
Income	Yes	Yes	Yes
Dealer	No	No	No

Effect on Basis. As we said in the discussion of basis at the beginning of the chapter, depreciation deductions reduce the taxpayer's adjusted basis in the property. Note that this reduction occurs whether or not the taxpayer actually takes the deduction. If the deduction was allowable—that is, the taxpayer was entitled to take it—the basis will be reduced. By reducing the basis, these deductions tend to increase the taxpayer's eventual gain (or reduce the size of any loss) on the resale of the property.

Repair Deductions

For most real estate other than principal residences and personal use property, expenditures for repairs are deductible in the year paid. A repair expense is one incurred to keep the property in ordinary, efficient, operating condition.

Repair expenses should not be confused with capital expenditures. As explained earlier, capital expenditures add to the value of the property and frequently prolong its economic life. Capital expenditures are not deductible in the year made, but rather are added to the taxpayer's basis. The resulting increase in the basis will affect the gain or loss on the eventual sale of the property. It will also increase the allowable depreciation deductions if the property is eligible for those.

Property Tax Deductions

General real estate taxes are deductible. Special assessments for repairs or maintenance are deductible. On the other hand, those for improvements (such as new sidewalks) are not. Special assessments for improvements are considered capital expenditures and their cost may be added to the property's basis.

Mortgage Interest Deductions

For most property, interest paid on a mortgage or deed of trust is usually completely deductible. However, there are some limitations on interest deductions for personal residences (principal residences or second homes).

A taxpayer may deduct interest payments on mortgage debt of up to $1,000,000 ($500,000 for a married taxpayer filing separately) used to buy, build, or improve a first or second residence. In addition, interest on a home equity loan of up to $100,000 ($50,000 for a married taxpayer filing separately) can be deducted without regard to the purpose of the loan. When the loan amount exceeds these limits, the interest on the excess is not deductible.

The deductibility of mortgage interest is one reason why homeowners often use a home equity loan to pay off credit card debt. The interest on credit cards isn't deductible, but the interest on the home equity loan is.

Deductibility of Points and Other Loan Costs. The IRS considers points paid to a lender in connection with a new loan (including discount points and the origination fee) to be prepaid interest, and the borrower is generally allowed to deduct them. This is true even if the points were paid by the seller on the borrower's behalf. (The borrower's basis in the property must be reduced by the amount of the seller-paid points.)

Note that fees a lender charges to cover specific services aren't deductible, even if the lender refers to them as points. This includes, for example, appraisal fees and document preparation fees.

If a seller paying off a loan is required to pay a prepayment penalty, the amount of the penalty is usually deductible. For tax purposes, a prepayment penalty is treated as a form of interest.

Chapter Summary

1. Any economic benefit realized by a taxpayer is treated as part of his income, unless there is a specific provision of the tax code that excludes it from income. The tax code provides for certain deductions from income before the tax rate is applied, and also for tax credits, which are subtracted from the amount of tax owed.

2. A gain or a loss is realized when an asset is sold. A gain is recognized (taxed) in the year it is realized, unless a nonrecognition or exclusion provision in the tax code applies.

3. A taxpayer's initial basis in property is the amount she originally invested in it. To determine the adjusted basis, capital expenditures are added to the initial basis, and allowable depreciation deductions are subtracted from it. The taxpayer's gain or loss is the difference between the amount realized and the adjusted basis.

4. Classifications of real property include principal residence property, personal use property, unimproved investment property, property held for the production of income, property used in a trade or business, or dealer property.

5. The tax code's nonrecognition provisions for real property transactions allow taxation of gain to be deferred in installment sales, involuntary conversions, and "tax-free" (Section 1031) exchanges. There is also an exclusion of up to $250,000 (or $500,000 if filing jointly) of gain allowed on the sale of a principal residence.

6. The tax deductions available to property owners include depreciation deductions, repair deductions, deduction of property taxes, and deduction of mortgage interest. Whether and to what extent these deductions are allowed depends on the type of property in question.

🔑 Key Terms

Income—Any economic benefit realized by a taxpayer that is not excluded from income by the tax code.

Deduction—An expense that can be used to reduce taxable income.

Initial basis—The amount of the taxpayer's original investment in the property; what it cost to acquire the property.

Adjusted basis—The initial basis plus capital expenditures and minus allowable depreciation deductions.

Realization—A gain or a loss is realized when it is separated from the asset; this separation generally occurs when the asset is sold.

Recognition—A gain is said to be recognized when it is taxable; it is recognized in the year it is realized unless recognition is deferred by the tax code.

Installment sale—A sale in which less than 100% of the sales price is received in the year of sale.

Involuntary conversion—When property is converted to cash without the voluntary action of the owner, as when it is condemned, destroyed, stolen, or lost.

Depreciation deductions—Deductions from the taxpayer's income to allow the cost of an asset to be recovered over a period of years; allowed only for depreciable property that is held for the production of income or used in a trade or business. Also called cost recovery deductions.

Repair expenses—Money spent on repairs to keep property in ordinary, efficient operating condition.

Capital expenditures—Money spent on improvements to property, which add to its value or prolong its economic life.

"Tax-free" exchange—When like-kind property is exchanged, allowing taxation of the gain to be deferred; also called a "1031 exchange."

Like-kind property—In a tax-free exchange, property received that is of the same kind as the property transferred; any two pieces of real estate are considered to be of like kind.

Boot—Something given or received in a tax-free exchange that is not like-kind property, such as cash.

Chapter Quiz

1. The basis of a principal residence would be adjusted to reflect:
   a) depreciation deductions
   b) expenses incurred to keep the property in good repair
   c) mortgage interest paid
   d) the cost of installing a deck

2. A married couple bought a home for $250,000. After living in the home for three years, they sold it for only $246,000. How much of this loss can they deduct on their federal income tax return?
   a) The full $4,000 loss
   b) Only $3,000
   c) Only $2,000
   d) None of it

3. Which of the following might the owner of unimproved investment property deduct on this year's federal income tax return?
   a) A loss on the sale of the property
   b) The depreciation of the land
   c) The entire amount of any capital expenditures
   d) Any of the above

4. Which of the following exchanges could not qualify as a "tax-free" exchange?
   a) An office building for a hotel
   b) An apartment house for a warehouse
   c) Timber land for farm equipment
   d) A city lot for a ranch

5. Under the federal income tax code, income is always taxed in the year it is:
   a) realized
   b) recognized
   c) recovered
   d) deferred

6. Munson just sold his principal residence. After deducting his selling costs, the amount of gain realized was $163,000. Munson will be allowed to exclude the entire amount of the gain from taxation only if:
   a) he is married and is filing a joint return
   b) he has never claimed this exclusion before, since it can only be used once in a lifetime
   c) the gain is not considered a capital gain
   d) he owned and occupied the property as his principal residence for two of the previous five years

7. Torino owns a triplex as an investment property. She paid $450,000 for it, including her closing costs. The allowable depreciation deductions for the property have amounted to $20,000, Torino has spent $50,000 on capital improvements, and the market value of the property has risen by 15%. What is Torino's adjusted basis?
   a) $537,500
   b) $500,000
   c) $480,000
   d) $430,000

8. Gillespie is buying a home that will be his principal residence. He is financing the purchase with a $200,000 mortgage loan. How much of the interest that he pays on the loan can he deduct from his income?
   a) All of it
   b) Up to $100,000 in interest
   c) 50%
   d) None of it

9. The Byrnes are selling some property on a five-year contract. Their gross profit ratio on the sale is 15%. This year, they will receive $4,775 in interest and $1,675 in principal. With installment sale reporting, approximately how much of that will be recognized and included in the Byrnes' taxable income for this year?

    a) $251
    b) $967
    c) $2,391
    d) $5,026

10. Sherrick is selling a lot for $72,000. Her adjusted basis in the property is $56,000. In addition to the 6% sales commission she'll be paying, she will also have to pay $2,500 in closing costs. For federal income tax purposes, what is the gain Sherrick will realize in this transaction?

    a) $6,820
    b) $9,180
    c) $16,000
    d) $22,820

Answer Key

1. d) The cost of installing a deck is a capital expenditure, which would be added to the taxpayer's basis. Remember that principal residences and personal use property do not qualify for depreciation deductions.

2. d) A loss on the sale of a principal residence or personal use property is never deductible.

3. a) If the owner loses money on the sale of the property, she may be able to deduct that loss. Depreciation deductions are not allowed for unimproved investment property, because land is not depreciable. Capital expenditures are not deductible; instead, they increase the taxpayer's basis.

4. c) The like-kind property requirement means that real estate must be exchanged for other real estate.

5. b) Income is taxed when it is recognized. It is often recognized in the same year it is realized, but that is not true if a nonrecognition provision applies.

6. d) To qualify for the exclusion from taxation, the taxpayer must have both owned and used the property as a principal residence for two of the previous five years.

7. c) The initial basis, plus the capital expenditures, less the allowable depreciation deductions, equals an adjusted basis of $480,000.

    $450,000 + $50,000 − $20,000 = $480,000

    (Ignore the increase in market value; it does not affect the taxpayer's basis.)

8. a) A taxpayer can deduct all of the interest paid on a loan of up to $1,000,000 used to purchase a first or second personal residence.

9. d) Multiply the principal payments by the gross profit ratio to determine the amount of principal that will be recognized this year. Then add that to the entire amount of interest received. (All of the interest is taxable.)

    $1,675 × 15% = $251.25 + $4,775 = $5,026.25

10. b) Sherrick will realize a $9,180 gain in the transaction. First subtract her selling expenses (the commission and closing costs) from the sales price to determine the amount realized; then subtract her adjusted basis from the amount realized to determine the gain.

    $72,000 × 6% = $4,320 commission

    $4,320 + $2,500 costs = $6,820

    $72,000 − $6,820 = $65,180 (amount realized)

    $65,180 − $56,000 = $9,180 (gain realized)

Civil Rights and Fair Housing

Chapter Overview

Civil rights laws are intended to promote fairness and freedom. In the real estate context, one of the main goals of these laws is equal housing opportunity. Anyone with the necessary financial resources should be able to choose a home or apartment in any neighborhood, regardless of race, religion, national origin, gender, or other characteristics that have historically been used as a basis for discrimination. There are also civil rights laws that affect nonresidential real estate.

Real estate agents must be familiar with both federal and state laws that prohibit discrimination in real estate transactions and related business activities. Complying with these laws—and encouraging others to comply with them—is an essential part of a real estate agent's professional duties. In this chapter, we'll look first at the federal antidiscrimination laws that affect real estate, then at the Washington laws.

Federal Antidiscrimination Legislation

Federal laws that prohibit discrimination in real estate transactions and related activities include:

- the Civil Rights Act of 1866,
- the Civil Rights Act of 1964,
- the federal Fair Housing Act,
- federal fair lending laws, and
- the Americans with Disabilities Act.

Civil Rights Act of 1866

The Civil Rights Act of 1866 states that "all citizens of the United States shall have the same right, in every state and territory as is enjoyed by white citizens thereof to inherit, purchase, lease, sell, hold and convey real and personal property." The act prohibits any discrimination based on race or color.

Enacted immediately after the Civil War, the act was largely ignored for almost a century. In the 1960s, during the civil rights movement, the act was challenged as an unconstitutional interference with private property rights. But the U.S. Supreme Court upheld the act in the landmark case of *Jones v. Mayer*, decided in 1968. The court ruled that the 1866 Act "prohibits all racial discrimination, private or public, in the sale and rental of property," and that it is constitutional based on the 13th Amendment to the U.S. Constitution, which prohibits slavery.

Someone who has been discriminated against in violation of the Civil Rights Act of 1866 can sue in federal court. The court could issue an injunction ordering the defendant to stop discriminating. The court could also order the defendant to pay the plaintiff both **compensatory damages** (to compensate for losses and suffering caused by the discrimination) and **punitive damages** (an additional sum to punish the defendant for wrongdoing).

Civil Rights Act of 1964

The Civil Rights Act of 1964 was one of the first attempts made by the federal government to promote equal opportunity in housing. The act prohibited discrimination based on race, color, religion, or national origin in many programs and activities for which the federal government offered financial assistance. Unfortunately, the effect of the act was extremely limited, because most FHA and VA loans weren't covered. In fact, it's estimated that less than 1% of all houses purchased were covered by the act. It wasn't until the Civil Rights Act of 1968 that major progress was made toward fair housing goals.

Federal Fair Housing Act

The federal Fair Housing Act is also known as Title VIII of the Civil Rights Act of 1968. It goes much further than either the 1866 Civil Rights Act or the 1964 Civil Rights Act, making it illegal to discriminate on the basis of **race, color, religion, sex, national origin, disability**, or **familial status** in the sale or lease of residential property or in the sale or lease of vacant land for the construction of residential buildings. The law also prohibits discrimination in advertising, lending, real estate brokerage, and other services in connection with residential real estate transactions. However, unlike the 1866 Civil Rights Act, the Fair Housing Act does not apply to nonresidential transactions, such as those involving commercial or industrial properties.

Exemptions. While the Fair Housing Act applies to the majority of residential real estate transactions, four types of transactions are exempt from it.

1. The law doesn't apply to the sale or rental of a single-family home by its owner, provided that:
    - the owner doesn't own more than three such homes;
    - no real estate agent is employed in the transaction; and
    - no discriminatory advertising is used.

    If the owner isn't the most recent occupant of the home, he may use this exemption only once every 24 months.

2. The law doesn't apply to the rental of a unit or a room in a dwelling with up to four units, provided that:
    - the owner occupies one of the units as her residence;
    - no real estate agent is employed; and
    - no discriminatory advertising is used.

    (This is sometimes called the **Mrs. Murphy exemption**.)

3. In dealing with their own property in noncommercial transactions, religious organizations or societies or affiliated nonprofit organizations may limit occupancy to or give preference to their own members, provided that membership isn't restricted on the basis of race, color, or national origin.

4. Private clubs with lodgings that aren't open to the public and that aren't operated for a commercial purpose may limit occupancy to or give preference to their own members.

These limited exemptions apply very rarely. Remember, the 1866 Civil Rights Act prohibits discrimination based on race or color in any property transaction, regardless of any exemptions available under the Fair Housing Act. In addition, there is no exemption for any transaction involving a real estate licensee. And for Washington residents, these federal exemptions don't really matter, because the exemptions in the Washington law governing discrimination in real estate transactions are narrower; these will be discussed later in the chapter.

Fig. 15.1 Fair housing poster

U. S. Department of Housing and Urban Development

EQUAL HOUSING OPPORTUNITY

We Do Business in Accordance With the Federal Fair Housing Law

(The Fair Housing Amendments Act of 1988)

It is illegal to Discriminate Against Any Person Because of Race, Color, Religion, Sex, Handicap, Familial Status, or National Origin

---

■ In the sale or rental of housing or residential lots

■ In advertising the sale or rental of housing

■ In the financing of housing

■ In the provision of real estate brokerage services

■ In the appraisal of housing

■ Blockbusting is also illegal

Anyone who feels he or she has been discriminated against may file a complaint of housing discrimination:
   1-800-669-9777 (Toll Free)
   1-800-927-9275 (TTY)

**U.S. Department of Housing and Urban Development
Assistant Secretary for Fair Housing and Equal Opportunity
Washington, D.C. 20410**

Previous editions are obsolete

form HUD-928.1 (2/2003)

Display of Poster. Regulations implementing the Fair Housing Act require a fair housing poster such as the one in Figure 15.1 to be prominently displayed at any place of business involved in the sale, rental, or financing of dwellings. This includes real estate offices, lenders' offices, apartment buildings, condominiums, and model homes in subdivisions. If a fair housing complaint is filed against a business, failure to display the poster may be treated as evidence of discriminatory practices.

Prohibited Acts. The Fair Housing Act prohibits any of the following acts if they are done on the basis of race, color, religion, sex, national origin, disability, or familial status:

- refusing to rent or sell residential property after receiving a bona fide offer;
- refusing to negotiate for the sale or rental of residential property, or otherwise making it unavailable;
- changing the terms of sale or lease for different potential buyers or tenants;
- using advertising that indicates a preference or intent to discriminate;
- representing that property is not available for inspection, sale, or rent when it is in fact available;
- using discriminatory criteria when making a housing loan;
- limiting participation in a multiple listing service or similar service; or
- coercing, intimidating, threatening, or interfering with anyone on account of his or her enjoyment, attempt to enjoy, or encouragement or assistance to others in enjoying the rights granted by the Fair Housing Act.

Also prohibited are the discriminatory practices known as blockbusting, steering, and redlining.

- **Blockbusting** occurs when someone tries to induce homeowners to list or sell their properties by predicting that members of another race (or disabled people, people of a particular ethnic background, etc.) will be moving into the neighborhood, and that this will have undesirable consequences, such as lower property values. The blockbuster then profits by purchasing the homes at reduced prices or (in the case of a real estate agent) by collecting commissions on the induced sales. Blockbusting is also known as **panic selling**.

  Example: Immediately after an African-American family moves into an all-white neighborhood, agents working for XYZ Realty start calling all the other homeowners in the neighborhood. The agents warn that several other African-American families are planning on buying homes in the neighborhood, and they claim that police have predicted a significant increase in crime, property values are expected to drop dramatically, and within months the owners will find it difficult to sell their homes at any price. Because of these "facts" made up by XYZ agents, several homeowners immediately list their homes with XYZ Realty. XYZ Realty is guilty of blockbusting.

- **Steering** refers to channeling prospective buyers or tenants toward or away from specific neighborhoods based on their race (or religion, national origin, etc.) in order to maintain or change the character of those neighborhoods.

  Example: The sales agents at PQR Realty are "encouraged" to show Latino buyers only properties in the city's predominantly Latino neighborhood. Non-Latino buyers aren't shown properties there, except by specific request. This is done on the principle that Latino buyers would be "more comfortable" living in the Latino neighborhood and non-Latino buyers would be "uncomfortable" there. PQR Realty is guilty of steering.

- **Redlining** is the refusal to make a loan because of the racial or ethnic composition of the neighborhood in which the security property is located.

  Example: A buyer applies to Community Savings for a loan to purchase a home located in the Cherrywood neighborhood. Cherrywood is a predominantly minority neighborhood. Community Savings rejects the loan, because it fears that property values in Cherrywood may suffer in the future because of possible racial tension. Community Savings is guilty of redlining.

The prohibition against redlining is enforced through the Home Mortgage Disclosure Act, discussed later in the chapter.

Disability and Familial Status. Originally, the Fair Housing Act did not prohibit discrimination based on disability or familial status; these classifications were added to the law in 1988.

Disability. Under the Fair Housing Act, it's illegal to discriminate against someone because he has a disability (referred to as a "handicap" in the statute). A disability is defined as a physical or mental impairment that substantially limits one or more major life activities. This includes people suffering from chronic alcoholism, mental illness, or HIV/AIDS. But the act does not protect those who are a direct threat to the health or safety of others, or who are currently using controlled substances.

A residential landlord must allow a disabled tenant to make reasonable modifications to the property at the tenant's expense, so long as the modifications are necessary for the tenant's full use and enjoyment of the premises. (The tenant can be required to restore the premises to their original condition at the end of the tenancy, however.) Landlords must also make reasonable exceptions to their rules to accommodate disabled tenants. For example, even if they don't allow pets, they can't refuse to rent to someone with a guide dog or other service animal. In addition, landlords may not charge a pet deposit for a service animal.

New residential construction with four or more units is required to comply with wheelchair accessibility rules under the Fair Housing Act. (This requirement has been in effect since 1991.) Doorways, bathrooms, and kitchens should be designed to accommodate wheelchairs. Wheelchair accessibility requirements do not apply to the upper stories of multi-story buildings, unless there is an elevator that would allow wheelchair users to reach those units.

Familial Status. Discrimination on the basis of familial status refers to discriminating against someone because a child (a person under 18 years old) is or will be living with him or her. Parents, legal guardians, pregnant women, and those in the process of obtaining custody of a child are protected against discrimination on the basis of their familial status.

While the Fair Housing Act doesn't override local laws limiting the number of occupants permitted in a dwelling, it's unlawful for anyone to discriminate in selling, renting, or lending money to buy residential property because the applicant is pregnant or lives with a child. "Adults only" apartment or condominium complexes are forbidden, and so are complexes divided into "adult" and "family" areas.

However, the law includes an exemption for properties that qualify as "housing for older persons." Children can be excluded from properties that fit into one of the following categories:

1. properties developed under a government program to assist the elderly;
2. properties intended for and solely occupied by persons 62 or older; or
3. properties that adhere to policies that demonstrate an intent to house persons 55 or older, if at least 80% of the units are occupied by at least one person who is 55 years old or older.

Enforcement. The Fair Housing Act is enforced by the Department of Housing and Urban Development (HUD), through its Office of Fair Housing and Equal Opportunity. Within one year of alleged discriminatory conduct, the aggrieved person may file a complaint with HUD or may file a lawsuit in federal or state court. If a complaint is filed with HUD, the agency will investigate the complaint and attempt to confer with the parties in order to reconcile their differences and persuade the violator to abide by the law.

If this doesn't resolve the dispute and the complainant's claims are found to have merit, an administrative hearing will be held, unless either party chooses to have the case decided in federal court instead. In an administrative hearing, HUD attorneys litigate the case on behalf of the complainant. If a case involves a "pattern or practice" of discrimination, the U.S. Attorney General can file suit in federal court.

When someone is held to have violated the Fair Housing Act, the administrative law judge or the court may issue an injunction ordering the violator to stop the discriminatory conduct, or to take affirmative steps to correct a violation. The violator may also be ordered to pay compensatory damages and attorney's fees to the complainant. A federal court can order the violator to pay punitive damages to the complainant. An administrative law judge can't impose punitive damages, but can impose a civil penalty, to be paid to the government; the maximum penalty ranges from $16,000 for a first offense up to $70,000 for a third or subsequent offense. In a case litigated by the Attorney General, the court can impose a civil penalty ranging from a maximum of $55,000 for a first offense up to a maximum of $110,000 for a third or subsequent offense.

In states such as Washington, where the state fair housing laws are very similar to the federal law, HUD may refer complaints to the equivalent state agency. (The state agency here is the Washington Human Rights Commission.)

Federal Fair Lending Laws

As we discussed earlier, the Fair Housing Act prohibits discrimination in residential mortgage lending. It doesn't apply to other types of credit transactions, however.

The **Equal Credit Opportunity Act** (ECOA) applies to all credit transactions, including residential real estate loans. The act prohibits lenders, loan brokers, and others involved in financing from discriminating based on race, color, religion, national origin, sex, marital status, age (as long as the applicant has reached the age of majority), or because the applicant's income is derived partly or wholly from public assistance.

The **Home Mortgage Disclosure Act** provides a way to evaluate whether lenders are fulfilling their obligation to serve the housing needs of the communities where they're located. The act facilitates the enforcement of federal laws against redlining.

Under the Home Mortgage Disclosure Act, large institutional lenders in metropolitan areas must file annual reports on the residential mortgage loans (both purchase and improvement loans) they originated or purchased during the fiscal year. The information is categorized by number and dollar amount, type of loan (FHA, VA, other), and geographic location by census tract or county. The reports may reveal areas where few or no home loans have been made, alerting investigators to possible redlining.

Americans with Disabilities Act

The **Americans with Disabilities Act** (ADA), which went into effect in 1992, is a federal law intended to ensure that people with disabilities have equal access to public facilities. The ADA requires any business or other facility open to the public to be accessible to the disabled.

Under the ADA, no one can be discriminated against on the basis of disability in places of public accommodation or commercial facilities. A **disability** is defined as any physical or mental impairment that substantially limits one or more of the individual's major life activities (the same definition used for the Fair Housing Act). A **public accommodation** is defined to include any nonresidential place that is owned, operated, or leased by a private entity and open to the public, as long as the operation of the facility affects commerce. Real estate offices are considered to be public accommodations, along with hotels, restaurants, retail stores, shopping centers, banks, and the offices of attorneys, accountants, and doctors.

To ensure the accessibility of public accommodations, the ADA requires each of the following to be accomplished, as long as it is "readily achievable":

- Both architectural barriers and communication barriers must be removed so that goods and services are accessible to people with disabilities.
- Auxiliary aids and services must be provided so that no one with a disability is excluded, denied services, segregated, or otherwise treated differently than other individuals.
- New commercial construction must be accessible to people with disabilities, unless that would be structurally impractical.

For example, the owner of a commercial building with no elevator may have to install automatic entry doors and a buzzer at street level so that customers of a second-floor business can ask for assistance. A commercial building owner might also be required to alter the height of a pay phone to make it accessible to someone in a wheelchair, add grab bars to restroom stalls, and take a variety of other steps to make the building's facilities accessible.

Washington Antidiscrimination Legislation

Real estate agents, sellers, landlords, and others involved in real estate activities must comply not only with the federal laws we've covered, but also with state laws that prohibit discrimination. The Washington Law Against Discrimination, the Washington Fair Lending Act, and the real estate license law all include provisions designed to promote fairness in real estate transactions.

Washington Law Against Discrimination

The Washington Law Against Discrimination declares that discrimination is a matter of state concern because it threatens the rights and privileges of state inhabitants and the foundations of a free democratic society. This state law is stricter than any of the federal antidiscrimination laws we've discussed; it covers more types of activities and extends protection from discrimination to more classes of people.

In real estate transactions, the Washington law prohibits discrimination based on **race, creed, color, national origin, sex, sexual orientation, marital status**, or **familial status; sensory, physical, or mental disability**; the **use of a trained guide dog or service animal**; or **honorably discharged veteran or military status**. Note that people infected or perceived to be infected with **HIV/AIDS** are protected from discrimination in the same manner as those suffering from any other physical disability.

To further the purposes of the Washington Law Against Discrimination, the Human Rights Commission was created and given the mission of eliminating and preventing discrimination in this state.

Prohibited Practices. The Washington Law Against Discrimination isn't just a fair housing law. It prohibits a wide range of discriminatory practices in employment, insurance, and credit transactions; in places of public accommodation and amusement (such as restaurants, movie theaters, hotels, stores, and most other commercial enterprises); and in regard to all types of real property.

Discrimination is prohibited in any real estate transaction. This includes the sale, appraisal, brokering, exchange, purchase, rental, or lease of real property; transacting or applying for a real estate loan; and the provision of brokerage services.

If based on discrimination against one of the protected classes we listed above (race, creed, color, national origin, etc.), it is against the law to do or attempt to do any of the following:

- refuse to engage in a real estate transaction;
- discriminate in the terms or conditions of a transaction;
- discriminate in providing services or facilities in connection with a real estate transaction;
- refuse to receive or fail to transmit a bona fide offer;
- refuse to negotiate;
- represent that property is not available for inspection, sale, rental, or lease when it is in fact available;
- fail to advise a prospect about a property listing, or refuse to allow the prospect to inspect the property;
- discriminate in the sale or rental of a dwelling, or otherwise make unavailable or deny a dwelling to anyone;
- make, print, circulate, or publish any advertisement, notice, or sign which indicates, directly or indirectly, an intent to discriminate;
- use any application form or make any record or inquiry which indicates, directly or indirectly, an intent to discriminate;
- offer, solicit, accept, or retain a listing with the understanding that a person may be discriminated against;

- expel a person from occupancy;
- discriminate in negotiating, executing, or financing a real estate transaction;
- discriminate in negotiating or executing any service or item in connection with a real estate transaction (such as title insurance or mortgage insurance);
- refuse to allow a disabled person to make reasonable modifications to a dwelling;
- refuse to make reasonable accommodations in rules or policies that would enable a disabled person to use a dwelling;
- fail to construct new multi-family dwellings in compliance with accessibility requirements imposed by the federal Fair Housing Act;
- induce, for profit, anyone to sell or rent by making representations regarding entry into the neighborhood of a person of a protected class (blockbusting);
- insert in a written instrument relating to real property any condition, restriction, or prohibition based on a protected class, or honor or attempt to honor such a provision (any such provision in a deed or any other conveyance or instrument relating to real property is void); or
- discriminate in any credit transaction (whether or not it is related to real estate) in denying credit, increasing fees, requiring collateral, or in any other terms or conditions.

In short, just about every form of discrimination in real estate transactions or any services associated with real estate transactions is unlawful if it is based on a person's status as a member of any of the protected classes.

Exemptions. The Washington Law Against Discrimination has few exemptions. Educational institutions may discriminate based on sex, marital status, or familial status in student housing. Private clubs and certain cemeteries and mausoleums operated by religious or sectarian institutions may discriminate based on religion. Discrimination based on familial status is allowed in connection with property that qualifies as housing for older persons under the federal Fair Housing Act.

The Washington law has no general exemptions for sellers or landlords in ordinary transactions. However, it does exempt transactions that involve sharing an owner-occupied dwelling unit, or the sublease of a portion of a dwelling unit occupied by the sublessor. For example, a homeowner who rents rooms in her own house does not have to comply with this law when choosing lodgers.

Of course, the Washington Law Against Discrimination has no exemptions for real estate licensees engaged in professional activities.

Fig. 15.2 Antidiscrimination legislation

Legislation	Prohibits Discrimination
Civil Rights Act of 1866	Based on race, in real estate transactions
Federal Fair Housing Act	In sale, lease, or financing of housing
Americans with Disabilities Act	Based on disability, in public accommodations
Washington Law Against Discrimination	In sale, lease, or financing of any real estate

Enforcement. For claims alleging an unfair practice in a real estate transaction, an injured party may file a written complaint with the Human Rights Commission within one year after the alleged discrimination took place. The Commission will then conduct an investigation. If the investigation reveals a reasonable basis for a belief that discrimination occurred, the Commission will act on the complaint.

First, the Commission will try to eliminate the unlawful discrimination by conference, conciliation, and persuasion. If that's unsuccessful, the Commission may schedule a hearing before an administrative law judge. If the judge finds unlawful discrimination, a cease and desist order may be issued. The judge may also require affirmative relief, payment of actual damages to the victim, and payment of a civil penalty to the government.

Either party may appeal the outcome of the administrative hearing to the superior court by filing an appeal within 30 days after being served with the final order.

As an alternative to an administrative hearing, the injured party may choose to have the attorney general enforce the law by bringing a civil action against the alleged discriminator.

Washington Fairness in Lending Act

The Washington Fairness in Lending Act prohibits redlining. Under this act, financial institutions may not deny single-family home loan applications solely because the home is located in a particular geographic area. They also may not vary the terms of the loan (such as by requiring a higher downpayment, higher interest rate, or shorter amortization term, or by deliberately undervaluing the property in an appraisal).

The act doesn't prevent a lending institution from using sound underwriting practices (including considering the borrower's creditworthiness and the market value of the property), but it outlaws the use of lending standards that have no economic basis.

Washington Real Estate License Law

Under the real estate license law, a licensee's violation of any federal or state antidiscrimination law is also a violation of the license law and grounds for disciplinary action (see Chapter 17). If a real estate licensee discriminates in sales or hiring activity, his license could be suspended or revoked. In addition, the licensee could face a substantial fine for each offense, and/or be required to complete an educational course in civil rights laws and nondiscriminatory real estate practices. Violations of the license law are also punishable as gross misdemeanors.

📖 Chapter Summary

1. Discrimination in real estate transactions is prohibited by the Civil Rights Act of 1866, the federal Fair Housing Act, the Washington Law Against Discrimination, and the real estate license law.

2. The Civil Rights Act of 1866 prohibits discrimination based on race or color in real estate transactions. The Civil Rights Act of 1964 prohibits discrimination based on race, color, religion, or national origin in programs and activities for which the federal government provided financial assistance.

3. The federal Fair Housing Act prohibits discrimination based on race, color, religion, sex, national origin, disability, or familial status. Unlike the Civil Rights Act of 1866, it applies only to transactions involving residential property.

4. The forms of discrimination prohibited under the federal Fair Housing Act include blockbusting, steering, and redlining. Blockbusting is attempting to obtain listings or encourage sales by predicting the entry of minorities into the neighborhood and implying that this will cause a decline in the neighborhood. Steering is the channeling of buyers or renters to specific neighborhoods based on race or other protected characteristics. Redlining is the refusal to make loans on properties located in a particular area based on the racial or ethnic composition of the area.

5. Federal laws that address discrimination in credit transactions include the Fair Housing Act, the Equal Credit Opportunity Act, and the Home Mortgage Disclosure Act.

6. The Americans with Disabilities Act guarantees people with physical or mental disabilities equal access to public accommodations.

7. The Washington Law Against Discrimination prohibits discrimination based on race, creed, color, national origin, sex, sexual orientation, marital status, or familial status; use of a trained guide dog or service animal; or honorably discharged veteran or military status. It applies not just to housing, but also to employment, insurance, and credit transactions; places of public accommodation; and all types of real property transactions.

🔑 Key Terms

Blockbusting—Attempting to induce homeowners to list or sell their homes by predicting that members of another race or ethnic group, or people suffering from some disability, will be moving into the neighborhood.

Steering—Channeling prospective buyers or tenants toward or away from particular neighborhoods based on their race, religion, or national origin, in order to maintain or change the character of the neighborhoods.

Redlining—Refusing to make a loan because of the racial or ethnic composition of the neighborhood in which the security property is located.

Familial status—Refers to those who have children (persons under 18 years old) living with them. It also includes someone who is pregnant or is in the process of securing custody of a child.

Disability—A physical or mental impairment that substantially limits one or more major life activities. Also called a handicap.

Public accommodation—A nonresidential place that is owned, operated, or leased by a private entity and is open to the public, such as real estate offices, restaurants, hotels, theaters, doctors' offices, pharmacies, retail stores, museums, libraries, parks, private schools, and day care centers.

Chapter Quiz

1. When a real estate agent channels prospective buyers away from a particular neighborhood because of their race, it is called:
   a) blockbusting
   b) steering
   c) redlining
   d) clipping

2. Rental of a room or unit in an owner-occupied dwelling is exempt from the federal Fair Housing Act if the dwelling contains:
   a) two or more units
   b) three units or less
   c) less than five units
   d) six units or more

3. A real estate licensee is helping the Jacksons sell their single-family home. Can this transaction be exempt from the federal Fair Housing Act?
   a) Yes, as long as the Jacksons own no more than three single-family homes
   b) Yes, as long as no discriminatory advertising is used
   c) No, because a real estate agent is involved
   d) No, the act applies to all residential sales transactions, without exception

4. The Gardenia Village condominium has a "No Kids" rule. This is not a violation of the federal Fair Housing Act:
   a) if the condo qualifies as "housing for older persons" under the terms of the law
   b) if no discriminatory advertising is used
   c) because age discrimination is not prohibited by the Fair Housing Act
   d) because condominiums aren't covered by the Fair Housing Act

5. Title VIII of the Civil Rights Act of 1968 prohibits:
   a) discrimination in housing
   b) discrimination in residential lending
   c) Both a) and b)
   d) Neither a) nor b)

6. Blockbusting is an acceptable practice:
   a) only under the supervision of real estate licensees
   b) only when approved by either HUD or the Justice Department
   c) only if the seller and buyer mutually agree
   d) under no circumstances

7. For violations of the Washington Law Against Discrimination, complaints should be filed with the:
   a) Department of Fair Employment and Housing
   b) Washington Human Rights Commission
   c) Washington Housing Council
   d) Washington Association of Realtors®

8. The Home Mortgage Disclosure Act helps to enforce the prohibition against:
   a) redlining
   b) steering
   c) blockbusting
   d) flipping

9. A landlord who is subject to the provisions of the federal Fair Housing Act must:
   a) permit a disabled tenant to make reasonable modifications to the property at the tenant's expense
   b) make reasonable exceptions to the landlord's rules to accommodate disabled tenants
   c) Both a) and b)
   d) Neither a) nor b)

10. Under Washington law, it would be permissible for a landlord to refuse to rent to a prospective tenant because the tenant:
    a) has a child
    b) was born in Germany
    c) has a low income
    d) None of the above

11. In comparison to the federal Fair Housing Act, the Washington Law Against Discrimination:

    a) protects more classes of people
    b) is narrower in scope
    c) provides exactly the same coverage
    d) has many more exemptions

12. Which of the following is not covered by the federal Fair Housing Act?

    a) A commercial property
    b) An eight-unit multifamily dwelling
    c) A triplex listed for sale with a real estate licensee
    d) A vacant lot intended for residential construction

13. A developer who intended to rent housing in a particular development only to persons 45 years of age or over would be in violation of the:

    a) Civil Rights Act of 1866
    b) Civil Rights Act of 1964
    c) Federal Fair Housing Act
    d) Americans with Disabilities Act

14. Under the Americans with Disabilities Act:

    a) real estate firms are exempt
    b) real estate firms may discriminate against people with disabilities when taking listings, if appropriate
    c) real estate firms must be accessible to people with disabilities
    d) only individual real estate agents are prohibited from discriminating against people with disabilities

15. Which of the following is prohibited by the Washington Fairness in Lending Act?

    a) Redlining
    b) Steering
    c) Blockbusting
    d) Panic selling

👉 Answer Key

1. b) Channeling prospective buyers or tenants away from (or toward) certain neighborhoods based on their race or other protected characteristics is called steering. Steering is a violation of federal and state antidiscrimination laws.

2. c) The Fair Housing Act exemption for rentals applies to owner-occupied dwellings with up to four units.

3. c) No residential transaction in which a real estate agent is employed is exempt from the federal Fair Housing Act.

4. a) The Fair Housing Act does not allow an apartment house or a condominium to discriminate on the basis of familial status unless the complex qualifies as "housing for older persons."

5. c) Title VIII of the 1968 Civil Rights Act (better known as the federal Fair Housing Act) prohibits discriminatory practices when selling, renting, advertising, or financing housing.

6. d) The discriminatory practice known as blockbusting is entirely prohibited by the Fair Housing Act.

7. b) The Washington Human Rights Commission is charged with enforcing the Washington Law Against Discrimination.

8. a) The Home Mortgage Disclosure Act helps to enforce the prohibition against redlining by requiring large institutional lenders to file an annual report of all mortgage loans made during that year. Loans are categorized by location, alerting investigators to possible redlining.

9. c) The Fair Housing Act requires a residential landlord to allow a disabled tenant to make reasonable modifications to the property. The landlord must also make reasonable exceptions to the rules to accommodate a disabled tenant.

10. c) A landlord may (and should) base a rental decision on whether the prospective tenant can afford the rent. However, the landlord cannot take into account the prospective tenant's national origin or familial status.

11. a) The Washington Law Against Discrimination protects several more classes of people than the federal Fair Housing Act.

12. a) The Fair Housing Act applies only to residential properties, not to commercial or industrial properties.

13. c) The developer's age limit would violate the Fair Housing Act. Housing for older persons is allowed, but 45 isn't the cutoff age.

14. c) Under the ADA, real estate firms must take reasonable actions necessary to make their accommodations accessible to people with disabilities.

15. a) The Washington Fairness in Lending Act prohibits redlining, among other discriminatory lending practices.

Property Management

Chapter Overview

Many real estate firms engage in property management to some degree, so all real estate agents should have a basic knowledge of property management principles. This chapter provides an overview of the property management profession. Since property managers primarily manage investment property, the first section of the chapter discusses the basics of investing in real estate. The next section describes some of the differences between types of managed properties. After that, we discuss the management agreement, the management plan, and the various functions of a property manager. The final section of the chapter looks at the laws that govern landlord-tenant relationships.

Introduction to Property Management

In this chapter, we'll use the term **property manager** to refer to someone other than the property owner who supervises the operation of income property in exchange for a fee. Until the 1930s, most real estate investors in the U.S. managed their own properties, perhaps hiring an assistant to collect rents. Then, during the Great Depression, countless borrowers defaulted on their mortgages, and many properties ended up in the hands of lenders. The lenders were saddled with management responsibilities for extensive property holdings, but they had little property management experience. Of necessity, some formed their own property management departments, and others came to depend on the real estate industry to provide the necessary expertise. Although the lenders eventually resold the properties they acquired during the Depression, the value of efficient property management had been discovered, and increasing numbers of property owners began to use the services of property managers.

Property management became even more important as construction and business practices changed. Better elevators and steel framing allowed the construction of taller structures, so apartment and office buildings became larger. Shopping centers replaced the corner store, and flourishing commercial activity led to the creation of industrial parks. It became increasingly difficult for property owners to manage all of their holdings, and professional, efficient, and effective outside management often became a necessity rather than a luxury.

Investing in Real Estate

A property manager's job typically begins after someone has decided to invest in income-producing property, such as an apartment building, an office building, or a shopping center. As we'll discuss later, the primary function of a property manager is to help the property owner achieve her investment goals. So before we go into the nuts and bolts of property management, let's take a brief look at general investment principles and at real estate as an investment. (A word of caution: real estate agents should not act as investment counselors; they should always refer clients to an accountant, attorney, or investment specialist for investment advice.)

An investment is an asset that is expected to generate a **return** (a profit). A return on an investment can take various forms, including interest, dividends, rent, or appreciation. An asset appreciates (increases in value) because of inflation, and may also appreciate because of a rising demand for the asset. For example, a parcel of prime vacant land appreciates as land suitable for development becomes increasingly scarce.

Types of Investments

Investments can be divided into two general categories: ownership investments and debt investments. With **ownership investments**, the investor takes an ownership interest in the asset. Real estate and stocks are examples of ownership investments. The return on ownership investments usually takes the form of dividends, rent, and/or appreciation.

A **debt investment** is essentially a loan that an investor makes to an individual or entity. For example, a bond is a debt owed to an investor by a government entity or corporation. The investor lends the entity money for a set period of time, and in return the entity promises to repay the money on a specific date (the maturity date), along with a certain amount of interest. An ordinary mortgage loan is another example of a debt investment for the bank.

Investors often choose to **diversify** their investments—that is, they invest in a variety of different types of investments, instead of putting all their eggs in one basket. The mix of investments that an investor owns is referred to as his **portfolio**.

Note that for tax purposes, investment income (such as interest, dividends, or rent) is usually distinguished from earned income (salaries, wages, or self-employment income).

Investment Characteristics

An investor evaluates any investment opportunity in terms of **safety**, **liquidity**, and **yield** (which is the total return on the investment, or **ROI**). These three characteristics are interrelated. Safety and liquidity tend to go together. On the other hand, for a high return an investor often sacrifices safety or liquidity, or both.

Safety. An investment is considered safe if there's little risk that the investor will actually lose money on it. Even if the investment doesn't generate the return she hopes for, the investor will at least be able to recover the money she originally invested.

Some types of investments are very safe, because they carry a guarantee. The federal deposit insurance that protects funds (up to $250,000) in a bank account is a simple example; it's highly unlikely that a depositor will lose any of the money he puts in the bank. On the other hand, some types of investments are inherently risky. For instance, an investor who puts his money into an uncertain venture such as a brand new company is likely to lose his investment if the company isn't a success.

Liquidity. A **liquid asset** is one that can be converted into cash (liquidated) quickly. Money in a bank account is extremely liquid: to convert it into cash, the investor has only to present the bank with a withdrawal slip or check. Mutual funds, stocks, and bonds are less liquid—they may take a little longer (perhaps a few days) to convert into cash. Other items, such as jewelry or coin collections, aren't considered liquid at all, because an investor might have to wait months to find a buyer and exchange those assets for cash. Real estate isn't a liquid asset.

As a general rule, the more liquid the asset, the lower the return. For example, the money in an ordinary savings account is very liquid, but it offers only a modest return, in the form of a low rate of interest. If you make a commitment to keep the funds deposited for a specified period (with a certificate of deposit), you'll get a slightly higher rate. A longer period generally means a higher rate of return.

Liquidity is an advantage because the investor can cash in the investment immediately if the funds are needed for an unexpected expense, or because a better investment opportunity has arisen. Money in a nonliquid investment is effectively "locked up" and unavailable for other purposes. Real estate and other nonliquid assets can be excellent investments, but their lack of liquidity has consequences that a prospective investor should take into account.

Yield. Investments that are both safe and liquid tend to offer the lowest returns. In a sense, investors "pay" for safety and liquidity with a low return. To get a high return, an investor usually must take the risk of losing some or even all of the money originally invested. The investor may also have to sacrifice liquidity, allowing the money to be tied up for a while.

Of course, except with the very safest investments, the yield isn't fixed at the time the investment is made. The yield can change with market conditions, such as an increase or decrease in market interest rates.

As a general rule, the greater the risk, the higher the potential yield needs to be. Otherwise investors won't be willing to make the investment. Investors also expect higher yields from long-term investments, as compensation for keeping their money tied up for longer periods of time.

With some types of investments, the return on investment will be much greater if the investor can afford to keep the investment for a long period of time and take advantage of healthy market conditions. This is true of real estate.

> **Example:** Jeanne and Harold each buy a piece of land for $20,000 in the same year. One year later, Jeanne desperately needs some cash. The market for land has taken a downturn, and Jeanne is forced to sell her property at a loss. She ends up with only $17,000 of her original $20,000 investment.
>
> Harold, on the other hand, is in no hurry to sell the property, so he can wait for optimal market conditions. He keeps the land for twelve years and then sells it at the peak of a real estate cycle, when property values are high. Because Harold could afford to choose when he sold the property, he walks away from the transaction with $60,000, an excellent return on his original $20,000 investment.

Advantages of Investing in Real Estate

People invest in real estate for many reasons. The advantages of investing in real estate can be broken down into three general categories:

- appreciation,
- leverage, and
- cash flow.

Appreciation. When property **appreciates**, that means it is increasing in value due to changes in the economy or other outside factors. Although real estate values fluctuate, over a period of several years real estate tends to appreciate at a rate equal to or higher than the rate of inflation. As a result, real estate has ordinarily been considered an effective "hedge" against inflation. And when buildable property becomes scarce, the value of properties in prime locations may increase more rapidly.

Fig. 16.1 Investing in real estate

Advantages of Real Estate Investment

- Appreciation
- Leverage
- Cash flow

Appreciation causes a property owner's equity to increase. **Equity** is the difference between the value of the property and the liens against it, so an increase in the property's value increases the owner's equity in the property. Also, each monthly mortgage payment typically increases the owner's equity, by reducing the loan's remaining principal balance. Equity adds to the investor's net worth and can also be used to secure an equity loan. So even though real estate isn't considered a liquid asset, equity in real estate can be used to generate cash funds.

Leverage. Real estate investors can take advantage of **leverage**, which means using borrowed money to invest in an asset. If the asset appreciates, then the investor earns money on the money borrowed as well as the money she invested.

> **Example:** Martha purchases a rental home for $215,000. She makes a $53,750 downpayment and borrows the rest of the purchase price. The rent generated by the property covers all the expenses of operating the property, plus the mortgage payment and income taxes. The property appreciates at 3% per year for five years. At the end of the five years, Martha sells the property for $249,000. She's made a $34,000 profit over five years on her $53,750 investment. This represents a 63% return over the five-year period. The property appreciated at 3% per year, but because she only invested 25% of the purchase price, Martha was able to generate a 63% return on the investment.

Cash Flow. Many real estate investments generate a positive cash flow, in addition to appreciating in value. **Cash flow** is spendable income—for income-producing property, it's the amount of money left after all the property's expenses have been paid, including operating costs, mortgage payments, and taxes. When a real estate investment generates a positive cash flow, the investor's monthly income increases. Thus, a real estate investment can increase both the investor's net worth (through appreciation) and his income (through positive cash flow). Investors sometimes use the term "cash on cash," which refers to a property's annual cash flow divided by the initial investment. It pinpoints the ratio between cash invested (equity) and cash received.

Rental income is one way a property can generate cash flow. Another way is through a **sale-leaseback** arrangement. In a sale-leaseback, the owner of a building used in the owner's business sells the building to an investor, but then leases it back from the investor and continues to use it. The money generated by the sale can be used for expansion, acquiring inventory, or investment elsewhere. At the same time, the seller can deduct the rent paid to lease the property from his income taxes as a business expense. Sometimes a sale-leaseback arrangement also includes a **buyback**

agreement, in which it's agreed that the seller will buy the property back for its fair market value after a certain number of years.

Types of Managed Properties

Now let's turn to our discussion of property management. We'll start with the different types of properties that a property manager may be called upon to manage. There are four basic types of income-producing properties:

1. residential rental property,
2. office buildings,
3. retail property, and
4. industrial property.

Each type of property has special characteristics and demands a different kind of management expertise, so property managers often specialize in one particular type of property. In the following paragraphs, we'll discuss some of the differences between property types.

Apartment buildings, which typically offer month-to-month or one-year leases, have a much higher turnover rate than industrial property, where leases often run for ten years or more. As a result, residential property managers tend to spend more of their time on marketing and leasing. Residential property managers also must fulfill the legal responsibilities imposed by the landlord-tenant laws, which are designed to protect residential tenants.

Office buildings have very different housekeeping requirements than residential buildings. Office buildings endure much heavier foot traffic; they have facilities that get continuous use (such as washrooms and elevators) and thus need frequent cleaning; and management is often responsible for cleaning the tenants' spaces as well as the common areas. Lease negotiations are also very different for office space than for residential space. Office tenants generally have more clout than residential tenants, and almost any aspect of an office lease might involve back and forth bargaining. Landlords commonly offer major concessions to attract office tenants, such as free rent for a limited period or extensive remodeling.

Leasing space to an appropriate tenant is a concern with any type of property, but it's especially important when managing a shopping center. The success of each tenant in a shopping center depends in part on the customers that each of the other tenants attract, so it's vital to lease to strong, compatible tenants. Also, a portion of the rent is often based on the store's income, so the owner has a vested interest in the financial success of each tenant. The tenant mix must appeal to the widest variety of potential shoppers, while avoiding too much direct competition within the shopping center itself.

Fig. 16.2 Income-producing properties

Types of Income Properties

Residential
(rental homes, apartments, condos)
Office
(office buildings and office parks)
Retail
(stores and shopping centers)
Industrial
(industrial parks)

These are only some of the ways in which property types differ. But even from these few examples, it's easy to see that the different types of properties require very different management plans. The advantages of specializing in one or two property types are clear.

However, there are general management principles that apply to any type of income property. Our discussion will focus mainly on managing residential properties, but most of the principles and practices we'll be describing apply to the other types of property as well.

The Management Agreement

The first step in the management process is for the property owner and the property manager to enter into a **management agreement**. This contract establishes and defines their working relationship. In the same way that a listing agreement creates an agency relationship between a seller and a real estate firm offering brokerage services, the management agreement creates an agency relationship between a property owner and a firm offering property management services. And in the same way a firm designates an affiliated licensee to work with a seller, a firm will also designate one or more of its affiliated licensees to provide management services for the property owner. For purposes of this discussion we'll use the term "property manager" to refer to the individual licensee who performs duties for the property owner on behalf of the real estate firm.

The management agreement must be in writing and signed by both parties, and the document should set forth all of the terms of their agreement. It's especially important for the exact duties and powers of the manager to be explicitly stated. What kinds of decisions can the manager freely make, and what kinds must be referred to the owner? For example, suppose several units in an apartment building needed new carpets. Could the manager replace the carpets without consulting the owner, or is this a decision that the owner wants to make? Other areas in which questions might arise include the authority to execute leases, make major repairs, choose an insurance company and policy for the property, or embark on a major advertising campaign.

At a minimum, the management agreement should include:

- the term of the agreement;
- the manager's compensation (a percentage of gross income, a commission on new rentals, a fixed fee, or a combination of all of these);
- the type of property and its legal description;
- the number of units or square footage;
- the manager's duties;
- the scope of the manager's authority; and
- how frequent and how detailed the manager's reports to the owner will be.

In most cases, the management agreement will authorize the property manager to collect rents and to hold and refund tenants' security deposits. It will usually also authorize her to pay expenses related to the management of the property, so that she can pay contractors for routine maintenance and repairs, purchase supplies, and so forth.

The property manager must bear in mind that after the management agreement is signed, an agency relationship exists between the manager and the owner, and thus the manager is bound by all the duties of an agent (see Chapter 7). Also note that, as with listing and buyer agency agreements, it is the firm who "owns" the management agreement, not the affiliated licensee.

The Management Plan

Once a manager has entered into a management agreement, the actual business of managing begins. The first (and often most important) step in managing a property is drawing up a **management plan**. A management plan outlines the manager's strategy for financial management and physical upkeep, and focuses on achieving the owner's goals.

The management plan should be designed to implement the owner's goals in the most effective manner possible. It's important to remember that there are many different reasons for investing in income property; different property owners have different management goals. For instance, one property owner may simply want a steady, reliable stream of income. Another owner may want a tax shelter. Another may want to increase the property's value as much as possible, in order to reap a bigger profit later on. An owner's goals can also change over the period of ownership.

> **Example:** When he's in his early 40s, Greg decides to purchase a small apartment building. He has other sources of income, so he's most interested in the long-term investment and tax shelter aspects of real estate ownership. However, as the years pass, Greg's needs change. When he retires, he becomes more interested in receiving a steady cash flow from his property.

Preliminary Study

A management plan can be created only after a comprehensive study of all of the facets of the property, including its location, its physical characteristics, its financial status, and its policies of operation. This preliminary study includes a regional analysis, a neighborhood analysis, a property analysis, and a market analysis.

Regional Analysis. Preparing a management plan begins with a study of the region (the city or metropolitan area) in which the property is located. The manager analyzes the general economic conditions, physical attributes, and population growth and distribution. Among the most significant considerations are trends in occupancy rates, market rental rates, employment levels, and (for residential property) family size and lifestyle.

Occupancy Rates. According to the law of supply and demand, when the demand for an item is greater than the supply, the price or value of the item increases. And when the supply exceeds the demand, the price or value of the item decreases. This basic rule applies to rental properties just as it applies to other commodities.

From a property manager's point of view, the supply of rental units is the total number of units available for occupancy in the area where the managed property is located. The demand for rental units is the total number of potential tenants in that area who are able to pay the rent for those units. When demand exceeds supply, rental rates go up; when supply exceeds demand, rental rates go down.

There is a **technical oversupply** of property when there are more units than potential tenants. There is an **economic oversupply** when there are enough potential tenants, but they are unable to pay the current rent. Likewise, there may be a **technical shortage** (when there are more potential tenants than units) or an **economic shortage** (when there are more able-to-pay tenants than units).

To set rental rates for a managed property, a property manager must determine the occupancy trend for the area. If the trend is toward higher occupancy levels, the value of the units will increase as space grows more scarce. It is during these times that managers raise rents and reduce services. On the other hand, if there is a trend toward higher vacancy rates, a unit's value will decrease. In periods of high vacancy, tenants are likely to resist rent increases or make more demands for services or repairs when leases are renewed.

Occupancy levels fluctuate constantly. The direction and speed of the changes have a significant impact on the property manager's operating and marketing policies.

Market Rental Rates. In addition to evaluating occupancy trends, a property manager should keep track of market rental rates, the rates currently charged for comparable rental units. The manager should set rental rates for the managed units at a level that will make them competitive.

Various published reports provide information about rental rates, such as the Bureau of Labor's statistics on rents paid for residential units. A property manager may also consult with other managers in the area to gather information on rental rates. Rental rates stated in classified ads can also be considered. These methods, while not precise, can give a manager a basic picture of market trends.

Labor Force. The property manager should be aware of local employment trends, since employment levels and the size of the labor force affect how many potential tenants can afford to rent. A property manager should also know whether earnings are increasing or decreasing, and about savings rates in the community. Clearly, if potential tenants can't afford a particular rental unit or would rather save than spend, the property manager's product isn't going to sell.

Family Size and Lifestyle. Family size has a great deal to do with the value of particular residential units. If the average family size were three (two parents and one child), five-bedroom units would have less appeal and two-bedroom units would be very attractive. Thus, the two-bedroom units would command a higher price per square foot than the five-bedroom units. A property manager needs to be aware of the national trend toward smaller and even single-person households, and also any local trends in family size and lifestyle.

Neighborhood Analysis. After the regional analysis, the next step in the preliminary study is to analyze the neighborhood where the property is located. The definition of a neighborhood varies considerably from one place to another. In rural areas, a neighborhood may consist of many square miles. In an urban area, a neighborhood may be only a few blocks.

The qualities of the neighborhood have a significant bearing on the property's value and use. Important neighborhood characteristics include:

- the level of maintenance (Are the buildings and grounds well cared for, or in poor condition?);
- a growth or decline in population; and
- the economic status of the residents.

A property manager should discover the reasons behind any neighborhood trends. Is the population density increasing because of new multi-family developments, or because single-family homes are changing into rooming houses? The building of new apartments is a sign of economic prosperity; rooming house tenancies are not.

A neighborhood analysis helps a property manager factor location into the management plan. No matter how effectively a property is operated, its location has a strong impact on its profitability. Realistic management goals must take location into account.

Property Analysis. Of course, to develop a management plan, the manager must become very familiar with the physical characteristics of the property itself. He will inspect the property, noting its architectural design, physical condition, facilities, and general layout.

The following characteristics are particularly important:

- the number and size of the living units, or the number of rentable square feet;
- the appearance of the property and the rental spaces (age, architectural style, layout, view, fixtures);
- the physical condition of the building (roof, elevators, windows);
- the physical condition of the rental spaces (floor coverings, stairways, shades or blinds, walls, entryways);
- the amenities provided (laundry room, recreational facilities);
- the services provided (janitorial services, repair services, or security);
- the relationship of the land to the building (Is the land used efficiently? Is there adequate parking?);
- the occupancy rate and tenant composition; and
- the size and efficiency of the staff.

Market Analysis. The last step in the preliminary study for a management plan is the market analysis, which provides information on competing properties. To do a market analysis, the manager must first define the pertinent market. The major divisions of the real estate market are residential, office, retail, and industrial. Each of these can be broken down into subcategories. For instance, the residential market can be divided into single-family rental homes, duplexes, townhouses, walk-up apartments, small multistory apartments, and large apartment complexes.

Once the manager has identified the market that the managed property competes in, several characteristics must be examined:

- the number of units available in the area;
- the average age and character of the buildings in which the units are located;
- the quality of the average unit in the market (size, condition, layout, facilities);
- the number of potential tenants in the area;
- the current price for the average unit; and
- the average occupancy rate.

The property manager compares the managed property to comparable properties in the neighborhood to derive an understanding of the managed property's advantages and disadvantages. Armed with this information, the manager can establish an effective management strategy.

The Management Proposal

After completing the preliminary study, the property manager develops a management proposal and submits it to the property owner for approval. The manager's proposal will include a rental schedule, income and expense projections, a schedule of day-to-day operations, and perhaps suggestions for physical changes to the property itself.

Rental Schedule. A rental schedule lists all the various types of units and their rental rates. For example, an apartment building may consist of studio apartments, one-bedroom apartments, and two-bedroom apartments. Some apartments may have views, others may not. Rental rates will vary accordingly.

Rental schedules are based on all the data collected during the regional, neighborhood, property, and market analyses. This information helps the manager determine the highest rent that can be charged while maintaining the optimum occupancy level. To set the rate for a particular type of unit, the manager can adjust the market rental rate for the average comparable unit up or down to reflect the differences between the comparable and the type of unit in question. Because this method of setting rates depends on market conditions, the rental schedule should be reexamined periodically to see if it's still current. Either an unusually high vacancy rate or an unusually low vacancy rate is an indication that the property's rental rates are out of line with the community. If the vacancy rate is high, the rent may be too expensive; if the vacancy rate is unusually low, the rent may be below the norm.

Budgets. The property manager also sets up a budget of income and operating expenses (see Figure 16.3). The manager lists the total value of all rentable space at the scheduled rental rates, then subtracts a figure for projected delinquent rental payments and vacancies (sometimes called a vacancy factor). Any other income sources, such as laundry facilities, vending machines, or parking, should also be listed.

Next, the estimated operating expenses—both fixed expenses and variable expenses—are listed. **Fixed expenses** include such items as property taxes, insurance premiums, and employee salaries. **Variable expenses** include utilities, maintenance, and repairs.

Finally, the manager deducts projected operating expenses from projected revenues to arrive at a cash flow figure.

Day-to-Day Operations. In addition to long-range financial planning, the management proposal should include the manager's plans for the property's day-to-day operations. The manager has to decide how much (if any) staffing will be required and what the employment policies and procedures will be.

Physical Alterations. In some cases, the property manager's proposal will include recommendations for remodeling, rehabilitation, or other physical alterations to the property. For instance, after a thorough examination of the property, the customer base, and the market, a manager might decide that the property would be worth much more if the building were altered to match current family size and lifestyle trends.

Example: An older building is made up of four- and five-bedroom units in a neighborhood predominantly made up of one- and two-person households. If the apartments were converted to smaller units, the owner's profits would probably increase significantly.

Fig. 16.3 Operating budget

	Jan	Feb	Mar	Apr	May	June	July	Aug	Sept	Oct	Nov	Dec	Annual
Income													
Scheduled Rents													
Less:													
Vacancies													
Rent Loss													
Effective Rent													
Miscellaneous Income													
Total Income													
Expenses													
Administrative													
Management Costs													
Other Adm. Costs													
Operating													
Payroll													
Supplies													
Heating													
Electricity													
Water and Sewer													
Gas													
Maintenance													
Grounds													
Maint. and Repairs													
Painting, Decorating													
Taxes and Insurance													
Real Estate Taxes													
Other Taxes, Fees													
Insurance													
Contract Service													
Total Expenses													
Net Operating Income													
Less Reserves													
Net Income													
Less Debt Service													
Cash Flow													

Owner's Approval. Once completed, the management proposal is presented to the property owner. When the proposal is approved, it becomes the management plan: the blueprint for managing the property.

Management Functions

Property managers must have the skills needed to perform a wide variety of management functions. They must be able to market the property, negotiate leases, and handle tenant relations. They must be able to keep detailed financial records and prepare regular reports for the property owner. They must also be able to arrange for the maintenance and repairs that will preserve the value of the property.

Leasing and Tenant Relations

The tasks involved in leasing and tenant relations include marketing the rental spaces, negotiating leases, addressing tenants' complaints, and collecting rents.

Marketing. Property managers generally use advertising to bring potential tenants to their properties. The more people who view a rental space, the more likely it is to be leased, and leased to a good tenant.

Different types of properties require different types and amounts of advertising. For some properties, advertising is necessary only when there's a vacancy to fill. In fact, if the property is attractive and in a prominent location, advertising may not be necessary at all. On the other hand, if the property is in an isolated location, continuous advertising may be required to generate enough interest to fill vacancies when they occur.

Successful advertising brings in a good number of potential tenants in the least amount of time for the lowest cost. Property managers often evaluate the effectiveness of their advertising in terms of the number of potential tenants for the advertising dollars spent. For example, based on experience, a property manager might have a general rule of thumb that the cost of advertising shouldn't exceed $30 per prospect. Thus, newspaper advertising that costs $300 should bring at least ten prospective tenants to the property.

To reach the greatest number of potential tenants for the lowest possible cost, the property manager must be familiar with the various types of advertising and know which will be most effective for the property in question. The manager may consider using signs, newspaper ads, Internet ads, a website, direct mail, or some combination of these tools.

Signs. Small, tasteful signs on the property are often used, whether there is a vacancy or not, to inform passersby of the name of the management firm and how to acquire rental information. The use of signs is most successful for office buildings, large apartment complexes, and shopping centers.

Newspaper Advertising. Newspaper advertising includes classified ads and display ads. **Classified ads** (relatively inexpensive line-type advertising that appears in the "classified" section of the newspaper) are the traditional way to advertise residential rental space, although in many cases newspaper advertising has given way to Internet advertising, as discussed below. **Display ads** are larger and more expensive than classified ads. A display ad often includes a photograph of the property, and it may appear in any section of the newspaper. Display advertising might be used to advertise space in a new office building, industrial park, or shopping center.

Internet Advertising. Classified ads can also be placed on the Internet, through online advertising websites. Internet classifieds have a number of advantages over newspaper classifieds; for example, they can include photographs of the property, and many websites allow listings to be posted free of charge.

Depending on the scope of her business, a property manager may want to maintain her own website to advertise all of the properties she's managing. In some cases, a website dedicated to a particular apartment complex, office building, or other property may be worthwhile.

Direct Mail. To be effective, direct mail advertising must be sent to potential tenants, not just to the general public. So a property manager who wants to use direct mail must compile or purchase a mailing list. With a good mailing list and a brochure designed to appeal to prospective tenants, direct mail can be an effective advertising method. Also, the same brochure can be handed out to those who visit the property.

Leasing. A prospect has seen an advertisement and comes to look at the available rental space. Now it's the property manager's job to convince the prospect that the rental space is desirable. They will usually tour the property together, and during the tour the manager will emphasize all of the property's positive qualities and amenities. The manager will point out traffic patterns and access to public transportation, the characteristics of the other tenants, the exterior and interior condition of the property, and its overall cleanliness. If it's commercial property, the manager and the prospect may discuss how the space could be altered to suit the prospect's needs, and how additional space could be incorporated if the tenant needs to expand.

After the tour, if the prospect is still interested in the property, it's the property manager's responsibility to make sure that the prospect is qualified to lease it. Although financial stability is a key consideration, it's not the only one. The manager must also decide whether the prospect is likely to be a responsible and cooperative tenant. At a minimum, this will involve checking the prospect's references and contacting the previous landlord. The manager can also use his own judgment, but must be very careful to avoid violating antidiscrimination laws (see Chapter 15).

If the manager decides in favor of the prospect, the next step is to execute a rental agreement or lease. The requirements for a valid lease are explained later in this chapter, in the discussion of landlord-tenant law.

Lease Renewal. Unless the tenant has caused problems, a property manager would much rather renew an existing lease than find a new tenant. Renewal avoids a vacancy between the time one tenant moves out and another moves in. A rental property has greater stability with long-term tenants, and it's usually easier and less expensive to satisfy the requirements of an existing tenant than improve the space for a new tenant.

A property manager should always be aware of which tenants are nearing the end of their lease term and notify them that their lease is about to expire. Then the manager should follow up on the notice, by phone or in person, to inquire whether the tenants want to renew. If so, the terms of the new lease must be negotiated.

Some leases contain an **automatic renewal clause**, which provides that the lease will be automatically renewed on the same terms unless one party notifies the other of his intent to terminate the lease. Absent a renewal of the lease, residential tenancies sometimes continue on a month-to-month basis.

Tenant Complaints. Of course, keeping tenants happy is a crucial part of the property manager's job. Making sure that the property is kept clean and in good repair is essential, and so is responding promptly and professionally to requests and complaints.

Rent Collection. Rental property can't be profitable unless the rents are collected when due. Careful selection of tenants in the first place is the most effective way to avoid delinquent rents. A high occupancy rate doesn't benefit the property owner unless the tenants meet their financial obligations.

The amount of the rent, the time and place of rent payment, and any penalties imposed for late payment should be clearly stated in the lease. The manager should consistently follow a collection plan that includes adequate recordkeeping and immediate notification of late payments. When all collection attempts fail, the manager must be prepared to take legal action to evict the tenant in accordance with the owner's policies.

Recordkeeping and Manager/Owner Relations

A property manager must account to the owner for all money received and disbursed. It's up to the owner to decide how frequent and detailed operating reports should be. This often depends on how involved the owner wants to be in the management of the property. For example, an owner with extensive property holdings who is also engaged in another full-time occupation may not want to be bothered with detailed, time-consuming reports. But a retired person with only one or two income-producing properties may want to be very involved in their management, and will therefore want a lot of information.

Statement of Operations. In many cases, the property manager's report to the owner takes the form of a monthly statement of operations. A statement of operations typically includes the following sections: a summary of operations, the rent roll, a statement of disbursements, and a narrative report of operations.

The **summary of operations** is a brief description of the property's income and expenses that makes it easier for the owner to evaluate the property's monthly financial performance. The summary is supported by the accompanying information in the rest of the statement of operations.

The **rent roll** is a report on rent collection (see Figure 16.4). Both occupied and vacant units are listed in the rent roll, as well as the total rental income, both collected and uncollected. The rent roll breaks down rental figures into the previous balance, current rent, total amount received, and balance due.

The information in the rent roll is obtained from the individual ledger sheets kept on each tenant and rental space. A ledger sheet typically shows the tenant's name,

---

Fig. 16.4 Rent roll

Rent Roll

Property _Magnolia Heights_   **Period** _April_

Owner _S.T. Jones_   **Prepared by** _M. Smith_

Unit Number	Occupant	Previous Balance	Current Rent	Date Received	Other Amounts	Description	Total Received	Balance Due
101	G. Tsui	0	900	4/1			900	0
102	F. Brown	700	700	4/9			1400	0
103	K. Plane	0	700	4/2	100	Parking	800	0
104	C. Flynn	0	850	4/1			850	0
105	P. Sneed	850	850	4/15			850	850
106	L. Hurt	0	850	4/1	100	Parking	950	0
107	E. Winn	0	700	4/2			700	0

unit, phone number, regular rent, other recurring charges, security deposit information, move-in date, lease term, payments made, and balances owed.

The **statement of disbursements** lists all of the expenses paid during the pertinent time period. A written order should be prepared for every purchase so that an accurate accounting can be made of all expenditures and the purpose of each one. Disbursements are usually classified according to type, which makes analysis easier. For example, maintenance expenses, tax and insurance expenses, and administrative expenses are each grouped separately.

In addition to the numerical accounts given to the owner, it's often helpful to include a **narrative report of operations** in the statement of operations. This is simply a letter explaining the information set forth in the other sections of the statement. The narrative report can add a personal touch, and it's especially important if the income was lower or the expenses were higher than expected. If there is a deviation from the normal cash flow, the owner will want a clear explanation. If the reason for a drop in cash flow is not explained, the owner may doubt the competence or integrity of the property manager.

Keeping in Touch. In addition to sending various reports and statements to the owner, the manager should contact the owner in person from time to time. A telephone call or an appointment to explain a particular proposal or problem or to ask a question is often much more effective than an email or a letter. A formal meeting is a good idea if the monthly report is especially unusual.

Maintenance

In addition to leasing, tenant relations, recordkeeping, and reporting to the owner, a property manager also supervises property maintenance. There are four basic categories of maintenance activities:

1. **Preventive maintenance:** This preserves the physical integrity of the premises and reduces corrective maintenance costs. (Cleaning the gutters is an example of preventive maintenance.)
2. **Corrective maintenance:** Actual repairs that keep equipment, utilities, and amenities functioning properly. (Fixing a leaking faucet is an example of corrective maintenance.)
3. **Housekeeping:** Cleaning the common areas and grounds on a regular basis (for example, vacuuming hallways and cleaning elevators).
4. **New construction:** This includes tenant alterations made at the beginning of the tenancy and when the lease is renewed, as well as cosmetic changes designed to make the building more attractive (for example, remodeling the lobby).

Most maintenance activities are handled by building maintenance employees or by outside maintenance services. However, a property manager must be able to recognize the maintenance needs of the property and see that they are fulfilled.

The property manager should direct the activities of the maintenance staff or independent contractors by giving them an inspection and maintenance schedule. First, the manager should inventory the building's equipment and physical elements (plumbing, furnace, roof, walls, and so on). Then a schedule of regular inspections, cleaning, and repairs should be set. For instance, walls and roofs should be scheduled

Fig. 16.5 Property maintenance record

Property Maintenance Record

Property *Magnolia Heights*

Date	Action	Location	by Whom	Time	Cost
4/12	inspect elevator	lobby	Elevator Express	1.5 hr.	contract
4/22	clean roof	roof	Johnson	5 hr.	contract
4/23	fix drain	Unit 104	Top Plumbing	1 hr.	$125

for periodic inspection, painting, and repairs. Elevators should be serviced on a regular basis.

The property manager should keep accurate records of when the various elements were inspected, serviced, replaced, or repaired (see Figure 16.5). These routine inspections and maintenance activities will help preserve the capital value of the building and prevent major repair expenses.

When managing commercial property, a property manager often has to alter the interior of the building to meet the needs of a new tenant. These alterations can range from a simple repainting job to completely redesigning or rebuilding the space. (If the property is new construction, the interior is often left incomplete so that it can be built out to fit the needs of particular tenants.) Property managers dealing with remodeling or new construction must be aware of federal laws requiring public accommodations and commercial facilities to be accessible to the disabled. (See the discussion of the Americans with Disabilities Act in Chapter 15.)

Landlord-Tenant Law

A property manager needs to understand the rules that govern the relationship between landlord and tenant. The landlord-tenant relationship is defined both by law and by the terms of the lease contract itself. We'll start with the requirements for a valid lease. Then we'll consider various landlord-tenant issues that are often addressed in a lease and discuss the impact of landlord-tenant law on leasing practices.

Requirements for a Valid Lease

A **lease**, or rental agreement, is a contract between a property owner (the landlord) and a tenant that gives the tenant possession of the property for a period of time, in exchange for rent. The lease must meet all of the requirements for a valid contract (see Chapter 6), and it must include an accurate description of the property.

In Washington, a lease for any fixed term must be in writing and signed by the property owner. If the term is over one year, the owner's signature must be acknowledged (notarized).

A rental agreement for a periodic tenancy, such as a month-to-month tenancy, does not have to be put in writing, unless the rental period is more than one year or the property is managed by a real estate firm. (All lease or rental agreements for property managed by a real estate firm must be in writing.) Of course, even when a written lease isn't legally required, it's preferable to have one.

A lease that should be in writing, but is not, creates a periodic tenancy instead of a lease for a fixed term. (See Chapter 2 for a discussion of the different types of leasehold estates.)

A written lease may be valid even if the tenant doesn't sign it; the tenant's acceptance of the lease is implied by occupancy and payment of rent. Even so, to protect both parties, it's better to have both property owner and tenant sign the lease.

In many cases, the management agreement authorizes the property manager to sign leases as the landlord's agent. Without such a specific authorization, the property manager's signature will not create a valid lease.

Lease Provisions

The following issues are commonly addressed by the provisions of a lease. As you'll see, the law also has a bearing on many of these issues. Some legal rules apply only when the lease doesn't address a particular issue; others override any contradictory provisions in the lease. The legal rules are especially likely to control in residential tenancies, which are governed by Washington's Residential Landlord-Tenant Act.

Payment of Rent. The consideration that the tenant gives the landlord for the lease is the promise to pay rent. Most leases state when the rent is to be paid, and they usually require payment at the beginning of the rental period. If a lease does not specify when the rent is to be paid, however, it is not due until the end of the rental period.

Use of Premises. Not surprisingly, the law restricts a tenant's use of the leased property to legal uses. Many leases place additional restrictions on the use of the property; for example, a lease for a space in a mall might have a provision restricting the rented space to a particular kind of retail use, in order to preserve the tenant mix. The restricting language must be clear. At a minimum, the lease should state that the premises are to be used only for the specified purpose and for no other. If there is no limitation in the lease, or if the language is not clearly restrictive, the tenant may use the premises for any legal purpose.

Security Deposit. Most property managers require a **security deposit** from the tenant when the tenant signs the lease. The deposit gives the landlord some protection against tenant default.

In Washington, a residential landlord (or property manager) can require a security deposit only if there's a written lease or rental agreement. The tenant must be given a written checklist describing the condition and cleanliness of the unit at the beginning of the tenancy. Both the landlord and the tenant must sign the checklist, indicating that they agree about the unit's initial condition.

The landlord or manager must place the tenant's security deposit in a trust account and give the tenant a receipt for the funds. At the end of the tenancy, the landlord or manager must return the entire security deposit to the tenant within 14 days after the lease terminates, or else inform the tenant of the specific reasons why all or part of the deposit is being retained.

The landlord may keep the deposit to cover unpaid rent, to pay for cleaning the premises, or to pay for repairing any damage to the property. But no portion of the deposit may be kept on account of normal wear and tear resulting from ordinary use of the property.

Any nonrefundable fee (such as a nonrefundable cleaning fee) must be designated "nonrefundable" in the lease. It may not be referred to as a deposit.

Entry and Inspection. A lease typically provides for inspection of the leased premises by the landlord during the lease term, under specified conditions. In Washington, a residential tenant may not unreasonably refuse the landlord's legitimate requests to enter the unit to inspect it, perform repairs, provide other agreed-upon services, or show the unit to prospective buyers or tenants. Except in an emergency, the landlord must give the tenant notice before entering the unit. Two days' notice is usually required, but only one day's notice is necessary if the landlord wants to show the unit.

Option to Renew. A lease may contain a provision that gives the tenant an option to renew the lease at the end of its term. Most options require the tenant to give notice of her intention to exercise the option on or before a specific date.

Maintenance. The tenant must return the premises to the landlord in the same condition in which they were received, with allowances for normal wear and tear. The landlord is usually responsible for making necessary repairs to common areas, such as the stairs, hallways, or elevators.

Transferring Leasehold Estates

A landlord can sell the leased property during the term of the lease, but the buyer takes title subject to the lease. This means the buyer must honor the lease for the remainder of its term.

The tenant can also transfer her leasehold estate to another party, through assignment, subleasing, or novation. The tenant has the right to assign or sublease without the landlord's consent, unless the lease provides otherwise. A novation always requires the landlord's consent.

In an **assignment**, the tenant transfers the leasehold estate for the entire remainder of the lease term.

Example: Landlord leases property to Tenant for a period starting January 1, 2015, and ending June 30, 2018. On July 1, 2015, Tenant transfers possession of the property to XYZ Corporation for a term starting July 1, 2015 and ending June 30, 2018.

The agreement between Tenant and XYZ is an assignment, because the transfer is for the balance of the unexpired term.

The assignee (the new tenant) becomes liable to the landlord for the rent, and the original tenant becomes secondarily liable for the rent. The assignee has the primary responsibility for paying the rent, but the original tenant is not fully released from the duty to pay it.

A **sublease** is a transfer of the leasehold estate for a period shorter than the unexpired term. The original tenant retains part of the leasehold.

Example: Landlord leases property to Tenant for a period starting January 1, 2015 and ending June 30, 2018. On July 1, 2015, Tenant transfers possession of the property to XYZ Corporation for a period starting July 1, 2015, and ending June 30, 2017, reserving the last year for himself. This agreement is a sublease, because the tenant has transferred less than the full balance of the lease term.

The sublessee (the new tenant) is liable for the rent to the original tenant, rather than to the landlord, and the original tenant is still liable to the landlord. This arrangement is sometimes referred to as a **sandwich lease**, since the original tenant is in the middle, sandwiched between the landlord and the sublessee.

A **novation** is an alternative to an assignment or a sublease. In a novation, a new contract is created and the old contract is extinguished. A landlord might agree to accept a new tenant in place of the original tenant, creating a new lease. The purpose of a novation is to terminate the liability of the tenant under the terms of the original lease.

Terminating a Leasehold Interest

As was discussed in Chapter 2, how a lease terminates depends on the type of tenancy in question. A month-to-month tenancy or other periodic tenancy ends when either party gives the other proper notice of termination. A lease for a fixed term terminates automatically at the end of its term, but it also may be terminated prior to the end of its term in any of the following ways.

Surrender. A landlord and a tenant may mutually agree to terminate a lease. This is known as surrender.

Breach of Covenant of Quiet Enjoyment. Every lease carries an **implied covenant of quiet enjoyment**, even if it is not actually stated in the lease. This covenant is the landlord's implied promise that the tenant's possession of the property will not be disturbed, either by the landlord or by a third party with a lawful claim to the property. The tenant is guaranteed exclusive possession and quiet enjoyment of his leasehold estate.

The covenant of quiet enjoyment is breached when the tenant is wrongfully evicted from the leased property. There are two types of eviction: actual and constructive.

Actual eviction occurs when the landlord actually expels the tenant from the property. **Constructive eviction** occurs when the landlord causes or permits a substantial interference with the tenant's possession of the property. For example, a landlord's failure to provide running water to a residence is a constructive eviction.

Breach of Warranty of Habitability. By law, all residential leases carry an **implied warranty of habitability**. This is the landlord's implied guarantee that the premises meet all building and housing code regulations that affect health and safety. If the premises do not meet these criteria, then the tenant must notify the landlord of the defective condition and the landlord must correct it within a certain time period prescribed by statute. If the landlord takes legal action to evict the tenant for nonpayment of rent, the tenant can use the poor condition of the premises as a defense in court.

Failure to Pay Rent. The tenant has a duty to pay rent as required by the terms of the lease. However, if the tenant fails to pay the rent, there isn't an automatic termination of the leasehold estate. The landlord is required by statute to give notice to the tenant of the nonpayment. After receiving notice, if the tenant still fails to pay, the landlord may file an **unlawful detainer action**, asking the court to evict the tenant.

If the court finds the tenant in default, it may issue a **writ of restitution** (or writ of possession), which requires the tenant to move out peaceably or be forcibly removed by the county sheriff.

Although unlawful detainer actions are given priority on the court's docket, the legal process of eviction may seem slow to a landlord or property manager. However, landlords and property managers should not take matters into their own hands. Someone who tries "self-help" eviction (forcing the tenant out with threats, or by cutting off the utilities) instead of using the legal process could end up facing a costly lawsuit.

Illegal or Unauthorized Use. If a tenant uses the leased premises in an illegal manner (for example, in violation of the zoning code), the landlord may demand that the tenant cease the illegal activity or leave the premises. Similarly, if a tenant uses the premises in a manner that isn't authorized by the lease, then the tenant has violated the lease and the landlord has the right to terminate the tenancy before the end of the term.

Destruction of the Premises. Destruction of the leased premises by a fire or other natural disaster generally terminates a lease. If the lease is for only a part of a building, such as an office, apartment, or retail space, the destruction of the building frustrates the entire purpose of the lease, so the tenant will be released from her duty to pay the rent. On the other hand, if the lease agreement is for the use of a building and the land it rests on (as is the case with a farm, for example), the destruction of the building may not terminate the lease, because the purpose of the lease is not entirely frustrated. The tenant isn't relieved from the duty to pay the rent through the end of the rental period.

Condemnation. Condemnation of property by a government entity can also result in the premature termination of a lease. (See Chapter 5 for a discussion of condemnation.)

Types of Leases

There are five major types of leases: fixed leases, graduated leases, net leases, percentage leases, and ground leases.

Sometimes called a flat, straight, or gross lease, a **fixed lease** provides for a fixed rental amount. The tenant is obligated to pay a fixed sum of money and the landlord pays the operating expenses (maintenance costs, taxes, and insurance). This type of lease is most commonly found in residential apartment rentals.

A **graduated lease** is similar to a fixed lease, but it provides for periodic increases in the rent, usually set at specific future dates and often based on the Consumer Price Index or some other measure of inflation. These increases are made possible by the inclusion of an **escalation clause**. A graduated lease is also called a step-up lease or an index lease.

A **net lease** requires the tenant to pay the landlord a fixed rent, plus some or all of the operating expenses. Commercial leases are often net leases.

Many retail businesses have **percentage leases**, especially in shopping centers. The rent is based on a percentage of the gross or net income from the tenant's business. Typically, the lease provides for a minimum rent plus a percentage of the tenant's business income above the stated minimum.

When a tenant leases land and agrees to construct a building on that land, it's called a **ground lease**. Ground leases are common in metropolitan areas; they are usually long-term, in order to make the construction of the building worth the tenant's while.

Chapter Summary

1. An investment is an asset that is expected to generate a return for the investor. Three basic characteristics of an investment are its liquidity, safety, and yield. The advantages of real estate investment include appreciation, leverage, and cash flow.

2. There are four main types of income-producing properties: residential, office, retail, and industrial. Property managers often specialize in one or two types of properties.

3. A property manager must have a written management agreement with the property owner. The agreement should include all of the terms of the management arrangement, including compensation, the manager's duties, the scope of the manager's authority, and provisions for reporting to the owner.

4. Before preparing a management plan, the manager should conduct a regional analysis, a neighborhood analysis, a property analysis, and a market analysis. The information gathered during this preliminary study will help the manager set a rental schedule, prepare a budget, and plan the day-to-day operations.

5. The functions of a property manager include marketing the property, leasing, handling tenant complaints, rent collection, recordkeeping, preparing reports for the owner, and arranging for the maintenance of the property.

6. A landlord-tenant relationship is governed by the terms of the lease and by landlord-tenant law. Unless otherwise agreed in the lease, assignment and subleasing are allowed without the landlord's consent, although the original tenant will not be released from liability.

7. A lease may terminate before the end of its term as a result of surrender, breach of the implied covenant of quiet enjoyment, breach of the implied warranty of habitability, failure to pay rent, illegal or unauthorized use of the premises, or the destruction or condemnation of the property.

8. The various types of leases include the fixed lease, graduated payment lease, net lease, percentage lease, and ground lease.

🔑 Key Terms

Investment—An asset that is expected to generate a return (a profit).

Portfolio—The mix of investments owned by an individual or company.

Liquidity—An asset's ability to be converted into cash quickly.

Yield—The return on investment (ROI) to an investor, stated as a percentage of the amount invested.

Appreciation—An increase in the value of an asset; generally due either to inflation or to an increasing scarcity of or demand for the asset.

Equity—The difference between a property's value and the liens against it.

Leverage—Using borrowed money to invest in an asset. If the asset appreciates, the investor earns money on the money borrowed as well as the money invested.

Cash flow—Spendable income; the amount of money left after all of the property's expenses (operating costs, mortgage payments, and taxes) have been paid.

Property management—When someone other than the property owner supervises the operation of an income-producing property.

Rental schedule—A list of the rental rates for units in a particular building.

Fixed expense—A property management expense that doesn't vary depending on rental income or current management needs (for example, property taxes).

Variable expense—A property management expense that varies depending on current management needs (for example, repair expenses).

Lease—A contract for possession of real estate in exchange for payment of rent.

Automatic renewal clause—A lease provision that ensures automatic renewal of the lease unless the tenant or the landlord gives the other party notice of termination.

Statement of operations—A periodic report showing the total money received and disbursed and the overall condition of the property during a given period.

Rent roll—A report on rent collections; a list of a property's total rental income, both collected and uncollected.

Statement of disbursements—A list of all of a property's expenses incurred during a specific operating period.

Preventive maintenance—A program of regular inspection and care to prevent problems.

Corrective maintenance—Ongoing repairs that are made to a building and its equipment to restore it to good operating condition.

Assignment—When a tenant transfers the entire remainder of her lease term to another person.

Sublease—When a tenant transfers only part of the remainder of the lease term to another person.

Novation—The substitution of a new lease obligation for an old one, or a new party for one of the original parties.

Eviction—The actual or constructive expulsion of a person (usually a tenant) from real property.

Unlawful detainer—A lawsuit filed by a landlord to evict a defaulting tenant.

∞ Chapter Quiz

1. The main disadvantage of investing in real estate is:

   a) the use of leverage to increase returns
   b) lack of liquidity
   c) uniformly low returns
   d) a constantly increasing supply, which decreases values

2. The difference between the value of real property and the liens against it is called:

   a) equity
   b) leverage
   c) portfolio
   d) cash flow

3. When population decreases, which type of oversupply results?

   a) Technical
   b) Economic
   c) Operational
   d) Constructive

4. A property manager's main purpose must be to fulfill:

   a) his career goals
   b) the owner's objectives
   c) the government's affordable housing goals
   d) the cash flow goals of his office

5. If a regional analysis shows that the typical family size is four, with two parents and two children, which of the following apartment units would be the most marketable?

   a) Studio
   b) Five-bedroom
   c) Three-bedroom
   d) It is unlikely that one type of unit would be preferred over any another

6. The type of property that ordinarily demands the most marketing is:

   a) residential
   b) office
   c) retail
   d) industrial

7. A property management agreement should always include the:

   a) manager's regional analysis
   b) manager's compensation
   c) owner's future plans for the property
   d) statement of operations

8. By completing a market analysis, a property manager discovers that the average rental rate for comparable residential units is $1,950. For the subject property, the property manager should set a rental rate of:

   a) $1,850 per unit, to undercut the competition
   b) $2,025 per unit, because tenants aren't very well informed and will probably pay a higher-than-average price
   c) $1,950 per unit, to remain competitive
   d) None of the above; a fixed rental rate should not be set, so the property manager can maintain flexibility when renting units

9. If it becomes necessary to evict a tenant, the landlord or property manager should:

   a) file an unlawful detainer action
   b) take legal action only after trying self-help methods, such as shutting off utilities
   c) breach the implied warranty of habitability
   d) use either leverage or a form of constructive eviction

10. Insurance premiums would be considered a:

   a) variable expense
   b) per diem expense
   c) fixed expense
   d) pro rata expense

11. A brief description of the property's income and expenses is called a:

    a) statement of operations
    b) summary of operations
    c) statement of disbursements
    d) rent roll

12. If a property owner wants to know which tenants are behind in their rent, she should examine the:

    a) rent schedule
    b) statement of disbursements
    c) narrative report of operations
    d) rent roll

13. The most effective way to reduce expensive repair bills is to:

    a) emphasize preventive maintenance
    b) put off repairs for as long as possible
    c) institute a policy of tenant-paid repairs
    d) find cheap repair companies

14. Repairs that return equipment to a functional condition are called:

    a) preventive maintenance
    b) corrective maintenance
    c) general housekeeping
    d) remodeling

15. A property manager is about to begin managing a new building. All of the following should be accomplished before she starts the actual management of the property, except:

    a) execution of a property management agreement
    b) preparation of a property management proposal
    c) preparation of a statement of operations
    d) completion of a market analysis

👉 Answer Key

1. b) The lack of liquidity is the main disadvantage of investing in real estate.

2. a) The difference between the value of real estate and the liens against it is the owner's equity.

3. a) A technical oversupply occurs when there are not enough potential tenants for the supply of a certain type of property.

4. b) A property manager must try to achieve the property owner's objectives.

5. c) The typical family would be more likely to rent a three-bedroom unit than either a studio or a five-bedroom apartment.

6. a) Because residential lease terms are relatively short, managing residential property tends to involve more marketing than managing other types of property.

7. b) A property management agreement should always include a provision that describes the manager's compensation.

8. c) Rental rates should not be much lower or much higher than the rates for competitive properties.

9. a) The legal process for evicting a tenant is called an unlawful detainer action.

10. c) Fixed expenses remain the same, regardless of rental income. Insurance premiums are fixed expenses.

11. b) A summary of operations is a brief summary of the detailed information in the other sections of the statement of operations.

12. d) A rent roll is a report on the collection of rent.

13. a) Preventive maintenance preserves the physical integrity of the property and reduces the need for corrective maintenance.

14. b) Repairs are classified as corrective maintenance.

15. c) A property manager cannot perform any management functions until she has a written management agreement. The market analysis and the management proposal should also be completed before the manager begins managing the property.

Chapter 17

Real Estate Careers and the Real Estate License Law

I. Real Estate as a Career
   A. Working as a real estate agent
   B. Real estate companies
   C. Professional associations and codes of ethics
   D. Related careers
II. Administration of the License Law
III. Real Estate Licenses
   A. When a license is required
   B. Exemptions from licensing requirements
   C. Types of licenses
   D. License qualifications and applications
   E. License expiration and renewal
IV. Regulation of Business Practices
   A. Agency relationships
      1. Creating agency relationships
      2. Duties owed by licensee
      3. Terminating agency relationships
      4. Vicarious liability
      5. Imputed knowledge
   B. Supervision and licensee responsibilities
   C. Affiliations and termination
   D. Office requirements
   E. Advertising
   F. Trust accounts
   G. Records
   H. Commissions
   I. Referral fees
   J. Handling transactions
V. Disciplinary Action
   A. Grounds for disciplinary action
   B. Disciplinary procedures
   C. Sanctions for license law violations
VI. Antitrust Laws

Chapter Overview

A successful real estate career requires not just hard work—it also requires a set of specific strengths and skills. We'll begin this chapter by discussing those requirements, as well as the professional associations that licensees can join.

Real estate careers are also controlled by the provisions of the state's real estate license law. As we explore these provisions, we'll explain who administers Washington's license law, when a real estate license is required, and the qualifications for licensure. Next, we'll discuss how the license law regulates the business practices of real estate professionals, controlling how firms form agency relationships, run their offices, supervise their sales agents, and handle client funds. Then we'll cover license law violations and disciplinary procedures. The final section of the chapter discusses how antitrust laws affect real estate agents.

Real Estate as a Career

Before discussing the real estate license law and how it affects all real estate agents—both new and experienced—we're going to briefly discuss real estate careers. Real estate is a flexible, lucrative, and enjoyable career for many people, but it's not for everyone. In this section, we'll discuss what it's like to work (and succeed) as a real estate agent, the different types of real estate companies an agent can work for, and the professional associations agents can join.

Working as a Real Estate Agent

Practically speaking (although not legally speaking), real estate agents work for themselves. Even though an agent must be affiliated with a brokerage firm and supervised by a designated broker, most firms expect their affiliated licensees to generate their own business. To a great extent, it's up to the individual agent to get new listings and find prospective buyers. An agent must therefore be self-motivated and disciplined to earn a good living.

Designated brokers usually don't require their agents to work on a fixed schedule, so agents have a lot of freedom. Experienced agents can generally choose how much to work based on their own financial needs, temperament, and ambition. However, a part-time effort generally isn't enough to get a new agent off the ground. It takes a big investment of time and energy to build a clientele.

Also, even though agents don't have a fixed schedule, that doesn't mean their time is their own. Since most home buyers and sellers hold down full-time jobs, a lot of real estate activity takes place outside of ordinary business hours. Agents often have to work evenings, weekends, and holidays, making themselves available when buyers and sellers want them.

In addition, real estate agents have to get along with all kinds of people. It may be necessary to spend a lot of time with certain clients or customers, some of them likable, some of them not. And because a real estate transaction is a very big deal for most people, it's not uncommon for buyers and sellers to be anxious, short-tempered, or demanding. Someone who doesn't honestly enjoy meeting and working closely with people will probably be miserable in a real estate career.

Real estate agents also must be able to tolerate uncertainty and rejection. There are a lot of ups and downs in the real estate business. Sometimes a listed property fails to sell. Sometimes a transaction falls through because of an unresolvable conflict. Sometimes an agent has to hear "no" dozens of times before getting to hear one "yes." A real estate agent must be able to handle all of this calmly or even cheerfully. An agent with the stamina and determination to keep going in spite of setbacks is likely to be well rewarded in the long run.

There are a number of other skills real estate licensees should acquire if they're going to be successful real estate agents:

- **Financial planning.** Most agents work on a commission basis, and in the early months of a real estate career, those commissions can take a long time to make their way into an agent's pocket. It's imperative for agents to use sound financial planning techniques if they want to survive that difficult time period. Real estate agents must be able to budget their income and expenses, and then live within that budget. They should also plan on saving extra money when times are good to help them survive the dry spells.
- **Marketing plans.** Real estate agents must be able to create and execute marketing plans, both for themselves and for the homes they list. They should be adept at using traditional marketing tools (such as yard signs and open houses), as well as newer techniques (such as websites and online social media).
- **Accounting.** Those who are paid on a commission basis (rather than a salary) have a lot more work to do with regard to financial recordkeeping and tax planning. If a new agent is unsure about how to go about setting up records and a tax payment system, she should consult an accountant.
- **Technology issues.** Technology is constantly changing, and real estate agents should make an effort to keep pace with innovations. While not all high-tech tools are necessary or even effective, many will help a licensee be more efficient. Today, most buyers and sellers want an agent they can freely contact by phone, text, and email.

Real Estate Companies

Although real estate agents work very independently, an agent's career can be strongly affected by the brokerage she works for. There's a lot of variety among real estate companies, and it's important for an agent to find a good fit.

Types of Companies. Real estate brokerage businesses range from sole proprietorships to very large companies with hundreds of agents and dozens of branch offices. Brokerages may be independent or part of a local or national franchise. Some companies work with all types of property and offer both traditional and nontraditional real estate services, such as sales, property management, escrow, investment counseling, or mortgage brokerage services. Other companies are very specialized, handling only certain types of property or certain types of transactions. For example, a commercial real estate firm might do nothing but tax-deferred exchanges; a residential brokerage might focus strictly on subdivision sales.

The particular type of company an agent should work for depends entirely on the agent's own preferences and interests. Bigger companies and franchises have some advantages, such as greater name recognition, but there are many small, independent companies with good clienteles and high profits.

Support for Agents. Another way in which real estate companies differ is in the services and support they provide for their agents. When deciding where to work, a new real estate agent should take the following considerations into account.

Training. Real estate is a complicated field, and there's a lot to learn about, from sales techniques to environmental issues. It's also essential to keep up with changes in the laws and regulations that affect real estate. So one of the most important services a company can offer an agent—particularly a new agent—is ongoing training. Some companies have a formal training program; others simply provide the opportunity to work closely with a more experienced agent. Designated brokers are required by law to review the transactions of brokers with less than two years' experience, but a good brokerage will provide mentoring that goes beyond the minimum requirement. A sink-or-swim approach, where new agents are given little or no guidance, can work out very badly for the agents and for their clients.

Facilities and Expenses. Most companies provide an agent with a telephone, a desk, and access to a computer, fax machine, and copier. It's very useful to have a pleasant office for meeting with clients and customers, where there's a receptionist, secretarial support, and other help, but an agent may have to pay for those advantages either directly (with a monthly desk fee) or indirectly (with a lower commission split). Even if a company does offer these amenities, individual agents are very likely to need some of their own equipment, such as a laptop computer and/or a smart phone.

Almost all companies require agents to pay for the expenses they incur in the course of their business activities, such as the cost of their business cards, car maintenance and gas, and cell phone service. In many cases, agents also bear the cost of advertising their listings and their services, including the cost of "For Sale" signs. An agent should ask about a company's policy in regard to all of these outlays.

Memberships. In most areas, membership in the local multiple listing service is essential, and some real estate companies provide MLS membership to their agents. Other firms require agents to pay their own membership fees. Some companies offer their agents membership in one or more professional trade associations. These associations typically give their members valuable information and training, and they're a good way to network with others in the real estate business.

Compensation. Some brokerage firms pay their agents with commission splits (for instance, the agent may get 60% of the firm's share of the commission), and other firms charge their agents a substantial monthly desk fee but let them keep 100% of the commissions they earn. Many firms use a combination of these methods. A few firms treat their agents as employees and pay them salaries. Agents should always have a good understanding of the compensation structures offered by the firms they're interested in working for.

Agent's Responsibilities. As we said earlier, real estate agents have a lot of freedom and generally don't have to work on a fixed schedule. However, many companies have some minimal requirements for their agents. For example, an agent might be expected to spend some time on **floor duty** each week. During the hours that an agent is assigned to floor duty, she must be at the office and handle all of the telephone calls and drop-in visits from prospective buyers or sellers. (This isn't just drudgery; if the callers or visitors don't ask to speak with a particular agent, the agent on floor duty can help them and, hopefully, retain them as clients or customers.)

Real estate companies differ in the extent to which they monitor their agents' levels of activity and productivity. (But remember, all new agents are subject to heightened supervision by their designated brokers.) Some designated brokers set specific sales goals for their agents to meet, and encourage competition among their agents. If an agent doesn't seem to be working hard enough or getting results, he may be let go. Other firms allow even new agents to set their own pace, with the understanding that those who aren't getting listings or making sales will eventually drop out on their own. In choosing a company, an agent has to judge whether she will thrive in a high-pressure office or do better in a low-key atmosphere.

Professional Associations and Codes of Ethics

There are numerous professional associations in the real estate industry. They provide their members with information, training, and opportunities for networking. In some cases, they also offer professional designations based on education and experience in particular areas of specialization. The general public often sees membership in a professional association as an indication of competence and trustworthiness.

Some professional associations have adopted codes of ethics for their members. A professional code of ethics sets standards of conduct for the members of a profession to meet in their dealings with the public and with other members of the profession. It provides guidance on how to handle ethical dilemmas with integrity and fairness. Failure to comply with an association's code of ethics can lead to expulsion.

For real estate agents, the code of ethics adopted by the National Association of REALTORS® (NAR) has been especially influential. NAR is the largest and best-known real estate professional association in the United States; there are also affiliated state organizations. Only licensees who belong to NAR can refer to themselves as REALTORS®.

Among the many other professional associations in the real estate industry are the National Association of Real Estate Brokers (NAREB®), the National Association of Exclusive Buyer Agents (NAEBA), the Real Estate Buyer's Agent Council (REBAC), the Appraisal Institute®, the American Society of Appraisers® (ASA), the Building Owners and Managers Association (BOMA), the Institute of Real Estate Management (IREM®), the American Society of Real Estate Counselors (ASREC), and the Real Estate Educators Association (REEA). There's also an organization for real estate regulators, the Association of Real Estate License Law Officials (ARELLO®).

Related Careers

If a real estate licensee decides that a career selling real estate is not right for him, there are several related fields that offer opportunities for someone with knowledge about real estate transactions. For instance, property management might be a good choice (and in some cases, also requires a real estate license). Title company employees, escrow officers, and mortgage loan originators all have important roles in real estate transactions, and any of these occupations might be a good fit for a real estate agent looking for another career. (Title insurance companies are regulated by the state insurance commission, and escrow officers and loan originators are regulated by the Department of Financial Institutions.) If a licensee is more interested in the nuts and bolts aspects of real estate, she could become a home inspector. Home inspectors must be licensed by the state, and are regulated by the Department of Licensing.

Administration of the License Law

Becoming a successful agent takes more than an outgoing personality and good business skills. Successful real estate agents also take their legal and ethical responsibilities seriously. So let's turn our attention to the real estate license law and the duties and obligations it imposes on real estate agents.

The real estate license law is administered by the Washington State **Department of Licensing**. The Director of the Department of Licensing supervises all divisions within the department, including the Real Estate Division. The Director and all Real Estate Division staff are employees of the state of Washington. They are not allowed to own any interest in a real estate firm.

The Director

The Director of the Department of Licensing is appointed by the Governor. The Director is charged with enforcing all laws, rules, and regulations relating to the licensing of real estate licensees. He has the authority to grant or deny licenses, and to hold disciplinary hearings and impose penalties for violations of the license law. And with the advice and approval of the Real Estate Commission, the Director also issues rules and regulations to govern the activities and practices of real estate licensees.

In fact, the term "real estate license law" is commonly used to refer not only to the statutory provisions adopted by the state legislature, but to the regulations issued by the Director as well. All real estate licensees are required to obtain a copy of the Director's regulations (available from the Department of Licensing), and to keep informed of changes in the regulations.

The Real Estate Commission

The **Real Estate Commission** is made up of the Director and six commissioners. The commissioners are appointed by the Governor to advise the Director on the real estate industry and profession.

The commissioners are generally required to have at least five years of real estate experience; they are usually real estate managing brokers. Each commissioner serves on a part-time basis for a six-year term. At least two commissioners must be from west of the Cascade mountain range, and two must be from east of the Cascades. The commissioners are paid a per diem stipend, plus travel expenses, for the days they spend holding public hearings, meeting with the Director, and conducting other Commission business.

The Commission prepares and conducts the real estate license examinations. It is also authorized to hold educational conferences for the benefit of the real estate industry. The Commission has created a **Center for Real Estate Research** to study real estate economics and concerns such as affordable housing. The Center advises the Director and the Commission about real estate education and related matters, and it also provides real estate information to the general public. The Center for Real Estate Research is funded through a surcharge imposed on real estate license renewals.

The Attorney General

The state Attorney General is the Director's legal advisor on matters relating to the license law. The Attorney General also acts as the attorney for the Director in any legal proceedings involving the Real Estate Division.

Real Estate Licenses

By requiring real estate agents to be licensed, the state tries to ensure that they have at least a minimum level of competence in handling real estate transactions. Licenses also serve as a tool for enforcement of real estate regulations; if an agent fails to comply with the law, her license can be suspended or taken away altogether.

When a License is Required

It's unlawful to perform real estate brokerage services without first obtaining the appropriate license.

The license law defines **real estate brokerage services** as follows:

"Real estate brokerage services" means any of the following services offered or rendered directly or indirectly to another, or on behalf of another for compensation or the promise or expectation of compensation, or by a licensee on the licensee's own behalf:

a) Listing, selling, purchasing, exchanging, optioning, leasing, or renting of real estate, or any real property interest therein; or any interest in a cooperative;

b) Negotiating or offering to negotiate, either directly or indirectly, the purchase, sale, exchange, lease, or rental of real estate, or any real property interest therein; or any interest in a cooperative;

c) Listing, selling, purchasing, exchanging, optioning, leasing, renting, or negotiating the purchase, sale, lease, or exchange of a manufactured or mobile home in conjunction with the purchase, sale, lease, exchange, or rental of the land upon which the manufactured or mobile home is or will be located;

d) Advertising or holding oneself out to the public by any solicitation or representation that one is engaged in real estate brokerage services;

e) Advising, counseling, or consulting buyers, sellers, landlords, or tenants in connection with a real estate transaction;

f) Issuing a broker's price opinion (a report of property value prepared by a licensee that is not an appraisal);

g) Collecting, holding, or disbursing funds in connection with the negotiating, listing, selling, purchasing, exchanging, optioning, leasing, or renting of real estate or any real property interest;

h) Performing property management services, which includes with no limitation: the marketing, leasing, and renting of real property; the physical, administrative, or financial maintenance of real property; or the supervision of such actions.

The main thrust of this definition is that it applies to anyone engaged in any of the listed activities: 1) on behalf of another person, and 2) for compensation. However, the law states that the definition also applies to "a licensee [acting] on the licensee's own behalf." Thus, real estate agents are required to comply with the license law even when they are buying, selling, or leasing property for themselves, not just when they are representing others.

In addition to more traditional real estate transactions, the license law covers business opportunities if an interest in real property is involved. The term **business opportunity** refers to the sale or acquisition of a business (either an existing business or the equipment, supplies, and services needed to start a new one, as in a franchise arrangement). A person who represents another in the purchase, sale, exchange, or lease of a business, a business opportunity, or the goodwill of a business must have a real estate license if the transaction involves real estate.

Also note that the definition of brokerage services may include a person who sells or leases a manufactured home before it has become attached to real property, so long as it is sold or leased at the same time as the land where the home is or will be placed.

Exemptions from Licensing Requirements

The following people are exempt from the real estate licensing requirement. They aren't required to have a license, even when their activities fall within the definition of real estate brokerage services.

1. Anyone buying or leasing property for herself, or on behalf of a group to which she belongs, or disposing of property she owns or co-owns.
2. An authorized attorney in fact acting without compensation.
3. An attorney at law, in the performance of his duties.
4. A receiver, trustee in bankruptcy, executor, administrator, or guardian, when acting in that capacity, or any person acting under court order, or a trustee selling under a deed of trust.
5. A secretary, assistant, bookkeeper, accountant, or other office personnel performing purely clerical duties.
6. Employees of a city, county, or other government, involved in acquiring property.
7. The owner or manager of a self-storage facility renting units in the facility.
8. A person who provides referrals to real estate licensees who is not involved in negotiation or execution of documents, and whose compensation is not contingent on the licensee receiving compensation.
9. Certified public accountants who do not promote the sale of a specific property.
10. Title companies, escrow companies, attorneys, financial institutions, or other persons or entities acting as escrow agents.
11. Investment counselors who do not promote the sale of a specific property.

12. Community association managers who do not promote the purchase, listing, sale, exchange, optioning, leasing, or renting of a specific property interest.

13. A person employed or retained by the owner of a property or a designated or managing broker who performs only limited property management tasks, such as delivering lease applications; receiving applications, security deposits, or rent payments; showing rental units or executing leases while acting under the owner or brokerage firm's direct supervision; providing information about rental units or leases; or carrying out administrative, clerical, financial, or maintenance tasks.

As we said, the license law defining real estate brokerage services applies to those who act on behalf of another and for compensation. Thus, someone who acts on her own behalf in a real estate transaction is exempt from the licensing requirement; this is the first exemption on the list above.

> **Example:** Matilda Thorn owns several pieces of property: three single-family homes, a duplex, an apartment building, and two vacant lots. If she decides to sell one of these properties, she can do so without having to obtain a real estate license.

In addition, someone acting on behalf of another but *without compensation* is also exempt; this is the second exemption on the list, the one for an authorized attorney in fact. An **attorney in fact** is not necessarily a lawyer; it is anyone a principal appoints to act as her agent through a power of attorney (see Chapter 3). As long as the attorney in fact is not compensated for services rendered, he is allowed to engage in the activities of a real estate broker without a license.

> **Example:** Suppose Matilda from the previous example is old and unwell. She gives her nephew, Truman, a power of attorney that authorizes Truman to sell Matilda's property for her. As long as Truman is acting without compensation, he doesn't need a real estate license to sell the property.

Unlicensed Assistants. The Real Estate Commission has issued detailed guidelines concerning the activities that an unlicensed assistant may engage in. (The guidelines are available at the Department of Licensing website.) According to these guidelines, an unlicensed assistant may help a licensee by carrying out various activities, including:

- providing information about a real estate listing or transaction, as written and approved by a real estate licensee;
- writing and placing advertising;
- gathering market analysis information;
- driving people to properties;
- greeting people at an open house and distributing preprinted material; and
- making keys, installing keyboxes, and placing signs on property.

Activities that an unlicensed assistant cannot perform include answering questions or interpreting information about a property or its condition (except by providing answers from preprinted material prepared by a licensee), filling in legal forms, and negotiating prices or other terms of sale.

Fig. 17.1 Types of real estate licensees

Real Estate Firm
• A business entity • Authorized to provide brokerage services and represent clients

Affiliated Licensees	
Managing Broker	**Broker**
• Works for and represents firm • May be designated broker or manage a branch office	• Works for and represents firm • Can't be designated broker or manage a branch office

Out-of-State Licensees. A real estate licensee who is licensed in another state may handle transactions concerning commercial real estate in Washington without obtaining a Washington license. However, the out-of-state licensee must have a written agreement with and work in cooperation with a real estate firm that is licensed in Washington. The Washington firm's name must be included on all advertising, and the Washington firm must have custody of the records for the out-of-state licensee's Washington transactions.

The out-of-state licensee must provide the Washington firm's designated broker with a copy of his license in good standing and must consent to Washington jurisdiction for any legal disputes that may arise from the transaction. For the purposes of this rule, commercial real estate is any property other than residential property with up to four dwelling units.

Types of Licenses

There are two basic types of real estate licenses in Washington: managing broker and broker. A real estate firm must also have a license.

Firm. A real estate firm is a business entity (such as a corporation, a partnership, or a sole proprietorship) that conducts real estate brokerage activities in Washington. The firm must name a managing broker as its designated broker (see below) who has the authority to act for the firm. The firm must also notify the Director of the names of the firm's owners and anyone else with the ability to control the operational and/or financial decisions of the firm.

A firm is authorized to employ managing brokers and brokers. Managing brokers and brokers are sometimes referred to as their firm's **affiliated licensees**. The law defines affiliated licensees as "the natural persons licensed as brokers or managing brokers employed by a real estate firm and who are licensed to represent the firm in the performance of any of the acts" for which a real estate license is required.

A commission or other compensation by clients or by other firms can be paid only to a firm, not directly to affiliated licensees. Managing brokers and brokers may only be paid by or through their own firm.

Managing Broker. A managing broker's license may be issued only to an individual. The licensee is authorized to work with and represent his firm, to manage other licensees, and to manage a branch office of the brokerage. A managing broker may also be appointed as a firm's designated broker.

A managing broker can be affiliated with only one firm at a time. We will discuss qualifications for a managing broker's license shortly, but to become a managing broker, one usually must have significant experience as a broker first.

Broker. A broker's license can be issued only to an individual. The license authorizes the broker to work with and represent her firm. A broker may be affiliated with only one firm at a time. A broker must be supervised by a designated broker or managing broker, and is not authorized to manage a branch office. A broker with less than two years of experience is subject to a heightened level of scrutiny by her managing broker, including the review of all her transaction documents within five days of the client's signature.

Designated Broker. As mentioned above, a firm license is issued to a business entity, and the firm must have a designated broker. If the firm is a sole proprietorship, the owner is the designated broker. If the firm is some other type of business entity (such as a corporation, a partnership, or a limited liability company), it must name one person to be its designated broker. The designated broker must have a managing broker's license and a controlling interest in the firm (in other words, the authority to control the firm's operational and financial decisions). He must obtain a designated broker's endorsement for his managing broker's license from the Department of Licensing.

Despite the fact that a managing broker can be the affiliated licensee of only one firm at a time, a managing broker may serve as the designated broker for more than one firm at the same time.

A designated broker has the final authority for all activities performed by the real estate firm. This includes ensuring that the firm's records are up-to-date and available to state auditors, that trust accounts are accurate and reconciled, and that procedures are in place to ensure compliance with all laws. A designated broker may delegate these duties to managing brokers and branch managers, but these delegations must be in writing and signed.

When a firm's designated broker changes, the outgoing and incoming designated brokers must submit a statement that lists all outstanding client trust fund liabilities, lists pending transactions, and certifies that sufficient funds are held in trust to cover all client liabilities. If a firm closes down, the designated broker is responsible for submitting a closing firm affidavit to the Director.

Licensing Qualifications and Applications

Applicants for real estate licenses must satisfy specified age and educational requirements and pass an examination. In addition, applicants for a managing broker's license are required to satisfy experience requirements. All education and experience requirements must be met before applying for the exam.

Managing Broker and Broker Qualifications. The qualifications for the managing broker's license and the broker's license are as follows.

Managing Broker. The managing broker must:

1. be at least 18 years old;
2. have a high school diploma or the equivalent;
3. have at least three years of experience within the last five years as a full-time real estate broker in this state or another state with similar licensing requirements;
4. have successfully completed 90 clock hours of approved real estate education courses within the previous three years, including one 30-hour course in advanced real estate law, one 30-hour course in brokerage management, and one 30-hour course in business management; and
5. pass the managing broker's examination.

An applicant who lacks three years' experience as a broker may be allowed to take the managing broker's exam if the Director of the Department of Licensing determines that the applicant has other education or experience that is a satisfactory substitute. Examples of experience that may qualify include:

- post-secondary education with an emphasis on real estate studies, together with one year of experience as a real estate broker or one year of experience from the other professional activities below;
- at least one year of experience as an attorney specializing in real estate transactions;
- five years' experience in closing real estate transactions for escrow companies or mortgage companies;
- five years' experience as an officer of a commercial bank, savings and loan association, title company, or mortgage company, involving all phases of a real estate transaction;
- five years' experience as a real estate appraiser;
- five years' experience in all phases of land development, construction, financing, selling and leasing residential or commercial buildings; or
- five years' experience in real estate investment, property management, or investment analysis.

If an applicant who is allowed to take the managing broker's exam based on alternative experience qualifications fails the exam, the applicant cannot re-take the exam without meeting all of the standard requirements.

Military training or experience may also be used to satisfy the three years' experience requirement, unless the Director determines that an applicant's training or experience is not a satisfactory substitute.

The 90 clock hours of approved courses required for the managing broker's license (number 4 on the list above) are in addition to any courses the Department required the applicant to take for other reasons. For example, if the applicant had to take a 30-hour course to fulfill the continuing education requirement to renew his broker's license, those 30 hours cannot be counted as part of the 90 hours required for the managing broker's license.

The Director may waive the 90 clock-hour requirement if the Director feels that the applicant has completed the equivalent educational course work in any institution of higher learning or degree-granting institution.

Broker. An applicant for a broker's license must:

1. be at least 18 years old;
2. have a high school diploma or the equivalent;
3. have successfully completed a 60 clock-hour course in real estate fundamentals and a 30 clock-hour course in real estate practices; and
4. pass the broker's examination.

Both courses must be completed within two years before applying for the broker's license examination.

The Director may waive the 90 clock-hour requirement if the Director feels that the applicant has completed the equivalent educational course work in any institution of higher learning or degree-granting institution.

A managing broker may apply to revert to a broker's license simply by completing the required form and paying any necessary fees. However, a former managing broker who reverted to broker status and now wishes to return to managing broker status must meet all managing broker requirements, including passing the examination and having three years of experience in the previous five years.

Real Estate Examination. The license law and regulations set forth the requirements for applying for and passing the real estate examination.

Exam Reservations. A person who fulfills the age, education, and experience requirements may make a reservation to take the exam. All examinations are by reservation only; there are no walk-in exams. Reservations must be made at least one business day prior to the desired test date. Candidates must bring the completed application and a candidate examination document with them to the test site. This document, which indicates completion of the required prelicense clock hours, must have been stamped and signed by a representative of the real estate school where the prelicense courses were taken. Applicants must also bring one piece of valid government-issued photo-bearing identification.

If an applicant fails to show up for the exam without providing adequate notice, she forfeits the exam fee. An applicant who fails either the broker's exam or the managing broker's exam may retake it (more than once, if necessary), but she will have to reapply and pay the fee again.

License applicants who have questions about the examination should contact the Department of Licensing for more information about the license application process.

Scope of the Examination. The real estate exam tests each applicant for an understanding of:

- real estate conveyances and the legal effect of deeds, finance contracts, and leases;
- real estate investment, property valuation, and appraisals;
- real estate agency relationships;
- real estate practices and business ethics; and
- the real estate license law.

In addition, applicants taking the exam are expected to have basic English language and math skills.

The real estate examination consists of two portions:

1. a national portion consisting of questions that test knowledge of general real estate practices, and
2. a state portion consisting of questions that test knowledge of Washington laws and regulations related to real estate licensing.

The state portion of the managing broker's exam also includes a section on the settlement (closing) process.

To pass, a real estate broker must get a score of at least 70% on each portion of the exam. A managing broker must get a score of at least 75% on each portion of the exam. When an applicant passes one portion of the exam but fails the other, the passing score is valid for six months. If the applicant retakes and passes the other portion of the exam within that six-month period, he can then apply for a license.

Fig. 17.2 Topics on the real estate exam

The Real Estate Exam

- Real estate conveyances:
  - deeds
  - mortgages
  - land contracts
  - exchanges
  - rental and option agreements
  - leases
- Real estate investments and appraisals
- Agency law
- Real estate practices and business ethics
- Real estate license law

Other basic requirements:
English language; arithmetic

Licensees from Other Jurisdictions. A license applicant who is actively licensed in the same or greater capacity in another jurisdiction is automatically eligible to take the state portion of the Washington exam. The applicant must submit an application to the Department along with evidence of licensure in the other jurisdiction. Once this evidence has been verified by the Department, the applicant may take the state portion of the exam. The additional requirements for licensure (education, experience, and passage of the national portion of the exam) are waived.

Obtaining a License. After the exam, the next step is obtaining the real estate license.

Application for License. After passing the exam, it's necessary to apply for the license itself. Examination results are only valid for one year. If someone passes the exam, but doesn't become licensed within one year after the exam date, she will be required to pass the exam again before a license can be issued.

An application for a managing broker's or broker's license must be signed by the designated broker that the applicant is going to work for. A branch manager may sign on behalf of the firm's designated broker for licenses issued to that branch office.

Applicants applying for a first broker's license must submit fingerprint identification as part of the application. Submission of fingerprints is also required every six years for all licensees, upon license renewal. If a fingerprint card is rejected by the director, the applicant must submit a new fingerprint card within 21 days of receiving written notice of the rejection.

If a firm is applying for a license, certain other information must be submitted, depending on how the firm is organized. For instance, if the firm is a corporation, the applicant will need to provide a copy of its articles of incorporation and a list of its officers and directors and their addresses. If it is a partnership, the applicant will need to list the partners and their addresses.

Interim License. An applicant for a broker's license who has been notified that he passed the exam may begin working on the date he mails or hand delivers the signed, dated, and completed license application form, license fee, and fingerprint card to the Department. The completed form serves as an interim license for up to 45 days after the postmark or hand delivery date.

There are no interim licenses for managing broker's license applicants.

License Expiration and Renewal

An individual's initial real estate license expires two years after the issuance of the license. The licensee must apply for renewal and pay a renewal fee. Thereafter, the license must be renewed **every two years** on that same date. If the renewal application is late, the licensee must pay a penalty (in addition to the renewal fee).

Licenses issued to firms must be renewed every two years. The renewal date for this type of license is the expiration date of the firm's registration or certificate of authority (which is filed with the Secretary of State).

Continuing Education. To renew their licenses, all brokers and managing brokers must submit proof that they have successfully completed a total of **30 clock hours** of approved continuing education courses.

As part of their 30 hours, licensees must complete a three-hour **core curriculum course**. The core curriculum course presents practical information on contemporary real estate issues. The three core curriculum hours may be taken as an independent course or included in a longer course.

A licensee can use a course to fulfill the continuing education requirement only if he began the course after issuance of his initial license. The licensee must have completed at least 15 of the 30 clock hours (including the three core curriculum hours) within 24 months before the renewal date. The remaining 15 hours can be completed up to 36 months before the renewal date. If the licensee exceeds the 30-hour requirement, up to 15 hours can be carried forward for credit in the next two-year renewal period.

A course the licensee used to fulfill prelicense requirements for either a broker's or a managing broker's license, or to fulfill the

Fig. 17.3 Education requirements for renewal

**License Renewal
(every two years)**

First renewal for broker:

- 30 clock-hour course in advanced real estate practices,
- 30 clock hours in real estate law, and
- 30 clock hours of other continuing education, including Core

Subsequent renewals:

- 30 clock hours of continuing education, including Core

requirements for reinstatement (see below), cannot also be used for the continuing education requirement.

Broker's First Renewal. When renewing for the first time, a broker must submit proof of completion of 90 clock hours: a 30 clock-hour course in advanced real estate practices, a 30 clock-hour course in real estate law, and 30 clock hours of other approved continuing education (including the core curriculum).

Cancellation and Reinstatement. If a license isn't renewed within one year after it expires, the license is **canceled**. (In other words, there's a one-year grace period between failure to renew and cancellation.) A license can be **reinstated** within two years after cancellation if the licensee:

- successfully completes 60 clock hours of approved real estate courses (including a 30-hour real estate law course) within one year before applying for reinstatement;
- pays all back renewal fees, plus penalties; and
- pays a reinstatement penalty.

Alternatively, the license will be reinstated if the licensee follows the procedures and satisfies the qualifications for initial licensure. That will mean passing the license exam again. (In some cases, starting over in this way would be less expensive than paying the back fees and penalties.)

If it's been more than two years since the license was canceled, the former licensee can't be reinstated unless she satisfies the qualifications for initial licensure again, including retaking and passing the exam.

Inactive Licenses. An inactive license is a license that has been turned over to the Director temporarily. (This may occur for a variety of reasons; some of these reasons are discussed later in this chapter.) The holder of an inactive license is generally deemed to be unlicensed. He is not permitted to engage in activities requiring a license, but is still subject to disciplinary action for violations of the license law.

Although an inactive license must be renewed on its renewal date, the holder is usually not required to comply with the continuing education requirement for renewal. (A licensee is not allowed to use inactive status simply as a means of avoiding the continuing education requirement, however.) Failure to renew an inactive license results in cancellation, just as with an active license.

To reactivate a license that has been inactive for more than three years, the holder must complete a 30 clock-hour real estate course. A single 30 clock-hour course in advanced real estate practices or real estate law may be used both for the reactivation of an inactive license and for the broker's first renewal.

A licensee may not reactivate an inactive license if proceedings to suspend or revoke his license have begun.

License Fees. Fees collected for licensing (application fees, renewal fees, etc.) are placed in the Real Estate Commission Account in the state treasury.

Regulation of Business Practices

Many provisions of the license law, as well as other state and federal laws, govern the day-to-day business practices of brokers and managing brokers. There are rules concerning:

- the relationship between licensees and their clients and customers;
- the relationship between a designated broker and his affiliated licensees;
- real estate firm offices, trust accounts, and business records; and
- how real estate transactions are handled.

Agency Relationships

One of a licensee's most important responsibilities is to comply with Washington's real estate agency statute. This law determines when and how an agency relationship is formed, the licensee's duties to clients and customers, when an agency relationship terminates, and liability for harm caused while acting as an agent. (For a more detailed discussion of the agency law, see Chapter 7.)

Creating Agency Relationships. The agency law describes how agency relationships are created. A seller's agent forms an agency relationship with her client when a listing agreement is signed. A buyer's agent enters into an agency relationship as soon as he performs any real estate brokerage services for a buyer, unless there is a written agreement to the contrary. If the seller's agent and the buyer's agent in a transaction are employed by the same firm, that brokerage firm is acting as a dual agent. A dual agency arrangement is unlawful without the written consent of both parties, and both parties must have a written agency agreement.

Agency relationships aren't affected by the payment of compensation. For instance, a buyer's agent may receive compensation from the seller without breaching any duty to the buyer.

Duties Owed by Licensee. Washington's agency law sets forth the duties a licensee owes to any party, and the special duties a licensee owes to a party she represents.

Duties Owed to Any Party. Any licensee owes a number of duties to any party when rendering real estate brokerage services, whether the licensee is acting as a buyer's agent, seller's agent, dual agent, or nonagent. The licensee must:

- exercise reasonable skill and care;
- deal honestly and in good faith;
- present all written communications to and from either party in a timely manner;
- disclose all material facts known to the licensee that wouldn't be readily apparent to a party;
- account in a timely manner for money or property received from or on behalf of either party;
- provide a pamphlet on real estate agency law to all parties; and
- disclose in writing to anyone she renders services to (before that person signs an offer) whether she's representing the buyer, the seller, both parties, or neither one.

The agency disclosure must be made before the party signs an offer in a transaction handled by the licensee. It must be either a separate paragraph entitled "Agency Disclosure" in the purchase and sale agreement, or a separate document entitled "Agency Disclosure."

An agent doesn't owe anyone the duty of independent inspection of the property, independent investigation of either party's financial condition, or independent verification of any statement reasonably believed to be reliable.

Duties Owed to Principal. In addition to the duties owed to any party, a licensee owes certain duties only to his client. The licensee must:

- be loyal to the client, by taking no action that is detrimental to the client's interest;
- disclose any conflicts of interest;
- advise the client to seek expert advice on matters that are outside the agent's knowledge;
- refrain from disclosing confidential information from or about the client; and
- make a good faith and continuous effort to complete the transaction.

Duties Owed by a Dual Agent. A dual agent owes the duties just listed to both clients, with one key exception. Since a dual agent cannot be completely loyal to both parties, she must instead refrain from taking action that is detrimental to either party's interest in the transaction. A dual agent owes the duty of good faith and continuous effort in both finding a buyer for the seller's property and finding a property for the buyer.

Terminating Agency Relationships. All of the duties owed by the licensee continue until the agency relationship terminates. This occurs upon:

- full performance by the licensee,
- expiration of the agreed-upon term,
- termination by mutual agreement, or
- termination by unilateral action.

The duties of confidentiality and accounting, however, do not expire upon the termination of the agency relationship.

No Vicarious Liability. Under Washington's real estate agency law, a principal isn't liable for harm caused by any act or omission of an agent or subagent. The two exceptions are: 1) when the principal participated in or authorized the wrongful act, or 2) when the principal benefited from the act and a court determines that the claimant could not enforce a judgment against the agent.

No Imputed Knowledge. A principal is not held to have notice of any facts known by an agent or subagent that are not actually known by the principal, unless the principal and agent have agreed otherwise in writing. For instance, suppose a property was due to be condemned to build a new freeway on-ramp. The seller did not know about the likely condemnation, but the listing agent did and kept silent about it. If the buyer sued, the seller would not be found liable for the buyer's financial losses caused by the condemnation, although the listing agent might be.

Supervision and Licensee Responsibilities

A designated broker is responsible for the proper supervision of all of his firm's licensees (brokers, managing brokers, and branch managers), whether they are independent contractors or employees. For branch offices, both the branch manager and the designated broker are responsible for all licensees working at the branch.

Any licensee who supervises other licensees must be a managing broker. A broker cannot be put in a position of supervising other brokers. For instance, if several licensees form a "team" within a firm, the licensee who supervises the team must be a managing broker, not merely a broker.

A **fee broker** is a licensed designated broker who does not own or manage a brokerage, but allows another person to operate a brokerage using her name and license, usually for a fee. This arrangement is a violation of the license law, even if the designated broker does not receive any compensation. A designated broker must actively manage and supervise the brokerage, and she can't avoid those responsibilities through any contract, agreement, or understanding with another person.

Liability for Violations by Affiliated Licensees. A designated broker who fails to supervise his affiliated licensees properly may be held responsible for their actions. If an affiliated licensee violates the license law, in addition to other possible consequences for the designated broker, the Director may suspend or revoke the designated broker's license (as well as the licensee's). The same sanctions could also be imposed on a branch manager or any other managing broker who failed to fulfill supervisory responsibilities in the case.

Broker's Responsibilities. Under the license law, a broker's responsibilities include:

- assuring that all brokerage services in which she participates comply with the license law, the real estate agency statute, and the Uniform Regulation of Business and Professions Act (URBPA);
- cooperating with the Department of Licensing in an investigation or audit;
- being knowledgeable about the license law, the agency statute, and URBPA;
- keeping the Department of Licensing informed of her current mailing address;
- following her firm's written policy regarding referral of home inspectors;
- being appropriately licensed;
- delivering brokerage service contracts and other transaction documents to the designated broker or the appropriate managing broker within two days of mutual acceptance by the parties; and
- following the license law rules regarding trust funds, advertising, and modifying or terminating contracts on behalf of the firm.

A broker who has been licensed for less than two years is subject to one additional responsibility: working under a heightened degree of supervision. This means the broker must participate in all required reviews of contracts by a supervisor (either the designated broker or a managing broker); obtain a supervisor's advice or assistance regarding matters beyond his expertise; and submit evidence of completion of required coursework to a supervisor. Brokerage service contracts involving a broker licensed for less than two years must be reviewed by a supervising broker within five business days after mutual acceptance by the parties, and documentary proof of review must be kept in the firm's records.

Managing Broker's Responsibilities. A managing broker has all of the same responsibilities as a broker, and may also have additional responsibilities delegated to him by the designated broker. Delegated responsibilities may include ensuring that:

- monthly trust account reconciliations and trial balances are completed, accurate, and show that the trust accounts are in balance;
- policies and procedures are in place for safe handling of client or customer funds and property;
- required records are properly maintained and kept up to date;
- advertising meets legal requirements;
- contracts and other transaction documents are submitted and reviewed in a timely manner;
- the Director's representatives have access to the firm's offices and records; and
- affiliated licensees are following the firm's written policies.

A managing broker serving as a branch manager is responsible for all activity within the branch office, including supervision of all licensees, with heightened supervision for brokers licensed for less than two years. The branch manager is responsible for hiring, releasing, and transferring licensees to and from the branch.

Designated Broker's Responsibilities. A firm's designated broker has additional levels of responsibility beyond those of a managing broker. The designated broker is responsible for ultimate oversight of the entire firm. Among many other responsibilities, this includes maintaining:

- up-to-date written delegations of managing broker and branch manager duties, signed by all parties to the agreement; and
- written policies concerning referral of home inspectors, supervision of the firm's brokers, managing brokers, and branch managers, and review of all contracts involving brokers licensed for less than two years.

Affiliations and Termination

A licensed broker or managing broker must be affiliated with a real estate firm in order for his license to be active. A broker or managing broker isn't allowed to engage in real estate activities except as a representative of a firm and under the supervision of a designated broker. The designated broker has custody of the licenses of her affiliated licensees.

The relationship between a designated broker and an affiliated licensee may be terminated at any time by either party. When an affiliation is terminated, the designated broker must notify the Director and surrender the broker's or managing broker's license without delay. (It isn't necessary to notify the Real Estate Commission.)

To give notice of termination, the designated broker signs the license and mails or hand-delivers it to the Department of Licensing, or the affiliated licensee surrenders the license himself. The termination date is the postmark date or the date the license is hand-delivered to the Department. The license is inactive until the broker or managing broker has found a new firm to work for and a new license is issued.

The designated broker has an absolute duty to surrender the license, so that the broker or managing broker can go to work for someone else. Failure to surrender a license promptly is grounds for disciplinary action against the designated broker. The designated broker cannot place any conditions on its surrender. For example, if a terminated licensee owes the designated broker money, the designated broker can't refuse to surrender the license unless the money is repaid. If the designated broker places conditions on surrender of the license, the broker or managing broker should notify the Department of Licensing in writing. The Department will process the license transfer, and the designated broker's conduct will be investigated.

If the license has been lost, the designated broker and the broker or managing broker must submit a **letter of release**. Transfer of the license is not allowed until the letter is filed with the Department.

When a broker or managing broker has been terminated because of conduct that would be grounds for disciplinary action under the license law, the designated broker must send the Director a written statement of the facts surrounding the termination.

If the firm itself is closing, the designated broker must provide a closing firm affidavit to the Department within five business days. The designated broker must also give written notice to all parties with pending transactions, and ensure that brokerage service contracts are terminated or transferred to another real estate firm with the parties' written permission.

Office Requirements

A firm licensed in Washington is required to maintain an office or records repository in this state. The location must be accessible to the Director's representatives. The office must be identified by a sign displaying the name of the firm or its assumed name.

The firm's license must be prominently displayed at the address appearing on the license, along with the licenses of all of the firm's affiliated licensees. If the firm has more than one office, the firm's license and the designated broker's license are displayed in the main office, and the licenses of affiliated licensees are displayed in the office where they work (which should be the address shown on the license).

If the location of a firm's office changes, the designated broker must promptly submit a change of address application to the Director, return all licenses (the firm's and those of any affiliated licensees), and pay a fee. The Department will issue licenses for the new address.

Two Businesses in the Same Office. It isn't unusual for a firm to be involved in other business activities that are related to, or at least not in conflict with, real estate brokerage activities. For example, in many regions it's common for a real estate brokerage to also act as an escrow agent or mortgage broker. A firm is allowed to operate two businesses out of the same office if the brokerage business is kept apart from other business activities, with its records kept completely separate.

Branch Offices. There is no limit on the number of branch offices a firm can have, but every branch office must receive a duplicate license. Every branch office is also required to have a branch manager, who must be a managing broker.

A separate license is not required for a branch office where sales activity concerns only a particular subdivision or tract. This exception applies only if the subdivision is within 35 miles of a licensed office.

Dual-State Licensees. Real estate licensees who are actively licensed in another state as well as in Washington and have an office in that other state aren't required to have their own office here. However, they must maintain a trust account in a Washington depository and keep records of their Washington transactions at a registered location in this state.

The licensee must notify the Department of Licensing of the location of the records and allow representatives of the Department access to them. The licensee is also required to give the parties involved in a transaction access to the records. The licensee's license should be displayed at the same place that the records are kept.

If a firm headquartered in another state is seeking a license to operate in Washington, it must obtain a firm license. The firm must appoint a designated broker, who must qualify as a managing broker in Washington and have a controlling interest in the firm (as is true for any designated broker).

Advertising

Advertising by real estate licensees must be truthful and not misleading, and must include the firm's name (or assumed name) as licensed. An ad without the firm's name, sometimes called a **blind ad**, violates the license law. There's one exception to this rule: if a licensee is advertising her own property for sale or lease, the firm's name doesn't have to appear in the ad. The ad must disclose that the seller or landlord holds a real estate license, however.

A real estate firm may advertise that it is able to pay referral fees to unlicensed persons, so long as the ad complies with all other advertising requirements.

A firm may use one or more assumed names in conducting its business. However, a firm may not use a name that is deceptively similar to that of another licensee or firm, nor one that creates the impression that the firm is a nonprofit organization, a research organization, or a public group. Note that all assumed names must be approved by the Department.

Advertising and the Internet. The Real Estate Commission has adopted guidelines to help licensees use the Internet to increase their sales while avoiding violations of advertising rules and regulations.

According to these guidelines, a licensee should be careful to fully disclose his licensed status in all Internet communications. A full disclosure would include the licensee's own name (as licensed) and the registered or assumed name of the firm with which he is affiliated. If the firm is not licensed in the state of Washington, the disclosure should also include the city and state in which the firm is located.

The guidelines include suggestions on how to meet the requirement of full disclosure for each of the following types of Internet communications:

- **Website:** Whenever a licensee or firm owns a website or controls its contents, every viewable page should include a full disclosure.
- **Email, newsgroups, discussion lists, bulletin boards:** Each should include a full disclosure at the beginning or end of each message, except when the licensee is communicating with a member of the public and the licensee's initial communication contained a full disclosure.

- **Instant messages:** Full disclosure is not necessary in this format if the licensee provided full disclosure in another format before providing or offering to provide real estate services.
- **Chat:** Full disclosure should be given before providing or offering to provide real estate services during the chat session, or it should appear in text visible on the same web page that contains the chat session if the licensee controls the website hosting the chat session.
- **Social media:** Full disclosure should be prominently displayed and be no more than one click away from any viewable page.
- **Multimedia advertising (such as executable email attachments):** Full disclosure should be visible as part of the advertising message.
- **Banner ads:** Each ad should link to (via a single click) a website that has a full disclosure, unless the banner ad itself has a full disclosure.

The Commission's guidelines also offer the following advice on prospecting over the Internet:

- If listings are maintained on a website, they should be removed in a timely manner when they have expired.
- If a licensee submits listing information to a third-party site, she should provide written communication of any change of listing status to the publisher in a timely manner.
- Licensees should not advertise the listings of other licensees without their written permission. If permission is given, licensees should not alter the online display or any informational part of the listing without the written permission of the listing broker.
- Metatags are descriptive words hidden in a website's code that search engines use to index the website. Occasionally, a website owner will insert the name of one of his competitors into the metatags, so that when a potential customer searches for the competitor's site, the owner's site will also come up as a match. Licensees should avoid this practice, as courts have ruled that it may constitute trademark infringement.
- Licensees should periodically review the advertising and marketing information on their website to make sure that it is current and not misleading.

Unsolicited Marketing. Federal and state laws regulate the methods licensees can use to advertise their properties. These restrictions are commonly called **Do Not Call** or **Spam** laws.

For example, real estate agents may not call individuals who have registered with the Do Not Call Registry maintained by the Federal Trade Commission. Violators of the law could be fined up to $16,000 per incident. (It's not a violation of the law to contact actual clients or to return calls from people who contacted the licensee first.)

There are also federal and state laws that apply to unsolicited email. The federal law that restricts unsolicited emails is known as the **CAN-SPAM Act** (short for Controlling the Assault of Non-Solicited Pornography and Marketing Act). Under this law, any unsolicited email must contain instructions on how to opt out of receiving future emails from the sender.

It's also a violation of Washington's Consumer Protection Act to send unsolicited or misleading email. Violators of the law can be subject to substantial fines.

Trust Accounts

A real estate firm must maintain one or more **trust accounts** (also called escrow accounts) if it holds any **trust funds**—money that belongs to clients or customers. Earnest money deposits are the most common example, but trust funds also include any other funds held temporarily on behalf of a client or a customer, as well as **advance fees** (fees a real estate licensee collects from a client in advance, before services are provided).

Trust fund accounts must be in a recognized financial institution in Washington State. They must be separate from the firm's general business and personal accounts, so that trust funds are not **commingled** (mixed) with the firm's own money. The trust accounts should be opened in the name of the firm as licensed, and specifically designated as trust accounts.

Fig. 17.4 Rules for handling trust funds

Trust Accounts

- Trust funds must be deposited by the first banking day after receipt
- Accounts must be interest-bearing
- Deposits of $10,000 or less:
  - must be placed in pooled account
  - interest is paid to State
- Deposits over $10,000:
  Customer or client chooses to put funds in:
  - pooled account with interest paid to State, or
  - separate account with interest paid to customer or client

All funds the licensee is given to hold until a transaction closes (such as earnest money) or until paid to a client (such as rents collected) must be deposited in a trust account no later than the **first banking day after receipt**, unless otherwise specified in the license law. For the purposes of this rule, Saturday is not considered a banking day.

Interest-Bearing Accounts. With the exception of property management trust accounts, brokerage trust accounts are required to be interest-bearing accounts that allow the designated broker to make withdrawals without delay (other than any minimum notice period required by banking regulations).

A firm is required to put all deposits of **$10,000 or less** into a **pooled account** called the **housing trust fund account**. The interest that accrues on this account, after deducting reasonable bank charges, must be paid to the state treasurer. It will be divided between the Washington **housing trust fund** (75%) and the **real estate education account** (25%).

For deposits **over $10,000**, the client or customer who is turning the funds over to the firm has a choice. With the written consent of the parties, the funds can be deposited in the pooled account, in which case the interest will be paid to the state. Alternatively, the firm can establish a separate trust account for the deposit, with the interest to be paid to the client or customer to whom the funds belong. The designated broker must inform the client or customer of these alternatives in writing.

Property Management Trust Accounts. The rules just outlined do not apply to trust funds that a licensee handles in property management transactions (such as rents or tenant security deposits). Property management trust accounts don't have to be interest-bearing accounts, and property management trust funds don't have to be placed in the firm's pooled account. However, a property management account can be interest-bearing, if the firm's written management agreement with the property owner provides for that, and if the firm follows certain special rules in the license law. If any commissions or property management fees are to be paid out of the trust account directly to the firm, they must be removed from the trust account at least once a month.

A firm that manages several rental properties for different owners does not have to open an individual trust account for each one, if all of the owners assign the interest accruing on their funds to the firm. When the management agreement between the owner and firm terminates, any trust funds associated with that owner that are left in the account will be disbursed according to the agreement's terms; security deposits are disbursed either to the owner or the next property management firm.

Trust Account Procedures. A firm must establish a system of records and procedures that provides an audit trail for all funds received and disbursed, identified to each client. The designated broker can either follow the procedures that are set forth in the Director's regulations, or submit an alternative system to the Department for approval. The system can be either manual or computerized.

Only trust funds may be maintained in the trust account. The only firm money that should be in the account is a "minimal amount" to open the account or maintain a minimum balance to keep the account open. If a client or customer has assigned the interest on a trust account to the firm (in writing), the firm must make arrangements with the financial institution to credit the interest to the firm's general account.

Trust Account Disbursements. As a general rule, a firm may not make any disbursements from a trust account before closing, or before a condition in the purchase and sale agreement has been fulfilled. There are three important exceptions to that rule, however. The designated broker may disburse funds:

1. with the written consent of all parties to the transaction;
2. when the transaction fails to close, if the purchase and sale agreement provides for disbursement without a written release in this situation; or
3. to the closing agent named in the agreement far enough in advance so that the checks will clear by the closing date.

A firm may not pay its own business expenses directly out of a trust account. That includes bank charges for the maintenance of the trust account; these should be paid out of the firm's general business account, not the trust account itself. If a client owes the firm money, the funds must first be transferred from the trust account to the firm's general business account before the firm can use them for business expenses. (See the note on commissions paid from trust accounts below.)

If the parties to a transaction cannot agree on who is entitled to the trust funds, the designated broker must notify all the parties of her intent to disburse the funds. The notice must include names and addresses of the parties, amount of money held, to whom it will be disbursed, and the planned date of disbursement.

Commissions Paid from Trust Accounts. Commissions payable to the firm and to other cooperating firms may be paid directly from the trust account. The designated broker must draw a separate check for each commission after the transaction closes.

Commissions the firm owes to its affiliated licensees may not be paid directly out of the trust account. These commissions are handled the same way as the firm's business expenses. Funds must first be transferred to the firm's general business account, and then the firm can pay its affiliated licensees with checks drawn on that account.

Records

The license law requires designated brokers to keep adequate records of the real estate transactions they handle for at least **three years** after closing. (It's wise to keep records for even longer than this minimum requirement, since the statute of limitations for some claims against a firm may not run out for several more years. Also, other state laws and regulations may require firms to keep records for longer than three years.)

Although a designated broker may delegate recordkeeping duties to someone else, she is still responsible for the custody and accuracy of the required records. She must make the records available to auditors from the Department of Licensing, and provide copies to the Director upon demand.

The designated broker must maintain an up-to-date log of all agreements and contracts for brokerage services that are submitted by the firm's licensees. She must also retain a copy of each agreement on file.

For each transaction, the designated broker must have a **transaction folder** that includes all of the following that apply:

- the listing agreement,
- the purchase and sale agreement,
- the lease or rental agreement,
- any modifications or addenda to those agreements,
- the settlement statement, and
- all other agreements or documents relevant to the transaction.

As we discussed earlier, brokers with less than two years' experience must have their contracts reviewed by the designated or managing broker. Documented proof of the review must be kept on file at the firm's record storage location.

The designated broker is also required to keep the following **trust account records**:

- a duplicate receipt book or cash receipts journal showing all receipts;
- prenumbered trust account checks with a check register, cash disbursements journal, or check stubs;
- validated duplicate bank deposit slips;
- a client's ledger summarizing all receipts and disbursements for each transaction, property management account, or contract or mortgage collection account;
- separate ledger sheets for each tenant, lessee, vendee, or mortgagor;
- a ledger for interest on the firm's pooled housing trust fund account; and
- reconciled bank statements and canceled checks, including voided checks. (Trust account checks must be prenumbered, so even voided checks must be kept to show that all checks are accounted for.)

A designated broker must keep all records for recent transactions at a location where the firm is licensed to have an office. Records for transactions that have been closed for at least one year can be kept at one central facility, as long as the facility is in Washington.

Older transaction records stored in a central location must be retrievable at the request of the Department. A list of all transactions for which records are stored at a remote facility must still be kept at the firm's licensed offices.

Records may be stored electronically, so long as the medium is nonerasable and doesn't allow the documents to be modified. The firm needs to have equipment available at its licensed office to view, retrieve, and print the documents, if Department representatives show up to inspect them.

Commissions

A valid real estate license is a prerequisite to collecting a commission (or any form of compensation) for brokerage services. A licensee cannot sue for a commission unless there is proof that she was properly licensed before she:

- offered to perform any act or service that requires a license, or
- procured a promise or contract for the payment of compensation for such an act or service.

This rule applies to lawsuits brought by one licensee against another (a broker's suit against his designated broker, for example), as well as to lawsuits brought by a firm against a client.

A firm may share a commission with or pay compensation to any firm that is licensed in the United States, in a U.S. possession, or in Canada, and to its own affiliated licensees. This includes compensation owed due to a transaction with a licensed manufactured or mobile home dealer, where the purchase or lease of land is part of the transaction.

A firm may not pay any compensation directly to a broker or managing broker licensed with another firm. Payment must be made to the other firm, which then pays its broker or managing broker.

Licensees may receive compensation only from their firm. They cannot collect a commission directly from a client or from another firm. They also are not allowed to share their compensation with other licensees. If two brokers are going to split a commission, for example, the split must be handled by their firm or firms.

Agency and management agreements are the property of the firm, not the licensee. In other words, a broker who changes to a new firm in mid-transaction cannot bring the transaction to the new firm with her; it belongs to the old firm.

Referral Fees

It's not uncommon for one real estate licensee or firm to pay another licensee or firm a fee for referring a potential customer or client. This type of agent-to-agent referral fee does not violate the prohibition against kickbacks and referral fees between settlement service providers contained in the federal Real Estate Settlement Procedures Act (RESPA). (See Chapter 13 for more about RESPA).

Example: Sheri, a broker with Whitehall Realty, specializes in commercial properties. When a potential client, Jordan, asks her about residential listings, she refers him to Larry, a broker with ABC Homes. In return, Larry agrees to pay Sheri one-third of any commission he receives from working with Jordan. This type of referral fee is permissible under RESPA.

Larry helps Jordan find a suitable home. When Jordan enters into a purchase and sale agreement, Larry recommends both an escrow agent and a title company to use in the transaction. If, in exchange for these referrals, Larry accepted a fee from either the escrow agent or the title company, this would violate RESPA.

A real estate licensee or firm may also pay a referral fee to an unlicensed person in exchange for referring a potential customer or client. However, as we mentioned earlier, the real estate license law prohibits such fees if they are contingent on the firm actually receiving compensation.

Handling Transactions

The Director's regulations include several rules governing how licensees serve their clients and customers in a real estate transaction, from preparation of a buyer's offer through closing.

Copies of Documents. A licensee is responsible for providing clients and customers with copies of any documents they sign (the listing agreement, escrow instructions, etc.) within a reasonable time after execution. Each licensee who participates in a transaction (the listing agent, the selling agent, and any other cooperating agents) must keep a copy of the purchase and sale agreement in his or her transaction records.

Earnest Money Deposits. A buyer's earnest money deposit may be in the form of a check that's payable to the brokerage firm as licensed, so it can be deposited in the firm's trust account. As explained earlier in the chapter, a licensee is ordinarily required to deposit trust funds by the end of the first banking day after receipt. But the licensee is allowed to hold an earnest money check without depositing it for a specific length of time or until a particular event occurs (for example, the seller accepts or rejects the offer) if that is what the purchase and sale agreement directs the licensee to do.

In some transactions, however, the agreement provides that someone other than the firm (for example, an escrow agent) will hold the earnest money deposit until closing. Unless the parties provide other instructions in writing, the licensee is required to deliver the check to the agreed-upon person within one banking day after the agreement is signed. The licensee should obtain a dated receipt to include in the transaction file.

The licensee who first receives the earnest money deposit is responsible for handling the funds in compliance with the license law (although of course the designated broker has ultimate responsibility). This licensee is usually the selling agent, who takes the earnest money check from the buyer. By law, the check should be made out to the real estate firm unless the parties have agreed that the deposit will be delivered directly to the escrow agent or another party. (The escrow agent is the choice in most transactions.)

It is a violation of the license law to accept an earnest money deposit in the form of a promissory note (or some other form that is not considered the equivalent of cash) unless the licensee discloses that fact to the seller before the seller accepts the offer; the purchase and sale agreement must also state the form of the earnest money.

Expeditious Performance. When a purchase and sale agreement or other contract obligates a licensee to perform a certain act (for example, ordering an inspection), that act must be performed as expeditiously as possible. Under the license law, a licensee's intentional or negligent delay is considered to be "conduct…that demonstrates bad faith, dishonesty, untrustworthiness or incompetency," and is therefore grounds for disciplinary action.

Closings. The licensee is responsible for ensuring that the parties to every transaction receive a complete, detailed settlement statement at closing. The licensee isn't required to prepare the statement (most are prepared by escrow agents—see Chapter 13), but making sure the parties receive it is one of the licensee's duties under the license law. The licensee also has to keep a copy of the settlement statement in the transaction folder, even if it was prepared by someone else.

Washington's Escrow Agent Registration Act allows a real estate licensee to close a transaction in which she is already representing the buyer or the seller (or both), if the licensee is designated as the closing agent in the purchase and sale agreement. Unless the licensee is a licensed escrow agent, however, she can't charge either party any fee (beyond her brokerage commission) for closing services. Only licensed escrow agents and attorneys can charge a fee for closing real estate transactions. (See Chapter 13 for information about the Washington Escrow Agent Registration Act.)

Property Management Agreements. A firm must have a written property management agreement with the owner or owners of each property it manages. The license law requires the agreement to state all of the following:

- the property manager's compensation;
- the type of property managed (for example, apartment or office building);
- the number of units or square footage;
- whether the firm is authorized to collect and disburse funds, and if so, for what purposes;
- whether the firm is authorized to hold and disburse tenant security deposits, and if so, how; and
- how often the firm is to provide summary statements to the owner.

Note that the property's physical condition does not have to be described in the management agreement.

A **summary statement** is a brief report showing the property's financial status over a certain period of time, such as one month or one quarter. The firm must provide a summary statement to the owner or owners for each property managed as often as the management agreement requires. A summary statement shows:

- the balance carried forward from the last statement;
- the total rent receipts;
- other itemized receipts (for example, from laundry or vending machines);
- contributions from the owner;

- itemized expenditures;
- the ending balance; and
- the number of units or square footage rented.

The firm must keep a copy of the management agreement and all summary statements in its records. The management agreement can be modified only in writing, and the modification must be signed by both the designated broker and the owner. For all rental properties managed by a firm, the leases or rental agreements must be in writing.

A firm may provide other services to the owner of a property that is being managed, such as janitorial and repair services, with the owner's consent. If the firm uses another company to provide these services, it must make a full written disclosure of its relationship with that company, and disclose the fees that are charged. (Property management is discussed in detail in Chapter 16.)

Disciplinary Action

The Director has the authority to investigate the actions of any real estate licensee and impose penalties, including license suspension or revocation. This is true regardless of whether the licensee was acting on behalf of another or on her own account, and regardless of whether her license is active or inactive.

Grounds for Disciplinary Action

A licensee or a license applicant may be subject to disciplinary action either for engaging in unprofessional conduct in violation of the **Uniform Regulation of Business and Professions Act** (URBPA) or for engaging in one of the activities specifically listed in the license law as grounds for disciplinary action. (The Uniform Regulation of Business and Professions Act applies to all types of professionals licensed by the state of Washington, not just to real estate licensees.)

Unprofessional conduct, as defined in the URBPA, includes any of the following conduct, acts, or conditions:

1. the commission of any act involving moral turpitude, dishonesty, or corruption relating to real estate activities, regardless of whether the act constitutes a crime;
2. misrepresentation or concealment of a material fact in obtaining or reinstating a license;
3. false, deceptive, or misleading advertising;
4. incompetence, negligence, or malpractice that harms another or creates an unreasonable risk of harm;
5. having any business or professional license suspended, revoked, or restricted by any government entity;
6. failure to cooperate with the Director of the Department of Licensing in the course of an investigation, audit, or inspection;
7. failure to comply with an order issued by the Director;
8. violating any license law provision or rule made by the Director;
9. aiding or abetting an unlicensed person to perform real estate activities that require a license;

10. practice or operation of a business or profession beyond the scope of practice or operation as defined by law;
11. any type of misrepresentation in the conduct of real estate activities;
12. failure to adequately supervise or oversee staff, whether employees or independent contractors, to the extent that consumers may be harmed or damaged;
13. being convicted of any gross misdemeanor or felony relating to real estate activities;
14. interference with an investigation or disciplinary action by willfully misrepresenting facts, or by threatening, harassing, or bribing customers or witnesses to prevent them from providing evidence; or
15. engaging in unlicensed real estate activities.

Further grounds for disciplinary action are specifically listed in the license law. One of the first items on this list is "Violating any provisions of [the real estate license law] or any lawful regulations made by the director pursuant thereto…" In other words, any violation of the license law is grounds for disciplinary action, and a licensee who failed to comply with any of the rules explained in this chapter could lose his license as a result.

Here is a brief summary of the items listed in the license law that have not been mentioned elsewhere in this chapter. A licensee is subject to disciplinary action for:

- being convicted of forgery, embezzlement, extortion, fraud, or similar offenses;
- making or authorizing statements that she knew (or could have known by the exercise of reasonable care) were false;
- converting trust funds (misappropriating them for her own use);
- failing to disclose information or to produce records for inspection upon request by the Director;
- selling real estate according to a plan that endangers the public interest, after the Director has objected in writing;
- accepting money from more than one party in a transaction without first disclosing this to all interested parties in writing;
- accepting a profit on expenditures made for a principal without disclosing it to the principal;
- accepting compensation for an appraisal contingent on reporting a pre-determined value;
- issuing an appraisal for property in which she has an interest without disclosing that interest in the appraisal report;
- falsely claiming to be a member of a state or national real estate association;
- directing a client or customer to a lending institution or escrow company in expectation of a kickback or rebate, without disclosing that expectation to the party he is representing;
- buying, selling, or leasing property (directly or through a third party) without disclosing that she holds a real estate license;
- any conduct in a real estate transaction which demonstrates bad faith, dishonesty, untrustworthiness, or incompetency; and
- discriminating against any person in hiring or in the provision of real estate brokerage services, in violation of antidiscrimination laws.

It is also a prohibited practice, under the license law, for a licensee who has a financial interest in a title insurance company to give a fee or kickback to another real estate licensee for placing business with or referring business to that title insurance company. (Such a kickback would also violate RESPA. See Chapter 13.) A licensee also may not accept or solicit anything of value from a title insurance company or its representative that it would be illegal for the company to give. In addition, a licensee may not require a client or customer to obtain title insurance from a title insurance company in which the licensee has a financial interest.

The Director is given the power to suspend the license of any real estate licensee who has been certified by a lending agency for nonpayment or default on a federal or state guaranteed education loan or service-conditioned scholarship. The same applies to any licensee who isn't in compliance with a child support or visitation order, as certified by the Department of Social and Health Services. License reinstatement is automatic upon repayment or compliance.

Disciplinary Procedures

The procedures for disciplinary action are designed to give the licensee notice of the charges and an opportunity to present a defense. The usual procedures include an investigation, a hearing, and, depending on the outcome of the hearing, either no action or some form of sanctions against the licensee. Either party (the licensee or the Department of Licensing) may appeal the result.

Statement of Charges. If, after investigation, the Director decides there is reason to believe there has been a violation of the license law, the licensee will be served with a statement of charges. The statement of charges must be accompanied by a notice informing the licensee that he may request a hearing to contest the charges. The licensee must file a request for a hearing within 20 days after receiving the statement of charges. If the licensee fails to request a hearing, the licensee will be considered in default and the Director may enter a decision based on the facts available at that time.

Hearing. Once a hearing has been requested, the Director will fix the time for the hearing. The time must be as soon as is convenient, but at least 30 days after the statement of charges was served on the licensee. The only exception to this rule is if the Director issued a summary (immediate) suspension or restriction, in which case the hearing may be held sooner.

The hearing may be conducted by the Director, but in most cases the hearing officer is an administrative law judge. The licensee and the Department of Licensing may each be represented by attorneys in the hearing. The Department and the licensee will each have an opportunity to present evidence and testimony, to cross-examine witnesses for the other side, and to present arguments to the hearing officer. A court reporter makes a transcript of the proceedings, just as in a trial.

If the accusation isn't proved by a preponderance of the evidence, no action is taken against the licensee and the case is dismissed. If the accusation is proved, the Director may impose any of the sanctions permitted by law (discussed below). An order imposing the sanctions will be filed with the Director's office and immediately mailed to the licensee. The sanctions called for in the order take effect as soon as the order is received by the licensee.

Appeal. A licensee who is dissatisfied with the outcome of a disciplinary hearing may file an appeal in superior court. The appeal must be filed within 30 days after the date of the Director's decision and order. The licensee will be required to post a $1,000 appeal bond to cover court costs—in case the judge decides against the licensee—and must also pay for a copy of the transcript of the hearing. Filing an appeal does not automatically stay the Director's order. In other words, if the Director suspended the licensee's license, it will remain suspended during the appeal process. However, the Director may choose to stay the sanctions during the appeal process, if it is appropriate to do so and any conditions necessary to protect the public are imposed.

Sanctions for License Law Violations

After a disciplinary hearing, if the licensee (or license applicant) is held to have violated the license law, the Director may impose any or all of the following sanctions:

- revocation of the license for an interval of time;
- suspension of the license for a fixed or indefinite term;
- restriction or limitation of real estate activities;
- the satisfactory completion of a specific program of remedial education or treatment;
- monitoring of real estate activities according to the Director's order;
- censure or reprimand;
- compliance with conditions of probation for a designated period of time;
- payment of a fine for each violation found by the Director, of up to $5,000 per violation;
- denial of an initial or renewal license application for an interval of time; or
- other corrective action.

All fines collected are placed in the Real Estate Education Account, to be used for education for the benefit of licensees. If a licensee fails to pay a fine, the Director may enforce the order for payment in superior court.

A **cease and desist order** is issued to stop a licensee (or an unlicensed person) from violating the law. After a disciplinary hearing, the Director might issue a cease and desist order to prevent continuation of an illegal activity. In special circumstances, the Director is also authorized to issue a temporary cease and desist order even before a hearing is held. The Director is allowed to do this only when a delay in issuing the order would result in irreparable harm to the public interest. The temporary order must advise the licensee that she has a right to a hearing to determine if the order

Fig. 17.5 Penalties after disciplinary action

Penalties for Violation of the License Law

- License suspension, revocation, or denial
- Restriction and/or monitoring of real estate activities
- Relevant real estate education
- Censure or reprimand
- Probation
- Fines (up to $5,000 per violation)
- Other corrective action

should be canceled, modified, or made permanent. If the licensee requests a hearing, one must be held within 30 days (unless the licensee requests more time).

Alternatively, the Director can ask a court to issue an injunction ordering a licensee or an unlicensed person to stop an ongoing violation. The Director can also ask the court to appoint a receiver to take over or close a real estate office operating in violation of the law until a hearing can be held.

Criminal Prosecution. Violations of the license law are gross misdemeanors. If the Director decides that criminal charges should be filed against a licensee, the prosecution would ordinarily be handled by the prosecuting attorney in the county where the violation is alleged to have occurred. If the prosecutor fails to act, the Director can ask the state Attorney General to prosecute instead.

Civil Liability. Anyone who has been injured by a licensee's actions or failure to act can file a civil lawsuit for damages. (See the discussion of tort suits in Chapter 7.) Note, however, that the Director of the Department of Licensing does not have the power to award damages to the victims of real estate fraud or other wrongful actions. Compensation for injured parties is handled through the court system, not by the Department of Licensing.

Notifying Department of Legal Action. A licensee is required to notify the Department of Licensing's real estate program manager within 20 days after learning of:

- any criminal complaint, information, indictment, or conviction in which the licensee is named as a defendant; or
- any civil court order, verdict, or judgment entered against the licensee if the case involves any of her real estate or business activities.

Antitrust Laws and Their Effect on Licensees

In addition to the real estate license law, federal antitrust laws impose certain restrictions on a real estate agent's behavior towards clients, customers, and other agents.

Federal antitrust laws are not new: the **Sherman Act** was passed in 1890, well over a century ago. The Sherman Act prohibits any agreement that has the effect of unreasonably restraining trade, including conspiracies. A **conspiracy** occurs when two or more business entities participate in a common scheme, the effect of which is the unreasonable restraint of trade.

At the foundation of antitrust laws is the notion that free enterprise is a part of our democratic society, and that competition is good for both the economy and society as a whole. While many people associate antitrust laws with big steel mills and telephone companies, in 1950 antitrust laws were held to apply to the real estate industry. In a landmark case, the United States Supreme Court held that mandatory fee schedules, established and enforced by a real estate board, violated the Sherman Act (*U.S. v. National Association of Real Estate Boards*).

If a real estate agent violates antitrust laws, she may be subject to both civil and criminal actions. If an individual is found guilty of violating the Sherman Act, she can be fined up to one million dollars and/or sentenced to ten years' imprisonment. If a corporation is found guilty of violating the Sherman Act, it can be fined up to one hundred million dollars.

The activities that are prohibited by antitrust laws can be grouped into four main categories:

- price fixing (fixing commission rates),
- group boycotts,
- tie-in arrangements, and
- market allocation.

Price Fixing. Price fixing is defined as the cooperative setting of prices or price ranges by competing firms. To avoid even the appearance of price fixing, two agents from different brokerages should never discuss their commission rates. It's a discussion between competing agents that is dangerous; a designated broker can discuss commission rates with his own licensees. One exception to this general prohibition is that two competing designated brokers may discuss a commission split in a cooperative sale (the split between the listing agent and the selling agent).

Even a casual announcement that a designated broker is planning on raising her commission rates could lead to antitrust problems.

> **Example:** Wood, a designated broker, goes to a dinner given by her local MLS. She's called on to discuss current market conditions and, in the middle of her speech, she announces that she's going to raise her commission rate, no matter what anyone else does. This statement could be viewed as an invitation to conspire to fix prices. If any other MLS members raise their rates in response to this announcement, they could be held to have accepted Wood's invitation to conspire.

Real estate licensees must understand that they do not have to actually consult with each other to be charged with conspiring to fix commission rates. The kind of scenario described in the example is enough to lead to an antitrust lawsuit.

Publications that appear to fix prices are prohibited as well. Any MLS or other association that tries to publish "recommended" or "going" rates for commissions could be sued.

Group Boycotts. A group boycott is an agreement between two or more real estate licensees to exclude other firms from fair participation in real estate activities.

> **Example:** Becker and Jordan are designated brokers of competing real estate firms. They have lunch together and begin discussing the business practices of a third designated broker, Harley. Becker says that Harley is just a "discount agent" and is dishonest and lazy. Becker states that he will never do business with him. Jordan laughs and agrees. She says that she never returns any of Harley's calls when he's inquiring about a listed property. She suggests that Becker do the same. Becker and Jordan could be found guilty of a conspiracy to boycott.

If a real estate licensee feels another licensee is dishonest or unethical, she may choose not to do business with him (as well as alert the Department of suspected misconduct). However, it isn't permissible for her to tell other licensees to do the same thing.

The purpose of group boycotts is to hurt or destroy a competitor, and they are automatically unlawful under antitrust laws.

Tie-in Arrangements. A tie-in arrangement is defined as "an agreement to sell one product, only on the condition that the buyer also purchases a different (or tied) product..."

> **Example:** Brown is a subdivision developer. Tyson, a builder, wants to buy a lot. Brown tells Tyson that he will sell him a lot only if Tyson agrees that after Tyson builds a house on the lot, he will list the improved property with Brown. (This is called a "list-back" agreement.)

The developer's requirement in the example is an illegal tie-in arrangement. Note, however, that a list-back agreement violates antitrust laws only if signing it is a required condition of the sale. Two parties may mutually agree on a list-back agreement without violating antitrust laws.

Market Allocation. Market allocation occurs when competing brokerage firms agree not to sell certain products or services in specified areas or to certain customers in specified areas. Market allocation between competing real estate firms is illegal, because it limits competition.

As with group boycotts, it's the collective action that makes market allocation illegal. An individual brokerage firm is free to determine the market areas in which it wants to specialize (if any); similarly, the firm can allocate territory to particular licensees affiliated with the firm. Allocation of territory between competing firms, however, is a violation of antitrust law.

> **Example:** ABC Realty assigns Agent Ava to handle all new customers in the luxury home market, and assigns Agent Paxton to all new customers in the vacant land market. This practice does not violate antitrust law.
> However, if ABC Realty and XYZ Realty agreed to allocate customers so that ABC Realty will handle all luxury homes and XYZ Realty will handle all vacant land, this would violate antitrust law.

Avoiding Antitrust Violations. There are several ways to prevent possible antitrust violations. Real estate licensees should:

- always establish their fees and other listing policies independently, without consulting competing firms;
- never use listing forms that contain preprinted commission rates;
- never imply to a client that the commission rate is fixed or nonnegotiable, or refer to a competitor's commission policies when discussing commission rates;
- never discuss their business plans with competitors;
- never tell clients or competitors that they won't do business with a competing firm, or tell them not to work with that firm because of doubts about its competence or integrity; and
- be aware of what actions may constitute an antitrust law violation.

Chapter Summary

1. Washington's real estate license law is administered by the Director of the Department of Licensing and the Real Estate Commission.

2. It's unlawful to provide real estate brokerage services without a license. There are several important exemptions from the licensing requirement, however, including someone buying or selling on his own behalf, and an uncompensated attorney in fact.

3. There are two types of individual real estate licenses: managing broker licenses and broker licenses. Real estate firms must also be licensed. Managing brokers and brokers may only work when representing a firm. A managing broker is also authorized to manage a branch office, and can be appointed as a firm's designated broker.

4. Any license applicant must be at least 18 years old, have a high school diploma, have completed certain real estate courses, pass an examination, and submit fingerprints. An applicant for a managing broker's license must also have three years of experience as a broker.

5. Licenses must be renewed every two years. For renewal, the licensee must complete 30 clock hours of approved continuing education courses, including the core curriculum. For a first renewal, a broker must have completed 90 clock hours of courses.

6. An agency relationship is formed when a licensee begins performing brokerage services for a client. An agent owes a number of duties to a principal, in addition to the duties any licensee owes to all parties in a transaction. An agency relationship can be terminated through full performance, expiration of the term, mutual agreement, or unilateral action.

7. A designated broker is responsible for the supervision of her affiliated licensees. A fee brokerage arrangement violates the license law. When an affiliation is terminated, the broker's or managing broker's license is returned to the Director; it is inactive until reissued for affiliation with another firm.

8. A firm is required to maintain an office in Washington that is open to the public, and may have one or more branch offices. Each branch office must be licensed, and each must be managed by a managing broker. An affiliated licensee's license must be displayed in the office where he works.

9. Advertising by real estate licensees must include the firm's name as licensed; blind ads are not allowed. An ad for the licensee's own property does not have to state the firm's name, but it must disclose the licensed status of the seller.

10. Trust funds must be placed in an interest-bearing trust account no later than the first banking day after receipt; deposits of $10,000 or less are placed in a pooled account, with interest paid to the state. (Property management trust accounts do not have to be interest-bearing accounts.) A designated broker may not pay business expenses or an affiliated licensee's share of a commission directly out of a trust account.

11. A firm is required to keep records (including a transaction folder and trust account records) for at least three years after a transaction closes.

12. A valid real estate license is a prerequisite to payment of a commission or other compensation for brokerage services.

13. In handling a real estate transaction, a licensee is required to provide copies to the parties after documents are signed; to perform expeditiously any acts she is obligated to perform by the purchase and sale agreement; and to make sure that the parties receive settlement statements.

14. When a licensee is accused of violating the license law, there is an investigation and then a disciplinary hearing. The possible sanctions include license suspension, revocation, or denial; fines; relevant coursework; restrictions on or monitoring of real estate activities; censure or reprimand; probation; or other corrective action. Violation of the license law is a gross misdemeanor and may lead to criminal prosecution.

15. Antitrust laws prohibit price fixing, group boycotts, tie-in arrangements, and market allocation. Real estate agents must be especially careful to avoid discussing commission rates with competing agents.

🔑 Key Terms

License law—The state statute that governs the licensing and business practices of real estate agents, along with the regulations issued by the Director of the Department of Licensing to implement that statute.

Real Estate Commission—A commission made up of the Director of the Department of Licensing and six commissioners who advise the Director.

Real estate firm—A business entity, such as a corporation or partnership, that is licensed to perform real estate brokerage activities in Washington.

Managing broker—A person who is licensed to represent a firm in real estate transactions and to supervise other licensees or a branch office.

Broker—A person who is licensed to work for and represent a firm in real estate transactions.

Affiliated licensee—A broker or managing broker who is licensed under a particular firm.

Designated broker—The person authorized to have full legal responsibility for a licensed real estate firm and its affiliated licensees.

Business opportunity—A business (including inventory and goodwill) that is for sale, where the transaction includes real property.

Interim license—The completed application form for a broker's license, which serves as a temporary license until the permanent license is issued.

Inactive license—A license in the possession of the Director of the Department of Licensing.

Fee broker—A designated broker who allows another person to use his license to operate a brokerage (which is a violation of the license law).

Blind ad—An advertisement placed by a real estate licensee that does not state the name of the firm as licensed (which is a violation of the license law).

Trust account—A specially designated bank account in a firm's name for funds held by the firm on behalf of clients, to keep those funds segregated from the firm's own money.

Commingling—When someone who is holding trust funds on another person's behalf intentionally or accidentally mixes those funds together with his own money.

Conversion—When someone who is holding trust funds on another person's behalf misappropriates the funds with the intention of using them for her own purposes.

Transaction folder—Part of the records a designated broker is required to keep; the contracts and other documents connected with a particular transaction.

Cease and desist order—An order issued by the Director of the Department of Licensing in a disciplinary action, to stop a violation of the license law.

Chapter Quiz

1. The members of the Washington Real Estate Commission are appointed by the:

   a) Governor

   b) Real Estate Program Manager

   c) Director of the Department of Licensing

   d) President of the Washington Association of Realtors®

2. The Morenos want to sell their house. They gave their friend Jessica Norwood a power of attorney, authorizing her to represent them in the transaction. Norwood doesn't have a real estate license. It's legal for Norwood to represent the Morenos:

   a) only if she's licensed to practice law

   b) only if she won't be compensated for her services

   c) as long as she obtains a real estate license before the transaction closes

   d) None of the above; it isn't legal for Norwood to represent the Morenos

3. Mark Cutler doesn't have a real estate license. Which of the following activities can he legally do, for a fee?

   a) Advise sellers in a real estate transaction

   b) Issue a broker's price opinion

   c) Oversee the management of an apartment building for its owner

   d) Lease units in a property he co-owns

4. Unlike a broker, a managing broker:

   a) must have at least three years' experience in real estate

   b) can accept compensation directly from a seller

   c) doesn't have to be licensed under a firm

   d) All of the above

5. Real estate licenses must be renewed:

   a) annually

   b) every two years

   c) every three years

   d) every five years

6. Paul Doren's real estate license expired last month, and now he wants to renew it. In order to do so, Doren will be required to:

   a) complete an additional 60 clock hours of approved real estate courses

   b) pass the license exam again

   c) pay a penalty in addition to the renewal fee

   d) All of the above

7. To renew a real estate license, a licensee must show that she has taken a certain number of clock hours of approved continuing education courses. The required total is:

   a) 30 hours commenced within 12 months preceding the licensee's renewal date

   b) 30 hours; at least 15 commenced within 24 months preceding the licensee's renewal date, and the remainder commenced within 36 months preceding the renewal date

   c) 20 hours completed within 24 months preceding the licensee's renewal date

   d) 20 hours completed within 36 months preceding the licensee's renewal date

8. For their first renewal, real estate brokers must complete:

   a) 30 clock hours of continuing education

   b) 60 clock hours of continuing education

   c) 90 clock hours of continuing education

   d) 120 clock hours of continuing education

9. Harrison's license has been canceled. Which of the following does he NOT need to do, in order to get reinstated?

   a) Complete 60 clock-hours of real estate courses, including 30 clock-hours of real estate law

   b) Pay all back renewal fees, plus penalties

   c) Pay a reinstatement penalty

   d) Re-take and pass the licensing examination

10. Jenkins, who lives in Portland, has a valid Oregon real estate license. She decides that she needs a Washington real estate license so she can show some of her Portland customers properties in Vancouver, Washington. Jenkins:

    a) must fulfill all the normal licensing requirements, just as if she were not already licensed in Oregon
    b) can apply for a Washington real estate license without taking the license exam
    c) only has to take the Washington portion of the real estate exam
    d) can get a special dispensation from the Director and receive a license upon completion of a 30-hour brokerage management course

11. Peterson hires an assistant to help him with his real estate business. His assistant answers phones, sets up appointments, and files paperwork. Peterson's assistant:

    a) need not be licensed
    b) must have a real estate license
    c) need not be licensed as long as Peterson has written authorization from his designated broker or branch manager to hire an assistant
    d) must have a real estate assistant license

12. Cortez has one year of experience as a real estate broker. He wants to become a managing broker. He may get the three-year experience requirement waived if he can show:

    a) post-secondary education with an emphasis on real estate studies
    b) six months' experience as an attorney specializing in real estate transactions
    c) three years' experience closing real estate transactions for an escrow company
    d) All of the above

13. Although Harper lacked three years' experience, she was still allowed to take the managing broker's exam because she had other professional experience that was deemed a satisfactory substitute by:

    a) Harper
    b) her firm's designated broker
    c) the Director of the Department of Licensing
    d) the Real Estate Commission

14. To pass the managing broker's exam, the applicant must score at least:

    a) 70%
    b) 75%
    c) 80%
    d) 85%

15. Which of the following may receive an interim license?

    a) A broker applicant who passed the exam
    b) A designated broker applicant who passed the exam
    c) A managing broker applicant who passed the exam
    d) All of the above

16. A dual agent may not:

    a) disclose a material fact that one party knows and wants to remain confidential
    b) disclose one party's intended negotiating position to the other party
    c) reveal a latent defect
    d) make his agency disclosure before either party has signed an offer in a transaction

17. A seller's broker notices some damage to the foundation of the seller's house, but doesn't tell the buyer about it. The seller won't be liable to the buyer for this failure to disclose if the broker:

    a) told the seller, and the seller let the broker decide whether to mention it to the buyer
    b) told the seller, and they mutually agreed not to mention it to the buyer
    c) didn't tell the seller, but the seller substantially profited from the deal, and the broker is now bankrupt
    d) never told the seller about the damage

18. Ellen Kendrick is a licensed broker. She wasn't getting along with her designated broker, so they decided to terminate their affiliation, and Kendrick's license was sent back to the Department of Licensing. Which of the following is true?

    a) Kendrick's license is inactive
    b) Kendrick may continue with real estate transactions that were in progress at the time of her termination
    c) Kendrick will be required to take the license exam again in order to reinstate her license
    d) All of the above

19. Which of the following statements is true regarding the supervision of brokers? A managing broker must review documents from:

    a) all brokers within three days
    b) all brokers within five days
    c) brokers with less than two years' experience within three days
    d) brokers with less than two years' experience within five days

20. The license of a broker who works at a branch office is:

    a) kept at her home address
    b) displayed at the firm's main office
    c) displayed at the branch office where she works
    d) kept at the Department of Licensing offices in Olympia

21. Trust funds received by a designated broker in a sales transaction must be placed in an:

    a) account that doesn't bear interest, by the third banking day after receipt
    b) interest-bearing account, by the second banking day after receipt
    c) account that doesn't bear interest, by the first banking day after receipt
    d) interest-bearing account, by the first banking day after receipt

22. The license law requires a firm to keep transaction records for:

    a) six months
    b) one year
    c) three years
    d) five years

23. A listing was submitted to a multiple listing service. The property was sold by a broker who doesn't work for the listing firm. How will that broker be paid a share of the commission?

    a) The listing firm must pay the broker's firm, who will then pay the broker
    b) The listing firm must pay the MLS, which will then pay the broker directly
    c) The listing firm may either pay the broker's firm or pay the broker directly
    d) The listing firm should pay the broker directly

24. Susan Kurosawa, a licensed broker, is advertising her own house for sale. The license law requires the ad to state:

    a) that the seller is a licensed real estate agent
    b) the name of Kurosawa's firm, as licensed
    c) Both of the above
    d) None of the above

25. A broker may manage a branch office for her firm:

    a) if the broker has at least two years of experience
    b) if the broker has taken an approved course in brokerage management
    c) if the office is in the broker's residence
    d) under no circumstances

26. A broker who is representing a seller is negotiating with a prospective buyer. Before the buyer signs an offer, the broker must:

    a) obtain the seller's written consent
    b) disclose to the buyer in writing that he's representing the seller
    c) explain to the buyer that he's acting as a dual agent
    d) have the buyer sign a buyer representation agreement

27. If a licensee accused of violating the license law does not request a hearing within 20 days after receiving the statement of charges:
    a) her license is automatically revoked
    b) the Director may enter a decision based on the available facts
    c) a hearing will automatically be scheduled for the licensee
    d) the Director will issue a cease and desist order

28. Howard Gray, a licensed broker, was involved in a traffic accident. The other driver (who was injured) sued Gray for compensation, and a judgment has just been entered against Gray. He is:
    a) required to notify the Department of Licensing within five days
    b) required to notify the Department of Licensing within 30 days
    c) not required to notify the Department of Licensing, because this was not a criminal charge
    d) not required to notify the Department of Licensing, because the lawsuit didn't involve Gray's real estate or business activities

29. A firm that is managing property must:
    a) have a written property management agreement with the owner
    b) keep a copy of all summary statements for the property in its records
    c) provide the property owner with a full written disclosure of its relationship with any firm providing services to the property, such as repair services
    d) All of the above

30. Barton, a real estate licensee, helps negotiate a sale. The purchase and sale agreement is contingent on a pest inspection, and Barton tells the parties he will arrange for an inspection to be done by August 19. But he forgets to request the inspection before taking his family on a planned vacation. When he gets back into town on August 18, he finally remembers to call the pest inspector. The inspector says she's very busy and won't be able to inspect the home until August 29.
    a) Since the pest inspection wasn't an important term in the purchase agreement, Barton hasn't done anything wrong
    b) Even though Barton was negligent in failing to perform his duty, he hasn't violated the license law
    c) The closing agent will cancel escrow immediately and terminate the sale
    d) Barton has failed to perform expeditiously, and may be subject to disciplinary action

31. Alberts is representing the seller in a transaction. She discloses this in writing to both the seller and the buyer. Later, Alberts decides that she can adequately represent both parties, and begins acting as a dual agent. Alberts:
    a) has done nothing wrong, as long as she acts in the best interests of both parties
    b) violated the agency disclosure requirement because she didn't act in accordance with her disclosed agency status
    c) has done nothing wrong, because dual agency isn't unlawful in Washington
    d) Both a) and c)

32. A licensee is taking a listing. In her discussion with the seller, which of the following statements suggests a violation of the Sherman Antitrust Act?

    a) "My office typically charges a 6% commission for this type of transaction"
    b) "I cannot charge less than the commission rate established by the local MLS"
    c) "You will owe me a commission, even if another agent finds a buyer"
    d) "My company's commission rates are lower than those charged by many other companies"

33. Federal antitrust laws apply:

    a) only to franchised firms, because of their ability to conspire to restrain trade
    b) only to large real estate firms that could actually affect the real estate market
    c) only to individual agents, not to real estate companies
    d) to all members of the real estate industry

34. Great County MLS publishes a monthly list of the commission rates charged by all member firms. The multiple listing association:

    a) could be found guilty of price fixing
    b) isn't guilty of price fixing, because it's simply reporting newsworthy information
    c) isn't guilty of price fixing, because no two competing firms are discussing rates
    d) isn't guilty of price fixing, because only real estate brokers can be guilty of price fixing, not multiple listing associations

35. A designated broker conducts a sales meeting once a week for her licensees. At one meeting, she discusses commission rates at length. She is:

    a) guilty of price fixing
    b) guilty of a tie-in arrangement
    c) guilty of a group boycott
    d) not guilty of any antitrust violation

Answer Key

1. a) The Governor appoints the members of the Real Estate Commission, which includes six commissioners and the Director of the Department of Licensing.

2. b) It is legal for an unlicensed person to represent another in a real estate transaction if authorized to do so by a power of attorney, as long as she is not acting for compensation.

3. d) The co-owner of a rental property can lease property on his own behalf without his actions falling under the definition of brokerage services.

4. a) The required qualifications for a managing broker's license differ from those for a broker's license in that at least three years of real estate experience in the previous five years is required. Just like a broker, a managing broker must be licensed under a firm and cannot accept compensation from anyone other than the firm.

5. b) Real estate licenses must be renewed every two years.

6. c) A real estate license can be renewed within one year after it expires if the licensee pays a penalty in addition to the renewal fee. After one year, the license is canceled, and there are several requirements for reinstatement.

7. b) Renewal requires a total of 30 clock hours of continuing education courses. At least 15 of the 30 hours must have been commenced within 24 months preceding the licensee's renewal date. The remaining hours must have been commenced within 36 months preceding the renewal date.

8. c) Brokers must complete 90 clock-hours of continuing education for their first renewal, with courses in advanced real estate practices, real estate law, and elective hours.

9. d) License reinstatement does not require retaking the license exam. A licensee must complete 60 clock-hours of course work, pay the back renewal fees, and pay a reinstatement penalty.

10. c) Those licensed in other jurisdictions must take the Washington portion of the license exam to obtain an equivalent Washington license.

11. a) Assistants need not be licensed, as long as they perform only clerical tasks. If an assistant were to engage in listing or selling activities, the assistant would have to obtain a license.

12. a) One year of experience plus post-secondary education in real estate studies may be sufficient to merit a waiver of the three-year experience requirement.

13. c) An applicant without three years' experience may still sit for the managing broker's exam if the Director of the Department of Licensing determines that her other education or experience is a satisfactory substitute.

14. b) A passing score for the real estate managing broker's exam is 75%. (A passing score for the real estate broker's exam is 70%.)

15. a) Only brokers receive an interim license; managing brokers do not.

16. b) A dual agent must not take any action that is detrimental to either party's interest in a transaction, unless it's something the agent is legally required to do (such as disclosing material facts).

17. d) Facts known by a real estate agent that aren't known by the principal are not imputed to the principal.

18. a)   When a real estate license is surrendered to the Director, it is inactive until the licensee finds another firm to work for and the license is reissued. In the meantime, it's unlawful for the licensee to continue any activities for which a license is required.

19. d)   A managing broker has the responsibility of reviewing documents within five days in transactions that involve a broker with less than two years' experience.

20. c)   A real estate license must be prominently displayed in the office where the licensee works.

21. d)   Trust funds must be placed in a trust account by the first banking day after receipt, unless the parties have instructed the firm in writing to handle the funds differently. Trust funds received in a sales transaction (or any trust funds other than property management trust funds) must be placed in an interest-bearing account.

22. c)   Transaction records and trust account records must be kept for at least three years after a transaction closes (or is otherwise terminated).

23. a)   A licensee can only receive compensation through her firm. The listing firm will have to pay the licensee's firm, who will then pay the licensee.

24. a)   When advertising their own properties, licensees are required to disclose their licensed status, but the firm's name does not have to be given. (The firm's name as licensed is required in ads for properties a licensee is advertising on behalf of someone else, however.)

25. d)   A broker can't manage a branch office; a branch office manager must have a managing broker's license.

26. b)   Before the buyer signs an offer, the selling agent must disclose to the buyer in writing which party he is representing. The agency disclosure may be a separate paragraph in the purchase and sale agreement, or it may be a separate document.

27. b)   If the licensee fails to request a hearing within 20 days, she will be considered in default and the Director may enter a decision based on the available facts.

28. d)   A licensee has to notify the Department of Licensing of a judgment in a civil lawsuit only if the case involves his real estate activities or other business activities. (With criminal charges, the Department of Licensing must be notified whether or not the charges involve real estate or business activities.)

29. d)   A firm that performs property management services must have a written management agreement with the owner, keep summary statements in its records, and fully disclose any interest in businesses that provide ancillary services.

30. d)   Real estate licensees must perform their duties as agreed, in a timely manner. Failure to do so may result in disciplinary action.

31. b)   Once a licensee discloses her agency status, she must act in accordance with the disclosure. A new disclosure is required if the licensee's representation in the transaction changes. In the situation described, Alberts would also need to obtain another agency agreement (one with the buyer) and written consent to the dual agency from both parties.

32. b)   The Sherman Antitrust Act prohibits price fixing, and referring to an agreement in the brokerage community to charge a standard or fixed commission rate is a violation of that act.

33. d)   Federal antitrust laws were extended to the real estate industry in 1950.

34. a) Even publishing a list of the "going rates" for
        commissions may be considered price fixing.

35. d) A designated broker may discuss commission
        rates with her own affiliated licensees without
        violating antitrust laws.

Real Estate Math

Chapter Overview

Real estate agents use math constantly: to calculate their commissions, to determine the square footage of homes they are listing or selling, to prorate closing costs, and so on. Electronic calculators make all of these tasks much easier than they once were, but it is still necessary to have a basic grasp of the math involved. This chapter provides step-by-step instructions for solving a wide variety of real estate math problems.

Solving Math Problems

We're going to begin our discussion of real estate math with a simple approach to solving math problems. Master this four-step process, and you'll be able to solve most math problems you are likely to encounter.

1. Read the question

The most important step is to thoroughly read and understand the question. You must know what you are looking for before you can successfully solve any math problem. Once you know what you want to find out (for example, the area, the commission amount, or the total profit), you'll be able to decide which formula to use.

2. Write down the formula

Write down the correct formula for the problem you need to solve. For example, the area formula is *Area = Length × Width*, which is abbreviated $A = L \times W$. Formulas for each type of problem are presented throughout this chapter, and there is a complete list at the end of the chapter.

3. Substitute

Substitute the relevant numbers from the problem into the formula. Sometimes there are numbers in the problem that you will not use. It's not unusual for a math problem to contain unnecessary information, which is why it is very important to read the question first and determine what you are looking for. The formula will help you distinguish between the relevant and irrelevant information given in the problem.

In some problems you will be able to substitute numbers into the formula without any additional steps, but in other problems one or more preliminary steps will be necessary. For instance, you may have to convert fractions to decimals.

4. Calculate

Once you have substituted the numbers into the formula, you are ready to perform the calculations to find the unknown—the component of the formula that was not given in the problem. Most of the formulas have the same basic form: $A = L \times W$. The problem will give you two of the three numbers (or information to enable you to find two of the numbers) and then you will either have to divide or multiply to find the third number, which is the solution to the problem.

Whether you'll multiply or divide is determined by which component in the formula is the unknown. For example, the formula $A = L \times W$ may be converted into two other formulas. All three formulas are equivalent, but they are put into different forms depending on the element to be discovered.

- ▶ If the quantity A (the area) is unknown, then the following formula is used: $A = L \times W$. The number L is **multiplied** by W. The product of L multiplied by W is A.
- ▶ If the quantity L (the length) is unknown, the following formula is used: $L = A \div W$. The number A is **divided** by W. The quotient of A divided by W is L.
- ▶ If the quantity W (the width) is unknown, the following formula is used: $W = A \div L$. The number A is **divided** by L. The quotient of A divided by L is W.

Thus, the formula $A = L \times W$ may be used three different ways depending on which quantity is unknown. For the examples below, assume the area of a rectangle is 800 square feet, the length is 40 feet, and the width is 20 feet.

$A = L \times W$	$L = A \div W$	$W = A \div L$
$A = 40' \times 20'$	$L = 800\ Sq.\ ft. \div 20'$	$W = 800\ Sq.\ ft. \div 40'$
$40' \times 20' = 800\ Sq.\ ft.$	$800\ Sq.\ ft. \div 20' = 40'$	$800\ Sq.\ ft. \div 40' = 20'$

After you've substituted the numbers given in the problem into the formula, you might have trouble deciding whether you're supposed to multiply or divide. It may help to compare your equation to the very familiar calculation $2 \times 3 = 6$. If the unknown component of your equation is in the same position as the 6 in $2 \times 3 = 6$, then you need to multiply the two given numbers to find the unknown.

If the unknown component is in the 2 position or the 3 position, you need to divide. You'll divide the given number in the 6 position by the other given number to find the unknown.

$$? \times 3 = 6 \quad becomes \quad 6 \div 3 = 2 \qquad 2 \times ? = 6 \quad becomes \quad 6 \div 2 = 3$$

Now let's apply the four-step approach to an example. Suppose a room is 10 feet wide and 15 feet long. How many square feet does it contain?

1. **Read the question.** This problem asks you to find the square footage or area of a rectangular room. So you'll need the area formula for a rectangle.

2. **Write down the formula.** *Area = Length × Width*

3. **Substitute.** Substitute the numbers given in the problem into the formula. The length of the rectangle measures 15 feet, and the width measures 10 feet: *A = 15' × 10'*.

4. **Calculate.** Multiply *Length* times *Width* to get the answer: *15' × 10' = 150 Sq. ft.* Thus, *A = 150*. The area of the room is 150 square feet.

Suppose the problem gave you different pieces of information about the same room: the area is 150 square feet and it's 10 feet wide. How long is the room? Again, follow the four-step approach.

1. **Read the question**. You're asked to find the length or width of a rectangle. You'll need the area formula again.

2. **Write down the formula**. *Area = Length × Width*

3. **Substitute**. Substitute the numbers given in the problem into the formula: *150 = L × 10′*.

4. **Calculate**. The length of the rectangle is the unknown. Thus, the basic area formula is converted into a division problem to find the length: *150 Sq. ft. ÷ 10′ = 15′*. The quotient of 150 divided by 10 is 15. The length of the rectangle, or of the room, is therefore 15 feet.

Decimal Numbers

To carry out a calculation, it's easier to work with decimal numbers than with fractions or percentages. So if a problem presents you with fractions or percentages, you'll usually convert them into decimal numbers.

Converting Fractions. To convert a fraction into decimal form, divide the top number of the fraction (the numerator) by the bottom number of the fraction (the denominator).

> **Example:** To change ¾ into a decimal, divide 3 (the top number) by 4 (the bottom number): *3 ÷ 4 = .75*.

> **Example:** To convert ⅔ into a decimal, divide 2 (the top number) by 3 (the bottom number): *2 ÷ 3 = .66667*.

If you don't already know them, it's useful to memorize the decimal equivalents of the most common fractions:

$$¼ = .25$$
$$½ = .5$$
$$¾ = .75$$

Converting Percentages. To solve a problem involving a percentage, you'll first convert the percentage into a decimal number, then convert the decimal answer back into percentage form.

To convert a percentage to a decimal, remove the percent sign and move the decimal point two places to the left. It may be necessary to add a zero.

Example:

98% becomes .98

5% becomes .05

32.5% becomes .325

17.5% becomes .175

To convert a decimal into a percentage, do just the opposite. Move the decimal point two places to the right, adding a zero if necessary, and add a percent sign.

Example:

.1 becomes 10%

.15 becomes 15%

.08 becomes 08%

.095 becomes 09.5%

The percent key on a calculator performs the conversion of a percentage to a decimal number automatically. On most calculators, you can key in the digits and press the percent key, and the calculator will display the percentage in decimal form.

Decimal Calculations. Calculators handle decimal numbers in exactly the same way as whole numbers. If you enter a decimal number into the calculator with the decimal point in the correct place, the calculator will do the rest. But if you're working without a calculator, you'll need to apply the following rules.

To add or subtract decimals, put the numbers in a column with their decimal points lined up.

Example: To add 3.75, 14.62, 1.245, 679, 1,412.8, and 1.9, put the numbers in a column with the decimal points lined up as shown below, then add them together.

$$
\begin{array}{r}
3.75 \\
14.62 \\
1.245 \\
679.0 \\
1,412.8 \\
+\quad 1.9 \\
\hline
2,113.315
\end{array}
$$

To multiply decimal numbers, first do the multiplication without worrying about the decimal points. Then put a decimal point into the answer in the correct place. The answer should have as many decimal places (that is, numbers to the right of its decimal point) as the total number of decimal places in the numbers that were multiplied. So count the decimal places in the numbers you are multiplying and put the decimal point the same number of places to the left in the answer.

Example: Multiply 24.6 times 16.7. The two numbers contain a total of two decimal places.

$$
\begin{array}{r}
24.6 \\
\times\quad 16.7 \\
\hline
410.82
\end{array}
$$

In some cases, it will be necessary to include one or more zeros in the answer to have the correct number of decimal places.

Example: Multiply .2 times .4. There is a total of two decimal places.

$$\begin{array}{r} .2 \\ \times\ .4 \\ \hline .08 \end{array}$$

A zero has to be included in the answer in order to move the decimal point two places left.

To divide by a decimal number, move the decimal point in the denominator (the number you're dividing the other number by) all the way to the right. Then move the decimal point in the numerator (the number that you're dividing) the same number of places to the right. (In some cases it will be necessary to add one or more zeros to the numerator in order to move the decimal point the correct number of places.)

Example: Divide 26.145 by 1.5. First move the decimal point in 1.5 all the way to the right (in this case, that's only one place). Then move the decimal point in 26.145 the same number of places to the right.

26.145 ÷ 1.5 becomes 261.45 ÷ 15

Now divide. *261.45 ÷ 15 = 17.43*

Remember, these steps are unnecessary if you're using a calculator. If the numbers are keyed in correctly, the calculator will automatically give you an answer with the decimal point in the correct place.

Area Problems

A real estate agent often needs to calculate the area of a lot, a building, or a room. Area is usually stated in square feet or square yards. The formula to be used for the calculation depends on the shape of the area in question. It may be a square, a rectangle, a triangle, or some combination of those shapes.

Squares and Rectangles

As stated earlier, the formula for finding the area of a square or a rectangle is $A = L \times W$.

Example: If a rectangular room measures 15 feet along one wall and 12 feet along the adjoining wall, how many square feet of carpet would be required to cover the floor?

1. **Read the question.** You're being asked to find the area (the square footage) of a rectangle.

2. **Write down the formula.** $A = L \times W$

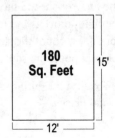

3. **Substitute**. *A = 15' × 12'*

4. **Calculate**. Since the quantity *A* is unknown, multiply *L* times *W* for the answer: *15' × 12' = 180 Sq. ft.* 180 square feet of carpet are needed to cover the floor.

Now take the problem one step further. If carpet is on sale for $12 per square yard, how much would it cost to carpet the room?

1. **Read the question**. You're first being asked to determine how many square feet there are in a square yard, and then to determine how many square yards there are in 180 square feet. A square yard is a square that measures one yard on each side. There are three feet in a yard.

2. **Write down the formula**. *A = L × W*

3. **Substitute**. *A = 3' × 3'*

4. **Calculate**. Since the quantity *A* is the unknown, multiply *L* times *W*: *3' × 3' = 9 Sq. ft.*

   So there are 9 square feet in a square yard. Now divide 180 by 9 to see how many square yards there are in 180 square feet: *180 ÷ 9' = 20 Sq. yd.*

   Now multiply the number of square yards (20) by the cost per square yard ($12): *20 × $12 = $240 Cost to carpet room.*

Triangles

The formula for finding the area of a triangle is:

$$\frac{\textit{Height} \times \frac{1}{2}\,\textit{Base}}{\textit{Area}} \quad \text{or} \quad \textit{Area} = \frac{1}{2}\,\textit{Base} \times \textit{Height}$$

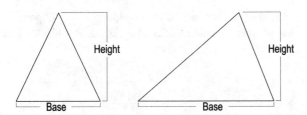

Example: If commercial building lots in a certain neighborhood are selling for approximately $5 per square foot, approximately how much should the lot pictured below sell for?

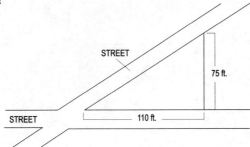

1. **Write down the formula**. *A = ½ B × H*

2. **Substitute**. *Area = 55' (½ of 110) × 75'*

3. **Calculate**. *75' × 55' = 4,125 Sq. ft.*

The order of multiplication doesn't matter. You can multiply 110 times 75 and then divide it in half. Or you can divide 110 by 2 and then multiply the result by 75. Or you can divide 75 by 2 and then multiply the result by 110. Whichever way you do it, the answer will be the same.

	Step 1	**Step 2**	**Answer**
a)	*110 × 75 = 8,250*	*8,250 ÷ 2 = 4,125*	*4,125 Sq. ft.*
b)	*110 ÷ 2 = 55*	*55 × 75 = 4,125*	*4,125 Sq. ft.*
c)	*75 ÷ 2 = 37.5*	*37.5 × 110 = 4,125*	*4,125 Sq. ft.*

The lot contains 4,125 square feet. If similar lots are selling for about $5 per square foot, this lot should sell for about $20,625.

4,125 Square feet
× $5 Per square foot
$20,625 Selling price

Odd Shapes

The best approach to finding the area of an odd-shaped figure is to divide it up into squares, rectangles, and triangles. Find the areas of those figures and add them all up to arrive at the area of the odd-shaped lot, room, or building in question.

Example: If the lot pictured below is leased on a 50-year lease for $3 per square foot per year, with rental payments made monthly, how much would the monthly rent be?

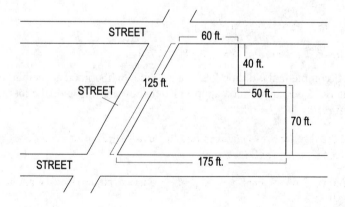

First, divide the lot up into rectangles and triangles.

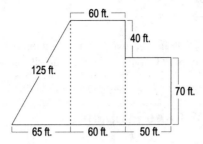

The next step is to find the area of each of the following figures. The height of the triangle is determined by adding together the 70-foot border of the small rectangle and the 40-foot border of the large rectangle, as shown above.

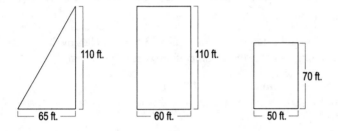

First, find the area of the triangle.

1. **Write down the formula.** *A = ½ Base × Height*

2. **Substitute.** *A = 32.5' (½ of 65') × 110'*

3. **Calculate.** *32.5' × 110' = 3,575 Sq. ft.*

Then, find the area of the large rectangle.

1. **Write down the formula.** *A = Length × Width*

2. **Substitute.** *A = 110' × 60'*

3. **Calculate.** *110' × 60' = 6,600 Sq. ft.*

Next, find the area of the small rectangle.

1. **Write down the formula.** *A = Length × Width*

2. **Substitute.** *A = 70' × 50'*

3. **Calculate.** *50' × 70' = 3,500 Sq. ft.*

Finally, add the three areas together to find the area of the entire lot: *3,575 + 6,600 + 3,500 = 13,675 Total square feet.*

The lot contains 13,675 square feet. At $3 per square foot per year, the annual rent would be $41,025.

$$13,675 \quad Square\ feet$$
$$\underline{\times \quad \$3 \quad Rent\ per\ square\ foot}$$
$$\$41,025 \quad Annual\ rent$$

The monthly rental payment would be one-twelfth of the annual rent: $\$41,025 \div 12$ $= \$3,418.75$. Thus, the monthly rental payment for this odd-shaped lot is $3,418.75.

Volume Problems

Occasionally you may need to calculate the volume of a three-dimensional space. Volume is usually stated in cubic feet or cubic yards. A formula for calculating volume can be stated as: *Volume = Length × Width × Height*, or $V = L \times W \times H$. It's the same as the area formula, except it has one added element: H, the height of the space being measured.

Example: The floor of a storage unit measures 13 feet 6 inches by 20 feet, and it has a 12-foot ceiling. What is the volume of the unit in cubic yards?

1. **Write down the formula**. $V = L \times W \times H$

2. **Substitute**. $V = 20' \times 13.5' \times 12'$

3. **Calculate**.

Step 1	Step 2
$20'$	270 *Square feet*
$\times 13.5'$	$\times 12'$
270 *Square feet*	$3,240$ *Cubic feet*

4. **Now convert the cubic feet into cubic yards**. As you saw earlier, a square yard measures 3 feet by 3 feet, or 9 square feet. A cubic yard measures 3 feet by 3 feet by 3 feet, or 27 cubic feet. Divide the volume of the storage area in cubic feet by 27 to find the volume in cubic yards: $3,240 \div 27 = 120$ *Cubic yards*. The volume of the storage space is 120 cubic yards.

Percentage Problems

Many real estate math problems involve percentages. This includes problems about brokerage commissions, interest on mortgage loans, property appreciation or depreciation, and capitalization.

Solving Percentage Problems

To solve percentage problems, you'll usually convert the percentage into a decimal number, calculate, and then convert the answer back into percentage form. As explained earlier, a percentage is converted into a decimal number by removing the percent sign and moving the decimal point two places to the left. If the percentage is a single digit (for example, 7%), it will be necessary to add a zero (.07). To convert a decimal number into a percentage, you reverse those steps: move the decimal point two places to the right and add the percent sign.

In a math problem, whenever something is expressed as a percentage "of" another number, that indicates that you should multiply that other number by the percentage. For instance, what is 75% of $40,000?

Step 1	**Step 2**
75% becomes .75	*$40,000*
	× .75
	$30,000

Basically, percentage problems ask you to find a part of a whole. The whole is a larger figure, such as a property's sales price. The part is a smaller figure, such as a broker's commission. The general formula might be stated thus: *A percentage of the whole equals the part.* This can be written as an equation: *Part = Whole × Percentage.*

Example: A house is listed for sale at a price of $172,000, with an agreement to pay a commission of 6% of the sales price. The property sells for $170,000. How much is the commission?

1. **Write down the formula.** $P = W \times \%$

2. **Substitute.** Change the percentage (6%) into a decimal number (.06) first: $P = $170,000 \times .06$.

3. **Calculate.**

> $170,000   *Sales price*
> × .06   *Commission rate*
> $10,200   *Commission*

The commission is $10,200.

In some percentage problems, the part is given and you're asked to calculate either the whole or the percentage. For those problems, you'll need to rearrange the percentage formula into a division problem. If the whole is the unknown, divide the part by the percentage: *Whole = Part ÷ Percentage.*

If the percentage is the unknown, divide the part by the whole: *Percentage = Part ÷ Whole.*

Notice that in either case, you'll be dividing the value of the part by either the whole (to determine the percentage) or by the percentage (to determine the whole).

Commission Problems

Like the example above, most commission problems can be solved with the general percentage formula: *Part = Whole × Percentage.*

The percentage is the commission rate, and the whole is the amount that the commission is based on. In most problems, this will be the sales price of a piece of property. The part is the amount of the commission.

Example: A listing agreement provides for a commission of 7% of the sales price. The managing broker has agreed to pay his broker 60% of the commission. How much will the broker receive if the property sells for $580,000?

1. **Write down the formula.** $P = W \times \%$

2. **Substitute.** Change the percentage (7%) to a decimal number (.07): $P = \$580,000 \times .07$.

3. **Calculate.** The part is the unknown quantity, so the percentage is multiplied by the whole.

$$\begin{array}{rl} \$580,000 & \textit{Sales price} \\ \times \ .07 & \textit{Commission rate} \\ \hline \$40,600 & \textit{Total commission} \end{array}$$

The total commission is $40,600. The broker is entitled to 60% of the total commission. Apply the percentage formula again to determine the amount of the broker's share.

1. **Write down the formula.** $P = W \times \%$

2. **Substitute.** Convert the percentage (60%) to a decimal number (.60): $P = \$40,600 \times .60$.

3. **Calculate.**

$$\begin{array}{rl} \$40,600 & \textit{Total commission} \\ \times \ .60 & \textit{Broker's percentage} \\ \hline \$24,360 & \textit{Broker's share} \end{array}$$

The following example illustrates another form that commission problems can take.

Example: A listing agreement provided for a two-tiered commission based on the property's sales price. The commission would be 7% of the first $100,000 and 5% of any amount over $100,000. If the commission was $8,250, what was the sales price?

1. **Read the question.** You're given the commission rates and the amount of the commission, and then asked to find the sales price. Your first step in the process is to find out how much of the commission amount is attributable to the first $100,000 of the sales price.

2. **Write down the formula.** $P = W \times \%$

3. **Substitute**, converting the percentage to a decimal: $P = \$100,000 \times .07$.

4. **Calculate.** $\$100,000 \times .07 = \$7,000$

So $7,000 of the commission is based on the first $100,000 of the sales price. Next, subtract to find the amount of the rest of the commission.

$$\begin{array}{rl} \$8,250 & \textit{Total commission} \\ - \ 7,000 & \textit{Commission from first \$100,000} \\ \hline \$1,250 & \end{array}$$

Now you know that out of the total commission, $1,250 is attributable to the part of the sales price in excess of $100,000. You can use that figure along with the second-tier commission rate (5% of the amount over $100,000) to determine by how much the sales price exceeded $100,000.

1. **Write down the formula**. $P = W \times \%$

2. **Substitute**, converting the percentage to a decimal: $1,250 = W \times .05.$

3. **Calculate**. The quantity W (the whole) is the unknown. To isolate the unknown, the basic formula must be turned into a division problem. The part divided by the percentage equals the whole: $1,250 \div .05 = $25,000.$

This shows that the portion of the sales price in excess of $100,000 amounted to $25,000. Thus, the total sales price is $100,000 plus $25,000, or $125,000.

Loan Problems

Loan problems include interest problems and principal balance problems. These can be solved using the general percentage formula: *Part = Whole × Percentage*. Here, the part is the amount of the interest, the whole is the loan amount or principal balance, and the percentage is the interest rate.

Example: Henry borrows $5,000 for one year and agrees to pay 7% interest. How much interest will he be required to pay?

1. **Write down the formula**. $P = W \times \%$

2. **Substitute**. $P = $5,000 \times .07$

3. **Calculate**.

$5,000 Loan amount
× .07 Interest rate
$350 Interest

Henry will pay $350 in interest.

Interest Rates. Interest rates are expressed as annual rates—a certain percentage per year. Some problems present you with monthly, quarterly, or semi-annual interest payments instead of the annual amount. In that case, you'll need to multiply the payment amount stated in the problem to determine the annual amount before you substitute the numbers into the formula.

Example: If $450 in interest accrues on a $7,200 interest-only loan in six months, what is the annual interest rate?

1. **Read the question**. You're asked to find the annual interest rate, but the interest amount given in the problem ($450) accrued in only six months. The annual interest amount would be double that, or $900.

2. **Write down the formula**. $P = W \times \%$

3. **Substitute**. For the part (the interest amount), be sure to use the annual figure ($900): $900 = $7,200 \times Percentage.$

4. **Calculate**. Rearrange the formula to isolate the unknown (in this case, the percentage). The part is divided by the whole to determine the percentage: *$900 ÷ $7,200 = .125.*

Convert the decimal number back into a percentage: .125 becomes 12.5%. Thus, the annual interest rate is 12½%.

Principal Balance. Some loan problems ask you to determine a loan's current principal balance at a certain point in the loan term.

Example: A home loan has monthly payments of $625, which include principal and 9% interest and $47.50 per month for tax and insurance reserves. If $27.75 of the June 1 payment was applied to the principal, what was the outstanding principal balance during the month of May? (Mortgage interest is paid in arrears, so the June payment includes the interest that accrued during May.)

1. **Write down the formula.** $P = W \times \%$. Once again, in this context the part is the amount of interest, the whole is the loan balance, and the percentage is the interest rate.

2. **Substitute**. First, find the interest portion of the payment by subtracting the reserves and the principal portion.

> | $625.00 | Total June payment |
> |---|---|
> | 47.50 | Reserves |
> | − 27.75 | Principal |
> | $549.75 | Interest portion of payment |

Next, multiply the interest portion by 12 to determine the annual interest amount: *$549.75 × 12 = $6,597.*

Now substitute the annual interest amount and rate into the formula: *$6,597 = W × .09.*

3. **Calculate**. Rearrange the formula to isolate the unknown, *W*. This is a division problem: *$6,597 ÷ .09 = $73,300.*

The outstanding principal balance for May was $73,300.

Profit or Loss Problems

Profit or loss problems ask you to compare the cost or value of a piece of property at an earlier point in time with its cost or value at a later point. They can be solved using a variation on the percentage formula. Instead of *Part = Whole × Percentage,* the formula is stated like this: *Now = Then × Percentage.*

The *Then* spot in the formula is for the value or cost of the property at an earlier time specified in the problem. The *Now* spot is for the value or cost at a later time. The percentage is 100% plus the percentage of profit or minus the percentage of loss.

The idea is to express the value of the property after a profit or loss (*Now*) as a percentage of the property's value before the profit or loss (*Then*). If there is no profit or loss, the *Now* value is exactly 100% of the *Then* value, because the value has not changed. If there is a profit, the *Now* value will be greater than 100% of the *Then* value, since the value has increased. If there is a loss, the *Now* value will be less than 100% of the *Then* value.

Example: Bonnie bought a house five years ago for $450,000 and sold it this year for 30% more than she paid for it. What did she sell it for?

1. **Write down the formula.** *Now = Then × %*

2. **Substitute.** To get the percentage, you must add the percentage of profit to or subtract the percentage of loss from 100%. In this case there is a profit, so you add 30% to 100%, then convert it to a decimal number (130% becomes 1.30): *Now = $450,000 × 1.30.*

3. **Calculate.** *$450,000 × 1.30 = $585,000*

Bonnie sold her house for $585,000.

Example: Paul sold his house this year for $840,000. He paid $1,050,000 for it two years ago. What was the percentage of loss?

1. **Write down the formula.** *Now = Then × %*

2. **Substitute.** *$840,000 = $1,050,000 × %*

3. **Calculate.** The percentage is the unknown quantity; thus, the formula is rearranged to isolate the percentage: *$840,000 ÷ $1,050,000 = .80 or 80%.*

The *Now* value is 80% of the *Then* value. Subtract 80% from 100% to find the percentage of loss: *100% – 80% = 20% Loss.*

Paul took a 20% loss on the sale of his house.

Let's look at another example, except this time there is a profit instead of a loss.

Example: Martha bought her home six years ago for $377,400. She sold it recently for $422,700. What was her percentage of profit?

1. **Write down the formula.** *Now = Then × %*

2. **Substitute.** *$422,700 = $377,400 × %*

3. **Calculate.** Once again, the percentage is the unknown quantity; thus, the formula is rearranged to isolate the percentage: *$422,700 ÷ $377,400 = 1.12 or 112%.*

The *Now* value is approximately 112% of the *Then* value. Subtract 100% from 112%, and you determine Martha received 100% of what she paid for the house, plus a 12% profit.

Let's try to solve one last variation of this type of problem.

Example: Ken sold his duplex for $280,000, which represents a 16% profit over what he paid for it five years ago. What did Ken originally pay for the property?

1. **Write down the formula.** *Now = Then × %*

2. **Substitute.** *$280,000 = Then × 116%*

3. **Calculate.** In this instance, the unknown is the price Ken originally paid for the duplex; so you isolate the *Then* part of the equation: *$280,000 ÷ 1.16 = $241,379.31.*

The price paid by Ken was $241,379.31.

Some profit or loss problems involve appreciation or depreciation that has accrued at an annual rate over a specified number of years. You solve this type of problem by applying the *Then* and *Now* formula one year at a time.

Example: A property that is currently worth $174,000 has depreciated 3% per year for the past four years. How much was it worth four years ago?

1. **Write down the formula.** *Now = Then × %*

2. **Substitute.** Because the property is worth 3% less than it was one year ago, the percentage is 97% (100% − 3% = 97%): *$174,000 = Then × .97.*

3. **Calculate.** Rearrange the formula to isolate the unknown, the *Then* value: *$174,000 ÷ .97 = $179,381.44.*

The property was worth $179,381.44 one year ago. Apply the formula to $179,381.44 to determine the property's value two years ago. Repeat the process twice more to find the value four years ago.

> *$179,381.44 ÷ .97 = $184,929.31*
> *$184,929.31 ÷ .97 = $190,648.77*
> *$190,648.77 ÷ .97 = $196,545.12*

The property was worth about $196,545 four years ago.

Capitalization Problems

Capitalization problems involve the capitalization approach to value, a method of real estate appraisal that is discussed in detail in Chapter 12.

The capitalization formula is another variation on the percentage formula. Instead of *Part = Whole × Percentage*, the formula is stated like this: *Income = Value × Capitalization Rate.*

The value here is an investment property's value, or the purchase price an investor should be willing to pay for the property in order to obtain a specified rate of return.

The specified rate of return is the capitalization rate. This is the percentage of return the investor desires on the investment. The desired rate of return varies according to many factors. A higher desired rate of return will mean a higher capitalization rate and a lower value for the property.

The income in the capitalization formula is the annual net income produced by the investment property.

Example: A property produces an annual net income of $26,000. If an investor desires an 11% rate of return, what should he pay for the property?

1. **Write down the formula.** *I = V × %*

2. **Substitute.** *$26,000 = V × .11*

3. **Calculate.** Rearrange the formula to isolate *V*, the unknown quantity: *$26,000 ÷ .11 = $236,363.64.*

The investor should be willing to pay approximately $236,364 for the property.

Example: If a property is valued at $1,000,000 using an 8% capitalization rate, what would its value be using a 10% capitalization rate? First, apply the capitalization formula to determine the property's annual net income.

1. **Write down the formula.** $I = V \times \%$

2. **Substitute.** $I = \$1,000,000 \times .08$

3. **Calculate.**

    $$
    \begin{array}{rl}
    \$1,000,000 & \textit{Value} \\
    \times\ .08 & \textit{Capitalization rate} \\
    \hline
    \$80,000 & \textit{Annual net income}
    \end{array}
    $$

The net income is $80,000 annually. Now substitute that figure into the formula to find the value at a 10% capitalization rate.

4. **Substitute.** $\$80,000 = V \times .10$

5. **Calculate.** Rearrange the formula to isolate V, the unknown quantity: $\$80,000 \div .10 = \$800,000$.

So the value of the same property using a 10% capitalization rate is $800,000, compared to $1,000,000 at the 8% rate. As you can see, a higher capitalization rate applied to the same net income results in a lower value for the property.

In some problems, it's necessary to deduct a bad debt/vacancy factor and operating expenses from gross income to arrive at the net income.

Example: A ten-unit apartment building has six units that rent for $800 per month and four units that rent for $850 per month. Allow 5% for vacancies and uncollected rent. Operating expenses include: annual property taxes of $7,200, monthly utilities of $2,475, and maintenance expenses of approximately $13,600 per year. The owner has an outstanding mortgage balance of $257,000 at 8% interest, with monthly payments of $2,150. If an investor requires a 7.5% rate of return, how much should she offer for the property?

1. **Write down the formula.** $I = V \times \%$

2. **Substitute.** Remember that the income referred to in the capitalization formula is annual net income. Thus, it's necessary to calculate the annual net income before substituting. The first step in that process is calculating the annual gross income.

    $$
    \begin{array}{l}
    \$800 \times 12\ \textit{months} = \quad \$9,600/\textit{year} \times 6\ \textit{units} = \$57,600 \\
    \$850 \times 12\ \textit{months} = \$10,200/\textit{year} \times 4\ \textit{units} = \underline{\$40,800} \\
    \phantom{\$850 \times 12\ \textit{months} = \$10,200/\textit{year} \times 4\ \textit{units} = }\ \$98,400
    \end{array}
    $$

The gross income is $98,400 per year.

Next, calculate the bad debt/vacancy factor and deduct it from the gross income to find the effective gross income. The bad debt/vacancy factor is 5% of the gross income.

$98,400 *Gross income*
× .05
$4,920 *Bad debts and vacancies*

Thus, the loss to be expected from uncollected rents and vacancies is $4,920 per year.

$98,400 *Gross income*
− 4,920 *Bad debts and vacancies*
$93,480 *Effective gross income*

The operating expenses must be deducted from the effective gross income to arrive at the net income. Remember, since you are trying to find annual net income, all the expenses must be annual also. The operating expenses add up as follows:

$7,200 *Property taxes*
$29,700 *Utilities (at $2,475 per month)*
+ $13,600 *Maintenance*
$50,500 *Annual operating expenses*

The annual operating expenses are $50,500. (The mortgage payments are not treated as operating expenses. See Chapter 12.) Subtract the operating expenses from the effective gross income to determine the annual net income.

$93,480 *Effective gross income*
− 50,500 *Annual operating expenses*
$42,980 *Annual net income*

Now, substitute the net income and the cap rate into the formula $I = V \times \%$: $42,980 = V \times .075$.

3. **Calculate.** Rearrange the formula to isolate V, the unknown quantity: $42,980 ÷ .075 = $573,067$.

The investor should be willing to pay approximately $573,067 for the property.

Example: Continuing with the previous example, if an investor paid $750,000 for the apartment building, what capitalization rate was used? (Assume that the property's income and operating expenses were the same.)

1. **Write down the formula.** $I = V \times \%$

2. **Substitute.** You already know the net income from the preceding problem: $42,980 = $750,000 \times \%$.

3. **Calculate.** Isolate the unknown quantity, the capitalization rate: $42,980 ÷ $750,000 = .0573$ or 5.73%.

The investor used a capitalization rate of approximately 5.7%.

A capitalization problem may give you the property's **operating expense ratio** (O.E.R.). The O.E.R. is the percentage of the gross income that is used to pay the annual operating expenses. The remainder is the annual net income.

Example: A property's annual gross income is $480,000, and its O.E.R. is 79%. If an investor wants a 10½% return on investment (ROI), how much is the property worth to her?

1. **Write down the formula.** $I = V \times \%$

2. **Substitute.** Calculate the annual operating expenses using the operating expense ratio. Then subtract the operating expenses from the gross income to arrive at the annual net income.

   $480,000 × .79 = $379,200   Annual operating expenses

   $480,000 − $379,200 = $100,800   Annual net income

   Now substitute the income and the cap rate into the formula: *$100,800 = V × .105.*

3. **Calculate.** Rearrange the formula to isolate *V,* the unknown quantity: *$100,800 ÷ .105 = $960,000 Value.*

The investor should be willing to pay $960,000 for the property.

Tax Assessment Problems

Many tax assessment problems can be solved using this formula: *Tax = Assessed Value × Tax Rate.* You may first have to determine the assessed value before you can carry out the rest of the calculations. Assessed value is a property's value for taxation purposes.

Example: According to the tax assessor, the property's market value is $292,300. The applicable assessment ratio is 85%. If the tax rate is 3%, how much is the annual tax amount?

1. **Multiply** the market value by the assessment ratio to determine the assessed value of the property: *$292,300 × 85% = $248,455 Assessed value.*

2. **Substitute** the assessed value and the tax rate into the formula: *Tax = $248,455 × .03.*

3. **Calculate.**

   $248,455   *Assessed value*
   × .03   *Tax rate*
   $7,453.65   *Annual taxes*

The annual taxes for this property are $7,453.65.

In some problems, the tax rate is not stated as a percentage of the assessed value. Instead, it is expressed as a dollar amount per hundred or per thousand dollars of assessed value.

Example: A property with an assessed value of $173,075 is taxed at a rate of $2.35 per hundred dollars of assessed value. How much is the annual tax amount?

1. **Divide** $173,075 by 100 to determine how many hundred dollar increments there are in the assessed value: *$173,075 ÷ 100 = 1,730.75 or 1,731 $100 increments.* (A partial $100 increment would be taxed as one $100 increment.)

2. **Multiply** the number of hundred dollar increments by the tax rate to calculate the annual tax amount.

$$
\begin{array}{rl}
1,731 & \text{\$100 increments} \\
\times\ \$2.35 & \text{Tax rate} \\
\hline
\$4,067.85 & \text{Annual taxes}
\end{array}
$$

The annual tax is $4,067.85.

In other problems, the tax rate is expressed as a specified number of mills per dollar of assessed value. A mill is one-tenth of one cent (.001). Ten mills equals one cent, and 100 mills equals 10 cents.

Example: The property's market value is $310,000 and the assessment ratio is 70%. The tax rate is 21 mills per dollar of assessed value. How much is the annual tax amount?

1. **Multiply** the market value by the assessment ratio to find the assessed value.

$$
\begin{array}{rl}
\$310,000 & \text{Market value} \\
\times\ .70 & \text{Assessment ratio} \\
\hline
\$217,000 & \text{Assessed value}
\end{array}
$$

2. **Multiply** the assessed value by the tax rate to determine the tax. In decimal form, 21 mills is .021.

$$
\begin{array}{rl}
\$217,000 & \text{Assessed value} \\
\times\ .021 & \text{Tax rate} \\
\hline
\$4,557 & \text{Annual tax}
\end{array}
$$

The annual tax is $4,557.

Seller's Net Problems

In a seller's net problem, you're told that a seller wants to take away a specified net amount from closing, after paying the real estate agent's commission and other closing costs. You're then asked to calculate how much the property will have to sell for if the seller is to receive the desired net.

Example: The seller wants to net $50,000 from the sale of her home. She will have to pay off her mortgage balance, which is approximately $126,500, and pay $1,560 for repairs, $2,015 for other closing costs, and a 7% commission. What's the minimum sales price that will net the seller $50,000?

1. **Add** the seller's desired net to the costs of sale, excluding the commission.

$$
\begin{array}{rl}
\$50,000 & \text{Seller's net} \\
126,500 & \text{Mortgage} \\
1,560 & \text{Repairs} \\
+\ 2,015 & \text{Closing costs} \\
\hline
\$180,075 & \text{Total}
\end{array}
$$

$180,075 is the amount that must be left to the seller after the commission has been paid, if she is to be able to pay all of the listed expenses and still have $50,000 left over.

2. **Subtract** the commission rate from 100%: *100% – 7% = 93%.*

3. **Divide** the total from step one by the percentage from step two. Since the commission rate will be 7% of the sales price, the seller's net plus the other costs will have to equal 93% of the sales price: *$180,075 ÷ .93 = $193,629.*

The property will have to sell for approximately $193,629 for the seller to net $50,000.

This may seem counterintuitive at first. At first glance, it may seem that you're applying the commission rate to the closing costs as well as the selling price. But you aren't. This is best understood by working backwards through the problem. By doing so, you'll see that, as in the real world closing process, the commission is subtracted from the selling price, and then the seller's closing costs are subtracted from those proceeds.

Start by calculating the cost of the 7% commission.

$$\begin{array}{ll} \$193,629 & \textit{Selling price} \\ \times\ .07 & \textit{Commission} \\ \hline \$13,554 & \end{array}$$

Now subtract the commission and the other closing costs from the gross proceeds, to find the seller's net proceeds.

$$\begin{array}{ll} \$193,629 & \textit{Selling Price} \\ 13,554 & \textit{Commission} \\ 126,500 & \textit{Mortgage} \\ 1,560 & \textit{Repairs} \\ -\ 2,015 & \textit{Closing costs} \\ \hline \$50,000 & \textit{Net proceeds} \end{array}$$

Proration Problems

Proration is the allocation of an expense between two or more parties. As was explained in Chapter 13, prorations are required in real estate closings, where a variety of expenses are prorated based on the closing date.

There are basically three steps in the proration process:

1. Calculate the per diem (daily) rate of the expense.
2. Determine the number of days for which one person is responsible for the expense.
3. Multiply the per diem rate by the number of days to determine the share of the expense that one party is responsible for: *Share = Rate × Days.*

To determine the per diem rate of an annual expense, divide the amount of the expense by 365 days, or 366 in a leap year. Some problems will instruct you to divide by

360 days instead, to simplify the calculation. (A 360-day year is sometimes referred to as a banker's year, as opposed to a calendar year.)

To determine the per diem rate of a monthly expense when you are prorating on the basis of a calendar year, divide the amount of the expense by the number of days in that particular month. Alternatively, to simplify the calculation, you may be instructed to base your prorations on a banker's year, which means that every month has 30 days, including February.

We'll present you with a series of examples concerning the proration of various expenses: property taxes, hazard insurance, rent, and mortgage interest. See Chapter 13 for more information about these expenses.

Property Tax Prorations

Property taxes are an annual expense. At closing, the taxes may or may not have been paid yet. If they've already been paid, the buyer will owe the seller a share of the taxes. If they haven't been paid, the seller will owe the buyer a share. Either way, the proration process is essentially the same.

Example: The closing date is August 3, and the seller has already paid the annual property taxes, which were $2,045. At closing, the seller is entitled to a credit for the tax amount covering the period from August 3 through December 31. The same amount will be a debit for the buyer. How much will the buyer owe the seller for the property taxes? Use a 360-day year with 30-day months for your calculations.

1. **Calculate the per diem rate** for the property taxes, using a 360-day year:
   $2,045 ÷ 360 = $5.68 per diem.

2. **Count the number of days** that the buyer is responsible for, using 30-day months.

28 days	*August 3 through 30*
30 days	*September*
30 days	*October*
30 days	*November*
+ 30 days	*December*
148 days	

3. **Substitute** the rate and number of days into the formula ($S = R \times D$), then calculate.

148	*Days*
× $5.68	*Per diem*
$840.64	*Credit to seller*

At closing, the buyer will be debited $840.64 and the seller will be credited $840.64 for the property taxes from August 3 through the end of the tax year.

In the following example, the taxes haven't been paid yet. You're given the seller's share of the taxes and asked to calculate the annual tax amount.

Example: The seller hasn't paid any portion of the annual taxes. The closing is scheduled for March 21. At closing, the seller will owe the buyer $663.60 for the taxes. How much was the annual tax bill? This time, use a 365-day year and exact-day months in your calculations. The buyer's responsibility for the taxes begins on the day of closing.

1. **Write down the formula.** $S = R \times D$

2. **Substitute.** First add up the number of days that the seller is responsible for.

$$
\begin{array}{ll}
31\ days & January \\
28\ days & February \\
+\ 20\ days & March \\
\hline
79\ days &
\end{array}
$$

   Substitute the seller's share and the number of days into the formula: *$663.60 = R × 79.*

3. **Calculate.** Rearrange the formula to isolate R, the unknown quantity: *$663.60 ÷ 79 = $8.40 Per diem.*

   The per diem rate is $8.40. Multiply that by 365 to arrive at the annual tax amount.

$$
\begin{array}{ll}
365 & Days \\
\times\ \$8.40 & Per\ diem \\
\hline
\$3,066 & Annual\ taxes
\end{array}
$$

The annual taxes were $3,066.

Insurance Prorations

A seller is entitled to a refund from the hazard insurance company for any prepaid insurance coverage extending beyond the closing date.

Example: The Morgans are selling their house, and the transaction is closing on May 12. They paid an annual hazard insurance premium of $810 that provides coverage through the end of October. If the insurance company does not charge the sellers for the day of closing, how much of the premium will be refunded to them? Base your calculations on a 360-day year.

1. **Calculate the per diem rate** for the insurance, using a 360-day year: *$810 ÷ 360 = $2.25 Per diem.*

2. **Add up the number of days** for which the sellers are owed a refund, using 30-day months.

$$
\begin{array}{ll}
19\ days & May \\
30\ days & June \\
30\ days & July \\
30\ days & August \\
30\ days & September \\
+\ 30\ days & October \\
\hline
169\ days &
\end{array}
$$

3. **Substitute** the rate and number of days into the formula ($S = R \times D$), then calculate.

$$
\begin{array}{rl}
169 & Days \\
\times\ \$2.25 & Per\ diem \\
\hline
\$380.25 & Credit\ to\ seller
\end{array}
$$

The insurance company will refund $380.25 to the sellers.

Rent Prorations

If the property being sold is rental property, the seller will owe the buyer a pro-rated share of any rent that has been paid in advance.

Example: A ten-unit apartment building is being sold, with the closing scheduled for April 23. Four of the units rent for $1,500 per month, and the other six rent for $1,200 per month. All of the tenants paid their April rent on time. What share of the prepaid rents will the seller owe the buyer at closing?

1. **Determine the total amount** of rent owed for April.

   $1,500 \times 4 = $6,000$

   $1,200 \times 6 = $7,200$

   $6,000 + $7,200 = $13,200$

2. **Calculate the per diem rate** for the month of April: $13,200 \div 30 = $440 Per diem.

3. **Determine the number of days** of rent the buyer is entitled to, beginning on the closing date. April 23 through April 30 is eight days.

4. **Substitute** and **calculate**.

$$
\begin{array}{rl}
\$440 & Per\ diem \\
\times\ 8 & Days \\
\hline
\$3,520 & Prorated\ rent
\end{array}
$$

The seller will owe the buyer $3,520 in prepaid rents at closing.

Mortgage Interest Prorations

Two different types of mortgage interest prorations are necessary in most transactions, one for the seller and one for the buyer. The seller typically owes a final interest payment on the loan he is paying off.

Example: The remaining balance on the seller's mortgage is $317,550, and the interest rate is 8%. The closing date is set for July 6. Because mortgage interest is paid in arrears, the mortgage payment that the seller paid on July 1 covers the interest that accrued during June. At closing, the seller owes the lender interest covering July 1 through the closing date. How much will that interest payment be? Base your calculations on a calendar year.

1. First calculate the annual interest, using the percentage formula.

   a) **Write down the formula.** *Payment = Loan balance × Interest*

   b) **Substitute.** *P = $317,550 × .08*

c)   **Calculate**.

> $317,550   Loan amount
> × .08   Interest rate
> _____
> $25,404   Annual interest

2. Next, find the per diem rate of the expense. Divide the annual rate by 365: *$25,404 ÷ 365 = $69.60 Per diem.*

3. Determine the number of days the seller owes interest for. The lender will charge the seller interest for the day of closing. Thus, the seller owes interest for six days, from July 1 through July 6.

4. Finally, substitute the numbers into the proration formula $(S = R × D)$ and calculate.

> $69.60   Per diem
> × 6   Days
> _____
> $417.60   Final interest payment

At closing, the seller will be required to make a final interest payment of $417.60.

The buyer also owes some mortgage interest at closing. This is prepaid interest (interim interest) on the buyer's new loan. Prepaid interest covers the closing date through the last day of the month in which closing takes place.

Example: The principal amount of the buyer's new loan is $230,680. The interest rate is 8%. The transaction closes on June 22. How much prepaid interest will the buyer's lender require the buyer to pay at closing? Base your calculations on a 365-day year.

1. Use the percentage formula to calculate the annual amount of interest.

   a)   **Write down the formula**. *Payment = Loan balance × Interest rate*

   b)   **Substitute**. *P = $230,680 × 8%*

   c)   **Calculate**. *$230,680 × .08 = $18,454.40*

2. Find the per diem rate of the expense. Divide the annual rate by 365: *$18,454.40 ÷ 365 = $50.56.*

3. Determine the number of days the buyer is responsible for. In prepaid interest prorations, the buyer pays for the day of closing. There are nine days: June 22, 23, 24, 25, 26, 27, 28, 29, and 30.

4. Substitute the daily rate and number of days into the proration formula *(S = R × D)* and calculate.

> $50.56   Per diem
> × 9   Days
> _____
> $455.04   Prepaid interest

The buyer's interest charge would be $455.04.

📖 Chapter Summary

Converting fractions to decimals:
Divide numerator (top number) by denominator (bottom number).

Converting percentages to decimals:
Move decimal point two places to the left and drop the percent sign.

Converting decimals to percentages:
Move decimal point two places to the right and add a percent sign.

Area formula for squares and rectangles:
Area = Length × Width
A = L × W

Area formula for triangles:
Area = ½ Base × Height
A = ½ B × H

Volume formula:
Volume = Length × Width × Height
V = L × W × H

Percentage formula:
Part = Whole × Percentage
P = W × %

Profit or loss formula:
Now = Then × %

Capitalization formula:
Income = Value × Rate
I = V × %

Proration formula:
Share = Daily Rate × Number of Days
S = R × D

1. Find annual or monthly amount;

2. Find daily rate;

3. Determine number of days; and

4. Substitute and calculate.

Chapter Quiz

1. Christine and Tom bought a condo one year ago for $168,500. If property values in their neighborhood are increasing at an annual rate of 7%, what is the current market value of their condo?

   a) $180,295
   b) $184,270
   c) $195,980
   d) $198,893

2. A home just sold for $183,500. The listing firm charged the seller a 6½% commission. The listing firm will pay 50% of that amount to the selling firm, and 25% to the broker who took the listing. How much will the listing broker's share of the commission be?

   a) $11,927
   b) $5,963
   c) $3,642
   d) $2,982

3. A rectangular lot that has a 45-foot frontage and contains 1,080 square yards has a depth of:

   a) 63 feet
   b) 216 feet
   c) 188 feet
   d) 97 feet

4. An acre contains 43,560 square feet. What is the maximum number of lots measuring 50 feet by 100 feet that can be created from a one-acre parcel?

   a) Six
   b) Seven
   c) Eight
   d) Nine

5. Felicia sold a client's building for $480,000 and received a commission of $33,600. What was her commission rate?

   a) 6.5%
   b) 7%
   c) 7.5%
   d) 8%

6. Jake bought a lot for $5,000 and later sold it for $8,000. What was his percentage of profit?

   a) 60%
   b) 75%
   c) 80%
   d) 85%

7. Diane wants to purchase an income property that has an annual net income of $16,000. If she wants at least an 8% return on her investment, what is the most she should pay for the property?

   a) $150,000
   b) $175,000
   c) $195,000
   d) $200,000

8. George purchases a building for $85,000. The building generates a yearly net income of $5,100. What is his rate of return?

   a) 5.5%
   b) 6%
   c) 6.5%
   d) 7%

9. How many square yards are there in a rectangle that measures 75 × 30 feet?

   a) 6,750
   b) 2,250
   c) 750
   d) 250

10. Mike is purchasing an apartment building. The closing date is September 15, and the seller has already collected the monthly rents in the amount of $13,960 for September. At closing, the seller will have to pay Mike a prorated share of the September rents, which will amount to approximately:

    a) $612
    b) $931
    c) $7,445
    d) $9,035

11. A triangular lot has a 40-foot base and a 30-foot height. What is the area of the lot?

   a) 500 square feet

   b) 600 square feet

   c) 750 square feet

   d) 650 square feet

12. What is the decimal equivalent of five-eighths ($5/8$)?

   a) .625

   b) .0825

   c) 1.58

   d) 1.60

13. Kay has obtained a $112,000 loan at 8.5% interest, as secondary financing to help with the purchase of a home. At closing, the lender will require her to prepay interest for April 26 through April 30. Assuming that the closing agent uses a 365-day year for the proration, how much will that prepaid interest amount to?

   a) $64.35

   b) $104.32

   c) $130.40

   d) $1,403.84

14. The Binghams are selling their house and paying off the mortgage at closing. The remaining principal balance on the mortgage at closing will be $168,301.50. They will also have to pay interest that accrued over the 7-day period between their last mortgage payment and the closing date. If the annual interest rate on the Binghams' mortgage was 10%, how much will they have to pay in interest at closing? (Use a 365-day year for the proration.)

   a) $85.21

   b) $322.77

   c) $409.86

   d) $694.41

15. Carol has just paid $460,000 for a building that will bring her a 9.75% return on her investment. What is the building's annual net income?

   a) $34,965

   b) $36,750

   c) $41,220

   d) $44,850

👉 Answer Key

1. a) The current market value of Christine and Tom's condo is approximately $180,295. The question asks you to determine the current value of the condo based on its earlier value, so the applicable formula is *Then* × *%* = *Now*. Here, the value has increased by 7%, so the appropriate percentage is 107% (100% + 7%), or 1.07 (as a decimal). *$168,500 × 1.07 = $180,295.*

2. d) The listing broker will get $2,982. This is a percentage question with two parts. First multiply the sales price by the listing firm's commission rate to determine the full commission. *$183,500 × .065 = $11,927.50.* Then multiply that number by 25% to determine the listing broker's share: *$11,927.50 × .25 = $2,981.88.*

3. b) The depth of the lot is 216 feet. The question asks you to determine the length of one of the sides of a rectangle, so the applicable formula is *Area = Length × Width*, *A = L × W*.

   First convert the area from square yards to square feet, so that it is in the same unit of measurement as the frontage. A square yard is a square that measures 3 feet on each side, or 9 square feet (3 × 3 = 9). Thus, 1,080 square yards is 9,720 square feet (*1,080 × 9 = 9,720*).

   Now substitute the numbers you have into the formula. *9,720 = 45 × L.* Isolate the unknown quantity, *L*, by changing to another version of the same formula: *L = 9,720 ÷ 45.*

   Divide the area, 9,720 square feet, by the width, 45 feet, to determine the length of the rectangle: *9,720 ÷ 45 = 216 feet.*

4. c) There are eight 50′ × 100′ lots in an acre, with one somewhat smaller lot left over. Use the area formula to determine the area of a 50′ × 100′ lot. *A = 50 × 100 = 5,000 square feet.* Thus, each lot will have an area of 5,000 square feet. Now divide the total number of square feet in the acre by the area of each lot: *43,560 ÷ 5,000 = 8.71.*

5. b) Felicia's commission rate was 7%. Use the percentage formula, *Part = Whole × Percentage, P = W × %.* You know the part ($33,600) and the total ($480,000), so switch the formula to isolate the percentage, then substitute and calculate.

   P ÷ W = %

   $33,600 ÷ $480,000 = %

   $33,600 ÷ $480,000 = .07

   Thus, the commission rate was 7%.

6. a) Jake's profit on the sale of the lot was 60%. The question asks you to determine what percentage of the original price (the *Then* value) the sales price (the *Now* value) represents. So use the formula *Now = Then × %*, switching it around to isolate the unknown quantity, the percentage:

   Now ÷ Then = %

   $8,000 ÷ $5,000 = 1.60 or 160%

   The *Now* value is 160% of the *Then* value—in other words, 60% more than the *Then* value. Thus, Jake's profit on the sale was 60%.

7. d)   Diane could pay $200,000 for the property and get an 8% return on that investment. This is a capitalization problem, so use the capitalization formula, *Income = Rate × Value, I = R × V*. You know the net income ($16,000) and the capitalization rate (8%), so switch the formula to isolate the unknown quantity, V:

$I \div R = V$

$16,000 ÷ .08 = $200,000

8. b)   George has a 6% return on his investment. This problem calls for the capitalization formula again, but this time it's the rate that is unknown. Switch the formula to isolate the rate, R:

$I \div V = R$

$5,100 ÷ $85,000 = .06 = 6%

9. d)   There are 250 square yards in a 75′ × 30′ rectangle. The area formula, *A = L × W,* will give you the area in square feet: *75 × 30 = 2,250 square feet*. Then you must convert that figure to square yards. There are 9 square feet in a square yard, so divide 2,250 by 9: *2,250 ÷ 9 = 250 square yards*.

10. c)   Mike, the buyer, is entitled to approximately $7,445 in rent for the period from the closing date through September 30. The proration formula is *Share = Rate × Days, S = R × D.* First determine the per diem rate for the rents by dividing the total amount by the number of days in the month: *$13,960 ÷ 30 = $465.33*. Next, determine the number of days for which the buyer is entitled to the rent: September 15 through 30 is 16 days. Finally, multiply the rate by the number of days to find the buyer's share: *$465.33 × 16 = $7,445*.

11. b)   The area of the lot is 600 square feet. Since the lot is triangular, the appropriate area formula is *Area = ½ Base × Height, A = ½ B × H*. Here, the base is 40 feet, so ½ the base is 20 feet. *20 feet × 30 feet = 600 square feet*.

12. a)   The decimal equivalent of ⁵⁄₈ is .625. To determine this, divide the numerator of the fraction (the top number, 5) by the denominator (the bottom number, 8). *5 ÷ 8 = .625*.

13. c)   The prepaid interest will be $130.40. First determine the annual interest, using the percentage formula: *Part = Whole × Percentage, P = W × %*. The principal (the whole) is $112,000 and the rate (the percentage) is 8.5%. *$112,000 × .085 = $9,520*. Next, divide the annual interest by 365 to determine the per diem rate. *$9,520 ÷ 365 = $26.08*. Multiply the per diem rate by the number of days for which Kay is responsible for this expense—five days. *$26.08 × 5 = $130.40*.

14. b)   The Binghams will have to pay $322.77 in interest at closing. To find the annual interest amount, use the percentage formula, *P = W × %*. *$168,301.50 × .10 = $16,830.15*. Divide that figure by 365 to determine the per diem rate: *$16,830.15 ÷ 365 = $46.11*. Finally, multiply the per diem rate by the number of days: *$46.11 × 7 days = $322.77*.

15. d)   The building's annual net income is $44,850. Use the capitalization formula, *Income = Rate × Value; .0975 × $460,000 = $44,850*.

The definitions given here explain how the listed terms are used in the real estate field. Some of the terms have additional meanings, which can be found in a standard dictionary.

1031 Exchange—See: Tax-Deferred Exchange.

Abandonment—Failure to occupy and use property, which may result in a loss of rights.

Absolute Fee—See: Fee Simple.

Abstract of Judgment—A document summarizing the essential provisions of a court judgment which, when recorded, creates a lien on the judgment debtor's real property.

Abstract of Title—See: Title, Abstract of.

Abut—To touch, border on, be adjacent to, or share a common boundary with.

Acceleration Clause—A provision in a promissory note or security instrument allowing the lender to declare the entire debt due immediately if the borrower breaches one or more provisions of the loan agreement. Also referred to as a call provision.

Acceptance—1. Agreeing to the terms of an offer to enter into a contract, thereby creating a binding contract. 2. Taking delivery of a deed from the grantor.

Acceptance, Qualified—See: Counteroffer.

Accession—The acquisition of title to additional property by its annexation to real estate already owned. This can be the result of human actions (as in the case of fixtures) or natural processes (such as accretion and reliction).

Accord and Satisfaction—An agreement to accept something different than (and usually less than) what the contract originally called for.

Accretion—A gradual addition to dry land by the forces of nature, as when waterborne sediment is deposited on waterfront property.

Accrued Items of Expense—Expenses that have been incurred but are not yet due or payable; in a settlement statement, the seller's accrued expenses are credited to the buyer.

Acknowledgment—When a person who has signed a document formally declares to an authorized official (usually a notary public) that he signed voluntarily. The official can then attest that the signature is voluntary and genuine.

Acquisition Cost—The amount of money a buyer was required to expend in order to acquire title to a piece of property; in addition to the purchase price, this might include closing costs, legal fees, and other expenses.

Acre—An area of land equal to 43,560 square feet, or 4,840 square yards.

Actual Age—See: Age, Actual.

Actual Authority—See: Authority, Actual.

Actual Eviction—See: Eviction, Actual.

Actual Notice—See: Notice, Actual.

ADA—See: Americans with Disabilities Act.

Addendum—An attachment to a purchase and sale agreement or other contract that contains additional provisions that apply to that transaction.

Adjacent—Nearby, next to, bordering, or neighboring; may or may not be in actual contact.

Adjustable-Rate Mortgage—See: Mortgage, Adjustable-Rate.

Adjusted Basis—For income tax purposes, the initial basis plus capital expenditures, less any depreciation deductions.

Adjustment Period—The interval at which an adjustable-rate mortgage borrower's interest rate or monthly payment is changed.

Administrator—A person appointed by the probate court to manage and distribute the estate of a deceased person, when no executor is named in the will or there is no will.

Ad Valorem—A Latin phrase that means "according to value," used to refer to taxes that are assessed on the value of property.

Adverse Possession—Acquiring title to real property that belongs to someone else by taking possession of it without permission, in the manner and for the length of time prescribed by statute.

Affidavit—A sworn statement made before a notary public (or other official authorized to administer an oath) that has been written down and acknowledged.

Affiliated Licensee—The individual licensee who is licensed under a particular brokerage.

Affirm—1. To confirm or ratify. 2. To make a solemn declaration that is not under oath.

After-Acquired Title—See: Title, After-Acquired.

Age, Actual—The age of a structure from a chronological standpoint (as opposed to its effective age); how many years it has actually been in existence.

Age, Effective—The age of a structure indicated by its condition and remaining usefulness (as opposed to its actual age). Good maintenance may increase a building's effective age, and poor maintenance may decrease it; for example, a 50-year-old home that has been well maintained might have an effective age of 15 years, meaning that its remaining usefulness is equivalent to that of a 15-year-old home.

Age of Majority—See: Majority, Age of.

Agency—A relationship of trust created when one person (the principal) grants another (the agent) authority to represent the principal in dealings with third parties.

Agency, Apparent—When third parties are given the impression that someone who has not been authorized to represent another is that person's agent, or else given the impression that an agent has been authorized to perform acts which are in fact beyond the scope of her authority. Also called ostensible agency.

Agency, Dual—When an agent represents both parties to a transaction, as when a broker represents both the buyer and the seller.

Agency, Exclusive—See: Listing, Exclusive.

Agency, Inadvertent Dual—Providing agency services to one party without disclosing that you already represent the other party; doing this inadvertently creates an agency with both parties.

Agency, Non-—When a licensee limits herself to the role of neutral intermediary in a transaction. Non-agency is typically limited to commercial transactions, but may occur in residential transactions as well.

Agency, Ostensible—See: Agency, Apparent.

Agency Coupled with an Interest—When an agent has a claim against the property that is the subject of the agency, so that the principal cannot revoke the agent's authority.

Agent—A person authorized to represent another (the principal) in dealings with third parties.

Agent, Dual—See: Agency, Dual.

Agent, General—An agent authorized to handle all of the principal's affairs in one area or in specified areas.

Agent, Special—An agent with limited authority to do a specific thing or conduct a specific transaction.

Agent, Universal—An agent authorized to do everything that can be lawfully delegated to a representative.

Agreement—See: Contract.

Air Lot—A parcel of property above the surface of the earth, not containing any land; for example, a condominium unit on the third floor.

Air Rights—The right to undisturbed use and control of the airspace over a parcel of land; may be transferred separately from the land.

Alienation—The transfer of ownership or an interest in property from one person to another, by any means.

Alienation, Involuntary—Transfer of an interest in property against the will of the owner, or without action by the owner, occurring through operation of law, natural processes, or adverse possession.

Alienation, Voluntary—When an owner voluntarily transfers an interest to someone else.

Alienation Clause—A provision in a security instrument that gives the lender the right to declare the entire loan balance due immediately if the borrower sells or otherwise transfers the security property. Also called a due-on-sale clause.

All-Inclusive Trust Deed—See: Mortgage, Wraparound.

Alluvion—The solid material deposited along a river bank or shore by accretion. Also called alluvium.

Amendment—A written modification to a contract that occurs after both parties have signed the document.

Amenities—Features of a property that contribute to the pleasure or convenience of owning it, such as a fireplace, a beautiful view, or its proximity to a good school.

Americans with Disabilities Act—A federal law requiring facilities that are open to the public to ensure accessibility to disabled persons, even if that accessibility requires making architectural modifications. The ADA also requires employers to make reasonable accommodations for disabled employees.

Amortization, Negative—When unpaid interest on a loan is added to the principal balance, increasing the amount owed.

Amortize—To gradually pay off a debt with installment payments that include both principal and interest. See also: Loan, Amortized.

Annexation—Attaching personal property to real property, so that it becomes part of the real property (a fixture) in the eyes of the law.

Annexation, Actual—When personal property is physically attached to real property, so that it becomes part of the real property.

Annexation, Constructive—When personal property becomes associated with real property in such a way that the law treats it as a fixture, even though it is not physically attached; for example, a house key is constructively annexed to the house.

Annual Percentage Rate (APR)—All of the charges that the borrower will pay for the loan (including the interest, loan fee, discount points, and mortgage insurance costs), expressed as an annual percentage of the loan amount.

Annuity—A sum of money received in a series of payments at regular intervals (often annually) over a period of time.

Anticipation, Principle of—An appraisal principle which holds that value is created by the expectation of benefits to be received in the future.

Anticipatory Repudiation—When one party to a contract informs the other before the time set for performance that she does not intend to fulfill the contract.

Antitrust Laws—Laws that prohibit any agreement that has the effect of restraining trade, including conspiracies.

Appeal—When one of the parties to a lawsuit asks a higher court to review the judgment or verdict reached in a lower court.

Appellant—The party who files an appeal because he is dissatisfied with the lower court's decision. Also called the petitioner.

Appellee—In an appeal, the party who did not file the appeal. Also called the respondent.

Apportionment—A division of property (as among tenants in common when the property is sold or partitioned) or liability (as when responsibility for closing costs is allocated between the buyer and seller) into proportionate, but not necessarily equal, parts.

Appraisal—An estimate or opinion of the value of a piece of property as of a particular date. Also called valuation.

Appraiser—One who estimates the value of property, especially an expert qualified to do so by training and experience.

Appreciation—An increase in value; the opposite of depreciation.

Appropriation—Taking property or reducing it to personal possession, to the exclusion of others.

Appropriation, Prior—A system of allocating water rights, under which a person who wants to use water from a certain lake or river is required to apply for a permit; a permit has priority over other permits that are issued later. Compare: Riparian Rights.

Appropriative Rights—The water rights of a person who holds a prior appropriation permit.

Appurtenances—Rights that go along with ownership of a particular piece of property, such as air rights or mineral rights; they are ordinarily transferred with the property, but may, in some cases, be sold separately.

Appurtenances, Intangible—Rights that go with ownership of a piece of property that do not involve physical objects or substances; for example, an access easement (as opposed to mineral rights).

Appurtenant Easement—See: Easement Appurtenant.

APR—See: Annual Percentage Rate.

Area—1. Locale or region. 2. The size of a surface, usually in square units of measure, such as square feet or square miles.

ARM—See: Mortgage, Adjustable-Rate.

Arm's Length Transaction—A transaction in which there is no family or business relationship between the parties. See also: Normal market conditions.

Artificial Person—A legal entity such as a corporation, which the law treats as an individual with legal rights and responsibilities; as distinguished from a natural person, a human being. Sometimes called a legal person.

Assemblage—Combining two or more adjoining properties into one tract. Also called assembly.

Assessment—The valuation of property for purposes of taxation.

Assessor—An official who determines the value of property for taxation.

Asset—Anything of value that a person owns.

Assets, Liquid—Cash and other assets that can be readily turned into cash (liquidated), such as stock.

Assign—To transfer rights (especially contract rights) or interests to another.

Assignee—One to whom rights or interests have been assigned.

Assignment—1. A transfer of contract rights from one person to another. 2. In the case of a lease, when the original tenant transfers her entire leasehold estate to another. Compare: Sublease.

Assignment of Contract and Deed—The instrument used to substitute a new vendor for the original vendor in a land contract.

Assignor—One who has assigned his rights or interest to another.

Assumption—When a buyer takes on personal liability for paying off the seller's existing mortgage or deed of trust.

Assumption Fee—A fee paid to the lender, usually by the buyer, when a mortgage or deed of trust is assumed.

Attachment—Court-ordered seizure of property belonging to a defendant in a lawsuit, so that it will be available to satisfy a judgment if the plaintiff wins. In the case of real property, attachment creates a lien.

Attachments, Manmade—See: Fixture.

Attachments, Natural—Plants growing on a piece of land, such as trees, shrubs, or crops.

Attorney General—The principal legal advisor for state agencies and employees, including the Department of Licensing.

Attorney in Fact—Any person authorized to represent another by a power of attorney; not necessarily a lawyer (an attorney at law).

Attractive Nuisance—A property feature that is dangerous and inviting to children, and a potential source of liability to the property owner.

Auditing—Verification and examination of records, particularly the financial accounts of a business or other organization.

Authority, Actual—Authority actually given to an agent by the principal, either expressly or by implication.

Authority, Apparent—Authority to represent another that someone appears to have and that the principal is estopped from denying, although no actual authority has been granted.

Authority, Implied—An agent's authority to do everything reasonably necessary to carry out the principal's express orders.

Automatic Renewal Clause—A lease provision that ensures automatic renewal of the lease unless the tenant or the landlord gives the other party notice of an intent to terminate.

Avulsion—1. When land is suddenly (not gradually) torn away by the action of water. 2. A sudden shift in a watercourse.

Backup Offer—An offer that's contingent on the failure of an existing sale to close; if a seller accepts a backup offer, the buyer will be able to purchase the property if the first transaction falls through.

Balance, Principle of—An appraisal principle which holds that the maximum value of real estate is achieved when the agents of production (labor, coordination, capital, and land) are in proper balance with each other.

Balance Sheet—See: Financial Statement.

Balloon Payment—A payment on a loan (usually the final payment) that is significantly larger than the regular installment payments.

Bankruptcy—1. When the liabilities of an individual, corporation, or firm exceed the assets. 2. When a court declares an individual, corporation, or firm to be insolvent, so that the assets and debts will be administered under bankruptcy laws.

Base Line—In the rectangular survey system, a main east-west line from which township lines are established. Each principal meridian has one base line associated with it.

Basis—A figure used in calculating a gain on the sale of real estate for federal income tax purposes. Also called cost basis.

Basis, Adjusted—The owner's initial basis in the property, plus capital expenditures for improvements, and minus depreciation or cost recovery deductions.

Basis, Initial—The amount of the owner's original investment in the property; what it cost to acquire the property, which may include closing costs and certain other expenses, as well as the purchase price.

Bearer—Whoever has possession of a negotiable instrument. See: Endorsement in Blank.

Bench Mark—A surveyor's mark on a stationary object at a known point of elevation, used as a reference point in calculating other elevations in a surveyed area; often a metal disk set into cement or rock.

Beneficiary—1. One for whom a trust is created and on whose behalf the trustee administers the trust. 2. The lender in a deed of trust transaction. 3. One entitled to receive real or personal property under a will; a legatee or devisee.

Bequeath—To transfer personal property to another by will.

Bequest—Personal property (including money) that is transferred by will.

Bilateral Contract—See: Contract, Bilateral.

Bill of Sale—A document used to transfer title to personal property from one person to another.

Binder—1. An instrument providing immediate insurance coverage until the regular policy is issued. 2. Any payment or preliminary written statement intended to make an agreement legally binding until a formal contract has been drawn up.

Blind Ad—An advertisement placed by a real estate licensee that does not include the brokerage's name.

Block—In a subdivision, a group of lots surrounded by streets or unimproved land.

Blockbusting—Attempting to induce owners to list or sell their homes by predicting that members of another race or ethnic group, or people suffering from some disability, will be moving into the neighborhood; this violates antidiscrimination laws. Also called panic selling.

Board of Directors—The body responsible for governing a corporation on behalf of the shareholders, which oversees the corporate management.

Bona Fide—In good faith; genuine; not fraudulent.

Bond—1. A written obligation, usually interest-bearing, to pay a certain sum at a specified time. 2. Money put up as a surety, protecting someone against failure to perform, negligent performance, or fraud.

Bond, Completion—A bond posted by a contractor to guarantee that a project will be completed satisfactorily and free of liens. Also called a performance bond.

Boot—In a tax-free exchange, something given or received that is not like-kind property; for example, in an exchange of real property, if one party gives the other cash in addition to real property, the cash is boot.

Boundary—The perimeter or border of a parcel of land; the dividing line between one piece of property and another.

Bounds—Boundaries. See: Metes and Bounds.

Branch Manager—A managing broker who is responsible for the operations of a firm's branch office; the branch manager is authorized to perform branch management duties under the supervision of the firm's designated broker.

Breach—Violation of an obligation, duty, or law; especially an unexcused failure to perform a contractual obligation.

Broker—A licensed individual acting on behalf of a real estate firm to perform real estate brokerage services, under the supervision of a designated and/or managing broker.

Broker, Designated—A person licensed as a managing broker, who has a designated broker endorsement added to his license by the DOL. May represent one or more firms, and will have ultimate responsibility for all firm activities.

Broker, Fee—A designated broker who allows another person to use his endorsement to operate a brokerage. This arrangement violates the real estate license law.

Broker, Managing—A licensed individual with at least three years' experience as a broker who has passed the managing broker exam; a managing broker performs brokerage services for a firm, under the supervision of a designated broker.

Brokerage—See: Real Estate Firm.

Brokerage Fee—The commission or other compensation charged for a real estate brokerage's services.

Broker's Price Opinion—Any oral or written report of property value prepared by a real estate licensee. For example, a competitive market analysis is a broker's price opinion.

Buffer—An undeveloped area of land that separates two areas zoned for incompatible uses.

Building Codes—Regulations that set minimum standards for construction methods and materials.

Building Restrictions—Rules concerning building size, placement, or type; they may be public restrictions (in a zoning ordinance, for example) or private restrictions (CC&Rs, for example).

Bump Clause—A provision in a purchase and sale agreement that allows the seller to keep the property on the market while waiting for a contingency clause to be fulfilled; if the seller receives another good offer in the meantime, he can require the buyer to either waive the contingency clause or terminate the contract.

Bundle of Rights—The rights inherent in ownership of property, including the right to use, lease, enjoy, encumber, will, sell, or do nothing with the property.

Business Opportunity—The purchase, sale, exchange, or lease of a business or a business's goodwill, inventory, or other assets. Generally, agents involved in a business opportunity transaction that includes real estate need a real estate license.

Buydown—When discount points are paid to a lender to reduce (buy down) the interest rate charged to the borrower; especially when a seller pays discount points to help the buyer/borrower qualify for financing.

Call Provision—See: Acceleration Clause.

Cancellation—1. Termination of a contract without undoing acts that have been already performed under the contract. Compare: Rescission. 2. Termination of a license that has not been renewed in the year following its expiration date.

Capacity—The legal ability or competency to perform some act, such as enter into a contract or execute a deed or will.

Capital—Money (or other forms of wealth) available for use in the production of more money.

Capital Assets—Assets held by a taxpayer other than inventory and depreciable real property used in the taxpayer's trade or business. Thus, real property is a capital asset if it is owned for personal use or for investment.

Capital Expenditures—Money spent on improvements and alterations that add to the value of the property and/or prolong its life.

Capital Gain—Profit realized from the sale of a capital asset. If the asset was held for more than one year, it is a long-term capital gain; if the asset was held for one year or less, it is a short-term capital gain.

Capital Improvement—Any improvement that is designed to become a permanent part of the real property or that will have the effect of significantly prolonging the property's life.

Capitalization—A method of appraising real property by converting the anticipated net income from the property into the present value. Also called the income approach to value.

Capitalization Rate—A percentage used in capitalization (Net Income = Capitalization Rate × Value). It is the rate believed to represent the proper relationship between the value of the property and the income it produces; the rate that would be a reasonable return on an investment of the type in question, or the yield necessary to attract investment of capital in property like the subject property.

Capitalize—1. To provide with cash, or capital. 2. To determine the present value of an asset using capitalization.

Capital Loss—A loss resulting from the sale of a capital asset; it may be long-term or short-term, depending on whether the asset was held for more than one year or for one year or less.

Capture, Rule of—A legal rule that grants a landowner the right to all oil and gas produced from wells on her land, even if it migrated from underneath land belonging to someone else.

Carryback Loan—See: Loan, Purchase Money.

Carryover Clause—See: Extender Clause.

Cash Flow—The residual income after deducting from gross income all operating expenses and debt service. Also called spendable income.

Cash on Cash—The ratio between the cash flow received from an investment in the first year and amount of the cash initially invested.

Caveat Emptor—A Latin phrase meaning "Let the buyer beware"; it expresses the idea that a buyer is expected to examine property carefully before buying, instead of relying on the seller to disclose problems. This was once a firm rule of law, but it has lost most of its force, especially in residential real estate transactions.

CC&Rs—A declaration of covenants, conditions, and restrictions; usually recorded by a developer to place restrictions on all lots within a new subdivision.

Cease and Desist Order—An order issued by the Director of the Department of Licensing in a disciplinary action, to stop a violation of the license law.

CERCLA—The Comprehensive Environmental Response, Compensation, and Liability Act; a federal law concerning liability for cleanup of contaminated property.

Certificate of Eligibility—A document issued by the Dept. of Veterans Affairs as evidence of a veteran's eligibility for a VA-guaranteed loan.

Certificate of Occupancy—A statement issued by a local government agency (such as the building department) verifying that a newly constructed building is in compliance with all codes and may be occupied.

Certificate of Sale—The document given to the purchaser at a mortgage foreclosure sale, instead of a deed; replaced with a sheriff's deed only after the redemption period expires.

Chain of Title—See: Title, Chain of.

Change, Principle of—An appraisal principle which holds that property values are in a state of flux, increasing and decreasing in response to social, economic, and governmental forces.

Chattel—An article of personal property.

Chattel Mortgage—See: Mortgage, Chattel.

Chattel Real—Personal property that is closely associated with real property; the primary example is a lease.

Civil Law—The body of law concerned with the rights and liabilities of one individual in relation to another; includes contract law, tort law, and property law. Compare: Criminal Law.

Civil Rights—Fundamental rights guaranteed to individuals by the law. The term is primarily used in reference to constitutional and statutory protections against discrimination or government interference.

Civil Rights Act of 1866—A federal law guaranteeing all citizens the right to purchase, lease, sell, convey, and inherit property, regardless of race or ancestry.

Civil Rights Act of 1964—A federal law prohibiting discrimination on the basis of race, color, national origin, religion, sex, handicap, or familial status in education, employment, access to public accommodations, and in many programs for which the government provides financial assistance.

Civil Rights Act of 1968—The federal Fair Housing Act, which strengthened the protections against discrimination in housing.

Civil Suit—A lawsuit in which one private party sues another private party (as opposed to a criminal suit, in which an individual is sued—prosecuted—by the government).

Civil Wrong—See: Tort.

Client—One who employs a real estate agent, lawyer, or appraiser. A real estate agent's client can be the seller, the buyer, or both, but is usually the seller.

Client Ledger—A separate accounting that a real estate firm must keep for each client that the firm is holding trust funds for. The account entries must include the date of deposit, the amount, and a description.

Closing—The final stage in a real estate transaction, when the seller receives the purchase money, the buyer receives the deed, and title is transferred. Also called settlement.

Closing Costs—Expenses incurred in the transfer of real estate in addition to the purchase price; for example, the appraisal fee, title insurance premium, brokerage commission, and excise tax.

Closing Date—The date on which all the terms of a purchase and sale agreement must be met, or the contract is terminated.

Closing Statement—See: Settlement Statement.

Cloud on Title—A claim, encumbrance, or apparent defect that makes the title to a property unmarketable. See: Title, Marketable.

Code of Ethics—A body of rules setting forth accepted standards of conduct, reflecting principles of fairness and morality; especially one that the members of an organization are expected to follow.

Codicil—An addition to or revision of a will.

Collateral—Anything of value used as security for a debt or obligation.

Collusion—An agreement between two or more persons to defraud another.

Color of Title—See: Title, Color of.

Commercial Bank—A type of financial institution that has traditionally emphasized commercial lending (loans to businesses), but which also makes many residential mortgage loans.

Commercial Paper—Negotiable instruments, such as promissory notes, sold to meet the short-term capital needs of a business.

Commercial Property—Property zoned and used for business purposes, such as a restaurant or an office building; as distinguished from residential or agricultural property.

Commingled Funds—Funds from different sources that are deposited in the same account and thereby lose their separate character; for example, if a spouse deposits cash that is his separate property in an account with funds that are community property, the entire amount may be treated as community property.

Commingling—Illegally mixing trust funds held on behalf of a client with personal funds.

Commission—1. The compensation paid to a brokerage for services in connection with a real estate transaction (usually a percentage of the sales price). 2. A group of people organized for a particular purpose or function; usually a governmental body, such as the Real Estate Commission.

Commission Split—A compensation arrangement in which licensees share a commission paid by the seller.

Commitment—In real estate finance, a lender's promise to make a loan. A loan commitment may be "firm" or "conditional"; a conditional commitment is contingent on something, such as a satisfactory credit report on the borrower.

Common Areas—1. The land and improvements in a condominium, planned unit development, or other housing development that are owned and used collectively by all of the residents, such as parking lots, hallways, and recreational facilities available for common use. Also called common elements. 2. In a building with leased units or spaces, the areas that are available for use by all of the tenants.

Common Elements, Limited—In a condominium, areas outside of the units (such as balconies or assigned parking spaces) that are designated for the use of particular unit owners, rather than all of the residents.

Common Law—1. Early English law. 2. Long-established rules of law based on early English law. 3. Rules of law developed through court decisions, as opposed to statutory law.

Community Property—Property owned jointly by a married couple in Washington and other community property states, as distinguished from each spouse's separate property; generally, any property acquired through the labor or skill of either spouse during marriage.

Co-Mortgagor—Someone (usually a family member) who accepts responsibility for the repayment of a mortgage loan along with the primary borrower, to help the borrower qualify for the loan.

Comparable—A recently sold and similarly situated property that is used as a point of comparison by an appraiser using the sales comparison approach.

Competent—1. Of sound mind, for the purposes of entering a contract or executing an instrument. 2. Both of sound mind and having reached the age of majority.

Competition, Principle of—An appraisal principle which holds that profits tend to encourage competition, and excess profits tend to result in ruinous competition.

Competitive Market Analysis—A comparison of homes that are similar in location, style, and amenities to the subject property, in order to set a realistic listing price. Similar to the sales comparison approach to value.

Completion Bond—See: Bond, Completion.

Compliance Inspection—A building inspection to determine, for the benefit of a lender, whether building codes, specifications, or conditions established after a prior inspection have been met before a loan is made.

Comprehensive Environmental Response, Compensation, and Liability Act—See: CERCLA.

Comprehensive Plan—See: General Plan.

Concurrent Ownership—See: Ownership, Concurrent.

Condemnation—1. Taking private property for public use through the government's power of eminent domain. 2. A declaration that a structure is unfit for occupancy and must be closed or demolished.

Condemnation Appraisal—An estimate of the value of condemned property to determine the amount of just compensation to be paid to the owner.

Condition—1. A provision in a contract that makes the parties' rights and obligations depend on the occurrence (or nonoccurrence) of a particular event. Also called a contingency clause. 2. A provision in a deed that makes title depend on compliance with a particular restriction.

Conditional Commitment—See: Commitment.

Conditional Fee—See: Fee, Qualified.

Conditional Use Permit—A permit that allows a special use, such as a school or hospital, to operate in a neighborhood where it would otherwise be prohibited by the zoning. Also called a special exception permit.

Condition Precedent—An event that must occur before a right or interest will be gained.

Condition Subsequent—An event that will cause a right or interest to be lost if it occurs.

Condominium—Property developed for concurrent ownership, where each co-owner has a separate interest in an individual unit, combined with an undivided interest in the common areas of the property.

Confidential Information—Information from or concerning a principal that was acquired during the course of an agency relationship, that the principal reasonably expects to be kept confidential, that the principal has not disclosed to third parties, that would operate to the detriment of the principal, and that the principal would not be legally obligated to disclose to the other party.

Confirmation of Sale—Court approval of a sale of property by an executor, administrator, or guardian.

Conforming Loan—See: Loan, Conforming.

Conformity, Principle of—An appraisal principle which holds that the maximum value of property is realized when there is a reasonable degree of social and economic homogeneity in the neighborhood.

Conservator—A person appointed by a court to take care of the property of another who is incapable of taking care of it on his own.

Consideration—Anything of value given to induce another to enter into a contract, such as money, goods, services, or a promise. Sometimes called valuable consideration.

Conspiracy—An agreement or plan between two or more persons to perform an unlawful act.

Construction Lien—See: Lien, Construction.

Constructive—Held to be so in the eyes of the law, even if not so in fact. See: Annexation, Constructive; Eviction, Constructive; Notice, Constructive; Severance, Constructive.

Consumer Financial Protection Bureau—A federal agency that enforces a number of consumer protection laws that affect the real estate business, such as the Truth in Lending Act.

Consumer Price Index—An index that tracks changes in the cost of goods and services for a typical consumer. Formerly called the cost of living index.

Consummate—To complete.

Contiguous—Adjacent, abutting, or in close proximity.

Contingency Clause—See: Condition.

Contour—The shape or configuration of a surface. A contour map depicts the topography of a piece of land by means of lines (contour lines) that connect points of equal elevation.

Contract—An agreement between two or more persons to do or not do a certain thing, for consideration.

Contract, Bilateral—A contract in which each party has made a binding promise to perform (as distinguished from a unilateral contract).

Contract, Brokerage and Affiliated Licensee—An employment contract between a brokerage firm and an affiliated licensee, outlining their mutual obligations.

Contract, Conditional Sales—See: Contract, Land.

Contract, Executed—A contract in which both parties have completely performed their contractual obligations.

Contract, Executory—A contract in which one or both parties have not yet completed performance of their obligations.

Contract, Express—A contract that has been put into words, either spoken or written.

Contract, Implied—A contract that has not been put into words, but is implied by the actions of the parties.

Contract, Installment Sales—See: Contract, Land.

Contract, Land—A contract for the sale of real property in which the buyer (the vendee) pays in installments; the buyer takes possession of the property immediately, but the seller (the vendor) retains legal title until the full price has been paid. Also called a conditional sales contract, installment sales contract, real estate contract, or contract for deed.

Contract, Oral—A spoken agreement that has not been written down. Also called a parol contract.

Contract, Parol—See: Contract, Oral.

Contract, Real Estate—1. Any contract pertaining to real estate. 2. A land contract.

Contract, Sales—See: Purchase and Sale Agreement.

Contract, Unenforceable—An agreement that a court would refuse to enforce; for example, because its contents can't be proven or the statute of limitations has run out.

Contract, Unilateral—A contract that is accepted by performance; the offeror has promised to perform her side of the bargain if the other party performs, but the other party has not promised to do so. Compare: Contract, Bilateral.

Contract, Valid—A binding, legally enforceable contract.

Contract, Void—An agreement that is not a valid contract, because it lacks a required element (such as consideration) or is defective in some other respect.

Contract, Voidable—A contract that one of the parties can disaffirm without liability, because of lack of capacity or a negative factor such as fraud or duress.

Contract for Deed—See: Contract, Land.

Contract of Sale—See: Purchase and Sale Agreement.

Contract Rent—See: Rent, Contract.

Contractor—One who contracts to perform labor or supply materials for a construction project, or to do other work for a specified price.

Contractor, Independent—See: Independent Contractor.

Contribution, Principle of—An appraisal principle which holds that the value of real property is greatest when the improvements produce the highest return commensurate with their cost (the investment).

Conventional Financing—See: Loan, Conventional.

Conversion—1. Misappropriating property or funds belonging to another; for example, converting trust funds to one's own use. 2. The process of changing an apartment complex into a condominium or cooperative.

Conveyance—The transfer of title to real property from one person to another by means of a written document, especially a deed.

Cooperating Agent—Any individual agent representing a party to the transaction.

A member of a multiple listing service who attempts to find a buyer for a listing.

Cooperative—A building owned by a corporation or association, where the residents are shareholders in the corporation; each shareholder receives a proprietary lease on an individual unit and the right to use the common areas.

Cooperative Sale—A sale in which the buyer and the seller are brought together by agents working for different brokerages.

Co-Ownership—See: Ownership, Concurrent.

Corner Influence—The increase in a property's value that results from its location on or near a corner, with access and exposure on two streets.

Corporation—An association organized according to certain laws, in which individuals may purchase ownership shares; treated by the law as an artificial person, separate from the individual shareholders.

Corporation, Domestic—A corporation doing business in the state where it was created (incorporated).

Corporation, Foreign—A corporation doing business in one state, but created (incorporated) in another state, or in another country.

Correction Lines—In the rectangular survey system, adjustment lines used to compensate for the curvature of the earth; they occur at 24-mile intervals (every fourth township line), where the distance between range lines is corrected to six miles.

Corrective Maintenance—Ongoing repairs that are made to a building and its equipment in order to restore it to good operating condition.

Correlation—See: Reconciliation.

Cost—The amount paid for anything in money, goods, or services.

Cost, Replacement—In appraisal, the current cost of constructing a building with the same utility as the subject property using modern materials and construction methods.

Cost, Reproduction—In appraisal, the cost of constructing a replica (an exact duplicate) of the subject property, using the same materials and construction methods that were originally used, but at current prices.

Cost Approach to Value—One of the three main methods of appraisal, in which an estimate of the subject property's value is arrived at by estimating the cost of replacing (or reproducing) the improvements, then deducting the estimated accrued depreciation and adding the estimated market value of the land.

Cost Basis—See: Basis.

Cost of Living Index—See: Consumer Price Index.

Cost Recovery Deductions—See: Depreciation Deductions.

Co-Tenancy—See: Ownership, Concurrent.

Counteroffer—A response to a contract offer, changing some of the terms of the original offer; it operates as a rejection of the original offer (not as an acceptance). Also called qualified acceptance.

Course—In a metes and bounds description, a direction, stated in terms of a compass bearing.

Covenant—1. A contract. 2. A promise. 3. A guarantee (express or implied) in a document such as a deed or lease. 4. A restrictive covenant.

Covenant, Restrictive—A promise to do or not do an act relating to real property, especially a promise that runs with the land; usually an owner's promise to not use property in a specified manner.

Covenant Against Encumbrances—In a warranty deed, a promise that the property is not burdened by any encumbrances other than those that are disclosed in the deed.

Covenant of Quiet Enjoyment—A promise that a buyer or tenant's possession will not be disturbed by the previous owner, the lessor, or anyone else making a lawful claim against the property.

Covenant of Right to Convey—In a warranty deed, a promise that the grantor has the legal ability to make a valid conveyance.

Covenant of Seisin—In a warranty deed, a promise that the grantor actually owns the interest he is conveying to the grantee.

Covenant of Warranty—In a warranty deed, a promise that the grantor will defend the grantee's title against claims superior to the grantor's that exist when the conveyance is made.

CPM—Certified Property Manager; a property manager who has satisfied the requirements set by the Institute of Real Estate Management of the National Association of Realtors®.

Credit—A payment receivable (owed to you), as opposed to a debit, which is a payment due (owed by you).

Credit History—An applicant's record of accruing debts and repaying loans, usually expressed in the form of a personal credit report.

Creditor—One who is owed a debt.

Creditor, Secured—A creditor with a security interest in or a lien against specific property; if the debt is not repaid, the creditor can repossess the property or (in the case of real estate) foreclose on the property and collect the debt from the sale proceeds.

Credit Union—A not-for-profit, cooperative depository institution intended to serve members of a particular group or profession, emphasizing small, short-term loans.

Criminal Law—The body of law under which the government can prosecute an individual for crimes, wrongs against society. Compare: Civil Law.

Customer—From the point of view of a listing agent, a prospective property buyer.

Damage Deposit—See: Security Deposit.

Damages—In a civil lawsuit, an amount of money the defendant is ordered to pay the plaintiff.

Damages, Compensatory—Damages awarded to a plaintiff as compensation for injuries (personal injuries, property damage, or financial losses) caused by the defendant's act or failure to act.

Damages, Liquidated—A sum that the parties to a contract agree in advance (at the time the contract is made) will serve as full compensation in the event of a breach.

Damages, Punitive—In a civil lawsuit, an award added to compensatory damages, to punish the defendant for outrageous or malicious conduct and discourage others from similar conduct.

Datum—An artificial horizontal plane of elevation, established in reference to sea level, used by surveyors as a reference point in determining elevation.

Dealer—One who regularly buys and sells real estate in the ordinary course of business.

Dealer Property—Property held for sale to customers rather than long-term investment; a developer's inventory of subdivision lots, for example.

Debit—A charge payable by a party; in a real estate transaction, the purchase price is a debit to the buyer, for example, and the sales commission is a debit to the seller.

Debtor—One who owes money to another.

Debt Service—The amount of money required to make the periodic payments of principal and interest on an amortized debt, such as a mortgage.

Decedent—A person who has died.

Declaration—A written description of a condominium development that addresses various issues, such as designating common areas, how dues are determined, and leasing restrictions.

Declaration of Abandonment—A document recorded by an owner that voluntarily releases a property from homestead protection.

Declaration of Homestead—A recorded document that establishes homestead protection for a property that would not otherwise receive it.

Dedication—A voluntary or involuntary gift of private property for public use; may transfer ownership or simply create an easement.

Dedication, Common Law—Involuntary dedication, resulting from a property owner's acquiescence to public use of her property over a long period. Also called implied dedication.

Dedication, Statutory—A dedication required by law; for example, dedication of property for streets and sidewalks as a prerequisite to subdivision approval.

Deduction—An amount a taxpayer is allowed to subtract from his income before the tax on the income is calculated (as distinguished from a tax credit, which is deducted from the tax owed).

Deed—An instrument which, when properly executed and delivered, conveys title to real property from the grantor to the grantee.

Deed, Administrator's—A deed used by the administrator of an estate to convey property owned by the deceased person to the heirs.

Deed, Bargain and Sale—See: Deed, Special Warranty.

Deed, Correction—A deed used to correct minor mistakes in an earlier deed, such as misspelled names or typographical errors in the legal description. Also called a deed of confirmation or reformation deed.

Deed, General Warranty—A deed in which the grantor warrants the title against defects that might have arisen before or during her period of ownership.

Deed, Gift—A deed that is not supported by valuable consideration; often lists "love and affection" as the consideration.

Deed, Grant—A deed that uses the word "grant" in its words of conveyance and carries certain implied warranties; rarely used in Washington.

Deed, Quitclaim—A deed that conveys any interest in a property that the grantor has at the time the deed is executed, without warranties.

Deed, Reformation—See: Deed, Correction.

Deed, Sheriff's—A deed delivered, on court order, to the holder of a certificate of sale when the redemption period after a mortgage foreclosure has expired.

Deed, Special Warranty—A deed in which the grantor warrants title only against defects that may have arisen during his period of ownership.

Deed, Statutory Warranty—A short form of the general warranty deed, in which the covenants are implied (by the use of language specified in the state statute) rather than spelled out.

Deed, Tax—A deed given to a purchaser of property at a tax foreclosure sale.

Deed, Trust—See: Deed of Trust.

Deed, Trustee's—A deed given to a purchaser of property at a trustee's sale.

Deed, Warranty—1. A general warranty deed. 2. Any type of deed that carries warranties.

Deed, Wild—A deed that won't be discovered in a standard title search, because of a break in the chain of title.

Deed Executed Under Court Order—A deed that is the result of a court action, such as judicial foreclosure or partition.

Deed in Lieu of Foreclosure—A deed given by a borrower to the lender, relinquishing ownership of the security property, to satisfy the debt and avoid foreclosure.

Deed of Confirmation—See: Deed, Correction.

Deed of Reconveyance—The instrument used to release the security property from the lien created by a deed of trust when the debt has been repaid.

Deed of Trust—An instrument that creates a voluntary lien on real property to secure the repayment of a debt, and which includes a power of sale clause permitting nonjudicial foreclosure; the parties are the grantor or trustor (borrower), the beneficiary (the lender), and the trustee (a neutral third party).

Deed Release Provision—See: Release Clause.

Deed Restrictions—Provisions in a deed that restrict use of the property, and which may be either covenants or conditions.

Default—Failure to fulfill an obligation, duty, or promise, as when a borrower fails to make payments, or a tenant fails to pay rent.

Default Judgment—See: Judgment, Default.

Defeasance Clause—A clause in a mortgage, deed of trust, or lease that cancels or defeats a certain right upon the occurrence of a particular event.

Defeasible Fee—See: Fee, Defeasible.

Defendant—1. The person being sued in a civil lawsuit. 2. The accused person in a criminal lawsuit.

Deferred Maintenance—Physical deterioration of a structure caused by postponed maintenance and/or repairs.

Deficiency Judgment—See: Judgment, Deficiency.

Degree—In surveying, a unit of circular measurement equal to $\frac{1}{360}$ of one complete rotation around a point in a plane.

Delegation Agreement—A written agreement in which a designated broker transfers some of her authority and duties to another managing broker, including a branch manager. The agreement doesn't relieve the designated broker of the ultimate responsibility for the delegated function.

Delivery—The legal transfer of a deed from the grantor to the grantee, which results in the transfer of title.

Demand—Desire to own coupled with ability to afford; this is one of the four elements of value, along with scarcity, utility, and transferability.

Density—In a land use law, the number of buildings or occupants per unit of land.

Department of Licensing—The state agency in charge of administering the real estate license law in Washington.

Deposit—Money offered as an indication of commitment or as a protection, and which may be refunded under certain circumstances, such as an earnest money deposit or a tenant's security deposit.

Deposition—The formal, out-of-court testimony of a witness in a lawsuit, taken before trial for possible use later, during the trial; either as part of the discovery process, to determine the facts of the case, or when the witness will not be available during the trial.

Deposit Receipt—See: Purchase and Sale Agreement.

Depreciable Property—In the federal income tax code, property that is eligible for cost recovery deductions, because it will wear out and have to be replaced.

Depreciation—1. A loss in value (caused by deferred maintenance, functional obsolescence, or external obsolescence). 2. For the purposes of income tax deductions, apportioning the cost of an asset over a period of time.

Depreciation, Accrued—Depreciation that has built up or accumulated over a period of time.

Depreciation, Curable—Deferred maintenance and functional obsolescence that would ordinarily be corrected by a prudent owner, because the correction cost could be recovered in the sales price.

Depreciation, Incurable—Deferred maintenance, functional obsolescence, or external obsolescence that is either impossible to correct, or not economically feasible to correct, because the cost could not be recovered in the sales price.

Depreciation Deductions—Under the federal income tax code, deductions from a taxpayer's income to permit the cost of an asset to be recovered; allowed only for depreciable property that is held for the production of income or used in a trade or business. Also called cost recovery deductions.

Dereliction—See: Reliction.

Descent—Acquiring property transferred by intestate succession. A person who receives property by intestate succession is said to receive it by descent.

Designated Broker—See: Broker, Designated.

Detached Residence—A home physically separated from the neighboring home(s), not connected by a common wall.

Developed Land—Land with manmade improvements, such as buildings or roads.

Developer—One who subdivides or improves land to achieve a profitable use.

Development—1. Any development project, such as a new office park. 2. A housing subdivision. 3. In reference to a property's life cycle, the earliest stage, also called integration.

Devise—1. (noun) A gift of real property through a will. 2. (verb) To transfer real property by will. Compare: Bequest; Bequeath; Legacy.

Devisee—Someone who receives title to real property through a will. Compare: Beneficiary; Legatee.

Devisor—A testator who devises real property in her will.

Directional Growth—The direction in which a city's residential neighborhoods are expanding or expected to expand.

Disability—According to the Americans with Disabilities Act and Fair Housing Act, a physical or mental impairment that substantially limits a person in one or more major life activities.

Disaffirm—To ask a court to terminate a voidable contract.

Disbursements—Money paid out or expended.

Disclaimer—A denial of legal responsibility.

Discount—1. (verb) To sell a promissory note at less than its face value. 2. (noun) An amount withheld from the loan amount by the lender when the loan is originated; discount points.

Discount Points—A percentage of the principal amount of a loan, collected by the lender at the time a loan is originated, to give the lender an additional yield.

Discount Rate—The interest rate charged when a member bank borrows money from the Federal Reserve Bank.

Discrimination—Treating people unequally because of their race, religion, sex, national origin, age, or some other characteristic.

Disintegration—In a property's life cycle, the period of decline when the property's present economic usefulness is near an end and constant upkeep is necessary.

Disintermediation—When depositors withdraw their savings deposits from financial institutions (such as savings and loan associations and commercial banks) in order to invest the funds directly.

Distressed Home—A personal residence that is in danger of foreclosure because the owner is delinquent on mortgage or tax payments.

Distressed Property Law—A state law intended to help protect financially distressed homeowners from foreclosure scams.

Domicile—The state where a person has his permanent home.

Double-Entry Bookkeeping—An accounting technique in which an item is entered in the ledger twice, once as a credit and once as a debit; used for settlement statements.

Downpayment—The part of the purchase price of property that the buyer is paying in cash; the difference between the purchase price and the financing.

Downzoning—Rezoning land for a more limited use.

Drainage—A system to draw water off land, either artificially (with pipes) or naturally (such as with a slope).

Dual Agency—See: Agency, Dual.

Due-on-Sale Clause—See: Alienation Clause.

Duplex—A structure that contains two separate housing units, with separate entrances, living areas, baths, and kitchens.

Duress—Unlawful force or constraint used to compel someone to do something (such as sign a contract) against her will.

Dwelling—A building or a part of a building used or intended to be used as living quarters.

Earnest Money—A deposit that a prospective buyer gives the seller as evidence of his good faith intent to complete the transaction.

Earnest Money Agreement—See: Purchase and Sale Agreement.

Easement—An irrevocable right to use some part of another person's real property for a particular purpose.

Easement, Access—An easement that enables the easement holder to reach and/or leave her property (the dominant tenement) by crossing the servient tenement. Also called an easement for ingress and egress.

Easement, Implied—See: Easement by Implication.

Easement, Negative—An easement that prevents the servient tenant from using her own land in a certain way (instead of allowing the dominant tenant to use it); essentially the same thing as a restrictive covenant that runs with the land.

Easement, Positive—An easement that allows the dominant tenant to use the servient tenement in a particular way. This is the standard type of easement (see the first definition of Easement, above); the term "positive easement" is generally only used when contrasting a standard easement with a negative easement.

Easement, Prescriptive—An easement acquired by prescription; that is, by using the property openly and without the owner's permission for the period prescribed by statute.

Easement Appurtenant—An easement that benefits a piece of property, the dominant tenement. Compare: Easement in Gross.

Easement by Express Grant—An easement granted to another in a deed or other document.

Easement by Express Reservation—An easement created in a deed when a landowner is dividing the property, transferring the servient tenement but retaining the dominant tenement; an easement that the grantor reserves for his own use.

Easement by Implication—An easement created by law when a parcel of land is divided, if there has been long-standing, apparent prior use, and it is reasonably necessary for the enjoyment of the dominant tenement.

Easement by Necessity—A special type of easement by implication, created by law even when there has been no prior use, if the dominant tenement would be entirely useless without an easement.

Easement in Gross—An easement that benefits a person instead of a piece of land; there is a dominant tenant, but no dominant tenement. Compare: Easement Appurtenant.

Economic Life—The period during which improved property will yield a return over and above the rent due to the land itself; also called the useful life.

Economic Obsolescence—See: Obsolescence, External.

Economic Rent—See: Rent, Economic.

Effective Age—See: Age, Effective.

Egress—A means of exiting, a way to leave a property; the opposite of ingress. The terms ingress and egress are most commonly used in reference to an access easement.

EIS (Environmental Impact Statement)—A written report analyzing a construction project's impact on the environment; required by Washington's State Environmental Policy Act (SEPA) for projects that are likely to have a significant impact on the environment.

Ejectment—A legal action to recover possession of real property from someone who is not legally entitled to possession of it; an eviction.

Elements of Comparison—In the sales comparison approach to appraisal, considerations taken into account in selecting comparables and comparing comparables to the subject property; they include date of sale, location, physical characteristics, and terms of sale.

Emblements—Crops that are produced annually through the labor of the cultivator, such as wheat.

Emblements, Doctrine of—The legal rule that gives an agricultural tenant the right to enter the land to harvest crops after the lease ends.

Eminent Domain—The government's constitutional power to take (condemn) private property for public use, as long as the owner is paid just compensation.

Employee—Someone who works under the direction and control of another. Compare: Independent Contractor.

Encroachment—A physical intrusion onto neighboring property, usually due to a mistake regarding the location of the boundary.

Encumber—To place a lien or other encumbrance against the title to a property.

Encumbrance—A nonpossessory interest in real property; a right or interest held by someone other than the property owner, which may be a lien, an easement, a profit, or a restrictive covenant.

Encumbrance, Financial—A lien.

Encumbrance, Nonfinancial—An easement, a profit, or a restrictive covenant.

Endorsement—When the payee on a negotiable instrument (such as a check or promissory note) assigns the right to payment to another, by signing the back of the instrument.

Enjoin—To prohibit an act, or command performance of an act, by court order; to issue an injunction.

EPA—The federal Environmental Protection Agency.

Equal Credit Opportunity Act—A federal law prohibiting providers of credit from discriminating based on race, color, religion, national origin, sex, marital status, age, or because the applicant receives public assistance.

Equilibrium—In the life cycle of a property, a period of stability, during which the property undergoes little, if any, change.

Equitable Interest or Title—See: Title, Equitable.

Equitable Redemption Period—The period between the initial complaint and the sale of a foreclosed property, during which time a borrower may redeem the property by paying the amount of the debt plus costs.

Equitable Remedy—In a civil lawsuit, a judgment granted to the plaintiff that is something other than an award of money (damages); an injunction, rescission, and specific performance are examples.

Equity—1. An owner's unencumbered interest in her property; the difference between the value of the property and the liens against it. 2. A judge's power to soften or set aside strict legal rules, to bring about a fair and just result in a particular case.

Erosion—Gradual loss of soil due to the action of water or wind.

Escalation Clause—A clause in a contract or mortgage that provides for payment or interest adjustments (usually increases) if specified events occur, such as a change in the property taxes or in the prime interest rate. Also called an escalator clause.

Escheat—The reversion of property to the state after no one with title to the property claims it. (For example, this can happen when a property owner dies without leaving a will and without heirs.)

Escrow—An arrangement in which something of value (such as money or a deed) is held on behalf of the parties to a transaction by a disinterested third party (an escrow agent) until specified conditions have been fulfilled.

Escrow Agent—1. A third party who holds money and documents in trust and carries out the closing process. 2. A company (not a natural person) that is licensed to engage in the escrow business.

Escrow Instructions—A written document that tells the escrow agent how to proceed and states the conditions each party must fulfill before the transaction can close.

Escrow Officer—A person licensed to work for an escrow agent.

Estate—1. An interest in real property that is or may become possessory; either a freehold or a leasehold. 2. The property left by someone who has died.

Estate, Fee Simple—See: Fee Simple.

Estate, Periodic—See: Tenancy, Periodic.

Estate at Sufferance—See: Tenancy at Sufferance.

Estate at Will—See: Tenancy at Will.

Estate for Life—See: Life Estate.

Estate for Years—A leasehold estate set to last for a definite period (one week, three years, etc.), after which it terminates automatically. Also called a tenancy for years or term tenancy.

Estate of Inheritance—An estate that can pass to the holder's heirs; especially a fee simple.

Estoppel—A legal doctrine that prevents a person from asserting rights or facts that are inconsistent with his earlier actions or statements.

Estoppel Certificate—A document that prevents a person who signs it from later asserting facts different from those stated in the document. In connection with a mortgage, for example, the term may refer to a document issued by the lender stating the unpaid principal balance of the loan, its interest rate, and so on. Also called an estoppel letter.

Et Al.—Abbreviation for the Latin phrase "et alia" or "et alii," meaning "and another" or "and others."

Ethics—A system of accepted principles or standards of moral conduct. See: Code of Ethics.

Eviction—Dispossession or expulsion of someone from real property.

Eviction, Actual—Physically forcing someone off of real property (or preventing them from re-entering), or using the legal process to make them leave. Compare: Eviction, Constructive.

Eviction, Constructive—When a landlord's act (or failure to act) interferes with the tenant's quiet enjoyment of the property, or makes the property unfit for its intended use, to such an extent that the tenant is forced to move out.

Eviction, Self-Help—When a landlord uses physical force, a lock-out, or a utility shut-off to evict a tenant, instead of the legal process. This is generally illegal.

Excess Land—That portion of a parcel of land that does not add to its value. For example, where the value of a property lies primarily in its frontage, additional depth beyond the normal lot size would not increase the property's value.

Exchange—See: Tax Deferred Exchange.

Excise Tax—See: Tax, Excise.

Exclusive Listing—See: Listing, Exclusive.

Exculpatory Clause—A clause in a contract that relieves one party of liability for certain defaults or problems; such provisions are not always enforceable.

Execute—1. To sign an instrument and take any other steps (such as acknowledgment) that may be necessary to its validity. 2. To perform or complete. See: Contract, Executed.

Execution—The legal process in which a court orders an official (such as the sheriff) to seize and sell the property of a judgment debtor to satisfy a lien.

Executor—A person named in a will to carry out its provisions.

Exemption—A provision holding that a law or rule does not apply to a particular person or group; for example, a person entitled to a tax exemption is not required to pay the tax.

Exit Interview—A final meeting between an agent and a representative of the firm, when the affiliated relationship is terminated; designed to gather feedback for the firm and achieve closure of the relationship.

Expenses, Fixed—Recurring property expenses, such as general real estate taxes and hazard insurance. In the property management context, the term may refer to a property expense that remains the same regardless of rental income.

Expenses, Maintenance—Cleaning, supplies, utilities, tenant services, and administrative costs for income-producing property.

Expenses, Operating—For income-producing property, the fixed expenses, maintenance expenses, and reserves for replacement; does not include debt service.

Expenses, Variable—Expenses incurred in connection with property that do not occur on a set schedule, such as the cost of repairing a roof damaged in a storm.

Express—Stated in words, whether spoken or written. Compare: Implied.

Extender Clause—A clause in a listing agreement providing that for a specified period after the listing expires, the brokerage will still be entitled to a commission if the property is sold to someone the brokerage dealt with during the listing term. Also called a safety clause or carryover clause.

External Obsolescence—See: Obsolescence, External.

Failure of Purpose—When the intended purpose of an agreement or arrangement can no longer be achieved; in most cases, this releases the parties from their obligations.

Fair Credit Reporting Act—A federal law requiring disclosure if a loan is rejected based on adverse information found in an applicant's credit history; the act also allows consumers to receive periodic free credit reports and to challenge incorrect information in credit reports.

Fair Housing Act—A federal law prohibiting discrimination in the sale or lease of residential property on the basis of race, color, religion, sex, national origin, handicap, or familial status.

Fairness in Lending Act—A Washington state law that prohibits redlining.

Fannie Mae—Popular name for the Federal National Mortgage Association (FNMA).

Feasibility Study—A cost-benefit analysis of a proposed project, often required by lenders before they make a loan commitment.

Fed—The Federal Reserve.

Federal Reserve System—The government body that regulates commercial banks, and that implements monetary policy in an attempt to control the national economy.

Fee—See: Fee Simple.

Fee, Defeasible—See: Fee, Qualified.

Fee, Qualified—A fee simple estate that is subject to termination if a certain condition is not met or if a specified event occurs. It may be a fee simple determinable or a fee simple subject to condition subsequent. Also called a conditional fee or defeasible fee.

Fee Broker—See: Broker, Fee.

Fee Simple—The highest and most complete form of ownership, which is of potentially infinite duration. Also called a fee or a fee simple absolute.

Fee Simple Determinable—A qualified fee that ends automatically, without legal action by the grantor, if the condition is violated or the terminating event occurs.

Fee Simple Subject to a Condition Subsequent—A qualified fee that terminates only if the grantor takes legal action to terminate it after the specified condition has come to pass.

FHA—Federal Housing Administration. See also: Loan, FHA.

FHFA—The Federal Housing Finance Agency. The FHFA regulates Fannie Mae and Freddie Mac.

Fidelity Bond—A bond to cover losses resulting from the dishonesty of an employee.

Fiduciary Relationship—A relationship of trust and confidence, where one party owes the other (or both parties owe each other) loyalty and a higher standard of good faith than is owed to third parties. For example, an agent is a fiduciary in relation to the principal; spouses are fiduciaries in relation to one another.

Finance Charge—Any charge a borrower is assessed, directly or indirectly, in connection with a loan. See also: Total Finance Charge.

Financial Statement—A summary of facts showing the financial condition of an individual or a business, including a detailed list of assets and liabilities. Also called a balance sheet.

Financing Statement—A brief instrument that is recorded to perfect and give constructive notice of a creditor's security interest in an article of personal property.

Finder's Fee—A referral fee paid to someone for directing a buyer or a seller to a real estate agent.

Firm Commitment—See: Commitment.

FIRPTA—The Foreign Investment in Real Property Tax Act; this federal law requires withholding funds from a sale of real property when the seller is not a U.S. citizen or a resident alien, in order to prevent tax evasion.

First Lien Position—The position held by a mortgage or deed of trust that has higher lien priority than any other mortgage or deed of trust against the property.

First Refusal, Right of—See: Right of First Refusal.

Fiscal Policy—The federal government's actions in raising revenue (through taxation), spending money, and managing its debt.

Fiscal Year—Any 12-month period used as a business year for accounting, tax, and other financial purposes, as opposed to a calendar year.

Fixed Disbursement Plan—A construction financing arrangement that calls for the loan proceeds to be disbursed in a series of predetermined installments at various stages of the construction.

Fixed Expense—See: Expenses, Fixed.

Fixed-Rate Loan—See: Loan, Fixed-Rate.

Fixed Term—A period of time that has a definite beginning and ending.

Fixture—An item that used to be personal property but has been attached to or closely associated with real property in such a way that it has legally become part of the real property. See: Annexation, Actual; Annexation, Constructive.

Foreclosure—When a lienholder causes property to be sold against the owner's wishes, so that the unpaid lien can be satisfied from the sale proceeds.

Foreclosure, Judicial—1. The sale of property pursuant to court order to satisfy a lien. 2. A lawsuit filed by a mortgagee or deed of trust beneficiary to foreclose on the security property when the borrower has defaulted.

Foreclosure, Nonjudicial—Foreclosure by a trustee under the power of sale clause in a deed of trust.

Foreign Investment in Real Property Tax Act—See: FIRPTA.

Forfeiture—Loss of a right or something else of value as a result of failure to perform an obligation or fulfill a condition.

For Sale by Owner (FSBO)—A property that is being sold by the owner without the help of a real estate agent.

Franchise—A right granted by a business to use its trade name and procedures in conducting business.

Fraud—An intentional or negligent misrepresentation or concealment of a material fact, which is relied upon by another, who is induced to enter a transaction and harmed as a result.

Fraud, Actual—Deceit or misrepresentation with the intention of cheating or defrauding another.

Fraud, Constructive—A breach of duty that misleads the person the duty was owed to, without an intention to deceive; for example, if a seller gives a buyer inaccurate information about the property without realizing that it is false, that may be constructive fraud.

Freddie Mac—Popular name for the Federal Home Loan Mortgage Corporation (FHLMC).

Free and Clear—Ownership of real property completely free of any liens.

Freehold—A possessory interest in real property that has an indeterminable duration; it can be either a fee simple or a life estate. Someone who has a freehold estate has title to the property (as opposed to someone with a leasehold estate, who is only a tenant).

Frontage—The distance a property extends along a street or a body of water; the distance between the two side boundaries at the front of the lot.

Front Foot—A measurement of property for sale or valuation, with each foot of frontage presumed to extend the entire depth of the lot.

Functional Obsolescence—See: Obsolescence, Functional.

Gain—Under the federal income tax code, that portion of the proceeds from the sale of a capital asset, such as real estate, that is recognized as taxable profit.

Garnishment—A legal process by which a creditor gains access to the personal property or funds of a debtor that are in the hands of a third party. For example, if the debtor's wages are garnished, the employer is required to turn over part of each paycheck to the creditor.

General Agent—See: Agent, General.

General Lien—See: Lien, General.

General Plan—A comprehensive, long-term plan of development for a community, which is implemented by zoning and other laws. Also called a comprehensive plan or master plan.

Gift Funds—Money that a relative (or other third party) gives to a buyer who otherwise would not have enough cash to close the transaction.

Ginnie Mae—Popular name for the Government National Mortgage Association (GNMA).

Good Faith Estimate (GFE)—RESPA requires loan originators to disclose accurate estimates of anticipated closing costs, using a standard GFE form published by HUD.

Goodwill—An intangible asset of a business resulting from a good reputation with the public, serving as an indication of future return business.

Government Lot—In the rectangular survey system, a parcel of land that is not a regular section (one mile square), because of the convergence of range lines, or because of a body of water or some other obstacle; assigned a government lot number.

Government Survey System—See: Rectangular Survey System.

Grant—To transfer or convey an interest in real property by means of a written instrument.

Grantee—One who receives a grant of real property.

Granting Clause—Words in a deed that indicate the grantor's intent to transfer an interest in property.

Grantor—One who grants an interest in real property to another.

Gross Income Multiplier—A figure which is multiplied by a rental property's gross income to arrive at an estimate of the property's value. Also called a gross rent multiplier.

Gross Income Multiplier Method—A method of appraising residential property by reference to its rental value. Also called the gross rent multiplier method.

Gross Rent Multiplier—See: Gross Income Multiplier.

Group Boycott—An agreement between two or more real estate agents to exclude other agents or firms from equal participation in real estate activities.

Growth Management Act—A Washington state law aimed at limiting sprawl and concentrating growth in existing urban areas.

Guardian—A person appointed by a court to administer the affairs of a minor or an incompetent person.

Guide Meridians—See: Meridians, Guide.

Habendum Clause—A clause included after the granting clause in many deeds; it begins "to have and to hold" and describes the type of estate the grantee will hold.

Habitability, Implied Warranty of—A warranty implied by law in every residential lease, that the property is fit for habitation.

Heir—Someone entitled to inherit another's property under the laws of intestate succession.

Heirs and Assigns—A phrase used in legal documents to cover all successors to a person's interest in property; assigns are successors who acquire title in some manner other than inheritance, such as by deed.

Highest and Best Use—The use which, at the time of appraisal, is most likely to produce the greatest net return from the property over a given period of time.

Historical Rent—See: Rent, Contract.

Holder in Due Course—A person who obtains a negotiable instrument for value, in good faith, without notice that it is overdue or notice of any defenses against it.

Home Mortgage Disclosure Act—A federal law requiring institutional lenders to make annual disclosures of all mortgage loans made, as a means of enforcing prohibitions against redlining.

Homeowners Association—A nonprofit association made up of homeowners in a subdivision, responsible for enforcing the CC&Rs and managing other community affairs.

Homestead—An owner-occupied dwelling, together with any appurtenant outbuildings and land.

Homestead Law—A state law that provides limited protection against creditors' claims for homestead property.

HUD—The U.S. Department of Housing and Urban Development.

Hypothecate—To make property security for an obligation without giving up possession of it (as opposed to pledging, which involves surrender of possession).

Implied—Not expressed in words, but understood from actions or circumstances. Compare: Express.

Impound Account—A bank account maintained by a lender for payment of property taxes and insurance premiums on the security property; the lender requires the borrower to make regular deposits, and pays the expenses out of the account. Also called a reserve account.

Improvements—Manmade additions to real property.

Improvements, Misplaced—Improvements that do not fit the most profitable use of the site; they can be overimprovements or underimprovements.

Imputed Knowledge—A legal doctrine stating that a principal is considered to have notice of information that the agent has, even if the agent never passed that information on to the principal. Washington does not apply this rule in the real estate context.

Income, Disposable—Income remaining after income taxes have been paid.

Income, Effective Gross—A measure of a rental property's capacity to generate income; calculated by subtracting a vacancy factor from the economic rent (potential gross income).

Income, Gross—A property's total income before making any deductions (for bad debts, vacancies, operating expenses, etc.).

Income, Net Operating—The income that is capitalized to estimate the property's value; calculated by subtracting the property's operating expenses (fixed expenses, maintenance expenses, and reserves for replacement) from the effective gross income. Also called net income.

Income, Potential Gross—A property's economic rent; the income it could earn if it were available for lease in the current market.

Income, Residual—The amount of income that an applicant for a VA loan has left over after taxes, recurring obligations, and the proposed housing expense have been deducted from his gross monthly income.

Income, Spendable—The income that remains after deducting operating expenses, debt service, and income taxes from a property's gross income. Also called net spendable income or cash flow.

Income Approach to Value—One of the three main methods of appraisal, in which an estimate of the subject property's value is based on the net income it produces; also called the capitalization method or investor's method of appraisal.

Income Property—Property that generates rent or other income for the owner, such as an apartment building. In the federal income tax code, it is referred to as property held for the production of income.

Income Ratio—A standard used in qualifying a buyer for a loan, to determine whether she has sufficient income; the buyer's debts and proposed housing expense should not exceed a specified percentage of her income.

Incompetent—Not legally competent; not of sound mind.

Independent Contractor—A person who contracts to do a job for another, but retains control over how he will carry out the task, rather than following detailed instructions. Compare: Employee.

Index—A published statistical report that indicates changes in the cost of money; used as the basis for interest rate adjustments in an ARM.

Index, Tract—An index of recorded documents in which all documents that carry a particular legal description are grouped together.

Indexes, Grantor/Grantee—Indexes of recorded documents maintained by the recorder, with each document listed in alphabetical order according to the last name of the grantor (in the grantor index) and grantee (in the grantee index); the indexes list the recording number of each document, so that it can be located in the public record.

Ingress—A means of entering a property; the opposite of egress. The terms ingress and egress are most commonly used in reference to an access easement.

In-House Sale—A sale in which the buyer and the seller are brought together by agents working for the same brokerage.

Injunction—A court order prohibiting someone from performing an act, or commanding performance of an act.

Installment Note—See: Note, Installment.

Installment Sale—Under the federal income tax code, a sale in which less than 100% of the sales price is received in the year the sale takes place.

Instrument—A legal document, usually one that transfers title (such as a deed), creates a lien (such as a mortgage), or establishes a right to payment (such as a promissory note or contract).

Insurance, Errors and Omissions—Insurance coverage that will pay for harm caused by an agent's (or firm's) unintentional mistake or negligence.

Insurance, Hazard—Insurance against damage to real property caused by fire, flood, theft, or other mishap. Also called casualty insurance.

Insurance, Homeowner's—Insurance against damage to the real property and the homeowner's personal property.

Insurance, Industrial—See: Workers' Compensation.

Insurance, Liability—Insurance coverage that will pay for physical harm to a person or property.

Insurance, Mortgage—Insurance that protects a lender against losses resulting from the borrower's default.

Insurance, Mutual Mortgage—The mortgage insurance provided by the FHA to lenders who make loans through FHA programs.

Insurance, Private Mortgage (PMI)—Insurance provided by private companies to conventional lenders for loans with loan-to-value ratios over 80%.

Insurance, Title—Insurance that protects against losses resulting from undiscovered title defects. An owner's policy protects the buyer, while a mortgagee's policy protects the lien position of the buyer's lender.

Insurance, Title, Extended Coverage—Title insurance that covers problems that should be discovered by an inspection of the property (such as encroachments and adverse possession), in addition to the problems covered by standard coverage policies. An extended coverage policy is sometimes referred to as an ALTA (American Land Title Association) policy.

Insurance, Title, Homeowner's Coverage—Title insurance that covers most of the title problems that an extended coverage policy covers, as well as some additional items, such as violations of restrictive covenants.

Insurance, Title, Standard Coverage—Title insurance that protects against latent title defects (such as forged deeds) and undiscovered recorded encumbrances, but does not protect against problems that would only be discovered by an inspection of the property.

Integration—In a property's life cycle, the earliest stage, when the property is being developed. Also called development.

Interest—1. A right or share in something (such as a piece of real estate). 2. A charge a borrower pays to a lender for the use of the lender's money.

Interest, Compound—Interest computed both on the principal and its accrued interest. Compare: Interest, Simple.

Interest, Future—An interest in property that will or may become possessory at some point in the future, such as a remainder or reversion.

Interest, Interim—See: Interest, Prepaid.

Interest, Prepaid—Interest on a new loan that must be paid at the time of closing; covers the interest due for the first month of the loan term. Also called interim interest.

Interest, Simple—Interest that is computed on the principal amount of the loan only, which is the type of interest charged in connection with real estate loans. Compare: Interest, Compound.

Interest, Undivided—A co-owner's interest, giving him the right to possession of the whole property, rather than to a particular section of it.

Interpleader—A court action filed by someone who is holding funds that two or more people are claiming. The holder turns the funds over to the court; the court resolves the dispute and delivers the money to the party who is entitled to it.

Interstate Land Sales Full Disclosure Act—A federal law requiring subdivision developers to make certain disclosures concerning the property to potential buyers.

Intestate—Without a valid will.

Intestate Succession—Distribution of the property of a person who died intestate to her heirs.

Invalid—Not legally binding or legally effective; not valid.

Inventory—The stock-in-trade of a business.

Inverse Condemnation Action—A court action by a private landowner against the government, seeking compensation for damage to property caused by government action.

Investment Property—Unimproved property held as an investment in the expectation that it will appreciate in value.

Inverted Pyramid—A way of visualizing ownership of real property; in theory, a property owner owns all the earth, water, and air enclosed by a pyramid that has its tip at the center of the earth and extends up through the property boundaries out into the sky.

Involuntary Conversion—For income tax purposes, when an asset is converted into cash without the voluntary action of the owner, such as through a condemnation award or insurance proceeds.

Involuntary Lien—See: Lien, Involuntary.

Joint Venture—Two or more individuals or companies joining together for one project or a related series of projects, but not as an ongoing business. Compare: Partnership.

Judgment—1. A court's binding determination of the rights and duties of the parties in a lawsuit.
2. A court order requiring one party to pay the other damages.

Judgment, Default—A court judgment in favor of the plaintiff due to the defendant's failure to answer the complaint or appear at a hearing.

Judgment, Deficiency—A personal judgment entered against a borrower in favor of the lender if the proceeds from a foreclosure sale of the security property are not enough to pay off the debt.

Judgment Creditor—A person who is owed money as a result of a judgment in a lawsuit.

Judgment Debtor—A person who owes money as a result of a judgment in a lawsuit.

Judgment Lien—See: Lien, Judgment.

Judicial Foreclosure—See: Foreclosure, Judicial.

Just Compensation—The compensation that the Constitution requires the government to pay a property owner when the property is taken under the power of eminent domain.

Kickback—A fee paid for a referral (for example, to an appraiser or inspector). The Real Estate Settlement Procedures Act prohibits kickbacks to settlement service providers in most residential mortgage loan transactions.

Laches, Doctrine of—A legal principle holding that the law will refuse to protect those who fail to assert their legal rights within a reasonable time.

Land—In the legal sense, it is the solid part of the surface of the earth, everything affixed to it by nature or by man, or anything on it or in it, such as minerals and water; real property.

Land Contract—See: Contract, Land.

Landlocked Property—A parcel of land without access to a road or highway.

Landlord—A landowner who has leased his property to another. Also called a lessor.

Landmark—A monument, natural or artificial, set up on the boundary between two adjacent properties, to show where the boundary is.

Land Residual Process—A method of appraising vacant land.

Latent Defects—Defects that are not visible or apparent (as opposed to patent defects).

Lateral Support—See: Support, Lateral.

Lawful Object—An objective or purpose of a contract that does not violate the law or a judicial determination of public policy.

Lease—A conveyance of a leasehold estate from the fee owner to a tenant; a contract in which one party pays the other rent in exchange for the possession of real estate. Also called a rental agreement.

Lease, Fixed—A lease in which the rent is set at a fixed amount, and the landlord pays most or all of the operating expenses (such as utilities, taxes, insurance, and maintenance costs). Also called a flat lease, gross lease, or straight lease.

Lease, Graduated—A lease in which it is agreed that the rental payments will increase at intervals by a specified amount or according to a specified formula.

Lease, Gross—See: Lease, Fixed.

Lease, Ground—A lease of the land only, usually for a long term, to a tenant who intends to construct a building on the property.

Lease, Net—A lease requiring the tenant to pay some or all operational expenses (such as taxes, insurance, and repairs), in addition to the rent paid to the landlord.

Lease, Percentage—A lease in which the rent is based on a percentage of the tenant's monthly or annual gross sales.

Lease, Sandwich—See: Sublease.

Lease, Straight—See: Lease, Fixed.

Leaseback—See: Sale-Leaseback.

Leasehold—A possessory interest in real property that has a limited duration, such as an estate for years or a periodic tenancy. Also called a less-than-freehold estate.

Legacy—A gift of personal property by will. Also called a bequest.

Legal Description—A precise description of a parcel of real property; may be a lot and block description, a metes and bounds description, or a government survey description.

Legal Person—See: Artificial Person.

Legatee—Someone who receives personal property (a legacy) under a will.

Lender, Institutional—A bank, savings and loan, or similar organization that invests other people's funds in loans; as opposed to an individual or private lender, which invests its own funds.

Lessee—One who leases property from another; a tenant.

Lessor—One who leases property to another; a landlord.

Less-than-freehold—See: Leasehold.

Leverage—The effective use of borrowed money to finance an investment such as real estate.

Levy—To impose a tax.

Liability—1. A debt or obligation. 2. Legal responsibility.

Liability, Joint and Several—A form of liability in which two or more persons are responsible for a debt both individually and as a group.

Liability, Limited—When a business investor is not personally liable for the debts of the business, as in the case of a limited partner or a corporate shareholder.

Liability, Vicarious—A legal doctrine stating that a principal can be held liable for harm to third parties resulting from an agent's actions.

Liable—Legally responsible.

License—1. Official permission to do a particular thing that the law does not allow everyone to do. 2. Revocable, non-assignable permission to use another person's land for a particular purpose. Compare: Easement.

License, Inactive—Any real estate license that has been turned over to the Director temporarily. The holder of an inactive license is not permitted to engage in activities requiring a license.

Lien—A nonpossessory interest in real property, giving the lienholder the right to foreclose if the owner doesn't pay a debt owed to the lienholder; a financial encumbrance on the owner's title.

Lien, Attachment—A lien intended to prevent transfer of the property pending the outcome of litigation.

Lien, Construction—A lien on property in favor of someone who provided labor or materials to improve the property. The term encompasses mechanic's liens and materialman's liens.

Lien, Equitable—A lien arising as a matter of fairness, rather than by agreement or by operation of law.

Lien, General—A lien against all the property of a debtor, rather than a particular piece of his property. Compare: Lien, Specific.

Lien, Involuntary—A lien that arises by operation of law, without the consent of the property owner. Also called a statutory lien.

Lien, Judgment—A general lien against a judgment debtor's property. The lien is created automatically in the county where the judgment was rendered and may be created in other counties by recording an abstract of judgment.

Lien, Materialman's—A construction lien in favor of someone who supplied materials for a project (as opposed to labor).

Lien, Mechanic's—See: Lien, Construction.

Lien, Property Tax—A specific lien on property to secure payment of property taxes.

Lien, Specific—A lien that attaches only to a particular piece of property (as opposed to a general lien, which attaches to all of the debtor's property).

Lien, Statutory—See: Lien, Involuntary.

Lien, Tax—A lien on property to secure the payment of taxes.

Lien, Voluntary—A lien placed against property with the consent of the owner; a deed of trust or a mortgage.

Lienholder, Junior—A secured creditor whose lien is lower in priority than another's lien.

Lien Priority—The order in which liens are paid off out of the proceeds of a foreclosure sale.

Lien Theory—The theory holding that a mortgage or deed of trust does not involve a transfer of title to the lender, but merely creates a lien against the property in the lender's favor. Compare: Title Theory.

Life Estate—A freehold estate that lasts only as long as a specified person lives. That person is referred to as the measuring life.

Life Tenant—Someone who owns a life estate; the person entitled to possession of the property during the measuring life.

Like-Kind Exchange—See: Tax-Deferred Exchange.

Limited Liability—See: Liability, Limited.

Limited Liability Company (LLC)—A form of business entity that offers both limited liability for its owners and certain tax benefits.

Limited Partnership—See: Partnership, Limited.

Liquidated Damages—See: Damages, Liquidated.

Liquidity—The ability to convert an asset into cash quickly.

Lis Pendens—A recorded notice stating that there is a lawsuit pending that may affect title to the defendant's real estate.

Listing—A written agency contract between a seller and a real estate brokerage, stipulating that the brokerage will be paid a commission for finding (or attempting to find) a buyer for the seller's property. Also called a listing agreement.

Listing, Exclusive—Either an exclusive agency listing or an exclusive right to sell listing.

Listing, Exclusive Agency—A listing agreement that entitles the brokerage to a commission if anyone other than the seller finds a buyer for the property during the listing term.

Listing, Exclusive Right to Sell—A listing agreement that entitles the brokerage to a commission if anyone—including the seller—finds a buyer for the property during the listing term.

Listing, Multiple—A listing (usually an exclusive right to sell listing) that includes a provision allowing the brokerage to submit the listing to its multiple listing service for dissemination to cooperating agents.

Listing, Net—A listing agreement in which the seller sets a net amount he is willing to accept for the property; if the actual selling price exceeds that amount, the real estate firm is entitled to keep the excess as its commission.

Listing, Open—A nonexclusive listing, given by a seller to as many brokerages as he chooses. If the property is sold, a brokerage is only entitled to a commission if it was the procuring cause of the sale.

Listing Brokerage—The brokerage that takes a listing, and thus represents the seller.

Listing Input Sheet—A form used to gather all pertinent information about a listed property, to expedite the process of inputting that data into a multiple listing service database.

Littoral Land—Land that borders on a stationary body of water (such as a lake, as opposed to a river or stream). Compare: Riparian Land.

Littoral Rights—The water rights of an owner of littoral land, in regard to use of the water in the lake.

Loan, Amortized—A loan that requires regular installment payments of both principal and interest (as opposed to an interest-only loan). It is fully amortized if the installment payments will pay off the full amount of the principal and all of the interest by the end of the repayment period. It is partially amortized if the installment payments will cover only part of the principal, so that a balloon payment of the remaining principal balance is required at the end of the repayment period.

Loan, Called—A loan that has been accelerated by the lender. See: Acceleration Clause.

Loan, Carryback—See: Loan, Purchase Money.

Loan, Conforming—A loan made in accordance with the standardized underwriting criteria of the major secondary market agencies, Fannie Mae and Freddie Mac, and which therefore can be sold to those agencies.

Loan, Construction—A loan to finance the cost of constructing a building, usually providing that the loan funds will be advanced in installments as the work progresses. Also called an interim loan.

Loan, Conventional—An institutional loan that is not insured or guaranteed by a government agency.

Loan, FHA—A loan made by an institutional lender and insured by the Federal Housing Administration, so that the FHA will reimburse the lender for losses that result if the borrower defaults.

Loan, Fixed-rate—A loan on which the interest rate will remain the same throughout the entire loan term. Compare: Mortgage, Adjustable-rate.

Loan, G.I.—See: Loan, VA-Guaranteed.

Loan, Guaranteed—A loan in which a third party has agreed to reimburse the lender for losses that result if the borrower defaults.

Loan, Home Equity—A loan secured by the borrower's equity in the home she already owns. Compare: Loan, Purchase Money.

Loan, Interest-Only—A loan that requires the borrower to pay only the interest during the loan term, with the principal due at the end of the term. Also called a term loan.

Loan, Interim—See: Loan, Construction.

Loan, Participation—A loan in which the lender receives some yield on the loan in addition to the interest, such as a percentage of the income generated by the property, or a share in the borrower's equity.

Loan, Permanent—See: Loan, Take-out.

Loan, Seasoned—A loan with an established record of timely payment by the borrower.

Loan, Take-Out—Long-term financing used to replace a construction loan (an interim loan) when construction has been completed. Also called a permanent loan.

Loan, Term—See: Loan, Interest-only.

Loan, VA-Guaranteed—A home loan made by an institutional lender to an eligible veteran, where the Dept. of Veterans Affairs will reimburse the lender for losses if the veteran defaults.

Loan Correspondent—An intermediary who arranges loans of an investor's money to borrowers, and then services the loans.

Loan Fee—A loan origination fee, an assumption fee, or discount points.

Loan Term—The length of time over which a mortgage will be repaid.

Loan-to-Value Ratio (LTV)—The relationship between the loan amount and either the sales price or the appraised value of the property (whichever is less), expressed as a percentage.

Loan Workout—An alternative to foreclosure in which a lender agrees to a new payment plan for a loan, or to reduction of the loan's interest rate or principal amount.

Local Market—See: Primary Mortgage Market.

Lot—A parcel of land; especially, a parcel in a subdivision.

Lot and Block Description—The type of legal description used for platted property; it states the property's lot number and block number and the name of the subdivision, referring to the plat map recorded in the county where the property is located. Sometimes called a maps and plats description.

LTV—See: Loan-to-Value Ratio.

Majority, Age of—The age at which a person becomes legally competent; in Washington, 18 years old. See: Minor.

Maker—The person who signs a promissory note, promising to repay a debt. Compare: Payee.

Managing Broker—See: Broker, Managing.

Maps and Plats—See: Lot and Block Description.

Margin—In an adjustable-rate mortgage, the difference between the index rate and the interest rate charged to the borrower.

Marketable Title—See: Title, Marketable.

Market Data Approach—See: Sales Comparison Approach.

Market Price—1. The current price generally being charged for something in the marketplace. 2. The price actually paid for a property. Compare: Value, Market.

Market Value—See: Value, Market.

Master Plan—See: General Plan.

Master/Servant Relationship—A legal term for a standard employer/employee relationship.

Material Fact—Information that has a substantial negative impact on the value of the property, on a party's ability to perform, or on the purpose of the transaction.

Maturity Date—The date by which a loan is supposed to be paid off in full.

Measuring Life—See: Life Estate.

Meeting of Minds—See: Mutual Consent.

Merger—1. Uniting two or more separate properties by transferring ownership of all of them to one person. 2. When the owner of one parcel acquires title to one or more adjacent parcels.

Meridian—An imaginary line running north and south, passing through the earth's poles. Also called a longitude line.

Meridian, Principal—In the rectangular survey system, the main north-south line in a particular grid, used as the starting point in numbering the ranges.

Meridians, Guide—In the rectangular survey system, lines running north-south (parallel to the principal meridian) at 24-mile intervals.

Metes—Measurements.

Metes and Bounds Description—A legal description that starts at an identifiable point of beginning, then describes the property's boundaries in terms of courses (compass directions) and distances, ultimately returning to the point of beginning.

Mill—One-tenth of one cent; a measure used to state property tax rates in some cases. For example, a tax rate of one mill on the dollar is the same as a rate of one-tenth of one percent of the assessed value of the property.

Mineral Rights—Rights to the minerals located beneath the surface of a piece of property.

Minor—A person who has not yet reached the age of majority; in Washington, a person under 18.

MIP—Mortgage insurance premium; especially a premium charged in connection with an FHA-insured loan.

Misrepresentation—A false or misleading statement. See: Fraud.

MLS—Multiple Listing Service.

Monopoly—When a single entity or group has exclusive control over the production or sale of a product or service.

Monetary Policy—The Federal Reserve Board's effort to control the supply and cost of money in the United States.

Monument—A visible marker (natural or artificial) used in a survey or a metes and bounds description to establish the boundaries of a piece of property.

Mortgage—1. An instrument that creates a voluntary lien on real property to secure repayment of a debt, and which (unlike a deed of trust) does not include a power of sale, so it can only be foreclosed judicially; the parties are the mortgagor (borrower) and mortgagee (lender). 2. The term is often used more generally, to refer to either a mortgage or a deed of trust. Note: If you do not find the specific term you are looking for here under "Mortgage," check the entries under "Loan."

Mortgage, Adjustable-Rate (ARM)—A loan in which the interest rate is periodically increased or decreased to reflect changes in the cost of money. Compare: Loan, Fixed-Rate.

Mortgage, Balloon—A partially amortized mortgage loan that requires a large balloon payment at the end of the loan term.

Mortgage, Blanket—A mortgage that covers more than one parcel of property.

Mortgage, Budget—A loan in which the monthly payments include a share of the property taxes and insurance, in addition to principal and interest; the lender places the money for taxes and insurance in an impound account.

Mortgage, Chattel—An instrument that makes personal property (chattels) security for a loan. In states that have adopted the Uniform Commercial Code (including Washington), the chattel mortgage has been replaced by the security agreement.

Mortgage, Closed—A loan that cannot be paid off early.

Mortgage, Closed End—A loan that does not allow the borrower to increase the balance owed; the opposite of an open-end mortgage.

Mortgage, Direct Reduction—A loan that requires a fixed amount of principal to be paid in each payment; the total payment becomes steadily smaller, because the interest portion becomes smaller with each payment as the principal balance decreases.

Mortgage, First—The mortgage on a property that has first lien position; the one with higher lien priority than any other mortgage against the property.

Mortgage, Graduated Payment—A loan in which the payments are increased periodically during the first years of the loan term, usually according to a fixed schedule.

Mortgage, Hard Money—A mortgage given to a lender in exchange for cash, as opposed to one given in exchange for credit.

Mortgage, Junior—A mortgage that has lower lien priority than another mortgage against the same property. Sometimes called a secondary mortgage.

Mortgage, Level Payment—An amortized loan with payments that are the same amount each month, although the portion of the payment that is applied to principal steadily increases and the portion of the payment applied to interest steadily decreases. See: Loan, Amortized.

Mortgage, Open—A mortgage without a prepayment penalty.

Mortgage, Open-End—A loan that permits the borrower to reborrow the money he has repaid on the principal, usually up to the original loan amount, without executing a new loan agreement.

Mortgage, Package—A mortgage that is secured by certain items of personal property (such as appliances or carpeting) in addition to the real property.

Mortgage, Participation—A loan made in exchange for a share of the borrower's equity in the property, and/or a share in the earnings of the property.

Mortgage, Purchase Money—1. When a seller extends credit to a buyer to finance the purchase of the property, accepting a deed of trust or mortgage instead of cash. Sometimes called a carryback loan. 2. In a more general sense, any loan the borrower uses to buy the security property (as opposed to a loan secured by property the borrower already owns).

Mortgage, Reverse Equity—An arrangement in which a homeowner mortgages the home to a lender in exchange for a monthly check from the lender.

Mortgage, Satisfaction of—The document a mortgagee gives the mortgagor when the mortgage debt has been paid in full, acknowledging that the debt has been paid and the mortgage is no longer a lien against the property.

Mortgage, Secondary—See: Mortgage, Junior.

Mortgage, Senior—A mortgage that has higher lien priority than another mortgage against the same property; the opposite of a junior mortgage.

Mortgage, Shared Appreciation—A mortgage in which a lender is entitled to a share of the increase in the value of the property.

Mortgage, Wraparound—A purchase money loan arrangement in which the seller uses part of the buyer's payments to make the payments on an existing loan (called the underlying loan); the buyer takes title subject to the underlying loan, but does not assume it. When the security instrument used for wraparound financing is a deed of trust instead of a mortgage, it may be referred to as an all-inclusive trust deed.

Mortgage Banker—An intermediary who originates and services real estate loans on behalf of investors.

Mortgage Broker—An intermediary who brings real estate lenders and borrowers together and negotiates loan agreements between them.

Mortgage Company—A type of real estate lender that originates and services loans on behalf of large investors (acting as a mortgage banker) or for resale on the secondary mortgage market.

Mortgagee—A lender who accepts a mortgage as security for repayment of the loan.

Mortgage Loan—Any loan secured by real property, whether the actual security instrument used is a mortgage or a deed of trust.

Mortgaging Clause—A clause in a mortgage that describes the security interest given to the mortgagee.

Mortgagor—A property owner (usually a borrower) who gives a mortgage to another (usually a lender) as security for payment of an obligation.

Multiple Listing Service (MLS)—An organization of brokerages who share their exclusive listings.

Mutual Consent—When all parties freely agree to the terms of a contract, without fraud, undue influence, duress, menace, or mistake. Mutual consent is achieved through offer and acceptance; it is sometimes referred to as a "meeting of the minds."

NAR®—National Association of Realtors®.

Narrative Report—A thorough appraisal report in which the appraiser summarizes the data and the appraisal methods used, to convince the reader of the soundness of the estimate; a more comprehensive presentation than a form report.

National Environmental Policy Act—See: NEPA.

National Market—See: Secondary Mortgage Market.

Natural Person—A human being, an individual (as opposed to an artificial person, such as a corporation).

Navigable Waters—A body of water large enough so that watercraft can travel on it in the course of commerce.

Negligence—Conduct that falls below the standard of care that a reasonable person would exercise under the circumstances; carelessness or recklessness.

Negotiable Instrument—An instrument containing an unconditional promise to pay a certain sum of money, to order or to bearer, on demand or at a particular time. It can be a check, promissory note, bond, draft, or stock.

Neighborhood Analysis—The gathering of data on home sizes and styles, topography, features, and amenities in a neighborhood, as part of the appraisal or property management process.

NEPA—The National Environmental Policy Act; a federal law requiring the preparation of an environmental impact statement before any governmental action that would have a significant effect on the environment.

Net Operating Income—See: Income, Net Operating.

Net Listing—See: Listing, Net.

Net Spendable—See: Income, Spendable.

Net Worth—An individual's financial assets minus her liabilities.

Nominal Interest Rate—The interest rate stated in a promissory note. Also called the note rate or coupon rate. Compare: Annual Percentage Rate.

Nonconforming Loan—See: Loan, Conforming.

Nonconforming Use—A property use that does not conform to current zoning requirements, but is allowed because the property was being used in that way before the present zoning ordinance was enacted.

Nonpossessory Interest—An interest in property that does not include the right to possess and occupy the property; an encumbrance, such as a lien or an easement.

Nonrecognition Transaction—A transaction for which a taxpayer is not required to pay taxes in the year the gain is realized.

Normal Market Conditions—A sale taking place in a competitive and open market, with informed parties acting prudently, at arm's length, and without undue stimulus (such as an urgent need to sell the property immediately).

Notarize—To have a document certified by a notary public.

Notary Public—Someone who is officially authorized to witness and certify the acknowledgment made by someone signing a legal document.

Note—See: Note, Promissory.

Note, Demand—A promissory note that is due whenever the holder of the note demands payment.

Note, Installment—A promissory note that calls for regular payments of principal and interest until the debt is fully paid.

Note, Joint—A promissory note signed by two or more persons with equal liability for payment.

Note, Promissory—A written promise to repay a debt; it may or may not be a negotiable instrument.

Note, Straight—A promissory note that calls for regular payments of interest only, so that the entire principal amount is due in one lump sum at the end of the loan term. Also called a term note.

Notice, Actual—Actual knowledge of a fact, as opposed to knowledge imputed by law (constructive notice).

Notice, Constructive—Knowledge of a fact imputed to a person by law. A person is held to have constructive notice of something when he should have known it (because he could have learned it through reasonable diligence or an inspection of the public record), even if he did not actually know it.

Notice of Cessation—A notice recorded when work on a construction project has ceased (although the project is unfinished), to limit the time allowed for recording construction liens.

Notice of Completion—A notice recorded when a construction project has been completed, to limit the time allowed for recording construction liens.

Notice of Default—A notice sent by a secured creditor to the debtor, informing the debtor that she has breached the loan agreement.

Notice of Non-Responsibility—A notice that a property owner may record and post on the property to protect his title against construction liens, when someone other than the owner (such as a tenant) has ordered work on the property.

Notice of Sale—A notice stating that foreclosure proceedings have been commenced against a property.

Notice of Value—A document issued by the Dept. of Veterans Affairs, setting forth the current market value of a property, based on a VA-approved appraisal. Also called a Certificate of Reasonable Value.

Notice to Quit—A notice to a tenant, demanding that he vacate the leased property.

Notice to the World—Constructive notice of the contents of a document provided to the general public by recording the document.

Novation—1. When one party to a contract withdraws and a new party is substituted, relieving the withdrawing party of liability. 2. The substitution of a new obligation for an old one.

Nuisance—A use of property that is offensive or annoying to neighboring landowners or to the community.

Obligatory Advances—Disbursements of construction loan funds that the lender is obligated to make (by prior agreement with the borrower) when the borrower has completed certain phases of construction.

Obsolescence—Any loss in value (depreciation) due to reduced desirability and usefulness.

Obsolescence, External—Loss in value resulting from factors outside the property itself, such as proximity to an airport. Also called economic obsolescence or external inadequacy.

Obsolescence, Functional—Loss in value due to inadequate or outmoded equipment, or as a result of a poor or outmoded design.

Offer—When one person (the offeror) proposes a contract to another (the offeree); if the offeree accepts the offer, a binding contract is formed.

Offer, Tender—See: Tender.

Offeree—One to whom a contract offer is made.

Offeror—One who makes a contract offer.

Officer—In a corporation, an executive authorized by the board of directors to manage the business of the corporation.

Off-Site Improvements—Improvements that add to the usefulness of a site but are not located directly on it, such as curbs, street lights, and sidewalks.

One-Time Agency Agreement—An agreement entered into by a FSBO seller and a buyer's agent: the seller agrees to compensate the agent for bringing him a particular buyer.

Open House—Showing a listed home to the public for a specified period of time.

Open Listing—See: Listing, Open.

Open Market Operations—The Federal Reserve's manipulation of the money supply through the purchase and sale of government securities.

Option—A contract giving one party the right to do something, without obligating him to do it.

Optionee—The person to whom an option is given.

Optionor—The person who gives an option.

Option to Purchase—An option giving the optionee the right to buy property owned by the optionor at an agreed price during a specified period.

Ordinance—A law passed by a local legislative body, such as a city council. Compare: Statute.

Orientation—The placement of a house on its lot, with regard to its exposure to the sun and wind, privacy from the street, and protection from outside noise.

Origination Fee—A fee a lender charges a borrower upon making a new loan, intended to cover the administrative costs of making the loan. Also called a loan fee.

"Or More"—A provision in a promissory note that allows the borrower to prepay the debt.

Overimprovement—An improvement that is more expensive than justified by the value of the land.

Overlying Right—A landowner's right to use percolating or diffused ground water.

Oversupply, Economic—A situation where there are more units available in a rental market than potential tenants who are able to pay the rent.

Oversupply, Technical—A situation where there are more units available in a rental market than potential tenants.

Ownership—Title to property, dominion over property; the rights of possession and control.

Ownership, Concurrent—When two or more individuals share ownership of one piece of property, each owning an undivided interest in the property (as in a tenancy in common or joint tenancy, or with community property). Also called co-ownership or co-tenancy.

Ownership in Severalty—Ownership by a single individual.

Panic Selling—See: Blockbusting.

Par—1. The accepted standard of comparison; the average or typical rate or amount. 2. Face value; for example, a mortgage sold at the secondary market level for 97% of par has been sold for 3% less than its face value.

Parcel—A lot or piece of real estate, especially a specified part of a larger tract.

Partial Reconveyance—The instrument given to the borrower when part of the security property is released from a blanket deed of trust under a partial release clause.

Partial Release Clause—See: Release Clause.

Partial Satisfaction—The instrument given to the borrower when part of the security property is released from a blanket mortgage under a partial release clause.

Partition—The division of a property among its co-owners, so that each owns part of it in severalty; this may occur by agreement of all the co-owners (voluntary partition), or by court order (judicial partition).

Partner, General—A partner who has the authority to manage and contract for a general or limited partnership, and who is personally liable for the partnership's debts.

Partner, Limited—A partner in a limited partnership who is primarily an investor, and who is not personally liable for the partnership's debts.

Partnership—An association of two or more persons to carry on a business for profit. The law regards a partnership as a group of individuals, not as an entity separate from its owners. Compare: Corporation.

Partnership, General—A partnership in which each member has an equal right to manage the business and share in the profits, as well as equal responsibility for the partnership's debts.

Partnership, Limited—A partnership made up of one or more general partners and one or more limited partners.

Partnership Property—All property that partners bring into their business at the outset or later acquire for their business; property owned as tenants in partnership. See: Tenancy in Partnership.

Party Wall—A wall located on the boundary line between two adjoining parcels of land that is used by the owners of both properties.

Patent—The instrument used to convey government land to a private individual.

Patent Defect—A problem that is readily observable in an ordinary inspection of the property. Compare: Latent Defect.

Payee—In a promissory note, the party who is entitled to be paid; the lender. Compare: Maker.

Payment Cap—A limit on the amount an ARM's payments can be increased, either during a given year, or over the entire life of the loan.

Percolation Test—A test to determine the ability of the ground to absorb or drain water; used to determine whether a site is suitable for construction, particularly for installation of a septic tank system.

Per Diem—Daily.

Periodic Tenancy—See: Tenancy, Periodic.

Personal Property—Any property that is not real property; movable property not affixed to land. Also called chattels or personalty.

Personalty—Personal property.

Personal Use Property—Property that a taxpayer owns for her own use (or family use), as opposed to income property, investment property, dealer property, or property used in a trade or business.

Physical Deterioration—Loss in value (depreciation) resulting from wear and tear or deferred maintenance.

Physical Life—An estimate of the time a building will remain structurally sound and capable of being used. Compare: Economic Life.

Plaintiff—The party who brings or starts a civil lawsuit; the one who sues.

Planned Unit Development (PUD)—A development (usually residential) with small, clustered lots designed to leave more open space than traditional subdivisions have.

Planning Commission—A local government agency responsible for preparing the community's general plan for development.

Plat—A detailed survey map of a subdivision, recorded in the county where the land is located. Subdivided property is often called platted property.

Plat Book—A large book containing subdivision plats, kept at the county recorder's office.

Pledge—When a debtor transfers possession of property to the creditor as security for repayment of the debt. Compare: Hypothecate.

Plot Plan—A plan showing lot dimensions and the layout of improvements (such as buildings and landscaping) on a property site.

Plottage—The increment of value that results when two or more lots are combined to produce greater value. Also called the plottage increment.

PMI—See: Insurance, Private Mortgage.

Point—One percent of the principal amount of a loan.

Point of Beginning (POB)—The starting point in a metes and bounds description; a monument or a point described by reference to a monument.

Points—See: Discount Points.

Police Power—The power of state and local governments to enact and enforce laws for the protection of the public's health, safety, morals, and general welfare.

Policies and Procedures Manual—Comprehensive handbook that describes a business's goals and objectives, code of conduct in workplace, and the manner in which employees should conduct business with third parties. Also called an employee handbook.

Portfolio—The mix of investments owned by an individual or company.

Possession—1. The holding and enjoyment of property. 2. Actual physical occupation of real property.

Possessory Interest—An interest in property that includes the right to possess and occupy the property. The term includes all estates (leasehold as well as freehold), but does not include encumbrances.

Potable Water—Water that is safe to drink.

Power of Attorney—An instrument authorizing one person (the attorney in fact) to act as another's agent, to the extent stated in the instrument.

Power of Sale Clause—A clause in a deed of trust giving the trustee the right to foreclose nonjudicially (sell the debtor's property without a court action) if the borrower defaults.

Preapproval—A process that allows a prospective borrower to submit a loan application to a lender and get approved for a loan before beginning the home-buying process.

Prepayment—Paying off part or all of a loan before payment is due.

Prepayment Penalty—A penalty charged to a borrower who prepays.

Prepayment Privilege—A provision in a promissory note allowing the borrower to prepay.

Prescription—Acquiring an interest in real property (usually an easement) by using it openly and without the owner's permission for the period prescribed by statute.

Preventive Maintenance—A program of regular inspection and care of a property and its fixtures, allowing the prevention of potential problems or their immediate repair.

Price Fixing—The cooperative setting of prices by competing firms; price fixing is an automatic violation of antitrust laws.

Primary Mortgage Market—The market in which mortgage loans are originated, where lenders make loans to borrowers. Also called the local market. Compare: Secondary Mortgage Market.

Prime Rate—The interest rate a bank charges its largest and most desirable customers.

Principal—1. One who grants another person (an agent) authority to represent him in dealings with third parties. 2. One of the parties to a transaction (such as a buyer or seller), as opposed to those who are involved as agents or employees (such as a real estate licensee or escrow agent). 3. In regard to a loan, the amount originally borrowed, as opposed to the interest.

Principal Meridian—See: Meridian, Principal.

Principal Residence Property—Real property that is the owner's home, her main dwelling. Under the federal income tax laws, a person can only have one principal residence at a time.

Prior Appropriation—See: Appropriation, Prior.

Private Mortgage Insurance—See: Insurance, Private Mortgage.

Probate—A judicial proceeding in which the validity of a will is established and the executor is authorized to distribute the estate property; or, when there is no valid will, in which an administrator is appointed to distribute the estate to the heirs.

Probate Court—A court that oversees the distribution of property under a will or intestate succession.

Procuring Cause—The real estate agent who is primarily responsible for bringing about a sale; for example, by negotiating the agreement between the buyer and seller.

Profit—A nonpossessory interest; the right to enter another person's land and take something (such as timber or minerals) away from it.

Progression, Principle of—An appraisal principle which holds that a property of lesser value tends to be worth more when it is located in an area with properties of greater value than it would be if located elsewhere. The opposite of the principle of regression.

Promisee—Someone who has been promised something; someone who is supposed to receive the benefit of a contractual promise.

Promisor—Someone who has made a contractual promise to another.

Promissory Note—See: Note, Promissory.

Property—1. The rights of ownership in a thing, such as the right to use, possess, transfer, or encumber it. 2. Something that is owned.

Property Held for Production of Income—See: Income Property.

Property Management Agreement—A document that creates an agency relationship between a property owner and property manager and establishes the terms and conditions of the relationship.

Property Management Plan—An outline for a property manager's strategy in meeting the owner's financial goals.

Property Manager—A person hired by a property owner to administer, merchandise, and maintain property, especially rental property.

Property Tax—See: Tax, Property.

Property Used in a Trade or Business—Real property and equipment owned by a taxpayer and used to carry out the taxpayer's trade or business.

Proprietorship, Individual or Sole—A business owned and operated by one person.

Proration—The process of dividing or allocating something (especially a sum of money or an expense) proportionately, according to time, interest, or benefit.

Public Offering Statement—A statement required by the Washington Land Development Act, that provides detailed information about the subdivision, such as whether there are any liens, the physical condition of the land, compliance with land use laws, and so on.

Public Record—The official collection of legal documents that individuals have filed with the county recorder in order to make the information contained in them public.

Public Use—A use that benefits the public. For a condemnation action to be constitutional, it must be for a public use.

Puffing—Superlative statements about the quality of a property that should not be considered assertions of fact.

Purchase and Sale Agreement—A contract in which a seller promises to convey title to real property to a buyer in exchange for the purchase price. Also called an earnest money agreement, deposit receipt, sales contract, or contract of sale.

Purchaser's Assignment of Contract and Deed—The instrument used to assign the vendee's equitable interest in a contract to another.

Qualified Acceptance—See: Counteroffer.

Qualifying Standards—The standards a lender requires a loan applicant to meet before a loan will be approved. Also called underwriting standards.

Quantity Survey Method—In appraisal, a method of estimating the replacement cost of a structure; it involves a detailed estimate of the quantities and cost of materials and labor, and overhead expenses such as insurance and contractor's profit.

Quiet Enjoyment—Use and possession of real property without interference from the previous owner, the lessor, or anyone else claiming title. See: Covenant of Quiet Enjoyment.

Quiet Title Action—A lawsuit to determine who has title to a piece of property, or to remove a cloud from the title.

Quitclaim Deed—See: Deed, Quitclaim.

Range—In the rectangular survey system, a strip of land six miles wide, running north and south.

Range Lines—In the rectangular survey system, the north-south lines (meridians) located six miles apart.

Ratify—To confirm or approve after the fact an act that was not authorized when it was performed.

Ready, Willing, and Able—A buyer is ready, willing, and able if he makes an offer that meets the seller's stated terms, and has the contractual capacity and financial resources to complete the transaction.

Real Estate—See: Real Property.

Real Estate Brokerage Relationships Act—A Washington state law that significantly changes traditional agency law in regards to real estate transactions. It governs when and how real estate agency relationships are created and terminated, the duties owed by real estate licensees to the parties to a real estate transaction, and when and how agency disclosures are to be made.

Real Estate Commission—A commission appointed by the Governor, consisting of the Director of the Department of Licensing and six commissioners; responsible for preparing and conducting the real estate licensing examinations.

Real Estate Contract—1. A purchase and sale agreement. 2. A land contract. 3. Any contract having to do with real property.

Real Estate Firm—A business entity that offers real estate brokerage services and is licensed by the state Department of Licensing, after having named a designated broker to represent the firm's interests; also known as a brokerage.

Real Estate Investment Trust (REIT)—A real estate investment business with at least 100 investors that qualifies for tax benefits if organized and managed in compliance with IRS rules.

Real Estate Settlement Procedures Act—See: RESPA.

Realization—For income tax purposes, when a gain is separated from an asset, and therefore becomes taxable.

Real Property—Land and everything attached to or appurtenant to it. Also called realty or real estate. Compare: Personal Property.

Real Property Transfer Disclosure Statement—See: Seller Disclosure Statement.

Realtor®—A real estate agent who is an active member of a state and local real estate board that is affiliated with the National Association of Realtors®.

Realty—See: Real Property.

Reasonable Use Doctrine—A limitation of water rights, holding that there is no right to waste water.

Recapture—An investor's recovery of money invested in real estate.

Receiver—A person appointed by a court to manage and look after property or funds involved in litigation.

Reconciliation—The final step in an appraisal, when the appraiser assembles and interprets the data in order to arrive at a final value estimate. Also called correlation.

Reconveyance—Releasing the security property from the lien created by a deed of trust, by recording a deed of reconveyance.

Recording—Filing a document at the county recorder's office, so that it will be placed in the public record.

Recording Numbers—The numbers stamped on documents when they're recorded, used to identify and locate the documents in the public record.

Rectangular Survey System—A system of grids, made up of range and township lines that divide the land into townships, which are further subdivided into sections; a property is identified by its location within a particular section, township, and range. Also called the government survey system.

Redemption—1. When a defaulting borrower prevents foreclosure by paying the full amount of the debt, plus costs. 2. When a mortgagor regains the property after foreclosure by paying whatever the foreclosure sale purchaser paid for it, plus interest and expenses.

Redemption, Equitable Right of—The right of a mortgagor to redeem property prior to the foreclosure sale.

Redemption, Statutory Right of—The right of a mortgagor to get her property back after a foreclosure sale.

Redlining—When a lender refuses to make loans secured by property in a certain neighborhood because of the racial or ethnic composition of the neighborhood.

Refinancing—When a homeowner takes out a new loan—usually to take advantage of lower interest rates—and uses the loan proceeds to pay off the existing loan.

Reformation—A legal action to correct a mistake, such as a typographical error, in a deed or other document. The court will order the execution of a correction deed.

Regression, Principle of—An appraisal principle which holds that a valuable property surrounded by properties of lesser value will tend to be worth less than it would be in a different location; the opposite of the principle of progression.

Regulation Z—The Federal Reserve Board's regulation that implements the Truth in Lending Act.

Reinstate—To prevent foreclosure by curing the default.

Release—1. To give up a legal right. 2. A document in which a legal right is given up.

Release, Lien—A document removing a lien, given to the borrower by the lender, once a mortgage or deed of trust has been paid off in full.

Release Clause—1. A clause in a blanket mortgage or deed of trust which allows the borrower to get part of the security property released from the lien when a certain portion of the debt has been paid or other conditions are fulfilled. Often called a partial release clause. 2. A clause in a land contract providing for a deed to a portion of the land to be delivered when a certain portion of the contract price has been paid. Also known as a deed release provision.

Reliction—When a body of water gradually recedes, exposing land that was previously under water. Also called dereliction.

Remainder—A future interest that becomes possessory when a life estate terminates, and that is held by someone other than the grantor of the life estate; as opposed to a reversion, which is a future interest held by the grantor.

Remainderman—The person who has an estate in remainder.

Remaining Economic Life—See: Economic Life.

Remise—To give up; a term used in quitclaim deeds.

Rent—Compensation paid by a tenant to the landlord in exchange for the possession and use of the property.

Rent, Contract—The rent that is actually being paid on property that is currently leased.

Rent, Economic—The rent that a property would be earning if it were available for lease in the current market.

Rent, Ground—The earnings of improved property attributed to the land itself, after allowance is made for the earnings attributable to the improvement.

Rent Roll—A report on rent collections; a list of the total amount of rent earned, both collected and uncollected.

Rental Schedule—A list of rental rates for the units in a given building.

Replacement Cost—See: Cost, Replacement.

Reproduction Cost—See: Cost, Reproduction.

Rescission—When a contract is terminated and each party gives anything acquired under the contract back to the other party. (The verb form is rescind.) Compare: Cancellation.

Reservation—A right retained by a grantor when conveying property; for example, mineral rights, an easement, or a life estate can be reserved in the deed.

Reserve Account—See: Impound Account.

Reserve Requirements—The percentage of deposits commercial banks must keep on reserve with the Federal Reserve Bank.

Reserves for Replacement—Regular allowances set aside by an investment property owner, a business, or a homeowners association to pay for the replacement of structures and equipment that are expected to wear out.

Residential Landlord-Tenant Act (RLTA)—A Washington state law that regulates landlords and tenants in most residential lease transactions.

Residual—The property value remaining after the economic life of the improvements has been exhausted.

Residual Income—See: Income, Residual.

Residuals—Commissions in the form of delayed payments (when a part of the commission is paid with each installment on an installment sales contract, for example).

RESPA—The Real Estate Settlement Procedures Act; a federal law that requires lenders to disclose certain information about closing costs to loan applicants.

Restitution—Restoring something (especially money) that a person was unjustly deprived of.

Restriction—A limitation on the use of real property.

Restriction, Deed—A restrictive covenant in a deed.

Restriction, Private—A restriction imposed on property by a previous owner, a neighbor, or the subdivision developer; a restrictive covenant or a condition in a deed.

Restriction, Public—A law or regulation limiting or regulating the use of real property.

Restrictive Covenant—See: Covenant, Restrictive.

Retainer—A fee paid up front to a licensee when entering into an real estate agency (usually a buyer agency) relationship.

Return—A profit from an investment. Also referred to as return on investment (ROI). See also: Yield.

Reversion—A future interest that becomes possessory when a temporary estate (such as a life estate) terminates, and that is held by the grantor (or his successors in interest). Compare: Remainder.

Reversioner—The person who has an estate in reversion.

Rezone—An amendment to a zoning ordinance, usually changing the uses allowed in a particular zone. Also called a zoning amendment.

Right of First Refusal—A right that gives the holder the first opportunity to purchase or lease a particular parcel of real property, should the owner decide to sell or lease it.

Right of Way—An easement that gives the holder the right to cross another person's land.

Riparian Land—Land that is adjacent to or crossed by a body of water. Compare: Littoral Land.

Riparian Rights—The water rights of a landowner whose property is adjacent to or crossed by a body of water. Compare: Appropriation, Prior.

Risk Analysis—See: Underwriting.

Rule of Capture—See: Capture, Rule of.

Running with the Land—Binding or benefiting the successive owners of a piece of property, rather than terminating when a particular owner transfers his or her interest. Usually said in reference to an easement or a restrictive covenant.

Rural Housing Service Loan—A loan made by the Rural Housing Service, a federal agency, to purchase, build, or rehabilitate homes in rural areas.

Safety Clause—See: Extender Clause.

Sale-Leaseback—A form of real estate financing in which the owner of industrial or commercial property sells the property and leases it back from the buyer; in addition to certain tax advantages, the seller/lessee obtains more cash through the sale than would normally be possible by borrowing and mortgaging the property, since lenders will not often lend 100% of the value.

Sales Comparison Approach—One of the three main methods of appraisal, in which the sales prices of comparable properties are used to estimate the value of the subject property. Also called the market data approach.

Sandwich Lease—See: Sublease.

Satisfaction of Mortgage—See: Mortgage, Satisfaction of.

Savings and Loan Association—A type of financial institution that emphasizes home mortgage loans.

Savings Bank—A type of financial institution that emphasizes consumer loans and home mortgages.

Scarcity—A limited or inadequate supply of something; one of the four elements of value (along with utility, demand, and transferability).

Secondary Financing—Money borrowed to pay part of the required downpayment or closing costs for a first loan, when the second loan is secured by the same property that secures the first loan.

Secondary Mortgage Market—The market in which investors (including Fannie Mae, Freddie Mac, and Ginnie Mae) purchase real estate loans from lenders; also called the national market.

Secret Profit—A financial benefit that an agent takes from a transaction without informing the principal.

Section—In the rectangular survey system, a section is one mile square and contains 640 acres. There are 36 sections in a township.

Securities—Investment instruments, such as stocks and bonds.

Security Agreement—Under the Uniform Commercial Code, a document that creates a lien on personal property being used to secure a loan.

Security Deposit—Money a tenant gives a landlord at the beginning of the tenancy to protect the landlord in case the tenant defaults; the landlord may retain all or part of the deposit to cover unpaid rent or repair costs at the end of the tenancy.

Security Instrument—A document that creates a voluntary lien, to secure repayment of a loan; for debts secured by real property, it is either a mortgage or a deed of trust.

Security Interest—The interest a creditor may acquire in the debtor's property to ensure that the debt will be paid.

Security Property—The property against which a borrower gives a lender a voluntary lien, so that the lender can foreclose if the borrower defaults.

Seisin—Actual possession of a freehold estate; ownership.

Seller Disclosure Statement—A form that state law requires a residential seller to give the buyer, disclosing problems with the property. Formerly called a transfer disclosure statement.

Selling Brokerage—The brokerage responsible for procuring a buyer for real estate; may represent either the seller or the buyer.

SEPA—The State Environmental Policy Act; a Washington state law analogous to NEPA that requires environmental impact statements before government actions that would have a significant effect on the environment.

Separate Property—Property owned by a married person that is not community property; includes property acquired before marriage or by gift or inheritance after marriage.

Servant—See: Master/Servant Relationship.

Setback Requirements—Provisions in a zoning ordinance that do not allow structures to be built within a certain distance of the property line.

Settlement—1. An agreement between the parties to a civil lawsuit, in which the plaintiff agrees to drop the suit in exchange for money or the defendant's promise to do or refrain from doing something. 2. Closing.

Settlement Statement—A document that presents a final, detailed accounting for a real estate transaction, listing each party's debits and credits and the amount each will receive or be required to pay at closing. Also called a closing statement.

Severalty—See: Ownership in Severalty.

Severance—1. Termination of a joint tenancy. 2. The permanent removal of a natural attachment, fixture, or appurtenance from real property, which transforms the item into personal property.

Severance, Constructive—When a landowner enters into a contract to sell an appurtenance or natural attachment, the contract constructively severs the item from the land—making it the personal property of the buyer—even before the buyer has actually taken it off the land.

Shareholder—An individual who holds ownership shares (shares of stock) in a corporation, and has limited liability in regard to the corporation's debts. Also called a stockholder.

Sheriff's Deed—See: Deed, Sheriff's.

Sheriff's Sale—A foreclosure sale held after a judicial foreclosure. Sometimes called an execution sale.

Sherman Act—A federal antitrust law prohibiting any agreement that has the effect of an unreasonable restraint of trade, such as price fixing and tie-in arrangements.

Shoreline Management Act—A Washington state law regulating development within 200 feet of coastal shores.

Shortage, Economic—A situation where there are more potential tenants who are financially able to rent than there are available units in a rental market.

Shortage, Technical—A situation where there are more potential tenants than units available in a rental market.

Short Plat—The subdivision of a parcel of land into four or fewer lots.

Short Sale—Selling a home for less than the amount owed, with the lender's consent. The lender receives the sale proceeds and, typically, releases the borrower from the remaining debt.

Site Analysis—The gathering of data about the physical characteristics of a property and other factors affecting its use or title, as part of the appraisal process.

Special Agent—See: Agent, Special.

Special Assessment—A tax levied only against the properties that have benefited from a public improvement (such as a sewer or a street light), to cover the cost of the improvement; creates a special assessment lien.

Specific Lien—See: Lien, Specific.

Specific Performance—A legal remedy in which a court orders someone who has breached to actually perform the contract as agreed, rather than simply paying money damages.

Special Warranty Deed—See: Deed, Special Warranty.

Spot Zoning—A proposed rezone that applies only to a small piece of property in an existing zone to benefit a particular landowner; illegal in Washington.

Square Foot Method—In appraisal, a method of estimating replacement cost by calculating the square foot cost of replacing the subject home.

Stable Monthly Income—A loan applicant's gross monthly income that meets the lender's tests of quality and durability.

State Environmental Policy Act—See: SEPA.

Statement of Charges—A document served on a licensee which contains a description of license law violations the Director of the Department of Licensing believes the licensee has committed.

Statement of Disbursements—A list of all of a property's expenses incurred during a specific operating period.

Statement of Operations—A periodic report that shows the total money received and disbursed during a given period, and also describes the overall condition of the property during that period.

Statute—A law enacted by a state legislature or the U.S. Congress. Compare: Ordinance.

Statute of Frauds—A law that requires certain types of contracts to be in writing and signed in order to be enforceable.

Statute of Limitations—A law requiring a particular type of lawsuit to be filed within a specified time after the event giving rise to the suit occurred.

Statutory Redemption Period—The period required by law (one year in Washington) following a sheriff's sale in which a foreclosed borrower may redeem a property.

Steering—Channeling prospective buyers or tenants to or away from particular neighborhoods based on their race, religion, national origin, or ancestry.

Stigmatized Property—A property on which some activity took place (for example, a crime, a death, or drug- or gang-related activity) which might make the property less attractive to certain buyers.

Stockholder—See: Shareholder.

Straight Note—See: Note, Straight.

Subagent—A person that an agent has delegated authority to, so that the subagent can assist in carrying out the principal's orders; the agent of an agent.

Subcontractor—A contractor who, at the request of the general contractor, provides a specific service, such as plumbing or drywalling, in connection with the overall construction project.

Subdivision—1. A piece of land divided into two or more parcels. 2. A residential development.

Subdivision Plat—See: Plat.

Subdivision Regulations—State and local laws that must be complied with before land can be subdivided.

Subjacent Support—See: Support, Subjacent.

Subject to—When a purchaser takes property subject to a trust deed or mortgage, she is not personally liable for paying off the loan; in case of default, however, the property can still be foreclosed on.

Sublease—When a tenant grants someone else the right to possession of the leased property for part of the remainder of the lease term; as opposed to an assignment, where the tenant gives up possession for the entire remainder of the lease term. Also called a sandwich lease.

Subordination Clause—A provision in a mortgage or deed of trust that permits a later mortgage or deed of trust to have higher lien priority than the one containing the clause.

Subprime Mortgage—A mortgage loan made to a borrower who doesn't meet the requirements for ordinary mortgage loans, because of problems with credit or financial qualifications, or a lack of documentation. The interest rates and fees for these mortgages are usually higher to offset added risks to the lender.

Subrogation—The substitution of one person in the place of another with reference to a lawful claim or right. For instance, a title company that pays a claim on behalf of its insured, the property owner, is subrogated to any claim the owner successfully undertakes against the former owner.

Substitution, Principle of—A principle of appraisal holding that the maximum value of a property is set by how much it would cost to obtain another property that is equally desirable, assuming that there would not be a long delay or significant incidental expenses involved in obtaining the substitute.

Substitution of Liability—A buyer wishing to assume an existing loan may apply for the lender's approval; once approved, the buyer assumes liability for repayment of the loan, and the original borrower (the seller) is released from liability.

Succession—Acquiring property by will or inheritance.

Sufferance—Acquiescence, implied permission, or passive consent through a failure to act, as opposed to express permission.

Summary of Operations—The key portion of a property manager's statement of operations, which summarizes income and expenses.

Supply and Demand, Principle of—A principle holding that value varies directly with demand and inversely with supply; that is, the greater the demand the greater the value, and the greater the supply the lower the value.

Support, Lateral—The support that piece of land receives from the land adjacent to it.

Support, Subjacent—The support that the surface of a piece of land receives from the land beneath it.

Support Rights—The right to have one's land supported by the land adjacent to it and beneath it.

Surrender—Giving up an estate (such as a life estate or leasehold) before it has expired.

Survey—The process of precisely measuring the boundaries and determining the area of a parcel of land.

Survivorship, Right of—A characteristic of joint tenancy; surviving joint tenants automatically acquire a deceased joint tenant's interest in the property.

Syndicate—An association formed to operate an investment business. A syndicate is not a recognized legal entity; it can be organized as a corporation, LLC, partnership, or trust.

Tacking—When successive periods of use or possession by more than one person are added together to make up the period required for prescription or adverse possession.

Taking—When the government acquires private property for public use by condemnation, it's called "a taking." The term is also used in inverse condemnation lawsuits, when a government action has made private property useless.

Tax, Ad Valorem—A tax assessed on the value of property.

Tax, Excise—A state tax levied on every sale of real estate, to be paid by the seller.

Tax, General Real Estate—An annual ad valorem tax levied on real property.

Tax, Improvement—See: Special Assessment.

Tax, Progressive—A tax, such as the federal income tax, that imposes a higher tax rate on a taxpayer who earns a higher income.

Tax, Property—1. The general real estate tax. 2. Any ad valorem tax levied on real or personal property.

Tax Credit—A credit that is subtracted directly from the amount of tax owed. Compare: Deduction.

Tax Deed—See: Deed, Tax.

Tax-Deferred Exchange—A transaction in which a piece of property held for investment or used in a trade or business is traded for a piece of like-kind property, thus deferring tax on the gain. Sometimes called a tax-free exchange or 1031 exchange.

Tax Sale—Sale of property after foreclosure of a tax lien.

Team—A group of real estate licensees and non-licensees, working in a real estate firm, who collaborate on transactions.

Tenancy—Lawful possession of real property; an estate.

Tenancy, Joint—A form of concurrent ownership in which the co-owners have unity of time, title, interest, and possession and the right of survivorship.

Tenancy, Periodic—A leasehold estate that continues for successive periods of equal length (such as from week to week or month to month), until terminated by proper notice from either party. Also called a month-to-month (or week-to-week, etc.) tenancy. Compare: Estate for Years.

Tenancy, Term—See: Estate for Years.

Tenancy at Sufferance—When a tenant (who entered into possession of the property lawfully) stays on after the lease ends without the landlord's permission.

Tenancy at Will—When a tenant is in possession with the owner's permission, but there's no definite lease term; as when a landlord allows a holdover tenant to remain on the premises until another tenant is found.

Tenancy by the Entireties—A form of joint ownership of property by husband and wife (in some states that don't use a community property system).

Tenancy for Years—See: Estate for Years.

Tenancy in Common—A form of concurrent ownership in which two or more persons each have an undivided interest in the entire property, but no right of survivorship. Compare: Tenancy, Joint.

Tenancy in Partnership—The form of concurrent ownership in which general partners own partnership property, whether or not title to the property is in the partnership's name. Each partner has an equal undivided interest, but no right to transfer the interest to someone outside the partnership.

Tenant—Someone in lawful possession of real property; especially, someone who has leased property from the owner.

Tenant, Dominant—A person who has easement rights on another's property; either the owner of a dominant tenement, or someone who has an easement in gross.

Tenant, Holdover—A lessee who remains in possession of the property after the lease term has expired.

Tenant, Life—Someone who owns a life estate. See: Estate for Life.

Tenant, Servient—The owner of a servient tenement—that is, someone whose property is burdened by an easement.

Tender—An unconditional offer by one of parties to a contract to perform his part of the agreement; made when the offeror believes the other party is breaching, it establishes the offeror's right to sue if the other party doesn't accept it. Also called a tender offer.

Tenements—Everything of a permanent nature associated with a piece of land that is ordinarily transferred with the land. Tenements are both tangible (buildings, for example) and intangible (air rights, for example).

Tenement, Dominant—Property that receives the benefit of an easement appurtenant.

Tenement, Servient—Property burdened by an easement. In other words, the owner of the servient tenement (the servient tenant) must allow someone who has an easement (the dominant tenant) to use the property.

Tenure—The period of time during which a person holds certain rights with respect to a piece of real property.

Term—A prescribed period of time; especially, the length of time a borrower has to pay off a loan, or the duration of a lease.

Testament—See: Will.

Testate—Refers to someone who has died and left a will. Compare: Intestate.

Testator—A person who makes a will.

Third Party—1. A person seeking to deal with a principal through an agent. 2. In a transaction, someone who is not one of the principals.

Thrift Institutions—A term used to refer collectively to savings and loan associations and saving banks.

Tie-in Arrangements—An agreement to sell one product, only on the condition that the buyer also purchases a different product.

Tight Money Market—When loan funds are scarce, leading lenders to charge high interest rates and discount points.

TILA—See: Truth in Lending Act.

Time is of the Essence—A clause in a contract that means performance on the exact dates specified is an essential element of the contract; failure to perform on time is a material breach.

Timeshare—An arrangement in which a buyer purchases a right to occupy a condominium unit, usually in a resort area, during a particular recurring period of time.

Title—Lawful ownership of real property. Also, the deed or other document that is evidence of that ownership.

Title, Abstract of—A brief, chronological summary of the recorded documents affecting title to a particular piece of real property.

Title, After-Acquired—A rule applicable to warranty deeds; if the title is defective at the time of transfer, but the grantor later acquires more perfect title, the additional interest passes to the grantee automatically.

Title, Chain of—1. The chain of deeds (and other documents) transferring title to a piece of property from one owner to the next, as disclosed in the public record. 2. A listing of all recorded documents affecting title to a particular property; more complete than an abstract.

Title, Clear—A good title to property, free from encumbrances or defects; marketable title.

Title, Color of—Title that appears to be good title, but which in fact is not; commonly based on a defective instrument, such as an invalid deed.

Title, Equitable—The vendee's interest in property under a land contract. Also may refer to the interest that a purchaser holds before closing. Also called an equitable interest.

Title, Legal—The vendor's interest in property under a land contract.

Title, Marketable—Title free and clear of objectionable liens, encumbrances, or defects, so that a reasonably prudent person with full knowledge of the facts would not hesitate to purchase the property.

Title, Slander of—Disparaging or inaccurate statements, written or oral, concerning a person's title to property.

Title Company—A title insurance company.

Title Insurance—See: Insurance, Title.

Title Report, Preliminary—A report issued by a title company, disclosing the condition of the title to a specific piece of property, before the actual title insurance policy is issued.

Title Search—An inspection of the public record to determine all rights and encumbrances affecting title to a piece of property.

Title Theory—The theory holding that a mortgage or deed of trust gives the lender legal title to the security property while the debt is being repaid. Compare: Lien Theory.

Topography—The contours of the surface of the land (level, hilly, steep, etc.).

Tort—A breach of a duty imposed by law (as opposed to a duty voluntarily taken on in a contract) that causes harm to another person, giving the injured person the right to sue the one who breached the duty. Also called a civil wrong (in contrast to a criminal wrong, a crime).

Total Finance Charge—Under the Truth in Lending Act, a loan's total finance charge includes the interest, the loan origination fee, any discount points paid by the borrower, any finder's fee or mortgage broker's fee, service fees, and mortgage insurance costs.

Township—In the rectangular survey system, a parcel of land 6 miles square, containing 36 sections; the intersection of a range and a township tier.

Township Lines—Lines running east-west, spaced six miles apart, in the rectangular survey system.

Township Tier—In the rectangular survey system, a strip of land running east-west, six miles wide and bounded on the north and south by township lines.

Tract—1. A piece of land of undefined size. 2. In the rectangular survey system, an area made up of 16 townships; 24 miles on each side.

Trade Fixtures—Articles of personal property annexed to real property by a tenant for use in his trade or business, which the tenant is allowed to remove at the end of the lease.

Transaction Folder—A record of all documents associated with a particular transaction, such as the listing agreement, the purchase and sale agreement, the settlement statement, and any modifications or addenda.

Transferability—If an object is transferable, then ownership and possession of that object can be conveyed from one person to another. Transferability is one of the four elements of value, along with utility, scarcity, and demand.

Trespass—An unlawful physical invasion of property owned by another.

Triggering Term—Under the Truth in Lending Act, a loan term which, if stated in an advertisement for consumer credit, "triggers" the requirement of full disclosure of repayment terms. Triggering terms include the amount of any finance charge, loan payment, or required downpayment, or the repayment period or number of payments.

Trust—A legal arrangement in which title to property (or funds) is vested in one or more trustees, who manage the property on behalf of the trust's beneficiaries, in accordance with instructions set forth in the document establishing the trust.

Trust Account—A bank account, separate from a real estate licensee's personal and business accounts, used to segregate trust funds from the licensee's own funds.

Trust Deed—See: Deed of Trust.

Trustee—1. A person appointed to manage a trust on behalf of the beneficiaries. 2. A neutral third party appointed in a deed of trust to handle the nonjudicial foreclosure process in case of default.

Trustee in Bankruptcy—An individual appointed by the court to handle the assets of a person in bankruptcy.

Trustee's Sale—A nonjudicial foreclosure sale under a deed of trust.

Trust Funds—Money or things of value received by an agent, not belonging to the agent but being held for the benefit of others.

Trustor—The borrower in a deed of trust. Also called the grantor.

Truth in Lending Act—A federal law that requires lenders and credit arrangers to make disclosures concerning loan costs (including the total finance charge and the annual percentage rate) to consumer loan applicants.

Unauthorized Practice of Law—Tasks undertaken by a real estate licensee that can be done legally only by a licensed attorney; for example, drafting special contract language for a client.

Underimprovement—An improvement which, because of deficiency in cost or size, is not the most profitable use of the land; not the highest and best use.

Underwriting—In real estate lending, the process of evaluating a loan application to determine the probability that the applicant would repay the loan, and matching the risk to an appropriate rate of return. Sometimes called risk analysis.

Undivided Interest—See: Interest, Undivided.

Undue Influence—Exerting excessive pressure on someone so as to overpower the person's free will and prevent her from making a rational or prudent decision; often involves abusing a relationship of trust.

Unenforceable—See: Contract, Unenforceable.

Uniform Settlement Statement—A settlement statement required for any transaction involving a loan that is subject to the Real Estate Settlement Procedures Act (RESPA).

Uniform Standards of Professional Appraisal Practice—Guidelines for appraisers adopted by the Appraisal Foundation, a nonprofit organization of professional appraiser associations.

Unilateral Contract—See: Contract, Unilateral.

Unit-in-Place Method—In appraisal, a method of estimating replacement cost by estimating the cost of each component (foundation, roof, etc.), then adding the costs of all components together.

Unity of Interest—In reference to concurrent ownership, when each co-owner has an equal interest (equal share of ownership) in the property. A requirement for joint tenancy.

Unity of Possession— In reference to concurrent ownership, when each co-owner is equally entitled to possession of the entire property, because their interests are undivided. This is a requirement for joint tenancy, but it is also a characteristic of all concurrent ownership.

Unity of Time—In reference to concurrent ownership, when each co-owner acquired title at the same time. A requirement for joint tenancy.

Unity of Title—In reference to concurrent ownership, when each co-owner acquired title through the same instrument (deed, will, or court order). A requirement for joint tenancy.

Universal Agent—See: Agent, Universal.

Unjust Enrichment—An undeserved benefit; a court generally will not allow a remedy (such as forfeiture of a land contract) if it would result in the unjust enrichment of one of the parties.

Unlawful Detainer—A summary legal action to regain possession of real property; especially, a suit filed by a landlord to evict a defaulting tenant.

Useful Life—See: Economic Life.

Use Value—See: Value, Utility.

Usury—Charging an interest rate that exceeds legal limits.

Utility—The ability of an object to satisfy some need and/or arouse a desire for possession; one of the four elements of value, along with scarcity, demand, and transferability.

VA—Department of Veterans Affairs.

Vacancy Factor—A percentage deducted from a property's potential gross income to determine the effective gross income; it serves as an estimate of the income that will probably be lost because of vacancies and tenants who don't pay.

VA Entitlement—The guaranty amount that a particular veteran is entitled to.

Valid—The legal classification of a contract that is binding and enforceable in a court of law.

Valuable Consideration—See: Consideration.

Valuation—See: Appraisal.

Value—The present worth of future benefits.

Value, Assessed—The value placed on property by the taxing authority (the county assessor, for example) for the purposes of taxation.

Value, Face—The value of an instrument, such as a promissory note or a security, that is indicated on the face of the instrument itself.

Value, Market—The most probable price which a property should bring in a competitive and open market under all conditions requisite to a fair sale, the buyer and seller each acting prudently and knowledgeably, and assuming the price is not affected by undue stimulus. (This is the definition from the Uniform Standards of Professional Appraisal Practice.) Market value is also called fair market value, value in exchange, or objective value. Compare: Market Price.

Value, Subjective—The value of a property in the eyes of a particular person, as opposed to its market value (objective value).

Value, Utility—The value of a property to its owner or to a user. (A form of subjective value.) Also called value in use.

Value in Exchange—See: Value, Market.

Value in Use—See: Value, Utility.

Variable Expense—See: Expenses, Variable.

Variable Interest Rate—A loan interest rate that can be adjusted periodically during the loan term, as in the case of an adjustable-rate mortgage.

Variance—Permission (from the local zoning authority) to use property or build a structure in a way that violates the zoning ordinance in a relatively minor way.

Vendee—A buyer or purchaser; particularly, someone buying property under a land contract.

Vendor—A seller; particularly, someone selling property by means of a land contract.

Verify—1. To confirm or substantiate. 2. To confirm under oath.

Vested—A person who has a present, fixed right or interest in property has a vested right or interest, even though he may not have the right to possession until sometime in the future. For example, a remainderman's interest in the property vests when it is granted (not when the life estate ends).

Vicarious Liability—See: Liability, Vicarious.

Void—Having no legal force or effect. See also: Contract, Void.

Voidable—See: Contract, Voidable.

Voluntary Lien—See: Lien, Voluntary.

Waiver—The voluntary relinquishment or surrender of a right.

Warranty, Implied—In a sale or lease of property, a guarantee created by operation of law, whether or not the seller or landlord intended to offer it.

Warranty Deed—See: Deed, Warranty.

Warranty of Habitability—See: Habitability, Implied Warranty of.

Washington Human Rights Commission—The state agency that enforces the Law Against Discrimination.

Washington Land Development Act—A Washington state consumer protection law that requires a subdivision developer to provide a Public Offering Statement (which contains information about the development) to prospective purchasers.

Washington Law Against Discrimination—A state law that is stricter than the Fair Housing Act in its prohibition against discrimination in housing and other transactions on the basis of race, creed, color, national origin, sex, sexual orientation, marital status, familial status, disability, military status, or use of a service animal.

Waste—Destruction, damage, or material alteration of property by someone in possession who holds less than a fee estate (such as a life tenant or lessee), or by a co-owner.

Water Rights—The right to use water from a body of water. See: Appropriation, Prior; Littoral Rights; Riparian Rights.

Water Table—The level at which water may be found, either at the surface or underground.

Wild Deed—See: Deed, Wild.

Will—A person's stipulation regarding how her estate should be disposed of after she dies. Also called a testament.

Will, Formal—A will that meets the statutory requirements for validity; it must be in writing and signed in the presence of at least two competent witnesses.

Will, Holographic—A will written entirely in the testator's handwriting, which may be valid even if it was not witnessed. Not recognized in Washington.

Will, Nuncupative—An oral will made on the testator's deathbed; valid only as to bequests of personal property worth under $1,000.

Without Recourse—A qualified or conditional endorsement on a negotiable instrument, which relieves the endorser of liability under the instrument.

Workers' Compensation—State-mandated insurance coverage for injured workers (also known as industrial insurance). Real estate brokerages must pay workers' compensation premiums on all their agents.

Wraparound Financing—See: Mortgage, Wraparound.

Writ of Attachment—See: Attachment.

Writ of Execution—A court order directing a public officer (usually the sheriff) to seize and sell property to satisfy a debt.

Writ of Restitution—A court order issued after an unlawful detainer action, informing the tenant that she must vacate the landlord's property within a specified period or be forcibly removed by the sheriff. Also called a writ of possession.

Yield—The return of profit to an investor on an investment, stated as a percentage of the amount invested.

Zone—An area of land set off for a particular use or uses, subject to certain restrictions.

Zoning—Government regulation of the uses of property within specified areas.

Zoning Amendment—See: Rezone.